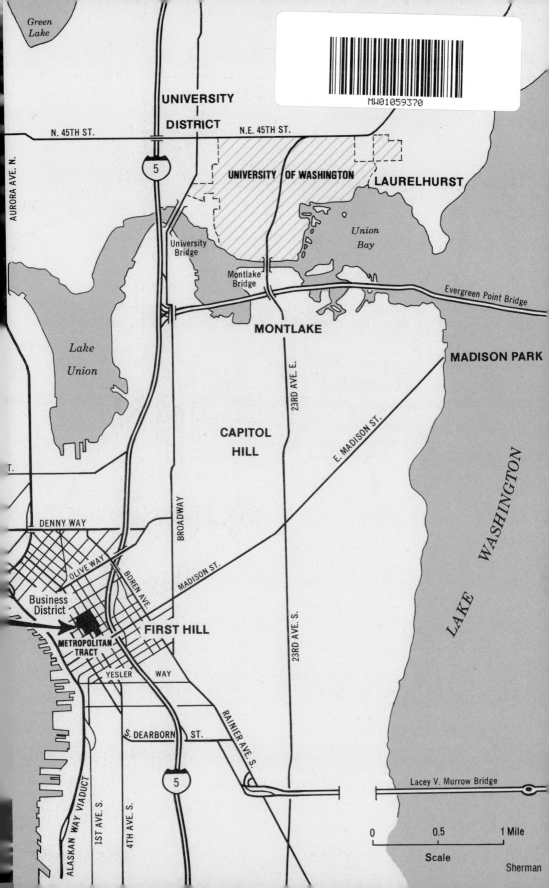

Green
Lake

UNIVERSITY

DISTRICT

N. 45TH ST.   N.E. 45TH ST.

5

UNIVERSITY OF WASHINGTON   LAURELHURST

AURORA AVE. N.

University
Bridge

Union
Bay

Montlake
Bridge

Evergreen Point Bridge

Lake
Union

MONTLAKE

MADISON PARK

CAPITOL
HILL

23RD AVE. E.

E. MADISON ST.

LAKE WASHINGTON

DENNY WAY

BROADWAY

OLIVE WAY

MADISON ST.

BOREN AVE.

Business
District

FIRST HILL

23RD AVE. S.

METROPOLITAN
TRACT

YESLER   WAY

RAINIER AVE. S.

S. DEARBORN   ST.

5

ALASKAN WAY VIADUCT

1ST AVE. S.

4TH AVE. S.

Lacey V. Murrow Bridge

0   0.5   1 Mile

Scale

Sherman

DENNY'S KNOLL

A History of the Metropolitan Tract
of the University of Washington

Denny's Knoll

*A History of the Metropolitan Tract
of the University of Washington*

Neal O. Hines

UNIVERSITY OF WASHINGTON PRESS
SEATTLE AND LONDON

Jacket illustration: front, from a painting by Emily Inez Denny, courtesy of
Photography Collection, Suzzallo Library, University of Washington; back,
photograph courtesy of Aerolist, Inc. Endpaper map by Helen Sherman.

Library of Congress Cataloging in Publication Data

Hines, Neal O
    Denny's knoll.

    Includes bibliographical references and index.
    1. Metropolitan Tract, Seattle—History.
2. Seattle—History. 3. Denny, Arthur Armstrong,
1882–1899. I. Title.
F899.S46M474   979.7'77   79–6760
ISBN 0-295-95718-2

PREFACE

This is the story of a piece of land—a plot of land once a campus and now a public property at the commercial center of a great American city.

The land lies where the city of Seattle, Washington, rises on steep slopes from its Puget Sound waterfront. In the modern urban landscape it is unrecognizable as a place with a singular and historic identity, for it is covered by buildings and its boundaries, unmarked, do not even fit neatly into the pattern of the downtown streets. But a singular identity the land has, and a history that reaches back into the formative days of the territory of Washington. Then it was a ten-acre bit of virgin forest—a perfect square, ten chains each way—staked out on a rough hillside to assure the establishment, at that spot, of a public university. The land was a private gift for a specific public purpose. It has remained ever since a public trust, a university land endowment still fulfilling, in an unexpected fashion, the intent of the givers.

That part of Seattle is what has been known for many years as the Metropolitan tract of the University of Washington.

The Metropolitan tract is a state property developed by private corporations under lease terms acceptable to the university's regents, whose control has been confirmed by the courts. The history is, in essence, a story of private commercial development with public oversight, a record of leasings and construction and of the necessary reconciliations between private plans and public policy. But it is more than that. The history of the Metropolitan tract reflects at every point the intersections and interactions of the economic, political, and social forces that have shaped the state of Washington, the city of Seattle, and the university itself. The state's interests have been legal and legislative, related to the status of the tract as a projection of the earliest hopes for the establishment and support of public higher education. The city grew up around the "old university grounds," the course of the growth strongly influenced thereby. As for the university, decisions about the tract have been made for eighty years by regents—some serving only briefly, a few for decades—whose responsibilities to the institution always have included that special responsibility for a property that not only is public in every sense but that also carries a great weight of historical association, sentiment, community symbolism and, of course, legend.

The circumstances of the founding of the university are behind all this, and the central figure, although he shared the honors, was Arthur Armstrong

v

Denny. When the territorial legislature passed in 1860 an act specifying that the university should be located in Seattle provided that "a good and sufficient deed to ten acres of land . . . be first executed," Denny was prepared to respond, for he had been persuaded that the university should be there and he already had determined to give a part of his land claim to get it. When the deeding was done, the following spring, there were two quitclaim deeds, not one, the land survey having demonstrated the need for condonors of the site Denny selected. But the impulse came from Denny, the success of the maneuver was his, and the deed of Arthur and Mary Denny to the territory set out the perpetual condition of the gift. The land was for the university, or beyond that, forever, for the uses of education. None could anticipate the university's move to a new campus in 1894–95, much less the tangle of events by which the land was transformed from campus to commercial center. But the wishes of the donors prevailed. Whatever the event, the university should have the benefit.

The story of the tract covers two principal epochs. The first was that of the Metropolitan Building Company—the company that left its name on the property—organized in 1907 to take over the lease of a faltering developer. The second is that of UNICO Properties, Inc., formerly University Properties, which won a new lease in 1953 and will continue to be the lessee until well into the next century. (There is, too, as not quite a separate matter, the story of the Olympic Hotel, which has passed through several epochs of its own and in 1980 is about to start another.) The periods are distinct, one beginning in Seattle's expansionist years—the years of grading, sluicing, filling, clearing, and building—and the other proceeding into this era of urban planning, environmental management, and historic preservation. Yet there has been continuity. From its earliest days the tract has been the scene of innovations in planning, architecture, community relations, management methods, leasing and lessor-lessee relationships. It was the dream of the Metropolitan Building Company to place on the tract something unheard of in 1907—a "city within a city," a ten-acre expanse of commercial buildings and apartments with garden courts, service areas, a plaza, all unified architecturally, a commercial acropolis in which would sit the commanders of Seattle's expanding interests in lumbering, railroading, manufacturing, shipping, and finance. That grand design never was fulfilled—although the White-Henry-Stuart Building, now gone, and the Cobb, which still stands, were the products of it—but the dream of unity never faded. It was still there when the new age, and several revolutions in styles of urban development, brought towers, malls, parking garages, sky bridges, and pedestrian concourses.

The Metropolitan tract has no counterpart. Its uniqueness as a property is less important, however, than the condition of the proprietorship under which boards of regents of seven members appointed for six-year terms have been answerable over the years for judgments affecting the character and appearance of a city's downtown area. In a situation that would seem to invite tensions there have been such moments, but they have been remarkably few. Even in disputes public policies were formed, the processes illuminating. And all who have parts in the story—lessees, regents, financiers, builders, legislators, planners—are members of a most interesting company.

The idea of a tract history arose almost seven years ago in discussions among regents and university staff members. The regents' minutes show who the leaders were, one of them Harold S. Shefelman, a member of the board since 1957 and chairman of the Metropolitan tract committee since 1960, and the other Ernest M. Conrad, then the university's vice president for business and finance. Even so early, with certain large tract developments still ahead, it was considered not too soon to encourage an effort to put together a comprehensive record. None knew quite what this should be, except, perhaps, that it should be rather more interpretative than technical. None knew who should make the attempt, or how long it would take, or what might result. When work on the project began in August, 1976, the story was indeed unfinished—readings of the records of the early years proceeding while the Rainier Bank Tower was going up, the White-Henry-Stuart Building coming down, and decisions about the Olympic Hotel and the Fifth Avenue Theater in suspense. If recent events are too recent for history, they are at least parts of the record. The timing now appears almost providential.

That this history exists is due to the interest and support of the regents who have served since 1973, and particularly, perhaps, of those who have been members of the Metropolitan tract committee—Harold Shefelman, James R. Ellis, and Robert F. Philip, the successive chairmen, and George V. Powell, Jack G. Neupert, R. Mort Frayn, Gordon C. Culp, Dr. J. Hans Lehmann, and Taul Watanabe. Yet the interest has been shared by all members of the board and to all of them the author's obligations are hereby acknowledged.

All along the way the draftings and reworkings of the text were assisted by persons whose contributions of information, suggestions, or critical comment were invaluable. Some read all or parts of draft chapters, some recalled personal experiences or impressions. Former regents who so contributed were Grant Armstrong, Dave Beck, Dorothy Bullitt, Dr. Donald G. Corbett, Beatrice Gardner, Charles M. Harris, and Robert J. Willis. From the university faculty were Brewster Denny, Solomon Katz, Vernon Carstensen, Philip Cartwright, and Warren Etcheson, and from the administrative staff Ernest Conrad, Fred Harlocker, James F. Ryan, James B. Wilson, and Barbara Zimmerman, secretary to the regents and custodian of the minutes and papers from which so much of the documentation is drawn. Help was at hand throughout from members of the university's archives and library staffs—from Richard C. Berner, archivist; Robert D. Monroe and Dennis Andersen, of the Special Collections Division; Andrew F. Johnson, of the Pacific Northwest Collection; and Gary Lundell, of the Records Center. Such support was provided also by members of the Metropolitan Tract Office staff, Marie Seidehamel, Arthur Cooperstein, and John S. Robinson, consultant.

There were many whose memories were wonderfully explicit and some who contributed papers or photographs. One was Arthur T. Lee, of Bellevue, the regents' Metropolitan tract representative from 1951 to 1955 and designer of the model of what became the University Properties lease of 1953. Others were James B. Douglas, of Seattle, and Neva Douglas, of Palm Desert, California, son and daughter of the J. F. Douglas who organized the Metropolitan Building Company. Officers of UNICO—James M. Ryan, Donald J. Covey, and Jack Dierdorff—were generous with information, as were Albert S. Kerry, Jr., Perry Johanson, William G. Reed, Norton Clapp, Sarah Hilmes, Edward L. Rosling, Arthur Simon, Irving Anches, Horace McCurdy, and F. E. Smetheram. Background materials came from, among others, George Stirrat, of Seattle; Jack Lines, of Yakima; and Loyal Treat Nichols, of Newport Beach, California. To all of these, and to the persons in libraries, historical museums, and newspapers who were consulted along the way, go the warmest thanks —and assurance that only the author is responsible for the uses to which their contributions were put. And there was, of course, first and last, Martha, whose enthusiasm for this work was surpassed only by her patience during the doing of it. May every toiler have such support.

This history is called *Denny's Knoll* for reasons that will not need explanation. Yet Arthur Denny's contemporaries thought his gift to the university was larger than land, and it is appropriate to remember here how his works were viewed when, upon Denny's death in 1899, a memorial service was held. A speaker on that occasion was Franklin P. Graves, president of the university, and the text of the Graves statement was rescued from old files in 1963 by a later president, Charles E. Odegaard, in the course of preparing a paper on the university for a Newcomen Society lecture. Of Denny and his gift Graves had said:

As far as any man could be the creator of an institution of learning, Arthur Denny was. . . . Such a creation can be attributed to but one other man, our great patriot and statesman, Thomas Jefferson, who founded the University of Virginia. But Jefferson was himself a scholar, while Arthur Denny never laid claim to any higher title than that of pioneer. That a hardy, rugged, and industrious pioneer, who had not the opportunity of early training, should seek to furnish this opportunity to the coming generation seems to me a far more glorious attribute.

In 1899 Denny's knoll was about to begin another life. With the words of President Graves let the story of it also begin.

Neal O. Hines

Hansville, Washington
March, 1980

CONTENTS

ILLUSTRATIONS

Photographs or illustrative materials not otherwise attributed in the captions are courtesy of the Photography Collection, Suzzallo Library, University of Washington.

Text Illustrations

Photographs   *following page 338*

DENNY'S KNOLL

A History of the Metropolitan Tract
of the University of Washington

CHAPTER 1

The Knoll: 1854 to 1894

The university established in Seattle in 1861 was the University of the Territory of Washington. That the university existed was something of a surprise, for the territory was very new, just eight years old, and there were at hand no students ready to attempt higher learning. The university was, nevertheless, the territory's. What was even more surprising was the university itself—the building a tall frame structure of dignity and character, finer than anything else in the region, situated on a hillside above Elliott Bay in a place which only five years before had been described as a "woods thronged with Indians." The University of the Territory of Washington had been founded in what was still a wilderness, the building more monument than university hall, a testimony to territorial aspirations in the realm of higher education, but one that expressed rather more explicitly Seattle's own aspirations and the mixture of idealism and political improvisation that had contributed to its creation.

There was now, in 1861, the question of support, the means not immediately discernible. A territorial university had been endowed by the U.S. Congress in a reservation of public lands, but the result had been beyond anticipation. Most of the lands for the endowment had been sold to build that splendid building, and the building itself stood on a ten-acre plot that had been donated by private citizens. All that happened thereafter flowed from these circumstances.

The beginning was in 1854, the year after Washington was carved out of what had been Oregon Territory. The new governor, President Fillmore's appointee, was Isaac I. Stevens, a thirty-five-year-old engineer, a graduate of the U.S. Military Academy at the head of his class, a veteran of the Mexican War, in which he was seriously wounded, and a former head of the U.S. Coast Survey. Stevens had an enthusiast's view of the Northwest and ideas about its development. On his way west he had conducted at his own request an exploration of a possible northern route for a transcontinental railroad. He was prepared to give the legislature his recommendations for the organization of the territory, and he did so, in February 1854, to legislators assembled in Olympia, which Stevens had designated the provisional capital. He spoke among other things of the need for schools—"The subject of education already occupies the minds and hearts of the citizens of this Territory," he said—and he had two proposals. Noting that Congress had made appropriations of land for the support of public schools, Stevens recommended that a "special com-

3

mission be instituted to report on the whole school system." Then the next
step: "I will also recommend that Congress be memorialized to appropriate
land for an university."[1]

Stevens was simply suggesting that Washington ask Congress for a university grant of the kind accorded other states and territories, most recently
Oregon. The donation or reservation of public lands for public purposes,
including the support of education, was as old as the nation, the principles
set out in the Ordinances of 1785 and 1787 relating to the survey and disposition of lands west of Pennsylvania and north of the Ohio River, the Old
Northwest. As new states and territories were organized, Congress had set
aside two sections of each township for the support of schools and two townships, some 46,000 acres, as endowments of universities. Oregon had received
its two townships, one to be south of the Columbia River, one to the north,
under the Donation Act of 1850. Now that Washington was a territory, Stevens
was suggesting a petition for equal treatment. The proposal needed no urging
in that first Washington legislature, and a memorial was quickly drafted and
sent on its way to Washington, D.C. By July 1854, Congress had passed a bill
providing: "There shall be reserved in each of the territories of Washington
and Oregon two Townships of land of thirty-six sections each, to be selected
in legal subdivisions for universities purposes under the direction of the legislatures of such Territories respectively."

Congressional grants from the public domain were general authorizations.
Selection of the land, once the surveys had been made, was left to local discretion, the selections to be recorded in the land office. The university township grants were viewed as true endowments, as sources of funds for the future.
The institutions they made possible were not necessarily to be situated on those
lands, but were to draw financial support from them, through leasing, perhaps, or by establishing endowment accounts when sales were advantageous.
In the case of a territory it was intended that lands reserved by Congress
should be withheld from sale until the new state, assuming responsibility
for university support, could make its own determination of the proper
course. The intention was not observed in every case, nor would it be in
Washington's.

With the congressional enactment of 1854, Washington Territory had its
two townships of land. But the selections were not immediately accomplish-
able, both because the land surveys were not sufficiently advanced and because
organization of the territory required the cultivation of other kinds of ground,
as in decisions with respect to the distribution of the offices and functions of
government. The congressional grant of university land had, predictably,
made the selection of the university's site a new element in the process of
political bargaining. The capital was the main prize, Olympia having only a
presumptive claim by virtue of its provisional status. But the site of a penitentiary had to be considered, as well as that of a land office. Now the site of
the university was also to be chosen.

In Washington Territory such bargaining went on, in successive sessions of the legislature, for six years—little enough time considering the sparseness of the settlement of so large a land. The legislature of 1854 had been meeting scarcely more than a dozen years after the U.S. Exploring Expedition conducted the first comprehensive survey of Puget Sound and the Northwest coast. There were not more than nine thousand settlers in the new territory, the largest number at Vancouver, on the Columbia River, where many families had clustered before the territorial separation. A few settlers lived east of the Cascade range, but most were scattered along the coastal side of the territory in small farming communities or in Puget Sound villages such as Port Townsend, Whatcom (which would become Bellingham), Seattle, and Tacoma. Olympia had a population of about eight hundred, and Seattle, less than three years old, had not yet a quarter of that number. And so new was the general population that almost every citizen was from somewhere else—from Oregon and California to Pennsylvania, New York, and Maine. Many settlers had come north after making the long trip to Oregon across the plains. Many had given up on California after taking passage around Cape Horn during the gold rush.

To such constituencies the winning of a university could not have seemed a major goal. Nevertheless, there were spokesmen for sites as far apart as Vancouver, which had political weight as a population center, and Cape Flattery, far to the northwest at the entrance to the Strait of Juan de Fuca. The legislature selected sites. The first law, in 1854, would have established a university of two parts (the still-unselected township lands to be divided between them), one "branch" in Seattle and the other at Boisfort Plains, to the south, in Lewis County. By 1858, Seattle had been dropped as a prospect and the university was placed at Cowlitz Farm Prairie, also in Lewis County. Thus there were enactments, but no university appeared and no lands were selected. Nor was the permanent site of the capital decided, although Olympia defended its preeminent claim, and Seattle, given a choice between a university and the capital, would have settled instantly for the latter. Community pride was a factor, but also economics. As the territorial capital, Seattle could anticipate commercial expansion and higher prices for real estate.

So it was in 1860 when two men came together in Seattle with talents, political and otherwise, that were perfectly combined to force decision. One was Arthur A. Denny, who had been there from the beginning. The other was a newcomer, Daniel Bagley, a Methodist minister and missionary who had moved north from Oregon in the hope that the Puget Sound climate might benefit his invalid wife.

Denny and Bagley, in their individual ways, were models of the pioneer, the one a busy and acquisitive builder, organizer, and public man, the other a driving, irrepressible idealist. The photographs of Denny and Bagley, made in their later years, are of men serene and patriarchal, the eyes of each gentle and wise, the faces interestingly lined above full but well-tended beards. But years earlier each had been hardened by long and dangerous wagon trips across the plains to Oregon and by their labors on the frontier, and in 1860 they were young enough (Denny thirty-eight, Bagley forty-two) to have ahead of them time enough to make something of the village on Elliott Bay. They shared a quality that Bagley once described in himself as "go-aheaditiveness." They plunged into things and were schemers in good causes. Neither had ever been to a university.

Denny was of a line that went back to the early days of the nation. His grandfather had served in the Revolution, and his father, John Denny, had been a Kentucky volunteer in the western battles of the War of 1812. John had followed, later, the classic route of the settlers moving from Kentucky through Indiana to Illinois. Arthur, born in 1822 near Salem, Indiana, had attended school in Illinois, where his father, as a member of the Illinois legislature of 1840–41, had been an associate and friend of Abraham Lincoln.

Arthur was married in 1843 to Mary Ann Boren, and two daughters had been born to them in Illinois before they decided, in 1851, to go west to Oregon. They started this trip in April, the train including the wagons of the Dennys, the Borens, and others, and by August they were at Portland, where John Denny remained for a time to try politics in the new land. In November 1851, Arthur and Mary Ann and their children took passage northward on a little vessel, the *Exact*, which put them ashore in Puget Sound on November 13, at what would be called Alki Point, off the south rim of Elliott Bay. With the Dennys were the Borens, the Lows, the Bells, and Charles C. and Lee Terry (twelve adults and twelve children). With that small party of immigrants the story of Seattle began.

Daniel Bagley had followed a similar route in a different way. Bagley was a Pennsylvanian, born in the western forests near Meadville in 1818. As a young backwoodsman he had met and married Susannah Whipple, whose parents had moved there from Massachusetts. In 1840, Bagley took his bride to Illinois, where the Dennys already lived, and there he farmed and taught school for two years until he was admitted to the Methodist ministry and began a decade of riding the circuit north of Springfield and getting deeply involved in antislavery activities with Owen Lovejoy, a celebrated leader in the movement. In 1852 Bagley was selected by his church as a missionary to Oregon. He and Susannah headed west in April of that year, and in that wagon train were men and women whom they would rejoin, years later, in Seattle: the Dexter Hortons, the Thomas and Aaron Mercers, and John Pike. For eight years Daniel Bagley toiled as a missionary in Oregon's Willamette Valley, establishing and building churches and traveling constantly, much of the time in the saddle. But Susannah was frail and Bagley's labors were undermining his own health. In 1860 they moved once again, riding north in a buggy from Salem to Seattle. There Daniel found the perfect outlet for his missionary zeal.

Denny had been in the legislature from the beginning, a participant in the maneuvering with regard to the capital. By 1860 he was a member of the

Legislative Council, the territorial senate, as one of two members from the six northern counties. His colleague was Joseph Foster, who shared Denny's hope that the capital would come to Seattle. Meanwhile, the territorial surveys had moved along. The 620,000 acres surveyed in 1859 brought the total to 2,000,000. The selection of the university's township grants could be made, and when the legislature met in November 1860, an allotment of the political plums seemed nearer. The plum soon allotted Seattle was the university. It was in this that Daniel Bagley, who was not even a member of the legislature, began to play a role of crucial importance, even though the details would be obscured thereafter by legend, sentiment, and the mists surrounding his handling, as a duly appointed commissioner, of the university's land endowment.

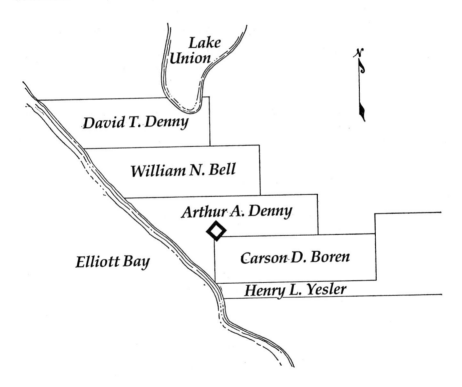

The position of the university's ten-acre tract at the edge of Arthur Denny's land claim, as shown in this simplified sketch of the claims along Seattle's waterfront in early territorial days (*adaptation of sketch in Special Collections, University Library*)

Denny, wanting the capital for Seattle, had looked upon the university as no more than a bargaining chip. Denny was one of the five original Seattle settlers (the others were Henry L. Yesler, Carson D. Boren, William N. Bell, and David Denny) whose claims covered all of the lower lands from the village to the south tip of what would later be called Lake Union and extended east from Elliott Bay into the forested hills. Somewhere in that primitive terrain, after clearing and improvement, a capitol might be built—not necessarily on Denny's land, although his claim occupied a central position. Denny must have held for years the vision of such a prospect.* Yet by 1860 it was the university that Denny wanted, and it was Bagley who, by every account, convinced him. And Bagley probably suggested how to get it.

Denny and Foster were participants in a plan, worked out that autumn with representatives from Vancouver and Port Townsend, by which the capital would go to Vancouver, the most heavily populated community, while Seattle would get the university and Port Townsend the penitentiary and, possibly, upon another memorial to Congress, the land office. The object could only have been to outflank the Olympians in the contest for the capital, perhaps with the thought of a later trade. But Denny had become serious about the university. Foster was quoted years later as having said:

He [Denny] and I thought my bill was a good thing, for we could trade the university off in one or two years and thereby get the territorial capital for Seattle. When I met Daniel Bagley I told him of the nice little plan that Mr. Denny and I had in view. Bagley knocked that plan into a cocked hat. . . . "Nonsense. You've got something a heap better than a capital. You go back to Olympia and get me and John Webster and Edmund Carr appointed regents or commissioners and I'll show you that a university is better."[2]

The quotation is from Edmond Meany, the university's teacher-historian and supreme sentimentalist, who was speaking in paraphrase almost half a century after the event. Yet Meany's account of Foster's recollection certainly contains the nub. The university was to be the prize, and two pieces of legislation set the stage for the winning of it. On December 12, 1860, the legislature passed "An Act to Relocate the Territorial University" in Seattle, *"Provided, a good and sufficient deed to ten acres of land, eligibly situated in the vicinity of Seattle, be first executed to the Territory of Washington for University purposes."* Then, on January 11, 1861—Bagley's advice presumably being followed now—a second act provided "for the selection and location of the land reserved for university purposes" and for the appointment of a board of commissioners to make the selections. In that bill, Bagley, John Webster, and Edmund Carr were indeed named commissioners, and they were given special powers. They were authorized to sell "any and all lands," when the

---

* It is part of the legend that Seattle's Capitol Hill, at the north end of the ridge between Elliott Bay and Lake Washington, was named by Denny when, hoping to anticipate or influence the decision of the legislature, he designated a part of his claim as the site of a future capitol. There are reasons to doubt this, one the simple fact that Denny's claim could not have reached so far. In a Seattle newspaper account of 1930 it is Foster, not Denny, who "set aside a tract of land near the city limits for the Capitol building and called it Capitol Hill." A pioneer reminiscence ascribes the naming to James A. Moore, the Seattle real estate promoter who developed Capitol Hill and whose career becomes a part of this story. See Sophie Frye Bass, *When Seattle Was a Village* (Seattle: Lowman and Hanford, 1947), p. 140.

selections had been recorded in the land office, for not less than $1.50 an acre (although the minimum price for federal land was $1.25 per acre), this to provide funds to have the university site cleared and improved provided that the cost "shall not at any time exceed the amount of available funds arising from the sale of lands or any donations made by individuals for that purpose." The commissioners also were authorized to "select, locate, and receive a title for ten acres of land within the vicinity of Seattle, that may be donated to the Territory of Washington for a site for the Territorial University."[3]

The package of legislation was a battle plan for what followed. Denny had decided to give ten acres, and the laws had been written accordingly: the commissioners were empowered to receive the ten-acre plot and to sell reserved lands to pay for its improvement. A possible difficulty went completely unnoticed. The commissioners' authority went beyond the legislature's power to grant and thus was extralegal. Neither of the pertinent federal laws —the organic act of 1853 or the university grant law of 1854—gave the territory the right to sell reserved lands. The territory could only select. But selling was what Bagley had in mind. When the commissioners met in Seattle on February 22, 1861, they elected Bagley president and authorized him to act for the board. The president was ready to act, but first he would pick the university site. Bagley conferred with Denny, and the two of them climbed through the woods above the town where the hillside was marked by a ter-

The corrected survey of the "10 Acre Lot" as reconstructed in 1926 at the request of the university regents

race, or bench, below the crest but commanding a superb view of Elliott Bay and the Olympic Mountains far beyond. That was the place. "Bagley," Denny said, "I'll give the knoll."

It happened that way, except that the survey showed that Denny's knoll covered not ten but about eight and one-third acres, and that it would be necessary to square off the ten-acre site by incorporating fractional pieces of adjacent properties owned by Charles C. and Mary Terry and Edward Lander, who had acquired parts of the Carson Boren claim, south of Denny's. The Terrys and Lander agreed to join in the gift, and thus on April 16, 1861, two quitclaim deeds were executed to the Territory of Washington, one by the Dennys, the other by their neighbors, transferring the land needed to fulfill the legislative stipulation.

The Denny deed—the language was echoed in the Terry-Lander instrument, which was written in the same hand—stipulated that the land should be dedicated forever to educational purposes. In the words of the Denny deed:

Provided Always and these presents are upon this express condition that if the said Territorial University by act of the Legislative Assembly or otherwise should not be located and built upon the ten acre lot of which the above described tract lot or parcel of land shall form a part according to the true intent and meaning of these presents then the said tract lot or parcel of land shall revert to and immediately vest in the Town of Seattle in King County aforesaid for the use and benefit of and as a site for a University, High School or College and for no other purpose.[4]

The Terry-Lander participation may have been fortuitous, but in any case the names of the codonors were already embedded in the history of the territory. Lander, a prominent attorney, had been a member of the territorial court in 1854, appointed to that office by President Fillmore at the time Stevens was named governor. Terry was one of the Seattle founders, a native of Waterville, New York, who, when not yet twenty years old, had sailed around Cape Horn to California in 1849 and had moved north to Oregon in time to join the Denny party aboard the *Exact*. The Terrys had been married at Port Madison, Washington, in 1856, and had become the parents of five children. Terry had prospered in Seattle, establishing a small business and investing in real estate. When he joined in the gift of land he was scarcely thirty-one years old, and soon he would serve briefly as treasurer of the university. But he was only thirty-seven when, in 1867, he died.

The university now had a fixed site, and Bagley, his "go-aheaditiveness" in full gear, immediately pressed on with plans and arrangements that would later astonish the legislature and with an enthusiasm that seems to have assuaged in Seattle any disappointment at the loss of the capitol. Even before the university deeds were accomplished, Bagley was having the university site cleared of trees and brush (paying up to $325 an acre for the work, since clearing then cost more than land itself), and enlisting the help of Seattle citizens in the project.[5] When the land, cleared and grubbed, was usable, the university building began to appear there.

No historian has been able to grasp firmly the facts or assess the ultimate significance to the university of the course on which Bagley had embarked. For the clearing and construction, money was required. To acquire funds, Bagley selected and sold off large parts of the lands Congress had reserved. Bagley acted for the commissioners under the authority of the legislature. Yet the legislature, even acting beyond its own authority in the matter of land sales, had thought only that lands would be sold as necessary to finance the clearing of the donated site. But Bagley meant to build, to put the university so firmly in Seattle, as his son said later, that there never again could be a thought of moving it. Bagley never needed apologists—he would be known forever as the "father of the university" for his work in those years—but his passion was for building, not accounting. Neither his ledgers nor the records of the land office ever yielded the full story of his financial management.

The building of the university was a revelation of the pride that Denny and Bagley had uncovered in their little waterfront village. Bagley was required to report to the legislature the activities of the commission, but until the legislature met again in December 1861—just ten months after the commission was organized—Bagley could go forging ahead. The clearing and deeding were done in March and April 1861. By May, the cornerstone of the new building had been laid in a program of speeches and community festivities. On November 4, the first classes were held. Asa Mercer, a young man from Ohio employed by Bagley as the first "principal," had rounded up sixteen "pupils" by hiring two Indians to take him by canoe to the nearer reaches of Puget Sound.

The university building was not quite finished in November 1861, but it stood majestically above the town. Near it was a "president's house," and there was even a dormitory for male students. The architect was John Pike, who had come west by wagon with the Hortons, the Bagleys, and the Mercers and who had conceived—with insufficient acknowledgement in history, as it turned out—something of an American classic. His design incorporated four graceful columns on a portico looking out toward the waters and mountains and a roof capped by an octagonal belfry in which would hang, by 1862, a bell cast in Troy, New York, and brought to Seattle around Cape Horn. A picket fence surrounded the new campus, including in the southwest corner a stand of maple trees which had been placed there to provide a shady spot.

The main building was 50 by 80 feet and two stories high. On the ground floor were six rooms separated by a 12-foot entrance hall running from front to rear. The second floor had four rooms, including a "grand lecture room" extending the full width of the structure. The president's house was another two-story building, 40 by 50 feet, seven rooms below and three above. The dormitory was a "plain box," 24 by 48 feet, designed for later expansion.

Materials were assembled from up and down the Sound: stone from Port Orchard, fir lumber from Port Madison and Port Gamble, pine from Seabeck, on Hood Canal, brick from Whatcom, hardware and fittings from as far away as Victoria, British Columbia. Into the construction went the work of men whose skills had been cultivated in distant parts of the country and whose names are known, in most instances, simply because they were paid for their work from the funds Daniel Bagley was accumulating through land sales. Edwin Richardson did the surveying, establishing the levels of the buildings. Hillory Butler, L. V. Wyckoff, Josiah Settle, and Thomas Mercer hauled materials to the site. John Dodge, John T. Jordan, and S. Thorndyke did the stonework at the foundations. Pike and Thomas S. Russell hammered at the framing, and D. C. Beatty, O. J. Carr, Settle, and Clarence Bagley—Daniel's son—floored and shingled. Franklin Matthias built window and door frames, Hugh McAleer shaped tin, and William W. White was the blacksmith. O. C. Shorey and Beatty built desks, and Shorey and A. P. DeLin shaped the four columns and put them in place. Many others painted or performed miscellaneous jobs of carpentry—Harvey Pike (John's son?), Jeff Hunt, Charles Gorton, J. E. Clark, Harry and W. B. Hitchcock, Martin Givler, J. W. Johnson, David Graham, Richard King, George Austin, Albert Pinkham, J. C. Purcell, Charles Harvey, James Kelley, and the new man from Ohio, Asa Mercer. The names were in Bagley's records.[6]

That the land was the university's was the contribution of the Dennys, the Terrys, and Lander; that the buildings stood there was Bagley's doing. Bagley had moved farther and faster than anyone had thought possible. By December 1861, Bagley reported to the legislature the sale of 20,524.70 acres of selected land, at $1.50 an acre, for a total of $30,787.05.[7] His expenditures for clearing the university site and erecting the buildings had been $30,400.69, and thus he was within the bounds of the legislative injunction that the costs of activity "shall not at any time exceed the amount of available funds arising from the sale of lands." But he was coming upon years in which he would suffer with dignified defiance humiliatingly pointed questions about his land sales and his informal accounting procedures. Arthur Denny had left the Legislative Council in 1861 to become register of the U.S. Land Office in Olympia—an appointment said to have been suggested to President Lincoln by Arthur's father, John Denny, who had come up from Oregon and was now himself a member of the legislature. The move almost certainly had something to do with the effort to put in order the record of Bagley's land sales. But Bagley himself, with the university a going institution, was busy with curriculum as well as paperwork. Bagley set up an office in the president's house, both because he needed an office and because he wanted the house to have a practical function. In one of the reports he shot off to the legislature, where there was only an indistinct realization of how much had transpired, he urged members to "come upon the grounds"—especially, he meant, any with tendencies to cavil—to see for themselves what had been created. So it occurred.

Early in the December session John Denny introduced a resolution creating a joint legislative committee to inspect the university and to report thereon. The visit was set for December 31, and the occasion, planned by Bagley, became a program of dedication. Seattle's citizens turned out in holiday mood.

The five-man legislative delegation was met at the Seattle wharf by a brass band and escorted to a platform on the campus where Mercer spoke and the visitors were called upon for responses. The chairman of the delegation accepted the university on behalf of the territory, and he and his fellow members, impressed by what they beheld and warmed by Seattle's hospitality, returned to Olympia with a favorable report that was quickly adopted.

Between January and December 1861—a momentous year in which, far to the east, a Civil War had erupted and other campuses were being converted to drill fields and tenting grounds—the University of the Territory of Washington had been established by statute, placed on its Seattle grounds and, now, formally blessed.

From 1861 until 1895—from the days of territorial organization into the beginnings of Washington's statehood, which came in 1889—the university occupied its ten-acre site. The period of thirty-four years was something like a prolonged adolescence, a painful season of growth, emotional turmoil, exaggerated hope, apprehension, dreaming, bravado—all to be remembered with wondering relief when adulthood arrived. The university was not without affection in those years, but it suffered deeply from misunderstanding, malnutrition, and what would be called, in later years, benign neglect.

Details of the experience may be passed over hastily, noted now only as they have some significance in the history of the land on which the university stood. As an institution, the university was at once too much and too little. Its troubles were organizational, curricular, financial, and political. A major part of the federal land endowment having been expended in the beginning, the balance became almost the sole source of support, because, it may be supposed, succeeding legislatures were content to let the university live as it had begun, the creature of federal bounty. Not until 1875 were funds appropriated, and then with a condition attached. As for academic leadership, Asa Mercer was followed, between 1863 and 1876, by a procession of presidents—Barnard, Whitworth, Hall, Hill, and Whitworth again—each of whom was forced to function in his own little wilderness of uncertainties. Two times the university was closed for lack of funds, first in 1866 and again in 1876, and once, in 1868, it was advertised for lease as a private school. At the level of curriculum, the university remained for an agonizingly long time little more than a somewhat pretentious adjunct to the system of common schools and predominantly a Seattle institution. In 1869 only thirty-eight students were enrolled, all for classes below the university level. The first collegiate degree was awarded in 1876. By 1878, enrollments were beginning to be above one hundred, but few students were there for work of university caliber.

One problem was getting consistency in governance. In 1862, in the burst of enthusiasm that followed the territory's acceptance of the institution, the legislature passed on January 24 "An Act to Incorporate the University of the Territory of Washington," and this measure, introduced by John Denny, created a board of regents of nine members elected by the legislature and serving, by threes, staggered terms of three years. Among the regents were Bagley and the other land commissioners, whose activities thus were incorporated into the flow of management, and whose land sales were the sole source of institutional support. The board had broad powers, to receive and hold property, to appoint officers and faculty, to determine curriculum, and to be responsible in all ways, financial and otherwise, for the welfare of the institution. Yet the board created so promptly in 1862 had been reconstituted twice within five years. In 1866 the membership was increased from nine to fifteen (one member the president of the Legislative Council), and in 1867 the membership was reduced from fifteen to five and the board of commissioners was abolished. That the regents were to meet in Seattle only once a year, oftener if it was found necessary, was a stipulation suggesting the consistency of attention considered reasonable.

The legislature's first appropriation of public funds for university purposes came with a cautious proviso that raised a question about the legal status of the ten-acre tract. The act of November 12, 1875, was "An Act Authorizing Necessary Repairs To Be Made Upon the Territorial University Buildings," and it appropriated $1,500 for such repairs, to preserve the buildings from "decay and waste": *"Provided,* That no part of said appropriation shall be expended until deeds shall be executed by the grantors of the Territory, conveying an absolute and unconditional title to the Territory, to the ten acres of land upon which the said university is located."[8]

The $1,500 may or may not have been spent for repairs. By one account it was, by another it was not. In any event, Denny and his fellow donors (the heirs of Charles Terry would now have been involved) did not then convey title as stipulated. The 1875 legislature seems to have thought that if it was going to appropriate public funds the territory should have a title unclouded by the possibility that the land might revert "to the Town of Seattle in King County aforesaid," as the original deeds suggested.

Within a decade the feeling was arising that the university could not continue much longer on the knoll. Not only was the university growing, though slowly, but Seattle—a city of forty thousand by the late 1880s—was growing around it. The campus was bounded now by Seneca Street on the south, Union on the north, with new buildings above Third Avenue and beyond Fifth. The growth of the university was not measurable simply in enrollment, which remained modest, or in financial support, for legislatures remained grudging and no biennial appropriation exceeded $10,000 in territorial days. The university gradually and inexplicably developed an institutional substance and a confidence that defied expectation. The more basic forms of training remained, and two-year courses were instituted, but university standards took shape. Teachers, poorly paid, were loyal. Library and natural history collections were enlarged. The last presidents to serve the university in territorial years—Anderson, Powell, and Gatch—brought the university along, somehow, through times in which loyalty and small cultural resources were (apart from its ten-acre tract and its buildings) almost the only resources the university had. Once, in 1882–84, when the legislature was stubborn about funds, the university was tided over with gifts of some $4,000 from Henry Villard, the railroad tycoon whose lines would soon connect Puget Sound to the Midwest but who also made gifts to the Universtiy of Oregon. In 1884 the legislature appropriated $3,000, and after that larger sums. Then came 1889, the watershed year. The university, high on its hill, was spared the fire that devastated the areas of Seattle's origins. In November, Washington became a state and the university, as a state institution, was about to acquire a new campus.

By 1889 the resolve to move the university to a new site was taking tangible form and actions thereafter were to that end. It was the legislature, somewhat uncharacteristically, that took the initiative. A legislative committee, having visited the university late in 1889, declared the ten-acre tract inadequate to the future needs of an institution serving "this great State of Washington," and recommended, accordingly, disposition of the old campus and acquisition of a new tract of "not less than forty acres" outside, but conveniently near, Seattle. The legislature responded. On March 7, 1891, after several changes of mind with respect to procedure, the legislature passed "An Act providing for the establishment, location, maintenance and support of the University of Washington."[9]

The act created a new Board of University Land and Building Commissioners. The board was a select body of five (the governor, Elisha P. Ferry, serving ex officio as president; a member of the board of regents; and three citizens appointed by the governor), and its mission was, as its name implied, to get the university moved to a new campus and installed there. The move was to be accomplished by March 1, 1893.

The act of 1891 was specific in its provisions. The board was to clarify the status of university lands, including the Denny tract, which it was authorized to sell. The board was to acquire a new site not exceeding 160 acres, and the site was specified as part of a fractional school section, described, "within a radius of six miles of the present site of the university"—the site on Lake Washington that eventually would be used. The board was to see that suitable buildings were constructed on the new site. All this was to be done, however—an echo of 1875—"as soon as practicable" after the state's title to the old grounds had been established clearly forever with the execution of quitclaim deeds by the original donors or their heirs and by the city of Seattle.

The framing of the act obviously had been accomplished only after a great deal of preliminary spadework. A special joint legislative committee headed by Edmond Meany, recently elected to the house of representatives, and L. F. Thompson, for the senate, had held an open meeting in Seattle on February 6 at which the question of the deeds had been approached directly. Arthur Denny agreed to the sale of the old grounds if the proceeds were used for the new university. The city passed an ordinance authorizing the mayor and the city clerk to execute a deed quitclaiming Seattle's interest. Inspections of several sites had been conducted before the Lake Washington site was confirmed. There was a general feeling that the old university grounds might bring $250,000 or more, which would do nicely as the new campus took shape.

It did not happen that way. The quitclaim deeds were executed early in 1891, the Denny deed on February 23; the Lander deed on February 28; the city of Seattle deed on April 15; and the deed by the heirs of Charles Terry on April 21. Little else went according to plan, although the board of commissioners tried mightily. Difficulties arose in economics and overoptimism. The old university grounds were not sold. Seattle was feeling the reverberations of the depression of the 1890s and there were no offers on the property and thus no funds of the kind so confidently anticipated. Designs of the new building proved, when the estimates came in, far too elaborate for any conceivable budget.

Not until 1893 was there forward motion. By an act of March 14, 1893, the legislature turned from the 1891 commission plan and placed on the board of regents the responsibility for seeing that the university's building was built after the governor had acquired the site.[10] The act set out procedures for procuring the Lake Washington tract, for getting architects' plans in open competition, and for construction on public bids. The act appropriated $150,000 for construction. With such guidelines before them, the regents moved as expeditiously as they could, once the site was acquired, to get a main building in place. Clearing of the land was begun in 1893, and early in 1894 the examination of architects' drawings began. The design selected was by Charles Saunders, of Seattle, who had been somewhat unhappily involved in the exuberant planning of 1891. Saunders's 1894 design was a building in French Renaissance style, the main rectangle of the structure capped by a belfry, marked by round towers flanking the entrance, and extended into rounded bays at the ends. The concept was a departure from John Pike's design for the original building, but the plan seemed almost extravagantly spacious, and it was pleasing in its symmetry.[11]

Thus in 1894 work on the new building began, and on July 4 of that year, in Masonic ceremonies conducted before a crowd of university professors and students and community leaders, the cornerstone was laid. But the economic recession of the 1890s was now at its deepest, and the regents were thinking that they should not try to sell the old grounds until conditions improved.

All of this had happened in just forty years from Isaac Stevens's address to the 1854 territorial legislature to the construction of the new building of the new university of the new state of Washington. The building, when it was finished, would be called Denny Hall. In the cupola would be hung the "Denny bell" of 1862. The bell had been both symbol and proof of Seattle's life. It had tolled when the news of Lincoln's death reached Seattle, it had been rung when distinguished visitors came to town or when fog-blinded ships needed guiding into the Seattle harbor, and it would continue to ring through the years on important occasions. But in 1894, when the new cornerstone was laid, the wonder was that the founders were still there. Denny spoke, and so did Bagley. But it was Daniel Bagley, the old Methodist circuit rider, who recalled the victories, political and spiritual, of 1860–61. It was an emotional moment. Denny, born in 1822, had almost five years more to live, Bagley, born in 1818, more than ten. The tough, visionary, scheming old gentlemen had built a university and had lived to see it built again. Construction of the new building went forward into 1895. Classes began there in September.

CHAPTER 2

Years of Decision: 1895 to 1902

There was, doubtless, an unaccustomed stillness north of Seneca Street in the autumn of 1895. The university on the knoll had never been a locus of more bustle and clamor than is generated by a small rural school, but its site had been as much a park as a campus, a place to welcome distinguished visitors, a public place even in times of trouble, as when the city government was moved there for a short time after Seattle's great fire of 1889. Now the old site was not even a campus. The main building stood quietly in its familiar solemnity, and near it were the president's house and the dormitory and two later structures, one the clubhouse and museum of the Young Naturalists, a natural history group organized in 1885 with young Edmond Meany as its moving spirit, the other the somewhat ornate two-story frame Armory Building, on Union Street near Third Avenue, under lease to the First Regiment of the Washington National Guard. But the scene had been shifted. The university was elsewhere. There had been some mutterings about the overgrown state of the old campus and the dilapidated condition of the fence around it.

To the question of what would be done with the property there was not, for the moment, even the beginning of a search for an answer. The year 1895 was a busy one for the members of the current board of regents, not only a year of new beginnings for the university, but a legislative year and a year of search for a new president to succeed Thomas Gatch, who had asked to be relieved. Some of the regents were active in Olympia (as was, of course, Meany, now secretary of the board). The new president turned out to be Mark W. Harrington, former professor of astronomy at the University of Michigan and more recently chief of the U.S. Weather Bureau, who came at a time of euphoria about the university's prospects.[1]

The initiative with respect to the future of the old grounds rested with the regents, and the expectation was that the property would be sold. The acts of 1891 and 1893 had anticipated this. The quitclaim deeds of Denny, Lander, the Terry heirs, and the city of Seattle had satisfied the condition considered essential to a sale of the land, as a single tract or in lots or parcels, to provide funds for the new university. The deeds were explicit and so was the legislation.

The Denny deed, the key document, had stipulated that the state "shall cause to be duly passed by its State Legislature and approved by its Governor proper enactments" to authorize purchase of new lands for the university "within a distance of Six miles of the present so-called University Site . . . , said land to be forever used exclusively for State University purposes," and that "said exactments shall further authorize the State of Washington . . . to contract the sale of the lands comprising the present so-called University Site. . . . That said enactments shall authorize the sale of lands hereinbefore described in such parcels and for such prices as may be most advantageous to the interests of the said State University." The proceeds of the sale, the deeds said, "shall be used," first, to buy the new university lands; second, to erect the buildings and improve the new campus; and third, to provide funds, from the balance, "to be invested in such manner as the State Legislature may prescribe: the interest arising therefrom to be used in the support and maintenance of said University."[2]

In such terms Denny and others had phrased their quitclaim deeds. The act of 1893, after authorizing the governor to acquire the new university site, had laid out the ground rules thus: "Sec. 7. After the purchase of the lands . . . the board of regents may, by decision of six-eighths of their number,* duly ascertained by aye and nay vote, which shall be recorded in their minutes, proceed to sell the ten acres in the city of Seattle known as the 'university grounds,' which have been deeded to the state by A. A. Denny and others, which deeds are hereby accepted and made part of this act. Such sale shall be made at public auction only, and the said board of regents may sell the whole of said tract of ten acres or it may cause the same to be subdivided into lots and blocks, with streets and alleys conforming to the plan of the said city adjoining." The grounds were to remain "in the charge and under the direction" of the regents until the university was moved: "*Provided*, That the board of regents may from time to time as parts of the university grounds are sold, in the manner herein provided, authorize the purchasers to take possession of the lot or lots purchased or may lease all unsold portions under such restrictions as the board of regents may provide."[3]

The regents, in short, were in control. They were authorized—were, in fact, expected—to sell the old grounds. They might lease "unsold portions" at their discretion, this to facilitate the ultimate disposition of the whole property, but disposition was the goal. The state had acquired the new campus (of 355 acres rather than the 160 acres originally anticipated) and the act of 1893 had appropriated $150,000 for the new building (although the low bid, in a recession year, had been only $112,000). But the state's expenditures were in the nature of an advance against the funds expected when the old campus was sold.

The principal expectations had been met. The new campus had been acquired, the new building had been built, the university had been moved. All that remained was to sell the old site and apply the proceeds advantageously "to the interests of the said State University."

---

* By 1890 the membership of the board of regents had been increased from five to seven and the state superintendent of public instructions made an ex officio, or eighth, member. Legislation of 1897 limited the membership to seven appointees.

Yet for almost three years after 1895 a decision concerning the old grounds —any kind of basic policy decision—was a matter of no more than philosophical import. With Seattle still suffering through recession and no bidders for the property in sight, the regents scarcely could have been considering with any intensity the large issues a possible sale might raise. Certain housekeeping obligations continued, and the Armory was being used, not only by the National Guard but increasingly as an auditorium for public meetings. At the university itself, however, other developments were intruding. The year 1897 was a disappointing year for the university at the legislature, but that was only the beginning. Membership of the board of regents was drastically altered when the new Populist governor, John R. Rogers, appointed four new members, all from Seattle, and the university entered, but not for that reason, an unhappy time of internal turmoil. President Harrington departed in March 1897, and was succeeded by William Edwards, of the faculty, who in turn was succeeded in October by Charles Reeves, also drawn from the faculty as an interim head. The situation would not begin to be stabilized until Franklin Pierrepont Graves became president in 1898. Even then difficulties continued.[4]

Records of the regents tended to be exceedingly cryptic in those years. As far as the downtown tract is concerned, it is difficult to make even a reasonable guess about what any of the regents were thinking concerning the old site. It seems likely, however, that they shared a feeling that delaying a decision was the wisest course. They were aware of the earlier estimates of the probable future value of the property. They held their meetings in a city that obviously was growing and was ready to grow faster once the recession ended.* Growth would mean a better price when the grounds were, at last, disposed of.

The earlier estimates may have been optimistic, but they were positive and impressive. The special legislative committee of 1891 had reported that the tract was "estimated to be worth from $250,000 to $300,000 and can be sold for that sum." The Board of University Land and Building Commissioners had said in 1892:

This ten acre tract is the most valuable piece of property which the state possesses. It should not be sold for less than one-half million dollars ($500,000). It ought to be held until it brings from $750,000 to $1,000,000.

Had the appraisement been made during the monetary depression of 1891 and the property been sold as the act contemplates, it is doubtful whether we could have realized one hundred and fifty thousand dollars ($150,000) from it. No member of the board would give his consent to the making of such a sacrifice, even for the purpose of building a new university.

---

* It is not always clear in the record *where* in Seattle the regents were meeting. Some meetings were held on the new campus, certainly. But the regents also seem to have used more convenient facilities downtown. In November 1899, the regents authorized an expenditure of forty dollars "to fit up a room in the old University Building for Board meetings." Frequently executive committee and other meetings were held in the offices of the president or chairman. The time came when lessees of the old grounds were asked to set aside rooms for board use.

Being situated in the heart of the largest city in the state, no other land owned by the state will grow so rapidly in value. With a population of one hundred thousand in Seattle this tract will bring a full million dollars. This increase of population will be realized within the next five years.[5]

Awaiting fulfillment of such predictions, the regents could not but know the difficulties that might attend development of the property. How could such grounds and buildings be converted to some other use? At what cost? To what purpose? The questions were quite as important to the city of Seattle as to the university and the state. The late campus was not merely a vacant lot awaiting an entrepreneur with sufficient funds to put a building on it. It was not just an empty field at the edge of the city available for some nondescript use. The university tract was a huge ten acres of parklike land high above Seattle's developing commercial district, which was spreading irregularly northward above and below First and Second avenues from the vicinity of lower Yesler at the core of the old town. It was bounded on the south by Seneca Street, on the north by Union, and its west and east boundaries split the blocks above Third Avenue and below Sixth. The land area approximated four city blocks, but no streets were yet cut across the planted grounds. If the property was to be incorporated into the pattern of the city, the regents would have to see that, as the 1893 law provided, the tract was "subdivided into lots and blocks, with streets and alleys conforming to the plan of the said city adjoining." The view from the site was magnificent, and residences and shops were covering the surrounding areas as far as First Hill, to the east. But none of the university buildings, not even the Armory, was adaptable to commercial uses. If no commercial use was immediately possible, perhaps a public use might be devised. But what use, and who would pay?

Seattle was a small city in 1897. But then, as later, it seemed bigger than its statistics. In 1880, Seattle was a town of fewer than 4,000 inhabitants; by 1890, the year after the great fire, the population had increased more than tenfold, to 43,000, and by 1896 the estimate was 61,250, even though there had been a slight dip in population in 1894, when the recession hit bottom. Seattle had the elements for growth. As a prime port on the Northwest coast, it was drawing to its deep-water harbor shipping from all over the world. It was linked to other parts of the continent by three railroads, the Great Northern, the Northern Pacific, and the Canadian Pacific. By ship and by rail it was exporting lumber and the products of Washington's farms and fisheries. It had the beginnings of a strong ship-building industry. The Moran brothers, Peter and Robert, "founders and machinists," were operating a plant at West Yesler Way and Railroad Avenue, on the waterfront (Robert had already been mayor of Seattle in 1889), and of the Moran Brothers firm more would be heard later.

Seattle was still rough-cut. Its commercial buildings were far from imposing, its hotel facilities meager, its waterfront improvised, its hillsides unconquered. Most of its streets were either unpaved or planked, its sidewalks were board walkways. Yet there was a preparatory bustle about the place that even the recession had not quelled. The city with unpaved streets was proud of its trolley lines. Hillside tracts to the north and east, even as far out as the new university, were dotted with homes. And there were assembling in Seattle many of the men who would move the city through its transitional stage. Some were the "capitalists," the builders and developers coming west in a period of national expansion. Some were the lawyers and other professionals plunging into the activities of a new state. Some were simply men who found in Seattle the outlets for their special kinds of genius. One of these was R. H. Thomson, who, after graduating from Hanover College, Indiana, in 1877, went on to become Seattle's city engineer in 1882, and for the next thirty years was director-in-residence of the grading, scraping, sluicing, draining, and filling that was necessary to bring the Seattle terrain under control. Rough it was, and unfinished, but Seattle was not unfamiliar with the leaders and builders of the nation. President Benjamin Harrison had spoken from a stand on the university grounds in 1891. The railroad magnates, Henry Villard in the 1880s and James J. Hill in the 1890s and later, were old acquaintances. And for all the roughness, Seattle was developing an air, an élan. Already it had fostered the organizations and clubs that reflected, in Seattle's special environment of lumbering and trade and shipping and agriculture, its business and social structures—the Chamber of Commerce in 1882, the Rainier Club in 1888, the Country Club in 1890, the Yacht Club in 1892, and the Athletic Club in 1893.

Two events transformed Seattle. One was the discovery of gold in the North. The other was the start of the Spanish-American War. Gold was found in the Klondike in July 1897. Soon thereafter the steamer *Portland*, carrying what was said to be a ton of gold, was cheered down Puget Sound to a Seattle dock. Within ensuing months Seattle became a transshipment and outfitting point for the Alaska gold fields. Seattle banks (there were ten, including Dexter Horton and Company) were equipped to weigh out gold dust. Seattle became the home of the "Yukon sled," and one company made two thousand the first season. Others were making pack saddles, tents, boots, and all kinds of mining gear. The U.S. Assay Office, opened in 1898, was said to have handled more business in a month than most of the other offices handled in a year. (By 1908 the office had purchased gold dust valued at $156 million.) Steamers plied the route north to Cape Nome, Skagway. Dawson, St. Michael, and "Yukon River points." In 1899, some 296 ships departed Seattle for the north and more than 35,000 persons "went and came," as a newspaper reported, over the Alaska route that year. It was not strange that, on another level entirely, Seattle was the headquarters for the Alaska Geographical Society, which listed among its honorary officers David Starr Jordan, president of Leland Stanford Junior University, Rear Admiral George Dewey, Professor John Muir, Sir Clements Markham, president of the Royal Geographical Society, London, and Professor Angelo Heilprin, president of the

Philadelphia Geographical Society. President Graves of the University of Washington was a vice-president.[6]

The gold strike occurred as Seattle was hoping to take advantage of new trade opportunities opening in the Orient and the central and western Pacific. The coming of the Spanish-American War brought change to the Pacific, but it also underlined Seattle's pivotal position in the region. The state of Washington mobilized twelve National Guard companies for the war, and by September 1898 the troops were on their way to the Philippines, where they went almost immediately into action. But the American flag had already been raised in Hawaii in the annexation of August 1898, and within a month five steam and sailing vessels had left Seattle for Honolulu with lumber, produce, and manufactured goods. The ships formed the vanguard of a fleet that extended Seattle's trade connections to Honolulu, Manila, and Tokyo.

The Seattle Chamber of Commerce published in 1898 a small booklet, *A Few Facts About Seattle, the Queen City of the Pacific,* in which certain community leaders—among them Mayor T. J. Humes, Edmond Meany, and J. W. Clise, a vice-president of the Chamber and manager of the Clise Investment Company—traced the outlines of Seattle's development. One of the authors was a J. A. Moore, whose leading article, "Reasons Why," presented fifteen reasons for Seattle's inevitable growth. Among the advertisements in the booklet was a full-page statement by the Moore Investment Company, 112 Columbia Street, quoting a number of well-known figures who agreed that Seattle had a splendid future: Jay Cooke, "Having been an interested spectator in the growth of cities, I can assure you that Seattle is to be one of the largest in the United States"; Andrew Carnegie, "That city is destined to be one of the great commercial centers in the country. If I were to go West I would go straight to Seattle." The J. A. Moore who had composed the article and the advertisement was James A. Moore, whose talent for real estate development would leave a permanent imprint on the city and the state and affect directly the history of the old university grounds.[7]

As 1898 gave way to 1899, Seattle lost Arthur Denny, who died on January 9, seventy-six years after his birth in Indiana. His death must have inspired in the city a feeling that the old century was already ended, for Seattle was pressing toward the new.

Time and circumstances were pressing, too, for a decision by the university regents on the future of the old campus, and two kinds of developments, slowly shaping, would soon converge to ignite the process. One was the evolution of legislation affecting the management of lands granted the territory and the state over the years. The position of the regents in relation to this would have to be clarified. The other was the emergence, through the mysterious workings of political appointment, of boards of regents that began to view the old grounds as a perpetual endowment and were disposed to explore the advantages to the university therein.

As for the legislation, the state had passed in 1893, 1895, and 1897 certain "land commissioners' acts" directed specifically at bringing order to the management of public lands. The first act, passed on March 15, 1893, had created a Board of State Land Commissioners having "full supervision and control" of all lands acquired for educational and other purposes and classifying these as granted lands, tide lands, shore lands, harbor lines and areas, and so on. Later acts of 1895 and 1897 had refined somewhat, but had not substantially altered, the powers of the commissioners to select, survey, inventory, and manage the thousands of acres under the control of the state—including not only what was left of the original 46,000 acres granted the territory for university purposes (by then about 3,000 acres) but also more than 100,000 acres granted subsequently for support of educational, charitable, and penal institutions. The legislation was necessary. Some such form of management was necessary. But it occurred to no one, then, that under such legislation the regents' right to control the old university site might become an issue.

As for the regents, who were they in 1899? They were Alden J. Blethen, John P. Hoyt, George H. King, and Richard Winsor, of Seattle; Charles M. Easterday, of Tacoma; Lincoln D. Godshall, of Everett; and James Z. Moore, of Spokane. To later generations the names may have no familiarity at all, but the bearers represented, in the main, something of a second wave of professional and political leadership in Washington. They differed in background—all of them had come west from other states—as they differed in experience and political leaning, and they were capable of voting quite independently on questions of university policy, as was demonstrated in their approaches to some of the issues troubling the university. But on the matter of the tract, their philosophical differences are not readily discernible in the record. They were knowledgeable men—one a newspaper editor, five of them lawyers, and two of the lawyers judges who had performed important services in the organization of the state.

The editor was Blethen, of the Seattle *Times,* and he had come to Seattle only in 1896. He was a native of Maine, a graduate of Wesleyan and Bowdoin, and early in his career he had been the principal of a private school and a member of the Maine bar. Not until 1880, when he was thirty-five, had he entered newspaper work as editor of the Kansas City, Missouri, *Journal,* but by 1884 he had moved to Minneapolis as part owner, editor, and manager of two newspapers, the *Tribune* and the *Journal,* and organized a bank, the New England Bank of Minneapolis. When fire destroyed the *Tribune* building, he built again, but then the bank was wiped out in the panic of 1893. So Blethen had moved on to Seattle to buy the *Times,* a small evening paper, to plunge into the political wars of 1896 (as a friend of William Jennings Bryan), and to begin to pay back—although it took years—the depositors of his failed bank.[8]

The judges were Hoyt and Moore, one from Ohio, the other from Kentucky, each full of experience he had begun to acquire long before reaching Washington Territory. Hoyt, born in 1841, served with Ohio regiments in the Civil War before getting a law degree in 1867 and moving to Michigan to set up a law practice and enter politics. By 1874 his political activities had made him speaker of the Michigan house of representatives and, without a doubt, a young man to watch. He was being watched, in fact, by the Grant administration, and by the time Hoyt had finished his term as speaker he was about to begin a most unusual career in the West. In 1876, President Grant, soon to leave office, appointed Hoyt secretary of Arizona Territory. The next year President Hayes made him governor of Arizona Territory and, in 1878, sent him north as governor of Idaho Territory. What then happened has not happened often in politics. Hoyt went to Idaho, but there he became convinced that the man he was to replace was being unjustly removed. He not only refused the office but made the long trip to Washington, D.C., to persuade Hayes to reinstate the former governor. Hayes was persuaded, apparently, and soon thereafter, in 1879, Hoyt, not yet forty years old, was sent to Washington Territory as a justice of the supreme court. In Washington—and in Seattle—he would live the rest of his life. He remained with the territorial supreme court until 1887, when he became manager of the Dexter Horton Bank in Seattle and, with Arthur Denny, opened the Denny and Hoyt Addition to the city, later the Fremont Addition. He was a King County delegate to the state constitutional convention of 1889 and was elected its president. When the state was born, he became a justice of the first state supreme court. He had left the bench only shortly before becoming a regent of the university.[9]

James Z. Moore had come to Washington Territory in 1886 and had set up a law office in Spokane when it was still called Spokane Falls. Although a Kentuckian, he had worked his way through Miami University in Ohio and, somehow, had gone on to Harvard Law School. He was admitted to the Ohio bar in 1868 and, as a lawyer active in politics, was a member of the Chicago convention that nominated James G. Blaine for president in 1884. No one knows, apparently, how he happened to move west, but he was a natural leader, as his contemporaries testified, a man of medium height, mustached, and a speaker of considerable presence. He was a newcomer to the territory and just forty-four years old when he went to Olympia as a member of the constitutional convention of 1889, "one of the leading members," an Olympia newspaper said, "as he is one of the ablest and most influential. And of his style, "he always commands the interest and attention of the audience, frequently electrifying them and inspiring them by his eloquence." At Olympia he had worked, undoubtedly, with Hoyt.[10]

Of Easterday, Godshall, and King less is known. The first was a Tacoma attorney who had served in the state senate and who had been named to the board by Governor Rogers, in 1897, with Hoyt and Winsor. Godshall, of Everett, would serve as a regent only two years, from 1898 to 1900, but in that time—when the Alaska gold rush and concurrent developments in Washington itself were stirring new interest in mining—Godshall presented to the regents the resolution by which the university's College of Mechanical and Mining Engineering became the College of Mining and Metallurgy, and Godshall also conducted personally in the college, with the thanks of the regents, a series of lectures on "Metallurgy, Assaying, and Analytical Chemistry." King was a fifty-three-year-old lawyer who had been practicing in Seattle since 1890 and who had come to the board in 1898 to succeed another Rogers appointee, S. M. Allen.[11]

Richard Winsor, at sixty, was the oldest of the seven regents of 1899. He was born in Ontario in 1839, but by 1856 he was in Michigan, where he studied law and went into politics more than a decade before Hoyt arrived there. In the Civil War years he was in the Michigan legislature, elected to his first term in 1862 as the legislature's youngest member. By 1867 he had been admitted to the Michigan bar, and for a number of years thereafter he practiced law, was elected prosecuting attorney, and served in the Michigan senate from 1868 to 1882. In 1889, at age fifty, he moved to Seattle, apparently following one of his sons, Amos, who had established a contracting business in the city in 1886. In any case, Winsor reached Seattle just before the fire, and his law library was said to have been one of the few to escape the flames. Winsor was perpetually active in politics, first as a Republican, then as a Populist, finally as a Socialist. In his Populist period, he was mentioned as possible candidate for the U. S. Senate. For nine years he was a member of the Seattle School Board, and he had been a member of the committee that framed the charter of the city of Seattle.[12]

These men—Blethen, Hoyt, King, Winsor, Moore, Easterday, Godshall— were the regents of 1899. They were men of experience and substance (their meetings were quarterly, with executive committee meetings in between), members of a body that would seem better prepared than most to decide what, in law and equity, should be done with the university's ten-acre property. Before the year was out the process of decision began.

Almost four years after the university's move the regents still had no offers for purchase of bits or pieces of the old grounds in the manner anticipated by the legislation. Seattle's expansion was evident everywhere, but no capitalists or enterprising developers had come forward with proposals for buying and improving parts of the property. In midyear, however, a proposal came— a proposal for the leasing of the whole tract—and this was a completely new thought. No one to that time had suggested leasing all of the ten acres, and the regents must have been both intrigued and puzzled. For the suggestion raised, of course, an entirely new set of considerations.

The suggestion came from a J. C. Levold, who was not, on the evidence, a capitalist. It must be presumed that he was simply a man with an idea. Levold submitted to the regents a "petition for renting the old University grounds for 20 years." The petition was discussed first by the executive committee—Winsor, Hoyt, and King—on July 25, 1899, and referred to the chairman of the committee on buildings and grounds, who was, probably, Blethen. The question was put before the whole board at the regular quarterly meeting on August 7, when the committee was asked to report at the next meeting "on the advisability of leasing."[13]

Leasing was no novelty. For years the regents had flirted with, or dabbled in, leasing and renting. In March 1884 the board had received a proposition from Seattle promoters who wanted to lease "certain portions of the grounds . . . with a view to erecting tenement houses thereon." In a year of pitifully small university appropriations, the regents toyed with this idea (by "tenement houses" only some form of multiple housing certainly was meant), and published a proposal to lease a north section of the tract, "the proceeds of such to be applied toward support of the University." Three responses were received, all rejected, and that idea died. The following year the board leased to the Young Naturalists for twenty-five years—at one dollar a year—the site for the clubhouse that would, after all, serve a function related to education. By 1888, the regents had also leased to the National Guard—for ten years, and also at one dollar a year, initially—a plot 80 by 180 feet at the northwest corner of the grounds. But that was when students were present. By 1899 there were none, although soon the university's new Law School, which had been established in May under the direction of John T. Condon, was housed on the old campus because there was no room on the new.[14]

As for renting, the regents had accumulated after 1895 some incidental experience by authorizing short-term arrangements with the Seattle Public Library and the Seattle Board of Education, but these arrangements had been informal and marginal, the returns modest. There were hints that the regents were not sure of their authority. The act of 1893 had given them the right to lease "unsold portions" of the grounds, this in the context of anticipated sale. In 1897 they asked an attorney general's opinion about renting—because funds were needed to replace a sidewalk on the campus. On September 16 they reported a response from Thomas W. Vance, who said that the board of regents "clearly [is] within its right and authority in collecting rent from the old University property and in applying it to make repairs as the necessity of the case may require." A subsequent report of income from the old building, covering the period from September 1897 to June 1899, showed receipts of $1,650, disbursements of $1,146.65, a net of $503.35.[15]

Thus neither leasing nor renting was a new thing, but leasing had been of an educational or public service nature and renting had been noncommittal, a way of keeping the property in condition and in appropriate use until it could be sold at a proper price. Now someone named Levold was proposing to lease all of the tract for twenty years. It is impossible to tell from the record just what the regents were thinking in the late summer and autumn of 1899, but long-term leasing of the whole ten-acre tract unquestionably was being seriously examined.

There were questions to be asked and weighed. Who was Levold? What were his plans for developing the property and his guarantee of performance? What income could accrue to the university over a span of twenty years? What were the regents' powers with regard to long-term leasing? What would be the impact on a future sale of the property?

As for the Levold petition of 1899, it was discussed—no more—and held in suspense. Two actions of the regents suggest, however, that the leasing idea was taking hold. On August 7, at the meeting at which the Levold petition was first discussed by the full board, the regents granted to the Armory Association permission to build an annex to the Armory "on condition that the building becomes the property of the state on the first of January, 1901." At that moment the regents still seemed willing to accept incidental developments on the tract. But in September the regents offered the use of the old main building to the Seattle Board of Education and then, four days later, at a special meeting of the executive committee, withdrew the offer. Something had happened to cause the regents to eschew long-term commitments. In the autumn of 1899 the regents were making up their minds.[16]

What the regents were deciding to do was to offer the whole tract for lease. They had accepted the Levold idea without accepting his proposal, for they felt obliged to open the leasing terms to public bidding. They were —and they could not have failed to realize it—going off on a course of their own. On December 27, 1899, the regents authorized publication of advertisements in two Seattle papers, the *Times* and the *Post-Intelligencer*—four weekly insertions in each newspaper—but the regents' action had a singular aspect. The act of 1893 had specified that "no sale of any part" of the tract should be made until the board had given notice "by publication for four successive weeks" in one daily newspaper in each of six communities—Walla Walla, Olympia, Port Townsend, Whatcom (Bellingham), Tacoma, and Seattle. The regents chose to advertise not in six newspapers but in two, and those in Seattle only.* In advertising the tract for lease rather than sale they seemingly did not feel bound by the 1893 law.[17]

The advertisements that appeared were two-inch legal notices published in the two newspapers in the four weeks of January 1900, over the signature of Clarke (*sic*) Davis, "Clerk to the Board of Regents," Clark Davis, a former regent himself, having become registrar of the university. The advertisement declared:

THE Board of Regents of the University of Washington will receive sealed proposals for leasing for a term of years the old university site, situated between Seneca and Union Street [*sic*], in the city of Seattle, Washington. Proposals must state fully the terms and conditions of the proposed lease, and must be indorsed "Proposal to Lease Old University Site," and be delivered to the undersigned on or before noon of

---

* The act of 1891 had required advertisements for sale of the property on an even larger scale. Such advertisements were to be placed for four successive weeks "in one paper in Spokane Falls, one in Walla Walla, one in Olympia, one in Port Townsend, one in Whatcom, two in Tacoma, and two in Seattle."

Saturday, February 4, 1900. All proposals must be accompanied by a certified check on some bank in Seattle for $500, same to be forfeited to the state if the bidder fails to enter into lease if awarded to him. The Board of Regents reserves the right to reject any and all proposals.[18]

The proposals were opened at the regents' regular quarterly meeting of February 14, 1900. Two proposals had been received, one from J. C. Levold, still in the game, and the other from James A. Moore, of the Moore Investment Company, 112 Columbia Street, the Moore whose "Reasons Why" of 1898 had stated the case for the "Queen City of the Pacific." Both bids were rejected, Levold's on its merits and Moore's because, presumably, it had not been received in time. The regents' first effort to lease the old university site had come to nothing. The matter might have ended there, but it did not. Certain aspects of the effort are noteworthy.[19]

With these brief notices in the Seattle *Times* and *Post-Intelligencer* the university regents first offered the old campus for lease in January 1900

THE Board of Regents of the University. of Washington will receive sealed proposals for leasing for a term of years the old university site, situated between Seneca and Union Street, in the City of Seattle, Washington. Proposals must state fully the terms and conditions of the proposed lease, and must be indorsed "Proposal to Lease Old University Site," and be delivered to the undersigned on or before noon of Saturday, February 3, 1900. All proposals must be accompanied by a certified check on some bank in Seattle for $500, same to be forfeited to the state if the bidder fails to enter into lease if awarded to him. The Board of Regents reserve the right to reject any and all proposals.   CLARKE DAVIS, Clerk to Board of Regents, University of Washington, Seattle, Wash.

In advertising the property the regents not only had ignored the mechanics set out in the 1893 law but they had announced publicly their willingness to lease and thus postpone for a period of years the sale that had been anticipated for almost a decade. They had tried for size a long-term policy in which a sale of the tract was not, as in the 1893 law, a specific goal. In considering a long-term lease they had been agreeable to an action which, if consummated, would put before them, and before their successors for years, entirely new questions in the realm of public accountability. They had opened, tentatively, a door that would not be closed again. Yet there was not then, apparently, a public reaction of any kind—a question in the legislature, a newspaper editorial of praise or inquiry. The old campus had been offered for lease and two proposals rejected.

Levold undoubtedly had submitted a proposal—a lease for twenty years—much like his petition of July 1899. The proposal, whatever its terms, nevertheless was discussed at length by the regents, in a long meeting lasting into the evening, before it was rejected and the certified check that accompanied it returned. Moore's proposal was returned unopened because of its lateness, although the regents, who seemed at one point ready to consider it anyway, must have done so with regret.*

The regents unquestionably knew Moore, who was an established figure in Seattle and a man whose confidence in the city's prospects was of missionary quality. Moore was, in fact, even then deeply engaged in development and building projects near both the old campus and the new. The university scarcely had moved to its new site before Moore was platting a University Heights section, west of the projected campus, and soon he would lay out University Park, to the north. In 1900, he was building at Fourth Avenue and Madison Street, within sight of the old grounds, a $250,000 apartment house, the Lincoln, described as "the first and finest apartment house west of Chicago." These were projects among many, and if Moore was late with his proposal he must have been uncharacteristically casual in his approach to an opportunity large enough to engage his interest. For Moore was a man who could see opportunities where others saw only difficulties. In the history of the university grounds, as in any chronicle of Seattle, Moore deserves more than passing attention.

James A. Moore had been in Seattle since 1886 or 1887. A native of Nova Scotia, born there in 1861, and of a family that moved there from Ireland in 1650, Moore was a builder and developer of daring and imagination, imbued by a conviction that Seattle was a promised land. He had been convinced of Seattle's future growth before the growth was fairly begun. He thought of Seattle land—any land—as a rare investment. He was not, however, a build-and-run promoter. He was well connected with financiers in Boston and elsewhere in the East. He meant to stay in Seattle, and he meant to build well.

Moore had made it on his own. Photographs of him at the turn of the century, when he was about forty, are of a handsome, well-turned-out man, with full mustache, the eyes confident. Yet Moore's education apparently had been limited to whatever public school instruction was available in Nova Scotia before 1880, and for some years after leaving high school he had worked in the shipping business operated by his father. Then the broke out of the family business and started for the American West, his route obscure, but one of the stops Denver, where in 1885 he married Eugenie Genevieve Jones. By 1889, the year of the Seattle fire, Moore had a real estate office in what was called the Safe Deposit Building on Front Street (later First Avenue) and a residence at Front and Stewart. He had already platted a Broadway Addition to Port Townsend, where certain iron smelting operations were blossoming.

---

* According to the regents' minutes of February 14, 1900, Moore had asked that his bid be returned unopened if the board decided not to consider it. Blethen nevertheless moved that Moore's bid be considered as if it had been received in time, and King, who was president, called Hoyt to the chair so that he could second Blethen's motion. There was a long discussion before the roll call, but the motion lost. Only Blethen and Godshall voted aye; Winsor, Hoyt, and King—who had seconded the motion—voted nay.

In 1890 his office was at 108 Columbia Street and from there he was developing Seattle's Latona Addition as "general agent, Latona Town Co." Throughout the 1890s he built and prospered, organizing by turn the Latona Land and Mortgage Company, the Seattle Rent and Collection Company, the Moore Investment and Mortgage Company, the Rainier Beach Improvement Company, and, finally, the Moore Investment Company. He developed the Brooklyn, Fremont, and Edgewater additions, and with two partners he had organized the Lake Union Transportation Company, which operated small steamers to these additions from the north terminus of Seattle's horse-car trolley system. Yet if any of this suggests that Moore was merely a quick-dollar operator, no such thought is detectable in any of the contemporary references to him or to his career. The testimony, in newspaper accounts as well as in the more flattering citations of the community histories, is that Moore was a man busy both in church activities and community affairs, an engaging man, with a sense of humor, well liked, a contributor to good causes. He and Eugenie were members of the Plymouth Congregational Church, and Moore was a member of the board of trustees and would be its chairman. As for his personal residences, he had moved, between 1890 and 1900, from Front and Stewart, to Third Avenue and Lenora (Mayor Robert Moran lived near Second and Lenora), to 1009 Marion, to 212 Olympia Place, below Queen Anne Hill, the not-yet-developed eminence north and west of the city. When the new apartment, the Lincoln, was finished, Moore and Eugenie moved into it in 1901. And by 1901 Moore was laying out that prime residential addition high on the ridge separating Puget Sound and Lake Washington, with views of the waters west and east. The new area he had named Capitol Hill—not, as has been thought, because it once might have been the site of the state's capitol, but simply because of Moore's memory of Capitol Hill in Denver.[20]

This was the Moore whose proposal to lease the old grounds was returned as not on time. Yet it was J. C. Levold who had first proposed a lease—who had, in fact, first interested the regents in such a possibility—and who actually became, within a few months, the first lessee of the old grounds. What did the regents know of him?

Whatever the regents knew, Levold left few traces. The record is puzzling, and tantalizing. Of all those associated in some way with the tract and the leasing of it, Levold is the least known. It would be supposed that a man with the imagination to initiate and conduct negotiations for a property so near the center of Seattle would have had some fixed address, some standing in the Seattle community or in another, some recognized business connections, some ready identification, if only for the newspapers. No such clues appear. In the regents' records Levold, like Moore, is mentioned only by name, but even the newspaper accounts of later transactions identify Levold only as a man representing interests in Portland, Oregon. A Seattle story published later by a Portland newspaper refers to "J. C. Levold, of Portland," yet Levold's name is not found in the *Portland City Directory* of that time. A J. C. Levold is listed six times in Seattle directories (three times as a real estate salesman, once as a bookkeeper, once as a broker, once as a promoter), no entry before 1900. No other reference is found in Seattle libraries and none in the vital statistics records of King County. Yet in his dealings with the board of regents Levold was represented by Seattle attorneys of considerable stature, one of whom would soon himself become a regent and, in time, a distinguished member of the bar. And before his involvement with the tract was ended, Levold would become, briefly, the associate of some of Seattle's prominent citizens in a final effort to put together a corporation that could develop the property. Levold must have been able to present acceptable credentials. Still, he remains a shadow.

Only one fragment of a record provides a faint clue to the manner in which Levold approached his initial petition of 1899. In an abstract of title to the university tract, prepared in 1921, is a notation of an agreement signed June 24, 1899, by Levold and two others wherein Levold presumably would undertake to obtain a lease to the ten-acre site, the partners then to form a corporation to put buildings on the land. Levold, according to this account, would be paid $50 on signing the agreement, $100 ten days later, and, upon the signing of the lease, another payment of $200 plus $500 for procuring a bond to the state for payment of three months' rent. In forming the corporation to erect the buildings, Levold and one of the partners would divide fourteen-sixteenths of the stock, the third partner holding two-sixteenths. In June 1900, after Levold had obtained, briefly, a leasehold, one of the partners sued Levold and the other partner, asking that the lease be declared held in trust for all three. The suit was dropped in December 1900, by which time Levold apparently was thinking of moving toward the lease from another direction.[21]

Such evidence is scant and inconclusive. There is the suggestion, however, that Levold's original petition to the regents grew out of an agreement in which the terms were essentially trifling and the participants, finally, quarrelsome. Can it be that such an action moved the university's board of regents to consider for the first time the prospect of a long-term lease of the ten-acre tract? Too little is certain. But Levold persisted. The regents had not heard the last of him.

As the new century began, the regents, whose first attempt to lease the old grounds had come to nothing, would try again—and again. They would award a lease—to Levold—and then cancel it for noncompliance. They would worry about their power to lease. They would sell to the U.S. government a tiny fraction of the land. They would return to leasing buildings on the property. They would be sued—by Levold. They would test in the courts their right to lease. They would lease, again, all of the property except for the fraction that had been sold. In time they would lease to James A. Moore, but even that would not be the end.

It is a complicated story, the details somewhat obscure. Moore fades from the narrative for a time after 1900, and it is Levold with whom the regents are repeatedly concerned, directly or in connection with other developments, until the course is set, finally, for almost half a century.

The Levold and Moore proposals were rejected in February 1900. On March 14 the board authorized the president and secretary—George King was president, Davis the secretary—to advertise for new proposals "in the Seattle Evening *Times*, the *Seattle Post-Intelligencer*, the *Tacoma Review*, and the *Spokane Review*." The notices now were not confined to Seattle, but they still failed to meet the requirements of the 1893 law. This time, however, the conditions for the leasing were somewhat more specific. A lease was to be for thirty years, and certain demands were made for space, these of a somewhat peculiar kind. The notice was published in ten consecutive issues of the newspapers—in the *Post-Intelligencer* from March 18 to 27—and the text announced:

PROPOSALS FOR LEASE—The Board of Regents of the University of Washington will receive sealed proposals up to noon of Wednesday, April 4, 1900, for leasing for a term of thirty (30) years the tract known as the Old University site, in Seattle, King County, Wash. The proposals must state the amount of rent to be paid for each period of five (5) years during said term, and agree that the lessee, if awarded the lease, will furnish a bond of $20,000 from a surety company satisfactory to the Board of Regents, for faithful performance of the conditions of the lease.

The term thus was fixed at thirty years, the rentals at intervals of five years. The requirements were as follows:

The lessee must also agree to furnish the university free of charge during said term the following: Two (2) rooms at least forty feet square, two (2) rooms at least fifteen feet square, one (1) room at least twenty feet square, and two sets of toilet rooms and cloak rooms, one each for male and female students. Said rooms need not necessarily be square in shape, provided the area of each room equals that of a square room as above given. Said rooms must be furnished with artificial heat free of charge and must not be higher than the second story of any building, unless the building is furnished with competent elevator service daily, except Sundays, between 8 A.M. and 8 P.M. Said rooms must be well lighted with a direct light from the outside.

Each proposal was to be accompanied by a certified check for $500 to assure performance. The regents reserved the right to reject all bids. The proposals were to be delivered to the president of the board at 53 Boston Block, which was King's office.

The notice reflected a considerable refinement of the regents' thinking since the abortive effort of little more than a month earlier. The lease term was established. A $20,000 bond was required. In asking free rooms and related facilities for thirty years the regents were thinking, as soon became apparent, of future housing for the new Law School, although a requirement that might confine the Law School to five rooms for thirty years seems, in hindsight, less than realistic. In any event, this leasing effort also ended in frustration.

The regents held a special meeting on April 11, 1900, to open the proposals.

Again there were two, one from Levold, the other from Harry Krutz, of Seattle. Krutz was a man who had come from New York with his brother, Thomas, to organize at Walla Walla the first mortgage loan business in the state, the Washington Loan and Trust Company. Krutz had been in Seattle only since 1897, but he had extensive real estate and other holdings in Eastern Washington and he was considered one of the state's leading financiers. Levold, nevertheless, was the winning bidder. The brief minutes of the April 11 meeting report that the proposals were discussed at length in the afternoon, when representatives of the Seattle City Council also appeared to propose a ten-year lease of the tract for a city park. It was Blethen who moved, Moore seconding, that the Levold proposal be accepted, but the meeting was adjourned at 5 P.M. for additional discussion later. When the board reconvened at 7:30 P.M., Levold's bid was unanimously accepted.[22] After three tries, Levold was the lessee. The arrangement did not last, but there was a moment, at least, of congratulation.

When J. C. Levold, a "Seattle broker," became the first lessee of the old university campus, this headline appeared in the *Post-Intelligencer* of April 13, 1900

The report of the regents' action appeared in the *Post-Intelligencer* of April 13, 1900, under the heading, "LEASED FOR THIRTY YEARS; Board of Regents Accept the Offer Made by J. C. Levold." The story identified Levold as a Seattle broker who said he represented "Portland capitalists, who are prepared to improve the grounds at a cost of upwards of $650,000." Rents for the thirty years would be, in the aggregate, $162,000. Levold, the story said, had shown the regents a "schedule of plans of the buildings he proposed to erect, together with a sketch of the grounds laid out with a park in the center, which he proposes to make part of the improvements." Provision was to be made for erection of "three or more substantial brick and stone apartment houses and store buildings on Union Street, and a number of frame residences." All buildings were to become the property of the state at the end of the thirty-year period. None was to cost less than $3,500; and none was to be leased "for a saloon or manufacturing site." Space was to be provided for regents' meetings and for the Law School, with elevators to rooms above the second floor. The National Guard was to have continued use of the Armory for five years at an annual rental of $350. A $20,000 performance bond was guaranteed.

The regents' action was public knowledge now and there seemed at the moment no discernible disposition in any quarter to quibble or criticize. The news report was appropriately felicitous in tone. The difficulty that developed was one that the regents probably could not have foreseen—unless, as experienced public servants, they might have guessed that Levold was, as is likely, a man undertaking a project that was too big for him. Levold paid his $500 deposit, but failed, so the regents said, to post his $20,000 performance bond. On June 25, the regents notified him that his lease agreement would be terminated unless he completed his contract by July 10. That is what occurred. The lease was canceled. The agreement, entered so auspiciously, was ended. The subsequent quarrel would go on for years.[23]

Whatever the regents' feelings about the Levold development—and disappointment must have been one—it seems suddenly to have occurred to them, that summer of 1900, that they needed to be certain of their right to lease. They had tried two times, but now they began to appear unsure.

On August 13, Hoyt introduced a resolution, seconded by Blethen and unanimously adopted, that "*Whereas*, it is deemed necessary to determine whether or not the Board of Regents have the power and authority to lease the property known as the 'Old University Site'," King, who had offered to do so, was authorized to institute a test case in the courts, "without expense to this Board except the necessary disbursements." No such suit was brought, then or later, yet board actions in the following months continued to show a somewhat belated uncertainty. On August 24 the board approved another resolution conveying "to the Armory Association such right of possession to the ground now occupied by the Armory Building *as we have a right to convey*, from year to year at an annual rental of $250.00 per annum" (emphasis added). Early in 1901 the board again discussed the possible use of the property by the City Library, and on March 25 the City Library Commission was exploring with the regents the purchase of the tract for the library "if the Regents have power to sell."[24]

It is possible only to guess at the reason for the regents' new doubts about their power to lease or even to sell. But a guess is possible. Early in 1899, Robert Bridges, then a member of the Board of State Land Commissioners, had raised a question about the legality of the university's title to the new site on Lake Washington. Bridges claimed, according to a contemporary newspaper account, that the state—through the board of regents, presumably—was in default on the payment of the remaining principal and interest on the purchase of land for the new campus. Bridges's inquiry was somewhat strange and the question was resolved somehow. But it appears, further, that when news of the Levold lease was published, Bridges wrote a letter to the regents in which he denied their right to make any lease to the ten-acre tract. Such a letter from a land commissioner would, not unreasonably, have occasioned some rethinking by members of the board.[25]

Doubts had to be resolved, and they would be. But the board of regents was in for two years of litigation and struggle with tract problems. The chain of events is an intriguing one. First, the regents were respondents in a legal action, *Callvert* v. *Winsor*, initiated by the state attorney general at the regents' own request to test whether the state land commissioners, rather than the regents, had the power to dispose of the old university grounds.[26] Second, having won the test case, their right to sell confirmed, the regents sold a corner of the tract to the U.S. government as part of a site for a new Seattle post office. Third, the regents were sued by J. C. Levold, who asked the court to require the regents to give him the thirty-year lease denied him in 1900. Fourth, the regents leased the tract, less the post office fraction, to a new corporation in which Levold again appears to have been a stockholder and mainspring, because the granting of the lease involved dismissal of Levold's suit.

The *Callvert* v. *Winsor* case was a milestone. Whether or not the Bridges letter had stirred doubts about the regents' power to lease, it nevertheless was necessary to get a determination of the board's power to sell, for opportunities for sale were arising. In February and March 1901, the city was hoping to get Carnegie funds for the City Library and was looking seriously for a library site. It is not clear when the federal government began its search for the post office site, but on April 11, 1901, the regents' executive committee met with Blethen at his *Times* office to consider offering to the government a plot of ground 240 by 256 feet, a plot of the size the government was seeking. But nothing could happen until the regents knew where they stood. Only a court test could decide the power of the regents to manage the property at all.[27]

Callvert v. *Winsor* was filed in King County Superior Court in the spring of 1901 by W. B. Stratton, attorney general, on behalf of S. A. Callvert, as commissioner of public lands, the action naming Winsor, president of the board, and his fellow regents.* The issue, simpy stated, was this: did the legislature's "land commissioners' act" of 1897, which repealed and superseded the acts of 1893 and 1895, remove from the regents the power to sell that had been given them by the university act of March 14, 1893? On July 15, 1901, Judge G. Meade Emory ruled for the regents on demurrer, declaring that they had full power to sell or lease. Stratton appealed immediately to the State Supreme Court, where the regents were represented by three of their number, Winsor, Hoyt, and King, the latter a partner, with Harry R. Clise, in the law firm of Clise and King. On November 27, 1901, in an opinion read by Justice White, his associates concurring, the ruling of the lower court was affirmed.[28]

---

* The name of the commissioner frequently appears as "Calvert," certainly a more usual spelling. The name is used here as it appears in the *Washington Reports*.

The Supreme Court's opinion incorporated a long and detailed review of the origins of the university site and the legislation affecting it, from the acts of 1861 and the original gift of the ten acres through the quitclaim deeds of the donors in 1891 to the "land commissioners' act" of 1897. The court examined the question whether land given by private persons to the territory or state, as in the Denny-Terry-Lander gift, could be considered "granted land" within the meaning of the acts giving the commissioners their power over land grants by the United States for public institutions and common schools. The court decided that the private donation was not so included. It examined whether the act of 1897, in repealing the "commissioners' acts" of 1893 and 1895, also had repealed the university act of March 14, 1893, and decided that it had not, either by specific reference or by implication. The court, having reviewed the legislation, the terms of the gifts and the deeds, and the pleadings, found the regents' power unimpaired.

By September 1901, even before the Supreme Court's ruling in *Callvert*, the regents were ready to move on the post office proposition. In June they had leased a part of the old main building to the City Library for one year at $150 a month. The Law School still used the building (it would do so until 1903), but the library use was compatible and the leasing may have been simply an effort to help the library pending the outcome of the legal test. But when the regents met in Seattle on September 20, they were ready to sell a bit of the university grounds to the government, and all members of the board were present—Hoyt, now president, Blethen, Easterday, King, Moore, Winsor, and James E. Bell, a new member. Bell, who had come to the board to succeed Godshall, was a pioneer lumberman, recently mayor of Everett, and president of the Bell-Nelson Mill Company there.

There had been preliminary exploration of the post office requirement, undoubtedly, after the executive committee had discussed it on April 11 in Blethen's office. The board had, in fact, considered offering for $200,000 a block of land on Union Street, between Fourth and Fifth avenues, large enough to meet the government's needs, and this would have removed from the tract at its north edge a piece of land of almost one and a half acres. But the government had apparently determined to place the federal building at Third Avenue and Union Street, some six blocks north of the post office then situated at Second and Columbia, and at Third and Union the government's representatives were exploring the purchase of property. The site was at the northwest corner of the campus, where the west boundary divided the block above Third Avenue, and the regents thus were having to decide to sell a much smaller strip of land—64 feet on Union Street by 240 feet along the northwest edge of the tract, about one-third of an acre—to complete the government's acquisition of the corner. That strip of land they sold. The price was $25,000.[29]

The proceedings of the sale were set out in the deed by which the land was conveyed on January 10, 1902, from the state of Washington to the Seattle real estate firm of Crawford and Conover, which on the following day conveyed the university land, as part of the larger post office site, to the federal government. When the board met on September 20, six of the seven regents voted for the sale, only Easterday voting against. Three appraisers were then appointed as prescribed by law—one by the regents, one by the mayor of Seattle, and one by the governor of the state, Henry McBride. The appraisers reported the value of the property, less improvements, at $22,000. The regents set the sale for October 20, 1901, and advertised—this time—for four successive weeks in seven newspapers, the Seattle *Times* and papers in Tacoma, Walla Walla, Port Townsend, Olympia, Spokane, and Whatcom. When the bids were opened on October 30, the "highest and best bidder"—the only bidder—was Crawford and Conover, and that firm's bid of $25,000 was accepted. Regents voting to accept were, again, Hoyt, Blethen, King, Moore, Bell, and Winsor.[30]

It can only be assumed from what is known of the transaction that Crawford and Conover, a well-regarded firm that had been in business for ten years, was assembling the parcels of land that would make up the new post office site. Four such parcels, including the university's, were needed, and for the four the government apparently paid $174,750 at prices ranging from $9,750 to $110,000.[31]

Certain procedural peculiarities are interesting. A minor one is that the deed attests that the offer to sell "was determined by a decision of six-eights [*sic*] of the members of said Board," although the board was of seven members, the eighth, ex officio, member, the superintendent of schools, having been dropped. Another is that although the conveyance was made in January 1902, it was not made by the regents, whose right to sell had been confirmed by *Callvert* v. *Winsor*, but by Governor McBride for the state of Washington, with the secretary of state, Sam H. Nichols, attesting. The fact seems to be that the U.S. district attorney, Wilson R. Gay, acting for the Treasury Department, refused to accept a deed from the board of regents—and in this he could only have been basing his judgment on the old act of 1891, which specified that a purchaser of any part of the university tract must receive a deed "to be executed by the Governor, and attested by the Secretary of State." The board of regents itself, after accepting the Crawford and Conover bid, had resolved on November 5, 1901, "that the President and Secretary of this Board be, and they hereby are, authorized to execute the necessary contracts, deeds and other conveyances to evidence the acceptance of said bid and consummate the sale of said property."[32]

The wisdom of the sale is not now a calculable thing. There would be a sequel half a century later. Yet the balances may be examined. If the regents were in fact offering the larger tract on Union Street for $200,000, they were asking (for 1.41 acres) about $3.25 per square foot—and this for land cut from the center of the north boundary of the campus. The strip actually sold (0.35 acre) brought about $1.63 per square foot, which the three appraisers thought a fair price. Five years later the regents would lease the balance of the property, at an appraised value of $500,000, for $1.19 per square foot; and on subsequent leases, as modified, rent would be paid at a rate of $4.76 per square foot. Whatever was fair or prudent in all this, the sale of that fraction of the ten-acre tract was an irrevocable act for which $25,000 seems, in retrospect, an inadequate recompense, especially if the government did indeed acquire from the university for $25,000 an essential strip of land that represented about one-third of the site for which the total cost was $174,750. However it was, a bit of the old campus was gone, at a price considered reasonable by the appraisers and in a sale conducted with due regard to the provisions of the authorizing legislation. The rest of the ten-acre tract awaited future decision —with a new federal building as a sturdy pinion at the northwest corner. The regents thought that a good idea.

The year 1902 was the year a policy finally took shape with regard to the development of the old grounds. The regents would decide, formally and by resolution, to lease the property rather than to sell. A course was set. The course, before and after, nevertheless was one of doubt, difficulty, and harassment.

To an extent only suggested in the sketchy records, there was continued involvement with Levold, who not only was undeterred but felt that the regents had done him less than justice in the matter of his performance bond. Levold, as the year advanced, presented new proposals, sued the board to try to force fulfillment of his aborted lease, and then had a somewhat mysterious role in the organization of the corporation which, upon dismissal of Levold's suit, was awarded a new thirty-year lease. For regents who could by no means devote full time to the problems of the new university, much less those of the old campus, the period must have been a bewildering one.

There were changes in the board that year. By the time the year was beginning—and it began with talk about the possible sale of another piece of the downtown property—Easterday had departed and in his place was William E. Schricker, of La Conner, a lawyer-banker-politician of considerable prominence. By May, when Hoyt resigned to join the faculty of the Law School, the second new regent would be John H. Powell, a thirty-six-year-old Seattle attorney who, before his appointment, had served briefly as Levold's attorney and who thus had to disqualify himself, quite properly, when the regents voted on Levold's proposals later. Schricker was a native of Iowa and a graduate of Iowa State College who, shifting from agricultural studies, had won his LL.B. in 1883, had taken additional law studies at Columbia, and had been admitted to the bar in both Iowa and Washington before moving to Seattle and then on to La Conner in 1886. In La Conner he had established the Skagit County Bank. He had been elected to the legislature in 1891 and 1893, and he would serve for years on La Conner's city council and school board.[33]

The regents' brief flirtation with a second sale is interesting chiefly as a reflection of how delicately balanced was the leasing-selling issue early in

1902. The regents met in executive sessions on January 21 and 22 to consider the City Library Commission's interest in acquiring a plot of ground extending 240 feet along Union Street at the northeast corner of the tract. This was just ten days after the deeding of the post office site, and the regents may have felt that things were looking up after all. To the government the regents had sold a third of an acre for $25,000; but on the library plot, which was about the size of the land originally offered for the post office, the regents fixed a price of $100,000 and authorized Hoyt, as president of the board, to so inform the library commission. Nothing more was heard of that.[34]

The library negotiation was not concluded. Had it been, the old campus might have had a federal building at its northwest corner and the library to the northeast, which would seem a not unattractive arrangement. There was no doubt that Seattle was growing. The population had passed the 100,000 mark that had been predicted so confidently ten years before. The major commercial buildings still were at the more accessible levels of the city— the Bon Marche at 1419 Second Avenue; Frederick and Nelson (until recently Frederick, Nelson and Munro) in the Rialto Building on Second Avenue between Madison and Spring; MacDougall and Southwick at 717 First Avenue; Stone, Stanford and Lane, ladies garments, at Second and Seneca; the Post-Intelligencer at Second and Cherry. New buildings were being erected, including the Lumber Exchange and the Arcade buildings, James A. Moore projects, the Marion Building, and others. Development was also creeping up the steep hills to the east. Moore's Lincoln Apartments stood at Fourth and Madison, the University Club at Madison and Boren. And Madison Street was being developed. Early in 1900 three city councilmen and three members of the board of public works had hiked, in a pouring rain, the four-mile length of Madison Street from First Avenue to Lake Washington— even struggling "through the ravines beyond Broadway"—to see for themselves the need for paving and improvement. By 1902, Madison had been improved (although not yet paved) and was the route of a new cable car line from the city to the lake. Crawford and Conover and John Davis and Company, another real estate firm, were advertising lots near Sixth Avenue and Pike Street at prices ranging from $8,000 to $13,500. The Davis company, with offices at 709 Second Avenue, had been offering lots "in the very cream portion of first hill [sic]" for some time. The Clise Investment Company was advertising Queen Anne Hill as "Seattle's choicest residential section," and the city was planning to build "roads" to the top. A city park on Capitol Hill had been named Volunteer Park to honor the men of those twelve companies of Washington soldiers who had gone off to Manila in September 1898. Seattle reached out. The regents of the university, seeing these changes, must have been encouraged to entertain briefly, again, the thought of selling off parcels of the old campus in the hope that the value of the property would rise with the flood tide of this expansion. If so, the impulse soon died. By March 1902, Levold was back.[35]

On March 13 the regents had a communication from Levold in which he tried to revive his lease of 1900. The regents, meeting on April 25, scheduled their regular quarterly meeting for May 7 to discuss the Levold situtation and, undoubtedly, leasing in general. When the regents met on May 7—Hoyt, King, Blethen, Schricker, Winsor, and Moore—John H. Powell appeared before the board on Levold's behalf. The board heard Powell, but the decision was to table Levold's petition and to direct the executive committee "to ask for bids for the leasing of the Old University grounds, or any part thereof, using the press of Seattle, Tacoma, and Spokane to do so." Levold must have felt he had been over that route before. As with his petition of 1899, the effort had led only to a general call for bids. On June 2, Levold filed suit.[36]

It was just at this juncture that the second change in the board occurred. Late in May, Governor McBride, seeking a successor to Hoyt, appointed Powell to the place, thus putting on the board the young man who so recently had acted as Levold's attorney. Powell was a native of Illinois, one of ten children in the family of a Methodist minister, and he had worked his way through the University of Michigan by teaching Latin and Greek while reading law in the evenings. Graduating from Michigan in 1888, he had come to Seattle in 1890 to enter the law office of a relative, Judge Julius Stratton, a leading member of the bar. Soon, however, Stratton had died and Powell had formed a partnership with William A. Peters, another young attorney. Powell had served one term in the legislature after 1897—one of two Republican members, it is said, in that Populist period. In 1902 the offices of Peters and Powell were in the Dexter Horton Building. On June 6, the day Powell's oath as regent was filed with the board, the regents referred Levold's suit to W. B. Stratton, the attorney general, their ex officio legal adviser.[37]

Levold's action was to compel the board to deliver to him "a good and sufficient lease of said premises for a period of thirty years." Levold, who had lost his lease because of a failure to file a performance bond, now alleged that he and the regents had agreed to delay any submission of the bond until their right to lease had been certified by the courts, as in the subsequent test in *Callvert*. He also said that he had indeed delivered his bond about September 1, 1900—although the *Callvert* action was not initiated until the spring of 1901—and that the regents had "wrongfully refused to approve" it. Whatever else it did, the Levold suit must have given the regents some nervous times, for as late as November and December 1902, Stratton was writing the board to urge searches of their minutes and records to find a copy of the bond, if any, or references to its delivery, or the wording of the resolutions concerning Levold's failure to deliver.[38]

In September 1902, the Seattle City Council sounded out the regents with regard to purchase of the tract. The board simply ordered the communication filed. A sale, any sale, presumably was no longer seriously considered. Blethen was president of the board now, but of course the regents had more than the problem of the tract on their minds. The university on the new campus was having growing pains, academically and administratively, of not unexpected kinds. Frank Pierrepont Graves had been succeeded by Thomas Kane as president of the institution. Meetings of the regents involved increasingly the handling of details regarding appointments and salaries and construction and revisions of the curricula. What the regents were thinking about the tract in that autumn of 1902 can only be surmised in the light of later developments. But Levold had been busy.

Levold's attorney in 1901 had been Powell, who now was a regent. His attorney in 1902 was L. C. Gilman, who, at forty-five, was already well known in Washington legal circles and who soon would become western counsel for the Great Northern Railway and eventually its vice-president. Whatever it meant, Gilman was the second attorney of prominence to take up Levold's case. On December 2, 1902, Gilman appeared at the regents' meeting to present a modified lease proposal, the details unknown. The regents on hand to discuss this were Blethen, Winsor, King, Schricker, Moore, and Powell. The discussion was particular in detail and came, at length, to a point. The regents might talk further with Gilman and Levold, but they did not feel committed. The question was one of policy, and they let this simmer for a week. When the board met again on December 9, 1902, the policy was decided, and it was Winsor who made the initial motion that established the course for the century. The minutes of the meeting contain these entries:

Regent Winsor moved that it is the sense of this Board that we adopt the policy of leasing the old University site in preference to selling. Motion seconded and carried unanimously.

Regent Winsor moved that, in case we lease this property, the amount of permanent improvements in buildings to be placed thereon by the lessee during the period of thirty years shall not be less than one million ($1,000,000) dollars. Carried unanimously.

Regent King moved that, in the event of our renting said property, in addition to the permanent improvements to be placed thereon, the money rental be not less than 3 percent of a valuation of $350,000, for the first ten years and thereafter at not less than three [*sic*] percent per annum on a valuation to be fixed by three appraisers to be chosen in the usual manner for each additional ten years up to thirty years, the lessee to pay all taxes and assessments on said property during the term of the lease, if any there be. Motion seconded by Regent Powell and carried unanimously.[39]

Since the regents had been trying for two years to lease the old campus—had, in fact, once leased it to the man who now challenged their cancellation of the agreement—the significance of their actions was that, in the context of new negotiations, they had put into the record their determination to lease and the terms they would accept. They acted in response to Gilman, who had attended the meeting as Levold's representative and who had "made a statement of a new proposition which was a modification of the original proposition, out of which has grown a suit at law." Winsor's motion was made after the regents had retired to executive session, and Gilman was then called back to hear the reading of it. Gilman said he would have another proposal, and this he brought to the board on December 10 at a meeting in Blethen's office. The discussions went on all afternoon and were continued in the evening.[40]

While the proposing and counterproposing were going on, a new corporation had been formed. It was called the University Site Improvement Company and its object was to lease and develop the university tract. Levold had a role in this without doubt, for his action then pending against the regents was an impediment to leasing. Levold was not, however, among the incorporators. For agreeing to dismiss his suit he was given a minority interest in the company. The incorporators were J. R. Stirrat, Herman Goetz, W. D. Hofius, and C. A. Riddle, and these, plus M. F. Backus, were trustees. The company was incorporated for fifty years for $1,000,000, to issue one million shares of stock at a par value of one dollar. The trustees were men of impeccable repute, all well known in Seattle—Stirrat and Goetz partners in a contracting and grading firm at 118 Columbia Street, Hofius a steel man who had been in Seattle since 1893, Riddle an attorney, and Backus a prominent banker.[41]

It was the University Site Improvement Company that now became the lessee of the tract. The details were worked out at a special meeting of the regents on December 11, 1902, in Blethen's office at the *Times*. In their resolution authorizing execution of the lease the regents stated explicitly that Levold had agreed to dismiss his suit "provided said lease be granted to the University Site Improvement Co." For the board of regents the lease was signed by Blethen, as president, and by William Markham, a member of the university's business office staff who had succeeded Clark Davis as secretary to the board. On the following day the regents approved the $20,000 performance bond submitted by the company.[42]

The new lease was for thirty years, the period the regents had specified in their resolutions of December 9. The rental terms, however, did not quite meet the expectations. And the regents could not know what turns lay in the road they had decided to follow.

CHAPTER 3

Call it Metropolitan: 1903 to 1907

The regents certainly believed, in that winter of 1902–3, that the lease to the new University Site Improvement Company was the best possible arrangement for all concerned, particularly for the university. The regents had retreated somewhat from the positions they had taken when they approved the motions of Winsor and King at the policy meeting of December 9. Then they had determined to ask that a lessee place on the tract not less than $1,000,000 in buildings over a thirty-year term. They had settled, instead, for $100,000 in improvements—grading, paving, sewers—in ten years. They had expected an initial rental of 3 percent on a valuation of $350,000, but they had accepted 2 percent of a valuation of $300,000. They had in hand, nevertheless, a thirty-year lease with a company that would seem incapable of failure to develop the tract at a time when the city's expansion continued in a rising tide.

Public announcement of the leasing appeared first in the Seattle *Times* of December 23, 1902, the heading on a small story on an inside page saying: "LEASE OF THE OLD GROUNDS; Regents Accept Offer of University Site Company; Modern Buildings To Be Erected Immediately Adjoining the New Federal Building." The *Post-Intelligencer* the following morning used a somewhat more extensive story—and the heading was the kind that would send shudders through other boards of regents in later years: "PLENTY OF MONEY FOR UNIVERSITY; Regents Sign a Lease on Grounds for Thirty Years; WILL IMPROVE AT ONCE; Business Blocks and Modern Flats to Be Erected on Union and Seneca Streets; WILL GRADE FOURTH AVENUE."

The report covered the lease arrangements in detail, and five of the regents —President Blethen, Powell, King, Winsor, and Schricker—were quoted at some length. The lead of the story set the tone:

The old university grounds are to be opened up and improved. Fourth Avenue is to be cut through, and sightly brick and stone buildings are to be erected on Union and Seneca Streets, none of which will be less than three stories in height.

This was made possible when a lease was given to the University Site Improvement Company yesterday morning by the regents of the state university to run for thirty years. The men composing the company are M. F. Backus, W. D. Hofius, and Stirrat & Goetz and they propose to begin the improvement of the property at once.

The terms were stated: five years' cash rental at 2 percent on $300,000, the next five years at 3 percent on that figure, 3 percent reappraisals thereafter,

44

grading and improving to cost not less than $100,000 in ten years. Improvements were to be of the "highest character," all buildings to become the property of the state. Space was reserved for the Law School until the close of the 1903 term, and the old main building, leased to the City Library, would continue to be so dedicated for two years. Meeting rooms were to be provided for the regents.

The new company had plans. Its first building would be a new "first class" business block at Fourth Avenue and Union Street, work to be initiated in the spring of 1903. And, as the *Post-Intelligencer* reported, the plans called for business buildings on Union Street from three to six stories high, for "flats" on Seneca, and, when Fourth Avenue was opened, for additional commercial buildings there. Such construction would, the story said, augment "the present Pike Street business district," and "in conjunction with the new Federal building," would "open up a district for business purposes which has not been available."

The regents' vote on the lease had been unanimous. But the public statements of the board members seemed to contain shadings of enthusiasm. Blethen said: "The property as it stands is practically dead and the state provided no funds with which to improve it. By the terms of this lease we have created a fund producer for the university that at the end of thirty years will be something magnificent." Powell's response was a touch more restrained: "I think it is a good thing to put the university grounds in such shape that they will yield a revenue. This arrangement will do this. Therefore I favor it." But from King: "In my opinion the leasing of the university grounds was the best thing that could be done for the university. That is the only statement I wish to make."

Winsor and Schricker had more to say. Each, in fact, argued the case. Winsor, whose motion had established the leasing policy, said in part: "In the first place I think we are on the flood tide and if we had not leased now, or within a reasonable time and at a reasonable figure, we are rapidly approaching a time when we could not have leased at all to advantage to the university. The terms of the present lease, fixing a rental on the appraised value of the property, will give the university a fund which will be added to as the property increases in value in the future. . . . It was my very best judgment to make this lease now and take no chance on not getting a valuation rental for a number of years later on." Schricker covered the same points and made a few of his own. He said that to carry out the provisions of the lease, the University Site Improvement Company would have to spend "from $1,000,000 to $1,500,000" on buildings. "If the state was to sell that property now," he said, "it could not possibly expect to get more than $350,000 for it. We will receive that much in rents . . . and at the end of the lease term will have the enhanced property with all of the improvements left." He estimated the rents for the second ten years at $30,000 a year and, for the final ten years, up to $60,000 a year.

All this, alas, was not to be. It is to be wondered why. The principals of the

University Site Improvement Company were men of experience in building and finance. They, no less than Moore, would have been familiar to the regents.

Manson F. Backus was a leading banker and already well into a career that would make him, long before he died thirty years later, the "dean of Seattle bankers." In 1902 he was forty-nine years old and president of what was then the Washington National Bank and would soon become the National Bank of Commerce. Backus was a native of New York, born in 1853, the son of a farmer turned manufacturer and banker. He was educated in public schools and in a Friends Academy at Union Springs, New York, where his father was president of the First National Bank. He was cashier of the bank for a time, then president of a gypsum company, and even postmaster of the little town. Then he studied law and by 1889 had been admitted to the bar at Buffalo, New York. But it was as banker, not lawyer, that he came to Seattle in 1889, just in time for the great fire. His Washington National Bank was established, it was said, in a half-finished building at Second and Cherry as Seattle dug out of the ruins. He was, by turn, cashier, vice-president, and president. He was president in 1902 when the University Site Improvement Company lease was negotiated.[1]

W. D. Hofius was wealthy, widely known and respected, and a self-made man of the classic type. In 1902 he was not yet fifty years old, but he had made a career in steel, beginning as a two-dollars-a-day pig iron handler in the mills at Sharpsville, Pennsylvania, and making his first plunge into the steel industry when he bought a Pennsylvania blast furnace from E. H. Harriman. Soon he had moved to Colorado, where he bought the Trinidad Rolling Mills, which he sold to a Colorado company and then moved to Los Angeles as the firm's agent there. By 1893 he had bought the Great Western Steel Company, in Kirkland, Washington, where an English millionaire, Peter Kirk, had tried to establish a steel manufacturing center. Soon he organized the W. D. Hofius Company, said to be one of the largest independent steel companies on the Pacific Coast.[2]

Of the incorporators of the University Site Improvement Company, James Raeside Stirrat and Herman Goetz were, if not the wealthiest, perhaps the most picturesque. In the newspaper reports of the leasing they were referred to simply as Stirrat and Goetz, which by then was their corporate identity, and this may simply have suggested the closeness of their partnership. Stirrat was president of the new University Site corporation, and the Stirrat and Goetz offices, which were moved about this time from 117 Columbia Street to the Washington Building, became the headquarters of the University Site company.[3]

Stirrat was a Scot, Goetz a German. Both had come to the United States as immigrants, Stirrat a twenty-two-year-old cabinetmaker and Goetz a somewhat younger bricklayer. Goetz had arrived first in Seattle, about 1888; Stirrat had lived for a time in Morristown, New Jersey, before moving west in 1889. They met, according to an account in a Seattle history, when they were employed to build a house on Jefferson Street for E. O. Graves, who was a founder, with Backus, of the Washington National Bank. Stirrat had hired himself out as an independent contractor to do the carpentry. Goetz, the mason, had been employed to build the chimneys. They became friends, and they went into business together. For a year, Stirrat and Goetz built houses, but soon they were partners as general contractors and graders. Arthur Denny was operating the Denny Clay Company, and Stirrat and Goetz joined Denny in developing concrete foundations on Union Street. Backus, who was for a time receiver of the street railway company, employed the firm to build a rail line on Second Avenue from Pike Street to Pioneer Square. Stirrat and Goetz also laid tracks on Pike Street. By 1902, the two partners were busy with improvements in Seattle—streets, sewers, curbs—and were investing modestly in real estate. Now they were associated with Backus in the University Site Improvement Company.[4]

Men such as these, with C. A. Riddle, the attorney, as secretary, had formed the new corporation and had won the lease. It all seemed right. There was no reason to believe that the University Site Improvement Company would not be able to follow through. It just did not work out that way. The company did indeed begin to build its first building, a "first class" structure on Union Street where Fourth Avenue abutted the old grounds. But the building finally had to be completed by others.

There was no mention in all this, in the press or elsewhere, of J. C. Levold. Yet it was Levold who had started the regents' leasing effort, and it was Levold who had withdrawn his suit when the lease was negotiated with the University Site company. Levold simply left the stage but not before a small final contest with the regents that seems, on the record, a pathetic flourish at the exit.

Almost immediately after the leasing Levold asked the regents to return the $500 deposit he had lost when his own lease was declared forfeited in 1900. At a meeting on January 27, 1903, the regents "laid over" the request. On February 11, they again took no action. On February 25, Levold appeared in person before the executive committee, and King, as chairman, asked the secretary to write the other regents to get their views and to pay Levold the $500 if there proved to be no objection. Apparently there was objection, for the board took up the matter again on March 25, when the vote was three to one to deny the payment, Powell declining to vote because he had been Levold's attorney. Still Levold was not through. When the board met on June 9, 1903, another attorney, a Mr. Jurey, spoke on Levold's behalf, and then L. C. Gilman took up the case again. It seems an unusual circumstance, but one about which it is useless to speculate. Gilman had become in 1903 the western counsel for the Great Northern, yet he went before the regents' executive committee on June 27 to ask the return of Levold's $500 deposit. The payment was made, finally, but not for another year. On June 14, 1904, when the regents again took up the Levold request, Winsor moved that the $500 be returned and the board "procure from him a receipt in full for all demands." The motion carried unanimously.[5]

LEVOLD LOSES HIS CLAIM

FAILS TO COMPLY WITH TERMS OF WASHINGTON UNIVERSITY.

Valuable Tract of Land in Seattle is Let to J. A. Moore—Fine Buildings to Be Erected.

SEATTLE, Wash., Nov. 15.—(Special.)
—The Board of Regents of the State
University has swept aside the claim of
J. C. Levold, of Portland, to the lease
of the old university site in the heart
of the City of Seattle and leased, the
grounds to James A. Moore. Ten acres,
belonging to the State University, lie
in the heart of the business district of
Seattle. About two years ago Mr. Levold secured a 30-year lease on the basis
of 3 per cent annually of the appraised
valuation, but failed to comply with the
terms. The regents of the university,
tiring of delays and failure to carry out
the terms of the lease, abrogated it and
gave Stirrat & Goetz a 30-year lease
with the provision that 3 per cent of
the appraised valuation of the property
should annually be paid as rental, a new
appraisement occurring every ten
years.

Stirrat & Goetz organized the University Improvement Company to handle the deal. Levold, on his claim,
threatened suit, and Stirrat & Goetz attempted a compromise, granting him a
monetary consideration and a minority
interest in the new company. This did
not end the trouble, and no development
work could be done. The regents of the
university daily found the chances for
the improvement of the property grow
less. Finally the company failed to
pay the quarterly rent due October 1.
Notification was given that the rent
must be paid, but the company refused
to comply with the demand.

November 1 the regents of the university, finding the old lessees would
not live up to the terms of the lease,
abrogated it. Then negotiations with
Mr. Moore were commenced. Now plans
are drawn for the investment of $1,000,-
000 in new steel and fireproof buildings
under the terms of a 50-year lease.

By 1904, J. C. Levold, now "of Portland," had lost his last chance to become a lessee and
James A. Moore had a fifty-year lease on the "old university grounds"; this account in the
Portland *Oregonian* of November 16

Levold, once the lessee of the tract, had won the final skirmish after a year and a half of trying. Whatever Levold's personal dream, he seems to have departed the leasing game at about the level he entered it.

The building begun by the University Site company was the Post-Intelligencer Building, a four-story brick structure that would be occupied by the newspaper for many years. The building replaced the old First Regiment Armory on a site that had been the scene of much Seattle history—the commotion after the fire, the drills and ceremonies during the Spanish-American War, and the political meetings, revivals, and mass meetings of all kinds. The Armory was moved to the corner of Terry Avenue and Stewart Street until a new Armory could be erected.[6]

The new construction was expected in 1903 to be merely the first step in a building program that would expand the "Pike Street business district" to the north and thus place the university property nearer the central city. The logic, from the city's view or the university's, was indisputable. The regents' biennial report to the legislature of 1903 contained a section on "University Lands" which reviewed not only the sale of the fractional acre to the U.S. government and the new lease to the University Site Improvement Company but also the status of all lands remaining from the original federal grants and other acquisitions.[7] The lands then included the 355 acres of the new campus; the 8.32 acres of the old; some 3,000 acres of the original 1854 grants, still unselected; a balance of 100,000 acres granted in 1889 for the support of education; and a tract of 320 acres near Tacoma that had been purchased in 1862. The regents urged action, and legislation if necessary, to place this collective endowment at the service of the university, and they congratulated themselves, understandably, on the actions they had taken with respect to the old campus. Of these they said in part:

The regents have sold to the United States a portion of the old university site of ten acres, in Seattle, being a strip 64x240 feet, for $25,000.00, which sum has been remitted to the State Treasurer. This strip of ground was needed to make the quantity required by the United States for a government building. The Regents considered that, in addition to the price received for the strip sold (which was its appraised value), this location of the government building would materially enhance the value of the remainder of the property. Subsequent events have shown that the judgment of the Regents in this respect was good. Two years ago the entire ten acres was conservatively valued at $200,000. Today a conservative valuation of the tract, exclusive of the strip sold to the United States, is $300,000.

The regents asked, in conclusion, that the university's endowment in lands be put in order and that the income from the old grounds, in particular, be devoted to university purposes under the regents' control: "This land was given to the University for university purposes, and the wishes of the donors should be respected in disposing of the proceeds of its sale or lease. We would, therefore, respectfully suggest that legislation be asked for, providing that such proceeds be devoted strictly to the acquisition of permanent improvements for the University."

Events moved swiftly—and, to the regents, perplexingly, undoubtedly —through 1903 and into the early months of 1904. After the clearing of the site, the construction of the new Post-Intelligencer Building was begun, but the University Site Improvement Company, in which Stirrat and Goetz now clearly were the principal figures, apparently began to realize that a thirty-year term was not sufficient to permit recovery of the investment required to accomplish the development to which they were committed. The realization set the stage for the return of James A. Moore.

On January 29, 1904, Stirrat and Goetz, accompanied by their attorneys, appeared before the regents to ask an extension of their lease from thirty to fifty years. The regents deferred action, according to their record, but appointed a committee—Schricker, Winsor, and Blethen—to examine the question and report at a meeting on February 25. Schricker made the report at the February meeting, and he accompanied it by a letter from the University Site company, "By J. R. Stirrat, its president," outlining the terms. In return for a lease of fifty years the company pledged construction of the building on Union Street costing not less than $60,000, construction of buildings all along the Union Street side of the grounds within six years, and rentals of 5 and 6 percent on the appraised values of the land for the two additional ten-year periods. The Stirrat letter struck a plaintive note: "We have deliberated long and seriously on what concessions in the amount of rent moneys we can afford to pay for the extended term of twenty years and we respectfully state in positive language, that in agreeing to pay 5 percent on the first valuation . . . and six [sic] percent on the second ten . . . we have gone to the extreme limits of our ability in that behalf. Our only object in asking for the proposed extension is to enable us to finance the project in order to carry out the object of the lease, and this object will be utterly defeated if we should be required to pay any greater rent than above stated."[8]

The regents' ensuing action seems strangely ambivalent. Schricker moved adoption of the report—acceptance of the proposal—and Winsor seconded. On the vote, Blethen, Winsor, Schricker, and Moore voted adoption, King and Powell against. After whatever discussion occurred, Winsor moved reconsideration, then indefinite postponement. That motion carried unanimously. It may simply be that, on a question of such long-term implication, the regents wanted a unanimous vote. In any case, the University Site petition had been, in effect, denied.[9]

Now Moore reentered. He had been in conversation, doubtless, with Stirrat and others of the University Site company. On June 14, 1904, Moore appeared before the board to ask if the regents would consider a fifty-year lease, the specifics to be negotiated, if he should acquire the University Site Improvement Company's leasehold. What Moore thought his prospects might be can only be guessed. He certainly counted on the regents' recognition of his record as a successful developer, for he was asking the same twenty-year extension that had already been postponed as a policy issue, and he apparently was not ready to outline his terms or plans for development. The regents "laid over" the inquiry, but they appointed King and Powell as a committee to confer with Moore.[10]

Whatever talks took place, Moore did not even wait for a board decision. On July 14, a month after his initial exploration, Moore paid the University Site company $40,000 for an assignment of its lease, although neither he nor the company bothered, at the time, to notify the regents about this. The company was becoming delinquent in its payments, but Moore apparently felt no obligation to take over the debts with the leasehold, and as far as the regents were concerned the debts still were the company's. On October 28, 1904, the regents held a special meeting at which they adopted a resolution to notify the University Site company that the lease would be declared forfeited if the payments were not brought up to date by November 1. The resolution noted that a copy was to be served "on J. A. Moore, the alleged purchaser or owner of the leasehold estate."[11]

The regents may have felt, with some reason, that the whole arrangement had become a shambles. The Post-Intelligencer Building was under construction, but its future seemed in doubt. Moore held a lease that had been given the University Site company, and the leasehold was producing debts, not income. But Moore was, presumably, the key figure, ready to pick up the pieces. The date upon which it happened was forever memorable in the history of the tract.

The regents called another special meeting on November 1, 1904. Not all members were there, but Schricker, now president, was in the chair, and Moore was present. The University Site Improvement Company's lease was declared forfeited for nonpayment of rent, and Moore immediately submitted a new lease offer based on a term of fifty years—to November 1, 1954. When the draft had been read and discussed, Powell moved its acceptance, King seconding, and the vote was unanimous. Schricker and Markham, the secretary, were authorized to draw up and execute the lease to Moore. It was so done. At the regents' regular quarterly meeting on November 25, members were informed that the lease had been executed and that Moore's bond of $15,000, the bond required, had been approved. Schricker and Markham had signed for the board, and the other regents—James Z. Moore, Winsor, Blethen, King, and Powell—joined Schricker in certifying approval.[12]

It mattered little in the practical sense, and it certainly did not touch the legality of the regents' actions, but the fact is that the board was experiencing a shuffling of membership in this period and thus was a little short-handed at the moments these decisions were being made.

In March 1904, Frederick A. Hazeltine, a South Bend newspaper publisher, was appointed by Governor McBride to succeed Bell, whose term had expired. Hazeltine attended his first meeting on March 25, and was listed as a regent in the university's *Catalogue for 1904.* But he failed to be confirmed by the state senate, and although he did not resign from the board until the next year, he took no part in the Moore negotiations and was not among the regents certifying the Moore lease.* Furthermore, although James Z. Moore was among the regents certifying the lease, his status by November 25 would seem to have been in doubt. Inserted in the regents' record immediately following the minutes of the November 1 meeting is this small paragraph: "Note: Nov. 15th news was received through the Daily Press that Gov. McBride had appointed Hon. F. A. Post of Spokane as Regent to succeed Hon. Jas. Z. Moore, whose term had expired."[13]

The action on the Moore lease was effected, it appears, by the stable core of the board. On November 1, the "unanimous" vote was by just five regents —Schricker, president, and Blethen, King, Powell, and Winsor. On November 25, only four were present. Surprisingly, Powell was among the absentees; Hazeltine and Post also were absent. It made no difference, for the regents really had no choice but to end the lease of the ineffective University Site Improvement Company and accept the presence of the successful James A. Moore, who had bought the University Site interests. Still, at a moment in which the future of the property was fixed for so many years, the board deserved full membership. Post, the Spokane appointee, was a regent only three months—apparently he too failed confirmation—and he resigned with Hazeltine in February 1905.[14]

Moore now had a fifty-year lease, and with it the obligation to finish construction of the Post-Intelligencer Building and to proceed with other developments. He had rents to pay, too, but he was, characteristically, involved in projects on other fronts.

As for the rental, the lease called for annual cash payments of $6,000 for three years, $9,000 for the next five, and percentage-on-appraisal payments thereafter—3 percent for ten years, 4 percent for the next ten, and 6 percent for the final twenty-two. Buildings were to become the property of the state, heights and construction requirements specified. Streets were to be of brick or asphalt, and all were to be "on the line of the present streets of the city of Seattle produced across said property." Sidewalks were to be of concrete.† The City Library, still occupying the old main building, was to be permitted to remain until 1905, the rents going to Moore. The "brick building now upon said premises"—the Post-Intelligencer—was to be kept in repair and rooms furnished for the use of the regents. And—a reflection of a state of the old campus in 1904—"no oak or maple shade trees upon said property shall be

---

* As will be seen, Hazeltine was returned to the board by another governor, in 1908, and served until 1913, twice as president.

† Generations accustomed to seeing cities paved and linked by countless miles of concrete may find it difficult to realize that concrete was only beginning to be used extensively in 1904. Streets in Seattle were still primarily graveled or planked, and board walks were everywhere. A city "progress report" at the end of 1902 showed that Seattle then had 132 miles of "streets, graded," 19 miles of "streets, planked," and—undoubtedly a sign of progress —5 miles of concrete walks. By 1907 Seattle had 88 miles of paved streets—all paving of wood, brick, or asphalt.

cut down or destroyed unless it shall be necessary to do so for the purpose of erecting a building or buildings or improving street or streets, or in doing necessary excavating or grading."[15]

The problem faced by Moore, which was the problem that had baffled the University Site Improvement Company, was how to generate income in the early, costly period of initial development. Moore moved ahead on this early in 1905. The first challenge was to get funds to complete the Post-Intelligencer construction, and to do so he formed another of the companies that seemed always trailing in his wake. Moore, well known in Boston and New York, turned naturally to the East, and the result was the organization of the Seattle Real Estate and Building Company, incorporated for $1,000,000, in which one of the associates was N. W. Jordan, president of the American Trust Company of Boston. To this company he assigned his leasehold, which then was mortgaged for $350,000 to the State Trust Company, of Rutland, Vermont. The new company sold stock and the proceeds were used to complete the Post-Intelligencer project. That, at least, had been accomplished.[16]

As for the cash flow, Moore's effort was to build temporary buildings to get income from rentals. The idea was not unreasonable, perhaps, except that such buildings by no means represented a firm step toward improvement. Soon the regents required him to tear them down. And soon Moore began to have second thoughts about the terms of the lease he had negotiated with the board. Through 1905 and into 1906 Moore gave the tract problem such attention as he could, presumably, although he was involved in other affairs of all kinds. To a man of Moore's temperament, the situation must have been exasperating, for he was accustomed to success. Moore had moved far since he had submitted that first, unopened lease proposal to the regents in 1900, and so had the city of Seattle.

By 1906, Moore's hand was evident in many places, in Seattle and elsewhere. He or his Moore Investment Company had dotted the city with buildings, at first the rather modest Estabrook, Seward, Whitcomb, and Curtis blocks, then the larger Arcade and Lumber Exchange buildings (and the Arcade Annex) on Second Avenue—"two mammoth structures," according to a contemporary account. He had taken over the old Denny Hotel, at Third and Stewart, a hotel that had been closed for ten years, and had refurbished it at a cost of $150,000, reopening it as the Washington, the first guests including President Theodore Roosevelt and members of his party. He was building the Moore and the Alexandria hotels, and the Moore Theater, where in 1907 he would receive a standing ovation on opening night. He was interested in the Lake Washington Ship Canal project, a plan to link the lake to Puget Sound, and apparently hoped to have a hand in the financing of it. He was involved in getting the city to attack the regrading of Denny Hill, one of the major programs conducted under the direction of R. H. Thomson, the ingenious city engineer—a project that would necessitate the demolition and replacement of the Washington.

Moore was thinking beyond Seattle, too. He financed a gold mining venture in Alaska. Having long before platted a subdivision in Port Townsend, he may even then have had his eyes on the steel operations at nearby Irondale, and perhaps was beginning to have visions of making that little mill town the steel center of the Northwest. He was without question thinking in 1906 about irrigating the rolling desert lands along the Columbia River near Pasco, and of building a model farm there. This interest arose in part, it was said, because Eugenie Moore had developed tuberculosis and Moore had looked about for a climate that would be comfortable for her.[17]

But it was Moore's Capitol Hill that seemed to epitomize him. With a vision far beyond his time, Moore developed that addition as an already-in-place residential area—spending $150,000 or streets, sidewalks, sewers, and ornamental lights—before offering lots for sale. In 1904 he built his own home there, a tall red-brick and stone mansion south of Volunteer Park, and among his neighbors were men who were the leading figures in Seattle industry and finance—E. A. Stuart, founder of what was then the Pacific Coast Condensed Milk Company, later the Carnation Company; Chester F. White, lumberman and capitalist; and C. H. Cobb, a financier with interests in lumber and other industries. In September 1904, not long after he had acquired the University Site Improvement Company's lease to the university grounds, Moore had sold to an Eastern firm, for $250,000 in cash, some eighty acres of unimproved land on Capitol Hill—the equivalent, the newspaper reported, of six hundred city lots.[18]

The Seattle that Moore was helping to build was changing in many ways between 1904 and 1906. The population was estimated by 1906 at 235,000, an incredible leap from the 4,000 of 1880. Seattle waters were filled with shipping, and yachts were racing on the Sound. The giant vessels of the Seattle-Orient trade, among them the S. S. *Minnesota* and *Dakota*, frequently lay majestically at anchor in Elliott Bay, but small steamers carried passengers and freight to towns about the Sound. In Lake Washington, the Mercer Hotel, on Mercer Island, was reached by the little vessels *Cyrene* and *Xanthus*. Within the city, the future of the downtown waterfront had already been decided when Judge Thomas Burke, a former State Supreme Court justice representing James J. Hill's Great Northern Railroad, had mobilized the public sentiment that prevailed in a controversy over the proposal of the Northern Pacific Railroad to build a $500,000 rail depot along the waterfront north of Madison Street. Seattle, supported by Hill, had even tilted with San Francisco over the question of what port would handle military shipping, the San Francisco newspapers charging that Hill and others were putting pressure on the "army ring" in Washington, D.C., to deprive San Francisco of military traffic. The new Federal Building, occupying land that had been acquired in part from the university, was in place at Third Avenue and Union Street, and Third Avenue was being graded. The Moran shipyard had produced its masterpiece, the battleship *Nebraska*, which was launched October 8, 1904, in ceremonies that caught up the whole city. Soon thereafter the Great Northern tunnel, which snaked under the central city below Fourth Avenue, was completed. The Alaska Building was hailed as "Seattle's first skyscraper." By 1906, the city was already looking forward to the Alaska-Yukon-Pacific Exposition, to be held in 1909 on the new university campus. It was hoped that the Lake Washington Ship Canal would be opened by then. The King Street Station was a model rail terminal. The $275,000 Carnegie Library had been finished at last, and a new twelve-story hotel, the $1,000,000 New Washington, was being built at Second and Stewart.[19]

In such times, and in such a city, the university's old campus was not, however, being developed. Not, that is, by James A. Moore. The only change that was occurring in 1905 and 1906 was the extension through the tract of Fourth Avenue, which had abutted the property to the north and south. On December 7, 1905, a city ordinance authorized the extension of the avenue through the property at an 84-foot width—the width now proposed for the whole length of the avenue—and on February 14, 1906, notice was filed in King County Superior Court of an action to determine damages to "lands and property rights" by such widening and extension. The regents received a copy of the summons and complaint, but their response was to refer the question to the state attorney general. In subsequent legal proceedings the award for the taking of property was "no dollars," but on December 6, 1906, the city and Moore's Seattle Realty and Building Company entered an agreement under which the company was to receive $15,000 for damages to "improvements" (presumably the Post-Intelligencer Building), plus one dollar for the taking of the 84-foot strip and one dollar for the grading of it. In the judgment, the Seattle Realty and Building Company was awarded $15,001. The $15,000 would seem to have been for damages to a building which, under the terms of the lease, actually was owned by the state of Washington. In any case, the university tract now was to be traversed by Fourth Avenue, and grading was about to begin.[20]

On December 15, 1904, the *Post-Intelligencer* published a photograph with an accompanying story headed, "Century Old Maples Victims of Ruthless Ax of Commerce." The photograph showed a pile of cordwood, all that remained, as the story said, of the grove of trees that had stood since the university's founding near the old main building which still occupied its original site. Two years later, in September 1906, another *Post-Intelligencer* photo-story— this time the text was by Edmond Meany—was a final salute to the "Last Living Tree on the Old University Campus." The tree had been planted when the first university dormitory was built in 1862.

In 1905 another lingering trace of the old years had disappeared. On April 25, Daniel Bagley died, at eighty-seven, six years after Arthur Denny. He had been living for some time with his son, Clarence, who was secretary of the city's board of public works. In all his years nothing had daunted Daniel Bagley—not the hardships of the trail from Illinois, not the rigors of circuit riding in Oregon, not the whims and doubts of territorial legislatures—and only the single tree on the old university grounds had outlasted him.

But the university tract was not being developed, and this was strange. Why could not a man of Moore's scope move forthrightly to improve a property that he knew well, that seemed to lie in the path of Seattle's growth, and that he held under a lease on terms he had himself devised? An answer may be that Moore simply was overextended—not financially, at the moment, but in the sheer volume of projects he had in mind. In September 1906, he bought under a court order, for $40,000, the Irondale mill property, then dormant and in receivership, and it was not long before he was borrowing capital in the east—$750,000, according to one source years later—and preparing also to invest his own funds in reconstruction and modernization of the plant. It may be, too, that Eugenie was now ill and Moore was thinking of Pasco, where he did in fact build in 1908 a magnificent mansion on the bluffs above the Columbia. Or perhaps the university property in Seattle, full of problems that even Moore had not foreseen, simply had lost its allure.[21] By 1906, in any case, events were coming to a head. The membership of the board of regents had been almost entirely changed, and soon John H. Powell was the only regent who had signed Moore's 1904 lease. And Moore was trying to get a modification of the 1904 lease terms. He wanted a fixed-rate rent schedule.

In 1905, Albert E. Mead had become the new Republican governor, and among his appointees were five new regents—A. P. Sawyer and John P. Hartman, of Seattle; Frank D. Nash, of Tacoma; J. F. Saylor, of Spokane; and S. G. Cosgrove, of Pomeroy. Schricker, James Z. Moore, Winsor, and Blethen were gone, and King was succeeded shortly by James T. Ronald, of Seattle. The new regents were, typically, men who had come from other states to build careers in Washington.

Nash, a Tacoma attorney, was a native of New York and a graduate of Cornell who had come west in 1889 and had served one term in the state legislature. Cosgrove was a lawyer too, but one with more specific political ambitions. He was from Ohio, a farmer's son and a young soldier in the Civil War who had worked his way through Ohio Wesleyan and had taught school and studied law until he was admitted to the bar in 1875. When Cosgrove moved to Washington in 1883 he brought his ambitions with him. He was a member of the state constitutional convention in 1889, and later—as a lifetime Republican and member of the Grand Army of the Republic—he was a McKinley and Roosevelt elector. From his law offices in Pomeroy, in Garfield County, Cosgrove (with his son, Howard, now in the firm) was working his way toward the governorship of Washington. He would succeed Mead as governor in 1909, after serving four years as a regent. But after all the struggle for the prize he would be governor for only a day. Elected to office in faltering health, Cosgrove immediately asked leave to go to California to recuperate. There he died, and his successor was Marion E. Hay.[22]

Hartman, born in Fountain County, Indiana, in 1857, went with his family to Nebraska in 1873, was graduated from the university, studied law in Kearney, and was admitted to the bar in 1883. He moved to Tacoma in 1891 and to Seattle in 1896, soon becoming prominent in law and Republican politics.

When the gold rush came, Hartman went north, but not for gold. Leaving a prosperous Seattle law practice, he moved to Skagway, where he was a member of a group that built what was known as the Brackett Wagon Road from Skagway to Log Cabin, and soon he helped build the White Pass and Yukon Railway and organize and finance the Northwest Commercial Company. He had resumed his practice in Seattle when he was appointed a regent. When the time came he would be a member of the board of the Alaska-Yukon-Pacific Exposition, and it was he who would draft the bill to establish Mount Rainier National Park.[23]

Ronald was a Missourian, born in 1855 into a pioneer family that had early ties among Virginia colonists, and he had come to the board of regents by an interestingly circuitous route. Ronald's formal education consisted of three years at the State Normal School at Kirksville, Missouri, but from Kirksville he went immediately to California to get a job as a teacher and to marry, in Stockton, a girl from his old Missouri neighborhood. While he taught school, Ronald studied law. By 1882 he had been admitted to the bar in California, but by this time he had his eye on Seattle as a place to go into practice. Ronald had little money, and Seattle at the moment had little use for another lawyer. Then, at a time when the prosecuting attorney for the district had his office at Port Townsend, Ronald was appointed deputy for King County at twenty dollars a month. Seattle was not large, but it had a seaport-town quota of bars and brothels, and on all such evidence of vice Ronald opened war, vigorously and persistently. Soon, as a Democrat in a normally Republican region, Ronald was elected prosecutor, then reelected. By 1892 he was mayor of Seattle, and as mayor he fought for municipal ownership of power and water systems and appointed young Thomson to the city engineer's office. In 1900, Ronald was the Democratic candidate for Congress, running powerfully but unsuccessfully. He had returned to law when Governor Mead, a Republican, appointed him to the university board.[24]

Sawyer was secretary of the *Post-Intelligencer* company, but his background was in politics and business rather than in newspaper work. A graduate of Yale in 1880, he had gone at once to Portland, Oregon, as a teacher of Latin and Greek in a private academy. Then, like Ronald, he had studied law. He had worked thereafter in a succession of jobs—as a mining broker, express agent for the Northern Pacific in Victoria, B.C., real estate salesman in Spokane—until in 1895 he became secretary to Washington's Senator John L. Wilson. When Wilson and a partner bought the *Post-Intelligencer* in 1899, Sawyer became a director and secretary of the company. As for the Spokane appointee, Saylor, he was a graduate of Iowa State College whose career was in secondary education. After serving as superintendent of schools in Red Oak, Iowa, and Lincoln, Nebraska, he had been superintendent in Spokane from the 1890s until 1903. He would be a regent less than two years, resigning in December 1906. Soon thereafter he established in Spokane a private school for boys that became, in 1917, Spokane Academy.[25]

Men such as these—men from elsewhere, their educational experiences as diverse as their origins—now were regents of the University of Washington, where Thomas Kane, who had succeeded Graves as president, was trying with some success to nourish a university spirit in an institution increasingly crowded for space but which now had on its faculty bright young scholars—Thomson, Padelford, Kincaid, Parrington, others—whose names would live on the campus. In 1907 the Seattle *Times* reported that twenty-nine students had been "expelled" from the university, where an unnamed professor had explained: "The University of Washington has taken its place among the best institutions of the country, and we are determined that a student shall do the work required of him or leave." The university enrollment was about 1,200, and housing was a problem. *Times* headlines were saying "STUDENTS CANNOT FIND LODGING AT THE UNIVERSITY," and "UNIVERSITY COEDS CANNOT FIND LODGING: PERSONS WITH ROOMS TO RENT DON'T WANT THEM."

Moore's unhappiness with his rental terms may have become evident in 1905. A possible reason will be examined later. In any event, the regents had been made aware of it by February 1906, and at an adjourned meeting on March 29 they discussed a proposal by Moore for a modification of a lease and then made some calculations of their own.[26]

The calculations are interesting, because in them the regents arrived at a graduated fixed-rate rental formula by working from a percentage-on-appraisal base. The calculations also are important because they established the levels of income the university would in fact receive until 1954. And whatever the later judgments on the regents' decision, it could not be said in fairness that they yielded more than they gained, for the final fixed-rent schedule tripled the aggregate rent payments Moore now was offering while sacrificing an unknown amount of additional income based on appraisals to be made far in the future.

The minutes of the regents' meeting of March 29, 1906, contain this entry:

The Special matter to come before the meeting was then stated to be the request of Jas. A. Moore, lessee of the old University Site in this city, for the modification of his lease by the substitution of the following definite amounts to be paid as rental, at the times stated, instead of the present terms of the lease, basing amounts of rental to be paid after the first eight years, on percentages of the appraised valuation of the property. . . .

Moore Proposition

Rental for the next two years					$ 6,000.00 per year	$ 12,000
"	"	"	five	"	12,000.00 " "	60,000
"	"	"	ten	"	18,000.00 " "	180,000
"	"	"	"	"	25,000.00 " "	250,000
"	"	"	"	"	30,000.00 " "	300,000
"	"	"	twelve	"	40,000.00 " "	480,000
					Total	$1,282,000

The regents obviously discussed the proposal in detail. It was Sawyer who, at length, proposed adoption of a resolution which, after an introductory summary, contained this recapitulation of the regents' counter offer:

Valuation	Per cent	Amt. per Annum	No. of Years	Total
$ 500,000	2	$ 10,000	7	$ 70,000
1,000,000	3	30,000	10	300,000
2,000,000	4	80,000	10	800,000
2,500,000	4	100,000	10	1,000,000
3,500,000	4	140,000	12	1,680,000
			Total	$3,850,000

Sawyer's resolution did not pass. Only Hartman joined Sawyer in voting approval. Saylor was absent, and Cosgrove, Nash, Ronald, and President Powell voted nay. Then on a motion by Cosgrove, seconded by Nash, the secretary was asked to inform Moore that his proposition was not accepted.

Moore had been rebuffed, but the regents had been through an exercise in forecasting. They—at least Sawyer—had visualized a $3,500,000 valaution for the old grounds after some thirty-seven years, or about 1943. They had tested, although rejecting it for the time, a 4 percent rental, $140,000, on such an appraisal. They had looked at a rent schedule that would produce $3,850,000 in income for the balance of the lease—three times as much as the $1,282,000 Moore had proposed, although perhaps $1,000,000 less than Moore might have to pay on his percentage-on-appraisal commitment. Somewhere in all this a pattern appears to have been established.

What happened in the next months is not altogether clear. Accounts prepared years later say that at some point the regents urged Moore to obtain the financial backing that would make it possible for him to proceed with development, that he did indeed go east to talk to certain capitalists—N. W. Jordan and Eugene D. Fess of Boston; G. H. Whitcomb of Worcester, Massachusetts; and C. D. Lord of Park River, North Dakota—and that his financial ability finally was assured by Seattle men, Chester F. White, E. A. Stuart, and C. H. Cobb among them, who appeared before the regents to say they were prepared to guarantee Moore's performance. The suggestion in this is that Moore now was in financial difficulty, perhaps already too deeply involved with his Irondale dream or in plans for his house and farm on the Columbia at Pasco. In any case, what the regents' minutes show is that Moore was back before the board on November 6, 1906, to present a case for a modification of the lease along the lines suggested by Sawyer on March 29. The regents seemed disposed to change their minds, but they wanted Sawyer's advice and Sawyer was in New York. So Hartman sent off a telegram to Sawyer asking for his present view, and Sawyer wired back that he was "strongly in favor" of changing the lease as he had proposed. The issue was still alive.[27]

On January 25, 1907, the regents, with Hartman now president, returned to the Moore matter. There had been a change in the board in December 1906, when Saylor, resigning, was replaced by D. L. Huntington, of Spokane, vice-president and general manager of the Washington Water Power Company and soon to be its president. By a vote of five to one—Ronald against and Powell absent—the board approved appointment of a committee to work out with Moore a modification of the lease on terms as stipulated—and the terms were remarkably similar to those that had been drafted by Sawyer and rejected by the board ten months before. The resolution asked:

That the president of this Board appoint a committee of three members with authority to prepare and submit to this Board for its approval, a modification of the present lease with James A. Moore, which modification shall contain a fixed yearly rental value in place of the rental values of the present lease, as follows:

For the term ending 1912	$ 15,000.00 per annum
For the next 10 years	40,000.00 " "
" " " 10 "	80,000.00 " "
" " " 10 "	100,000.00 " "
" " remaining 12 years	140,000.00 " "

The modification, "to embody such further conditions as to improvements," was to be drafted for the board's approval, then submitted to Moore, who would "have until the 10th day of February, 1907, to sign same."[28]

Hartman named Sawyer, Ronald, and Nash as members of the special committee. Rather than modify the existing lease, the committee drafted a new instrument that incorporated the modified rental schedule and made certain other minor changes regarding improvements. The new lease was signed on February 1, 1907, for the board by Hartman and Markham, the secretary, and by the Moores, James A. and Eugenie. On February 7, all of the regents—Hartman, Cosgrove, Nash, Huntington, Powell, Ronald, and Sawyer—certified their approval.[29]

The terms of the Moore lease of 1904 had now been modified in 1907, and, as far as the rental was concerned, the terms had been established for almost half a century. There remained, however, a final test—a test of the whole leasing question, really—before Moore, with appropriate flashes of newspaper publicity, surrendered to others the development of the university tract.

The regents met again on March 7, 1907, a month after they ratified the Moore modification. Hartman announced that the question before the board was the approval or disapproval of the amended lease, the lease they had already signed. Cosgrove offered a resolution to approve. The resolution carried, but this time on a split vote—Hartman, Cosgrove, Huntington, Nash, and Sawyer voting to ratify, Powell and Ronald voting against. The Moore lease modification had been approved for the second time, but this time not unanimously.[30]

Why this? What had happened between the meetings of February and March? Supposition must take over. Later accounts of the development of the tract say that at some point in the period of Moore's difficulties the regents were subjected to intense public pressure to abandon leasing and sell the property so that money could be made available immediately for new construction on the Lake Washington campus. The needs of the university undoubtedly were great. Classes were being held, it was said, in whatever space could be found, including a patched-up tool shed. Hartman was reported to have been taken to the university campus one day to visit a chemistry class meeting in the shed. Prices of up to $750,000 were suggested as obtainable for the old grounds, and sketches of a desirable new building were prepared as posters for display in downtown store windows, the legend: "$750,000 Will Build This Building at the University. Does the University Need Such a Building? If So, Urge the Regents to Sell the Downtown Property."[31]

Perhaps it was in this period that the campaign took place or that its re-verberations still were felt. In any event, the Moore lease of February 1 had been reviewed and reaffirmed and, beyond that, the leasing policy. And the reaffirmation had come from regents who had not been members of the board when the original Moore lease was signed in 1904. They had held to the idea that the greatest benefit to the university lay not in a sale for $750,000 or some other figure, but in a lease that would be binding until 1954—a year that none of them could expect to live to see.

On March 8, 1907, the day after the meeting, the *Post-Intelligencer*—which now occupied its new building—published a lead story headed: "MIL-LIONS FOR THE STATE UNIVERSITY; Secures Heavy Rental and Buildings Under Terms of Moore Lease; TO IMPROVE OLD CAMPUS; Lessee Announces Plans for Several Fire-Proof Structures on the Property." The report was based heavily on statements by Moore. The opening paragraph gave the flavor:

Negotiations were completed yesterday by James A. Moore and the regents of the University of Washington, modifying the terms of the lease under which Mr. Moore holds that tract of ten acres, lying to the south of Union Street, which was formerly the campus of the University of Washington. This modification makes the terms more satisfactory to both parties than the lease under which Mr. Moore has been holding the property; and directly following the conclusion of the transaction Mr. Moore was able to announce building plans providing for the ultimate improvement of the entire property with fireproof structures of the first class. The first of these, costing half a million dollars, are to be erected within the next four years.

The Moore planning, however, was a little vague. In his references to this Moore said in part: "For the past two years I have had almost constant calls for the construction of buildings on the property. There is room in that vi-cinity for a high class of business construction, and the buildings we shall erect there will be absolutely first-class and absolutely fireproof. The exact details have not yet been decided. Work on the leveling of the property will com-mence almost immediately, or as soon as the details can be arranged."

On July 22, 1907, a new company came into existence, organized under the laws of the state of Washington for a term of fifty years and with an authorized capital of $5,000,000. The company was established to take over the Moore leasehold, and the man who had mobilized the resources—who had, in fact, conceived the idea—was a thirty-two-year-old attorney, John Francis Douglas.

The assignment of the lease to the Metropolitan Building Company had been discussed with Moore. Douglas had also assembled, in the East as well as in Seattle, a group of men interested in the university tract development, some of them the men who had been willing to assure Moore's ability to meet his commitments. In this group was Chester F. White.

On August 1, 1907, although a leasehold interest had not yet been formally acquired, the new company conveyed its prospective interest to the Washington Trust Company, of Seattle, as security for a mortgage bond of $5,000,-000, the proceeds to be used to acquire Moore's leasehold for $250,000 and the balance for construction of new buildings on the tract. By September 20, 1907, Moore and the Metropolitan Building Company had concluded an agreement outlining the terms of the sale and assignment of the lease. Although the assignment had not yet been made, the news of the projected development was public, and it was Moore who was again, momentarily and finally, the central figure. On September 22, 1907, the *Post-Intelligencer*'s story reported the organization of a "syndicate" of "rich men" to improve the tract. The story was redolent of the Moore touch. The lead proclaimed:

A $5,000,000 corporation, composed of Seattle and Eastern capitalists, representing more than ten millions of money, and having $1,000,000 paid in, for the development of the old university tract, is the latest promotive achievement of James A. Moore.

Mr. Moore announced yesterday that he had completed the formation of the syndicate, articles having been filed at Olympia, and that work would be commenced this fall on the first two of the series of fireproof buildings that is to [be placed on] the university tract. He recently secured a modification of the original terms of the lease of this tract, making it more advantageous to holders contemplating permanent improvements.

The story noted the incorporation of the Metropolitan Building Company, listing Moore, with White, Cobb, and others as incorporators, and identifying Douglas as a "heavy investor in Seattle property." "This concern," the story said, "is the largest ever organized in Seattle for the development of real estate."

The lease agreement was filed for record on October 2, 1907. Moore's assignment of the lease was made on December 3, and on the following day the company filed Moore's assignment and the trust deed to the Washington Trust Company. Chester F. White was listed as president of the company, Douglas its secretary. Moore was one of the eighteen stockholders because he had received, in payment for his leasehold, $90,000 in cash, $150,000 in bonds at par, and $10,000 in stock.[32]

The Metropolitan Building Company completed its payments to Moore on February 1, 1908. It was not until February 29, however, that Douglas, in a letter to Hartman, notified the regents officially of the transfer of the lease from Moore to the company on December 3, 1907. The regents considered this at their meeting of March 31, 1908, when they also had before them the $25,000 bond of the new lessee. The assignment and the bond were approved. The new Metropolitan Building Company was in charge.[33]

But what was metropolitan about the company or, more specifically, about the property it had undertaken to improve? Little enough, in 1908. On the old campus stood, north of Seneca, the original building, and below it was the huge, muddy slash where Fourth Avenue was being graded across the tract. On Union Street was one new building, the Post-Intelligencer, and the new company had not built that. The company, nevertheless, was the Metropolitan Building Company, and the name had been given it by J. F. Douglas.

Douglas had a promotional sense, as he later demonstrated, and by 1907, when he set about organizing the company, he had learned the appeal of a name to the men he hoped to interest, especially the Eastern capitalists who would be asked to put their funds into a project they had not seen in a city they had not visited. Early in his career, Douglas, seeking Eastern investors for an apartment building, had named the building the Manhattan. Later, financing a hotel, he called it the Waldorf. Now, for the organization that would undertake to develop the old campus, he chose a name that carried the same suggestion of cultivated elegance and that certainly expressed his plans for the place. His $5,000,000 corporation was called the Metropolitan.

Douglas intended to make the old university grounds the business and financial center of the new Seattle metropolis.

CHAPTER 4

The Transformation Begins: 1908 to 1911

The history of the Metropolitan Building Company's association with the old university site began in a year that would be remembered primarily as the first year of a sharp, short economic recession called the panic of 1907. Of all the years after the depression of the 1890s that year would seem the least auspicious for launching an enterprise of the kind now contemplated at a site where two lessees had already failed. Yet the new company moved ahead with a great show of confidence, and with a flexibility and ingenuity that can only be appreciated by a careful reading of the chronology of events. The Metropolitan Building Company had personal and financial ingredients that had not been present before, and enough momentum to enable it to brave the panic, which arrived in the Pacific Northwest as not much more than a diminishing shock from an economic turbulence far to the east. The principal new ingredients were, without doubt, Chester F. White and J. F. Douglas.

The Metropolitan Building Company had been incorporated in July 1907, as has been seen, to take over the James A. Moore leasehold. By August, two months before the lease agreement was filed for record, the company's interest had been mortgaged to secure the funds to buy out Moore and begin operations. By September, Seattle had learned through the press that a powerful new combination of capitalists was behind the move to develop the university tract. What also would soon become known was that a leading New York architectural firm already was at work on a "master plan"—although it was not yet called that—for the development of the site. The plan, with accompanying architectural sketches of the projected new buildings, was ready for public announcement even before the university regents formally considered the transfer of the leasehold at their meeting of March 31, 1908. All this was the work of Douglas, and Douglas—somewhat like Daniel Bagley, but in a different time and for different reasons—had moved farther and faster than anyone expected.

The time was, in fact, a good time for a man with ideas—a wonderfully exciting time, not only in Seattle and the Northwest, but in the nation that was emerging as a new world power. It was a time of peace with only faint portents of the shattering changes the twentieth century would bring. In the Far East, it was true, there were rumblings of international adjustments resulting from

The new Metropolitan Building Company's first bond offering was made in a prospectus of 1907–08 showing its leasehold property in an artist's sketch of Seattle's downtown area—the only building then on the tract the Post-Intelligencer, at Fourth and Union, begun by the University Site Improvement Company and finished by James A. Moore the Russo-Japanese War, but Europe's coming troubles were not yet on the horizon. The newspapers dutifully chronicled developments abroad, but what they also chronicled were notes on the arrival of what was recognized everywhere as a revolutionary age. Evidence accumulated daily. If it was not yet possible to assess the significance of the advent of the automobile, the airplane, and the wireless, it was certain that old ways of living were soon to be altered irrevocably.

Preening itself in its far Northwest corner of the country, Seattle had a feeling of nearness to all this in 1907 and 1908. The panic of 1907 was, after all, the "bankers' panic," but Seattle's own banks had deposits of more than $60,000,000 compared to only $4,652,000 just a decade before. Klondike gold dust continued to come in—the U.S. Assay Office said the total now had passed the $156,000,000 mark—and Seattle, knowing Alaska, was interested to read that Congress had considered authorizing a $1,000,000 wagon road to Valdez, a tiny little port, north on the Gulf of Alaska, that was experiencing a copper boom. Seattle had twelve hundred "manufacturing establishments" with seventeen thousand employees, an annual payroll of $15,000,000, and an annual production of $60,000,000. The population by 1908 was estimated at 276,462.[1]

As usual, the statistics did not fully reveal what Seattle was experiencing. The Pacific cable had reached Hawaii from the West Coast in 1902 and was being unrolled, beyond, to the Orient. In 1908, President Roosevelt's Great White Fleet arrived in Puget Sound with William Howard Taft, secretary of war, who would soon be the Republican nominee for president. In the fleet was the cruiser *Washington*, the state's own, which was given a welcome devised by the Seattle Commercial Club, cheered and displayed at all of the ports of the Sound while the other vessels were anchored in sixteen fathoms off Discovery Point, halfway between Seattle and Bremerton, where the Navy Yard took care of coaling and support operations. Even while the flotilla had been plunging northward along the west coast of South America, the United Wireless Company's University Station in Seattle had picked up faint signals from the fleet's transmitters, a small but significant suggestion of what was happening in communications. In September 1907, the Seattle *Times* contained a dispatch headed, "New Giantess of the Sea Breaks All Records." The new giantess was the transatlantic liner *Lusitania* on her maiden voyage. The newspapers noted that Wilbur and Orville Wright, demonstrating their new Flyer for the U.S. Army at Fort Myer, Virginia, had attained speeds in the air of over 39 miles per hour. A Seattle man had invented a new airship with "adjustable propellers" by which the direction of an airship might be controlled. And Seattle, like all of America, was welcoming the automobile— the Winton, the Stanley, the Studebaker, the Cadillac, the Duryea, and other exotic machines—and those Seattleites sufficiently wealthy to afford to be pioneers were being photographed for the newspapers in, or upon, their vehicles. The Seattle papers began to have Sunday automobile pages. In March 1908, the *Post-Intelligencer* carried stories headed "Auto Industry Booming"

and "Washington Has the Auto Craze," and the following month the newspaper, in an editorial entitled "Speeding Must Stop," suggested penal treatment for drivers who ran down pedestrians or caused other damage by reckless
behavior at the wheel.[2]

Culturally as well as physically, Seattle was maturing. Early in the century
Judge Thomas Burke, Edmond Meany, Clarence Bagley, and a few others
had met to organize a historical society. By 1908 the Seattle Symphony was
a "permanent institution," the newspapers said. Alexander Pantages, a
theater builder and vaudeville producer, was coming to full flower as a rival
of John Considine, an earlier entrepreneur, and the city's theatrical scene
was exceedingly busy on a dozen dramatic and variety stages—many below
Third Avenue on Cherry, Madison, and Seneca streets—and in six theatrical
agencies. Just beginning to be recognized as a serious photographer-historian-
ethnologist, although he had held his first exhibit in Seattle in 1904, was a
singular genius, Edward S. Curtis, who had dedicated himself since 1897 to
recording the lives, languages, and culture of the North American Indians.
Curtis's work and his classic publication, *The North American Indian*, ultimately cost $1,500,000, half of this paid by J. P. Morgan, the New York
financier, whom Theodore Roosevelt interested in the project. But when, in
1907, Curtis was searching for funds to begin publication, a group of twenty
Seattle men subscribed $50,000 to support the effort. The University of Wash-
ington Library became in time a repository of a set of the volumes and of
twenty portfolios of photogravures.* The university in 1908 was graduating
a class of 123. More than half the graduates were women, most of whom were
completing the "normal"—teacher education—courses. The university faculty
now had 113 members—more than twice the number of 1901. Seattle looked
to the campus more and more, now, because the campus, in 1909, would be
the site of the Alaska-Yukon-Pacific Exposition for which everyone had been
waiting for almost three years. The Exposition buildings would become the
property of the university when the fair was over. The regents had signed the
lease with the AYP board in 1906 (the space at no cost), and the legislature had
appropriated $1,000,000 for Exposition purposes, $600,000 to be used toward
construction of buildings of permanent use to the university. There had
already been a considerable purchase of (or speculation in) lots in James A.
Moore's University Heights Addition near what would become the Exposition grounds. Downtown, by 1908, the city was considering a plan for the

---

* On June 24, 1908, the regents noted receipt of a letter from Edmond Meany saying
that "twenty gentlemen" had subscribed $50,000 "to enable Mr. Ed S. Curtis to defray the
expenses of publishing the first volumes of his monumental work on the North American
Indians," and that "Mr. Curtis, out of gratitude for such help, had agreed to present a
set of the work . . . to the Library of the University in the name of the twenty friends." Among
the subscribers were several men whose careers touched in some way the story of the university tract. The twenty were F. W. Baker, P. H. Frye, John W. Roberts, A. J. Blethen,
John P. Hartman, Fred E. Sander, J. S. Brace, Samuel Hill, A. J. Smith, J. E. Chilberg, William H. Lewis, Charles D. Stimson, J. W. Clise, J. D. Lowman, Frederick S. Stimson, C. H.
Cobb, James A. Moore, H. F. Strickland, Miller Freeman, and C. E. Patton (Regents Record,
4:564, June 24, 1908).

improvement of Pioneer Place, that historic center of the original town, the plan including construction of "an open iron shelter, equipped with seats, where people may wait for street cars."[3]

The Metropolitan Building Company now proposed to do for the old university tract what was being done all over the city—to build, to convert idle property to productive and money-making uses. Douglas's plans were already far along in 1907. There were problems to be solved, among them the most basic one, the reduction of Denny's knoll to a manageable contour. The land not only was unimproved but the surface of the ground was, on the average, twenty-five feet above street level, and the property was accessible only on Union Street, at its northern boundary. Beyond that was the need to construct buildings that would attract the stores and shops and office-space renters essential to profitable operations. It all had to be done rapidly, and synchronized and made plausible. In the mind of Douglas it had to be done with a flair.[4]

Chester F. White was president of the new company because it was he who, approached by Douglas and persuaded of the possibilities of the site, had made an initial pledge of financial support and had enlisted or suggested others who might be similarly interested. Investors in the company had purchased $100 debenture bonds bearing 6 percent interest, each bond entitling the holder to a share of stock. No brokerage was involved, then or later. With White and Douglas, as stockholders of the company, were eighteen of the "rich men" listed in the *Post-Intelligencer* story. One of them was Moore, who received stock as part payment for his leasehold. Most of the other stockholders were men who were making fortunes in lumber in Seattle or elsewhere in the state. Seattle stockholders were Manson F. Backus, president of what was now the National Bank of Commerce and listed as treasurer of the new company; and Thomas Bordeaux, James Campbell, C. H. Cobb, James H. Douglas, Austin E. Griffiths, H. C. Henry, E. E. Hess, W. D. Lane, Patrick McCoy, and R. D. Merrill. Those from other Washington communities were W. J. Patterson, of Aberdeen; Alexander and Robert Polson, of Hoquiam; and Neil Cooney, of Cosmopolis. The list also included N. W. Jordan, of Boston, already associated with the Seattle Realty and Building Company, and C. D. Lord, president of the Bank of Park River, North Dakota. Lord was on the list (and it is interesting to recall that he was among the "Eastern" financiers who had been approached by Moore) because he was a North Dakota friend of the Douglas family who had advised young J. F. Douglas to seek his fortune in the West.[5]

White, the head of the new company, was another of the men who had found in Seattle the culmination of their transcontinental adventures, and White's course had been as full as any of turns and zigzags. White had been born in 1852 near Boston, the son of a shoe manufacturer, but when he was still a youth, his father, who must have been something of an adventurer himself, took his family to San Francisco, not across the country by rail or around

Cape Horn but by way of the Isthmus of Panama. In San Francisco, White finished his education in the public schools and in 1871, not yet twenty, he left home and, reversing traditional procedure, went east to enter the lumber business—in, somewhat improbably, Keokuk and Montrose, Iowa. Lumber then became his life. In 1885, he moved to Shelton, Washington, where, while he worked with a lumber company, he served as postmaster. When the lumber company failed in the recession of the 1890s, White went off to San Francisco, it is said, to get a job with Pope and Talbot, giant in the lumber field, and that company sent him back to Cosmopolis to manage its Grays Harbor Commercial Company, which became one of the largest mills in the Northwest. Soon he was in Tacoma as head of the Pacific Mill Company, and by 1896 he had offices in Seattle where he continued as manager of the Grays Harbor Company and supervised other interests. He was an organizer and first president of the Seattle Commercial Club, and he had been a leader in a fight by lumbermen against a 25 percent rate increase imposed by the transcontinental railroads on eastbound lumber. In 1907, White was fifty-five, a figure in the Northwest as well as in Seattle, and the kind of person to whom a man like young Douglas would turn with a plan for a major development. White was, obviously, a man who would respond.[6]

Not all of the other Metropolitan Building Company founders were so well known, but undoubtedly they formed a harmonious society. All were self-made men, even though several had college training.

McCoy and Bordeaux were from Canada. McCoy, born in 1854, had come to Washington in 1882 and had made whatever wealth he had acquired by engaging in lumber operations in the Skagit River country and in British Columbia. Bordeaux was one of two French-Canadian brothers who had come west—Thomas himself by way of California gold fields in 1875, Joseph as a "bullwhacker" and logger about 1883—to seek their fortunes in a land where they literally did not know the language. Although they spoke little English, they were tough and hard-working and for years cut cordwood and drove the logging wagons that hauled lumber for the Northern Pacific's railroad ties. They also saved their money, and by 1892 had formed the Mason County Logging Company at Shelton and were operating a sawmill near Olympia. By 1904 they had extended their lumber interests and were in banks and other enterprises and had transferred their headquarters from the Shelton area to Seattle, where Thomas had built a fine residence on Capitol Hill.[7]

Cobb, a native of Maine, was born on his father's farm near Lincoln, in Penobscot County, where his father was a partner in a logging firm. Cobb grew up with logging, driving ox teams and getting a little schooling at the Lee Normal Academy. Before he was twenty-four he was a junior partner and manager in his father's business. When he struck out for the West he had lumbering in mind, but he went first to California with a party of sixteen young Maine men in April 1876, then north to Seattle on the coastal steamer *Dakota*. To get his start he worked in harvest fields near Seattle, then as a timber cruiser and timber buyer. It was not until the 1890s that success began to come, but by then he was in business on his own, incorporating the Port Susan Logging Company, the Suquamish Logging Company, the Eby Logging Company, and the International Timber Company. He was in railroading as an incorporator of the Marysville and Arlington Railroad Company, a short line north of Seattle; in real estate investment as an organizer of the Cobb-Haley Investment Company; and in banking with the Dexter Horton Bank.[8]

James Douglas and W. D. Lane were partners of J. F. in the law firm of Douglas, Lane and Douglas. James was a younger brother of J. F.'s and a graduate of the University of Washington Law School. Lane was a native of Iowa, and he had clerked in a general store to save money for college. At Northwestern University he earned a B.S. degree in three years, was elected to Phi Beta Kappa, was a student orator, and won a letter in track. He also worked as a student assistant in English to earn money for law school, and at the University of Minnesota he won his law degree in eighteen months. He had practiced law in South Dakota for six years, serving two terms as state's attorney, before moving to Seattle and into the Douglas firm.[9]

Merrill and Griffiths had Michigan connections—University of Michigan connections, at any rate—although their origins were quite different. Griffiths was a lawyer and a prominent citizen who had been defeated for mayor of Seattle, but who had been a city councilman whose interest in public causes had led him to sponsor the development of municipal playgrounds for Seattle children. A native of Worcester, England, he was a graduate of the University of Michigan Law School in 1888 and had been practicing law in Seattle since 1897. Merrill, like Cobb, was from a Maine lumbering family, but the family had moved to the Great Lakes region in 1856. Born in Saginaw, Michigan, in 1869, Merrill was graduated from the University of Michigan in 1892 and moved west in 1898 to manage the Washington and British Columbia properties of Merrill and Ring, a leading lumber firm. He lived some years in Tacoma and Hoquiam before moving to Seattle in 1906, and in Hoquiam had established connections with the Polson Logging Company, in which the principals were the Polson Brothers, Alexander and Robert, now also with the Metropolitan Building Company.[10]

Campbell, like so many others, had worked with his hands in a long climb to affluence. Born in Nova Scotia in 1853, he was the son of John and Mary Renton Campbell, his mother a sister of the Captain William Renton for whom the town of Renton, southeast of Seattle, eventually would be named. Campbell had become a carpenter, then had gone to sea for three years before he arrived in Seattle in 1879. For a while he was a millwright at the Port Blakely Mill Company, on Bainbridge Island, across the Sound from Seattle, where Captain Renton was principal owner. By 1888 he and his brother, John A. Campbell, had built a mill at Port Blakely which for two years cut more lumber, it was said, than any other mill in the world. He eventually sold the mill to San Francisco interests, and invested in timberland and logging operations. By 1907 he was an exceedingly wealthy man, provident, charitable, still making money.[11]

But it was Horace C. Henry who most nearly approached, perhaps, the beau ideal of the adventuring, successful, and cultivated man of affairs. Henry was not a lumberman, banker, or lawyer, but a railroad builder— not a railroad financier, but a railroad contractor. Thus he was not a Villard or a Hill, but he was a man at home in such company and one to whom experience and success had given a gentlemanly polish.

By 1907–8, Henry had been in the state of Washington almost two decades, and in later photographs—a somewhat aquiline face carrying close-cropped Burnside whiskers, the coat and cravat immaculate—he appears as a handsome man who savors, but is modest about, his success. The facts were that Henry, born in Vermont in 1844, had been a cadet at Norwich Military Academy at the outbreak of the Civil War; he had left Norwich with his classmates to enlist in the Northern army in 1862, when he was eighteen; he had taken part in the Battle of Gettysburg; he had entered Williams College in 1864, hoping to get a degree, but had transferred to Hobart when his family moved to Geneva, New York; and he had given up on college, finally, to go to Minneapolis to work for a family friend who was a railroad contractor and by whom Henry was employed for ten years. Then he went out on his own. From 1878 until 1890 Henry built railroad tracks, tunnels, grades, and bridges throughout the Midwest, many for rail companies (the Minneapolis and St. Louis, the Wisconsin Central, the Diagonal) long since absorbed or vanished, but also for longer lines. In 1890, when he came to Washington, Henry had been engaged by the Great Northern to build the first beltway line around Lake Washington. After that he was busy with a number of Great Northern projects, most of them local and shortline (Seattle to Bellingham, Auburn to Palmer, Hoquiam to the sea), but including the difficult road from Everett to the crest of the Cascade Mountains. By 1906 the Chicago, Milwaukee and St. Paul had decided to extend its line to the coast, and Henry had received a $15,000,000 contract to build five hundred miles of rails across Montana and Idaho, an undertaking that employed ten thousand workers and required, it was said, $1,000,000 for explosives alone. Henry was and would be a capitalist, moving into banking and countless enterprises, but he also was a generous man, public spirited, the president of clubs, the head of civic organizations, and—never forgetting Gettysburg—always a member of the Grand Army of the Republic.[12]

Men such as these, representing "more than ten millions of money," the newspapers said, now were joined in a company to see what might be made of the university tract.

By the time the regents approved the assignment of the Moore lease in March 1908, the situation had changed, positively and dramatically. The regents—with A. P. Sawyer, of the *Post-Intelligencer*, as president of the board

—were dealing not with Moore, the brilliant promoter so full of other pre-occupations, but with a "syndicate" headed by White and guided by Douglas, to whom the development of the tract was a single, absorbing, consuming goal. To use an analogy that would not have been inappropriate even in 1908, it was as if, with the score tied at zero in the third quarter, a bright young quarterback suddenly had led the first team onto the field. The situation could not have been unpleasing to the regents, for the board had been looking for seven years for a capable and imaginative lessee, and the Metropolitan Building Company, new though it was, had experience, weight, and depth. The organizers not only were successful men, but many were those whom the Seattle regents, at least, undoubtedly encountered in their own business or professional lives, at the Chamber of Commerce, perhaps, or in connection with planning for the AYP Exposition, or socially, as at the Rainier Club, that center of financial-professional mingling. The irony was that the new company presumably had taken over the Moore lease with only a minimum of consultation with the regents, if any. And the fact seems to be that Douglas had been dreaming about the tract for perhaps two years before the leasehold was acquired, his "master plan" under development six months before the transfer was formally approved.

Douglas had been in Seattle only since 1900, a young man with a law degree, a wife, little money, and a large ambition. As Moore had before him, Dougas was cultivating a taste for building, but his first houses had been ones he had built himself, by hand. He had built and sold houses. He had organized companies to finance and erect the Manhattan "flats" and the Waldorf Hotel, at Seventh and Pike, getting investment money in New York and Boston. But whereas Moore's ideas exploded all over the landscape, Douglas's were concentrated and focused totally on the university tract. When Douglas began to dream of obtaining a lease on the tract, his whole mind embraced that rough place, and he already could see it graded, unified, with handsome buildings on it—a gem of commercial development.

Douglas fits no comfortable pattern. He was more than a developer, far less than a capitalist. If he was not a genius, his was at any rate the genius that created a tract forever after called Metropolitan. Douglas was an innovator, imaginative in business affairs, willing to take chances, intense in all he did. Yet he was essentially a modest and almost self-effacing man, preferring that others take the bows. He was an affectionate father and family man, and not without humor, but while his children called him "Pop," and to other intimates he was "Frank," Seattle and his business associates knew him only as J. F.—or, later, Major—never as John, much less Jack. He was the companion of the rich and he traveled and lived comfortably, always fascinated by automobiles (his first cars a series of Model T Fords), but he seems not to have profited greatly from the Metropolitan. Some of his truest friends and admirers were Metropolitan employees or former employees with whom he kept in touch for years. For more than two decades he was the central figure in the management of his company, yet in all that time he seemed content to be "Secretary Douglas." In a milieu in which the conduct of business affairs frequently was followed by a relaxing conviviality, Douglas, who neither smoked nor drank, remained his own man, convivial but abstemious.[13]

Douglas was born in Ontario in 1874, one of eight children of James A. Douglas, an Irishman who moved his family to North Dakota in the early days, to a farm near Park River. In due course, the father became a delegate to the North Dakota constitutional convention and a member of the legislature. Working on the family farm in summer and getting his first schooling in Park River, Douglas by age fifteen was in the University of North Dakota's Preparatory School and two years later at the university, where, as a six-foot two hundred pounder, he was something of an athlete as well as a campus leader, a quarter-miler in track, member of the baseball team, and editor of the campus newspaper. A classmate from Preparatory School days was Neva Bostwick, just his age, whose family had moved from Iowa to North Dakota and whom Douglas soon would marry. But first, after graduating from the University of North Dakota in 1896, Douglas went to the University of Minnesota Law School (there he perhaps met Lane, who would become his law partner) and on to Yale Law School, from which he was graduated in 1898. Then he came back to marry Neva, who had been teaching "grammar school."[14]

Briefly, and restlessly, Douglas practiced law in Grafton, North Dakota. He was elected justice of the peace. He was involved in community affairs, including organizing a campaign for funds to welcome home and help the Spanish-American War veterans. But already he was deciding to go west. It was C. D. Lord, the banker, who suggested Seattle. Douglas, traveling on a railroad attorney's pass, it is said, arrived in Seattle in July 1900, and there, enchanted by the mountains, the waters, and the grooming of the Sunday afternoon strollers in Madison Park, on Lake Washington, he determined to stay. He opened a law office with furniture bought on credit from D. E. Frederick, of Frederick and Nelson (who still sold used furniture as well as new), and in October 1900, Neva joined him.[15]

Douglas prospered, but only because he undertook, with Neva's help, an incredible amount of work. He went after law clients by making himself altogether visible, and this he did by joining and becoming secretary of every lodge he could find and by engaging furiously in community and church activities. Before 1900 was out he was deacon of the First Presbyterian Church and chairman of the building committee, and by 1901 he was vice-president of the West Seattle Improvement Club, this while he was helping improve West Seattle by building his own first house there. With the gold rush in full flower and vacancies almost nonexistent, J. F. and Neva were living in a rooming house. In the spring of 1901 they had taken a ferry to West Seattle and had bought an "impossible" place that nevertheless had a view of the Sound and the Olympics beyond. For a year and a half they lived there, commuting by ferry or sometimes walking home along an abandoned railroad trestle. Then they sold that home and built others, five in the Fremont district, three closer

to the city, saving their profits, hiring workmen, Douglas meanwhile expanding his law practice. As for the law, the gold rush helped, for new mining
and prospecting companies were forming and Douglas was preparing incorporation papers and working with corporate problems. Improbable as it
seems, Douglas found time to write a small book, *Douglas on Washington
Corporations*, published in 1904 by a local printing company, for which
Neva herself was to become the principal salesperson.* The Douglases hired
a man to sell the book, but he soon gave up, abandoning a shipment of
copies in Spokane. Neva took a train to Spokane, sold copies there and, later,
in Aberdeen, and the edition then was sold out by mail with orders still un-
filled. When she was over eighty and her husband long dead, Neva Douglas
remembered selling the book. "It was not that I was so smart as a saleswoman,"
she wrote. "I had typed it twice and had worked on it until I could recite it."[16]

Douglas was a lawyer. Douglas's brother James and W. D. Lane had joined
him by 1905 in the law firm of Douglas, Lane and Douglas. But at some
moment that year—or perhaps it had happened earlier—Douglas began to
think about the university tract. He had gained experience in building. He
was acquainted with Eastern sources of financing. Douglas-the-builder spent
days walking over the old university grounds and imagining the kinds of
developments that might be possible there, and Douglas-the-lawyer, studying
the lease held by James A. Moore, became convinced that Moore could not
possibly develop the property under the lease terms as they existed. The key
to Moore's difficulty was a rental schedule based on future appraisals, for
large lenders of money were fearful of such uncertainties. Douglas might have
waited until Moore gave up, but that was not in his nature. At some point,
perhaps early in 1906, Douglas went directly to Moore to discuss the lease.
Moore was the legendary developer, breathing success. Douglas was a thirty-
one-year-old newcomer. But Moore was impressed. Whether or not it was
the talk with Douglas that inspired him, it was in February 1906 that Moore
went to the regents with his first proposals for the lease revision. When the
regents eventually modified Moore's lease to incorporate the new fixed-rent
schedule, Moore presumably had played the game as long as he cared to and
Douglas, with his eye on the university property, had set the stage for the
gamble of his life. Moore told Douglas in July 1907 that he would be willing
to sell his leasehold for $250,000. That was the opening Douglas wanted.
He took a sixty-day option on the lease—an option expiring September 20—
and set about raising money.[17]

The annals of American finance are filled with stories much like Douglas's.
Yet his story is his own, and it is revealing to recall what he had become and
what he risked in 1907. Douglas, Lane and Douglas was a successful firm,
occupying new offices, employing two secretaries. J. F. and Neva had moved

---

* The copy in the Seattle Public Library is indexed thus: *The Law of Private Corporations Based Upon the Statutes of the State of Washington, and the Decisions of the Supreme
Court of the State of Washington, with the General Constitutional and Legislative Provisions of the State of Washington, and the Forms Most Commonly Used by Washington
Corporations. By J. F. Douglas, Seattle, Wash., Tribune Printing Co., 1904.*

in 1906 into one of the new Manhattan "flats," where Neva was manager. A son, John, had been born in 1905, and by 1906 there was a daughter, Neva. J. F., in the meantime, had become interested in a company that was buying a six-hundred-acre tract of land at Renton, where railroad freight yards were to be constructed, and at that place, near what was called Earlington Station, the company had converted an old farm house into a country club and had surrounded it by a residential community. The Douglases were soon living there, Neva helping to get Carnegie funds for a new Renton library. But also in 1906, when refugees from the San Francisco fire were being moved by train to temporary care even as far north as Seattle, it was J. F. Douglas who had dropped everything else for six weeks to help organize housing and feeding and, where necessary, temporary work for the displaced.[18]

In 1907, Douglas had two months to raise $250,000. The effort was a hair-breadth thing. Chester White, who undoubtedly could share Douglas's vision, subscribed $100,000, and some of the Northwest capitalists came in for smaller shares. Douglas nevertheless had to go east again, to Boston and New York, seeking to scrape together the funds he needed before the option expired. The story is that at 4 P.M. on the sixtieth day he still was $25,000 short (Neva Douglas remembered that it was $10,000), and that Douglas finally turned again to White, who came in for the final pledge, securing the leasehold. With that, Douglas could turn his attention to the organization of the Metropolitan Building Company. But White's name, naturally, would go on the first building.[19]

By the autumn of 1907 the new company's plan for transforming the university tract was in the process of creation. It is not easy to appreciate fully, so many years after the fact, the scope and intensity of the interest inspired in Seattle by the plan that would soon be disclosed. Skeptics there were, and some who felt that J. F. Douglas and his associates were overreaching themselves. But with the plan there could be no quarrel. Suddenly it became possible to visualize, skeptically or not, how almost ten acres of sloping land, idle for so long and hedged about by "business blocks" and residences, might become the site of a grand, new, totally integrated commercial center. Seattle, a little weary of the old campus and of the original building still standing there, could see in its mind's eye the strong, block-long façades of the new ten- and twelve-story "skyscrapers" that were already on the drawing boards.

The new idea was in the comprehensiveness of the planning, with unity the theme. No other city of Seattle's size—no other city of any size, probably—had near its center a plot of land so ready for development. The response to the opportunity was new for its time and, considering the challenge, brilliant in its expression. The development was conceived as a whole, the buildings to be designed not only with regard for function but in relation to each other—all executed with dignity and style, in brick, terra cotta, and marble, and with courts and open spaces. Quite early the Seattle project attracted the attention of architectural journals. Almost from the beginning the plan was described

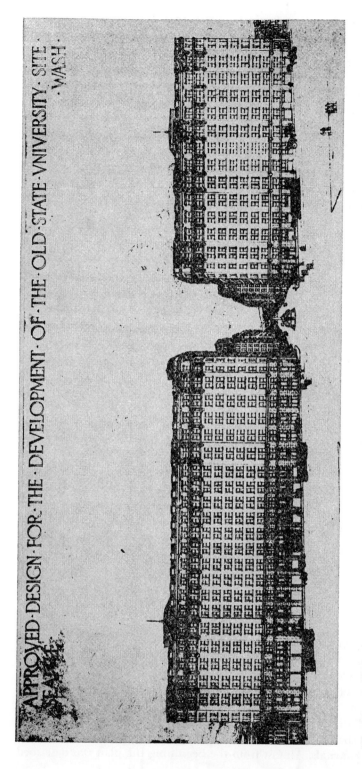

APPROVED · DESIGN · FOR · THE · DEVELOPMENT · OF · THE · OLD · STATE · VNIVERSITY · SITE · SEATTLE · WASH ·

The Metropolitan Building Company had before it in 1907 this vision of the future university tract, and the "approved design" worked out by the architectural firm of Howells and Stokes was something unique in its time—a master plan for a unified and architecturally harmonious commercial development near the heart of a growing city; the design was exhibited in New York even before it was displayed in Seattle early in 1908 as a plan to build a "city within a city." The phrase may have been used first by a writer who was later quoted in a report in the *American Architect* in 1916:

The completion of the Metropolitan developments will produce in effect a city within a city. No greater task has fallen to any body of men, no greater chance to accomplish great results with few mistakes. Symmetry, beauty, adaptability and economy in construction should be easy to attain under these conditions. It is seldom given to any group of city builders to act as a unit in the building of the very center of a large city; seldom that a tract of so many acres can be found unimproved with the retail district of 200,000 people bounding it on two sides, and a better portion of the residence district abutting on the other two sides.[20]

The plan as it was executed was the work of Howells and Stokes, a New York architectural firm that would serve the Metropolitan Building Company for almost two decades. How much of the original concept came from Douglas cannot be known, but even the architects themselves apparently regarded Douglas as the guiding hand. He had leased the tract as a whole and it was as a whole that he expected to develop it, to make it a commercial success, a place desirable to tenants who wanted to be identified with the best accommodations Seattle had to offer. Whatever ideas Douglas had accumulated by 1907 he would entrust, undoubtedly, only to architects he considered capable of improving upon them. When he turned to New York to find such architects, he found in Howells and Stokes what came to be seen, in retrospect, an ideal connection—a young firm whose principals were already launched on long careers in which they would win reputations as architectural historians and critics as well as designers of noteworthy university and commercial buildings.*

Howells was John Mead Howells, the son of William Dean Howells, novelist and editor of the *Atlantic Monthly*, while Stokes was I. N. Phelps Stokes, the son of Anson Phelps Stokes, a prominent New York banker and philanthropist. The two had been classmates at Harvard, graduating in 1891, and both had been students at the École des Beaux Arts in Paris, Howells as a candidate for a French government diploma, which he won in 1897, and Stokes (having given up banking for architecture) for a year of study abroad after graduate work at Columbia. By 1907, when Howells and Stokes undertook the Seattle project, the firm was ten years old.* Stokes, with an interest in mass

---

* In subsequent years, even while the firm still was represented in Seattle, Howells and Stokes designed such buildings as Woodbridge Hall at Yale; St. Paul's Chapel at Columbia; the Music School at Harvard; the Stock Exchange Building in Baltimore; and the Royal Insurance Company buildings in Baltimore and San Francisco. Howells, in association with Raymond M. Hood, one of the designers of Rockefeller Center, developed plans for the Daily News Building in New York and the Tribune Tower in Chicago, the latter the winner in a competition involving some two hundred architects from all over the world. Howell's interests included the preservation and restoration of colonial buildings, and he wrote extensively on early American architecture.

* Douglas apparently sought out the firm even before he was sure of his leasehold. Neva remembered accompanying J. F. on one of his fundraising expeditions to New York during which they were entertained by William Dean Howells and Anson Phelps Stokes.

housing, had been appointed by Theodore Roosevelt in 1900 as a member of the New York Tenement House Commission that drafted legislation governing such construction. Howells was becoming known for his use of Gothic themes and decoration in skyscraper design. The partners were quite willing to make Seattle their West Coast address, and soon the firm of Howells and Stokes was a fixture in the Seattle professional scene, carrying on the Metropolitan Building Company's design programs with the help of an associate, A. H. Albertson, sent out to supervise construction.[21]

The Metropolitan Bulletin

Issued Bi-Weekly by The Metropolitan Building Company

SEATTLE, WASHINGTON, JULY 18, 1908

White Building as it will appear when completed.

The White Building still was not finished when the Metropolitan Building Company's new biweekly publication, the *Metropolitan Bulletin,* presented this sketch in July 1908 of the first of the projected "skyscrapers"

The first public announcement of the Metropolitan Building Company's plan was made early in March 1908, three weeks before the regents were to meet to approve the transfer of the lease from Moore. The *Post-Intelligencer*'s report of Sunday, March 8, was accompanied by drawings displayed under a page-wide heading: "APPROVED DESIGN FOR THE DEVELOPMENT OF THE OLD UNIVERSITY SITE." The drawings were the Howells and Stokes sketches, the larger a "View of Fourth Avenue Frontage, Looking Up University Street," and the other a ground plan of the buildings then projected. Office buildings were to be placed west of Fourth Avenue, one wrapped around the new Federal Building at the northwest corner of the tract. Other office buildings, backed by service courts, were also planned on Seneca and Union streets, but the area above Fifth Avenue was to be lined by apartment houses with garden-court entrances. But the most striking developments were to be on University Street. To the south would be a new department store occupying half of the block between Fourth and Fifth avenues, and across University Street, to the north, a twelve-story "University Hotel." In the center of the street, between the department store and the hotel, would be an attractively planted yard, its sides set back from the street lines, to be called "University Place."

The planning and designing had been done with remarkable speed. Stokes had visited Seattle in the autumn of 1907 to go over the ground with Douglas, White, and others. The sketches had been developed during the winter while the Metropolitan Building Company was arranging to complete its payments to Moore. The construction plans for the first building, the White, had been finished in time to permit work to begin in March. Space in the White Building was being leased, and it was hoped that the building could be opened by February 1, 1909. Douglas was quoted as saying that the company had planned to move next to construction of the hotel, but that the demand for offices was so great that the second office building now was contemplated south of, and adjoining, the White. "It is our intention," Douglas said, "to go ahead with buildings as fast as the separate units are finished. We expect to complete about two buildings a year, and hope to have the entire group finished within seven years."[22]

Yet if any of what was done in those first months was done in consultation with the university's regents it is not apparent in the record. J. F. Douglas, driven by his own kind of "go-aheaditiveness," seems to have moved too fast for consultation with a board, although of course he was only doing what the regents had expected earlier lessees to do. The regents, nevertheless, appear to have been the last to be informed. Long before the public announcement in Seattle, the Howells and Stokes plans were put on display in New York City at the annual exhibition of the Architects League of America, where they drew admiring attention. On March 16–18, 1908, after the public announcements, Douglas held a local showing of the drawings at an invitational exhibit in the banquet room in Seattle's most fashionable hotel, the Butler. At length, on March 25, 1908, Douglas told the regents officially what was already known to almost everyone including, without doubt, the regents themselves. In a letter to Sawyer, Dougas said, "We now have the completed drawings for the development of the University Tract in our office." Could it be that the regents had not been invited to the preview exhibit at the Butler?[23]

A BUSINESS BUILDING for BUSINESS MEN

The White Building in Metropolitan promotion, 1908

The grand design was there in 1908 for all to see, and so too, at the beginning of construction of the White Building, was the evidence of its anticipated realization. By summer 1908, the foundations of the new buildings were laid and the structural steel was rising toward its eleven-story height. The steel frame at the corner of Fourth Avenue and Union Street towered above the drab, four-story brick Post-Intelligencer Building, across Fourth Avenue, where the regents held their meetings in a room provided under the terms of the Moore lease. The regents, meeting there, needed only to look across the street to note the progress of construction on the first truly dynamic building on the property of which they were the custodians. The White Building was the centerpiece, in its way, of all that was going on in Seattle that year. It was not the only large project taking shape. A new National Guard Armory was being built at Western Avenue and Lenora Street, to the north; the Arctic Club was beginning a new building at Third Avenue and Jefferson Street, to the south; and the Sisters of Providence had announced plans for a $1,000,000 hospital at Eighteenth and Jefferson, at the very crown of the heights between Elliott Bay and Lake Washington. The university tract nevertheless had a special charm, a historic interest, a sentimental attraction. It was easy to feel the romance of it all, the new replacing the old. The wonders that could be wrought by American capital were romantic, too. Howells and Stokes, the firm that had drawn up the plan, worked in such a glow. Looking back at these beginnings, in an article prepared only four years later, the architects said:

The start of the development of the University Tract in Seattle, Wash., is one of business boldness amounting almost to romance. About ten years ago the growth of the city was so great in one direction as to threaten to grow around and encircle the ten-acre campus of the State University of Washington, and it looked as if this large academic tract must either drive the development in another direction or itself become the heart of a new business district.

A group of Pacific Coast financiers was formed, which took over from the State a fifty-year lease of this land, with a rental graded heavily upward during that period. The Metropolitan Building Company, thus formed, was, however, held in its turn to cover the entire tract of twelve city blocks of street frontage with high-class, ten or twelve story buildings. At the expiration of fifty years the entire property, including the buildings and all other improvements, under the lease, will be turned over to the University of Washington as a well co-ordinated unit in the heart of the city, when it will probably be the largest commercial development of its kind undertaken in any part of the world.[24]

Romance aside, the Howells and Stokes statement phrased precisely the tactical situation faced by the Metropolitan Building Company in that era—from 1908 to 1910, for a beginning. Either the university tract would become the center of the Seattle commercial district or it would not. If it was to become the center, it must be made attractive, so that commercial activity would be pulled into it—which meant pulling the development uphill to the difficult knoll and thus actually changing the course of the city's growth, which had flowed northward along First and Second avenues, and more recently on Third, at the more accessible levels of the city's steep hillside. And all had to be done at the earliest moment—the land and the streets graded, buildings built, the tenants and sublessees brought into the tract as soon as possible so that a cash flow could be started.

Ideas rolled out of Douglas in those early years, but his problem was the one that had defeated his predecessor—how to build a "city within a city" from a standing start. The period from 1908 to 1910 was for Douglas a time of quick, almost frantic, forward motion, although not always along the lines so carefully laid out, and it was a time in which the Metropolitan Building Company and the board of regents began to get a feeling for the relationship that now existed between them.

The realities of the situation are glimpsed in the record of Douglas's responses. Before the White Building was well started the company had already decided to build a second, adjoining office building, which became the Henry Building, but it also had put aside the idea of the hotel on "University Place," and the reason may be surmised. Office space would bring to the tract the steady, long-term business tenants the company sought to lure to its premises. A hotel, even an apartment hotel, would not. So the Henry Building followed the White, and both were completed in 1909—the White ahead of its February 1 target date, early evidence of Douglas's impatience to get his plans in motion. The White cost $610,000, the Henry, $520,000. The construction firm was the Stone and Webster Engineering Corporation, of Boston.

But already Douglas and his associates had concluded, as had Moore before them, that something had to be done about income. Not only was the construction expensive, but so was the grading and preparation of the ground. When the White Building was started, Fourth Avenue, on which it stood, was still a muddy ditch where the city was joining the ends of the avenue abutting the tract at Seneca Street on the south and Union on the north. This work was the city's, and the contractor, C. J. Erickson, was keeping steam shovels on the job sixteen hours a day to meet the construction deadlines.* But before the White's foundations were laid it had been necessary

---

* Seattle's conquest of its hills remains one of the engineering marvels. Clarence Bagley, writing in 1928, recalled that in the years of Seattle's beginnings the "builders of the new

to core the soil to check moisture loss and potential settling, and the building had to be erected, while the grading was in progress, at what would be the new, lower street level. Where the city was not grading, it was necessary for the Metropolitan Building Company to do so. The preparation of the tract called for the removal, it was said, of 10 million cubic feet of earth.[25]

The company's idea about solving the income problem was the same as Moore's. It proposed to build temporary buildings, quickly, to establish a cash flow, then remove them as soon as work could proceed on the larger, grander units of the Howells and Stokes plan. On June 1, 1908, when work on the White Building was only begun, the company asked the regents to permit it to erect one-story buildings on the tract, these to be removed in five years. On June 24, the regents approved the petition—but for seven years, not five—and authorized the president, Sawyer, to see that the lease was appropriately modified. Moore had built temporary buildings and had been ordered to tear them down, but the new company now had clear authority to proceed along this line.[26]

This small transaction, it cannot be doubted, made possible all of the development that came later. Even in 1908, no company, whether or not it represented "more than ten millions of money," could have afforded to place on the tract—in the seven years, as Douglas hoped—all of the buildings laid out in the Howells and Stokes plan.* It is not known why the company asked for five years rather than seven, or why the regents approved seven years rather than five. Doubtless there had been consultations between June 1 and June 24. At the meeting on June 1 the board had appointed Hartman and Powell as a committee of two with power to act. Hartman and Powell had settled on seven years and the board approved their decision.

That modification of the lease was the first of several that would be made over the years with the regents' approval. The occasion also was the first in which the regents found themselves having to respond to modification re-

---

town were greatly surprised at the number of steep hills that were gradually exposed as the forest disappeared." Before the new century began, and under the direction of R. H. Thomson, the city engineer, Seattle was beginning to attack the hills with water, washing down millions of cubic yards of soil, which was used, after a few false starts, to build up the low tidelands of the waterfront. Howells and Stokes, writing in 1916, said, "Hydraulic regrading has been brought to such development in Seattle, as we all know, that it is said that if they do not like a hill in Seattle they do not hesitate to wash it away," but they noted that "the University Tract did not lend itself to this method" ("Some Work, Away from New York," *American Architect*, June 21, 1916, p. 403). By 1928, according to Bagley, the city engineer's office estimated that more than 37 million cubic yards of earth had been washed away, not counting the leveling and grading done privately.

* In the University of Washington Library is a copy of a printed folder, "Bondholders of the Metropolitan Building Company, Seattle," undated, but certainly published in 1908, listing fifty-three persons and firms holding Metropolitan bonds totaling $825,000. C. F. White's share, $150,000, was by far the largest, although N. W. Jordan, of Boston, held $95,000. Most of the holdings were of $5,000 to $10,000. The name of James A. Moore was not listed, nor were those of four of the originals—James H. Douglas, W. D. Lane, Austin Griffiths, and E. E. Hess.

quests from the Metropolitan Building Company. There would be many more, many not approved. The company was back with a new request early in 1909. This one the regents denied. It was a request of the kind the regents would deny again and again.

On January 26, 1909, the company asked the regents to extend the lease for ten years beyond 1954, the rental for the additional term to be 4 percent of the appraisal in 1954. The Moore lease acquired by the company now had about forty-one years to run, and Douglas probably felt that the company deserved a fifty-year period in which to improve on its investment. In any case, the regents thought the proposal deserved study. The request was referred to the Seattle members of the board—Hartman, Powell, Ronald, and Sawyer—copies of the proposal to be sent in the meantime to each regent pending the calling of a special meeting. The president of the board now was Nash, the Tacoma attorney appointed a regent in 1905 by Governor Mead, and Nash was asked to call the meeting. On February 10, 1909, the regents met in the evening in the Tacoma Hotel, in Tacoma, and the request for extension was unanimously denied.[27]

There was a foretaste in this of the cautious sparring—the action and reaction—that would characterize relations between the board and its lessee in later years. The company would press, the regents would respond, searching for a policy. And slowly a policy emerged, a guide for the regents no matter what the board's membership. The regents seemed willing—too willing, some thought later—to accommodate the company's plans within the term of the lease. But any extension beyond 1954 they resisted. The 1909–10 period, when this was beginning, must have been a time of trial for Douglas, who was starting to develop the one-story temporary buildings, who was having to arrange the details of construction and financing of the White and Henry Buildings, and to whom forty years was beginning to seem not enough time to do what needed to be done to get the Metropolitan Building Company on a paying basis.

Suggestions of the urgency in which Douglas was working are found in the regents' records of those years. Rebuffed in February 1909, Douglas presented another request for a ten-year extension on October 26. This was denied. New requests were presented on January 7 and February 23, 1910; these were rejected by the board on April 26, 1910. Douglas finally was proposing a fifty-year extension of the lease for any parts of the tract upon which the company constructed buildings of the White-Henry type, the rental to be 4 percent of the 1954 appraisal—and one offer was of a 4 percent rental "plus an amount that would be equivalent to the taxes assessed against the ground if the ground was held in private ownership." To none of these proposals would the regents accede.[28]

The question of taxation had been called to Douglas's attention in August 1909. Early in the month the county assessor, A. E. Parish, had placed an assessment of $480,000 on the Metropolitan leasehold—this calculated at 48 percent of a $1,000,000 valuation—and was insisting that the company pay taxes. On August 18, the assessment was sustained by the board of equalization after a hearing at which Douglas testified for the company. The testimony, as it was reported in the Seattle *Star*, is revealing. Douglas said that he considered the assessment "arbitrary" and declared, apparently, that the Metropolitan Building Company would take the tax question to the courts. But he seems also to have mobilized for his testimony every conceivable argument. He said that the land was "some blocks distant from the business center," the adjoining streets never had been business streets, two and a half years of the lease had already expired, the company had spent $148,000 in grading, the lease had "numerous restrictions" that curtailed its value, and the company was obliged to furnish for the regents "an office suite with private toilet free of cost." When a member of the equalization board asked, "What was the valuation of the leasehold, in your estimation, on March 1?" Douglas responded that the company would sell "for a couple of hundred thousand dollars." Another member said, according to the *Star*, that he "thought the company could not be jarred loose from the lease with dynamite." To this Douglas responded: "I agree that the value of the property will increase in value rapidly. We went into it to make money. That we have failed to do so far, and we cannot until the property is further improved. . . . The only inducement for us to take the leasehold was that it would be exempt from taxation."[29]

Douglas, resisting the assessment for taxes in 1909, was offering the regents, in 1910, "an amount that would be equivalent to the taxes assessed" if the lease were extended. It was a measure, perhaps, of the anxiety Douglas was feeling.

The tax problem was one that would continue to hover about the leasehold. But while Douglas was first fretting about this, legal actions were under way which, although they affected directly neither the university's interest nor the company's lease, raised questions about the dimensions of the tract.

Years earlier, in 1873, the regents of that time had granted a petition of residents living to the east and west of the old campus "to appropriate so much of the University grounds as may be necessary to make a street fifty feet wide on each side, inclusive of the alleys; provided such residents shall erect a good and substantial fence on the grounds, as good at least as the one first erected, within five months next ensuing." Thirty-five years later, in 1908, the regents revoked that 1873 resolution. At a meeting in the Post-Intelligencer Building on February 27, Sawyer in the chair, the regents approved unanimously a resolution by Powell to "disclaim and deny" any rights presumed to have been acquired and now being "asserted by certain property owners."[30]

How the rights were being asserted is not known, but on March 9, 1908, ten days after the regents' action, the state brought suit in King County Superior Court against the city of Seattle and the owners of the properties ad-

The beautifully detailed Howells and Stokes plans for university tract buildings incorporated front and profile projections of Indian faces "symbolic of the characteristics of the American Indian, and indicative of the strength and vigor of the West"; these faces, molded in terra cotta and placed high in the frieze lines of the White-Henry and the Cobb, were devices of a continuing Metropolitan theme

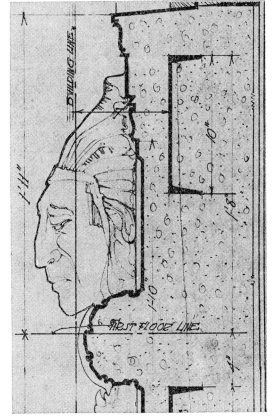

joining the tract to quiet title to the two fifty-foot strips. The state asked that its title to the entire ten-acre tract, less the part sold to the government, "be decreed good and valid, and free from all manner of interest, or easements." The board of regents was not a party to the action, but on January 26, 1909, the matter of the suit "for an alley on the westerly side of the University Tract" was referred to a committee composed of Powell, Hartman, and Ronald. At a meeting on March 25 Powell moved that the president of the board, Nash, authorize the attorney general to enter a stipulation that would end the claims of property owners on the west edge of the tract and effect a compromise on the fifty feet in question—thirty of the fifty feet to be the state's—that is, within the tract—and twenty feet, for an alley, to be the city's. Powell's motion, approved by the regents, rested on the premise that "the Metropolitan Building Company shall enter into a contract with this Board to the effect that the lease . . . may be modified in accordance with the terms of said stipulation." No such modification appears to have been made, but the stipulation was filed by attorneys for the state and the city on July 10, 1909, the final decree was entered by the Superior Court two days later, and an appeal to the Supreme Court was sustained on March 10, 1910.[31]

What had happened was that a twenty-foot strip had been sliced off the west side of the tract, from the south end of the Federal Building to the south property line at Seneca Street, to become an alley between Third and Fourth avenues. The loss was minor, and an alley had been gained. The state's—the university's—title to the rest of the land, east and west, had been confirmed. But that small adjustment proved to be the first of several, some relating more specifically to the boundaries and effective acreage of the land the Metropolitan Building Company held under lease.

Another such problem had arisen in 1908 in the widening of Union Street at the north side of the tract. An examination of the Denny deed of 1861 and of subsequent plats filed by Denny led to the conclusion that the ten-acre property as originally dedicated extended to a line six feet farther north than had been thought—six feet beyond the south line of Union Street and six feet beyond the line described in the Denny deed. The city, preparing to widen the street, filed condemnation proceedings in the Superior Court in 1908, and the court's order subsequently took from the tract a strip five feet wide at the north edge, thus leaving, as one writer later pointed out, a net addition to the tract of a strip of land one foot wide. Neither the White Building nor the Post-Intelligencer was affected, since each had been constructed with the future widening in view. The court, recognizing nevertheless the interests of the state, the regents, and the Metropolitan Building Company, awarded compensation in amounts totaling, with interest, $52,546.49.[32]

The question of the disposition of these payments would be examined many years later, but at the time Seattle had other things on its mind. The year 1909 was the year of the AYP Exposition, and it was a busy year at the university, where the regents were dealing repeatedly with matters related to the presence of the Exposition on the campus—in January, the placement of the

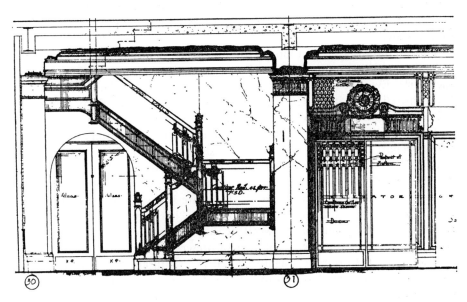

Howells and Stokes 1908 plans for the Henry Building, showing a lobby with marble walls, and bronze trimmings and grilles for the stairs and elevators

Women's Building; in the spring, questions of management; in August, the decision on which AYP buildings should be kept permanently for university purposes.

The Exposition was a complete success. On the slope of the campus, below Denny Hall and above Lake Washington, Exhibition buildings had been placed around a beautiful new mall, with a pond and fountain at its center, a spectacular corridor of buildings oriented toward Mount Rainier seventy miles away. All of Washington's industries were represented in the displays. Special exhibits honored the pioneers, the railroad builders, the loggers and lumbermen, the fishermen, the shipping and navigation companies. Attention was of course given to Alaska and the Yukon—to the gold rush, to mining, to the future of the vast lands to the north. There were exhibits from the Eastern states, and states nearer by had special "days" at which their governors or other dignitaries were speakers or honored guests. Seattle had a chance both to show off and to see itself in what it confidently believed was the beginning of an unlimited growth. The exhilarating effects of the fair would be felt for decades.

There had been some thought that the original university building, which stood on the downtown tract, might be moved to the campus for the Exposition. Edmond Meany, writing as chairman of an alumni association committee, had asked the regents to approve such a plan—a daring one, certainly, since the old building would have to be taken from its knoll and hauled, somehow, by land and water to a new site. The regents were sympathetic, but feared the costs. On a motion by Powell, the regents had given the alumni association permission to move the building, "to be located at such point as the Board of Regents may approve of and without expense to the university or the state."[33]

The old building was not moved from the tract. It was demolished in 1910, only the classic columns preserved and erected on the new campus as a memorial. Even before that, to make room for grading, the building had been shifted from its original site to an empty lot above Fifth Avenue.* When the demolition finally began, the Howells and Stokes representative, A. H. Albertson, took time to prepare a report on the condition of the structure—a report that he thought of as "the last chapter in the history of the Old University Building." The admiration that Albertson felt for the structure clearly showed, for he found its condition astonishingly good, the wood scarcely touched by dry rot or moisture (C. F. White had said the wood was fir), the framing and siding perfect—the framing "hard as bone." The doors, stairs, and flooring were all in excellent shape except for wear; the window frames were "in such an excellent state of preservation that L. B. Gullet, the wrecker, expects to use them again." Finally: "All in all, this historic building, now forty-nine years old, is in better condition as to durability than the casual observer expects of this type of construction. Aside from plastering, parts of the finish floor, front doors, and parts of the sleepers, this building would have been good for forty-nine more years."[34]

Architect John Pike and his fellow builders of 1861 would have been pleased. Howells and Stokes, of New York, had found their work good.

But 1909 and 1910 brought not just the AYP Exposition and the ensuing expansion of facilities on the university campus. The years also brought changes in the board of regents and, on the part of Douglas and his associates, the beginning of a rush of construction and planning for construction that would at last set the Metropolitan Building Company on its way.

The board of regents was undergoing one of its periodic major shifts in membership. The board of 1908–9 (the board that first declined to extend the term of the Metropolitan Building Company lease) had been composed of Nash, as president, and Sawyer, Hartman, Powell, Ronald, and Cosgrove, plus Huntington, the newest member, from Spokane. Soon the alignment was altered. Cosgrove resigned in November 1908, "on account of being elected governor of the State," as the regents' minutes quaintly put it, and he was replaced by F. A. Hazeltine, the South Bend newspaper publisher whose earlier appointment by Governor McBride, in 1904, had not been confirmed.†

* As the building was going down, J. F. Douglas wrote, "At Professor Meany's request we have kept the building in its former condition for nearly three years, thinking that funds might be raised for its preservation." At Douglas's request, Meany wrote a short paper on the history of the building (Metropolitan Building Company, *Metropolitan Bulletin*, March 12, 1910).

† Hazeltine must have been an interesting person. A graduate of Oberlin College in 1889, he had spent a year in South America, later writing a book about his travels while

·UTAH·BUILDING·COMPANYS·DEVELOPMENTS·

Proposed department store, which failed to find a lessee—one of three of the major buildings originally visualized in the Howells and Stokes master plan that never were constructed

When Cosgrove died soon after being sworn in as governor and Marion Hay became his successor, there were changes in the political winds. Before the year was out Ronald, Sawyer, Powell, and Huntington had resigned (Ronald on March 27, Sawyer on July 29, Powell on July 31, and Huntington on November 18), although Powell, the senior member, said simply that he had served six years and needed to devote more time to his business affairs. The new regents were Howard G. Cosgrove, of Pomeroy, the son of the late governor; John C. Higgins, of Seattle, who succeeded Ronald; M. F. Backus, who succeeded Sawyer; Alexander F. McEwan, of Seattle, who succeeded Powell;

he worked for the Spokane *Chronicle.* By 1890 he had bought an interest in the yearling *Journal* in the one-year-old town of South Bend. On his visit to South America he had met on shipboard an Amy Wood, the Argentine-born daughter of a U.S. consul, missionary, and former president of Valparaiso College in Indiana. In 1895, young Hazeltine returned to South America, from his little newspaper office in South Bend, to marry Amy in Callao, Peru. The marriage was contested, it is said, because it had been performed by a Protestant minister in a Catholic country, so the bride's father took the issue to court and won a change in Peruvian law. By the time Hazeltine became a regent he was a leader in politics and in community and church work—and a prohibitionist so ardent that his county, Pacific, was the first to vote "dry" under local option legislation. Amy Hazeltine apparently fitted perfectly into her life as the wife of an activist Washington publisher, and some years later she was secretary of the Washington State Federation of Women's Club. See Herbert Hunt and Floyd C. Kaylor, *Washington, West of the Cascades,* 3 vols. (Chicago and Seattle: S. J. Clarke Publishing Co., 1917), 2:228–30.

and A. L. Rogers, of Waterville, who succeeded Huntington. By 1910, John A. Rea, a Tacoma real estate and insurance agent, would succeed Nash.[35]

The personalities were changing. Cosgrove, like his father, was a lawyer—he had been his father's partner in Pomeroy—and the first alumnus of the university, the newspapers noted, to be named to the board. Higgins was a Seattle lawyer, a native of Michigan with an A.B. from the University of Oregon and an LL.B. from the University of Washington, who was also secretary and a director of Frye and Company, a packing firm. McEwan was another Michigan native, president of the Seattle Cedar Lumber Manufacturing Company, which he had founded in 1890. It could not have been a surprise that Manson Backus was appointed to the board, for Backus, although not yet the "dean" of Seattle bankers, was a leader in the financial community, a distinguished citizen, and a cultivated man. Still, Backus had been associated with two of the university tract lessee companies—first the University Site Improvement Company and then the Metropolitan Building Company—and publicly identified as treasurer of the second. A question about these associations arose later in the state senate, but the committee looking into the matter confirmed the appointment after it was satisfied that Backus had long since sold his interest in the Metropolitan Building Company and had never actually served the company as treasurer.[36]

Douglas found the new regents no more amenable than their predecessors to the idea of extending the lease. But he was authorized to build temporary buildings, and this he proceeded to do, while trying in every way to move forward with the major buildings envisioned in the comprehensive plan. Douglas was not facing the problems alone, surely, for he had with him a team whose members included such stars as White, Cobb, and Henry. But it cannot be doubted that it was Douglas about whom the problems swirled and from whom the ideas and plans were emanating.

The record of the Metropolitan Building Company to 1910 is, in the sheer volume of building activity, a little dizzying. By 1909 the company had finished work on the White and Henry buildings, had started work on the Cobb Building, the third new major structure and named for one of the original investors. The Cobb was not an extension of the White-Henry. It was across the street at Fourth and University and was further evidence of J. F. Douglas's flexible genius. Plans for a "Grandin Building" next to the White-Henry had been prepared by Howells and Stokes, but construction was stalled. The problem never quite comes clear, but it may have been related to financing or to the width of what was visualized as "University Place." In any case, Douglas had learned of the development in the East of buildings constructed entirely for physicians and dentists—buildings in which every office and facility was designed for the use of the professional practitioner. Douglas sent company representatives east and went himself to Cleveland, Ohio, it is said, to examine such a medical-dental center. The Cobb Building was designed as the first such building in the West.[37]

The temporary buildings were also going up. These were the seven-year buildings, each representing a negotiation by Douglas and a set of designs by Howells and Stokes. Five were erected in 1909–the Sawyer and the Seattle Art Company buildings at Fifth and Union; the Olympic Motor Car and Metropolitan Garage buildings on Fifth, north of the Sawyer; and the Greeley

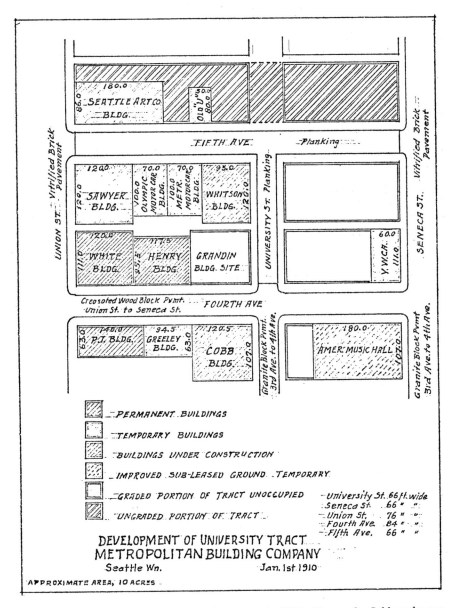

DEVELOPMENT OF UNIVERSITY TRACT
METROPOLITAN BUILDING COMPANY
Seattle Wn.   Jan. 1st 1910

In January 1910, the new permanent buildings were the White-Henry, the Cobb under construction; the old university building had been moved to a plot east of Fifth Avenue, which now was planked, where grading had only begun; the block between University and Seneca streets held just one building, the temporary YWCA (*Metropolitan Bulletin*, 1910)

Building, on the west side of Fourth between the Post-Intelligencer and the Cobb buildings. Soon there would be a Whitson Building at Fifth and University, named for M. J. Whitson, manager of Stone and Webster and a company stockholder, and a Uhl Building on Union Street to house the Uhl Brothers company, a West Coast wallpaper firm.

The hotel project had been dropped at the start, but meanwhile Howells and Stokes had been busy with the department store idea. In July, 1909, the idea was not only alive but a plan was ready for public announcement. The *Post-Intelligencer* front-page story of July 31, which was accompanied by a three-column sketch of the projected building, said that Howells had arrived from New York only the day before with the completed drawings for a $750,000 store that would cover the half block west of Fourth Avenue between Seneca and University streets. This was not at University Place, but the scope of the project had not been diminished and the newspaper report was, as usual, slightly effusive:

The latest plan of the Metropolitan Building Company, the company now improving the old University tract with modern business buildings, is to erect an immense department store structure for one tenant on the half block facing the west side of Fourth Avenue. . . .

This building has not been rented, although efforts are being made to secure a tenant.

The officers of the company believe that a large department store is logically the next step in the development of the old University tract.[38]

The store was not built, despite the seeming confidence of the Metropolitan Building Company. The officers may have believed the plan logical, but prospective tenants did not. The range of J. F. Douglas's lessee explorations is not known, but he must have tried, at the very least, to induce one of the large Seattle stores—Frederick and Nelson, the Bon Marche, the Standard, or MacDougall and Southwick—to move there. Perhaps he also made overtures in the East, although in 1909 no established merchandising company was ready to think about a move, a branch store, or a chain. The announcement of the projected store building may have been, simply, a casting of bait. If so, there were no nibbles. The difficulty was that the university tract was too high above what Seattle had thought of until then as its proper shopping area. Shoppers are pedestrians, and it was impossible for a merchandiser to imagine them climbing the hill from Second Avenue to Fourth. The Bon Marche, at least, was planning to move northward at the lower level, not eastward up the hill. Frederick and Nelson would do the same. The department store idea died for want of a second.

The first challenge before the Metropolitan Building Company had been to make the tract tractable, so to speak, by lowering the crest of the knoll, putting streets there, and making the property accessible. The second was to bring people to it, especially long-term lessees. A hotel would not do that. A department store did not. The Douglas response to the second challenge was inherent, nevertheless, in the concept of the comprehensive plan. Douglas struggled from the beginning to implant the idea that the tract had a special identity because of its historic associations and university connections, and that the tenant of a Metropolitan Building Company building was acquiring a prestige address.

The facets of this idea were numberless, and Douglas perfected them over the years. The buildings would not merely be "absolutely fireproof" (any new building was supposed to be that). They would offer conveniences and amenities—conference rooms, lounges, food services, and auditoriums—not found elsewhere. The tract would have the unity of the "master plan," the buildings readily identifiable as parts of the tract. Yet each building would have its own character. Its façade would be given a unique treatment and its accommodations tailored to the requirements of the tenants. The tract would have a quiet dignity appropriate to a place where major companies made major decisions and to which they would be bringing clients or customers from New York, Chicago, San Francisco, or the Orient. No garish commercial signs would be permitted anywhere, and no signs would project over the sidewalks. The street-level shops would be leased only to tenants who needed no tasteless, oversize advertising displays. University Place would be a beautifully planted plaza. There would be courts and arcades. The tenants would be grouped by buildings, insofar as grouping was useful and comfortable, so that lumber companies, for example, would have lumber company neighbors, as in the White Building and the Henry. And of course, doctors and dentists would have a new kind of professional grouping in the Cobb.

The Douglas idea was based on the themes of unity, identity, neighborliness, and pride. Douglas knew the men he served in the Metropolitan Building Company, the stockholders, the wealthy and tough-minded men whose big new homes were on First Hill and Capitol Hill and, beginning in 1908, in the Highlands, where certain wealthy merchants and financiers were developing an exclusive residential enclave far to the north of the city, with a magnificent view of Puget Sound. The leader in this was C. D. Stimson, president of the Stimson Mill Company since 1892 and in 1904 an organizer of the South Seattle Land Company. Douglas knew these men, and he knew too, the kinds of men he wanted as tenants in the tract—the men whose companies were significant in the commercial development of the Northwest. Douglas tried incessantly to create an atmosphere irresistible to them.[39]

Quite early, as a way of reinforcing the spirit of unity he wanted, Douglas established a biweekly news publication for tenants of the tract, the *Metropolitan Bulletin*, a small printed paper of four or more pages full of notes on the progress of construction, company plans, new tenants, and even the goings and comings of people of the tract—a Metropolitan equivalent of the small-town newspaper. The techniques of such communication, internal and external, have been thoroughly explored since 1908–9, but there could have been few such papers when Douglas started his, and surely none serving so specialized a clientele in the heart of a major city. How much of the text was by Douglas is not clear, but the tone is pure Douglas. On December 4, 1909, the lead story was "Second Anniversary," a review of developments since the Metropolitan Building Company had come into possession of the Moore lease in December 1907, just after the "panic." Douglas viewed the progress and the future with satisfaction, saying in part:

In spite of the disturbed condition of the times, the Metropolitan Building Co. has proceeded with the work of developing the University Tract just as rapidly as plans could be prepared and contractors could execute the work. As soon as our Company took over the lease, it had a comprehensive plan of development prepared by Messrs. Howells & Stokes of New York. With this plan of development in mind, we proceeded to improve the property in a manner that has excited the admiration of the entire City of Seattle and in a way that has given us wide and favorable publicity. The development that we have in hand is the largest development of its kind that has ever been undertaken in this country.

Later, on the theme of service:

Any group of men can plan buildings and, if they have the money, build them. No scheme such as we have in hand could be successful unless it rests on a money basis, so that, in order to justify our faith in the enterprise, it was necessary to have the buildings well rented at remunerative rates as the work of building progressed. This we have been able to do. . . . The business tenant of today, however, demands more than a good structure. He demands service of the highest kind—consistent, every day, high-grade service. . . . We believe that we have also met this requirement, so that today what is known as "White Building Service" represents the highest standards of office building service in the city.

Turning to the Henry Building:

Within the past week, a number of important leases have been closed up for space in the Henry Building. . . . The Henry Building is very nearly rented, and the space has been rapidly taken by very large business firms. Every tenant in the Henry Building would be considered a star tenant in any building in town. For some reason or other, the very best class of tenants seem attracted to our buildings. . . .
    The tenancy in the Henry Building, like the White Building, largely runs to lumbering, as will be seen in a few days when we publish a building directory. . . . A close reader of the Bulletin must long ago have come to the conclusion that all lumber roads lead to the White and Henry Buildings. . . .

And of the Cobb Building, then under construction:

Since the last issue of the Bulletin, we have had the worst weather we could possibly have for construction purposes. Nevertheless, we have proceeded rapidly. . . . Whether it rained or shined, we have kept the men at work and we have done everything we possibly could to expedite the construction work.

A meeting had been called by tenants to consider organizing a "Social Club," and Douglas had a suggestion about this:

We trust that if such a club is organized it will be called the "Lumbermen's Club." We are aware that a former Lumbermen's Club in this city came to grief. This was not due to the name, but was due to the fact, as we understand it, that the membership was too much restricted. The lumbering industry is the greatest industry in the Pacific Northwest and has attracted to it an exceedingly fine type of men. A Lumbermen's Club should attract to its membership as nonresident members practically every lumberman in the Pacific Northwest. . . .

As we said before, if a Lumbermen's Club is organized, it should be open to the same class of members as are eligible, say, to the Rainier Club, but the majority of the directors should always be lumbermen.[40]

Personal items appeared in a column, "Among Our Tenants," with other notes scattered throughout the paper. Examples from issues of 1909–11:

Mr. W. H. Talbot of San Francisco has been spending some time in the city inspecting his various interests.

The many friends of Miss May Walker regret to learn of her resignation as Secretary of the Y.W.C.A. We trust that success will follow her in her new work.

Stirrat & Goetz have the steel partly erected for the top five stories of their office building on the northeast corner of Fourth Avenue and Pike Street.

As we have previously mentioned in the Bulletin, Fourth Avenue is getting to be quite a "Club Street." The Seattle Athletic Club, the Rainier Club, and the Metropolitan Club all have quarters in this street. The Elks Club has purchased the corner at Fourth and Spring for a site for its new building. The College Club . . . is meeting with very good success. It has taken quarters in the Colman Building on Fourth Avenue and Marion Streets. In other words, five of the important clubs of the city are located on Fourth Avenue.

The above picture [an architectural sketch] will give our readers a very good idea of the new Plymouth Congregational Church as it will appear when completed. The building will cover a site on University Street between our property and Sixth Avenue.

A son arrived at the home of Secretary J. F. Douglas on the 15th inst.

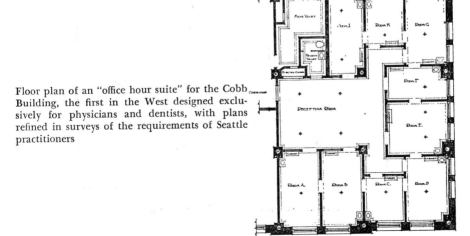

Floor plan of an "office hour suite" for the Cobb Building, the first in the West designed exclusively for physicians and dentists, with plans refined in surveys of the requirements of Seattle practitioners

The son born on August 15, 1911, was James B. Douglas, who years later would carry many of his father's ideas into the development of Seattle's Northgate shopping mall.

The style of the *Bulletin* reporting was homey, and any touch of salesmanship was merely a sharing of interests and enthusiasms. The *Bulletin* became, in fact, an intimate and believable record of what was going on not merely within the tract but in the surging downtown area. Many issues carried photographs of buildings at various stages of construction or of the streets as grading proceeded, and the news notes provided glimpses of Seattle that probably are to be found nowhere else, as when Douglas (who else could have been so excited by the prospect?) reported in December 1909:

The first street car that has ever passed over Fourth Avenue is just going up the street as the matter is being prepared for the Bulletin. The first car is a construction car that is putting the trolley wire connections in condition for use. Unless something unforeseen occurs within a few days, we will have regular passenger service on Fourth Avenue.... The regular operation of cars on the street will be a great factor in bringing it to the front as a first-class business thoroughfare.[41]

The offices of the Metropolitan Building Company were now in a suite on the first floor of the White Building (114–117), and it is possible to imagine Douglas looking out a window at the streetcar and seeing it as the flagship on his sea of expectations.

To Douglas—to the Metropolitan Building Company—the tract still was the "University Tract" in 1910, but the buildings were beginning to carry the names of the company's pioneers—the men who pledged major support

The Metropolitan Building Company

invites you to be present

at the opening of the

Cobb Building

on Wednesday evening, September the Fourteenth,

nineteen hundred and ten

at seven-thirty o'clock

Fourth Avenue and University Street

Formal invitation to the Cobb Building opening

when funds were being accumulated to cover the costs of construction. The White Building, the first, certainly could have been given no other name, for Chester White was the man whose original pledge had enabled Douglas to begin to organize the company. Thereafter each major building would bear the name of the leading participant in the financing (the "bell cow," as someone irreverently put it), the member of the company whose pledge was sufficiently large to bring along the others. The pledging process was entirely informal, it is said, because it was among gentlemen whose commitments needed no guarantees. It is recalled that the records of these transactions were kept only in a small black notebook which Douglas would circulate about the table at the meetings of officers and directors, each member simply jotting down and initialing the amount of money he was prepared to make available.[42]

Throughout 1910 and 1911 the affairs of the Metropolitan Building Company must have been at a difficult stage. Funding for the "Grandin" was proving doubtful, and temporary buildings stood where permanent buildings had been planned. The land above Fifth Avenue was almost entirely ungraded, and Fifth Avenue itself was planked, as was University Street above Fourth, where Howells and Stokes had designed "University Place." Union and Seneca streets were paved with brick, Fourth Avenue with creosoted wood blocks.

In January 1910, the Metropolitan made an offering of $500,000 of first-mortgage 6 percent sinking-fund bonds to raise money for the "Grandin." The bonds were secured by the leasehold mortgage, to the Washington Trust Company, of August 1, 1907. The Metropolitan's prospectus showed (with map) the area of the leasehold. It projected rental income to 1954. And it contained notes on certain matters, including the tax situation, that would raise questions later in circles larger than the circle of potential investors. "The land," the prospectus said, "is owned by the State of Washington and is exempt from taxation," although the taxability of the company's leasehold "is now in the courts." The advantages to the investor were the low rental rates (on an appraisal of $3,000,000), the freedom from taxation, and the "management and maintenance of a large property under one management." The net annual earnings, after interest charges and operating expenses, were placed at $235,000. In addition: "The officers and stockholders of the Company are men of wide business experience. They are also men of large means, and their financial interest in the enterprise is such as to assure it of able and honest management."[43]

New money seems to have come into the company soon after. One of the new investors was a newcomer to Seattle, Oliver D. Fisher, with a background in lumber and merchandising; and it may have been about that time that E. A. Stuart became an investor. The Grandin name apparently was associated with the tract, however briefly, because of the interest of Oliver Fisher. A precocious young businessman, Fisher had come west in 1907 to begin to take up options on timberlands in the Cascade Mountains, inspired to do so, it was said, because he realized that the San Francisco fire of the year before was creating new markets for lumber. Fisher was a native of Missouri and had already managed a lumber company at Birch Tree, Missouri. He had founded, with two brothers, a chain of general merchandise stores, the Golden Rule Stores, throughout the west and southwest.* In Seattle, Fisher organized what was called the Grandin–Coast Lumber Company, in which his associates were J. L. and E. B. Grandin, wide-ranging Boston financiers. Soon he was a director of the First National Bank of Seattle, recently acquired by a Missouri-Montana-Washington group, and a member of the board, through his association with Horace Henry, of a new Metropolitan Bank in the university tract. He invested in the Metropolitan Building Company, and by 1910 he was organizing the Fisher Flouring Mills Company (of which his father, O. W., was the president) and building a mill capable of producing two thousand barrels of flour a day. But it was Oliver Fisher's connection with the Metropolitan Building Company that interested his Grandin colleagues. According to a history of the Fisher family, J. L. Grandin,

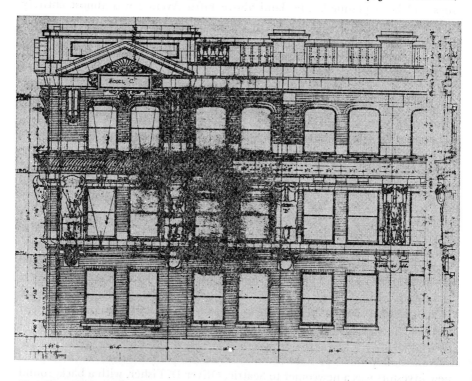

Howells and Stokes plans for the "Grandin Building," which became the Stuart, incorporating details of the proposed façade

* A clerk at one of Fisher's Colorado stores was J. C. Penney, who went on to establish his own system of general merchandising outlets. Fisher and Penney, close friends for life, had made a pact, it was said, to celebrate their one-hundredth birthdays together. Neither reached one hundred, but each came wonderfully close: Fisher died in 1967 at ninety-one, Penney in 1971 at ninety-five.

visiting Seattle to look for investment opportunities, concluded that he wanted to invest in the company—but with a safeguard. Calling on Fisher, he said, "Ollie, come along with me to their office. E. B. and I are prepared to put a million dollars apiece into Metropolitan, but only on condition that you are elected vice president and treasurer."[44]

Was this just talk? The "Grandin Building" idea—the Grandin name—faded, although O. D. Fisher was a stockholder, director, and officer of the Metropolitan Building Company until the leasehold passed to others forty years later. The new building that eventually joined the White and the Henry was the Stuart, named for E. A. Stuart. Whatever the financing, local pride may have been the key. E. A. Stuart was from Seattle, not Boston, and his Carnation company was already revolutionizing an industry.

But nothing by 1911 really had solved the Metropolitan's need for additional capital. J. F. Douglas was improvising, and hoping. On March 21, 1911, Douglas sent a letter to the regents asking approval of a five-year sublease with the Uhl Brothers company—a lease, already negotiated, that would run to May 1916, eleven months beyond the end of the seven-year temporary building agreement of June 24, 1908. Of this he wrote:

This company [Uhl] would not take a lease for a shorter time. All of the local members of the Board of Regents were out of the city, and we were unable to reach them. We felt that it was to our interest and to the interest of the University Tract to secure this business. . . .

It was not our intention to violate the terms of this agreement, but it was necessary for us to act in the matter, and we thought your Board would agree with us that it was for the best interests of everybody concerned to secure this business for the University Tract.[45]

Douglas also asked, in the same letter, for a three-year extension of the seven-year modification. He stated the case for the temporary buildings, which he himself certainly saw as compromises with the original "master plan":

In view of our experience with Uhl Bros., and in view of our experience with the tenants who rented our other temporary buildings, we think we ought to take up with your Board the matter of making some modification of this temporary agreement.

So far as the Metropolitan Building Company is concerned, at the time we asked for permission to put up the temporary buildings we did not realize how necessary it was to have some kind of business structures on the University Tract. It would be very difficult to rent large permanent structures to advantage if these structures were isolated. By building temporary buildings we were able to develop some of the land quickly and thus make a continuous line of businesses, and be able to take many tenants in the temporary buildings that could not afford the rents required in the permanent structures.

The logic was impeccable. The regents appointed a subcommittee—Higgins, Rea, and McEwan—to confer with the company. When the Uhl Building lease question was taken up on October 25, 1911, the building had already been in place since May. Higgins's subcommittee was asked to draw up an agreement covering the lease extension, and this it did, for five years rather than for the three years Douglas had asked. The regents, again, had been disposed to be understanding. The agreement was signed on January 8, 1912.

By that time there was a new building on the tract. It was a permanent building, and the regents had approved it, but it was a building that departed utterly from the original concepts of what the tract should become.

The new building was a theater, the Metropolitan. Neither in the early planning nor during the subsequent shifts and gropings had anyone, apparently, thought of a theater for the tract. This may have been because Douglas was so intent on creating a commercial center or because a theater seemed inappropriate to a place so hallowed by its historical association. The cost-income calculations would have argued against it, in any case.

In recent years, however, Seattle had become one of the capitals of the theater arts in the United States. A city with such freewheeling innovators as Pantages, Considine, and John Cort could be nothing less. Its established theaters included the Seattle, the Moore, the Third Avenue, and the Grand Opera House—all "legitimate." Among the variety and vaudeville houses were the Rockefeller, the Strand, the Central, the Pantages, the Orpheum, and the Princess. In this period the Metropolitan came to Seattle. How it happened was, according to contemporary testimony, simply fortuitous. The beginning was in 1910.

Marc Klaw, one of the most prominent of the New York theatrical producers, riding a train south from Vancouver, B. C., to Portland and San Francisco, disembarked in Seattle—a city he had never seen—to have dinner with a "New York–Seattle friend." The friend met him at the Union Station with his "60-horse power motor car" and took him for a quick tour of the downtown streets before dinner at the Rainier Club. Excited by the tour and warmed by the dinner, Klaw sent off a telegram to his New York associates, Charles Frohman and Abraham Erlanger: "Seattle wonderful city. Have decided best to build our own theater. City warrants expenditure up to half million." [46]

Whether or not the Metropolitan Theatre was thus conceived, that was the account of it in the *Post-Intelligencer* on the day before the opening. Whatever the case, the events thereafter had proceeded expeditiously to the opening of the theater on October 2, 1911, and a recitation of developments would be unnecessary except that, out of the processes of subleasing, approving, and building, there came a lingering question about the legal status of "University Place."

The Metropolitan Building Company had the approval of the regents, in the lease modifications, to build one-story temporary buildings. It also needed their approval of the theater—not because it was a theater, but because it was a permanent building that departed from the stipulation laid down in the Moore lease of 1907 (clause 1, article 2) that major buildings were to be at least five stories, others no less than three, and all "constructed with foun-

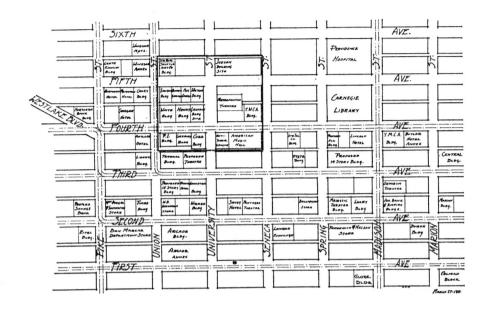

Much construction was proceeding or proposed in the Seattle of 1911: on the university tract, the Metropolitan Theatre was being made ready for its opening in October, and a "Judson Building" was planned at Fifth and University, although this project was abandoned and the Arena ultimately occupied the space (*Metropolitan Bulletin*, 1911)

dations and walls sufficient to carry at least six stories." The theater would be the equivalent of three stories, which was tolerable, but it would be an entity unto itself, outside the six-story office-building requirement, and certainly not a White, a Henry, or a Cobb.[47]

It was on September 28, 1910, that the Klaw and Erlanger sublease was signed with the Metropolitan Building Company. The Cobb Building had been open only a week, ablaze with lights from top to bottom on the night of the opening. On September 27, the regents had a note from Douglas asking them to appoint a committee to consult on the theater sublease, and the regents obliged by referring the matter to the Seattle members, Backus, Higgins, McEwan, and Cosgrove (the last-named having moved from Pomeroy to practice law in Seattle), thus simply continuing the local "lease committee" appointed earlier to handle questions relating to the tract. The committee was given power to act on the theater question, but the committee became, as it proved, a committee of three, because Backus, having been briefly connected with the Metropolitan Building Company, seems to have withdrawn from participation in review of the matter. (Earlier in the year Backus had abstained from voting on one of the company's lease-extension proposals.)[48]

Douglas's note to the board of September 27 invited examination of plans that were already being prepared. He wrote:

The Metropolitan Building Company has leased a tract of ground to Klaw & Erlanger of New York, on which Klaw & Erlanger propose to erect a theatre.

The plans for the theatre are partially prepared, but before completing the plans, we would like to have a committee from your Board pass upon the plans and ascertain whether or not they are in conformity to all the terms of the lease.

We would like also, to take up with the committee from your Board certain matters that effect [sic] the building of the Grandin Building. . . .

Kindly give this matter your immediate consideration, and oblige. . . .[49]

The consultations between the Metropolitan Building Company and the regents' committee—McEwan, Higgins, and Cosgrove—were initiated. When the regents next met on October 25, President Hazeltine in the chair, McEwan made a verbal report "on the request of said company to sublet ground on the University Tract for the erection of a theatre which, as a building, would not strictly conform to the requirements of the company's lease from the University, and also for permission to widen University Street between Fourth and Fifth Avenues." No mention had been made in Douglas's note of a proposed widening of University Street, but the question now was presented in McEwan's statement. On motion by Rea, seconded by Rogers, the committee simply "was continued with power to act."[50]

Two other meetings were held by the regents in 1910, one on November 29, the other on December 21. At neither was there a mention in the minutes of the Metropolitan Building Company. Following the record of the November meeting, however, the minutes contain a transcript of a resolution, signed by the committee members, modifying the company's lease to permit the construction of a theater "providing the building is a first-class building, well constructed of good materials . . . that shall conform to the type of construction and the standard of materials and workmanship of the said " 'White,' 'Henry,' and 'Cobb' buildings." Peculiarly, the committee referred to the time of its appointment as the regents' "regular monthly meeting on the eighth day of November, 1910," although no meeting of the regents was held on that date. Furthermore, the resolution is dated December 6, 1910, a week after the November 29 meeting and two weeks before the meeting of December 21. Since a public announcement of the plan to build a theater had been made on November 17, it must be presumed that the regents' committee, having the power to act, had checked all the bases on November 8 and had drawn up a resolution incorporating what they knew would be the board's decision.[51]

Neither the regents' discussions as reflected in their minutes nor the text of the resolution had touched the question of the widening of University Street. Yet on December 9, 1910, shortly after the filing of the resolution on the theater, the regents received from Douglas, and Secretary Markham received from Cosgrove, information about the Metropolitan Building Company's plan to widen University Street by fifteen feet on each side, between Fourth and Fifth avenues, and so to create an attractive "University Place." Douglas sent to the regents a copy of a notice that he was filing with the city and county to announce his intention and to declare that setting back the buildings on University was not a dedication of the land to street purposes. Douglas wrote:

You will see from the notice that we intend to erect all buildings of a permanent character fifteen feet back from the present lines of University Street, produced. . . . This is done for the purpose of making more attractive the entrances to the buildings, and in order that the city may not at some future time claim prescriptive rights in these fifteen foot strips we have filed a notice with the auditor of the County and the City Comptroller to the effect that this action is purely voluntary on our part, and that by our action we do not intend to dedicate even the leasehold interest in these strips. Of course, no action on our part could be presumed as a dedication on the part of the State. We agree with you, however, that no building of a permanent character shall be erected . . . on either side of said street, within fifteen feet of the present line . . . without your written consent.[52]

There the matter rested for the moment. The regents, who had repeatedly turned down the Metropolitan Building Company's requests for extension of the lease, had been perfectly willing to make accommodations within the existing lease term. In fact, on October 25, the day they had received McEwan's committee report, the regents had denied a new Metropolitan request for a lease extension. The regents could be flexible, perhaps even a little casual, on intermediate matters. But the term of the lease was fixed.[53]

The theater, when it was built, was set back fifteen feet from "the line of University Street, produced." That had been anticipated in the Klaw and Erlanger sublease. The entrance court was indeed attractive. Who could object? But the question of the street lines would arise again later.

The Metropolitan was, as a building, "first class," and as a theater it was a cut or two above—as it was meant to be—anything else Seattle could offer. The design was by Howells and Stokes and the construction by Stone and Webster under contract to Klaw and Erlanger. The original contract was for $221,325 for the building itself, but the final cost was said to approach $500,000, although the sum may have been exaggerated in newspaper accounts, for it fitted almost too neatly the figure attributed originally to Marc Klaw. In any case the theater was, from the standpoint of the Metropolitan Building Company, an almost perfect counterpoint to the theme the company had been developing. It gave the university tract a cultural as well as a commercial interest. And it brought people to the tract by night as well as by day.[54]

The theater occupied the midpart of the half block on University Place where the Howells and Stokes plan of 1907 had put the now aborted department store. The design had been adapted, the newspapers said, from the Palace of the Doges in Venice. That alone was enough to stir Seattle's imagination. The building was, undeniably, a gem—a structure of brick, terra cotta, and marble, with three arched window bays above a wide marquee that jutted over the sidewalk toward a planted plaza in the street. The patterned brickwork was executed by a mason of such a rare and specialized talent that architects and builders had come from the East and South, it was said, to inspect the design. The entrance was through "heavy oaken doors" to a rotunda walled in "pure white Italian marble, black Belgian mosaics, and terrazzo panels." There were ladies lounges with mirrored walls and parquet floors, and smoking rooms for gentlemen. There were seats in the theater for 1,650, the sweeping first balcony carried farther forward than had been the

Howells and Stokes sketch of 1911 dramatizing the Venetian façade of the Metropolitan Theatre being built that year; the buildings shown flanking the theater were symbolic only, for until the Olympic Hotel was erected in 1924 the Metropolitan stood tall among the temporary buildings surrounding it

practice elsewhere and in what was said to be the new European mode. The gilded proscenium arch curved above a 70-foot stage.[55]

Elegant and Venetian in tone it may have been, but the theater did nothing to disturb the general architectural harmony of the tract. Howells and Stokes had seen to that. The University Street front had dignity and unobtrusive style. Klaw and Erlanger had built the building, but the Metropolitan company was paying the costs of the stonework, paving, and planting to improve the setting. News reports stressed the importance of the theater to the development of the tract as a civic center, an angle that Douglas undoubtedly was emphasizing. The *Post-Intelligencer*'s story welcoming the theater said: "Just as the new Metropolitan theater marks the center of the 'Old University Tract,' it marks also the new center of Seattle. It is the heart of the town. . . . If it is to be the civic center, then it must be made also the civic beauty spot, and thousands of dollars are still to be spent in carrying out this idea. There are to be parking strips and parkways; an electric fountain amid bright flower beds, bay trees and boxwood hedges. . . . The new theater is beautiful within; there is to be even greater beauty without." The hotel idea was still alive, too. Or perhaps revived. The report concluded with this paragraph: "Before a year has passed, the Metropolitan will be flanked on the west by a huge hotel which the Metropolitan Building Company is now planning, and on the east by another big office structure of the type of the Henry and White buildings. Ultimately the hotel will be connected with the White and Henry buildings, and with a third structure to go up at the corner of Fourth and University, by an arcade which will serve to tie the blocks of structures into one harmonious whole, architecturally and otherwise."[56]

Not for years would a hotel be there, and for years the theater was flanked not by tall buildings but by a tea garden and by squat, temporary structures. But J. F. Douglas and Howells and Stokes were keeping the larger plans before them.

On September 30, 1911, which was a Saturday, the Metropolitan Theatre was opened first for a public reception attended by "about 6,000 persons," the company said, and that evening the officers and trustees were hosts at a tract-wide reception for members of the Seattle Rotary Club and their wives, the guests strolling through the White-Henry and Cobb buildings (refreshments in the White and then into the new theater). All this was preliminary. On October 2, 1911, the Metropolitan's first-night crowd—dress clothes "the order of the hour" on the first floor—saw Edna Wallace Hopper in a comedy, *Jumping Jupiter*. Miss Hopper was charming, the newspapers said, and her leading man, Richard Carle, a well-known comic actor, was described by the *Post-Intelligencer* reviewer as "gracefully awkward and appealingly loose-jointed." The crowd was there not so much to see the play, however, as to be dazzled by the theater, and the beginning was delayed for half an hour to allow the patrons to wander about and marvel at the splendors. The names of all who attended were published in the newspapers the following day, and they included, of course, the names of persons everyone knew—the Alden

Blethens, the James D. Hoges, the Henry Brodericks, the H. C. Henrys, the O. D. Fishers, the E. A. Stuarts, the members of the board of regents and, from other theatrical enterprises, the Alexander Pantages and the John Considines. The Metropolitan had only four boxes (this, too, in the newer European style, it was said), and among those for whom the boxes were reserved were Mr. and Mrs. Chester White, Mr. and Mrs. J. F. Douglas, Mr. and Mrs. W. H. Talbot, Mr. and Mrs. Manson Backus, President and Mrs. Thomas Kane, of the university, and John C. Higgins, president of the regents, and Mrs. Higgins. Some members of the crowd, the papers said, had attended the opening of each of the twenty-two theaters that had preceded the Metropolitan, from the Seattle Theater in 1892 to the "palatial" Orpheum that had been opened only recently, in May 1911, but the first person to enter the doors on the Metropolitan's opening night was a Tom McDermott, identified as a Yesler Way businessman, who was not, it is supposed, in white tie. When at length the inspection of the theater was over and the crowd was seated, there was another revelation before the play began. The red velvet curtain, drawn aside, disclosed Douglas, Higgins, and Marc Klaw seated in chairs on the stage for a brief ceremony of dedication. Douglas welcomed the audience, related events leading to the building of the "Northwest's best theater," and read congratulatory telegrams. Higgins traced the history of the university on the site. Klaw promised, briefly and wittily, to bring to Seattle the "very best plays we can get." The speeches brought "prolonged applause." The orchestra played the national anthem. Then, at last, the curtain rose on *Jumping Jupiter*.[57]

What James A. Moore thought of all this can only be guessed. Moore had built a theater, among so many things, and the Moore had been opened in 1907 with *The Alaskan*. On the evening of the Metropolitan opening the Moore Theater was playing *Saison des Ballets Russes*, "direct from the Winter Garden in New York," a production with its own orchestra and a corps de ballet of one hundred and fifty. But Moore's brilliant career in Seattle was cresting by 1911. Eugenie Moore had died in 1908, just as Moore was building, for his model farm at Pasco, a tall, white mansion overlooking the Columbia, a house faced at the front by two-story columns that rose above columned verandas. The house incorporated, it was said, materials taken from Moore's old Washington Hotel when the hotel was torn down to clear the land for the Denny Regrade. Moore's offices were still in Seattle—in the Hoge Building, at Second Avenue and Cherry Street—but he was also becoming more deeply involved in the Irondale project near Port Townsend. The Irondale dream consumed him. He was trying, characteristically, to sell lots there. His dream cost him a fortune—millions, by later accounts. Moore was said to have been worth $15,000,000, although the fortune and the loss may have been overstated. But it was Moore's theater, not Irondale, that lasted. The Moore was still a landmark in Seattle years after the new Metropolitan had disappeared.

October 1911, was a memorable month for Seattle, for the university, and for J. F. Douglas. Seattle was preparing for a short visit—another visit—by William Howard Taft, now president of the United States. The Puget Sound Bridge and Dredging Company, under a $200,000 contract with the U.S. Corps of Engineers, was starting to build the new locks at the Puget Sound end of the Lake Washington Canal. The university, where the enrollment was nearing 2,500, was getting ready to hold, from November 3 to 8, an academic golden jubilee commemorating its founding by Daniel Bagley. Edmond Meany was chairman, of course, and his committee included such faculty members as F. M. Padelford, Henry Landes, and J. Allen Smith. Charles F. Spooner, a Seattle attorney recently named a regent to succeed Backus, was arranging a program for the official visitors from Northwest institutions and from Yale, Harvard, Michigan, Minnesota, Chicago, and other major universities.

As for Douglas, who had presided at the opening of the Metropolitan Theatre on October 2, he then had been honored on October 10 in a special way. Douglas had been president in 1911 of the Potlatch Association, sponsor of a huge community-wide pageant and celebration, and when members met at the Rainier Club to elect new trustees, Douglas was given a silver dinner service encased in a large mahogany chest, the presentation made by Judge Burke. By October 24, Douglas was in New York and departing for Europe on the North German Lloyd steamer *Kaiser Wilhelm der Grosse*. It was a business trip, but exploratory only, and Douglas made interesting contacts in England and Scotland, and particularly with officers of the Century Insurance Company, of Edinburgh. "The Metropolitan Building Company is not offering any of its bonds for sale at this time," he wrote upon his return in December, "but I spent some time looking into conditions in London to see whether there would be a market for our bonds in case we were to offer any in the future." That time came soon.[58]

CHAPTER 5

To Build a Center: 1912 to 1917

The first modification of the Moore lease as assigned to the Metropolitan Building Company was in the agreement of June 24, 1908, permitting the erection of temporary, one-story buildings that were to be removed by June 24, 1915, seven years from the date of the signing.

Next had come the modification of 1910 permitting the company to build the Metropolitan Theatre, and the Uhl Building negotiation of 1911 which produced the modification of January 1912 extending by five years the agreement covering temporary buildings. Such developments took place in a climate of concord between the regents of the university and the officers of the Metropolitan Building Company. The climate continued to prevail for a time. Yet the year 1912 may be seen in retrospect as the beginning of a period in which the climate would change, subtly at first and then markedly, because of an inevitable spread of public interest in what was happening at the university and, as a concomitant, in what was happening at the university tract.

The events between 1912 and 1917 were tangled. The company continued to ask modifications of its lease and to build temporary buildings. There were studies of the tax-free status of the leasehold. A new governor, as the result of a crisis on the university campus, installed what was virtually an entirely new board of regents. The White and Henry buildings were joined, at last, by the Stuart, but only after a prolonged struggle for funds, and then only under a special sanction concerning its cost. A long and sometimes tense dispute occurred over whether one of the Metropolitan Building Company's new buildings was permanent or temporary—a peculiar question, but one that involved larger issues that stirred the community and that continued to hover over the tract for a decade.

With the outbreak of the war in Europe in August 1914, issues of many kinds began to be seen in new perspectives. In Seattle, as elsewhere in the nation, movements already in process could only run their course until, with America's entry into the war, many things were changed forever.

By 1912 there had appeared, in Seattle and in other parts of the state, reactions critical of the university tract lease and of the circumstances under which the leasehold had come to the Metropolitan Building Company. As early as June 1909, months before Douglas's *Bulletin* had celebrated the company's second anniversary, the Spokane *Spokesman-Review* had published a long and detailed analysis of the leasing and the lease terms, a report charging that, since the increasingly valuable property was free from taxation, the state was making an "annual gift" to the company of $418,000 or a cumulative gift of $15,221,000 over the duration of the leasehold. The regents had leased to Moore, the newspaper said, without a proper effort to find a lessee who would offer better terms and, with the assignment of the lease to the Metropolitan Building Company, "millionaires" were now "in control." Apparently there had also been some legislative interest in the lease. Or should have been, the *Spokesman* thought. The newspaper said that a "legislative investigating committee has overlooked an opportunity to expose a deal entered into a few years ago by the regents of the state university by which that institution and the state have been deprived of a resource the value of which is greater than all the appropriations ever made" to the university. But Sawyer, of the *Post-Intelligencer*, the former regent who had been a leading figure in the drafting of the Moore lease modifications, promptly denied the imputations. In a 1,200-word letter to the *Spokesman-Review* in July 1909 (a letter read and supported by Spokane's own D. L. Huntington, who also had been a regent at the time), Sawyer reviewed the whole history of the lease negotiations from the Stirrat and Goetz days to the Metropolitan Building Company's, pointing out that the percentage-of-appraisal lease had been held "valueless" by the "gentlemen in Seattle" whom the regents had consulted—gentlemen "competent to pass upon the question"—and that the regents' studies throughout 1906 had included a conference with Governor Mead and with members of the State Tax Commission, who had approved a lease along the lines ultimately adopted. "Your correspondent insinuates," Sawyer wrote, "that the making of this new lease was done in secret and that there was some mystery about the transaction." Not so. The minutes of the board were open to inspection. The terms of the lease had been covered in the daily press and published in university bulletins. As for taxes, neither the land nor the improvements were taxable, because they belonged to the state, but the lessee was subject to all local assessments. The regents' prime reason for altering the percentage arrangement was to establish a "credit asset" to the university—"to have it in such form as to enable the board to borrow money . . . for the purpose of erecting needed buildings . . . without laying upon the taxpayers of the state additional burdens."[1]

But the new buildings on the tract were becoming, in some eyes, monuments to the Metropolitan's alleged margin of advantage over competitors or evidence of how "millionaires" were profiting at the expense of the state. The tax question was an irritant. Even the Metropolitan's own statements and prospectuses—such as for the bond offering of 1910—naturally mentioned the tax situation and thus called attention to it. The proliferation of temporary buildings raised questions, too, about the course of development the company was pursuing and about the concessions the regents could be presumed to be making. To cap it all, the growing university was itself desperate for additional buildings, even though the AYP residues had augmented the usable space, and many persons in the university community could see nothing good about a downtown lease that produced what seemed a pitifully small income even though the Metropolitan Building Company's annual rental would soon rise from $15,000 to $40,000.

To J. F. Douglas all this was baffling, no doubt, for Douglas was developing a huge tract in the center of the city, not just erecting and renting individual buildings. But stirrings continued. In 1910, the taxation committee of the Seattle Chamber of Commerce, nudged by the proprietors of other Seattle properties, made a study of the tax savings that would accrue to the Metropolitan because of the tax-exempt status of the tract. The study concluded that the tax savings alone, projected for the term of the lease, would build the White, Henry, and Cobb buildings. By 1911, the state legislature was on the verge of action, although nothing really happened. A bill introduced in the senate in January 1911 would have required approval by the senate of any "lease . . . modification, cancellation, or extension of any lease, or any act affecting or involving the title or possession" of the university tract. The bill was reported out of committee, passed by the senate, read in the house, and reported out there with recommendation for passage. Then it died—apparently never brought to a vote. Whatever all this meant, public scrutiny of a new dimension was beginning to be focused on the tract, on the regents, and on the company's lease.[2]

The scrutiny seemingly was not lost on the regents. John C. Higgins was president of the board in 1911–12, his fellows still Hazeltine, Cosgrove, McEwan, Rogers, Rea, and Spooner. When they approved on January 8, 1912, the five-year extension of the temporary-building agreement (this the result of the Uhl Building petition of 1911), they incorporated, this time, a condition. The regents could appreciate the Metropolitan's need for intermediate income, but they also wanted the company to get along with major construction. The regents inserted a quid pro quo—for the five-year extension, a new major building:

Whereas, The Regents of the University of Washington may be unwilling to have said [temporary] buildings stand longer than the time fixed [seven years] . . . unless the Metropolitan Building Company does some act of value to the University Tract not required by the original lease,

Now, THEREFORE, It is agreed that if the Metropolitan Building Company shall, in lieu of the kind of buildings provided in the aforesaid lease, build upon the University Tract, prior to the 24th day of June, 1915, at a cost of not less than five hundred thousand dollars ($500,000.00), a fire-proof building or buildings of the kind and description hereinafter provided, then the Metropolitan Building Company shall, for and in consideration of building said superior building or buildings, be entitled to an extension of five (5) years' time in which it shall have the right to erect and maintain the kind of buildings specified by the agreement hereinbefore named and dated the 24th day of June, 1908. . . .[3]

The regents were asking a "superior" building of the White-Henry or Cobb style. The company had until June 24, 1915—the ending date of the seven-year agreement—to get the building in place and earn its five-year extension to June 1920, although a six-month grace period was allowed if the building was more than 50 percent complete. The cost was to be at least $500,000, which was less than the cost of the White, the Henry, or the Cobb. J. F. Douglas had three years to do it all, and he still was thinking of a "Grandin" Building, the plans for which were not yet formulated. But the new modification agreement had scarcely been signed when the regents were getting new requests, and the requests began with the trivial.

The tract lease stipulated that liquor could be dispensed only in hotels. On January 18, 1912, Douglas wrote the board to ask a waiver of this provision so that liquor could be sold in the "buffet" of the Metropolitan Club, a new tract tenants' lounge in the Henry Building. The regents had granted such a waiver for the Press Club in 1911 and they quickly approved this new request. Meanwhile, the company had begun construction of two new temporary buildings, one for the College Club, at Fifth Avenue and Seneca Street, and the other the Hippodrome, an auditorium for meetings and exhibits, at Fifth and University. The College Club, like the Metropolitan, wanted to operate a "buffet," and Douglas, writing the regents about this on March 21, 1912, also asked the regents for permission to put a second story on the College Club Building, even though the temporary buildings were to be one-story only. "We feel," Douglas said, "that it can make no difference to the Board of Regents if we build two-story buildings, provided they come under the terms of the temporary building permits." It did, of course, make no difference. The regents approved, in a single resolution, both the buffet and the two-story building.[4]

By April 1912, however, the Metropolitan was beginning to face up to its commitment to build the "superior" building. The company had been planning a four-story "mill-type" building on Fifth Avenue, the Judson, but on April 25 Douglas wrote the regents to say that the Judson idea had been dropped and the company now proposed to erect a building at Fourth and University adjoining the Henry. Douglas linked this announcement with another request—a request of the kind rejected in 1910. He asked that the company be given a fifty-year lease on the site the new building would occupy, the rent to remain the same as for the whole tract until 1954, after that 4 percent of the appraised value of that single plot plus "an amount that would be equivalent to the taxes assessed against the ground if the ground was held in private ownership." The request not only echoed the earlier one, it asked a modification of the main lease for the "superior" building that would validate the temporaries. It was, too, another reminder that the tract was not taxed as in "private ownership." The regents promptly turned down the proposal.[5]

J. F. Douglas's problem was that any new permanent building erected by 1915 would have a life of less than forty years under the lease, and Douglas was not certain that major investors would accept such a term. Whatever the scope of his financial soundings in that spring of 1912, Douglas decided to go back to Scotland and England to talk again to the potential investors he had met there in 1911, just six months before. On July 23, 1912, Douglas attended the meeting of the regents to tell them about his plans, and he must have felt that he could persuade them to extend the ground lease if necessary. An informal memorandum for the regents gave the "gist" of Douglas's statement on that occasion: "He said he was going to London to try to raise money for the Grandin Building. That if he could get the money on the present terms of the lease, he would ask nothing further from the Board of Regents, but if he could not he would cable the Board and ask them to so modify the lease as to allow a full fifty-year term for that part of the ground to be occupied by the Grandin Bldg."[6]

Douglas went abroad that summer, taking his family with him. He got investment money from the Century Insurance Company, of Edinburgh, where he already had firm friendships, and the Douglases stayed in Europe for seven months, touring, studying, and being entertained. There were trips to France, Switzerland, and Italy, but London was a triumph for the young couple from the American West. Douglas was a guest of the Inaugural Luncheon Club at the Savoy and the speaker at a luncheon meeting of the London Chamber of Commerce at the Trocadero. Neva Douglas was invited to join the American Women of London, a club whose meetings were frequently attended by the Duchess of Marlborough. It had been a dazzling expedition, a complete success, and no need to cable the regents.[7]

The Metropolitan could not have been in 1912 the money-making enterprise that many then believed it to be, although its record was amazingly good and it certainly was totally solvent. In just four years the company had built four large and impressive buildings, one an innovative medical-dental center, one a beautifully designed theater. In addition, it had built eight temporary buildings, all of brick and reinforced concrete, the YWCA, the Sawyer, the Seattle Art Company, the Greeley, the Olympic Motor Car, the Metropolitan Garage, the Whitson, and the Uhl, and it was building two more, the two-story College Club and the Hippodrome. As for the company's finances, there is a memorandum reference to a statement signed by Douglas "early in 1912" in which he said that the funds in the business were the proceeds of the sale of the 6 percent thirty-year gold bonds; that the company had spent about $2,500,000 on improvements, principally office and store buildings, all well rented; and that the gross income was nearly $400,000 a year, the net $75,000 after bond interest. Many improvements had been made out of earnings, Douglas said. All construction bills had been paid promptly and no money was owed to banks. Now the fifth major building was in prospect, and if it was completed by 1915, the temporary buildings could remain until June 24, 1920.[8]

Douglas had moved fast and far in a dozen years. The young man who in 1900 had bought office furniture on credit from D. E. Frederick had become by 1912 a person of importance in Seattle with connections on the Eastern

Seaboard and in Europe. Photographs of him in that year, when he was thirty-eight, show him as handsome, clean-shaven, with an aristocratic brow and a thick shock of well-tended hair, the eyes calm and confident. Douglas was a member of the Rainier Club, the Arctic Club, the Press Club, the Athletic Club, the Yale Club, and the Canadian Club, of which he was president. He had helped organize the Metropolitan Club and the College Club. He was a director of the Charity Organization of Seattle and secretary of the Anti-Tuberculosis League. In 1909 the Douglases had taken the train east to attend the Taft inauguration. (They were scheduled to ride in the inaugural parade as the guests of Senator Stiles, but when Washington, D.C., produced a major storm they watched the parade from a hotel window.) Douglas had become a man to whom Seattle turned when things needed doing, such as the Golden Potlatch, an early version of Seattle's Seafair. When businessmen decided in 1910 that a pageant would stimulate the local economy, Douglas was made president and chief of the ensuing carnival that became a reminiscent celebration of the arrival of the 1897 gold ship, the *Portland*, with a grand ball, a masked ball, military and athletic events, exhibition airplane flights by Eugene Ely and Eugene Witmer, aviation's leading stunt men, and a marine parade in which the old *Portland* herself was escorted into Elliott Bay by lines of Navy ships and private yachts. It was for this that Douglas had been given his silver dinner service amid laudatory speeches by Judge Burke and others. And after the Potlatch the Seattle Ad Club took over the Metropolitan Theatre for a hometown production of parodies and songs, in one of which, to the tune of "I Wonder Who's Kissing Her Now," Douglas was singled out:

> . . . and we wanted a leader with force.
> Who was the man to be first at the wheel?
> We know it was Douglas, of course.
>
> *Chorus*
>
> No wonder we're boosting him now,
> No wonder we're toasting him now . . .[9]

Douglas was president and lifetime member of the Earlington Country Club, where tennis had been the principal sport, but after the visits to Scotland a golf course was laid out on the lower slopes of the 600-acre property. He was also the head of a small Seattle contingent of North Dakota Douglases—two brothers, James H. and Walter, the former in the law firm, the other attending the university; and a sister, Florence, who taught English at Whitworth College before becoming manager of the Metropolitan Commercial College on the tract. Amid it all, Douglas remained the builder with a developing grasp of management and employee relations. He was holding regular management staff meetings. The eighty service employees—janitors, window washers, painters, electricians, elevator operators—were beginning to reap employment benefits, unusual in 1912, such as paid vacations, accident insurance, and company parties. Douglas sought to encourage feelings of identity and pride among Metropolitan employees. Members of the service staff were in Metropolitan uniforms. Then, or soon after, the company established a Puget Sound beach camp where employees and their families could enjoy summer holidays. At the Metropolian's Christmas parties there were gifts for all, the tree surrounded by presents for the children.[10]

The Seattle of those years before World War I was in what soon would seem a golden time even to those who were not sharing significantly in the money being made. It was a time when men who would become legends were on hand, some with the Metropolitan Building Company, some not. These were men whose names would go on banks or buildings or who would be shaping or polishing a still-formative Seattle—the Fishers, J. D. Hoge, Joshua Green, C. D. Stimson, Harry W. Treat, Albert S. Kerry, Laurence Colman, James D. Lowman, and many others. The social structure was financial and professional, but singularly of Seattle's kind—a mix of business opportunism and philanthropy, of competition and community leadership, of first families and successful representatives of the later waves. Hoge, for example, had been in Seattle since 1890, had been a coowner of the *Post-Intelligencer* when he was in his twenties, had made money in business and banking, and in 1911–12 was erecting the eighteen-story Hoge Building on Second Avenue. Green was on his way to becoming the legend among legends, a Mississippian who had come West with his parents in 1886, had worked as a youth with pick and shovel on survey crews, and had risen from purser on a paddlewheel steamboat to the presidency of the Puget Sound Navigation Company. In 1912 Green, like Douglas, was one of the "younger crowd" of entrepreneurs, really just well started on a career that would not end until, more than six decades later, he died at 105.[11]

The Seattle of those years also had Treat and Stimson. Harry W. Treat (the W for Whitney) left his own name nowhere in Seattle, yet two names still imprinted there, Loyal Heights and Golden Gardens, were among his legacies—those and memories of a man who brought dash to his financial ventures and, to all he did, a superb style.

Treat, not yet forty, had come to Seattle in 1904, for no better reason, apparently, than confidence that he could expand his financial talents in a growing western city. A native of Wisconsin and a graduate of Cornell University and Harvard Law School, he had served a business apprenticeship with Marshall Field and Company, then had moved to New York in the 1890s to establish his own Wall Street investment and real estate firms. He had been, it is said, "secretary" to John D. Rockefeller, although a more likely role was an agent or associate. He was, in any case, wealthy, strikingly handsome, an expert horseman and amateur sportsman, widely traveled, an intimate of the Rockefellers and the Vanderbilts—his wife had her own associations in such families—and the father of two daughters, Priscilla and Loyal.

Harry Treat was not of the Metropolitan Building Company, but he was a figure in the Seattle that was being stretched into new shapes in that pre-World War I era. Treat's first act had been to build on Queen Anne Hill a huge brick personal residence with views commanding the whole of Seattle's land and water scene. But then to business, and at a time when fortunes were being made in the tideflats and fill-lands south of the city, Treat went north beyond Ballard, the little incorporated town in which C. D. Stimson's mill was the sole industry. Treat bought hundreds of acres on the bluffs above the Sound and hundreds of feet of waterfront below. He called the lowlands Golden Gardens, and to make the park there accessible he constructed a trolley line (the fare, three cents) from downtown Ballard. He established his own farm in the forested lands above, and he sold lots in what he called Loyal Heights, named for his younger daughter. And from 1906 to 1918, when it was incorporated into the Seattle transit system, Treat's trolley line was the Loyal Railway.

While Harry Treat was around—until he was killed in 1922 when his car plunged off a mountain road in British Columbia—Seattle had a man to be watched with amazement. A lover of fine horses, Treat was a daring rider and an impeccably turned out master of the Seattle Hunt, which probably was his own invention. His Queen Anne home as well as his farm had accommodations for his coaches, carts, and horses, the coaches including a tallyho pulled by blooded horses he had purchased from the Vanderbilts, from whom he also lured their coachman, Gooch.* It was natural that Treat, with his love of horses and of the theatrical, should be a friend and admirer of W. F. (Buffalo Bill) Cody, whose "Wild West" show toured America for years. Cody was a guest now and then at the Treat home, and on Priscilla's ninth birthday Treat arranged for Cody to bring to Queen Anne Hill the whole "Wild West" troupe. From Treat's talks with Cody came, it is said, his most significant monument. In 1915, Treat and Cody, meeting in the Treat mansion on Queen Anne Hill, set in motion plans for what would become the Buffalo Bill Museum in Cody, Wyoming.[12]

C. D. Stimson was not among the originals of the Metropolitan Building Company—his leadership therein would come later—but he was an original in another sense. He was a man who had so mastered a handicap that it became no handicap at all. Born in 1857, he had lost his right arm in blood poisoning when as a boy he had been scratched by a fence wire near a swimming hole in his native Michigan. With a mother who refused to let him do any less, Stimson grew up learning to use his other arm for all the chores, sports, and classroom work of his youth. The family was in lumbering and that was to be his life. After attending private schools, including Racine College, he was in charge of a lumber mill in Chicago. In the meantime he had married

---

* In 1909, Treat used his coach and four to take friends to the AYP Exposition. In 1910, he instituted for a few days a similar service from downtown Ballard to the Seattle Golf Club, the fares going to charity. There is a story about an occasion when Joshua Green and a friend (Green had something of a reputation for practical joking) dressed themselves as masked road agents and staged a mock holdup of the Treat coach on its way to the club, frightening two prominent young lady guests from the East. Gooch, who had been the Vanderbilt coachman, remained in Seattle and operated a pet store there in the years before World War II.

a New York girl, then joined a Stimson family survey of the nation's timberlands that culminated in 1890 when he and his brothers established their mill in Ballard. By 1907, when J. F. Douglas was putting together the Metropolitan Building Company, Stimson was fifty, well to do, busy with his mill and various real estate interests, very much involved in social and community affairs, and living in a large and gracious home that he had built on First Hill in 1901, his family now including a son, Thomas D., and a daughter, Dorothy. Even then the time had come when Stimson and the self-made men of his generation wanted a place out of town where they could golf and be together after work. It was Stimson who, thoroughly accustomed to fighting his way through uncut timberlands, fought his way through those northeast of Harry Treat's new Loyal Heights to make the first layout of what would become the Highlands, where the homes would be placed on five-acre plots arranged around a golf club and with accommodations for the yachtsmen among them. When the Highlands was organized, Stimson was president, Harry Treat, vice-president, Frederick A. Wing, secretary, and Frederick S. Stimson, treasurer. Among the first members were Manson Backus, Joshua Green, Horace Henry, James Hoge, Chester White, Albert Kerry, and Harry Krutz, who had been the unsuccessful bidder on the university tract lease. By 1912, many had built homes there.

With only one arm to serve him, Stimson did it all, asking help from no one. He was golfer, horseman, yachtsman, businessman, at ease anywhere. (Stimson and Henry were among those with Taft when the president played the Seattle Golf Club course, probably in 1909.) He sometimes went by horseback from his First Hill home to the mill at Ballard. He acquired much later a large power yacht, the *Wanda*, built to his specifications. He did all the routine things—"everything but tie a white tie, which had to be right the first time," his daughter recalled—but he did not play cards, simply because he didn't care to.[13]

It is risky, looking at the Metropolitan Building Company of that period, to try to visualize why things happened as they did. The company had authority to build and use temporary buildings until 1920 if it built a major building by 1915. Douglas had been successful in getting investment money in Scotland and England for a building he still thought of as the Grandin. Yet within six months after his return from abroad—in May 1913—he again went to the regents to ask a second extension of the agreement covering temporary buildings, this to permit their construction and use to June 24, 1925. Douglas appeared before the board on May 14, 1913, and with him were C. H. Cobb, who was succeeding Chester White as president of the Metropolitan, and two Grandins—J. L. Grandin, who once presumably had been willing to put $1,000,000 into the company, and G. W. Grandin, of Cleveland, Ohio, a stockholder. The regents approved the new five-year extension, and certainly the Grandins joined in urging it. The regents' resolution, accepting the Metropolitan Building Company's assertion that "in order to secure additional money for permanent buildings" it should have longer use of the temporary ones, said that the board "deemed it best for the interests of the State of Washington to extend the time . . . and to make the said five years' extension ten years." The resolution also noted, specifically this time, that the company was to build "the Grandin or other buildings . . . at a minimum cost of $500,000."[14] Thus, even before the new "superior" building was started, the Metropolitan had the right to use temporary buildings until 1925.

Douglas could build buildings, but the regents had a problem of a different kind before them. The time was one of stress at the university itself, a bewildering time that would come to a head in a drastic restructuring of the university administration at the highest levels, first in the forced termination of Thomas Kane's presidency and then in the creation, almost overnight, of a new board of regents. The episode was too sweeping to be remembered solely for its relevance to the story of the downtown tract. But when the regents of 1913 dismissed President Kane and a new governor dismissed most of the regents, events at the tract were about to enter a new phase.

President Kane had served the university since 1903. He had brought to the campus many of the stars of the young faculty, and had reorganized departments, encouraged graduate education, presided over what was for the time a remarkable expansion of university facilities, and consulted consistently, internally, on matters of governance. Kane was also widely respected in the larger circles of higher education. But by 1911 the regents were feeling an impatience with President Kane. His tendency to consult appeared to some an indication of indecision, whereas what the university needed was a "strong" administrator. By 1912, Kane was suffering the ordeals of a university president who must deal with internal questions that have external significance. The questions were the sort that would trouble many university administrations in Washington and elsewhere—student discipline, political activities within the university community—but the difficulties were exacerbated by the approach of the election of 1912, for the political action issues touched the campus. In November 1912, Ernest Lister, a Democrat, was elected to succeed Hay as governor. The new governor had his own ideas about the university situation, but he did not immediately press them. By mid–1913 the regents had made their decision about President Kane. When at length they began their discussions with the president, they were prepared to offer him a year—until August 1, 1914—to find another place. Kane refused to resign, both because he believed that his record was sound and because he felt that the university would suffer if its president could be discharged for what might be regarded as political manipulation.

There was a tragic inevitability about it all. Kane was a tool of the regents to some, a victim of a reactionary board to others. While in May 1913 Douglas was beginning to plan his new building, Thomas Kane was nearing what proved to be a confrontation with the regents, and the regents must have felt themselves plunged into action on two fronts. They may indeed have felt more comfortable with the downtown lease questions, for to these business matters they had given thought and study. Rogers said later that he had been appointed to the board by Governor Hay "to guard and protect the best interests of the University under the original lease." But now every decision was being scrutinized as a new governor opened many matters to fresh review.[15]

A clue to the public mood—and to the governor's—may be found in a letter that Lister addressed to Cosgrove, now president of the board, on August 13, 1913:

My attention has been called by the newspaper fraternity to the fact that it is the policy of the Board of Regents of the State University to make all meetings of the Board executive sessions.

While I appreciate that there are occasionally matters which any board or commission, having the administration of public affairs in charge, desires to discuss in executive session, I am opposed to the "star chamber" idea as a hard and fast policy. The conduct of the business of the public is a matter regarding which the public has a right to be advised, and executive sessions accomplish anything but the confidence of the public. I would suggest that the policy of the Board of Regents in this connection be changed hereafter and that newspaper men or anyone else who may care to be present at the meetings of the Board, be allowed to attend.[16]

Lister was taking what was, for the time, an exceedingly liberal view of the question of the public's right to know. It is possible to think, however, without doubting his sincerity, that he was feeling the pressure of public and political interest in what was going on at the university, and was coming to the belief that the board's discussions with Kane could not be contained. The discussions were not contained, of course. There was a small change in the membership of the board in October 1913, when Spooner moved from the state to take up the practice of law in New York with his father, former Senator John C. Spooner of Wisconsin, and another Seattle attorney, George H. Walker, was appointed by Lister to fill the vacancy. But on November 19, 1913, Cosgrove wrote the governor asking to be relieved on December 1, and the newspapers, reporting this, said that a "complete reorganization" of the board was expected. A week later, on November 26, the regents held what proved to be a final meeting with President Kane—in executive session. When Kane refused to resign, he was informed that he was dismissed as president as of January 1, 1914.[17]

With that, the reorganization of the board began. Walker, who had served less than three months—just long enough to be cordially welcomed by the *Washington Alumnus*—resigned. Late in December, Governor Lister sent letters to McEwan, Hazeltine, Rogers, and Higgins asking for their resignations, and as 1914 arrived the governor announced his appointments. The new regents were Oscar A. Fechter, of North Yakima; Charles E. Gaches, of Mount Vernon; and Winlock W. Miller, William T. Perkins, and William A. Shannon, of Seattle. Rea remained, as did Eldridge Wheeler, of Montesano, who had been named by Lister to succeed Walker and who had taken no part in the Kane affair.

Fechter became president of the board. The regents' first move was to select an acting president of the university, and their choice was Henry Landes, a professor of geology and the dean of the recently created College of Sciences.

The board of regents not only was new—the members new to each other—but it faced an entirely new set of demands upon it. Kane's successor had to be selected, and everyone wanted the new president to be a man powerful enough to pull together a university community that was divided and exhausted emotionally and to rally the state behind an institution that was undersupported, overcrowded, and seriously in need of additional buildings. The regents might, in fact, have to woo rather than simply find the right man, for men of stature or promise might prove reluctant to come to a university where the recent upheaval suggested so clearly, as Kane had predicted, that educational leadership was at the mercy of politics. Until such a man was found, however, the problems—the finances, the crowding, the budget requests—lay between Landes and the regents, five of whom were recently appointed.

Governor Lister, drastic as was his action in the creation of the new board, nevertheless had made appointments that were admirably balanced politically. Shannon and Miller were Democrats; Fechter, Gaches, and Perkins, Republicans. Some of the appointments, viewed in the longer perspective, would seem admirable in other ways as well. Among the new regents were men of strong mind.

Shannon was a Seattle physician whose offices (as Douglas noted in an early issue of the *Metropolitan Bulletin*) were in the Cobb Building. Perkins was in finance, mining, and railroading, president of the Northern Securities Company and secretary of the Northwestern Exploration and Development Company and the Alaska Midlands Railroad. Wheeler was at once mayor of Montesano and superintendent of the little city's schools. Rea was a Tacoma real estate man. The leadership of the board was in Fechter, however, and much of its strength, as soon became apparent, was in Miller and Gaches.[18]

Fechter, president of the new board, appears to be almost forgotten now, but if that is the case he deserves better, for on the evidence he was a small-town banker of unusual intellectual scope and a man who had brought to the West an early touch of the Wisconsin-German liberal tradition.

Fechter was a native of Manitowoc who had worked his way through the University of Wisconsin, earned his law degree in 1887, and moved to Yakima in 1888 when the town was scarcely two years old. It was not law, however, but banking and business—and public service—that engaged him from then on. He started in real estate, but by 1904 he was manager of the Yakima Valley Bank, and soon its president. In the meantime he had served eight one-year terms as mayor of Yakima—drafted repeatedly for additional terms, it is said, after announcing plans to retire. Fechter was tough physically. Yakima was familiar with his hikes of five miles on weekdays and fifteen on Sunday. He was an avid reader, a student of economics, and a translator from the German of works by Goethe and Max Müller. Fechter had been a regent less than a year when he went out to the university to talk to the faculty on "University Control," a response to a book by a Columbia University professor whose conservative ideas had stimulated faculty discussion. Fechter roamed over the sensitive subjects of academic freedom and tenure—subjects much debated in President Kane's unhappy time—and he must have electrified his academic audience when he said:

I believe it is the duty of the members of the board to visit the university; to familiarize themselves with the work that is being done and the methods that are employed; to become acquainted with the members of the faculty; to learn their wants, to listen to their grievances. . . .

The board of regents does not restrain, does not limit your academic freedom, does not destroy your initiative. It leaves you free agents to perform the great work which is your mission, as great or greater than any other in the field of human endeavor. . . . Speaking for myself, I would discharge the professor if he didn't teach what he believed whatever heresy might be involved. . . .

If there is one thing in the world that is free, that never has been enslaved, it is intellect; intellectual freedom can never be restrained for any length of time; it cannot be domineered over. If you rest under the domination of a college president it is because he is a bigger intellectual force that you are; if he is not, he cannot rule you for a day. If you rest under the domination of a governing body, it is because the members of that body are of lesser intellectual caliber than you are and are carried away by their authority. . . . If a combination of president and governing body is directed against you, then it lies within your power to combine and to stand as one man for your rights.[19]

Thus spoke Fechter, who would serve the university as a regent far longer than he served Yakima as mayor. But one of his new colleagues, Miller, would serve even longer (he would even be serving again when the 1907 university tract lease expired in 1954), and the other, Gaches, one of the youngest regents ever appointed, would help find the new university president and would stand firmly with Miller in an approaching tumult over one of the new buildings on the downtown tract.

As for Miller, there was little in his career before 1914—he was forty-three when he came to the board—to suggest the kind of a man he was. He was of pioneer Washington stock. His father, William Winlock Miller, had been the first mayor of Olympia. His mother, who managed the family affairs after the death of her husband, had become the first woman director of a Washington bank before the territory became a state. Yet Miller went east to college, graduated from Yale in 1894, and read law for a time but never practiced before the bar. He simply took over from his mother the management of the family properties (in 1914 he was secretary of a family corporation, Mary M. Miller and Sons, Incorporated) and whatever his inclinations to that time, neither politics nor public service seems to have been among

them. The fact is that Miller as a regent began to make the university's affairs his most consuming interest.[20]

Gaches was thirty-three when he became a regent. His parents, like Miller's,
had been pioneers of Washington Territory, his father one of the early merchants of La Conner, far north of Seattle on Puget Sound, and his mother a
lifelong activist in community and church affairs. Gaches had graduated
from the university in 1901, when he was only nineteen—a good student,
something of an athlete (a pole vaulter), and a lieutenant in the cadet corps.
For a year after graduation, and despite his youth, Gaches was an instructor
at the university, then he went to Korea for two years with a mining project.
Home again by 1904, Gaches thought of politics while serving incidentally
with the National Guard. He was elected to the legislature for the session of
1907, but he was headed for banking, business, and farming. He was also
headed, liks so many others, for military service, but sooner than most. He
would leave the board of regents in 1916 to become one of Pershing's officers
on the Mexican border, and when America entered Word War I he would
serve as an infantry officer.[21]

Men such as these were the regents of 1914. Only Rea had any experience
at all with the recurring questions associated with development of the university tract.

A reading of the record before 1914—the regents' record primarily—pro-
duces an inescapable impression that the Metropolitan Building Company
had indeed been asking persistently, if understandably, for lease modifications or waivers large and small. The impression is equally strong that the
regents, apart from their consistent refusal to extend the basic lease, had
proved receptive, if not pliant, regarding modification requests. But it was
as if both sides were caught up in a movement that neither had the power
to change. The company—Douglas, White, Cobb, and the others—had to
develop the tract or lose all. The regents faced a similar problem. If the
company failed to complete the development of the tract, the university—
the state—would be back in the business of trying to lease an unfinished
property. Whatever the regents thought of the lease itself, the lease existed.
The arrangements had been worked out in earlier years by earlier boards, and
the basic terms—the lease to 1954, the rental schedule—were fixed and immutable. The regents could feel, perhaps, that they were doing the best they
could with a lease for which their predecessors had been responsible—that
in permitting the Metropolitan Building Company some freedom of action
they were simply helping to assure the success of a venture in which the university, like the company, had a considerable stake.

The relationship between the board and the company appears to have been
correctly formal, before 1914, as between landlord and tenant having common objectives. Douglas's letters to the regents were explicit if sometimes
short on detail. In his visits to the regents' meetings Douglas must have dis-

cussed freely—as when he announced his projected visit to London—the condition of the company and its plans for action. Yet there had been occasions when the company seemed to be asking—or assuming—approval of lease modification proposals that went to the farthest notch.

The Metropolitan Theatre lease modification, for example, had been approved by the regents without an explicit consideration of the projected widening of University Place, even though the widening was an already negotiated condition of the sublease with Klaw and Erlanger when the proposition was presented by the company and even though such a widening had implications with regard to the size and placement of other buildings adjoining, and across from, the theater. It is true that the widening was an aspect of the earliest plan to beautify the tract (the widened University Place between Fourth and Fifth avenues had been clearly indicated on the first Howells and Stokes drawings), and Douglas later had informed the regents, and had filed a public notice, that the widening was not a dedication of the space for street purposes. It was also true that by 1910 the company had already built the one-story Whitson Building at Fifth Avenue and University, this temporary structure placed on the line of the street, not fifteen feet back from the line. But nowhere in the regents' records is there an indication that the board even discussed the University Place widening or gave thought to its potential long-term meaning to the platting of the tract as a whole.

It would be hard to say that the regents were making "concessions" in such things. But there was an air of casualness about the proceedings. It seemed so in the case of the Uhl Building, the one-story temporary building constructed by the company under a lease running eleven months beyond the seven-year agreement then in effect, and in the case of the addition of a second story to the College Club Building. The regents approved the Uhl lease as they approved the first five-year extension of the agreement covering temporary buildings. They approved the elevation of the College Club as they approved the sale of liquor in the club buffet. They had asked, at last, that the company build one new permanent building, but even in the granting of the modifications relating to temporary buildings they had been somewhat unclear about the ultimate disposition of the buildings themselves. The main lease stipulated that all buildings erected on the tract were to become the property of the university. The modifications said that the temporary buildings were to be removed by the company in a specified number of years. The modifications left untouched, however, the section of the original lease covering university ownership of the buildings; thus they left untouched the question of the residual value of the one-story buildings that were dotting the tract.[22]

But all this had been done by former boards. Now, in 1914, there was a new one. What difference did it make? Soon the tests would come. The Metropolitan Building Company was asking approval of additional extensions and modifications.

On April 24, 1914, Douglas appeared before the board to present, with explanatory letters and statements, three new matters.[23] He asked, first, that the board ratify—or consider "just the same as if we were making an application"—the construction of a State Fisheries Commission Building that already was completed and ready for opening the following week. He asked also that the board permit the construction of a Women's University Club Building next to the College Club Building, the two buildings "considered as one" and exempt from the condition that temporary buildings were to be removed if the Metropolitan Building Company had not added $500,000 in permanent improvements by 1915. He was asking, in effect, a waiver for two temporary buildings, one not yet constructed.

The third request concerned the $500,000 commitment itself. Douglas's written statement, "Improvements Required for the Extension of Permit Time on Temporary Buildings," described the status of the company's efforts to build that building:

It is necessary for the Metropolitan Building Co. to build $500,000 of fireproof improvements upon the University Tract, prior to June 24th, 1915. If, however, we have this amount of improvements 50% completed, we can have six months' additional time in which to complete the improvements. It may be necessary for us to come before the Board at a later date and ask for some extension of time on this agreement. In the meantime, however, we are making strenuous efforts to raise the balance of the money necessary to comply with the conditions fixed by your Board.

And of the projected building—now the Stuart, not the Grandin:

We have plans prepared for a building to be called the Stuart Building. The building will adjoin the Henry Building on the south and will complete the block front of which the White and the Henry Buildings form a part.

And of University Place:

In order to make a central plaza on the University Tract, University Street was widened fifteen feet on each side with the approval of your Board. The widening of University Street will cut down by fifteen feet in width the size of the Stuart Building. We propose to build the Stuart Building in the same manner as our other buildings have been built, except in this, the Cobb Building, which is the latest building built by us, has reinforced concrete girders and floors, but has steel columns. We propose to build the Stuart Building with reinforced concrete floors and girders and with reinforced concrete columns. In other respects, so far as we know at present, the building will be of the same character as our other buildings.

Then, the prospect:

On account of the low price of materials at the present time, it might be that the cost of the building will fall a *little* [Douglas's emphasis] below $500,000. We would like to have a resolution passed by your Board to the effect that if we build the Stuart Building along the lines that I have indicated, that it will be considered a compliance with requirements for $500,000 of improvements. The White Building which occupies the other end of the block cost a little over $600,000 and the Henry Building a little over $500,000. We know of nothing that could be gained if we are able to build this building for less than $500,000 by requiring us to put a few thousand dollars into some other permanent improvement.

Douglas added that the plans for the Stuart Building were prepared and that "they can be turned over to you for your consideration."

Douglas's proposals were interestingly diverse. Two—the State Fisheries and Women's University Club proposals—were of some urgency, especially since one of the buildings had already been built. The regents, new to all this, did on that day, April 24, 1914, what the other regents probably would have done. They decided that the erection of the Fisheries Building, "although not in accordance with the provisions of the lease," should be approved for a period of three years. Then Perkins moved that other questions be referred to the "permanent standing committee" on the lease, to which Fechter now appointed Shannon, Perkins, and Miller, their report to be made at the next meeting of the board.[24]

What was happening was interesting simply as a foretaste of what was to come. The Fisheries Building came to the regents more as an accommodation to a state department than as a company proposal for augmenting rental income. The State Fisheries Commission needed offices in Seattle, and Alden Blethen, the former regent, who now was chairman of the industrial committee of the Chamber of Commerce, had urged the building on university property. The rental was exceedingly modest. The regents could not but think the arrangement a good one. Douglas had even noted that the building was the kind that could be moved to some other part of the tract if there should be another need for the space, which was below Fourth Avenue between Seneca and University streets. The regents immediately voted approval.

The matter of the Women's University Club was a similarly bland proposal, except that in this case a breaching of the three modification agreements was involved. The Women's University Club and the College Club were to be considered "as one" to allow the former to have an authorized sublease of at least seven years, as Douglas asked, regardless of the outcome of the Stuart Building projections. When the regents met again on May 20, 1914, the "permanent standing committee" made its report, recommending approval of the Women's University Club Building "providing that the granting of this request does not in any way grant an extension of or modify the agreements in force, except as respects the building contemplated." The report was signed, however, only by Shannon and Perkins. The third member, Miller, submitted a minority report, probably the first such report in the history of the leasehold. Miller wrote: "I beg to disagree with the majority report of the Committee above named, believing it to be inadvisable at this time to extend the lease, or any portion of it, for the purpose named, especially in view of the fact that the matter will automatically adjust itself within one year."[25]

Miller meant, quite simply, that the Metropolitan Building Company should be held to its commitment to build the Stuart. If the new building was constructed in 1915, the company had all the time it needed for the Women's University Club sublease. If the Stuart was not built, all bets were off anyway. On the regents' vote, Gaches and Wheeler stood with Miller; the others—Fechter, Perkins, Rea, and Shannon—voted to accept the majority report. Miller lost.

There remained the proposition about the Stuart, the suggestion that since the new building might cost a "little" less than $500,000, a structure of a lower cost be accepted as in compliance with the regents' requirement in the agreement of 1912. Douglas had asked, in conversations with the "permanent standing committee," that a building costing $450,000 be considered in compliance. The committee accepted this. At the regents' meeting of June 16, 1914, a report—this time again signed only by Shannon and Perkins—recommended that a building costing $450,000 be accepted. Rea moved approval, Perkins seconded, Gaches voted no. Fechter and Miller were absent. The approval was granted.[26]

In these spring and early summer months of 1914 the new board of regents was beginning to get a taste of what it meant to have a downtown property to consider. Fechter, the banker, was president of the board and voting with the majority. Miller and Gaches were exhibiting what must have seemed an unexpected independence of mind. The board was beginning to look seriously for a university president to succeed Kane, and was, with the help of Acting President Landes and Herbert T. Condon, the university's bursar, putting together a budget request to be presented to the legislature of 1915, a request of $1,163,794 for operations and $300,000 for new buildings. The university enrollment was now approaching 3,800 and the space problem was acute. Landes prepared a "statement to the people of the state" which, published later in the *Washington Alumnus* was headed: "THE UNIVERSITY NEEDS BUILDINGS. . . . . It needs them badly! Washington is so poorly housed that a large percentage of entering students may be turned away next year if proper facilities are not provided to care for an increased enrollment."[27]

All the while the days ticked away until August 1914, when Germany invaded Belgium and the Great War began. In Seattle, a new play, *Strongheart*, was opening July 1 at the Metropolitan Theatre. On July 4, the new wonder, the forty-two-story L. C. Smith Building, was opened to the public for the first time and 4,400 visitors rode the elevators to the observation deck, where the view from the "tallest building west of New York" was better, the newspapers said, than the view from any of the three taller buildings in the Eastern metropolis. The *Post-Intelligencer* now carried a daily log, "Wireless Reports from Ships at Sea," as the ships reported their positions to the Marconi Company's North Pacific Station. Elsewhere, preparations were being made for the opening of the Panama Canal on August 3; in Washington, D.C., the "suffragists" were planning to "bombard" Congress again in behalf of votes for women; and Francisco "Pancho" Villa was organizing an army for his revolt against Carranza's Mexican government. The European war finally came in a torrent of black headlines—"British Fleet Sails under Sealed Orders for Unknown Destination," "Kaiser Strikes First Blow," "England Declares War," "Battle on North Sea"— and the news reports noted that thousands of American tourists were stranded in Europe, scores from the Seattle area, unable to get aboard ships to bring them home. One small story struck a cheerful note. The headline: "New York Banker Says War Will be Advantageous to America." The banker was not identified.

In the summer of 1914 the construction of the Stuart was under way. Douglas had solved the financing problem, and the "superior" building would not have to cost $500,000, because the regents had accepted a lower figure as in compliance. And all—the regents, the Metropolitan Building Company, and the city of Seattle itself—had reason to rejoice that the Fourth Avenue frontage would soon be complete and there would be at last a White-Henry-Stuart façade of the kind depicted by Howells and Stokes when the "master plan" of the university tract was drawn up in 1907–8. Since the building was to be called the Stuart, there undoubtedly had been another of those meetings of the Metropolitan trustees and bondholders at which the financing had been finally solicited and committed.

The new building carried the name of a man who, in a most adventurous way, had made a circuit of the West in the course of beginning to establish not merely a fortune but a singularly important American industry—not in lumbering or transportation or mining, but in, of all things, milk.

E. A. Stuart (the initials were for Elbridge Amos) was by 1914 a successful man whose greatest success still lay ahead. He was not, however, one of the Metropolitan's original investors, but a later enlistee. Photographs of him in those years of middle age suggest the well-established attorney or prominent school man—his face, with clipped mustache, just a touch austere above a high collar, pince nez on a rather long nose. But all his life Stuart had been facing up to adversity and even occasional danger with a spirit that reflected absolute determination, deep idealism, a salesman's confidence, and a gambler's feeling for the long chance.

Born in North Carolina in 1856, Stuart had spent his early youth on a farm in Indiana to which his family had moved at the outbreak of the Civil War. As a boy he had only the schooling he could get when not needed on the farm, and by the time he was in his teens he had been afflicted so severely by rheumatism that he could get around only on crutches. A physician uncle in Kansas offered help, and to Kansas young Stuart went, literally working his way to health with farm jobs, railroad construction jobs, and clerking in stores. From 1875, when he was nineteen, he made his own way. He began to have ideas about merchandising, and he thought he saw opportunity in the Southwest, particularly in El Paso, Texas. With a friend, S. H. Sutherland, he got financial backing from a Kansas merchant, and as Stuart and Sutherland the two young men went into business in El Paso with a store—a tent, because lumber was too expensive—to which their goods had to be hauled 150 miles by mule team from the railhead at San Marchial, New Mexico.

Stuart and Sutherland made money. The firm made much money, in fact, even in a border town still so raw that the law-abiding citizens had to organize a vigilante committee and walk the streets, Stuart among them, to maintain order. The San Marchial–El Paso mule-team run remained hazardous, however, and in 1894 Stuart sold out. He had spent fourteen years in the Southwest, he was only thirty-eight, he was moderately well off, and he sought other fields.

The fields Stuart found were near Kent, Washington, sixteen miles from Seattle. He had heard in 1899 of a chance to buy up a failed condensed milk company there. Why this attracted him no one ever really understood, apparently, for Stuart knew nothing of the Northwest, the plant was in disrepair, and the idea of condensing milk was in disrepair too. The technique was not perfected and grocery stores everywhere were skeptical of the product. But Stuart was fascinated by this challenge and confident that he could make a success where everyone else had met discouragement or failure. He apparently came to believe that in the future all milk, properly processed, would be sold in cans.

Stuart began production of milk on September 6, 1899, in the rehabilitated plant of what now was called the Pacific Coast Condensed Milk Company. The first operations were as bleak as every knowledgeable observer had predicted they would be. Stuart had his own initial failures with the canning process. He overcame them. When sales were almost nonexistent, Stuart packed his own cases of samples and visited stores up and down the Northwest coast, selling cans in any numbers, however small. When his partner, discouraged, wanted to leave the company, Stuart bought him out with a deposit of $5,000 and a large bank loan. He was then, it was said later, $140,000 in debt. But Stuart's imagination never flagged. Soon he was selling not just condensed milk but "Carnation Cream," the cans attractively labeled in red and white.* He tried in every way to prove that Carnation Cream was totally resistant to spoilage. He sent shipments of cans to the frozen Yukon, where condensed milk became a staple among the gold rush miners and prospectors. He sent cartons of cans on a round-trip voyage to Japan to demonstrate that months at sea had no deleterious effect on the quality. He advertised Carnation Cream in widening markets, from Seattle to Tacoma to Portland, Oregon. In 1902 he opened a new plant at Forest Grove, Oregon. By 1903 the plant in Kent was showing a profit for the first time.

If there was romance in business—and that was a fundamental American credo—Stuart's story epitomized it. He had surmounted physical handicaps and hardships that would have induced most reasonably hardy men to withdraw from competition. But he was winning. Behind the spectacles and placid

---

* The story is that Stuart picked red and white for eye appeal on grocery shelves; that, liking flowers, he asked his patent attorney to search the trademark files for a flower name still unclaimed; and that he came across "Carnation" himself one day—on a box of cigars displayed in a store window. When the attorney found the name unpatented. Stuart adopted it. There was an additional contemporary appeal, it was said, because President McKinley invariably wore a carnation in his buttonhole and thus had given the flower a measure of popularity.

face of the photographs was a mind tuned by years of exercise. Yet it was in the development of the dairy herds that produced the milk that Stuart's special genius was most apparent.

In the first years, the milk for Carnation Cream came from the well-fed but undistinguished cattle grazing in the pastures of Western Washington. Stuart soon felt that he needed something better, so about 1906 he bought sixty-five young registered Holsteins and distributed them at cost to the farmers from whom he was buying milk, hoping in this way to improve the Washington herds. The infusion of new blood was not signally successful, but the farmers liked the idea and Stuart was inspired to open a small breeding farm near Seattle where experiments in stock improvement could be conducted. The new federal Pure Food Law made it impossible for Stuart to market his Carnation product as "Cream," for cream now had to contain 18 percent butterfat, a level that could not be achieved in the can. Carnation Cream became Carnation Evaporated Milk produced by the Carnation Milk Products Company.

When the panic of 1907 struck the West, Stuart's farmer suppliers, among others, were demanding cash for every transaction because banks were tottering and checks were suspect. Stuart demanded of his bank, and received in sacks, $60,000 in gold pieces that he hauled to Kent in a buggy and used to pay off his bimonthly milk bills. The gesture solved the immediate crisis in confidence, but the incident probably reinforced Stuart's growing feeling that the industry he was creating needed its own stable and superior sources of milk supply. The company was expanding. New plants had been placed in nearby Washington cities—Chehalis, Mount Vernon, Ferndale—and Stuart was looking farther afield, soon to the Wisconsin-Illinois markets of the Chicago area. The production of milk from his own herds became of supreme interest.

In 1910, Stuart began the development, in the Snoqualmie Valley, east of Seattle, of his Carnation Milk Farms. The first small plot of fifty acres— the original experimental farm—became in succeeding years a huge 1,500-acre establishment of fine dairy barns set in lush, fenced fields, and the breeding of Holsteins became both a Stuart passion and a theme of the company's production and sales efforts. Stuart brought to the farms the finest Holsteins he could buy (eventually he paid $106,000 for a young bull, a record price at the time), and at Carnation Farms his managers developed Holsteins that repeatedly set milk production records. Stuart was describing the beauties of the farms, one day—the peaceful Snoqualmie Valley pastures where streams came down from snow-capped mountains—to a young woman copywriter for his Chicago advertising agency. The young woman created in that moment one of the classic phrases of American industrial promotion: "Carnation Milk . . . from Contented Cows." [28]

When the Stuart Building was finished in 1915 the Carnation Company occupied offices on the eleventh floor. Stuart, who had fought so many battles from Indiana to Kansas to New Mexico to Texas to California to Washington, was not yet sixty years old, and even then the Carnation Company was only on the verge of an expansion that would make it, after World War I, a worldwide enterprise. Stuart's own office was in the building that carried his name.

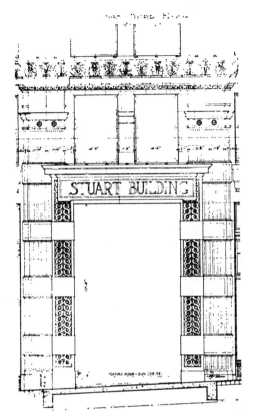

Howells and Stokes sketch of the entry of the Stuart Building

The Stuart Building was accepted by the board of regents on May 8, 1915, as in full compliance with the Metropolitan Building Company's obligation to build a first-class fireproof structure. The building differed somewhat in its specification from the White and the Henry, but Carl Gould, of the university's architectural firm of Bebb and Gould, had filed two reports late in 1914 pronouncing the construction thoroughly sound and well conceived. By completing the building before June 24, the company had assured the ten-year extension of its permit to build and sublease temporary buildings, the extension to June 24, 1925. The Stuart had been set back fifteen feet from the line of University Street to accommodate the widened University Place, but the regents had long since accepted that idea. There was a difference in the cost, it turned out: the Stuart, originally supposed to be an improvement of "not less than $500,000," this figure reduced to $450,000 in the 1914 amendment, actually cost, in the end, just $421,845.90, according to the company's report to the board. Although the "improvement" of the tract had not even met the reduced cost expectation, a fine new building was in place and everyone was pleased.[29] The regents were pleased about something else, too. They were about to conclude their search for a new president of the university.

The new president was Henry Suzzallo, since 1909 professor of the philosophy of education at Columbia University. Suzzallo's name had been suggested a year earlier by Franklin Graves, Kane's predecessor, who, though going on to other posts, had continued his interest in university affairs. Suzzallo was a rising star, well known in the East because of his association with Columbia, and already mentioned for several other college or university posts. But a special strength as far as Washington was concerned—an element noted by his supporters—was that Suzzallo was a native of San Jose, California, a graduate of Stanford University, a Western man with national credentials. It was Charles Gaches who had spearheaded the regents' inquiries about Suzzallo, visiting him in New York and talking to university people East and West. Early in May 1915, about the time the Stuart Building was up for acceptance, the regents had decided to invite Suzzallo to Seattle. Suzzallo arrived soon after, and by the middle of May the negotiations were concluded. After almost a year and a half, Kane's successor had been selected.[30]

It was a time of satisfaction. The university was grateful to Landes, who had served the university well as its interim head, but glad that there now was a man of Suzzallo's energy at the helm. Suzzallo came to Seattle in June 1915 to begin to pick up the reins. He was with the regents at their June meeting, which began on June 14. Also with them was J. F. Douglas, for the regents were to have before them, apart from matters related to university administration, a matter that took their minds back to the downtown tract— a request from the Metropolitan Building Company for another modification of its lease. The request was of the kind an earlier board had faced regarding construction of the Metropolitan Theatre. This time the company wanted to build an auditorium, and the preliminary construction work apparently was already started.

For some years Douglas had entertained the idea that the tract should have a building sufficiently large and flexible in design to accommodate both large pubic meetings and the automobile and boat shows that were becoming increasingly popular. He had mentioned such a need in the *Metropolitan Bulletin* as early as 1909, but the one-story, temporary Hippodrome Building had not filled the bill and was not supposed to. By 1915 another plan had matured.

At that June 14 meeting, Douglas visited the board of regents to discuss it. He asked then, in preliminary fashion, that the lease be modified "so as to permit his company to construct an auditorium building on the vacant space on Fifth Avenue, between University and Seneca Streets, and to have the same accepted as a permanent building." Miller immediately moved, seconded by Gaches, that no modification of the lease be granted. On the vote, Fechter joined Miller and Gaches in support; Perkins, Rea, Shannon, and Wheeler were against the motion. Miller's motion lost. The proposed modification was alive, and the issue was referred to the standing committee on the lease—Shannon, Perkins, and Miller.[31]

Two days later, the regents still in session but Wheeler absent, Douglas returned with preliminary sketches of the proposed building and a long letter in which he outlined the company's plan in detail.[32] Douglas said that the company "is about to erect a building of the auditorium type," that a building of the kind projected could not be amortized within the ten years of the temporary-building permit, and that the company desired, as an alternative, to build a permanent building which, like the Metropolitan Theatre, would be approved as an exception to the provisions of the lease requiring structures of at least three stories with walls and foundations strong enough to carry six. The company asked again, in short, to be allowed to build a special-purpose building departing from the lease stipulations but "permanent and useful . . . and in every way a creditable improvement to the University Tract," a building that would grace the tract to 1954 and after.

Douglas's letter covered the company's thinking on the question. It was needless to settle for a cheap "mill-type" or "loft" building, he wrote, when the permanent building, costing more and amortized over the longer period, could be of the "Metropolitan Theatre type." The city badly needed such an auditorium, he said, for events that could not be accommodated in the increasingly busy National Guard Armory. Douglas was candid about the arrangements the company had already made to build and rent the building. The numbered paragraphs of his letter included, in part, the following ones:

9. We have rented the auditorium building for the five winter months for the next ten years at a monthly rental of $2,000.00 net, which is evidence that a building of this type will bring in a large revenue. We propose to use the building for auditorium purposes during the summer months, which is the season when it will be most in demand in Seattle. . . .

10. If your Board will permit a change in type of the building that we are required to build under our lease, we will build a much better building, costing a larger sum of money, than if we build under our ten year permit. We will agree to use a very much better grade of mortar; to build the structure itself entirely of brick, reinforced concrete and steel. . . .

Douglas asked a resolution of approval of the board. He asked appointment of a committee to "pass on plans and specifications of a building that would be accepted by your Board as a permanent building." Then he urged haste, for a completion date was already set:

13. In the lease that we have made we have agreed that we will use our best endeavors to have the building finished prior to October first. It will be impossible to get the plans and specifications for the building completed and to get the work started earlier than July fifteenth—ten weeks only will remain in which to get the building finished prior to October first. On that account we would appreciate it if we could have immediate action by your Board so that the committee could confer with our architects.

Douglas had been candid, and he was there to answer the regents' questions. The building was to be used for ice skating and hockey in winter months, for assemblies or exhibits in summer. It is possible only to draw inferences about what the regents were thinking, yet to at least some of them the proposition must have seemed a little presumptuous. The company had leased for five years a building that had not been built and of a kind requiring a lease modification despite the Metropolitan Theatre precedent, a permanent building of Metropolitan Theatre quality that the company had undertaken to have finished by October 1—within three and a half months—even before the board had been consulted. At that meeting of June 16, the proposal came to a tie vote because Wheeler was absent. It was Shannon who moved that the board approve the modification to allow such a building "of permanent construction and superior quality" and that the plans and specifications be submitted to the lease committee with power to act. Perkins and Rea voted with Shannon for approval. Fechter, Gaches, and Miller voted against. The motion was lost, and approval, for the moment, was withheld.[33]

The key word then and later was "permanent." Was the new auditorium, which would be called the Arena, a permanent building? The Metropolitan Building Company unquestionably could have erected a reasonably satisfactory structure under the temporary-building agreement it then had, although another waiver regarding height might have been necessary. But there was the question of amortization. The company, wanting the longer lease term, offered a "permanent" building of "Metropolitan Theatre type," even as the pressure to get along with construction was mounting. Construction apparently was proceeding into the early weeks of July 1915, while the regents' approval was in suspense; but perhaps, under the pressure, compromises were made. In any case, the building was nearing completion by the time the lease modification was signed. Events then moved forward along a fascinatingly erratic course.

The preliminary motions of June having failed, the regents had the Arena question before them when they met on July 23, 1915. Douglas was with them again. This time, according to the regents' minutes, he had brought "plans," although these must have been no more than additional sketches. Miller moved, again, that the "plans" not be accepted, but again only Gaches and Fechter joined him, and the motion was lost. Shannon moved "that the plans of the building submitted to the Board be accepted for a permanent building under the terms of the lease, subject to submission to and approval of the Attorney General." Gaches then offered as an amendment, somewhat surprisingly, the idea that the university be allowed free use of the auditorium for ten days each year. But when it came to the roll call, Gaches joined Miller and Fechter in voting against the motion he had amended; Perkins, Rea, Shannon, and Wheeler voted for it. The "plans" were approved. The attorney general would review the modification agreement. The university would get ten days use of the auditorium each year. If the meaning of this small parliamentary gavotte is not entirely clear, it is at least as clear as some of the later developments.[34]

Soon after the July 23 meeting Douglas sent to the regents a copy of the proposed modification agreement, and this was forwarded on August 1 to the attorney general for review. On August 5 the City Building Department issued a permit for erection of the Arena, now well along. When the attorney general responded to the regents on August 25, he sent with his letter a slightly modified form of agreement in which he, having assumed that there could be no other way, specified that the company "is hereby permitted and allowed to erect and maintain . . . a building . . . according to plans and specifications filed with and approved by the said Board of Regents." The new draft did not say, as had the earlier one, that the building "shall be considered and accepted as complying with the terms of said lease for the full term thereof." The modified form was approved by the regents on September 24, 1915—Gaches and Miller voting nay—and the final signing took place on September 29, Fechter for the regents and C. H. Cobb for the Metropolitan Building Company.[35]

It was October, now, and the new Arena, nearly completed, was stretching along the slope above Fifth Avenue between University and Seneca streets, a long brick structure, two tall stories at the lower end, not quite so high at the other, a line of twenty-two arched windows extending the length of the building at the second level, and the roof a low, auditorium-style crown scarcely visible from the street. The Arena was not another Metropolitan Theatre—the feeling was utilitarian—but the brickwork had certain Metropolitan Theatre touches and it was both structurally innovative and capable of multiple uses, whether for skating or for automobile shows. A 75-ton refrigeration plant would chill floor pipes in the winter ice skating season. A covering floor would be laid for other events. The Arena had no posts or pillars to block the view of the thousands to be seated at public meetings. The acoustics were superior. The interior was to be brightened by huge murals on Northwest themes. The building was not quite finished in October 1915, but J. F. Douglas was said to be very proud of it.

But on October 6 a member of the regents' standing committee dropped by to inspect the Arena. This was Miller, who had voted repeatedly against the company's proposal, and he did not like what he saw. He thought that the building clearly was not fireproof, a condition basic to its acceptance as permanent. He had no recollection of seeing plans suggesting the kind of building the Arena had turned out to be. He informed the other regents that in his opinion the new building fell short of the requirements of the resolution authorizing its construction. He and Gaches, exchanging letters, turned to Markham, secretary of the board, for confirming information on the details of the regents' actions. Almost immediately the regents asked Bebb and Gould, their architectural consultants, for a professional opinion on the building. This time Charles Bebb responded:

Complying with your request, I beg to state that I have examined this building by personal inspection. In no sense can this building be classed in the Standard Class "A" fireproof buildings. The foundation and walls are concrete and masonry construction. The roof is carried on steel trusses resting on steel columns built into the masonry. The roof itself is only of wood construction, the roofing being what is known as Carey roofing. . . . As a guess I should say there are several hundred thousand feet of lumber used in the building. . . . The Arena building might come under the classification of mill building, but could not be described as a fireproof building.[36]

The regents turned to the Seattle Building Department. The superintendent, T. Josenhans, responded on October 11:

You ask if the building conforms "to the established standard of a Class 'A' fireproof building." In answer I will say that the building does not conform in several respects. The roof sheathing is of wood, as are also the steps on which the seats are to be placed. . . . The features however are expressly permitted by the building ordinance.[37]

The regents met on October 29, 1915, to receive the report of the standing committee. The parliamentary proceedings were made interesting this time by the delayed appearance of Shannon, the physician, who had to be called from his office, where he was attending a patient, to break a tie vote. Miller, of course, made the initial motion: "That the Metropolitan Building Company be notified that the resolution of the Board of Regents covering the matter of modification of their lease has not been complied with either in letter or spirit in so far as plans and specifications of the auditorium building under construction have not been filed with the secretary of the Board, and in so far as said building is not being erected in the manner as represented by J. F. Douglas, representative of the Company to the Board at the time that said resolution was passed." Rea moved, as an amendment, that Douglas be asked to come to the board to "make explanation." With Shannon absent, the amendment and the motion lost on tie votes—Perkins, Rea, and Wheeler voting one way, Gaches, Miller, and Fechter the other. Rea then moved that Douglas be asked before the board to "answer questions," Miller amending this to require that the meeting be open to "interested persons." It was then that Shannon entered, and he joined the losing side. Gaches, Miller, Perkins, and Fechter voted for the open meeting. The main motion carried. Rea moved that the meeting with Douglas be held the next day. So ordered.[38]

All of this got into the newspapers, of course, and with far more detail than appeared in the official records. The *Post-Intelligencer*'s report the following morning (October 30) was headed, "ARENA BUILDING CAUSES DISPUTE AMONG REGENTS. Gaches, Miller and Fechter Oppose Accepting Structure as Permanent Improvement. . . . J. F. Douglas, Secretary of the Metropolitan Company, Is Requested To Be Present to Explain Attitude Assumed by Corporation." If the newspaper account were even moderately accurate, the emphasis on the disputatious spirit of the regents' meeting was not misplaced. There had been sharp exchanges, even between Shannon and Rea, apparently, and Miller and Gaches had stood foursquare against accepting the Arena as permanent. Miller and Gaches denied that anything but an "elevation drawing" of the building ever was shown the board, and Miller recalled that the Arena had been leased, and the materials for it ordered, before the Metropolitan Building Company asked permission to build it.

"The Arena cannot by any manner of means be classed as a permanent building," Gaches was quoted as saying, "and therefore it would be extremely unwise to modify the university lease. The control of the valuable half-block which the building occupies would virtually pass from our hands until 1953 [*sic*], when the university lease expires. . . . On the other hand, at the end of ten years the building must either come under the rental readjustments, with other temporary buildings on the tract, or be razed to make way for a better improvement."

The regents' meeting of October 29 had been something of a test—of the regents among themselves and of the regents in their relationship to the lessees of a university property. In the newspaper report, the issue within the board came down to an exchange between Rea and Miller.

Rea said, at one point, that objections of the kind raised by Gaches, Miller, and Fechter "would lead to the bankruptcy of the Metropolitan Building Company." Miller's reply had a ring to it. "I am not here to guard the interests of the Metropolitan Building Company," he said. "Whether they succeed or fail is their lookout. I am looking out after the best interests of the university." When Rea persisted, saying that business would "swing away from the tract in the future," reducing the value of the tract as a real estate holding, Miller responded: "We are interested in Seattle's future as much as you are. We believe that the university tract will always be an extremely valuable property." Miller had said "we." It was Gaches, Fechter, and Miller at the barricades.

The *Post-Intelligencer* had even called President Suzzallo, who had attended the regents' meeting in June, to ask his view on the issue now before the board. Suzzallo replied forthrightly that his view "coincided" with that of Gaches, Miller, and Fechter. He opposed a modification of the lease and he had said so when Douglas first visited the board with the company's proposal.

What, in its essentials, was the issue that now divided the regents? To Miller it was simply that the Metropolitan Building Company had built a temporary building that it wished declared permanent, which meant that for thirty-nine years—until 1954—the company could lease it and alter it and use it as opportunities arose and turn it back to the university after it had been drained of any possible future usefulness or value. There were other matters —such as the leasing of the building before it was approved and the question whether "plans" actually had been submitted for the regents' approval—but a building such as the Arena, in Miller's eyes, was merely one of the temporary buildings that were to be removed and, it was to be hoped, replaced by permanent improvements by June 24, 1925.

The open meeting at which Douglas was expected was scheduled, this

issue hanging in the air, for October 30, 1915, the day after the "dispute."
The regents had been meeting for some time now in the Henry Building,
and the newspapers were announcing that Douglas was to appear. Douglas
did not appear, and he certainly could have been given only the most inadequate notice, if any. Instead of appearing, Douglas sent a letter to the
board—"To the Honorable, The Board of Regents of the University of Washington."[39] Douglas wrote:

I understand that I am expected to appear before your Board today to answer questions with reference to construction of the Arena Building. I have learned from
reading the morning paper that some members of your Board claim that the Arena
Building does not conform to their expectations.
    Immediately after your Board agreed to accept the Arena Building as a permanent
building, we changed our policy with reference to the building and we have built
the building in accordance with our understanding with you and in some particulars
we have exceeded what we understood had been promised you.

Douglas said that the contractor and the architects would testify regarding
the change in "policy," and that the lessee would testify that he got a better
building than he expected. The point he made, however, was that the regents
should put in writing their view of where the company had failed. Of this,
he said:

Believing as we do that we have complied with our promises to your Board, we feel
that before the matter is discussed that the issues between us should be clearly defined. We suggest therefore, that your Board prepare a statement showing the particulars in which the building fails to conform to our agreement. As soon as this
statement is prepared we will examine it carefully, and I will then go before your
Board prepared to discuss the issues involved in an intelligent manner.
    There is no disposition on our part to dodge any issue. . . . We regard the accep-
tance of the Arena as a closed matter from a legal and technical standpoint. We are
willing, however, to waive any rights that we have and have the subject opened up
for a full and free discussion.

Rea moved that the board comply with Douglas's request. There was not
even a vote on the motion. Rea and Miller again had a "tilt," the *Post-
Intelligencer* reported, but the meeting adjourned without action on the
Arena, and members of the board were guests of university alumni at a dinner
at the Butler Hotel, where President Suzzallo was the speaker.
    It was the university's alumni association that now came strongly into the
contest, and it was to the regents that the association soon addressed a letter
asking that the board defer action until an association committee could make
its own study of the case. When the association's report was filed, it proved
to be a long analysis of some four thousand words—addressed to the regents
and stinging in its tone—demanding not merely rejection of the Arena as a
permanent building but an end to "favors" to the Metropolitan Building
Company at the expense of the university.
    The initial letter to the board was submitted on November 25 by King
Dykeman, president of the alumni association, and Jerry D. Riordan, execu-

tive secretary. Dykeman was widely known and respected—a lawyer in Seattle from 1903 to 1906, then the city's assistant corporation counsel, and a superior court judge since 1911. Dykeman had appointed a special committee to conduct the study, but the report itself was signed by Dykeman, Riordan, and the seven members of the executive board, and it spoke not only of the Arena case but of what the editor of the *Alumnus* called "a principle that must endure in the matter of the University Tract."[40]

The association statement reconstructed in minute detail the actions of the regents with regard to the Arena—the motions, the amendments, the discussions, the correspondence, the tie votes, the failure to insist on plans—and it declared that the Arena must not be accepted as permanent. It went into the whole matter of the lease, too, including the tax-exempt status of the property, and spoke bluntly:

This attempted modification of the Metropolitan Building Company lease to permit the erection of the Arena Building is the fourth time in eight years the original lease has been altered. We have already shown that the instrument as it was first drawn was too liberal in its terms . . . by not bringing the University a fair return for the use of its property. But we are not clamoring against the original lease. It is a binding agreement, however unfortunately entered into from a University standpoint. . . . But the alumni do demand that this everlasting tinkering with the original lease be stopped.

In every case the modifications of the lease have been made at the request and in the interests of the Metropolitan Building Company. A search of the record will not disclose a single alteration proposed by the Board of Regents for the sole good of the University and agreed to by the Company. The question has always been, "Will it benefit the Metropolitan Building Company?" If it did, the modification was promptly agreed to. The majority of the Board has apparently never concerned itself with the query, "Will the University be benefited?"

The statement then made a singular charge:

It is common knowledge that the Metropolitan Building Company has asked and is going to ask again for an extension of the lease from fifty to one hundred years. In fact, the report is current that the company has already advertised and boasted that it was certain to get this extension. If this last suggestion is agreed to, the lands might just as well be deeded to the company at once, for practical ownership, without the necessity of paying taxes, would be the ultimate result of such a concession. . . . We respectfully suggest that at this feast on the Old University Tract, the building company has already been bountifully helped; that if you insist on keeping its plate heaped to overflowing with this Arena alteration, you might just as well relinquish your seat at the head of the table and allow the company to hereafter carve and serve.

We, the alumni of Washington, insist that the question now before you is a bigger, broader and a more far reaching one than the mere acceptance or non-acceptance of the Arena Building as a permanent improvement to the tract. It goes to the very ownership of the property, for if the Metropolitan Building Company is allowed to cut here, slice and shave there, ultimately there will be no lease at all and the University in the last analysis will lose the property which should be its principal means of support.[41]

This was rough talk to a board of regents by a body of alumni leaders, well-known citizens all, whose own leader was the highly regarded Judge Dyke-man. The sting must have been felt by Miller, Gaches, and Fechter as well as by others, for while the alumni supported their stand with regard to the Arena, the statement was addressed to the board as a whole, which had indeed allowed the project to proceed without creating, at the least, a reasonably coherent official record of its views and actions. In their failure to insist on seeing plans the regents seemed particularly vulnerable. As the statement pointed out, Douglas had written the board on November 4, 1915, to imply that the members had seemed not much interested in plans. In the course of a long letter reviewing events, Douglas had said: "At the time . . . that the agreement was signed, the building was practically completed. When I delivered a copy of the agreement to you I stated that there was not much use in filing plans and specifications as required by the agreement, as the members of the Board could inspect the completed building and pass on it instead of examination [*sic*] of the plans and specifications."[42]

The alumni had expounded a "principle"—that members of the board of regents were trustees of a property, not its proprietors, and that their first obligation was to the university. The alumni were not even critical of the Metropolitan Building Company as such. They believed that it was the duty of the regents to be on guard against too much pressure from a lessee. The statement, widely publicized, was accompanied by editorials in the *Washington Alumnus* applauding the "courageous stand" of Gaches, Fechter, and Miller and saying, "The regents are stewards of this property. . . . Future citizens of the state will be affected by their decision. . . . Public policy is involved that will reach out ten college generations." Resolutions protesting "tinkering" with the lease were adopted by several alumni groups, including the Pierce County alumni association in Tacoma, Rea's home town, where Judge Dykeman and President Suzzallo had addressed the alumni meeting. The Arena issue apparently drew more alumni attention there than did Gil Dobie, Washington's great football coach, who had recently resigned and was being feted throughout the state.[43]

When the regents met again on December 27, 1915, the test vote came. The key motion was Miller's, and by a vote of four to two the regents declared the Arena temporary. It was Rea, who had sparred so many times with Miller, who changed his position and cast his vote with Miller, Gaches, and Fechter. Perkins and Shannon still held out. Wheeler was kept from the meeting by the serious illness of his daughter. The meeting was open to "interested persons," and these included not only Dykeman, Riordan, and their alumni colleagues, but Charles Denny, son of Arthur Denny. The report in the Seattle *Times* the following day, headed "REGENTS WON'T ACCEPT ARENA AS PERMANENT," described the proceedings and quoted Douglas as saying:

I have felt that the worst that could happen to us was that at the end of ten years' time we would be required to spend a few thousand dollars in putting two extra floors across the building, making it a three-story structure as our original lease calls for. We felt that we had complied with all the requirements of the board of regents to make the Arena a permanent building and legally we believe we could hold the regents to this.

It has never been our policy, however, to get into legal controversies with our landlord. We feel that a molehill has been made into a mountain. . . . At a later date, when the heat of discussion has passed away, I think the regents will accept the Arena for the kind of building it really is, a first-class, A-1 structure, better than is required under the terms of the lease.[44]

Douglas felt aggrieved, and for a moment he was tempted to let it show. On December 24, just before the regents' meeting, President Suzzallo had written Douglas to indicate the dates that the university would like to use the Arena under the free-use terms of the agreement, and in his statement after the regents' decision Douglas said that the company now was, in any case, "relieved of its obligation" in that regard. But when Suzzallo then wrote to withdraw his request, Douglas had thought better of it. He sent a note to Suzzallo saying that the company would find it "agreeable . . . to give the University some free time as a sort of free will offering."[45] Douglas was too sanguine about what might come later. The stage had been set for another showdown in 1925.

The year 1916 was a transitional year in the affairs of the Metropolitan Building Company as in those of the university. At the university, the Suzzallo administration was installed formally with the inauguration of the new president in March. Columbia University's Nicholas Murray Butler was a speaker, and Rea, Perkins, and Wheeler represented the regents in preparations for the event. In March the university established for the first time a University of Washington Building Fund—a fund authorized by the legislature of 1915 in an effort to respond to the university's obvious need for new classroom and laboratory space. Custodian of the fund was Herbert T. Condon, now comptroller of the university rather than "bursar." The new title had been bestowed by the regents at the meeting at which they acted on the Arena. Into the building fund would go the tuition and matriculation fees and the $40,000-per-year rentals from the university tract. Condon estimated that by 1918 the fund would contain $117,420, and the first building would be a new Home Economics Building designed by Bebb and Gould and situated in what was visualized as a "Collegiate Tudor" quandrangle below, but related to, the pivotal mass of Denny Hall.[46]

The Great War went on in Europe, with America hoping to preserve neutrality. But Francisco Villa's revolutionary army had been making terrorist raids into towns along the Rio Grande and General Pershing had taken troops to the border to guard United States territory. In July 1916, Charles Gaches, now thirty-five and a member of the National Guard, was given a leave of absence from the board of regents to serve under Pershing's command as a lieutenant in the Second Infantry. In the autumn he was home again, and on December 1 he was elected president of the regents as the successor to Fechter.

But America's participation in the war was approaching. The university faculty had already approved compulsory military training.

By 1917, ten years after it had taken over the Moore lease, the Metropolitan Building Company had created a commercial center where the old university had been. The center was not the splendidly integrated area that Howells and Stokes had visualized. Only the White-Henry-Stuart and the Cobb buildings suggested the grandeur of the original plan, and these, plus the Metropolitan Theatre, stood in sharp contrast to the temporary buildings about them—fifteen now, including the Arena. But only one space in the university tract was not occupied, and that was a corner lot on Fifth Avenue, between the Arena and the theater, where a small park called Totem Gardens had been created. The YWCA was gone (to be replaced off the tract), and the new temporary buildings included the Kennard, the Olympic, the Curran, the Neyhart, and the Otis.[47]

However short of the dream, the Metropolitan Center was busy. There was a Metropolitan Bank, and Horace Henry was president. The Metropolitan Business College was training young people, mostly women, for secretarial or other employment with tenant firms. The J. F. Douglas management ideas were flowering, and Douglas himself was more than ever at the center of community activities—chairman of the industrial committee of the Chamber of Commerce, member of the executive committee of the new China Club, secretary of the Washington Art Association, an honorary director of the Symphony Association, a member of the advisory board of the YWCA. He had been cited by the Japanese government (and given a fine Japanese screen) for his work in promoting friendly relations. For members of the Art Association he was hanging pictures in Metropolitan buildings and sponsoring exhibits and one-man shows in a gallery that he had created on the tract. On January 31, 1916, long-distance telephone service had been inaugurated between Seattle and New York in a three-night celebration in which the telephone company had taken over the Metropolitan Theatre and had installed five hundred receivers at seats in the lower floor where subscribers heard voices from New York and even the sounds of waves breaking on Atlantic beaches. President Suzzallo had spoken to New York the first night and J. F. Douglas, who was chairman of it all, had spoken on the second. But in that year, 1916, Douglas knew that his Metropolitan company was at a critical stage. Thirty-eight years remained before the lease would expire, but even if he could build more buildings of the White-Henry-Stuart style by 1918, the financing would be difficult, perhaps impossible, with fewer than thirty-six years to amortize buildings costing $500,000 each. Douglas determined to try once again to obtain a modification of the lease that would give the Metropolitan a full fifty-year hold on any permanent buildings that might follow the Stuart. If the regents would not agree, Douglas would go directly to President Suzzallo.[48]

On December 14, 1916, Douglas wrote Suzzallo asking for an appointment

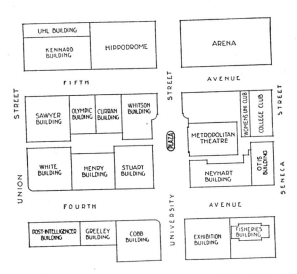

In this plat, published just before the United States entered World War I, the permanent buildings were the White-Henry-Stuart, the Cobb, and the Metropolitan Theatre; the status of the Arena, which the company considered permanent, later would be in dispute

to discuss "questions with reference to the University Tract lease," but saying that since he realized the president was busy preparing for the 1917 legislature, he would await Suzzallo's wishes. Nothing seems to have happened. On February 20, 1917, Douglas met with Shannon and Miller, who composed the regents' building committee, to ask if they would "name or suggest the terms upon which such further development of the property [under a lease modification] could be made." Shannon and Miller, declining to discuss terms, said that any proposal should come from the company. On March 12, Douglas wrote the regents to ask them to appoint a committee to confer, and to this Secretary Markham replied briefly that Shannon, Miller, and Perkins (Seattle regents) constituted a standing committee. Douglas had been over that path before. He determined now to approach Suzzallo formally, and he would enlist the support of Horace Henry, who was a key figure in the Metropolitan but whose leadership in the community was so widely acknowledged that he was above any thought of private motive.[49]

Thus in April 1917, President Suzzallo received letters from Douglas and Henry—Douglas's letter written April 16, and Henry's three days later.[50] The letters were cordial, explicit, developed at length. They were written at a time when the world was being overturned and the Metropolitan was about to lose its founding financier. Since April 6 the United States had been at war with the Central Powers. And Chester White, who had been the first investor in the Metropolitan, was lying fatally ill in his home in the Highlands, where he would die on April 26. None of this shows. What comes through in the language of the letters is the great dream of a university tract developed to the potential visualized in 1907.

Douglas, addressing the president of the university, touched briefly on his contacts with the regents and on the instruction to him to consult the building committee or to give it a specific proposal. Then he went on:

It is difficult for us to submit a proposal for the reason that the Company has no financial interest in the matter. As far as we know, our Company can carry out the provisions of the lease. Any modifications that the Board of Regents might make in the lease would not bring one penny of gain to this Company unless they were to lower the rental on the property, a thing that we have never asked or considered. The Company has nothing before it at this time except an ideal. We would like to develop the ten acres of ground belonging to the University in such a way that it would be the best piece of city property in the world, in so far as the character of the improvements is concerned. From the beginning we have had in mind a plan for the development of the property that, if carried out, will accomplish this result. . . .

It will take ten years, and perhaps twenty years, to complete the development of the University Tract if the remainder of the property is improved with buildings of the same high character as those that have already been put upon the property. It is axiomatic that high grade structures should not be built on leaseholds running less than fifty years. If we erected another building now there would be only about thirty-six years of lease time left. If we are to continue to make improvements under the present lease with the same character of improvements that we have already put upon the property and it should take ten years to complete these improvements, the last building would be erected at a time when there were only twenty-six years of lease time left. We have reached a point when it is absolutely necessary for the Board of Regents to find some way that will permit of a high class development, if the property is to be adequately improved.

If the Board of Regents believe that it makes no difference what kind of improvements are put upon the University Tract, then it is a waste of their time and ours to consider a modification of the lease. If, on the other hand, the Board of Regents believe that it is desirable to have the undeveloped portion of the property improved with high class structures, some modification of the lease must be made. As we see it, any citizen of the State has the right to make suggestions regarding the lease. I thought perhaps you, as President of the University, might give this subject consideration and that you might make some suggestion that would appeal to us, to the Board of Regents, and to the citizens of the State. We feel certain that there is some modification that would allow the development work to go on and would be to the best interests of the State. We do not know what this plan is and we do not pretend to know it. It is our theory that no plan can be worked out except after long consideration and as a result of conferences between the Board of Regents and ourselves.

Henry's letter to President Suzzallo was friendly, even more specific:

The building specifications in the lease demand structures of quite an ordinary type. A building of the exterior character of the P.I. building, five stories high, with concrete floors and basement able to carry six stories, would fill every requirement. A building of this sort frequently repaired might be made to last out the time of the lease, but certainly not beyond. Buildings only three stories high are called for, except fronting Union and Fourth Streets. Please contrast the P.I. building with the White, Henry, Stuart and Cobb, splendid modern structures, built of brick, and stone, and steel, fireproof, and nearly timeproof. These four buildings, which will revert to the University in 1954, the end of the lease, cost over $2,200,000. I venture to say that no city in this country can boast of four finer buildings upon the same limits of ground. . . . What the Metropolitan Building Company would like, if the action of the regents and the growth of the city makes possible, is to continue erecting these fine, durable buildings so the university at the end of the lease will have in hand a magnificent income producing property worth many millions of dollars. Another matter should be taken into consideration. If the company is compelled to relapse into the construction of buildings of ordinary type, the city will be much more likely to grow away from the district, as it already has in some sections, to be followed by great depreciation in the value of the whole tract. Moreover, as the life of the lease approaches its end in the year 1954 all construction, even the cheapest, must cease, [unless] some provision is made for extending the time on individual units. . . .

Facing these conditions, the modification the Metropolitan Building Company asks is this: That whenever it is able to secure funds to erect a firstclass, fireproof building, that the time of the reversion of the ownership to the university of that particular building shall be at least fifty years from the time of its completion.

Douglas called on President Suzzallo a few days later to discuss the proposal, the letters having been submitted as background for such a chat. But then in his written responses Suzzallo could only be noncommittal. It was the regents, he pointed out, who were responsible for policy, but he would consult others in the community, he promised, to make himself better acquainted with such financial considerations.[51] In a short follow-up note, Henry urged consultations, but caution in the choice of consultants. Some of those happy to consult might be friends neither of the university nor of the Metropolitan Building Company.

There the episode closed, a sadly strange end to an era already disappearing. The nation was mobilizing for war and on the Saturday night following the declaration Suzzallo was the speaker at a huge mass meeting and patriotic rally at which Seattle pledged itself to support the war effort. The rally was held not at the National Guard Armory but at J. F. Douglas's new Arena.

The university had too much on its mind that summer to do more than note the death in Wyoming of Asa Mercer, who had been its young first "president" in 1861. Asa died August 10 at seventy-eight—years away from Seattle, years spent in Oregon, Texas, and Wyoming as newspaperman, editor of a livestock journal, and author of a book on the Wyoming cattle wars. The regents of 1917 planned to appoint a subcommittee to draft a resolution expressing the university's regret at Asa's passing, but no such resolution appeared in their minutes.[52]

CHAPTER 6

The Center in Place: 1918 to 1925

Nothing was more important in 1917 and 1918 than winning the war. Three years of grinding, bloody fighting on the Eastern and Western fronts had taken ten million lives, according to contemporary estimates—60 percent of that among the military forces and civilian populations of the Allied nations. Now American men were going into the slaughter and American women of all ages were enrolling for war work, including work in factories. Thousands of National Guardsmen—many of them, like Regent Charles Gaches, veterans of the police action along the Mexican border—were held in service or recalled to active duty with their units. Seattle, its population now about three hundred thousand, was a pivot of mobilization and war preparation in the Northwest. Ship construction and outfitting were turned to full speed at Seattle yards and at the Navy Yard at Bremerton. Recruits poured into Fort Lawton and Camp Lewis, near Tacoma. People not otherwise involved were caught up in rallies, Liberty Bond drives, Red Cross services, and entertainment for soldiers and sailors.

The university campus, like campuses elsewhere, became a training center. More than two thousand men were enrolled in navy and marine units and in the new Student Army Training Corps. The university was the only institution on the Pacific Coast offering training to all three branches. The trainees went to classes in university buildings and lived in barracks and tent cities constructed at middle- and lower-campus sites. So thoroughly converted was the university campus that the regents' biennial report to the governor incorporated a map showing how buildings and open spaces had been dedicated to military training. One of the newer research installations was an "aerodynamical laboratory," equipped with a four-foot wind tunnel, given to the university in 1916 by William E. Boeing, a young scion of a Michigan lumber family who had gone into airplane manufacturing with his Pacific Aero Products Company and now had established the Boeing Airplane Company. More than 1,500 students and faculty members were in military service, and by autumn 1918 the university had only 207 regularly enrolled male students. President Suzzallo, ever the leader, was chairman of the State Defense Council, which was involved in activities ranging from war bond sales to surveys of farm production and settlement of labor disputes, and he served with a number of federal agencies, including the National War Labor Board and, as chairman, the National Metal Trades Board, which adjusted disputes in the munitions industry. Gaches, having served briefly as president of the board of regents, went off to war again as an infantry officer. Perkins succeeded Gaches as president of the board, but Gaches's successor as a regent was a woman, Ruth Karr McKee, of Hoquiam. Mrs. McKee served the war effort as the woman member of Suzzallo's State Defense Council.[1]

Many of that circle of financiers then composing the Metropolitan Building Company were deep in war work. One was C. D. Stimson, who simply turned his private affairs over to others to serve as a dollar-a-year manager of the Northwest campaign of the American Red Cross, a Washington-Oregon-Idaho-Alaska campaign so successful that it was almost immediately over-subscribed. J. F. Douglas, in those early months, worked with the Red Cross as chairman of a King and Kitsap County Committee to get Red Cross pledges, then he headed a second drive that enlisted teenagers in a Christmas campaign—the first prize an automobile, the second a pony with saddle and bridle.[2]

The University tract, by the time America entered the war, was at mid-point. Douglas had struggled with it for ten years, and in 1917 he had told President Suzzallo that it would take another ten years, perhaps twenty, to fill the tract with the permanent buildings that everyone wanted. But the tract had, nevertheless, not merely identity but a quality that amounted to personality. That achievement was Douglas's. The place was alive with his ideas.

Those who knew Douglas best, the members of his family, remembered the absolute concentration he focused on the tract in the years before the war and for a dozen years thereafter. Douglas, it was recalled, was forever roaming the streets and the buildings looking for ways to improve what he had called "White Building service," or to devise new attractions or conveniences for tenants, or to support the interest and morale of the company's employees. Douglas talked about the tract constantly—to his family at breakfast and dinner, to his associates at lunch, and to tenants as he visited them in their offices or met them in the streets. Douglas became a man who seemed almost to carry the tract in his head. He knew it foot by foot. With him, frequently, as he paced the halls and looked at the buildings, was his young daughter, Neva, who remembered, many years later, climbing with her father about the scaffoldings of the new construction and visiting the Metropolitan offices in the White-Henry-Stuart or the Cobb. In 1917, Neva was not yet twelve years old, but she was her father's companion in his incessant wanderings about the property that was at the center of his life.[3]

The special problems of the war years Douglas met, according to contemporary testimony, with a steady hand. Although costs of operations were rising, the Metropolitan Building Company imposed no rent increases during the war. The leases of sublessees who were called into military service were canceled voluntarily. Douglas insisted on keeping services and maintenance at the highest standards possible in wartime, even though in some buildings—as in the Cobb, where many physicians left for military duty—

offices were standing empty and the company was losing money on them.[4]

In the decade before America entered the war Douglas had perfected his management themes. He had proved himself an innovator, and he was recognized as something of an authority in the field of office building management. Occasionally he read a paper before the Seattle Building Owners Association or the larger Pacific Coast group. He was proud of the tract. He wanted the tenants to be proud of it. He regretted the temporary buildings, perhaps, but he was proud even of them. A promotional booklet of about 1917 had this to say: "Under the direction and by the expenditures of the Metropolitan Building Company, the University Tract has been almost wholly covered with buildings. A number of these are called 'temporary buildings,' not that they are of flimsy construction, but in order to differentiate them from the buildings of greater size, and because of the purpose of the Metropolitan Building Company to replace them with larger buildings as the needs and requirements of the district are further developed. All of these so-called temporary buildings are of substantial construction, specially designed to the uses to which they are being put by tenants until such time as their present sites must be cleared again for the greater work to come."[5]

The tract had such interests. It had, too, its own amenities and conveniences. In the White-Henry-Stuart were a tenants' dining room and a tearoom and lounges for women. At the top was a roof garden lined by benches and screened and shaded by trees and shrubs in planter boxes. The building had been heavily populated from the beginning by lumbermen, but when it began to attract lawyers and law firms as lessees, Douglas installed a law library for their common use. The idea had been carried over, undoubtedly, from the Cobb Building, for the Cobb not only epitomized Douglas's idea of grouping tenants but carried to the ultimate the corollary concept of accommodations and services tailored to the tenant's requirements.

The Cobb Building may or may not have been, as the company said in 1917, "the finest physicians' and dentists' building that has ever been erected in any part of the world," but it had been brought to a high level of development. The eleven stories of the Cobb provided offices for some two hundred doctors and dentists. Each office had light, water, gas, compressed air, and power circuits adaptable to individual needs. The corridors of the building were wide. The elevators, of hospital size, were operated night and day. There were medical lavatories and sinks in every office and heavy-duty ventilating systems. X-ray facilities incorporated a gallery for developing color X-ray film. Design features for cleanliness included washable walls and a system for cleaning offices by vacuum. There were operating rooms, medical laboratories, and medical and dental supply stores. There was, of course, a medical library (later it would be the library of the Washington Medical Library Association), and there was also a garden on the roof, as at the White-Henry-Stuart Building, but with an even better view of Elliott Bay. And to the doctors and dentists taking offices in the Cobb, the Metropolitan Building Company offered a service that became general throughout the tract. The company would help a new tenant plan the layout of his quarters, making suggestions about the placement of reception areas, equipment, examination rooms, operating rooms, desks, partitions, even about color schemes. "We put ourselves in the tenant's place, and tried to figure out what he'd want," Douglas told an interviewer some years later. "We came to him with suggestions for planning his office. In some cases he would have an idea where he wanted his desk or what tone he liked, and we would simply build around that. Gradually we developed a force of experts who furnished and decorated the office in our buildings."[6]

As far as the tenants of the Metropolitan company were concerned, Douglas must have seemed at once a stern, helpful, admonitory, sympathetic, and ever-inquiring presence. Douglas from the beginning had need of tenants for the buildings. But he wanted tenants of the "best class"—lumbermen, shippers, merchants, builders. Even so, he had not hesitated to publish a little lecture, in a 1914 issue of the *Metropolitan Bulletin*, on "Prompt Payment of Rent." Douglas pointed out that credit rating companies were curious about such behavior: "We think we show pretty good discretion in this matter. . . . It is not our policy to keep tenants who do not pay their rent promptly. . . . On one thing our policy is fixed, that we endeavor at all times to do as much good as we can for our tenants. We have never been too busy and we never expect to be too busy to take up any matter that has been suggested to us in the interest of our tenants. It is easy to understand, therefore, that we are put in a very difficult position when we are asked to make a statement with reference to a tenant that might reflect on the tenant's business standing. . . . There are certain accounts that ought to be settled promptly and among those accounts is the monthly rental account."[7]

The time came when Douglas was, in fact, selecting tenants, expecting them to deserve the kind of attention the company provided. His assistance to tenants went far beyond normal practice, however, and far beyond helping them plan and decorate their offices. New tenants who needed help finding apartments or establishing local banking connections got that kind of assistance too. But Douglas, with an eye on rental payments, was curious about how they ran their affairs. One story is that Douglas saved a tenant from failure by calling in the tenant and his creditors, analyzing the company's expenses and space needs, and making adjustments that got the firm on a paying basis. Another is that Douglas devised a percentage lease plan, perhaps the first in the nation, when he discovered in a street-corner conversation that a drug store was about to give up its lease because its rental payments were proving unbearable. Douglas inquired into the rental arrangement and studied the rent as a percentage of the store's anticipated gross income. The result was a revision of the lease to permit payments that were calculated, above a fixed minimum, on the monthly gross income reported by the store and subject to audit. The percentage lease later was offered to other tenants conducting retail businesses, the monthly reports of income always open to review by Metropolitan representatives.[8]

Service to tenants was an obsession with Douglas, who invited complaints, sent out questionnaires asking for suggestions, and posted two girls at office telephones solely so clear up troubles. The elevators in the main buildings were operated by young women who were expected to know the names and office numbers of every tenant firm so that they could quickly refer callers to the right building or floor. "Elevator operation is an extremely important part in building management," Douglas told an interviewer. "The company employs only women elevator operators, because we have found that they are nicer to passengers and that they are more careful in running the cars. Most of them are high-school girls. They have to take an examination every month on the rules of the company and the names and offices of the tenants. . . . The papers are graded and the standings of the girls posted on the bulletin board. They turn in excellent papers, too." Tenants had at their call the Metropolitan's staffs of electricians, carpenters, plumbers, painters, and even window dressers to serve the street-level shops. Fireproof storage vaults were available through a subcontractor. Rug cleaning was on call. Tenants could have, without fee, the services of the company's advertising department, which would provide help with any project from the layout of a booklet to the design of an advertising campaign. The Metropolitan Service Department coordinated it all. But Douglas expected proper behavior on the part of the tenant, too. He once terminated the lease of a Cobb Building dentist who had abused a window washer for interrupting a conference. Hearing of the incident, Douglas called the dentist to his office and told him he must leave the tract. Recounting the incident later Douglas said: "We insist on the employees in our buildings being respectful to tenants, but we also insist upon tenants being courteous to employees." [9]

Douglas never wavered in his insistence that the buildings and store fronts of the tract be free of projecting signs. He made an exception for the Metropolitan Theatre, where the traditional marquee, extending over the sidewalk toward University Place, added a classic touch, but he would refuse a lease to a prospective lessee company that felt it needed such display. Douglas demanded dignity. Repeatedly, the photographs illustrating the *Metropolitan Bulletin* emphasized the clean and uncluttered lines of the buildings along Fourth Avenue.

J. F. Douglas was forty-three when America entered the war in 1917, the youngest of the Metropolitan circle perhaps, but seemingly too old for service in uniform. Before the war ended Douglas was in uniform nevertheless, and his military rank became the title he bore for the rest of his life.

Until 1918 Douglas was engaged in home-front activities. The tract was on a wartime basis, and soon the law firm of Douglas, Lane and Douglas was dissolved when J. F.'s brother-partner, James, went off to Washington, D.C., for government service. But in 1918, J. F. was commissioned a major in the Army Quartermaster Corps and stationed in Seattle as acting deputy quartermaster (the depot quartermaster in San Francisco) in charge of a force of 150 officers, civilians, clerks, and dock workers handling supplies and war materiel passing through Seattle's Bell Street Terminal. Douglas's commission came late—not long before the Armistice in November 1918—but he remained with the Bell Terminal into the months of postwar readjustment. The terminal continued to handle shipments to military destinations and Douglas was engaged in housing surveys and even with an organization called "Hotel Liberty," developed to house, feed, and find public service jobs for men thrown out of work at the war's end. When Douglas went back to the Metropolitan, he installed in the company a young woman who had been a telephone operator at the Bell Terminal. It was she, the story goes, who perpetuated Douglas's rank. Knowing him only as Major Douglas, she continued to refer to him that way when calls came to the Metropolitan switchboard. To Seattle, thereafter, J. F. was "Major" Douglas.[10]

Seattle shared with the nation the economic letdown of 1919 and 1920. Seattle's case was worsened because, among other things, shipbuilding was at a full stop. Curiously, James A. Moore, who had left Seattle about 1914, had returned for a visit in 1918 and had urged Seattle's businessmen to begin immediately to forestall depression by organizing a steel industry—the steel industry that Moore had failed to create. Moore was now in Los Angeles, and certain Seattle leaders apparently had invited him to return. He declined because of his health, but in a long letter published by the *Post-Intelligencer* he urged Seattle to look to its future in ships and steel. Moore was not yet sixty, but his own career was on the wane. Having lost his fortune at Irondale, he had moved to Florida to try, characteristically, to create a new town. This would be Moorehaven, on Lake Okeechobee. Moore was selling properties and was even vice-president of a "Palm Beach and Everglades Railroad" company that would provide rail service between Moorehaven and West Palm Beach. Moorehaven was said to have had two hundred residents when a hurricane swept across central Florida and wiped it out with losses of life. Moore, much shaken, returned west—but never again to Seattle.[11]

For the university, as for the Metropolitan Building Company, the years of postwar recession were difficult. Trying to return to something approaching normal operations, the university was having to schedule classes in the barracks and temporary buildings constructed for wartime training. There had been no change in the board of regents since McKee had succeeded Gaches in 1917. Perkins, president of the board in 1918–19, was succeeded by Miller, president for 1919–20. Fechter was still a regent, as were Rea, Shannon, and Wheeler, who became president in 1920. But there had been a change in the governorship. Governor Lister, his health weakened by strenuous activity in the war period, died in June 1919, and was succeeded by Lieutenant Governor Louis Hart. But Ruth McKee, Lister's last appointment to the board, had proved herself something of an addition.

Governor Lister had wanted to appoint a woman to the board of regents, and in this he seems to have been as farsighted as in his opposition to the executive meetings he once had asked the regents to abandon. In McKee he found what certainly was the ideal nominee—the daughter of a pioneer, a university graduate with an advanced degree, a woman already widely recognized for her leadership in community affairs.

Ruth Karr had been born in a log cabin on the Hoquiam River, one of twelve children of James A. and Abigail Boutwell Walker Karr, the first permanent settlers of Hoquiam, a village near the Washington coast, then a two-day trip from Seattle by paddlewheel river boat, stage, and Puget Sound steamer. Her father was from Indiana, her mother from Oregon, and the parents were so determined that their children be well educated that for many months of the year they conducted their own family school in the frame house that ultimately succeeded the cabin. When Ruth was fifteen, the father hustled her and two of her sisters off to the university. Because the sisters arrived late for the fall term of 1889, President Gatch (who had taught Latin to Ruth's mother thirty-five years before) became their special tutor for a few weeks. Ruth caught up. She was elected to Phi Beta Kappa in her senior year and, after winning her B.A. in pedagogy (1895), stayed two years to get a master's degree. She taught school three years—as "preceptress" and instructor in "ancient and modern languages" at the Puget Sound Academy in Snohomish—and then went off to Hawaii, "for a year of travel and study," where she met and married a Canadian, J. S. McKee, who took her to Ontario, then to Seattle, and later back to Hoquiam, where he became mayor. By 1914 she had been president of the Washington State Federation of Women's Clubs and was widely known and respected for her acquaintance with public affairs.[12]

By 1920, Seattle was beginning to talk about having a new hotel big enough and grand enough to accommodate the visitors and national meetings the city was certain it would attract. The idea was in part a response to slack times, a search for a revival of business. But it was also a time of new hotels all across the country—a time of replacement of older hostelries that had served the "commercial traveler" and railroad tourist trade in the earlier years of the century. In many other cities the building of new hotels had become community-action projects.

On two occasions late in 1920 the regents discussed with representatives of the Metropolitan Building Company what were described in the regents' minutes as "the proposed additions and extensions to buildings" on the tract. The record contains no mention of a hotel. At a September 3 meeting with the company's directors the regents had been joined by several members of the university's alumni association, including Nelson Hartson, the president, and at a meeting on November 26 the regents' Metropolitan lease committee had taken up the question of the "proposed modifications of lease in relation to proposed new buildings," and had decided that there should be a conference with the alumni association committee. Whatever this meant, the alumni were again taking a direct and continuing interest in tract developments.[13]

In any event, Seattle's hotel idea had matured by 1921 and it was not surprising that the leaders of the Metropolitan Building Company, with E. A. Stuart now president, should be the leaders of such a venture. On May 13, 1921, Stuart and Douglas addressed a letter "To the Hon., The Board of Regents of the University of Washington" saying that the company and its stockholders were "willing to cooperate with the citizens of Seattle" in a hotel development.[14] Rea was now president of the board of regents. Wheeler's term having expired, Governor Hart had appointed to succeed him a well-known Republican newspaper publisher, Werner A. Rupp, of the Aberdeen *World*.

Stuart and Douglas said that the company proposed to build a twelve-story hotel costing, with furnishings and equipment, $3,200,000. The hotel would be erected between Fourth and Fifth avenues and University and Seneca streets, wrapped around the Metropolitan Theatre. The project would include the building of a below-ground power plant on Fourth Avenue between University and Seneca. It would also include a "remodeling of the Arena Building in order to make said building into a suitable convention hall."

The Stuart-Douglas letter described the plans for financing. The Metropolitan Building Company would form a hotel company to build the hotel and equip it at a cost of $3,200,000, the company having that amount in capital stock, $800,000 of common and $2,400,000 at 7 percent preferred stock redeemable over a period not to exceed forty years. (Sinking-fund bonds might be issued instead of the preferred stock if this proved "advisable.") The Metropolitan would lease the hotel site to the hotel company at cost, would subscribe for the $800,000 of common stock for cash (releasing up to 50 percent to other investors), and would pledge that its "present stockholders and associates" would buy $700,000 or more of the preferred stock or bonds. In addition, the company would remodel the Arena Building and build the heating plant at its own expense, these improvements being considered "an essential part of the hotel development." The letter went on to describe certain contingent considerations:

The lease on the University Tract expires on November 1, 1954, and the temporary building agreement permitting us to use one story buildings expires on June 26 [*sic*], 1925.

It will not be possible to raise funds to make the improvements above described on a lease-hold running for only thirty-three years. Investors would not be willing to put money into the erection of the hotel unless they would be assured of at least fifty years use of the grounds.

The hotel structure will replace four temporary buildings. We ask your Board for the following modifications of the lease on the University Tract:

1. That the lease on the block on which the hotel is to be located and that half block on the West side of Fourth Avenue between University and Seneca Streets and of the site where the Arena stands be extended for a period of nineteen years from November 1, 1954, conditioned on the erection and furnishing of a hotel structure, costing in the neighborhood of $3,200,000.00.

2. That upon the erection of said hotel structure, the permit time on our temporary buildings be extended for a period of ten years.

If the terms were accepted, Stuart and Douglas said, the company would pledge itself to pay rental on the segments of the tract "above described" for the additional nineteen years of the lease at levels determined by "appraisers chosen in the usual manner . . . one year before the expiration of the present lease." The four temporary buildings would be replaced. In short, the Metropolitan Building Company was asking (1) an extension of nineteen years on its lease of the block to be occupied by the new hotel, including the land already occupied by the Metropolitan Theatre (2) lease extensions of nineteen years on those parts of the tract occupied by the Arena Building, as remodeled, and the proposed new power plant, and (3) an extension of ten years—to June 24, 1935—of the company's permit to erect temporary one-story buildings. There would be no adjustment of rental payments until 1954.

The newspapers heralded the hotel proposal at once, and there was jubilation in Seattle. There was an excitement in the thought, soon expressed by various leading citizens, that a hotel of the dimensions projected—609 rooms, with associated banquet rooms, lobbies, foyers, and courts, all enveloping the Metropolitan Theatre and adjacent to an enlarged Arena convention hall—would give Seattle the only facility it needed to become one of the great centers of commerce and tourism. Furthermore the project seemed a sure-fire investment. The Metropolitan Building Company and its stockholders were committed to almost half the cost—more than half, if the remodeling of the Arena and the construction of the power plant were included—and now Seattle citizens could help their city while earning a respectable return on their stocks or bonds.

The Seattle *Times* of May 15, 1921, carried a story—under the headline "$3,200,000 HOTEL ASSURED SEATTLE"—which said that the Metropolitan Building Company's proposal opened the way to the building of "a gigantic hotel that will rank among the palaces of the West," the announcement accompanied by a six-column layout of architects' sketches and floor plans. The impetus for the development came from the Chamber of Commerce and the Commercial Club, the *Times* said, and the Chamber would be preparing at once to organize a public campaign for funds to match the Metropolitan Building Company's commitment. For the company's role in the venture the *Times* had high praise, with a nod to the investment potential:

The Metropolitan Company will sublease the site of the new hotel to the hotel company for exactly the same rental it pays to the University of Washington. It will make no profit on the sublease. The rental for the first ten years will approximate only $16,000, a figure that helps make the hotel proposition one of the best investments ever brought before the Seattle public.

The Metropolitan Building Company's decision to waive any and all profit on the sublease is regarded in all circles as one of the most liberal and public-spirited decisions known in Seattle's history. By the decision the company provides a site at a nominal cost for the huge hotel, opening wide the way to immediate action.

Thus launched, the hotel idea inevitably gathered momentum. The idea also was being attributed to the Metropolitan Building Company, and enthusiasm grew even as the final decision on the project necessarily was held "in abeyance," as the *Post-Intelligencer* pointed out, until the meeting of the university regents on May 26. The newspapers reported in the intervening days that Seattle was "swinging into line" behind the proposal. C. D. Stimson, then chairman of the Chamber of Commerce hotel committee, announced that he was prepared to invest in the hotel company. "I am enthusiastic about the plan," he told the *Times*, "and the best way to tell you what I think about the proposition is to point out that I will take $100,000 worth of the company's stock. . . . I do not know of any fairer proposition for all parties concerned than the proposal to build a $3,200,000 hotel on the university tract."

The trustees of the Chamber of Commerce, meeting on May 17, received recommendations on the hotel from Manson Backus, A. S. Eldridge, a local automobile dealer, and John C. Higgins, who spoke for the hotel committee. Eldridge, like Stimson, was a stockholder in the Metropolitan Building Company, Backus and Higgins former regents. In the Seattle weekly, the *Argus*, a commentator called the Stroller noted: "There seems to be no question that Seattle is at last to have a new hotel, and one of which this city can be proud. The men behind the proposition do things. They have a proposition which is entirely feasible."[15]

Of course there were "knockers" and skeptics. Some already had been heard. To these the Stroller responded: "Seattle needs and must have just such a hotel, and the men behind this are men who do things right. The new hotel will be the biggest kind of a benefit for the city. It will be worth more to Seattle than a shipyard employing ten thousand men. . . . The only thing which stands in the way . . . of this hotel is the consent of the Board of Regents of the University of Washington to an extension of the lease on the block of ground which it is to occupy. The men who have worked out this plan have done a thorough job. They have a business proposition to put up to the regents and as business men they can hardly turn it down. . . . Hurrah for the new hotel. And now what shall we name it? I will suggest the University."

The regents—Rea, the president, and Fechter, Shannon, Miller, McKee, and Rupp—met at 10 A.M. May 26, 1921, in President Suzzallo's office on the university campus. Perkins was absent because he had gone to Washington, D.C., to discuss with federal officials the prospect that the university might acquire for its Marine Biological Station the 484-acre tract of land that was occupied by the Point Caution Military Reservation near Friday Harbor in the San Juan Island group.[16] The regents' morning session was devoted to routine business, the meeting open "as usual," the minutes noted. In the afternoon the board took up the Metropolitan Building Company's hotel proposal. The *Times's* evening edition of that day, in a front-page story headed "EXPECT REGENTS TO PROMOTE BIG HOTEL PROJECT," said, "There is every prospect that the board will grant the extensions." The regents continued their meeting, however, until the following day, May 27. At noon the announcement was made. The regents had rejected the hotel proposal. The *Times* hurried to press with a brief page-one report, "REGENTS OPPOSED TO HOTEL PROJECT." Then the thunder of community outrage began to roll.

The thunder rolled primarily from the editorial offices and newsrooms of the *Times* and the *Post-Intelligencer*, for the Seattle *Star* took a more restrained view, as did certain other journals in and out of Seattle. Yet it must have been true that the regents' denial of a "proposition" so widely acclaimed before the event seemed, to the man in the Seattle street, an unbelievable betrayal of the community's will. Six members of the little board, four from out of town, had met for two days only to approve, finally—and unanimously—a long and declamatory report drafted in secret by a Metropolitan lease committee (Fechter, Miller, and Rupp) that boggled on an abstraction, a lease extension. How could it be?

In the days immediately following the regents' meeting the newspaper headlines, news reports, and editorials were blistering in tone. The *Post-Intelligencer's* account of May 28—the heading, "SEATTLE'S CHANCES FOR FINE HOSTELRY MEET OBSTRUCTION"—used in full the text of the regents' statement, but managed to suggest not too subtly that it had been drafted "behind closed doors" and thus somehow illicitly. Twinned with the report was a long, 2,000-word "clause by clause" reply to the regents by John C. Higgins, now chairman of the Chamber of Commerce hotel committee, who began by saying that the regents' statement was "neither accurate nor fair" and moved on from there to conclude, "The decision of the regents is a grave mistake, seriously detrimental in its consequences to the University, the city and the state." Higgins certainly had an affection for the university, for it was he who, as president of the regents in 1911, had spoken of the university's history at the opening of the Metropolitan Theatre. But to him, now, the regents' decision was a "blunder." The *Times* of that day, May 28, was suggesting that an irate citizenry was searching for a way to correct the mistake. The headline said: "GOVERNOR MAY BE ASKED TO REMOVE BOARD OF REGENTS." The story, flanked by an editorial, "Regents Board Must Reconsider Hotel Plan Veto," bore hard, without naming them, on the Seattle regents, Shannon, Miller, and, by implication, Perkins, although Perkins had not been present to vote. The news lead said:

Everywhere in Seattle citizens, astounded by yesterday's action of the University Board of Regents on the hotel plan, are asking: "What kind of Seattle men are those on the board who voted against this plan? Have they no loyalty to the city in which they live, to say nothing of the great educational institution that they administer?"

There is the strongest kind of talk in Seattle of circulating petitions requesting

Gov. Louis F. Hart to remove all members of the board who voted against a project which meant so much of benefit to the university, to Seattle and to the entire state.

By May 29, which was Sunday, both the *Times* and the *Post-Intelligencer* were using stories under six-column banner lines—in the *Times*, " 'RECALL' REGENTS, CITY'S DEMAND," and in the *Post-Intelligencer*, "REJECTION OF HOTEL PROJECT AMAZES BUSINESS MEN." The *Times*'s page-one editorial "University Loses Millions Through Action of Regents," argued that the regents were putting aside to 1954 the proper development of the tract; that the tract, where it was not already improved, "will be covered only with small, temporary structures that will be mere shacks by 1954"; that a hotel would tremendously increase the value of the whole property; and that the board can "INSIST upon a NEW RENTAL for his block BASED ON THE VALUE OF IMPROVEMENTS for the nineteen additional years the lease . . . is to run." The *Times* said that "minor, short-sighted objections urged by the Regents are puerile and unconvincing." The *Post-Intelligencer* said that the "general opinion" in the city was that the regents had been "piqued" into a show of authority because so many had expected them to approve the plan. The *Post-Intelligencer*'s editorial, "Regents Should Reconsider," called the regents' action "ill-advised, premature, hasty," specifically:

If the board of regents should stand fixed in the decision announced yesterday it means the end of development of the university tract, thus far improved only by five buildings that may be called first-class. By the end of the present lease, in 1954, the university will come into the ownership of these few buildings, and of whatever may happen to be left of the one-story temporary structures now spread over the area.

By contrast, if the regents make possible the construction of the splendid hotel proposed, they will bring about the improvement of the whole tract with buildings of the best kind. A spacious convention hall is immediately assured; and, without any change in the terms of the lease as they affect other portions of the tract, the temporary structures must soon give way to buildings of the most modern type. Then when the leaseholds terminate, partly in 1954 and wholly nineteen years later, the University will come into a magnificent heritage.

The thunder rumbled for some days. But not invariably about the heads of the regents. The Seattle *Union Record*, a labor paper, was saying on May 30, in a long editorial covering the presumed financial balances, including the tax-exempt status of the tract, that the regents simply were defending the university from the greedy:

Through the single item of tax exemption alone the hotel promoters are handed back the total of their investment in the hotel and $2,096,000.

In addition, the date for the turning over to the University of the Metropolitan theater is extended for 19 years.

To make the deal "attractive" to the Metropolitan Building Company it is also proposed to extend the time for the use of land to house a central heating plant.

All of this is done in the name of "patriotism." Those who oppose this looting of University resources are branded as unpatriotic.

The regents were right when they turned down this proposal. They ought to be supported. . . .[17]

The stand the regents had taken on May 26 was, at its center, the stand they had taken many times before. They opposed any extension of the lease, even on fractions of the tract. Other boards had been doing this since 1912, when Douglas had said he was going to Europe to try to raise money for the Grandin Building, which he hoped would have a fifty-year term. This time the decision had to be made in the glare of public interest. But the precedents existed. The lease committee considered that a policy had been established.

The decision had been announced in open meeting on May 27, the second day of the long session. The initial discussion had been conducted with and in the presence of Stuart, Douglas, and Stimson, of the Metropolitan Building Company; Higgins, of the Chamber of Commerce committee; Harold Crary, of the Commercial Club; and Judge Dykeman, now chairman—Gaches was a member—of the permanent alumni association committee on the Metropolitan lease, which had been conferring for some months with the regents and with representatives of the Metropolitan company. Reporters from the *Times* and the *Post-Intelligencer* were also present. But the regents' response to the hotel proposal had been drafted by Fechter, Miller, and Rupp on May 26 for action by the board the following day. The *Post-Intelligencer* account of May 28 made something of this procedure:

The action of the board was taken after an evening session of the committee to which the proposal was referred, consisting of O. A. Fechter, of Yakima, W. A. Rupp, of Aberdeen, and Winlock W. Miller, of Seattle, during which the committee arrived at its decision to recommend the rejection of the proposal. Yesterday morning was spent by the committee in instilling its conclusions into other members of the board in an informal session behind closed doors, and in drafting its argument for justification. The doors were opened and the report read before representatives of the press at the close of this star-chamber session. On motion of Rupp, seconded by Ruth Karr McKee, of Vancouver, Wash., the report was accepted by a roll call vote. There was no dissenting vote.

The statement read by Fechter and adopted by the board reflected without question determinations evolved in earlier consultations with the alumni committee.[18] The preamble held that "the proposals of the Metropolitan Building Company to amend the contract existing between the University and the company must be considered in the light of the welfare and advantage of the University solely." The statement went on:

No concessions should be made to the company, quite regardless of the civic or other motives which prompt them to erect a much-needed hotel for Seattle, unless equivalent advantages are guaranteed to the University. . . . The downtown tract of the University was a gift for the benefit of the children of the State of Washington. It is, in effect, a perpetual endowment held as a public trust and the board is bound to proceed with that conservation which is properly associated with the administration of a public trust.

The statement then ticked off the four "concessions" the university was asked to make—three of them the postponement until 1973 of the university's "possession" of the Metropolitan Theatre lot, the hotel site, and the power plant location, and the fourth the extension to 1935 of the company's permit to build temporary buildings. If they approved such terms, the regents said, the university would receive only "a speculative increase in the land value of the tract (not realizable at all until 1954)," and "that doubtful increase in rentals from 1954 to 1973 on part of the tract, based on the theory that a land rental from the Metropolitan Building Company on appraisal in this period would be greater than the University's return from possession of both buildings and land in the same period." And in conclusion:

The hotel proposal provides for no increased revenues or rentals to the University, prior to the expiration of the present lease in 1954. It proposes, on the other hand, that the present lease, which admittedly does not bring the University an adequate revenue, shall be continued for 19 years on the proposed hotel and heating plant sites. The proposal, in short, gives the University nothing additional before 1954 and asks instead that the University shall subsidize the hotel project and postpone for 19 years beyond 1954 the time when it can hope to regain control of the property.

So that there may be no misunderstanding, let it be remembered that the rentals on the Metropolitan tract are fixed by the present lease, up to the year 1954, that only $40,000 yearly is paid now for the whole tract of nearly ten acres and that under the terms of the existing lease the Metropolitan Company will never pay more than $140,000 annually, that both the tract and the buildings are tax exempt, except for a small tax on the leasehold, and that after thirty or forty or more years of use the buildings . . . will be of doubtful value when the University receives them. . . .

We therefore recommend that the Board of Regents reject the present proposals . . . and we further recommend as a permanent policy, in line with the well established precedents of this and previous Boards of Regents, that no extension of the lease be granted.

In the long view it may be recognized that the whole incident, angry though it was, cleared an atmosphere that was in need of a refreshing wind. The regents, holding the line on the lease extensions, forced a widened public appreciation of the status of the tract as a public property. There were peculiar sputterings and reverberations for a time, but the regents came out of the affair with their statures wonderfully enhanced. The alumni backed them solidly. Dykeman was the author of a long, analytical article in the *Washington Alumnus* for May 1921, "Why University Regents Rejected Proposal of Metropolitan Building Company," in which he hit hard at the Metropolitan Building Company's tax advantage—the company was paying, he said, only $14,710, on a leasehold valuation of $200,000—but in which he also said that the Arena Building proposal was a rerun of the 1915 effort to have the building declared permanent, that it was "absurd" to devote half a block to a power plant that would contribute a 125-foot smoke stack to the Seattle skyline, and that a large part of the cost of the hotel would be paid from $100,000 in annual rentals received from the temporary buildings in the course of the proposed extension of the company's permit. By the time Dykeman's article appeared, the regents' decision had been made, of course, and thus there was room for alumni applause. The *Alumnus* editorial entitled "Be Fair to the University," in the same May 1921 issue, ended, "HAIL TO THE REGENTS," and the editor in a special note cheered both the regents and the hotel:

Let's go. The city of Seattle needs a hotel, a splendid hotel that will be a credit to the entire Pacific Northwest. And we will be tickled to death to see it constructed on the downtown property of the University of Washington. . . . We will be glad to see the Metropolitan Building Company build the hotel, for then we will be assured of a first-class hostelry. . . .

We want that hotel as quickly as possible.

But we do not want it under the terms and conditions proposed by the Metropolitan Building Company several weeks ago. . . .

The Board of Regents were right when they rejected the proposal. We admire their decision. We admire their nerve. We admire their attitude of respectable silence maintained during the storm of almost abusive newspaper comment that followed their decision. May the University always be blessed with a Board of Regents of similar character.

The echoes of the 1921 hotel affair died slowly. Whatever Seattle's view of the regents' verdict, the passing days brought some realization that the case had not been as simple as it seemed. But the city wanted and needed a hotel. Everyone agreed on that. And before that original dream faded, the Metropolitan Building Company seems to have had another thought about it. The thought became—and not within the company alone—an idea for challenging the regents to assume responsibility for seeing that a hotel was built, whether under the regents' direct control or under public auspices. The circumstances are not altogether unclouded, but a simple recitation of the sequence of events suggests the degree of feeling that the hotel issue had aroused.

John Higgins, in his "reply" to the regents of May 28—the day after their rejection of the hotel proposal—had touched on the new thought: "Fortunately there still is a chance of saving the institution from the consequences of this blunder. The Metropolitan Building Company has offered to turn this hotel tract over to the public at cost, on the sole condition that a hotel of a class equal to that proposed by the building company be financed and erected on the site. If the regents are not mere obstructionists, if they have real faith in their declaration that a hotel can be erected on this property under terms more favorable to the University, let them justify their faith by getting others to finance and erect a hotel under better conditions and a shorter lease! If the regents are real friends of the University . . . they will at least make the attempt." [19]

Higgins was writing with a knowledge of the company's present assessment of the case. On May 24, two days before the regents' meeting of May 26–27, Stuart and Douglas had addressed a letter to Higgins, as chairman of the Chamber of Commerce committee, in which they said: "While the Metropolitan Building Company is willing to co-operate with the Chamber of Commerce Committee in the matter of financing and erecting a hotel for Seattle, we will be very glad if other arrangements can be made for financing the hotel. We will be willing to sub-lease the proposed hotel site (at cost) provided the citizens of Seattle will erect thereon a hotel commensurate with the needs of the city. Your committee then could make whatever arrangements they see fit with reference to the extension of the lease on the hotel site. If this arrangement is satisfactory to the Hotel Committee, the Metropolitan Building Company will be very glad to withdraw entirely from the hotel enterprise."[20]

It is to be wondered, of course, why the Metropolitan Building Company, even before the regents had acted, was offering to "withdraw entirely from the hotel enterprise" that it had initiated, simply leasing the land and leaving to others the problem of lease modification if a modification seemed necessary. The fact is that the company's offer was soon translated, after the regents had acted, into an alternative approach to the problem. The *Times* of May 31 used a front-page story (headline: "WOULD FORCE REGENTS' HANDS IN HOTEL ROW") to announce that the regents were to get a new proposal.

In preparing to submit the proposal, the *Times* said, the Metropolitan Building Company was acting at the request of the hotel committee of the Chamber of Commerce and Commercial Club, whose members had met that day with Stimson and Douglas. The company's letter, which would "have the effect of reopening the question of erecting a mammoth hotel on part of the university's downtown tract," contained terms mirroring those of the Stuart-Douglas letter of May 24 and Higgins' "reply" of May 28. The *Times* now noted, however, that "precisely the same offer was made several weeks ago by the Metropolitan Building Company to the Chamber of Commerce," when the Chamber committee was exploring financial arrangements, but the company had asked the nineteen-year lease extension "so that the hotel would have a business life of 50 years." The offer seemed a fair one, as the *Times* pointed out. That was the view of the *Argus*, too, on June 4, when the editor said that the regents, having been faithful to their trust, now had "an opportunity to make every possible effort to see that his hotel is erected on terms more favorable to the University." The regents had balked at lease extensions, however, not at a hotel, and it is possible that if a different proposition had been put before them, they might have spared themselves the agonizing days of public excoriation.[21]

The Metropolitan Building Company letter, signed by Stuart and Douglas, was sent to the board on May 31 as the *Times* had said. The terms and the condition—that "you procure the financing and erection of a hotel . . . of a class equal to the one we planned to erect"—were as specified. If the regents discussed this, no record shows. When the board met again, on July 8, 1921, with the letter before it, the regents simply directed Markham, the secretary, to acknowledge it.[22]

There was, by 1921, a Douglas Building. It was not new. It was, in fact, the decrepit old Post-Intelligencer Building, now largely gutted and rebuilt and made presentable. The Douglas stretched along Fourth Avenue from Union Street to the Cobb Building, making it possible for visitors to walk indoors, as the Metropolitan company pointed out, from Union Street to University. That it carried Douglas's name was appropriate, for it was the first building on the tract, and although Douglas had not built it, it had been the starting point for all that had happened since.

What had happened was prelude, played in fortissimo. There would come now, in the development of the main theme, a long and complicated series of maneuvers that molded for decades the character of the university tract and the nature of the leasehold. First, Seattle would get its hotel, which would be called the Olympic. Second, the state legislature would enact in 1923 a law forbidding the regents to make any contract "modifying or extending" the tract lease without specific legislative approval. Third, the Metropolitan company would build five new permanent buildings to replace, at last, the temporary ones—these the addition to the Cobb Building in 1922, the additions to the White and the Stuart in 1923, and the new Stimson and Skinner buildings in 1925 and 1926. Fourth, there would be another dispute over the Arena Building—a dispute in which the regents, standing firm again, established a point, but in which Douglas preserved the building in an eleventh-hour reconstruction project sufficiently ingenious to win wide attention.

The board of regents could not attempt to finance a hotel or even undertake a search for appropriate financial sponsorship. No one thought it could. But the Seattle Chamber of Commerce was prepared to do so. A new hotel was at the top of any list of community priorities, and whatever else the recent uproar had accomplished, it had (1) ignited a small blaze of community determination and (2) fixed firmly in the minds of all the idea that the university tract was the perfect hotel site, a place where a Metropolitan Theatre–hotel complex would transform a whole block in the center of the city into the tourist and convention center that Seattle wanted so much. It would take a community effort of the kind Seattle well remembered (the campaign to make certain that the Moran Brothers company got the contract to build the battleship *Nebraska*, the mobilization of resources for the AYP Exposition of 1909), but the leadership for this new effort was present and ready to go.

Through the winter and spring of 1922 planning went forward under Chamber of Commerce auspices. By June the plans were in place. On June 28 a Community Hotel Corporation was organized under the laws of Washington, the term fifty years and the capital $270,000, the 27,000 shares of stock to be offered at a par value of ten dollars. The trustees named as incorporators were C. D. Stimson, Horace Henry, J. F. Douglas, Frank Waterhouse, Thomas Burke, C. S. Wills, George Donworth, W. L. Rhodes, Worrall Wilson, Reginald Parsons, and Andrew Price. On June 29 the newspapers carried full-page advertisements headed "SEATTLE'S NEW HOTEL PROJECT," announcing the organization of the company and describing the offerings of stocks and bonds. The advertisements, and a prospectus published at the same time, described the proposed financing, the plan for public subscriptions, the potential for investment, the concept of the hotel as a community project, the lease arrangement with the Metropolitan Building Company, and the peculiar advantages of the hotel site, among these the tax advantage—"This property is State property and exempt from taxation, except that the State has the right to tax the use." As for the details, the company proposed to offer $3,000,000 in twenty-five-year 7 percent gold bonds secured by a first mortgage on the hotel property. The mortgage provided for a sinking fund—4 percent to 1942, 6 percent to 1947—for bond retirement. For each $100 invested, the subscriber would receive a $100 bond at $90 and a share of stock at par. The total subscription would be $2,700,000, the final $300,000 of bonds not to be issued "except in the case of some unforeseen contingency requiring the additional money." In its contract with the Metropolitan Building Company—the sublease running to November 1, 1954—the corporation agreed to pay $25,000 a year in rent, its proportionate shares of assessments and taxes, and $75,000 to cover "the unamortized portion of the improvement put upon the block." This meant it would pay the company $75,000 for the unamortized portions of the Otis, College Club, Women's University Club, the Neyhart buildings that would have to be removed.[23]

The bond subscription campaign, the Community Hotel Corporation announced, would be held the following month, from July 17 to 25, 1922. The general chairman, who also headed the corporation, was Frank Waterhouse, president of the Chamber of Commerce.

The corporation-campaign lineup was a mobilization of the business and professional men, bankers, and industrialists who were the city's acknowledged leaders. With Waterhouse, president of the corporation, were C. J. Smith, vice-president, and Manson Backus, treasurer. A key figure was W. L. Rhodes, an increasingly successful department-store owner, who would direct the citizens' committee. Behind these men (although many members were serving in dual capacities) were a board of directors of twenty-two, an executive committee of thirty-two, and an advisory committee of fifty-two, the lists studded with names of men everyone knew: C. D. Stimson, A. S. Kerry, J. F. Douglas, Laurence Colman, H. C. Henry, James D. Hoge, C. B. Blethen, Joshua Green, J. D. Lowman, Dr. P. W. Willis, Judge Thomas Burke, W. E. Boeing, D. E. Frederick, E. A. Stuart, C. H. Cobb, Judge J. T. Ronald, O. D. Fisher, and many others. It was a small army of such leaders that Waterhouse would head, and Waterhouse had his own impressive background.

Waterhouse was not yet fifty-five in that summer of 1922, yet he had put together a spectacular and wide-ranging career in shipping and industry since coming to the United States from Great Britain in 1882 as a fifteen-year-old farm hand, hod carrier, and itinerant handyman. After young Waterhouse worked seven years in Minnesota and Manitoba, he returned to England for four years and then came back to the United States and to the Puget Sound country as a stenographer for the Northern Pacific Railway. He was with a shipping company briefly, but when the Klondike rush started, he went back to England to organize Frank Waterhouse and Company, Limited, to promote British Columbia ports and establish trading posts on the Yukon River. During the Spanish-American War, Waterhouse chartered to the United States a fleet of ships carrying mules and war supplies to the Philippines, and by 1901 he had bought out his British associates and begun operation of his American firm, Frank Waterhouse and Company, which established the first shipping lines linking Puget Sound ports to Australia,

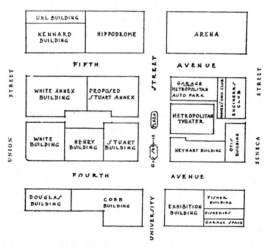

In this plat of 1922, the White Building Annex was in place, the Stuart Annex proposed; the refurbished Post-Intelligencer Building had become the Douglas and was linked to the Cobb, and the Metropolitan Theatre still was surrounded by temporary buildings, which soon would vanish when ground was cleared for the new Olympic Hotel

to England through the Suez Canal, and to the Malay Peninsula. He was a pioneer in the shipping trade with the Hawaiian Islands, the Philippines, and North China. His companies had developed farms in Eastern Washington, coal fields on the east shore of Lake Washington, and docks and storage facilities, an automobile agency, and taxi services in Seattle. Since before the world war, Waterhouse had been chairman, officer, or director of virtually every important community enterprise from the Red Cross to the Washington State Harvesters' League. Now he was to head the drive to build Seattle's new hotel.[24]

Preparations for the drive moved rapidly in 1922 and the period was an interesting one. There was an oil "boom" in Alaska, and anchored for a time in Seattle's Elliott Bay was a huge white steam yacht of classic lines owned by Edward L. Doheny, the Los Angeles oil millionaire, who told the press he was going to Alaska on vacation but also admitted he might look into the oil possibilities there. Seattle was still building, school buildings among other things, including Roosevelt and Garfield high schools. The university tract was, however, at the focal point. The annex to the Cobb Building was being completed and work was well along on the new additions to the White and the Stuart. The *Times* on July 16 used a five-column aerial photograph, "snapped by Aviator Smith," of the "Metropolitan Building Company's Expansive Civic Center." The caption noted that the photograph "shows plainly the block surrounding the Metropolitan Theatre where within the next two years Seattle's big $2,700,000 hotel will rise." An accompanying story said that the Metropolitan company would soon be finishing its "program," and that the company planned to widen University Street at Fifth Avenue (the old Whitson Building was down now and the Stuart Annex was being set back fifteen feet), the widened space to become a plaza, with a fountain or a clock tower, of the kind found in Europe. The new Municipal Market at Pike Street—the Public Market, which had been visited in April by Marshal Joffre, the French war hero—was being prepared for a "grand opening." In that time of burgeoning prosperity, but nevertheless a time in which international concerns were about equally divided between questions of rearmament and war reparations, the Boeing Airplane Company was turning out a plane a day on a new War Department order for two hundred MB-3A biplane fighter aircraft for the army. And even as the hotel campaign was being put together, Seattle indulged itself in a three-day celebration of the twenty-fifth anniversary of the Klondike gold rush, with a parade, exhibits, and speeches at the Arena, all sponsored jointly by the *Times* and the Yukon Order of Pioneers.[25]

Then came the hotel campaign. By July 1, 1922, two days after the preliminary announcements, forty team captains had been assigned to eight divisions under Rhodes, and the drumbeat of publicity had begun. On July 15, two days before the opening, 440 campaign workers met at dinner in the Masonic clubroom in the Arcade Building, and there the battle plan was explained. Waterhouse and members of his executive committee would take the solicitation to three thousand selected businessmen; Rhodes and his citizens' committee, working only from assignment cards, would try to reach fifteen thousand others. The campaign headquarters would be in Koller's skating rink at Third Avenue and Union Street. A huge scoreboard, 9 feet high and 42 feet long, would carry the daily totals reported by the division leaders. The goal was $2,700,000 by July 25. The *Times*, meanwhile, was sponsoring a contest to find a name for the new hotel.

The financial drive was successful, of course—on paper. At the end of the first day, Monday, July 17, the subscriptions totaled $1,600,000. By the second the total was $1,842,600. On following days newspaper advertisements again appeared. The first, headed "The Man Who Says 'I Won't,'" decried the slacker. The second struck the same note from the positive side, saying "The Man Who Says, 'I Will' . . . That is the type of man Seattle welcomes . . . There are just two kinds of men in Seattle, the 'I Will' men—and those who just live here." The message in each case: "The new hotel WILL pay . . . BUY BONDS." By July 20, with pledges totaling $2,434,400 the goal already seemed within sight, but then there came a lull. "Hotel Campaign May Be Forced into Next Week," the *Times* reported. But by July 25, the final day, which was Tuesday, the division reports totaled $2,854,900, and $3,000,000 seemed assured.[26]

As at its other fine moments, Seattle distributed congratulations all around. While the Community Hotel Corporation now moved to get the hotel built and managed, the *Times* was announcing on September 1 that the new structure would be called the Olympic, the name selected by the Community Hotel board of directors from more than four thousand suggestions submitted in the newspaper's public contest. The name had been proposed by Robert Ellzey, a real estate broker, who thus made a large, if only briefly acknowledged, contribution to history.[27]

It had been the idea from the beginning that management would be—under sublease—by a hotel company with appropriate experience. Four such firms were said to be interested. By October an arrangement had been consummated. On October 12 the Community Hotel Corporation executed a lease on the projected hotel to Frank A. Dudley, of Niagara Falls, New York, president of the United Hotels Company of America. A week later a new corporation, the Olympic Hotel Company, was organized under the laws of Delaware, and to this corporation Dudley's lease was assigned. When Seattle got the news on October 20, it learned that its new hotel would be under the management of two stars of the hotel world—Dudley, whose United Hotels operated seventeen hostelries in the eastern states and Canada, and Roy Carruthers, managing director of New York's Waldorf-Astoria, who had earlier experience in Seattle and on the West Coast and who would now be manager of the Olympic. The Olympic Hotel Company was to issue 15,000 shares of stock, 7,500 preferred at $100 and 7,500 common at no par value.* The company was to pay the $25,000 in ground rent assumed by the Community Hotel Corporation in its lease from the Metropolitan. It was also to pay interest charges on the bonds, sinking-fund payments, all taxes, insurance, or assessments levied against the Community corporation, plus $2,500 for the hotel corporation's clerical expenses. Finally, it would pay a

---

* Under the agreement, 50 percent of the common stock would be assigned to the United Hotels Company and 20 percent to Roy Carruthers for assuming management of the Olympic. The balance of the common would be reserved for distribution with the 8 percent cumulative preferred stock, three shares of common as a bonus with every ten shares of preferred. (Douglas to Waterhouse, Stimson, Hoge, and Kerry, May 25, 1923, A. S. Kerry file).

quarter of its net proceeds—after payment of all charges and of 8 percent dividends on the preferred stock—but not to exceed $17,500 in any year. When the organization of the Olympic Hotel Company had been completed, Dudley was president, C. D. Stimson was first vice-president, Carruthers was second vice-president and managing director, and James D. Hoge was treasurer. The nine directors included four from Seattle, Stimson, Douglas, A. S. Kerry, and Waterhouse.[28]

The Olympic Hotel Company had assumed responsibility for management, but it remained for the Community Hotel Corporation to see that the hotel was built. The corporation soon employed a leading hotel architectural firm, George B. Post and Sons, of New York, to begin to work out the details, and by the end of October 1922, a principal of the firm, J. Otis Post, was in Seattle to discuss plans—he was interviewed in the office of J. F. Douglas—and Post was visualizing a hotel of some 600 rooms that could be expanded by 250 or more when business justified the enlargement. Post would cover the property with a U-shaped ground floor built around the Metropolitan Theatre and containing a lobby, a ballroom, and dining, kitchen, and service facilities, the guest rooms on floors above Fourth Avenue and Seneca Street and a Fifth Avenue wing to be added later. Post was delighted by the site, and by the interesting challenge of the sloping terrain, and he pronounced it an "excellent location from every standpoint." Bebb and Gould would be the local firm involved in the designing.[29]

Things simply could not continue to go so well, of course. As weeks went by, the machinery of community action began to sputter a little. The Olympic Hotel Company's Seattle office was in the White Building, the Community Hotel Corporation's in the Chamber of Commerce headquarters in the Arctic Building, and as the year 1923 advanced the office in the Arctic Building was a place where Waterhouse and his associates faced one difficulty after another.

It seems now almost predictable that $2,700,000—actually $2,250,000 in the preliminary calculations—would be far short of the sum needed to build a hotel of the kind Seattle visualized. When the construction bids came in, the total was $3,900,000, or $1,650,000 more than had been allocated. The corporation took the problem to the holders of bonds and stock, asking permission to issue up to $2,000,000 in additional 6 percent first mortgage bonds. The subscribers approved overwhelmingly, by 87 percent, but 13 percent wanted their money back. The Olympic Hotel Company then signed a new lease incorporating the former terms but undertaking also to pay the interest on the new issue and for retirement of the bonds on a fixed sinking-fund schedule. Meanwhile, the start of construction had been set back, both by a delay in shipments of steel from the East Coast (James A. Moore may have appreciated this), and then by the need to redraft the hotel plans to reduce costs. These costs were calculated at $3,250,000 plus $600,000 in carrying charges, a total of $3,850,000. Late in 1923 the whole project was struggling in deep waters. When Waterhouse filed his annual report on December 4, he said that the corporation had spent $534,757 for materials, architects' fees, ground rent, campaign expenses, amortization of buildings and so on, while it had $1,185,242 in cash, treasury certificates, and "good" unpaid subscription balances due February 15, 1924. But the corporation had to sell its new bonds—at least $1,700,000 of them—and the bond market had been in an "unfavorable condition." It was the hope, Waterhouse said bravely, that the hotel would be completed by October 1, 1924.[30]

The Community Hotel Corporation had entered 1923 with a board of directors of twenty-five members, with Waterhouse, C. J. Smith, and Backus serving as president, vice-president, and treasurer. When 1924 arrived, a December election had modified the composition of the board slightly, but there had been drastic changes in the leadership.* The new president of the corporation was A. S. Kerry, and with him as vice-presidents were Stimson, Smith, and A. W. Leonard, Backus continuing as treasurer and J. F. Douglas the new secretary.[31]

The changes at the top were nowhere viewed as a criticism of the leadership of Waterhouse, whose triumph in organizing the bond drive had been followed by a series of troubles with the financing arrangements. But Kerry began in December 1923 with a determination to get the job done. Under Waterhouse there had been, in addition to the large board of directors, an eight-member executive committee that was supposed to approve all bills and make decisions on financing. Thus no one was really in charge. Kerry took the presidency only on the understanding that the executive committee would be abolished and he would "be allowed to handle the hotel matters in exactly the same way as the affairs of any commercial organization are handled." He moved at once to accelerate construction (part of the steel was now coming from San Francisco) and to place the new issue of bonds with a major investment house. By February 1924, construction had been started in earnest, and the prime contractor was Grant Smith and Company, a national firm based in Seattle, whose representative was George E. Teufel. Kerry promised that the building would be ready to turn over to the Olympic Hotel Company by November 1, 1924.[32]

Albert S. Kerry, like Waterhouse, had been deeply involved in the hotel project from the beginning, and like Waterhouse he was a man who had worked hard to win a place among Seattle's financial elite. Born in Canada in 1866 (he was a year older than Waterhouse), and one of a family of eleven children, Kerry was in Washington before he was twenty, tallyman in a sawmill when Seattle was a village, and soon the foreman of the plant. By 1897 he had founded the Kerry Mill Company, supported financially in the venture, it is said, by C. J. Smith, now one of the senior leaders of the hotel

---

* The board of 1923 had been composed of Backus, Burke, Donworth, Douglas, F. A. Ernst, Gilman, Henry, Hoge, Otto F. Kegel, Kerry, A. W. Leonard, Lowman, R. H. and W. H. Parsons, John H. Powell, Andrew Price, W. L. Rhodes, C. J. Smith, A. B. Stewart, Stimson, Moritz Thomsen, Waterhouse, C. W. Wiley, C. S. Wills, and Worrall Wilson. In 1924, Donworth, Hoge, R. H. Parsons, Powell, Price, and Thomsen had been succeeded by E. G. Ames, M. A. Arnold, A. S. Eldridge, Victor Elfendahl, and R. D. Merrill.

movement. The Kerry Mill plant was destroyed by fire two times, and each time Kerry rebuilt it. By 1903 he had established the Kerry Timber Company, which he was to head the rest of his life. In 1913 he had built the Columbia and Nehalem River Railway to reach his timber holdings near Kerry, Oregon, a project that was said to have presented seemingly insuperable engineering problems. By 1924, when he took over the hotel project, Kerry not only was a wealthy man (in that year he sold 750 million feet of Oregon timber for $2,200,000), but was active in other community affairs, as was his wife, Katherine, a founder of the Music and Art Foundation, a member of the first board of the Seattle Symphony, and one of the first governors of the English Speaking Union. Kerry, a fine amateur golfer, was something of a national figure in the sport and in later years a committeeman of the U.S. Golf Association.[33]

Unencumbered by an executive committee and firmly supported by a board that included Waterhouse, Kerry simply drove the hotel into existence. He had troubles collecting from certain subscribers to the original first mortgage bonds, which became second mortgage bonds when it was found necessary to develop the new $2,000,000 issue. When such subscribers wanted their money back, Kerry saw that they were paid, with interest, although he remembered such persons as lacking the "Seattle spirit." The bonds of the second issue were underwritten by a national firm (Blyth, Witter and Company), widely advertised throughout the United States and in Canada, offered by representative bond houses and banks, and sold successfully. Kerry had to move fast—and put on a brave front—because in the months of little progress even those citizens with the "Seattle spirit" had become a little restless. He was also working on exceedingly narrow margins, and delays meant increased costs. Kerry was determined to make the November 1 deadline, because, as he said later, "to have carried our construction on through November would have cost an additional forty thousand, and we didn't have the forty."[34]

Through the summer of 1924 the Olympic rose about the Metropolitan Theatre. As the raw steel framework took shape, huge signs were suspended there to tell the world how things were going:

SEATTLE SPIRIT IN THE SADDLE AGAIN
This Is the Biggest Job We Have Ever
Tackled. Four and One-half Million
Dollar Hotel Building Financed by
3050 Loyal Citizens.
OUR FINANCING IS DONE—WATCH US GO
Community Hotel Corporation.

OLYMPIC HOTEL
These Giant Trusses, Forty-five Tons Each,
Support the Upper Nine Stories of the Olympic
Hotel. Directly Below is the Ballroom, 116
Feet Long.

NOTICE TO BONDHOLDERS
Your Second Mortgage Bonds, With Interest,
Will Be in the Hands of Your Trustee,
DEXTER HORTON NATIONAL BANK, Ready for You
on February Fifteenth.
Community Hotel Corporation.

By June 1924, the exterior of the Olympic was completed. Kerry and the corporation arranged a public inspection and published a small promotional booklet that described the hotel and its financing and issued an invitation to buy common or preferred stock. By October 31 the building was finished, as Kerry had promised, except for furnishing, which would be done by the Olympic Hotel Company as lessee. The cost had been $4,574,000. Furnishing would add about $1,000,000 to the cost. On the evening of October 31, 1924, Kerry stood at a switch panel in the *Times* Building to press a button that would sound a whistle announcing to the city that construction was, at last, complete. As Kerry sounded the whistle, lights were turned on in every room of the hotel. The newspapers photographed the Olympic thus illuminated, brilliantly, for the first time. Kerry gave the keys of the building to W. P. Taylor, Jr., who would be the resident manager.[35]

The Olympic Hotel Company—Carruthers and Taylor on the scene—now took over the job of getting the hotel into operation. It was estimated that gross annual income would be $1,779,775, gross expenses $1,300,077, and net profits $479,698. (Estimated income included $995,255 from hotel rooms, $165,420 from stores, shops, and concessions, and $619,000 from the restaurants, lunchrooms, and soft drink sales.) But Kerry made a short talk when he turned over the building to the company and, although he had compliments for all who had been faithful, he had nothing good to say of those who had failed to keep the faith:

We started out to build a hotel to cost not to exceed $2,700,000 . . . and found that the class of hotel that we needed would cost $4,500,000 exclusive of the furnishings. . . .

We have built it; it has cost $4,574,000. We have paid every bill the day that it was due; paid our second mortgage bondholders $200,000 in cash for interest; have the finest hotel of its size in the world according to the architect's statement; have the cash in the bank to pay every dollar that we owe, and will turn the building over to the Olympic Hotel Co. without a dollar's indebtedness with the exception of the bonded debt.

Some of our newer citizens, not familiar with our achievements of the past, may be harboring the thought that the successful completion of this community enterprise . . . is to set a mark in community endeavor. . . . [But] raising a bonus for the building of the battleship *Nebraska*, the financing of the A.Y.P. Exposition, and all other community undertakings of the past were proportionately as big as this one. The same men who backed the others backed this. . . .

But there had been some who had not backed this undertaking, and Kerry, emerging triumphantly from the community hotel battle, could not help remembering:

In this instance we had the additional incentive of having some of our early subscribers quit in the middle of the stream. While past experience had reconciled us to the fact that there were certain men of means in the city who were a bit shy of either civic duty or public spirit, we were willing again to hold the umbrella over them and forget it, but to find that we had fallen heir to a new crop of quitters got under our skin, and not only aroused the Seattle Spirit but the spirit of our ancestors. Anybody who knows the old Seattle crowd . . . surely knows that they won't quit. Besides this, we have a lot of newcomers with us who not only have the same spirit but are about a lap ahead of the "Old Guard." When the small group quit, reducing our public subscription from $2,600,000 to $2,400,000 . . . we decided that we would complete the job without appealing to the public for another dollar and we have done it.[36]

Seattle, its population 350,000, finally had a hotel of imposing proportions, a hotel of 609 rooms, a solid, sumptuous-looking building of stone and brick with a grand ballroom, dining rooms, service facilities, shops—"the finest hotel of its size in the world," Seattle was certain. Later, when the city had come into its own as a tourist center, more rooms would be added above the Fifth Avenue wing.

The Olympic stood on the spot where the original university building had looked out over Elliott Bay.

While the Olympic was going up, other construction and proposals had come along too. First the annex to the White Building was added along Union Street to Fifth Avenue. Then the Stuart Annex was built on University, where the temporary Whitson had stood. Although they lacked the height of the main buildings, these annexes were permanent buildings, their plans approved by the regents. But in that early-1920s time of a brightening economy and incipient growth, relations between the Metropolitan company and its lessor were under strain. Evidence was seen in the regents' determination to seek legislative protection from what they apparently regarded as importunings by the Metropolitan. The action, whatever its presumed necessity, would plague the university for years. And there would be another showdown over the Arena.

It is not difficult to see what, in the 1922–23 period, was causing tension. Douglas was managing the university property with dash and imagination, but the regents had been through the wringer in the hotel imbroglio. The membership of the board had changed slightly in this period. Perkins, resigning, had been succeeded by Roger R. Rogers, president of the Vermont Loan and Trust Company, of Spokane; and when Rea's term expired in April 1922, he was succeeded by James H. Davis, a Tacoma insurance man. But the board's attitude seems to have remained, as far as the Metropolitan was concerned, a trifle jaundiced.

In February 1922, for example, the regents had recalled that the university was not getting the ten days' free use of the Arena each year, as promised in the clause inserted by Gaches in the 1915 agreement, and they referred to the attorney general the question whether the Metropolitan was guilty of violating its obligation. No answer ever came. Douglas, meanwhile, was having thoughts about altering the Arena. In April 1922, he sent to the board the plans and specifications for converting the Arena into a garage and store building—"a better building than is called for by the lease," he wrote—but the regents referred the plans to Bebb and Gould and got a negative judgment: "If it is the intention that this building when altered shall fully comply with all the terms of the lease, the proposed alterations do not fill the conditions." The Metropolitan came back in June with new plans. These were also found unsuitable. The effort languished for a while.[37]

None of these emerging projects—the hotel under its new auspices, the building of annexes to the White and the Stuart, the alteration of the Arena —involved proposals to modify the Metropolitan Building Company's lease. But many such proposals there had been—the last the one that had brought on the hotel confrontation—and with the Arena situation in flux it could be suspected, perhaps, that the company would still like to extend its permit to use temporary buildings, which Douglas had been quoted as saying, in 1921, were earning $100,000 a year. In those months there must have arisen a feeling—perhaps within the board, almost certainly among the alumni leaders who had been disturbed by the hotel pressures—that the regents, as appointed guardians of public property, needed the support of the public's elected representatives. When the regents had permitted lease modifications, they had been accused of allowing "tinkering" with the terms. When they stood fast, they had been subject to obloquy. Perhaps the state legislature should become a backstop. By 1923, the idea had been followed to its conclusion.

When the legislature met in January 1923, the senate had before it Senate Bill No. 56, "An Act Relating to and Limiting the Powers of the Board of Regents of the University of Washington." It was declared later that "limiting the powers" was not exactly what the regents had in mind if that meant removing from them the "initiative" for dealing with proposals to modify or extend the lease. But the bill said:

The Board of Regents . . . shall not sell, lease, re-lease or make any other disposition of, or extend or modify the present lease upon, that certain tract . . . or any part thereof, unless and until authorized and empowered so to do by statute enacted by the Legislature, and any contract . . . extending or modifying the present lease . . . made or attempted to be made by said Board of Regents shall be null and void unless and until the same has been approved, confirmed and ratified by statute. . . .[38]

The bill, passed by the senate on January 25, 1923, was approved by the house on February 21 and signed by Governor Hart on March 1. Its effective date was June 7, 1923.

None could know it in 1923, but the regents and the Metropolitan Building Company were on a collision course once more. The relevance of the new legislation to what actually occurred is debatable, but the regents were to find themselves approving a modification of the Arena that amounted to a modification of the lease, and this (although the point was not apparent at the time) without the authority of the legislature as now required. The action they eventually took with regard to the Arena Building both clarified what had become an exceedingly complex situation and set the stage for what Douglas made a triumph of engineering ingenuity.

The developments concerning the Arena—the significant developments after the initial explorations of 1922—covered a period of just over two years, from April 1923 to June 1925. The developments are difficult to trace with confidence (and the details are not of fundamental interest, in any case), because the regents for the most part were simply acting and reacting with respect to Metropolitan Building Company plans and proposals for making the Arena not merely a "better building" but a building of three stories, or perhaps four, that could support six. Behind all considerations was the unmentioned fact that the Arena had been declared a temporary building in 1915. If it was not made a permanent building, the regents could take it over in the name of the university after June 24, 1925.

McKee was president of the regents for 1923–24, Miller vice-president, but Shannon had been succeeded in March 1923 by Judge George Donworth, a senior attorney of distinction. Born in Maine in 1861, Donworth had been in Seattle since 1888, when his first law work was as clerk and errand boy for L. C. Gilman. Donworth was widely known and respected, professionally and otherwise: he had been a Taft appointee to the U.S. District Court in 1909, decorated by the Italian government for his interest in Italian history and literature, and in 1923 a civilian aid to the secretary of war. The regents of that year thus were McKee, Miller, Rogers, Rupp, Fechter, Davis, and Donworth, four of them veterans of the hotel confrontation, three newer appointees.

On April 6, 1923, the Metropolitan Building Company obtained a city building permit which, as a note said, authorized "the altering of this building [Arena] into a three story garage" and provided for "the construction of 3 additional stories." A copy of the permit with a new set of plans was sent to the regents by A. H. Albertson, the architect, with a note saying, "You will notice by the copy of the permit, that the permit for the six story building also operates as a permit for the lower three stories." The plans were again referred to Bebb and Gould. The architects, now reporting favorably (the revised plans "are drawn for a six story building of mill construction . . . and conform with the conditions of the Metropolitan Lease"), said in a final paragraph: "In the interest of the University of Washington we wish to point out that it may be advisable that the building permit when applied for should be 'For the alteration of the Arena Building for a future six story building, three stories of which are to be constructed at the present time.' If this is done there will be no question in the future as to the addition of the remaining three stories."[39]

There was, however, a question about how many stories were contemplated.

On May 26, 1923, the regents approved the modified plans "on the condition that the fourth floor be constructed as a ceiling for the third floor," which meant, to the regents, that the Arena's existing roof trusses, built only to support the shallow wooden crown, should be replaced by concrete slabs. But by July, Albertson was writing again to say that the company did not want to "wreck the roof" to install slabs that would have to be covered by planking (for wiring, piping, and drainage) and asked a "reconsideration of our conditional approval" of the company's plans. The new legislation "limiting the powers" of the regents had become operative on June 7, 1923, but it held no meaning to the regents in their present efforts to solve matters of slabs and floors. On July 9, the board, having in mind the favorable report of Bebb and Gould, approved the Arena as "a permanent building of six stories but to be built only to the height of three stories at this time."[40]

The building permit, issued for a year, would expire April 5, 1924. Until March 1924, the Metropolitan Building Company did nothing, and then it changed the plans again. Or rather it asked the board's approval of plans that were being changed. On March 8 (the regents were to meet on March 14) the company sent to the regents a letter saying that to convert the Arena to what was considered "the last and most improved type of garage building" it now planned to change interior framing from mill construction to reinforced concrete, to change floors to reinforced concrete slabs, to install reinforced concrete columns strong enough to carry two additional stories, to change the floor levels (to "increase the amount of floor area about 14,400 square feet"), and to place in "that portion of the building used for garage purposes what is known as the deHumy Ramp"—an improved and patented automobile ramp on which the company was paying a use fee. "The plans are not entirely completed," the company said, "but have been approved in their outline by the City Building Department. They will be completed and approved about the first of April. We are anxious to start construction as soon as we can get a permit for the building which will probably be before the meeting of the Board of Regents in April." The plans were not complete, but the idea was. The company had already announced it in the *Metropolitan Bulletin* of March 7, 1924.

Solving the parking problem for tenants of Metropolitan Center who use automobiles as well as for the great number of visitors who will be passing through the Olympic Hotel, the Arena Building will be remodeled into the latest type of garage, and will be opened in the early fall.

The Arena Garage marks a new epoch in the type of garage construction, and is built after what is known as the ramp plan. The d'Humy Motoramps, a patented method of construction involving a combination of ramps with staggered floors, will be used in the Arena. . . .

The advantage of the ramp type over the several level entrance type is the centralized control of the entire garage. It gives full protection to cars and gives greater service to patrons.

And as for the building itself:

The entire frontage of Fifth Avenue will be made into stores. These will conform to other store spaces in Metropolitan Center, having the same high type of construction and finish.

On March 13, the day before the regents met, the City Building Department did indeed write the regents to say that although final plans were not before it (the preliminary plans had been submitted that day), a permit would be issued upon the submission of final plans modified to call for installation of automatic sprinklers, standpipes, automatic fire doors, fireproof partitions, and fire curtains. Considering all this, the regents referred the Arena matter to the committee on buildings and grounds—Miller and Rupp —with power to act. Again the firm of Bebb and Gould was consulted and again the architects approved, saying the changes seemed "distinctly advantageous." By March 29, 1924, Miller and Rupp had reported that they had inspected the revised plans and specifications and had "authorized the Metropolitan Building Company to proceed with the reconstruction of the Arena Building." Construction had proceeded immediately. The arena, the temporary building of 1915, now was a new garage of the latest type, with d'Humy Motoramps, additional floor area, and Fifth Avenue stores. No one seems to have wondered whether the converted building was classifiable as permanent. What else could it be?[41]

The garage—the new garage in the old Arena shell—was called at first the Metropolitan. Across Fifth Avenue from it was the twelve-story mass of the new Olympic Hotel, which was being completed in 1924. On the other side of the hotel, across Fourth Avenue, work was going forward on the new Stimson Building, named, naturally, for C. D. Stimson, vice-president of the Metropolitan Building Company, and this was to be another physicians' and dentists' building linked to the Cobb by a pedestrian corridor under University Street. There also existed in University Place, as a somewhat anomolous facility, an automobile service area—a "gas station," actually—operated under lease to an oil company and situated between the Metropolitan Theatre and the Stuart Building where only flowers and shrubs once had made a beauty spot in the center of the tract.

By 1924, much was happening, not only on the university tract but on the university campus, where a great new library, a towering Gothic structure, was rising. Horace Henry had given the university $18,000 for the modeling and installation, on the library's façade, of the figures of the eighteen men who, in the judgment of the faculty, were the major contributors to mankind's growth in the arts and sciences. At the tract, the squat temporary buildings were disappearing in the rush of construction. The Hippodrome Building at Fifth and University, which had been the site of so many meetings and conventions while the Arena was used as a skating rink, was scheduled for demolition and replacement. J. F. Douglas, busy with plans, now had as his assistant his brother Walter. Another brother, George S., much younger, was on the company staff. E. A. Stuart was still president of the Metropolitan; the vice-presidents were Stimson, Cobb, W. H. Talbot, Langdon C. Henry, son of Horace, and O. D. Fisher, who also served as treasurer. The Metropolitan had created by this time what it called a "junior board," organized in 1923 "from the sons, sons-in-law and brothers of men who are directly interested in the company" and serving as an "advisory" body to the trustees. Members of this group were Walter and George Douglas, Scott Bullitt, William Edris, Edward Middleton, Gilbert Skinner, Thomas Stimson, Elbridge H. Stuart, F. C. Talbot, and H. C. Stibbs. At such a time and in the face of such a lineup it may have seemed almost a niggling thing when the regents, at their meeting of May 28, 1924 (the same meeting at which they noted and filed a "further report on approval of plans" for the Arena), observed that the Metropolitan Building Company apparently had been careless about the filing of lien bonds, as required by the lease, "on the various new buildings now being erected." The bonds were to assure that there was money to pay construction workers and so on. The regents asked Herbert Condon, the comptroller, to get figures on the "outstanding liabilities" while the regents prepared to insist that bonds be filed at minimums of $50,000 on the Olympic, $75,000 on the Stimson Building, and $15,000 on the Arena. By July 19, the bonds had been filed.[42]

If this showed anything, it was that the regents were reading the lease with considerable care. It may have shown something else, too, although there can be only speculation about it. On June 16, 1924, shortly after the regents' May meeting, George Donworth resigned from the board. Since Donworth had served only fifteen months, it may be that he felt himself in some fundamental disagreement with the way things were going. But how things were going in 1924 can only be guessed by examining the events of 1925. In any case, Donworth's successor was John T. Heffernan, not a lawyer but another Seattle "capitalist," owner of the Heffernan Dry Dock Company and the Heffernan Machine Works in West Seattle.[43]

Other changes, larger and smaller, were coming in that season of 1924–25. The new governor of Washington was Roland H. Hartley, a hard-hitting, economy-minded Republican millionaire-politician, a native of Canada who had come from Minnesota in 1902 to seek out timber investments and who had been mayor of Everett and a one-term state legislator on his way to the governorship. At another level entirely, the position of secretary to the board of regents was getting a new incumbent. William Markham, who had served successive boards for almost twenty-five years, was in his late seventies and, because of trouble with his eyes, had offered to resign. By February 1925, Markham had departed with the thanks of the regents and in his place was Herbert Condon, who would come to occupy a unique niche in university recollections as bursar and comptroller, registrar, secretary to the regents, and dean of students, always a gentle figure, profoundly loyal to the university. Markham's place in the records seems to be marked only by his signature in the board's minutes, yet he had memories like no other's to sustain him. Markham, as a young volunteer, had ridden with George Armstrong

Custer's Michigan cavalry in the Civil War. In 1923 the regents had given him a rare leave of absence (Markham made the notes) "to attend the 27th annual, and probably last, reunion of the Civil War veterans of the Custer Mich. Cavalry Brigade at Grand Rapids, Mich., June 5 and 6 . . . he having served as a member of the Co. C, 7th Mich. Cavalry under Gen. George A. Custer in 1864 and 1865."[44]

In the spring and summer of 1925 things were booming everywhere. Calvin Coolidge was president of the United States, business was good, and the nation was at peace. Seattle reflected the times and added a few touches of its own. The Seattle summer was hot and dry and a water shortage threatened. But industry was strong, the Boeing Airplane Company was expanding modestly but surely, and analysts were predicting that Seattle would be an important center of air traffic when the coming air age had matured. On June 27 the whole city celebrated the opening of the Montlake Bridge connecting the Capitol Hill–Montlake area and the University District—a handsome new drawbridge carrying trolley rails and spanning the channel between Lake Washington and Lake Union. The city had awaited such a bridge for years (the regents of 1916 had adopted a resolution urging it), and at the opening ceremonies a university coed dressed in academic robes had shaken hands with the president of the Chamber of Commerce to symbolize the linkage between the city and the university community. King Dykeman, the judge so intimately associated with university affairs, left the bench in June to become publisher of the *Post-Intelligencer*, and President Suzzallo was among the guests at the Chamber of Commerce luncheon at which Dykeman was honored.[45]

Amid such interesting developments what else could matter in 1925? To the regents, it mattered that June 24 was the expiration date of the Metropolitan Building Company's final, ten-year permit covering temporary buildings —the permit that had been extended a decade before upon acceptance of the Stuart Building and the permit the board had refused to extend to 1935 when the hotel proposal was first being considered. June 24 was a deadline that the regents felt they could not ignore. They also felt they needed professional help if they were to make any comprehensive judgment of the performance of the Metropolitan Building Company with regard to its leasehold. There was also curiosity about the current value of the leasehold for tax purposes. To make a study of the status of tract developments the regents employed in 1925 a local consultant, Roy H. Dodge.

Dodge, from what can be sifted from contemporary accounts, was an expert appraiser specializing in long-term leaseholds, a Seattle consultant with earlier experience with leading firms in Ohio. The regents may have approached Dodge in February 1925, because an initial letter-report was filed in mid-March. In any case, at a regents meeting of March 20—a meeting attended by Governor Hartley—the lease committee was authorized to make arrangements with Dodge "or some other suitable person" to "furnish facts" on alleged violations of the lease. Someone obviously thought that there had been violations. By May 1, pursuant to a resolution approved in April, the board had entered into a formal agreement by which Dodge was employed to the end of the year, at one hundred dollars a week, "to use his best skill and knowledge in investigating all the terms, conditions and modifications of that certain lease . . . and to examine all the facts concerning questions of compliance and non-compliance with said lease and its modifications, and . . . also the valuation of such property and leasehold."[46]

The Dodge report of March 12, 1925, was followed by another—undated—statement concerning the status of the Arena Building. The March letter cited five "violations and non-performances" of the lease by the Metropolitan Building Company: (1) the failure to post indemnity bonds while building on the tract; (2) the widening of University Street, forbidden under the lease clause on "Streets and Alleys"; (3) construction and operation of a gasoline service station on University Street, forbidden in two paragraphs of the lease; (4) construction of the tunnel under University Street between the Cobb Building and the new Stimson Building; and (5) reconstruction of the Arena Building, the existence of which, after June 24, 1925, would be "in direct violation of the modification agreement under which it was permitted" by the temporary building modification of 1908. Dodge went further. He said that certain sums, "illegally collected by the lessees, are recoverable by the Board of Regents." One such sum was the $52,545.51, plus interest, received by the company as a condemnation award upon the widening of Union Street in 1910, an award based on the taking of "real property owned by the University." He said that the regents could claim, with accumulated interest, the $75,000 paid by the Community Hotel Corporation for the temporary buildings (the Women's University Club, the former College Club—later the Engineers Club—and the Otis and the Neyhart buildings) that formerly occupied the hotel site and that were, in fact, the university's. Dodge said that the university was entitled to certain sums—$6,750 in one case, $2,500 in another—received by the Metropolitan Building Company when other temporary buildings were sold.[47]

If this was not enough, Dodge's analysis of the Arena Building case made two points that apparently had occurred to no one else. Dodge had inspected the Arena himself and had considered it in relation to the lease modifications, the regents' actions, and the city's ordinances and codes. One of his conclusions was that the Arena, "as it stands today," failed to meet the height specifications of the original lease, of the subsequent modification, or of the regents' conditional approval of 1924. There was another point, however, that must have jarred the regents a little. Dodge concluded: "No authority is contained in [the] original lease or any modifications thereof, which would permit Lessees to remodel, or change a temporary building into a permanent one, without special permission granted by the Board of Regents prior to 6 June 1923, when act of Legislature became effective."[48]

It was a nice question. The legislature had not been consulted, even though all the conclusive actions had occurred in 1924, months after the 1923 legislation limited the regents' powers of decision. Miller and Rupp, with "power to act" as members of the buildings and grounds committee, had authorized the company in March 1924 to proceed with the Arena conversion and to make the building permanent. On May 28 the regents had merely noted a "further report" on the plans. But the regents' approval of the conversion of a temporary building to a permanent one—a permanent building of a new type that did not meet the height requirements—appeared to Dodge to be a lease modification in violation of the legislative mandate.

How high was the building? That was the critical question. The problem existed because of the slope of Fifth Avenue, downward from Seneca Street to University, a slope on which any building necessarily was taller at the lower end than at the upper. A building clearly of four stories would have satisfied, or even one of three stories to hold six. But what was the converted Arena? The regents had Dodge's opinion. They turned to Robert L. Proctor, the city's superintendent of buildings, for additional information. When the regents met on June 16, 1925, they had Dodge's report and Proctor's response before them. Proctor said that the building was two stories at the highest point of the site on Seneca Street, three stories at Seneca Street and Fifth Avenue, and four stories on University. But the regents also had before them, for the first time, a copy of the building permit issued to the Metropolitan Building Company on April 30, 1924—more than a year earlier—specifying, "Change existing building to garage, containing four floors; plans being checked for two additional stories. . . . Building is 240 x 120 and 4 stories in height in addition to no basement." Whatever the building was, the regents thought, it was not that.[49]

The regents—Rogers, Heffernan, Miller, Rupp, Fechter, Davis, and McKee —thus faced on June 16, 1925, the question of what to do about the remodeled Arena. Only eight days remained before the expiration of the Metropolitan Building Company's permit to use temporary buildings. In a sense, the meeting was a replay of the meeting of December 1915, when the regents of that day (only Fechter and Miller now remained) first declined to accept the Arena as permanent. There was a long discussion, the minutes say. The regents must have thought they were choosing between accepting the building as it stood, and thus perhaps modifying the lease in a way that was legally beyond their power, or taking from the Metropolitan Building Company, in the name of the university, a building which, whatever its inadequacies, was a welcome part of the new Olympic Hotel–garage complex. Either way, it must have seemed, lay calumny of the kind the regents had experienced in 1921. Ultimately, Rupp moved, Miller seconding, that the board choose the second course: "Resolved that the Metropolitan Building Company be notified that investigation reveals that the building formerly known as the Arena Building, located on Fifth Avenue between Seneca and University Streets, does not conform with the terms of the lease and, therefore, is classed as a temporary building, and as such the Board will exercise the rights conferred on it relating to temporary building, on and after June 25, 1925."[50]

The regents' letter to the company stated the determination concerning the Arena. It also cited two other complaints: the first that the gasoline station in University Place was in violation of the lease, the second that although insurance policies on tract buildings had been made payable to the state, as required, the policies themselves had not been surrendered.

The regents must have had a feeling that whatever the merit of their decision—and to whatever extent the crisis had been forced by the Metropolitan Building Company's delay and changes of plan since 1922—an ultimatum delivered only a week before the deadline would be regarded as unworthy. Presumably they simply had reached a point at which, as in 1921, unpleasantness seemed preferable to retreat. There seem to have been some persons who thought that the regents were trying to break the lease (why else the instruction to Dodge to inquire into, among other things, questions of "compliance and non-compliance"?). Whatever the motives, the regents had looked at a deadline and had delivered an ultimatum. But not even Miller and Fechter, the most experienced of them, could realize the extent of J. F. Douglas's resourcefulness.

The letter from the regents must have struck the Metropolitan Building Company with the force of a thunderbolt. As it happened, Douglas was far from Seattle, visiting an island in the St. Lawrence with his daughter. He had to relay questions and decisions to his brother Walter, who was in charge. But if there was hesitation over what the response should be, it could not have lasted more than hours, for there was little time to weigh choices. (It was said later that the company considered for a moment taking the issue to court, but rejected the idea because a court action could lead only to a prolonged and minute review of the history of the company as leaseholder.) The Douglases and the Metropolitan directors decided to try to add a story to the Arena and thus make it a three-story building at the southerly, Seneca Street end. Such a building would meet without question, after a decade of doubt, the height stipulations of the lease. By June 19, 1925—two days after the regents' letter arrived and five days before the deadline—arrangements had been made for what would have seemed an impossibly fast remodeling effort.

The Arena-become-garage, whatever its height, was a massive structure, covering half a hillside city block. As an ice-skating rink it had been both a center of amusement and the home court of a Seattle hockey team. As an auditorium it had seated thousands at community meetings and political rallies. As a garage, with floor levels adjusted and the d'Humy ramps installed, it was able to accommodate more than 450 automobiles. At a normal pace, the addition of a story to such a building, from the awarding of the contract to completion, would have taken weeks, perhaps months. The Douglases and the Metropolitan got it done in four and a half days. The work was accomplished so swiftly (almost half of it on a weekend, and where so much other building had been done), that Seattle seems scarcely to have been aware of what was going on.

What was going on was a construction project that can have had few parallels. By 10 A.M. on Saturday, June 20, 1925, the third day after the regents' letter had been received, the construction contract had been accepted by Grant Smith and Company, the national firm that had built the Arena in 1915 and converted it into a garage in 1924 even as it was building the Olympic. By noon of that day the 1924 floor plans of the building were being modified in the drafting rooms of Hall and Stevenson, Seattle structural engineers, while two construction supervisors were organizing teams of workers—concrete men, steel handlers, bricklayers, plumbers, electricians—called from other Grant Smith work sites or mobilized by various union hiring halls. By that Saturday evening, some eight hours after the awarding of the contract, 250 men were starting to work through the night under floodlights. On Sunday and Sunday night, 300 followed them, and more than 200 continued the work on twelve-hour shifts from Monday to Wednesday. The wooden roof was removed from the Seneca Street end of the building, a concrete floor was installed, and new walls went up. The weight was supported on concrete columns that had been thickened by ten inches for added strength. The wooden roof at the north end of the building was left in place, but the walls were heightened to provide an unbroken roofline.

There were certain crises along the way. The swiftness of the effort was possible only because a new quick-drying, 24-hour cement—Lumnite—had recently become available. The local distributor had supplied 600 barrels of Lumnite—500 ordered by telephone and barged in from Bremerton—while the Pacific Coast Steel Company was rounding up steel for the reinforced slabs and roof trusses. By Monday, however, the Lumnite was running out and more steel was needed. At that moment—and by pure chance—the U.S.S. *Iowan* docked at Seattle with a cargo that proved to include a load of Lumnite being consigned to a $1,500,000 dock project at Bremerton's U.S. Navy Yard. The *Iowan's* captain was prevailed upon—at what risk to his career history does not say—to lend 150 barrels of the new cement, and these were trucked to the garage site just as the mixers were running out. Meanwhile, additional steel was being sent in by the Hofius Steel and Equipment Company, one of the sixteen suppliers and subcontract firms that contributed to the effort. By the evening of Wednesday, June 24—the last day of all the days of temporary buildings—the converted Arena had been lifted toward permanence. On the following day the newly installed garage floor was receiving automobiles, including those of delegates to the Foreign Trade Council meeting that was opening in Seattle. The Metropolitan Building Company's contractor had established what a regional engineering journal said was thought to be a "speed record for reinforced concrete work in commercial building."[51]

But it was only with puzzling slowness that the people of Seattle and the state began to realize what had happened. Neither the statements of those most immediately concerned nor the reports published after the fact did much to improve understanding. It is not at all obvious what the regents thought they meant when they notified the Metropolitan Building Company that "the Board will exercise the rights conferred on it relating to temporary building." They could not have wished to operate the building themselves in the name of the state, yet that was hinted, and they certainly could not have wanted the building torn down, yet Condon soon was quoted as saying that if the Arena "was a temporary building on June 25, it should have been demolished." What is clear is that the regents were feeling, before and after the floor was added to the Arena, both a creeping apprehension and a need for legal guidance as differentiated from the expert-appraiser judgments they had received from Dodge.

On June 23, even as the Arena work was in process, Condon was writing the out-of-Seattle regents—McKee, Rupp, Rogers, Davis, and Fechter—to tell them that since the board might need the services of a "first class legal counsel," he and Miller had made a trip to Olympia to discuss with John Dunbar, the state attorney general, the appointment of a deputy to represent the regents in any discussions with the Metropolitan Building Company. The company's own counsel, they knew, was Judge Donworth, who had resigned as a regent only a year before, and Condon and Miller had a man in mind—"one of the very best lawyers in the state," as Condon put it— John H. Powell, the young lawyer-regent of 1902-9 and now a leading member of the bar. Powell not only was a prominent lawyer, but he had been a regent during virtually all the early negotiations relating to the tract lease. Dunbar had approved Powell's appointment instantly, and the out-of-town regents had approved it enthusiastically, when their responses to Condon's letters came trickling in. The regents were glad about Powell. They also, unanimously, wanted to be prepared.[52]

There was no confrontation, as it proved. The Metropolitan Building Company simply assumed that it had won, and there the matter hung for some weeks. But information was given the public haltingly and confusingly. The weekend after the Arena job, Walter Douglas was saying, somewhat ingenuously, that the garage had been expanded simply because business was so good the company felt it could afford to provide the additional space. But "gossip" had it, the Seattle *Star* said, "that a lease notice served on the company by the university board of regents had something to do with the rush." By that time the newspapers were using photographs of the Arena with its new story while giving the news a variety of interpretations. The *Times*, having called Fechter at Yakima ("I wish it to be distinctly understood that there is no controversy," Fechter said), was assuring its readers that no building on the tract but the Arena was involved in the "issue," whatever that was. The *Star*'s story, filed from Olympia and headed "U. OF W. LEASE FIGHT ON," said that the regents had "appealed to the state for aid in a controversy that has sprung up with the Metropolitan Building Company," and by this was meant the appointment of Powell. The *Post-Intelligencer*'s story, at least, was local, quoting Walter Douglas as saying that he thought the Arena had met the lease requirements even without the added story and that the gasoline station had been removed because it, too, was a temporary building. The *Post-Intelligencer* reported that there would be a new building on the Hippodrome site and that more would be known about this when "Major J. F. Douglas, manager of the company" returned from the East, where he had been investigating "types of buildings considered suitable."[53]

If there remained an "issue" concerning the Arena, it was soon abated. Powell abated it. And at almost the same moment the future of the Hippodrome site was also determined. On September 26, Powell submitted to the regents a seven-page opinion related principally to the questions that had been raised by Dodge.[54] Addressing the Arena case, Powell wrote: "This building was constructed originally under an agreement between the Board and the company, dated September 29, 1915. It would serve no useful purpose to recite here the subsequent negotiations over its construction and alteration. In my opinion the only remaining question with reference to this building is whether it now conforms either (a) to the terms of the original lease or (b) to the terms of the resolution passed by Board on May 26, 1923. This is a question of fact, primarily for an architect or an engineer, or both."

The resolution of May 26, 1923, was of course the resolution approving the third-floor concrete slabs, the regents' last action on the Arena before the new state legislation went into effect. Powell said further: "If it should be determined that the building as it now stands does not conform . . . the Board could then determine what other steps, if any, it desires to take. It may be questioned whether the company had the right, by alterations or additions, to convert the temporary Arena Building into a building that would conform to the requirements of a permanent building. In my opinion the company had such right."

The old Arena—the new garage—finally was sanctified. The regents accepted it. Even as Powell was sending forward his memorandum the Metropolitan Building Company was announcing that a new corporation, the Fifth Avenue Building Company, had been organized to erect on the Hippodrome site an eight-story "motion picture, office, and studio building to cost in the neighborhood of $1,500,000."

Officers of the new company were William Edris, president; Thomas D. Stimson and Paul H. Henry, vice-presidents; Walter Douglas, treasurer; and George S. Douglas, secretary. The motion picture theater, with a seating capacity of three thousand, would be leased to Washington State Theatres, Incorporated, a new subsidiary of a $25,000,000 Motion Picture Capital Corporation. The Fifth Avenue Building Company would itself be a subsidiary of the Metropolitan Building Company. The company's decision in this "closes," the company said, "the major development of the University Tract."

The new theater-office-studio building was completed in 1926. It was named the Skinner Building for D. E. Skinner, a Metropolitan Building Company trustee. Its sandstone façade, considerably higher than that of the Metropolitan (Arena) Garage, rose along Fifth Avenue from University to Union streets, covering the 355-foot half block upon which had stood the Hippodrome, the Kennard, and the Uhl buildings. It did not quite "close" the development of the tract, as the company had said. The construction of the Fifth Avenue wing of the Olympic Hotel did that. But the university tract had achieved, after almost twenty years, the shape it would have for almost another twenty.

Little note had been made of it at the time, but the man who made the motion establishing the regents' policy on leasing had lived long enough to see the tract in that nearly completed state. Richard Winsor, the regent of 1902, had died December 2, 1923, at his home in the University District. He was eighty-five.

CHAPTER 7

Good Times, Hard Times, War:
1926 to 1943

The university tract was the "Metropolitan Center" by 1926. The quotation marks were being used by the Metropolitan Building Company as if the center concept was being advanced only tentatively. The nicety was unnecessary. The Metropolitan Center was a fact. The development of the old university grounds—the "act of business boldness amounting almost to romance," as Howells and Stokes had called it—was fulfilled.

Not that the original plan was fulfilled. Some of the new permanent buildings stood where apartment houses or the department store had been visualized, others on the site once reserved for a "University Hotel." But the one-story temporary buildings were gone forever, and the hotel that Seattle now had, the Olympic, had risen majestically around the Metropolitan Theatre, dwarfing it, and Seattle had watched with satisfaction as it grew. The aggregate cost of construction on the tract had exceeded $11,500,000. Excluding the theaters and the hotel, the rental area in the buildings—the Douglas, the Cobb and its annex, the Stimson, the Skinner, and the White-Henry-Stuart and its annexes—was 825,000 square feet, more than 18 acres of store and office space. The center had evolved in its own way, but solidly.[1]

The center by 1926 possessed—even with the converted Arena considered something of an aberration—more than enough unity of style to set it apart from the city about it. It had the J. F. Douglas style, too, for Douglas's ideas were in full flower. It was not just that the center was a busy place, the shops the kind Douglas wanted, the office-space tenancy high. Even the roof gardens flourished, and tearooms and food service facilities. Service was the watchword. The service organization of the Metropolitan Center was now a staff of "232 technical and practical persons"—from the elevator operators to the maintenance men—all wearing uniforms or work clothes carrying the MBC badge. Every statement by the company, every piece of promotional literature, stressed the unique character of the center and its attractions as a place where selected tenants conducted important business. The "city within a city" theme was emphasized too. When the Stimson Building joined the Cobb in the expanded medical-dental complex, the Metropolitan Building Company was saying, for example:

Some twenty years ago a tract of unimproved land belonging to the University of Washington stood midway between Pine and Madison Streets, a few blocks from the harbor of Elliott Bay. For thirty-three years, the original University Building, erected in 1861, had witnessed the tread of students through the historic halls, had seen graduated the men and women who are a part of Seattle's history.

But in 1894 the University of Washington was moved to the grounds overlooking Lake Union [*sic*]. The paths which led across the meadow land of the University grew green, the beautiful old structure itself was finally demolished. The ten acres became a boggy pasture, an unimproved spot in the heart of what was to be a great city.

And then to a small group of men was given a vision of what was to be. They conceived the pasture land as a "city within a city," its ten acres of offices and shops rising with a symmetry, beauty and adaptability which should serve as models of business construction. A lease on the land was secured, and in 1907 the plan for "Metropolitan Center" was born.

This building group was destined to be unique among such enterprises in the business world.[2]

Themes were everywhere. In the decorative terra cotta of the White-Henry-Stuart Building was the bas-relief head of Chief Seattle, the friendly Suquamish patriarch for whom the city was named. On the façade of the Cobb were terra cotta Indian faces "symbolic of the characteristics of the American Indian," the company said, "and indicative of the strength and vigor of the West." When the Stimson Building came along there was suspended from the ceiling of the two-story Sienna-marble lobby a large bronze lamp that had hung for years in the Peacock Alley of New York's Waldorf-Astoria Hotel— a touch undoubtedly arranged (with the help of Roy Carruthers) by Douglas, whose first major project in Seattle had been the building of the Waldorf Apartments. Among the interesting new tenants of the Stuart Building was the Japan Society—the life members including Manson Backus, Judge Burke, and J. F. Douglas—the society occupying new clubrooms in which the floors were covered by Oriental rugs, the furniture was overstuffed, and the walls were paneled "in taupe damask, surrounded by an ivory trim." The expanded medical-dental complex represented a theme in itself. To doctors or dentists who might have hesitated (if any could have) to commit their professional prospects to offices in the city's center, the company gave this reassurance:

You may be proud of your office in the Stimson Building. More than in any other profession the medical man requires an office which indicates his standing. Equipment and appointments being correct, there must be the intangible feeling of reliability, integrity, and prestige, which is given emphasis by correct location.

For many years the Cobb Building has been established as *the medical building* of Seattle, not only in the minds of the profession, but in the consciousness of people generally. The linking of the Stimson Building to the Cobb Building by a subsurface corridor increases the facilities of both buildings, and permanently locates the *medical center* at Fourth Avenue and University Street.[3]

There was action in the Metropolitan Center. The assembly halls were busy with business and professional meetings of various kinds. The Seattle

Press Club had new quarters in the Stuart. The White-Henry-Stuart had become a capital of the lumber industry. More than 150 lumber and forest-products firms had offices there, and with them were the offices of dozens of railroad and shipping companies doing business in lumber, the railroads including the New York Central, the Green Bay, the Chicago, Burlington and Quincy, and the Chicago, St. Paul, Minneapolis and Omaha. The Metropolitan National Bank had moved to new and larger quarters in the White. Beneath the Stuart Building was the Metropolitan Garage, with room for 150 automobiles, and the old Arena was now the Olympic Building, office space augmenting the garage. The eleventh floor of the Stuart was still the major headquarters of the Carnation Company, and Carnation was beginning to take its operations abroad. Before World War I the company founded by E. A. Stuart had established new plants in the rich dairy regions of Wisconsin and Illinois. After the war, Stuart had organized a General Milk Company, capitalized at $1,500,000, to sell evaporated milk everywhere in the world outside the United States and Canada. Early overseas sales offices had been set up in London, Paris, and Essen. By 1923, condensing plants had been put into operation in Carentan, France, and Neustadt, Germany, and others were about to follow in Germany, Holland, Scotland, South Africa, Peru, and Mexico. Stuart was almost seventy, his eyesight failing, and in 1926 his son, Elbridge H. Stuart, became executive vice-president of the Carnation Milk Products Company, with headquarters at Oconomowoc, Wisconsin. The heart of the Carnation empire remained, nevertheless, in Seattle's Metropolitan Center, and so did E. A. Stuart, the presiding genius. Stuart had become interested some years before in the breeding of fine harness horses, and for a while there were annual horse shows at Carnation Farms, society events at which Stuart himself, sitting erect in an immaculate four-wheel cart, reins in hands, would put a favorite horse through its show-ring paces.[4]

The opening of the Olympic had given Seattle not merely a grand new hotel but a magnet for society functions, from dinners and balls to a regular Monday luncheon at which Seattle's business leaders and members of their families met in a dining room sometimes so crowded that tables had to be set in the halls. The handsome new Skinner Building, named for a man who had become one of the Northwest's leading industrialists, contained a theater that was wonderfully and authentically Chinese in its decor. D. E. Skinner, who was another Michigan man, had come west in 1906, had headed a number of enterprises, including the Port Blakely Mill, and then in 1916 had been joined by John W. Eddy in forming the Skinner and Eddy Shipyard to build steel steamers for wartime shipping service. The first of the Skinner and Eddy ships, the *West Haven*, had been built in sixty-four days, then a record, and thirty-one other vessels were built before the war's end. Skinner was a director of the Metropolitan and, of course, a leader in the financing of the last office building in the university tract.

But it was the Fifth Avenue Theater, rather more than the Skinner Building itself, that brought excitement to Fifth Avenue. In an era in which new

THE SKINNER BUILDING

"East is East and West is West,"
And here the twain shall meet.

—in shops where are marketed together
foreign wares and domestic merchandise;
in offices, where are administered busi
nesses with extensions over the Seven
Seas; in the theatre, where are combined
the arts of the Old World and the New
to work a magic of delight—here, in this
stately edifice, the twain *do* meet.

At the Gateway to the Orient the Skinner Building stands dedicated to
the commerce and trade of two great Continents.

The Skinner Building of 1926, shown here in a contemporary sketch, contained shops at
the street level, office suites above, and that most exciting feature, the Fifth Avenue Theater,
all of the designing by Robert C. Reamer

motion picture and vaudeville houses were of an Art Deco mode or of Holly-wood-style imitation grandeur, Seattle's sought genuinely to express the city's view of itself as the "Gateway to the Orient." The auditorium was a replica of the Ming dynasty throne room and audience hall in Peking's Forbidden City, the theme suggested by Julian Arnold, U.S. commercial attache in China, and developed under the direction of Robert C. Reamer, architect of the Skinner Building. The dome was a nearly exact copy of the throne room original, but twice to scale, and from the mouth of a coiled Great Dragon was suspended the "Pearl of Perfection" chandelier. The decorative details—paintings, carvings, fixtures—were executed with the aid of hundreds of photographs and sketches sent from China, the installations by Gump's, San Francisco's premier importer of Oriental art. When the theater was opened on the evening of September 24, 1926, the crowd that jammed Fifth Avenue was the largest since Seattle celebrated the Armistice.[5]

J. F. Douglas—"Major Douglas," as he was invariably called in the press and elsewhere—was fifty-one now, mature, handsome, square-jawed, a determined man with the look of success about him. The young attorney who had written a small book on Washington corporate law had become a figure in corporations that were exceedingly important in Seattle. He had achieved what was becoming a national reputation in property development and management. In 1924 he had been interviewed by an up-and-coming young feature writer, John Monk Saunders, and the result was a story in the November 24 issue of the *American Magazine*, one of the major national family publications of the period, which appeared under the title, "A Western Builder Who Changed the Face of a City," the subtitle: "Twenty years ago J. F. Douglas was a struggling lawyer; to-day he is manager of one of the biggest building companies of its kind in the world—How he transformed ten acres of pasture land into Seattle's office-building center." Douglas's story was the kind America loved.

The Metropolitan of 1926 had an administrative staff whose members would go far with the company. Andrew Steers was manager of the rental department, his assistants L. S. Forbes and E. A. Hart. Sarah A. Hilmes, assistant treasurer, was a woman who had been a navy staff member when Douglas was at the Bell Street Terminal. She had joined the Metropolitan about 1920, as Douglas's secretary and assistant, and would be for years the principal custodian of the company's financial records. Other women were occupying important positions. Freda Tilden was advertising manager and Katherine Wilson, who was in charge of publicity and publications, was giving the *Metropolitan Bulletin* a handsome, 1920s Art Deco format. A. G. Schille was assistant manager of the Service Department. With the Metropolitan also was Robert Reamer, an Ohioan who had come to the company in 1920, whose Skinner Building would win an American Institute of Architects award, and whose architectural ingenuity would mark Seattle for generations. Reamer's designs would include, in addition to those of the Seattle Times, Great Northern, and 1411 Fourth Avenue buildings, the University District's

Edmond Meany Hotel, a remarkable little tower in which, it was truly said, "Every room is a corner room."[6]

The flowering of the Metropolitan Center encompassed, or at least was associated with, a flowering in the arts as well. The Edward Curtis studio had been established on the university tract years before, and J. F. Douglas, as a patron of the Seattle Art Association and other such cultural assemblies, had provided encouragement to Northwest artists in the form of rooms and wall space in Metropolitan Center buildings for the display of their works, now and then purchasing a painting himself. It was in this time that Eustace P. Ziegler came to the scene. Ziegler was a wonderfully productive artist who seemed preeminent among those seeking to catch the color of the Northwest and who still had more than forty years of work ahead of him. A graduate of the Detroit and Yale Schools of Fine Arts, Ziegler, in his early twenties, had gone immediately to distant Alaska to draw and paint, and he had been there sixteen years when, in the early 1920s, the Alaska Steamship Company invited him to Seattle to execute a set of murals for its offices. In Seattle Ziegler stayed, exhibiting in 1925 and 1926 and on into the 1930s. Years later, Metropolitan Building Company Christmas greetings bore reproductions of Ziegler's works.[7]

But at the University of Washington the year 1926 was one of shattering change, politically engineered change, a year to be long remembered with bitterness. The irony could only be appreciated fully after the fact, for the situation that developed, involving clashings of strong personalities, was, like the Kane situation of 1913, too broad and too complex to be assessed simply in regard to its effect on a leasehold. But irony was there. In a year of climactic success at the Metropolitan Center, the university itself was seriously wounded. Regents then serving were swept away. New regents were seated. The new regents discharged the president of the university. The Metropolitan Building Company's performance under its lease came under intense examination. And the new regents would find themselves, before long, presiding over an institution chilled by the first cold winds of the Great Depression.

The activating agent of what happened in 1926 was Roland Hartley. By May, Hartley had been governor for sixteen months, every month augmenting incrementally an administrative tension that had begun on the day of his inaugural address. Whatever Hartley's motivations, it is needless to try to search for them now. His political text was economy. He was capable of demagoguery, but he was not the simple demagogue. He was, rather, an independent force. He broke with most of the officials of his own administration. He bullied the legislature. He began by advocating the reduction of election costs, the state printing of textbooks, revision of procedures for selling state timberlands, a slowing of road and reclamation projects. Soon he took aim at the costs of education. Political enemies had quoted him as saying that the state should not be responsible for education beyond the eighth grade. Whether or not that story was true, Hartley's own formal education may have stopped at about that level, for he had been one of a family of twelve children, a bullwhacker in the Canadian woods by the time he entered his teens and a man who had fought his way to wealth in both lumbering and farming long before he had come to Washington from Minnesota in 1902. Hartley was a driven man, and ambitious. It may be that he saw in Henry Suzzallo a potential rival for a higher political post. Some thought so. Or perhaps he merely felt uncomfortable in the presence of Suzzallo's intellectual force. However, it was, when Hartley began taking aim at the costs of education he also was taking aim at the president of the University of Washington.[8]

Suzzallo was an educational leader who, because the state, the times, and the university were what they were, lived at the edge of the political arena. Long before Hartley came to the governor's chair, Suzzallo had wrestled with the university's needs for faculty, buildings, and funds, representing his institution before the legislature with spirit and ingenuity and keeping his own vision of its future. In World War I and the depression years that followed he had been called into national service to deal with problems, including labor problems, larger than the university's, yet it was primarily in behalf of the university that his political talents were exercised. But Hartley now turned the screws a little tighter, and the scope of his intent became plain almost immediately. On April 24, 1925, the regents then sitting saw fit to adopt a resolution: "Resolved, that [the board] records its complete faith and confidence in Dr. Henry Suzzallo, President of the University. That under his wise and economical administration the University has grown on the material side to that point where it is one of the largest universities in the land. . . . That the long continuance of Dr. Suzzallo in the Presidency of the University is a matter of vital importance to the State as well as to the University, and we pledge ourselves to that end."[9]

The resolution was approved unanimously—by Rogers, Heffernan, Miller, Rupp, Fechter, Davis, and McKee—and it was, as they said, a "pledge" to support Suzzallo. It was their measure of Hartley, certainly, that they pointed to Suzzallo's "economical" administration and his development of the university on the "material side." Suzzallo would hope to be remembered for other things. In 1915, in his talk at the students' first fall assembly, Suzzallo had said: "This University is dedicated to the liberal life. It is the institutional expression of all that is best in human aspiration. Whatever truth the world has not been able to find, it is here sought by scientific means. Whatever of human morals it has not been able to implant among grown men, it here tries to develop in plastic youth. Here it expects that human action shall be finer, kindlier, and more efficient."[10]

There has been something of a mixed prophecy in Suzzallo's inaugural address the following spring. When he took the university presidency Suzzallo had discussed leadership in a democracy: "I have assumed, of course, that leaders are as necessary in a democracy as elsewhere. There are some few doctrinaires who think we ought to fear strong men. But strong men are no more to be feared than ignorant ones. What the former are in size, the latter will make up in mass. One may be done to death as readily by a mob as by a highwayman. It is the nature of our political past that has given us a traditional fear of large personalities. Enough has happened in our present life to give us a very rational fear of uncontrolled crowds."[11]

But the board of regents that supported Suzzallo in 1925 had little more than a year to live. Various matters relating to the Metropolitan Center came before it, these in addition to business of more direct significance to the welfare of the university. The regents had approved the plans for the Skinner Building and, recalling the earlier unfortunate experiences with plans, had followed the advice of Bebb and Gould and put copies of the plans on file "for future record." They also required a bond of $150,000 on the Skinner. When the Metropolitan Building Company suggested that the new Fifth Avenue Building Company would deal with the board directly, the regents refused this arrangement, saying that the board "looked solely" to the Metropolitan, not to a subleasing company, in matters concerning improvements. The regents made a new contract with Dodge to enable him to finish his studies of "violations" of the Metropolitan Center lease, and they received additional reports from Powell regarding insurance on the downtown buildings. There had also come an adjustment in the regents' organization when Miller, even as an active member of the board, was made secretary, Herbert Condon being appointed as his assistant. The officers of the board in the spring of 1926 thus were Rupp, president; Heffernan, vice-president; and Miller, secretary. This board, in March 1926, received a note from Horace C. Henry offering to the university "all of my private Collection of Paintings except a very few retained for family reasons and a building to house the same costing not over one hundred thousand dollars provided its construction be commenced at a very early day." The Henry collection even then was valued at several hundred thousand dollars. The regents accepted the gift gratefully, and the construction of the gallery was expeditiously arranged.[12]

But there then began, in May 1926, a summer of shock at the university that proceeded into an autumn of emotional stress in which Suzzallo, departing his presidency, was both victim and hero and Hartley, as governor, simply rode out the storm he had created. By the time the regents were to meet on May 6, 1926, Governor Hartley had made four appointments. To succeed Rogers and Miller, whose terms had expired, the governor had named Roscoe A. Balch, of Spokane, secretary of the F. M. Rothrock Company, which operated a cattle and sheep ranch at Sprague, and Sidney B. Lewis, who was the Weyerhaeuser Timber Company representative in Seattle and general manager of the Clearlake Lumber Company at Clearlake. But also (and he had a recent State Supreme Court opinion confirming his right to do so) Hartley had appointed new regents to replace Davis and Rupp. These were Alvah H. B. Jordan, of Everett, president of the Everett Pulp and Paper Company and the American Telechronometer Company, and Paul H. Johns, of Tacoma, president and general manager of the City Lumber Company. The four new regents attended the meeting, and the sitting regents present were Rupp, president of the board, Heffernan, the vice-president, and McKee, Fechter, and Davis. Thus nine regents attended a meeting of a board of seven. The situation obviously had interesting potentials. In Miller's absence, Condon recorded the proceedings.

Rupp and Davis had determined to fight their case in the courts, to institute quo warranto proceedings, with the support of the alumni association, to retain their places. Because Rupp felt that he could not take the chair "under the circumstances," Heffernan presided. Rupp and Davis presented a statement protesting their removal from the board, and Rupp submitted two additional communications. One was from Governor Hartley telling the regents that the university appropriations of $547,750 must "be not expended" because they had been irregularly approved, this a reference to the fact that the legislature had passed certain funding bills over his veto.* The other was a letter from the attorney general, John Dunbar, declaring the appropriations legal. Jordan and Johns, there to succeed Davis and Rupp, presented their commissions and asked to know who were to sit as regents. Heffernan, presiding, but unable to do anything but recognize the commissions, consented to adjournment to executive session for an election of officers. Jordan, with the votes of Johns, Lewis, and Balch, was elected president of the board. Johns was elected secretary, Condon to be his assistant. McKee and Heffernan simply remained for a while.[13]

This bit of juggling may have had certain comic opera aspects, but it was a prelude to what became deadly serious warfare between Governor Hartley and the friends of the university, the alumni particularly, but also members of the legislature who were affronted by the governor's assumption of power over state appropriations. The university went about its business in that pre-commencement season of 1926, but amid a rising clamor. The University of Washington *Daily's* May 7 report of the regents' meeting—the banner heading, "HARTLEY CHANGES WILL BE CONTESTED"—described the presentation of the Davis-Rupp statement, Rupp's yielding of the chair to Heffernan, and the results of the "star chamber" executive session in which Jordan was elected president. It was reported even then that petitions asking Hartley's recall would be circulated, and the Seattle newspapers were full of stories about the case. (The political temperature was suggested by the headlines: "HARTLEY DARES PEOPLE TO RECALL HIM," "RUPP FAVORS COURT TEST OF HARTLEY POWER OVER SCHOOLS," "CONSTITUTIONAL LEAGUE TO DISCUSS DISMISSALS," and "LIES POISON PUBLIC MIND, SAYS HARTLEY.") Suzzallo was already seen as a Hartley target. When Hartley mentioned Suzzallo's name in an address at Seattle's

---

* The appropriations bill (chap. 83, *Laws of 1925*) had been approved by both houses and vetoed by the governor on December 24, 1925. The senate voted to override the veto, the house to sustain it. House rules to that time had made it impossible to reconsider such a vote, but proponents of the appropriations won a change in rules to allow reconsideration, and the house then joined the senate in voting to override. The university's stake in the action included $231,750 in funds for operations, $150,000 for construction and equipment of the Mines Building, and $81,000 for completion of the new library.

Eagles' Auditorium he was interrupted by pro-Suzzallo demonstrations. It may have seemed to university partisans an almost providential bit of timing that the president of the alumni association was Charles Gaches, so long a leader in university affairs. Gaches, now prominent in banking as well as farming, was one of Suzzallo's great friends—it was he who had first interviewed Suzzallo on behalf of the regents in 1915—and he was quoted as saying: "The governor can see no difference between managing penitentiaries, insane asylums, and logging camps and [managing] universities, colleges, and public schools." When the regents met again on June 3, 1926, the new regents in the majority, they voted to "retain" Suzzallo for a year, renewing his salary at $18,000. The salary was the highest paid by the state, a point that Hartley emphasized when he sought to show the "extravagance" represented by the university's administration under Suzzallo. In the week following, nevertheless, an anti-Hartley mass meeting was held in the University District under the sponsorship of the "Constitutional Government League" and the alumni association. Gaches was among the leaders and speakers.[14]

For several weeks the situation simmered. By August, however, Fechter was gone from the board, succeeded by another Hartley appointee—also a Yakima man—J. M. Perry, president of an ice and cold storage company that bore his name. There were five Hartley appointees now, Heffernan and McKee a residual minority. In the fall, with the university just opening its autumn session, the denouement came.

The regents met on October 4, 1926, presumably to work on the university's budget request for the 1927 legislative session. What they did, however, was to dismiss Suzzallo, the president they had voted to "retain" four months before. The *Daily*'s black headline announced the action: "REGENTS OUST PRESIDENT: Suzzallo Evicted by 5 to 2 Vote of Board." As had the board in Kane's time, the regents had asked Suzzallo's resignation. When he refused, they voted him from office, extending his salary to December. The regents' discussions—in another "star chamber" session, the *Daily* said—had been prolonged; at least, Heffernan and McKee had tried vainly to defer the judgment. When the decision had been made, McKee immediately resigned in protest. She and Heffernan were speakers several days later at a downtown rally in support of Suzzallo—a mass meeting at which McKee described in some detail the processes by which the board had arrived at its determination. (An interesting aspect of the case was that none of the Hartley appointees had yet been confirmed by the state senate.) Through it all, Suzzallo remained calm, viewing the developments philosophically, even hopefully, while the emotions subsided and the university carried forward in the autumn months under the interim administration of David Thomson, dean of faculties, a gentle, scholarly man who had been named acting president. On October 19, Hartley appointed a regent to replace Heffernan, who had resigned, and this was John D. Farrell, of Seattle, a widely known and respected pioneer railroad builder and Catholic layman. Farrell had just passed his seventieth birthday, but his career had been of the kind Seattle knew well. A native of New York state, Farrell had started as a water boy on a Chicago and Northwestern track-laying crew, then rose over the years to become general superintendent of the railroad and, among other things, assistant to the president of the Great Northern, president of the Great Northern Steamship Company, and vice-president of the Union Pacific. In 1927 Governor Hartley appointed another regent, Joseph E. Lease, a prominent Centralia school man-become-banker who had served a term in the legislature from Lewis County. Lease had come west from Pennsylvania in 1889 and had been a high school principal and county superintendent. By 1902 he had joined John A. Field in organizing the Field and Lease Bank, later the First Guaranty Bank, and he had acquired extensive property interests. Lease would be reappointed a regent but would die in 1930 after serving only half of his six-year term; his successor was another Hartley appointee, Ward C. Kumm, a Seattle attorney. But by 1927, little more than a year after he had turned his attention to the university, Governor Hartley had transformed the board of regents—all of the appointments were his—and the effort to recall him had faded away.[15]

Perhaps the least important aspect of the agony through which the university had passed was its effect on the institution's relationship, as lessor, with the Metropolitan Building Company. The University of Washington had been "politicized," as the word was, and its condition was so viewed throughout higher education from coast to coast. There had been no time for matters of leasehold, and Governor Hartley was considered to hold the university, as much else, under tight control. Even with President Suzzallo gone—and perhaps simply because he was gone—the governor kept the university under a close and personal scrutiny.

The results of the seating of the new board of regents seem, so far as the Metropolitan Center was concerned, both expectable and a little surprising. The minutes of the board's meetings in 1927 and after show almost no entries relating to affairs at the university's downtown tract. There was not even a Metropolitan lease committee, although the regents frequently were dealing with matters affecting university lands and, once, with the question of the legality of an expenditure from the University Building Fund, to which Metropolitan Building Company rents were assigned.

Yet Hartley, campaigning for reelection as governor in 1928, cast himself in the role of defender of the university—and of the taxpayers' interest in it—against alleged machinations of the Metropolitan Building Company under its leasehold. And although the regents' minutes do not reveal it, new studies were indeed going forward at the university in 1928 and 1929 of the status and dimensions of the tract as a property and of what had been asserted were the Metropolitan's lease violations.

It is small wonder that the new board had little time for matters not directly concerned with the university itself. Not only were there problems of

A Building Vision, Realized

Metropolitan Center

A TEN-ACRE tract of fine business blocks at the heart of Seattle's downtown business section. The city's smart shopping and fine theater district. Office headquarters for the Lumber Industry, the great Life Insurance agencies, and all Transportation Lines of the Pacific Northwest.

AN improvement project begun twenty years ago, its final completion was one of this year's outstanding building events. This group of fine edifices, built on ground leased from the University of Washington, will ultimately revert to ownership by the State's great educational institution, a perpetual source of income and revenue.

Constructed and Operated by

Metropolitan Building Company
1301 Fourth Avenue
Seattle

The Metropolitan Center as idealized in Metropolitan Building Company advertising of 1927 when, with the Olympic Hotel and the Stimson and Skinner buildings in place, the development of the university tract was "A Building Vision Realized" budget and building—the new library was being brought to completion and other campus developments were coming—but Suzzallo's successor was to be selected and the regents seemingly wanted no one with what they considered Suzzallo's propensity for uncomfortable activism. The new president turned out to be a man from the campus, M. Lyle Spencer, dean of the College of Journalism, whose selection was confirmed at a meeting of July 23, 1927. The truth was, however, that the Hartley board was a group of seven persons new to it all—new to the university and without a single member with any experience in matters relating to the downtown tract. The regents were from business backgrounds, and undoubtedly competent. Later, in 1928, Sidney Lewis was succeeded by James V. Paterson, of Seattle, a distinguished marine architect who had become president of the Moran Shipbuilding Company in 1908 and of the Seattle Construction and Drydock Company in 1912. But the experience that the new members brought to the board had to be polished in the university setting. Whatever the attitudes or predilections possessed by earlier regents—such as Perkins, Rea, Gaches, Powell, McKee, Wheeler, Miller, Shannon, Fechter, Davis, and Rupp—they had functioned, even in their disagreements, from points of view that would be absent now for a time.[16]

In 1928 the board as it was then organized included Jordan as president, Farrell as vice-president, Johns as secretary (with Condon as his assistant), and Lease, Perry, Balch, and Paterson. In reference to the Metropolitan Center the board had inherited two important studies of developments there. One was Dodge's detailed analysis of the regents' actions with regard to the Metropolitan company's management of its leasehold, and the other was John H. Powell's report of 1925 which quieted the question of the Arena but which touched on a number of other issues. Dodge had been assisted along the way by a member of the faculty of the university's Law School, Professor Leslie J. Ayer, who may be presumed to have acquired his own working knowledge of the history of the leasehold.[17]

Dodge's preliminary reports had raised disturbing questions about the university tract and had inspired the earlier board to declare the Arena unacceptable as a permanent building. Dodge had proceeded under contracts with the regents to make a thoroughgoing examination of the whole history of the tract, from the time of the original gift to the Metropolitan Building Company's development of the property to 1926. Dodge's paper was in two forms. One was a running account called, awkwardly, "Chronology of Events and Facts Relating to the University 10 Acre Tract in Seattle." The other was a somewhat longer statement, "The University '10 Acre Tract' in Seattle," of ten chapters and more than 50,000 words, incorporating Dodge's extended judgments and opinions. The fact that there were two papers was a result of the regents' action in February 1926, when the board asked Dodge to prepare one report giving the "facts" on the lease and another giving "said Dodge's interpretation on said facts." In any case, Dodge had spent months examining the deeds of gift, the legislation, the leases, the modifications, the judicial rulings, the building permits, and the records of the regents from the beginning. Questions raised by Dodge were those addressed by Powell when the latter was appointed to advise the regents in 1925. Some of these matters were still in suspense when a third study was made by Professor Ayer in 1929.[18]

Dodge had fault to find with the early proceedings of the tract leasings. The advertising had been irregular or absent altogether, as in Moore's acquisition of the University Site Improvement Company lease and, of course, his sale to the Metropolitan Building Company. Dodge noted that the most critical decisions on leasing—such as the one on November 1, 1904—had been made with less than a full board present to vote, and that the decisions between 1904 and 1907 had been made at a time when changes in the board were so sweeping that John H. Powell was the only regent who participated in all of them. Dodge went through hypothetical calculations of income to the university based on the three leases—the University Site lease, the Moore lease of 1904, and the Moore lease as modified in 1907—and arrived at the conclusion that if the 1904 percentage lease had been in effect in 1926, the university would be receiving not $80,000 a year on the fixed schedule but $240,000 a year, at 4 percent of a "conservative" $6,000,000 appraisal of the value of the tract as then established. Dodge made calculations, based on a variety of assumptions, of the "millions lost in revenue" because the Moore lease of 1907, as transferred to the Metropolitan Building Company, provided only for a fixed rental schedule on a property free of taxation. But his point was not to prove that the earlier regents had been either obtuse or less than honest in accepting such terms. His point was that the regents who approved the lease—who "could not know, in 1907, that such increases in land value would happen in these later years"—had counted on the lessee, Moore, improving the property by constructing permanent buildings that would have compensating value at the end of the lease term. The regents has approved a lease that specifically provided: "No buildings shall be erected abutting upon Union Street or Fourth Avenue of less than five stories in height. . . . All buildings erected on said premises shall be constructed with foundations and walls sufficient to carry at least six stories." When Moore sold his leasehold to the Metropolitan Company, Dodge noted, the long history of petitions for lease modifications began—a history of erosion of what the regents had seen as the compensating value of the improvements.[19]

In any case, the regents of 1926–27 possessed reports by Dodge and the opinions of Powell on certain questions. There is no evidence that the regents gave them any immediate consideration, but the questions formed a background to what erupted occasionally into renewed public interest in the affairs of the Metropolitan Building Company, as when the city of Seattle appealed unsuccessfully to the State Tax Commission, in 1925, in an effort to raise the assessed valuation of the leasehold from $600,000 to $3,003,000.*

---

* Dodge testified as an expert witness at the State Tax Commission hearings in Olympia in 1925, supporting the city's attempt to increase the valuation of the Metropolitan Building

The questions in themselves were of slight public interest, relating more to principle—to the company's possible "violations" of its lease—than to developments in the general view. The Metropolitan Center was being polished. The new Fifth Avenue elevation of the Olympic was going up. Seattle was getting the big and important meetings it wanted. Technical questions of the Metropolitan's performance under its lease were, perhaps, only technical questions. They remained to be proved. Still, if there had been violations of the lease, what then? Serious violations could become grounds for cancellation. But were any persons—in particular, any members of the board of regents—thinking of cancellation as possible? The record is inconclusive. Whatever the force of the idea, it died in a sputter, and on the weakest possible issue, in 1929.

The three examinations of the company's performance were those of Dodge, Powell, and Ayer between 1925 and 1929. Dodge was the principal examiner because he worked under contract with the regents to conduct a most careful scrutiny of all the records. Powell was working from another view, with only Dodge's preliminary findings before him. In any case, Powell's assignment was not to scan the records but to give the regents his judgments on the information presented. When Ayer came along, much later, he had Dodge's complete studies and he was familiar with Powell's report. There was an uneven overlapping of judgments and opinions. Dodge, who surely brought to his task a prejudiced eye, nevertheless was the investigator who had devoted the most time and thought to the lease questions. The two attorneys, Powell first, then Ayer, had somewhat different reactions. And before Ayer made his analysis in 1929, there had been an election in which Roland Hartley, winning his campaign for reelection as governor, made an issue of his opponent's one-time connection with the Metropolitan Building Company. Perhaps a time had come, now that the center was an accomplished fact, for an inevitable recapitulation of what had happened, why it had happened the way it had, and whether there had been, along the way, lapses in responsibility or obligation—in short, violations. What were these alleged violations? The principal charges were these:

First, that the Arena Building still did not qualify as permanent, and thus existed as a violation of the lease terms, even if—a separate question—

Company leasehold. Dodge admitted, a newspaper account said, that he had been employed by certain persons, some of whom were "competitors" of the company, to make a financial analysis of the company's operations under the lease, an analysis that presumably had been facilitated by access to financial data given him by stockholders (Seattle *Times*, "Metropolitan Company Rivals Press Tax Suit," August 28, 1925). Dodge's employment by the "competitors" apparently took place just before he made his agreement with the regents, for a regents' minute of June 16, 1925, refers to "a group of Seattle citizens who had employed Mr. Dodge from October 23, 1924 to April 30, 1925." While the significance of all this is somewhat obscure, Dodge evidently came to the regents' assignment with a background of earlier study of the lease. The regents' agreement with Dodge of May 1, 1925, duly said that Dodge would "accept no other employment during the term of this contract." Regents Minutes (Dodge's prior employment), 6:324, June 16, 1925; (Dodge agreement), 6:315–17, May 15, 1925.

the Metropolitan Building Company had the right to attempt the conversion.

Second, that the company had wrongfully used for its own purposes the $52,545.49 awarded in condemnation proceedings upon the widening of Union Street.

Third, that in widening University Street between Fourth and Fifth Avenues the company had proceeded without the express authority of the regents, who may not, in any case, have had the power to approve such widening.

Fourth, that the company had no right under the lease to build under University Street the tunnel connecting the Cobb and the Stimson buildings.

Fifth, that the company, in permitting the erection of a "gas station" in University Place, not only had violated the lease terms concerning building but had collected rentals that properly belonged to the university.

Sixth, that in selling off for $75,000 and lesser sums the temporary buildings removed to make way for the permanent ones, the company had received allowances for buildings that were university property.

Seventh, that insurance on the buildings on the tract had not been made payable to the board of regents as required, and that the regents never had received the policies.

Eighth, that the company never had complied with the lease provision requiring that a bond be filed before construction of a building was begun.

All inquiries into such matters sprang from—or followed, at least—Dodge's preliminary report to the regents of March 12, 1925. Since this report was filed even before his contract with the regents was signed in May, Dodge obviously came to the scene with some other acquaintance with the problems. Nevertheless, Dodge had raised questions that no one else had examined before—questions concerning the Arena, the University Street widening, the gas station, the Union Street condemnation award, the bonds, the sale of temporary buildings—and he had closed his memorandum with the thought that cancellation would have been contemplated already if both the lessor and lessee had been private companies. In Dodge's words: "Without a complete analysis of the lease, it cannot be stated positively whether there have been other violations. It is my opinion, however, that the above would constitute sufficient grounds for cancellation long since had the contract been drawn between two private parties. The lease made by the Metropolitan Building Co. with the Community Hotel Corporation, for example, calls for forfeiture and re-possession should the lessee company's rent be in arrears for *ten days* [Dodge's emphasis]."[20]

In short, the regents, as representatives of the lessor, had been far less careful to protect the university's interests than the Metropolitan Building Company had been in protecting its own interests in leasing to a closely related corporation. Even in 1926, after the Arena had been converted and the gasoline station removed, Dodge still felt that the regents had ample grounds for cancellation. Powell made no such judgments. Professor Ayer tended to support Dodge, but Ayer was submitting his opinions three years after Dodge completed his studies, and apparently informally, in response to an inquiry by J. D. Farrell, who was vice-president of the board. The regents' records show no formal consideration of Ayer's reports or his views.

So there were questions. And what were the responses of the three men most qualified by experience and training to supply answers?

First, what about the Arena Building, the focus of controversy since 1915? Powell, after Dodge raised the question, had said that whether the converted Arena actually qualified as permanent was for an architect or engineer to determine but that, in his opinion, the Metropolitan Building Company had the right to make the conversion. Dodge disagreed altogether. He said the building was not permanent, no temporary building should remain, and the legislature should share any decision concerning disposition:

The important question, however, has not to do with the engineering details of the building. From the time the first letter from Levold was written, in 1900, the Board of Regents has had the sole authority and responsibility for modifying the existing lease contract at any time. By its enactment of the law of 1923, the legislature thereby assumed joint responsibility and authority with the Board of Regents for the protection of the State's reversionary interests in the leased premises.

It seems doubtful, therefore, whether the legislature can escape the responsibility for its passive attitude in the matter of extending for a period of 29 years, the lessee's limited right to use and occupation of buildings constructed under its joint supervision with the Board of Regents. Clearly there was not authority, behind Douglas' assumption in the matter, that these temporary buildings could ever remain on their site after the definite termination of the modification under which they were built. And if the matter of consideration contained in the modification agreement of 1908, namely, the total removal on June 24, 1925, is not enforced by the State, some other consideration must accrue to the State in lieu of their removal.[21]

Professor Ayer, when he came to the question, was back in the architect-and-engineer field, but he clearly felt that violations had occurred. Retracing the history of the Arena, and citing section 7 of the lease concerning defaults, he wrote:

As the Act of the legislature provided that there could be no modification of the then existing lease, and as the lease with the modification existing at the time provided only for the removal of the Arena Building if classed as a temporary building, some question might be raised as to whether the building could be remodeled into a permanent building. If in fact it does conform to the requirements for a permanent building it would probably be contended that the change was ameliorating waste only. This however would not dispense with the necessity of accounting for the property used in remodeling. . . .

But the much more serious question arises, that the building did not satisfy the requirements of a permanent building on June 25, 1925, and that the building still does not satisfy these requirements. Following the notice received from the Board of Regents, the Metropolitan Building Company hastily constructed what may be questionably called another story on Seneca Street. At this time it also attempted to reinforce the columns for the purpose of carrying a six-story structure. It is doubtful whether the added story really is a story; it is further doubtful whether the columns as reinforced will carry any additional weight; and, it is questioned whether the walls will carry the additional story. This, however, represents a problem for the engineer and architect.

But there was, in any case, Ayer felt, an overriding meaning to the default clause prescribing that improvements were to be "strictly in accordance" with the lease terms. "One of the main restrictions in the lease," Ayer concluded, "is the restriction as to the character of the buildings to be constructed, and it is not altogether free from doubt that the Building Company in this violation, along with its many other violations, has not subjected itself to a termination of the lease under this clause, which seems to be explicit enough to cover same."[22]

Second, what of the Metropolitan Building Company's use of the $52,546.49 awarded after the Union Street condemnation? The matter was ancient history, for the actions had taken place a decade and a half before. Yet Dodge, Powell, and Ayer were in substantial agreement. The company had been wrong: it should have paid the assessment from its own funds, and some shares of the award represented claims still unpaid to the university and the state. Dodge stated the case. He found, quite simply (but in an exceedingly detailed description of events), that four warrants totaling $49,857.57, with interest of $2,698.62, had been drawn by January 10, 1911, from the City of Seattle Condemnation Fund and made payable to the State of Washington, the board of regents, the Metropolitan company, and the Washington Trust and Savings Bank. The awards, Dodge pointed out, were for taking of real property in the widening of Union Street and to cover the costs of "readjusting or moving" adjoining buildings. The real property did not belong to the Metropolitan Building Company, however, and the jury in the condemnation hearing had held that the "remainder of said tract is not damaged," for no building was readjusted or moved. For some reason, nevertheless, the awards had been paid to the Metropolitan Building Company—for the loss of land it did not own and for moving costs not incurred—and the company had used the funds to pay assessments for improvements, such assessments being the company's clear obligation under its lease. The case was not a simple one, for while most of the award was paid on December 9, 1910, the balance on one warrant was withheld for a time "for lack of funds." On the central issue, the university's right to its share of the award, Powell agreed with Dodge, and so too, later, did Ayer. "It therefore appears," Ayer wrote, "that the substantial part of this award with interest should be accounted for and paid to the University."[23]

Third, how about the widening of University Street, with or without the regents' permission? No other problem was quite as important as this one, for the widening of a street affected permanently the plan of the tract, the placement of buildings, the utilization of useful space, and the rights or obligations of the city with regard to the use and maintenance of public thoroughfares.

Powell, necessarily basing his judgment on the more recent history, saw

The Metropolitan Bulletin

THE METROPOLITAN   BUILDING COMPANY

| VOL. XI | SEATTLE, WASHINGTON | MAY, 1929 | NUMBER 6. |

Metropolitan Bulletin logotype, with the face of the American Indian, which had identified major Metropolitan buildings since 1908, still a company symbol in the late 1920s

the question in two parts, "(a) whether the Board of Regents consented to this widening, and (b) if so, whether they had the power to do so." He felt that, with the construction of the Olympic and the Stuart Annex, the board had consented to the widening of an entire block that had been widened only by half when the Metropolitan Theatre and the Stuart Building were erected. He felt it enough, too, that the consent "was given long before the Act of 1923, depriving the Regents of the power to modify the lease." In Powell's eyes, the widening was, by 1925, a fact of life.[24]

Not to Dodge. Dodge traced the whole development of University Place from the original sublease to Klaw and Erlanger, which clearly promised a widened court in front of the Metropolitan Theatre, through the regents' sketchy and casual "approval" of the idea, to the ultimate construction of the Stuart Building and its annex on a line fifteen feet back from the line of University Street "as produced." Such setbacks on University Street were not possible under the terms of the lease, Dodge said, and the regents' approvals had been by assent rather than explicit. Dodge noted that the original Whitson Building, which preceded the Stuart Annex, had been built on the street line, as had the Metropolitan Auto Park, east of the theater, before the Fifth Avenue wing of the hotel took its place. Thus there had been for a time a widening of University Street only halfway up the block from Fourth Avenue, a widening that was extended to Fifth Avenue with only the inferred approval of the regents when the Stuart Annex and the hotel were erected on the fifteen-foot setbacks. The widening to create University Place was not a dedication of the ground to street purposes. Douglas's public notice had taken care of that. But the ground was not dedicated to buildings, either, as the lease required. In Dodge's view the regents not only had not approved the widening, but had no power to do so. Of this he said: "And had the Board given consent to such widening and vacation of 7,410 square feet of ground which is not graded and improved, and bare of buildings, with no reversionary building rights accruing to the University in 1954, such consent would have been beyond the power of the Board of Regents to give, as being specifically prohibited by the "University Acts" of 1891 and 1893, according to the Supreme Court's interpretation."[25]

Dodge was resting his argument, finally, on the early laws which, although drafted in anticipation of the sale of the tract, had said that the regents might lease "unsold portions" that had been subdivided "into lots and blocks conforming to said city adjoining." When Professor Ayer looked at the case, he doubted that the regents of 1914 had possessed the power to approve the setback of the Stuart Building—the only setback they ever specifically approved. But he based his case on the lease itself and he pointed to the adverse effects of the setbacks on the university's future use of its property:

> Whether or not the University is subject to the prescriptive use acquired in the use of public highways, every step should be taken to protect the University and its right to build on these strips which will in the course of time represent an enormous value. . . .
>
> These violations may seriously injure the rights of the lessor in the future enjoyment of the property. They clearly violate the lease and the spirit of the lease in that the lease evidently contemplated not only a reversionary interest in all buildings constructed but further that the construction of all buildings would be on the street line. A comparison with the allowance made in condemnation proceedings for the small strip on one side of Union Street suggests the possibility of the values involved.[26]

The fourth, fifth, and sixth "violations"—the tunnel under University Street, the leasing of the gasoline station, and the selling off of the temporary buildings—what of these? Powell had addressed the tunnel issue only incidentally, finding the tunnel "does not damage or render unsafe either the street or any of the buildings." Dodge sailed into this matter with customary references and documentations, however, declaring that the forfeiture clause of the lease forbade improvements "whether buildings, street improvements, sewers, water mains, *or of any nature* [Dodge's emphasis] except strictly in accordance with the terms" of the lease, which had not anticipated an underground traffic corridor. He said that while the plans for the Stimson Building had shown the tunnel under University Street, no permission to build it was asked of or given by the regents, who were by that time under the 1923 legislative stricture in any case. He thought that the state might indeed become involved in actions resulting from personal injuries sustained in use of the tunnel. With this general thesis Ayer subsequently agreed—although with more brevity and less heat—and he agreed with Dodge, too, about the Metropolitan company's obligation to account for the $2,500 annual income for the lease of the gasoline station (and income from a taxi stand placed on University Street), and for the $75,000 and other sums received for the sale of temporary buildings.[27]

Finally, what of the seventh and eighth questions—what of the matters of insurance and idemnity bonds? Powell had told the regents that in neither instance had the company been complying with terms of the lease and that it should be required to do so. On the bonds, Dodge and Ayer were in agreement, although Ayer termed the possible injuries "nominal," adding tersely that "it is not customary to so regard the direct violations of the express provisions of a lease." By the time Ayer wrote, the company had been required to post bonds of $50,000 on the new wing of the Olympic Hotel, $75,000 on the Stimson Building, $15,000 on the Arena, and $150,000 on the Skinner. But with regard to the insurance, it was Dodge who made a thorough analysis, finding that there were four forms of insurance in effect (on the Metropolitan company's buildings, on the Metropolitan Theatre, on the Olympic Hotel, and on the Skinner Building) and that the Metropolitan company's policies were so drawn—to the company *"and/or* the State of Washington," loss payable to the company *"and* the Board of Regents of the University, *as their respective interests may appear"*—that the state and the university virtually were at the mercy of the company with regard to claims or estimates of value on the buildings. Furthermore, Dodge said, the policies were not in the possession of the university. All fire insurance policies were on deposit with the Dexter Horton National Bank, successor to the Washington Trust Company as trustee for the Metropolitan Building Company's original $5,000,000 bond issue. The policies of the Community Hotel Corporation, the sublessee, named the corporation and/or the state of Washington as *owners* of the hotel building, the "loss, if any, payable to the Community Hotel Corporation of Seattle *and* the Board of Regents. . . . *Mortgagees,* as their respective interest may appear." Two signatures were thus required to validate any drafts for losses under the policies.[28]

There was more from Dodge, much more, on this and the other topics. The regents had wanted information on possible violations of the lease, and Dodge gave them information, and views, in plenty. It was Dodge who discovered that because of the original six-foot difference between the Denny plat and the description of the land as donated, the tract actually was larger than had been thought, the boundary line a foot farther north along Union Street even after the five-foot condemnation. (The difference may have been trivial, but it was in fact some 462 square feet of tract land not earlier accounted for, or about 2,700 square feet including the land condemned for the Union Street widening.) Dodge ended his assignment for the board a somewhat unhappy man, it would seem (there was a difficulty over payment of his fees and expenses), for in a letter to the regents in the spring of 1926 he said, "I cannot hope to leave this job with any feeling of great satisfaction, nor of appreciation of work well done. I will venture to say, however, that no more complete record . . . could have been compiled, and I am confident it will be found accurate." As for his record, he was certainly right. Where Dodge found what he thought were violations by the Metropolitan Building Company, he found reasons to be critical of the regents, too—not of individuals, not even of boards as they had been constituted at various times, but of a way of doing business in which the lessor was, for reasons inherent in the Seattle milieu, less vigilant than the lessee. Dodge suggested that if the role had been reversed—if the Metropolitan Building Company had been leasing to the state and the university—few "violations" would have been permitted to occur. The Metropolitan Building Company would not have permitted the university to build an Arena Building and then convert it in questionable fashion. The company would not have allowed the university to fail to post lien bonds, or to sell off temporary buildings without accounting for them, or to sequester insurance policies on company property, or to build a tunnel under University Street without seeking some compensation for the privilege, or to lease a gasoline station where it had no right to build one. The boards of regents and the Metropolitan Building Company had been too much the products of their common environment, Dodge thought, too parallel in view, sometimes sharing the same advisers, who were not always unprejudiced. But, "searching the record of the past 19 years of Metropolitan Building Company control, not one instance can be found where the State's reversion was ever harmed, nor the lessee's estates enlarged, by an intelligent and analytical study, on the part of the Board of Regents, of any lease modifications or extension propounded by the Metropolitan Building Company."

In short, when the regents had stood fast, their position supported by "analytical study," the university's interests had been protected, at least as well as could be under a lease that had been hopelessly bad from the beginning. And the best example of that had been the regents' stand in the hotel case of 1921, when they had dared the fire of the company and of the community at large. If the regents had been of that mood and mettle throughout, Dodge said, "few, if any, of the attempts to abrogate the lease contract would have been successful." [29]

That was Dodge in 1926. Perhaps the very success of the Metropolitan Building Company opened it to criticism or suspicion. There was, naturally, a certain mistiness about the details of the company's operations—its tax situation, the huge profits it was supposed to be making—and room for suspicion, too, that questions about such matters were inspired by competitors, or, as was once hinted, by one of the company's own stockholders who "had a grouch on." But soon Governor Hartley had his turn, and Hartley inserted himself into the discussions of the Metropolitan lease by way of an attack on his opponent in the 1928 gubernatorial campaign. [30]

The Democratic candidate for governor in 1928 was A. Scott Bullitt, a native Kentuckian who, although something of a newcomer to the state of Washington, was already a rising figure in an opposition party that had become badly demoralized in the Hartley-Coolidge period. Bullitt was of distinguished lineage, distantly related to Patrick Henry on his father's side and to John Marshall on his mother's, and a political leader of much promise—young (about forty), a former athlete (swimmer, oarsman, lightweight amateur boxer, high school football coach), a graduate of Princeton and of the University of Louisville law school, and an orator and campaign speaker of considerable skill and magnetism. In Louisville he had been appointed to a six-month term as sheriff of Jefferson County to clean up an election-fraud mess. This had been followed by a term as county attorney. That Bullitt was in the West at all was simply because he had gone to Seattle in 1916 to attend the wedding of his brother and had met Dorothy Stimson, the daughter of C. D. Stimson. Within six months he had married Dorothy and taken her back to Louisville. By 1919 (Bullitt served with the adjutant general's office of the army during the war) the couple had decided to live in Seattle, where Bullitt soon became prominent in professional and Democratic party affairs and was widely perceived as a man with a future in state and possibly national politics. In 1924, Bullitt was a Washington delegate to the Democratic convention in New York. By 1926 he was his party's candidate for the U.S. Senate against the Republican Wesley L. Jones. And until about that time, as has been noted, he had been associated with the Metropolitan Building Company, first as a member of the "junior board" and then as a trustee of the Fifth Avenue Building Company. Bullitt thus could be accused of having—or having had—ties that were too tempting to be ignored by a politician of Hartley's stamp.[31]

It may be doubted whether, in that final season of prosperity before the Great Depression, the issue of the Metropolitan company's prosperity, if such it was, would have affected the outcome of an election. But on the eve of the balloting Hartley published over his name a long campaign statement, "Scott Bullitt and the Metropolitan Building Company," in which he attacked Bullitt on the very question he said Bullitt had been raising— that the governor of the state had no control over the Metropolitan lease— and moved then into his own recitation of the history of the company's development under what he considered inexcusable tax advantages. Hartley made himself the champion of the outsider, referring in the beginning to Bullitt as "the son-in-law of C. D. Stimson, and . . . at one time himself interested in the company." Hartley disclaimed any feeling of ill will toward the developers of the university tract. He spoke only, he said, on behalf of the university and the taxpayers of the state. It is enough to give the flavor:

The Metropolitan Building Company is an issue in this campaign. The property belongs to the University of the State of Washington, and the people of this state are entitled to know all the facts concerning the lease.

At the outset it should be made plain that it is not my purpose to attack the individuals who have their money invested in the Metropolitan Building Company. I recognize as well as anyone the important part this company has had in the upbuilding of Seattle. I realize this was a pioneer project and its promoters, for that reason, were entitled to more than ordinary profits. The returns, however, have been, and will continue to be during the remaining years of the life of the lease, way far in excess of any reasonable amount.

The present Metropolitan lease is a transaction of the past. It is to the future we must look to protect the interests of the state university and the taxpayers of the commonwealth of Washington.

Look to the future and to Roland Hartley, that is, for Hartley already had forestalled a creeping conspiracy:

For more than ten years there has been a movement under way to extend the life of the Metropolitan lease an additional twenty-five or fifty years. The promoters of

MAY, 1928

By the late 1920s the designs and sketches of Eustace P. Ziegler, a prolific and highly-regarded Seattle artist, were appearing on Metropolitan publications, as on this *Metropolitan Bulletin* cover of 1928

that scheme were dominant factors in the political control of the state university under the leadership of Dr. Henry Suzzallo as president of the institution, as well as guiding spirits in the recall movement when, as governor, I undertook the reorganization of the university.

The activities to secure a renewal of the lease became so pronounced that the friends of the university brought the question before the state legislature in the session of 1923. At that time a law was passed prohibiting any modification or extension of the lease, except by the act of the legislature. The sponsors of the measure were advised that it was clearly unconstitutional, and it was enacted with that understanding, on the theory that it would have a deterrent effect on any board of university regents in any efforts to change or extend the life of the lease.

Regardless of how this act might be construed by the courts, it must be perfectly clear to anyone that the university regents constantly pass upon questions involving interpretations of the terms of the lease. The regents are appointed by the governor, as are members of the State Tax Commission, which has the power to increase or decrease the leasehold taxes.

It should also be remembered that the governor has the power of approval or veto of acts of the legislature.[32]

Hartley went on from there. He made his own calculations of the savings to the Metropolitan company under the fixed-rate lease of 1907 (about $3,000,000 "allowing nothing for increases in the valuation of the land between the years 1926 and 1954"), and the savings in taxes the company was enjoying ("the Metropolitan Building Company is receiving the use of the university land for $10,355,186 less than it would produce in taxes on the basis of its present valuation"). The central point of all this was clear enough. A governor of the state did indeed, in Hartley's opinion, have a "control" over the lease—by appointment, by veto—and only a governor untainted by connections with the Metropolitan Building Company could be trusted to exercise it wisely.

The year 1928 was a Republican year. Herbert Hoover won the presidency and, in the state of Washington, Roland Hartley defeated Scott Bullitt even though Bullitt ran 60,000 votes ahead of the Democratic ticket. But it was in 1929, after all the years of studies and reports, that there came a single, anticlimactic effort by the board of regents to gather a shell from a strewn beach, as it were. As it happened, the shell was picked up and thrown back by a lawyer who not more than five years before had been a regent himself.

The regents had decided to try to collect from the Metropolitan Building Company a part of the sum—Dodge had put it at $52,546.49—awarded in the condemnation proceedings upon the widening of Union Street years before. On April 29, 1929, A. H. B. Jordan, now president of the board for the third year, addressed an official letter to J. F. Douglas which put the request thus:

An award was made for the taking of the part of the property of the University in eminent domain proceedings brought by the City of Seattle in 1908 for the widening of Union Street.

The amount of this award was $52,540.80, for which the City on December 9th, 1910, issued its warrants payable to the State of Washington, University of Washington Board of Regents, Metropolitan Building Co., and Washington Trust Co. No part of this amount was received by the Board of Regent or by the state. . . .

It is the opinion of the Board of Regents, under the terms of the lease, that the lessee was bound to pay the whole of the assessment . . . and that amount of compensation awarded by the judgment should have been equitably apportioned . . . and the amount belonging to the State determined and paid into the State Treasury. . . . There is no reason why the amount of the compensation should not now be apportioned and the lessee required to pay the amount which shall be found to belong to the State, and I have been authorized by the Board of Regents to request that this be done.[33]

An ultimatum? Well, in a way. But no question was raised about the Arena's status, or about the widening of University Street, or the possible residual values of the temporary buildings that had been demolished and removed. This was just a request for an "equitably apportioned" part of that old judgment of 1910. Douglas referred the letter to George Donworth, of the law firm of Donworth, Todd and Holman, who wrote Jordan directly to say that he would be in the East for some weeks, but he hoped it would be agreeable "to you and to the Board of Regents to let the matter stand until my return." He said that at that time he would "be glad to take up the matter with you personally, or with such representatives of the university as you may wish."[34]

If it was true, as some thought, that the regents' persistent interest in possible lease violations flowed from a hope that the lease might be broken, it may be wondered why their approach was on grounds that seem so old and so fragile. The monetary gain would appear scarcely worth the effort. None of the more substantial issues would be solved. Whatever their thoughts, the regents found how weak was the base on which they rested their request.

The George Donworth who was now to act for the Metropolitan was the George Donworth who had been a regent until June 16, 1924. Not even when he returned from the East, apparently, did he turn immediately to the regents' letter, for it was in November 1929 that J. V. Paterson sent Donworth another note saying that the board had instructed him "to pursue this matter." When Donworth replied on November 22, it was with an eight-page letter in which he simply buried the regents' request, beginning with a reminder that the "suggestion of the existence of a possible claim . . . seems to have arisen from a report made by one Dodge something over four years ago." Donworth examined the whole record in detail—the language of the lease with regard to improvements, the nature of the assessment, the record of payment by warrants, the endorsements of the attorney general in 1910. His conclusion was that the judgment had only covered costs incurred by the Metropolitan. The company had in fact been forced to move the footing of the White Building, which was under construction in 1908. The company had lost for forty-four years the rental on the condemned land. It was true that the university had lost its reversionary interest in the Union Street strip, but the company had a claim for the reduced rentals, a claim it had not pressed.

"Surely," Donworth wrote, "a reasonable, business-like, and honorable action all around." And, in any case, it was ancient history:

If this solemn and businesslike adjustment made nineteen years ago through the Board of Regents and the Attorney-General is now to be opened up and an attempt made to set it aside, I would like respectfully to propound the following question: "Do the present Board of Regents and the present Attorney-General have any greater authority than that possessed by their predecessors in 1910, and of what use is it to make a settlement and adjustment with these responsible public officials if the settlement and adjustment go for naught?"

I am satisfied that if you [Paterson] and other members of the Board will consider this matter in the light of the records you will come to the conclusion there is no just or lawful reason for opening any phase of the transaction.[35]

Paterson wrote Donworth the next day "to thank you for your courtesy and for the fullness of your letter." On that note, and on that insignificant issue, the question of the Metropolitan's possible lease violations expired. That November, in any case, the world was about to be overturned again.

The Depression that settled upon the world after 1929—the business failures, unemployment, political unrest, searches for economic restoratives, readjustments in philosophies, savage humors—came to Seattle and to the state of Washington with differences only in kind.

With banks tottering and credit vanishing, there was less talk of business profit. Whatever thoughts there had been about the profits of such institutions as the Metropolitan Building Company, or about the company's alleged lease violations, were lost amid the larger apprehensions. The University of Washington was in trouble too, state finances being what they were, and the annual rentals from the university tract—currently $80,000, soon to be $100,000—seemed more important than ever to an institution that needed every dollar it could get.

An epoch was ended in 1929, but two of the men whose careers had represented Seattle in its happiest, most booming times did not live to see it. On May 21, James A. Moore died—of overwork, it was said—in the Palace Hotel in San Francisco. Someone found among Moore's papers a note that he had saved: "Make no little plans; they have no magic to stir men's blood. Make big plans; aim high and hope and work." On August 29, C. D. Stimson died at his home in the Highlands. Moore's rule had been Stimson's too. Neither had made little plans, neither Moore, the developer whose name had entered university history by way of a lease, nor Stimson, the lumberman, community leader, and philanthropist who had headed the lessee company. Although their careers had been vastly different, Moore and Stimson had each contributed to the establishment of what A. S. Kerry had called the spirit of the "old Seattle crowd." They did not live to see the tests that were coming.[36]

Prospects had seemed bright for the Metropolitan in 1929. On June 28— Stimson had lived long enough to participate—leaders of the Metropolitan had formed what was called the Metropolitan Company, which would provide a centralized management for the Metropolitan Building Company and related activities, existing or to be acquired. The development of the university tract now completed after twenty-two years, including construction of the new Fifth Avenue wing of the Olympic, the directors of the Metropolitan thought it time to form a company "that would unite through stock holdings a number of companies, the stock of which is largely held by the same people." The articles of incorporation were filed September 29, 1929, in Reno, Nevada, and the people were indeed the same. Stimson had been elected president, but upon his death had been succeeded by J. F. Douglas. O. D. Fisher and D. E. Skinner were vice-presidents, Walter Douglas secretary, and Sarah A. Hilmes assisted Fisher as treasurer. Directors, apart from the officers, included C. H. Cobb, William Edris, A. S. Eldridge, R. D. Emerson, and D. E. Frederick. On the eve of the Depression, the Metropolitan group was looking toward a consolidation of management for the Metropolitan Building Company, the Metropolitan Investment Company, the Fifth Avenue Building Company, and certain subcompanies (the Metropolitan Service Corporation was one), and it soon acquired the Brooklyn Building, in the University District, and had other plans in mind. On December 10, 1929, the directors even approved an employees' stock ownership plan, probably another instance of the J. F. Douglas touch. But the future did not prove so subject to management.[37]

Hard times changed the political climate, and Scott Bullitt in 1930 was one who was looked to. Bullitt's defeat by Hartley had only further seasoned him

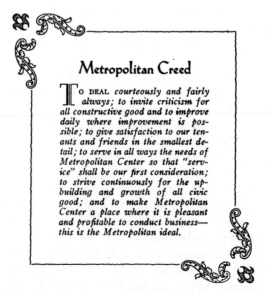

Metropolitan Creed

To DEAL *courteously and fairly always; to invite criticism for all constructive good and to improve daily where improvement is possible; to give satisfaction to our tenants and friends in the smallest detail; to serve in all ways the needs of Metropolitan Center so that "service" shall be our first consideration; to strive continuously for the upbuilding and growth of all civic good; and to make Metropolitan Center a place where it is pleasant and profitable to conduct business—this is the Metropolitan ideal.*

Emphasis on "White Building service"—the J. F. Douglas theme—which characterized Metropolitan management from the beginning, as expressed in this 1929 statement of the company's "creed" for political leadership on some larger scale, and soon he was a member of the Democratic National Committee, busy in the party's councils on the national level. Yet by 1932 Bullitt was gone. In the spring—just as he was expected to play a role in the coming campaign but before the role had been decided—he died suddenly after a trip to Washington, D.C., where he had been stricken by what seemed to be influenza but which was, in fact, cancer. His loss was widely mourned, in the state of Washington and elsewhere. In November 1932, in the election that made Franklin Roosevelt president in a landslide, Washington chose as its new governor a wealthy rancher and milling company owner, Clarence D. Martin. What this meant—particularly to the university—became apparent almost at once.

Martin's home ground was the little Eastern Washington community of Cheney, where he had been a student at what then was Cheney Normal School before getting his degree at the University of Washington. Martin had gone into the milling business with his father, expanding later into cattle-raising and ranching, meanwhile serving ten years as a member of Cheney's city council, three times as Cheney's mayor, and two years as chairman of the state's Democratic committee. As a Democrat, Martin meant to sweep out the vestiges of the Hartley administration. But Martin had been trained as a teacher, and it certainly seems a measure of him that he moved so soon to try to shore up the struggling university. Again the familiar scenario was followed—the appointment of a new board of regents, the installation of a new university president. But in years that saw so many changes everywhere, these changes came with an air of hope. It was the university, its finances inadequate, its campus in disarray, its programs static, that now needed help. There was no time to worry about the fortunes of the Metropolitan Building Company.[38]

Martin had been governor less than a month when he announced his appointment of seven regents. The names were revealed on January 25, 1933, and the news reports contained instant speculation that the sweeping change in the board would mean the end of the presidency of Lyle Spencer. If this was unfair, it was a pattern with which the university was familiar. Spencer had served steadily and faithfully, from that earlier time of Suzzallo's dismissal into the new time of the university's financial agony. Faculty salaries had already been cut 10 percent and might be cut more. Even a Spencer reorganization plan, combining schools and colleges into four units, had caused unhappiness on the campus and among alumni. The new board would have to decide about such things.[39]

Spencer did, in fact, resign immediately. But who now were the regents? Two of them were—was it surprising?—Winlock Miller and Werner Rupp, the veterans of the pre-Hartley years, back now to begin new terms. With them were five men of wide repute: Lewis B. Schwellenbach and Philip D. Macbride, Seattle lawyers; Edward P. Ryan, a Spokane investment banker; Robert L. Montgomery, a Puyallup newspaper publisher; and Alfred Shemanski, a Seattle businessman. When Martin had selected his regents he put a charge before them. There must be a "new era" at the university.* There would be no interference from the governor's office, but: "You have the job of prescribing for the intellect of the state. In selecting you I wanted to select men who would carry out your responsibilities without interference from this office. This institution must be restored to its former standing. I'm inclined to believe it has been drifting for some time, and it's up to you to build it up. I know you can do it. I feel we are starting a new era. And I have full faith in your abilities to make it so." Four of the regents were from Seattle, but only four (Miller, Schwellenbach, Ryan, and Montgomery) were Democrats. When the board chose its officers, Schwellenbach became president, Ryan vice-president, and Herbert T. Condon, again, the board's secretary.[40]

Martin had installed what came to be recognized as a blue-ribbon board. Most of the members would serve for the next decade, some longer. Miller and Rupp, who had been there before, may have formed a core of experience in university affairs, but their new associates in the "new era" brought to the board an interesting diversity.

Schwellenbach had been Martin's opponent in the party primaries of 1932. He was not yet forty when he went to the board in 1933, and he would serve only briefly—little more than eighteen months—because by the following year he had been elected to the U.S. Senate and was embarked on a career that took him from the Senate to a federal judgeship to a cabinet position, as President Truman's secretary of labor. But Schwellenbach knew the University of Washington. He had waited on restaurant tables to earn his way to a law degree there before serving overseas in World War I.[41]

Ryan, whose career as a regent would cover precisely the 1933–43 decade, was something more than a mortgage and investment man. A native of East Mauch Chunk, Pennsylvania, he had won his law degree at New York University in 1909, had practiced five years in Brooklyn, had managed a mine at Wallace, Idaho, and had then moved to Spokane to establish his investment firm, to get into other banking and mining enterprises, and to become a prominent Catholic layman and a leader in practically every community and charitable activity in the Spokane region.[42]

Shemanski had come to America in 1897 as a twenty-three-year-old immigrant. In 1900 he had established in Seattle a small store, the Eastern Outfitting Company. By 1933 he was both a successful businessman—Eastern Outfitting had become a West Coast chain of stores—and a leader of the Jewish community whose philanthropies extended beyond his Congregation

---

* One result of Martin's "new era," a climax of an episode now little remembered, was the return to the campus of the alumni association office, a fugitive since early in the Hartley regime. In 1925, when Hartley had demanded an audit of university records, a team of twenty or so alumni association men went to the campus one evening and hauled away in boxes the alumni records, an act that not only astonished the regents but was described in somewhat dramatic detail in their minutes. For as long as Roland Hartley was governor the association maintained off-campus quarters in the University Bank Building nearby, but in 1933 the records were hauled back again, at the invitation of the new regents, in what was now regarded as a friendlier atmosphere.

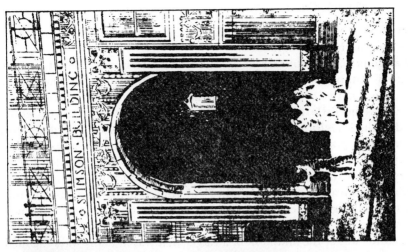

Eustace Ziegler etchings of the Cobb, Henry, and Stimson Building entrances, commissioned by the Metropolitan Building Company for its Christmas cards

Temple de Hirsch to touch Seattle's hospitals, museums, and general cultural and charitable programs.[43]

Montgomery, as publisher of a Democratic newspaper, almost certainly balanced Rupp, the Republican publisher. Although Montgomery, like Ryan, was a native of Pennsylvania, he had graduated from Whitworth College when the little institution was in Tacoma, and soon thereafter had founded the *Puyallup Valley Tribune*, his editorials widely quoted. Montgomery was a practicing Democrat—three years as mayor of Sumner and ten as Puyallup's postmaster—but he was, above all, a colorful character, big and hearty, forever dressed in a "tail-coat" with a rose in the lapel, author of a number of privately printed "studies" of American political and military leaders, a willing public speaker with an uninhibited style, and the kind of man who would be called the "Sage" of Puyallup.[44]

Macbride was at the midpoint of a career that was in many ways the model of the professional-business-public service ideal. Born in Iowa City, he was the son of a former president of the University of Iowa and a graduate of that university. Macbride was admitted to the bar in Montana in 1908 and then moved on to Seattle. When J. F. Douglas was launching the Metropolitan Building Company, Macbride was becoming an organizer of the Kitsap County Transportation Company, which established the first ferry service between Seattle and Bainbridge Island across the Sound. He was also an organizer of the Puget Sound Freight Lines, a vice-president and director for many years, and by 1933 was associated with a variety of business enterprises.[45]

The new board of regents was a strong board called to action in a difficult time. Among its first tasks, as had been the case with certain other boards, was to select a new president of the university.

The nature of the decade then beginning—the decade that extended from 1933, when the Depression was at its depth, to 1943, when the fighting was approaching its bitterest in the new world war—needs to be recalled here only to provide perspective. While Governor Martin was appointing his new board of regents, President-elect Roosevelt was putting together his New Deal, and almost at that moment, in Germany, a bristling little nonentity, Adolph Hitler, was becoming chancellor—and suddenly an entity. And if the political lines then only starting to emerge were lines that eventually would converge in war, there was as yet small notice because there was so much immediate hardship. The years wore on in an unremitting search for "recovery"—a search ended only when the lines converged and war came. All this was reflected in what went on in the state of Washington and in Seattle, where the university's new era was not the dynamic thing so widely anticipated.

Throughout that time, from 1933 until the nation was at war again, the Metropolitan lease entered the regents' considerations only in relation to efforts to scrape up funds to sustain the university. Such occasions were few, although the new regents had their own tilts with reality.

On January 27, 1933, even as the board was being organized and President Spencer was resigning, the regents authorized the executive committee to get a legal opinion "on the usage to which the rentals of the Metropolitan Tract could be put under the deed of gift." A week later the executive committee reported. Its own examination of the deeds, the committee said, had made it "apparent that the rentals . . . could not be used for any other than building operations." The committee thought it "not worth while seeking legal opinion." Miller had another idea, but it went nowhere. Miller moved that the board ask the legislature "for permission to use for building purposes [in] 1933–35 those funds derived from Metropolitan Tract and student fees" —all nontax funds. The suggestion was a strange one, however, because such funds had been put into the university building fund since 1915. And it must simply have been a reflection of the intensity of the Depression that another strange proposal was entertained briefly the following year—in October 1934 —about the time Schwellenbach resigned to make his run for the U.S. Senate. Macbride reported that a Seattle bank had asked an agreement whereby the bank would be notified "if any default occurred in the terms of the Metro- politan Building Company's lease, this to be the basis of a proposed loan by the bank to the Metropolitan Building Company on leasehold." Macbride said the executive committee thought any such agreement would be in viola- tion of the 1923 legislation prohibiting lease modifications without legislative approval. Nothing more was heard of that.[46]

As far as the tract was concerned, in the 1930s, it was as if the university and its lessee were simply waiting out the Depression years. There were changes—the university got its new president, the Metropolitan Building Company new management—but the relationship was frozen into a lease pattern that had been established decades before.

The new university president was Lee Paul Sieg, a University of Pittsburgh physicist—a tall, craggy, kindly man—whose undergraduate years had been spent at Iowa when Macbride's father was president there. The search had taken more than a year—the dean of the College of Forestry, Hugo Winken- werder, had taken over from Spencer as acting president—for the university still bore the stigma of its "politicization" and its financial situation was felt to be unpromising. Schwellenbach, Macbride, and Miller were the leaders in the search, and they had turned to Suzzallo, who by then was president of the Carnegie Foundation for the Advancement of Teaching (and whose inter- est in the university was undiminished), and to Nicholas Murray Butler, of Columbia University, who had suggested Suzzallo to Gaches so long ago. Suzzallo, tragically, did not live to see the choice made, and it was Butler who proposed Sieg's name.* Sieg was at first not eager for the Washington posi-

---

* Suzzallo died, by sheer chance, in Seattle, the city in which he had reached the peak of a dynamic career. In the summer of 1933 he talked to Schwellenbach and Miller in San Francisco, then sailed north to visit friends in the Northwest before returning to New York. In Seattle, an illness that had bothered him for some time suddenly became acute and he died on September 25, 1933. See Charles M. Gates, *The First Century at the University of Washington, 1861–1961* (Seattle: University of Washington Press, 1961), p. 181.

tion, for at Pittsburgh he was building a new graduate program in engineering while he held a triple deanship—of the College, of the School of Education, and of the Graduate School. In the end it was Macbride who persuaded Sieg to visit Seattle, and on June 1, 1934, Sieg accepted the university presidency. The new era was at least a step closer.[47]

There had been, soon after, a significant change in the board of regents. Schwellenbach, resigning in October 1934, was succeeded by Thomas Balmer. This appointment brought to the stage a man who would become a major influence in the history of the Metropolitan tract. Balmer was the forty-six-year-old general counsel for the Great Northern Railway Company, soon to succeed L. C. Gilman as resident vice-president of the railroad. A native of Danville, Illinois—he had come to Seattle with his family in 1900—Balmer had begun his career as a stenographer and law clerk with the Great Northern in 1907, working meanwhile to get a law degree at the University of Washington. Admitted to the bar in 1909, at the age of twenty-one, Balmer had then served the Great Northern until 1926 as assistant attorney in Spokane, as attorney in Idaho, Oregon, and Western Washington, and as assistant general counsel in St. Paul, Minnesota. He had also won a master of laws degree from Gonzaga University along the way, and had been a part-time teacher there in his Spokane years. Balmer was a careful, thoughtful man, judicial in mien but with a gentle sense of humor, and widely known and involved in business affairs. Somewhat in the Winlock Miller manner, he was prepared to make his membership on the board of regents a large part of his life.[48]

But in the middle 1930s even a board with such members as Macbride, Miller, Rupp, and the others, and now Balmer, could do little more than keep the university going—and as for the Metropolitan lease, let it run. The university's era was no paler than the times. But faculty salaries were down, and so were enrollments, and students went to classes in buildings that were sadly in need of maintenance and repair. In Seattle itself—the population about 370,000—certain unpredictable successes were being achieved anyway. The Boeing Airplane Company, still designing new types of pursuit aircraft for the Army Air Corps, was also developing mail planes and civilian transports including a four-engine flying boat, the Clipper, and accumulating experience against the time it would build the B-17 bomber of World War II. In 1934 William E. Boeing was awarded the Guggenheim medal for his contributions to air transportation. In another realm, Dave Beck, an organizer for the International Brotherhood of Teamsters, was making himself a leader of labor in the decade that produced the Wagner Act, which revolutionized employer-labor relations. But, simply because half a century had passed since the city—and the university—had felt the surges of early growth, many of the men who had been the movers and shakers of the boom years, some of the members of the "old Seattle crowd," were leaving the scene. Waterhouse and Powell had died in 1930, neither much past sixty. George H. King died in 1931, A. P. Sawyer in 1933, and Manson Backus in 1935. Oscar

Fechter also died in 1935, in Yakima, his passing apparently unnoted by a university he had served as regent for fourteen years.

The death that shook the university and affected the state, however, was Edmond Meany's. Meany was already such a legend that it was hard to believe him only seventy-two. He had continued to teach, and he died of a stroke on an April morning of 1935 as he was preparing, seemingly in perfect health, to meet a class in Canadian history. Whatever Meany's stature as a historian, he had devoted himself to the history of the state and of the Northwest and he had helped make some of it. To generations of students he had represented the kind of excitement in learning that a university was supposed to inspire, principally because he never lost his own sense of excitement.

In a singularly personal way, Meany had been the custodian of the university's pride in its origins. When he died, all history classes were dismissed until after the funeral and other classes did not meet that day.[49]

The Metropolitan Building Company must have shared, in its way, the economic troubles of Seattle in the 1930s. The details are not known. There never was, and it seems inconceivable that there should have been, a delay in the rental payments to the university, which had risen to $100,000 a year in 1932. The company may have lost tenants because of business failures or consolidations. Yet it would seem to have had a margin of security in the fact that the company had always sought, in line with J. F. Douglas's earliest concept of the tract, to bring to its buildings tenants of the "best quality." Tenants of that caliber would tend to have a high incidence of survival.

Yet changes came to the company and to the tract. For one thing, Douglas, who had brought the Metropolitan Center to its current stage of development, was being wooed away after almost thirty years, and the active management of the company was passing to other hands. For another, the Olympic, completed in 1929, was in trouble.

Douglas's departure was far from abrupt. As early as 1927, E. A. Stuart, his eyesight and hearing failing, had called on Douglas to lend his talents to Carnation, on a part-time basis, when the company was expanding its operations into Wisconsin. Douglas must have enjoyed this, feeling that his creation of the Metropolitan Center was substantially complete. Douglas was chairman of Carnation's finance committee, then vice-president. When, late in 1930, Carnation moved its main office to Milwaukee, Douglas moved there, taking the Nevas, wife and daughter, with him. Even then he continued as a director of the Metropolitan while his brother Walter remained with the center as vice-president and manager. The other vice-presidents were O. D. Fisher, who was also treasurer, and Stuart, Cobb, Langdon C. Henry, and James H. Douglas, the Douglas brother who had been practicing law in New York since 1917. The Metropolitan Company, in the period of the consolidated management, was trying its diversification. It was managing the 1411 Fourth Avenue Building, which had been built by C. D. Stimson across Union Street from the Douglas, and several other buildings including the Crary on Union Street, the Walker on Second Avenue, the Emily Walker, the Empress, and, in the University District, the Brooklyn.[50]

Douglas did not really leave the Metropolitan. He was too much the pillar of it. When he went to Milwaukee he left the Metropolitan's offices and a new home in the Highlands—a home he would not occupy again until 1940. And when Carnation moved its world headquarters to Los Angeles, Douglas moved there. He was in Seattle now and then, vice-president of the Metropolitan and in touch with Walter's management of it. But if in Seattle he was not the presence he had been, he was a large presence elsewhere. While he was in Milwaukee he was familiar with business leaders and belonged to all the clubs—the Country, the University, the Wisconsin, in Chicago the Union League, and in New York, the Bankers. In Los Angeles, later, J. F. was similarly in touch with things, organizing business affairs, serving as trustee of the Los Angeles Arboretum. And he was handling, for Carnation, financial operations that were, in fact, worldwide.[51]

D. E. Skinner was president of the Metropolitan in 1932–33, and upon his death in 1933 he was succeeded by Langdon Henry. Walter Douglas's management of the company continued only until 1936, for in May of that year he died suddenly of a heart attack while he was in the offices of a Cobb Building physician. Walter was only forty-six, and he had spent much of his life in J. F. Douglas's shadow. But not altogether. He had attended the University of Washington and the University of Michigan, but he had not taken the law-degree trail as his brothers had, and he had created a life outside the Metropolitan company. He had helped organize Seattle's Arboretum Foundation and was its president, and he was a director of two private schools, the Lakeside School for Boys and the Helen Bush School for Girls. He was identified with many community activities, including, of course, those of the Chamber of Commerce. He was also president of the University Theatere Company, which now operated the Metropolitan Theatre, and he was vice-president of The Olympic, Incorporated, organized to take over the hotel. The theater and hotel companies had come into being to facilitate reorganizations during the depths of the Depression. The Olympic, in particular, was a major problem.[52]

Hotels all across the country were casualties of the Depression. Hundreds of new hotels, in cities large and small, financed and built in the optimism of the 1920s (many, like Seattle's, the products of community campaigns), now came upon unexpected lean years. Tourism, travel, vacationing, conventioneering, and restauranteering faded. Hotels were among the first of the community institutions to feel the pinch. New hotels could not be demolished, and they were, in any case, necessary. Most were refinanced. But investors suffered. Thus it was with the Olympic, so recently completed. The new company, The Olympic, Incorporated, which was incorporated in Delaware at the end of 1933, became the successor to the Community Hotel Corporation and the Olympic Hotel Company, which had been organized only slightly more than a decade before. The Olympic, Incorporated, was authorized to issue two classes of no-par common stock—24,000 shares of class A and 12,000 shares of class B. With the Community and Olympic Hotel companies entering receivership, the first and second mortgage bonds of the Community corporation and the preferred and common stock of the Olympic company were selling for about 2.5 cents on the dollar. Under the plan of reorganization by The Olympic, Incorporated, however, an exchange was worked out. Each $100 of the Community corporation's 7 percent bonds could be exchanged for one share of class A stock in The Olympic, Incorporated, and thirty-three and one-third shares of common could get one share of The Olympic, Incorporated, class B stock. It was a painful squeeze for many investors, and for all it was dealing in futures with the future exceedingly obscure. Among the investors was the Metropolitan Building Company, lessor of the land on which the hotel stood, which held securities in the Community and Olympic Hotel companies totaling more than $731,000 and which exchanged them, in due course, for stock in The Olympic, Incorporated.[53]

The Metropolitan Theatre, an institution in Seattle for more than two decades, had its troubles too. On November 23, 1932, the University Theatre Company was organized to take over the old lease that had been made by the Metropolitan Building Company in 1911 with Charles Frohman, Marc Klaw, and A. L. Erlanger—a lease that was supposed to run to November 1, 1954. The Metropolitan Theatre Company became the University Theatre Company—with a capitalization of only one hundred shares of no-par common stock—and on February 8, 1933, the new company had acquired the lease and was in charge. All of the common stock was owned by the Metropolitan Building Company, which was lessor of the land and was receiving $5,500 in rentals and 4 percent in taxes on the fraction of the leasehold.[54]

The Metropolitan Company, that central-management holding corporation created in 1929, had vanished by 1938. In that year the assets, which included those of the Fifth Avenue Building Company, had been transferred back to the Metropolitan Building Company, which again was the prime corporate agency. An effort of the 1920s to consolidate success had proved, in the Depression, only ill-starred and confusing.[55]

And for the first time, in the late 1930s, there was a Metropolitan Building Company without a Douglas actively in charge. Walter Douglas's successor was Andrew Steers, who had been with the company since 1926. There was a Stimson as president, however, and this was C. W. "Cully" Stimson, long prominent in lumbering, real estate, and finance, a director of the C. D. Stimson Company, and a member of the Metropolitan board since 1931. The membership of the board was changing slowly. The names of many members were familiar—O. D. Fisher, E. A. and E. H. Stuart, R. D. Merrill, F. C. Talbot, A. S. Eldridge—but the directors now also included Paul Pigott, president of the Pacific Car and Foundry Company; William Edris, of Skinner and Eddy, owner of hotels in Seattle and elsewhere and widely involved in other business interests; John A. Baillargeon, an officer of several major industries, including the C. D. Stimson Company; and William G. Reed, the young president of the Simpson Investment Company. The Metropolitan on the eve of World War II still reflected, nevertheless, the management philosophies that J. F. Douglas had originated a quarter of a century before. E. A. Hart, who had taken over the rental department, was a Douglas man, and R. W. Kidwiler's service department was maintaining what Douglas once had thought of as "White Building service." The young women operating the elevators, dressed in their MBC uniforms, were still expected to know the Metropolitan Center tenants and the offices they occupied.[56]

There was, before World War II erupted, a final, brief burst of public interest in the operations of the Metropolitan Building Company. The focus was the old Arena again, that building that had been a periodic center of controversy.

What was said was said primarily by a newspaper columnist in search of a story. What was done was done by the state senate, which, as a legislative body, was not averse to having a committee look into things, especially things touching the Metropolitan tract. But the fact that the Arena got any attenion at all, after all those years, must have had a base in feelings among friends of the university that the Arena still existed as a deviant from the Metropolitan's mandate to build only "permanent" buildings. On February 27, 1939, the senate, on a resolution introduced by three Democratic members, ordered an investigation of the Arena, appropriating only $100 of the costs because, as the committee said, a "university alumnus" had offered to defray costs beyond that. The affair got scant attention in the press. The Seattle *Times* said that a "probe" had been ordered of the Metropolitan company's lease. The University of Washington *Daily* headed its lead story, "University May Get Large Added Rents for Business Area," saying that the senators had charged "that $700,000 in rentals rightly belonged to the University as the result of lease violations which the board of regents cited to the Metropolitan company in 1925." Again, nothing happened, although the mood did not die for a while. A year later Herbert Condon reported to the regents that the senate committee appointed in 1939 had announced its "intention of taking the matter up at a very early date." But 1940 was no time to be raking up ancient history.[57]

When war came, Seattle, so long a point of commerce and communication with the Orient, felt the special shocks of the war in the Pacific. Every war-making or support facility, military or civilian, was under stress. But Boeing was already turning out heavy bombers, the B-17 Flying Fortresses, and soon these were followed by the B-29 Super Fortresses. William E. Boeing, who had retired in 1934 as chairman of the company's board, returned as a consultant. Seattle was jammed with thousands of servicemen training at nearby military bases or loading on transports bound for theaters of war. The widened part of University Street became "Victory Square," scene of war-bond rallies.

Eustace Ziegler etching of University Street in its wartime "Victory Square" period, designed for the Metropolitan Christmas card of 1942

Even the depths of the war period produced, nevertheless, developments of significance to the university and to the future of its downtown tract. One of these was an interesting change in the board of regents, another the passage of legislation protecting the regents forever from removal on political whim, and the third a change in control of the Olympic, which was feeling the revival of activity that the war had brought.

The new governor of Washington, Clarence Martin's successor and the only Republican elected to state office in 1940, was Arthur B. Langlie, a native of Minnesota but a Washingtonian since childhood, a graduate of the university, where he had earned his own way to a law degree, a Seattle city councilman in 1935 and mayor in 1938 and, at barely forty, a winner over former Senator C. C. Dill in one of the closest elections in the state's history. Langlie had wartime problems on his hands, but he also would be appointing university regents to succeed Ryan and Montgomery, whose terms were expiring. His appointees, in June 1942, were persons of far more than local stature, both deep in business, educational, and community affairs, and one was a woman.

Montgomery's successor was Eugene A. White, of Tacoma, manager of the Tacoma Smelter, the largest plant of the American Smelting and Refining Company and the largest single industrial unit in the state until the war brought the Boeing expansion. In one prewar year the plant had produced gold, silver, and copper valued at $51,000,000. A native of Iowa, White had attended Iowa State College in 1903 before coming West with his family and winning his degree in mining engineering at the university in 1908. White was a business leader of prominence, outside the state as well as within; his wife was identified with the American Association of University Women, and the family was consistently involved in university alumni activities.[58]

Eva Greenslit Anderson, of Chelan, was the first woman regent since Ruth Karr McKee. What was important, although events had to prove it so, was that Eva Anderson was approaching service to the university that would reach a climax when she, more than a decade later as a legislator, would help make a decision vital to the university's interests at the Metropolitan tract. Langlie, like Lister before him, had appointed a woman of extraordinary breadth. In 1942, Eva Anderson was already a wonder—the holder of a Ph.D degree, an author, involved in more educational activities than anyone could count, and with it all the happy wife of a Chelan automobile dealer, L. O. Anderson, with whom, when they fished, she "liked to row the boat." She was known in Chelan and elsewhere as "Mrs. Andy."

Mrs. Anderson was a figure in the state, but it might not have been so. Until she was twelve she had been almost blind—her eyes affected by a childhood attack of measles—and unable to go to school. When she could finally see, she seems to have exploded into learning, not only catching up but charging ahead into graduate work to get her Ph.D. Nothing made her withdrawn or bookish, however, nor quenched her sense of humor. She had been a teacher in rural schools, county superintendent in Douglas County, instructor in summer sessions at the University of Oregon, president of the Washington Education Association, officer of the Inland Empire Education Association, president of the State Administrative Women in Education, vice-president of the Washington Federation of Women's Clubs, and a National Education Association delegate, in 1925, to the NEA's World Conference in Edinburgh. She had written five books; one, *A Child's Story of Washington*, was used as a text in thirty-six Washington counties. When she attended her first regents' meeting, reporters had questions for her. "Working on a board of regents is what I've always wanted to do," she said. "I'm accustomed to working with men. I was raised with six brothers." Was she "thrilled"? "Festival queens and beauty contest winners are thrilled," she replied. "I'm happy to serve. You can say that I'll serve with my last red corpuscle."[59]

White and Anderson had scarcely joined the board, in that first year of America's participation in the war, when matters pertaining to the tract came up. At the very next meeting of the regents a spokesman for the Metropolitan Building Company appeared before the board to say that the company wanted to place war damage insurance on the buildings, the university to share the expense. The regents decided that the university was under no obligation to share—insurance was the company's problem—and that the board "would decline to consider such a proposal if made." But the next month, July 1942, the company did make proposals—three, actually—and the regents accepted one. There could be blanket coverage on the tract buildings, the loss payable to the company and the regents "as their interests may appear," but the Metropolitan was to pay the premiums. By November 1942, the future of the Olympic was on the agenda. A. S. Eldridge and two others came to the regents to suggest that it would be helpful in the refinancing of the hotel if there could be an extension of the lease, possibly with the authority of the legislature meeting in 1943. But on this matter the regents were firm. Their decision was that the Olympic is "part of the larger problem involved in the administration of the Metropolitan lease, and that in view of the length of time yet remaining the University will not be justified in presenting recommendations to the 1943 legislature."[60]

What came from the 1943 legislature, however, was the law that ended the implied "control" by a governor of the boards of regents of the state's institutions of higher education. It had been a long time coming, but at last there was a law stipulating that a regent could be removed only for "misconduct or malfeasance in office" and stipulating that removal could be accomplished only after the filing of a petition for removal, a proof of service of the charge, and a public hearing by a tribunal composed of three Superior Court judges appointed by the chief justice of the State Supreme Court. The legislation (Senate Bill No. 22) had joint alumni support, by legislators from the university and from Washington State College, in senate and house.* A wartime legislature had seen to it. Never again could there be, at the university or its sister institutions, the wholesale replacement of regents that had been so traumatic at certain moments in the university's history.[61]

As for the Olympic, that question was also settled, for the moment, at least, in 1943. In July, with the war at midpoint, William Edris purchased from the Metropolitan Building Company its block of stock—a block representing 23 percent of the total—and thus acquired a controlling interest in the hotel.

Edris, by 1943, had become in two decades a substantial presence among Seattle's "capitalists." A native of Eugene, Oregon, he had served two years in the army during World War I, then had come to the University of Wash-

---

* Chap. 59, *Laws of 1943*. S.B. 22 passed the senate on February 2 and the house in February 26 and was signed by Governor Langlie on March 3, 1943. Sponsors in the senate were Ernest Huntley, an alumnus of Washington State College, and Robert T. McDonald, a university alumnus. In the house the bill was sponsored by Asa Clark, of Washington State College, and Edward F. Riley, a university alumnus.

ington to earn a law degree in 1922. Joining Skinner and Eddy, Edris had been a member of the "junior board" of the Metropolitan and then president of the Fifth Avenue Building Company that had built the Skinner Building. He had been investing all along in business buildings, hotels, and theaters in Seattle and Spokane. He already had a base of stock in the Olympic, but his control could not be complete until November 1, 1943, because until then the control of the hotel was vested equally, under a federal court order, in the holders of stock and in the holders of certain first mortgage and debenture bonds—some $2,000,000 of these—that had been issued in 1936 when the Community Hotel company and the Olympic Hotel Company were reorganized in bankruptcy. By November, as it proved, the bonds had been retired on schedule and Edris, holding the majority of the stock, was in command. The sale price was not made public when C. W. Stimson announced on July 14, 1943, that the Metropolitan directors had approved the transaction. The price was, in fact, $240,000, and the stock Edris bought was the stock that the Metropolitan had obtained in its own exchange of Community Hotel and Olympic Hotel securities, which originally had represented an investment of $731,000.[62]

The war went on, the university again the site of war-related training and research activities. The Metropolitan Center was managed under a lease that still had ten years to run. The university's income from rentals had reached, at last, $140,000 a year, the maximum level under the lease executed in 1907. Even then there were some persons who considered it not too early to begin to think about what should be done with the downtown tract in 1954.

CHAPTER 8

Moving Toward Decision–Again: 1944 to 1950

Neither the city of Seattle nor the university community at large had time in the World War II era to recall that forty years had passed since an all-but-forgotten board of regents had given to James A. Moore the first fifty-year lease on the university's old campus, the lease modified and reassigned to the Metropolitan Building Company in 1907. To a university hard pressed for funds, the lease was a relic of little charm, a hand of the past laid on the present, an instrument that limited to $140,000 a year the income from a property worth many millions. To any who then considered the lease, the passage of forty years meant only that ten years remained—or that only ten years remained—until its expiration.

Yet some there were who gave thought to the lease and particularly to the kinds of calculations and judgments that would have to be made before its expiration in 1954. Among these were members of the board of regents—in 1944, Alfred Shemanski, president, Thomas Balmer, vice-president, and Winlock Miller, Philip Macbride, Eugene White, Werner Rupp, and Eva Anderson. Beginning to be involved also were members of a newer generation of leadership in the alumni association.

If it is wondered why the lease question attracted alumni attention at what proved to be the midpoint of the war, one answer is that the question had never been far from the focus of interest among alumni, including alumni in the legislature. There was a real—almost traditional—sense of baffled restlessness at the lease's inflexible rental terms. Now, amid war, and ten years before the lease was to expire, there was arising a positive impulse to help the university get ready to capitalize at last on its downtown property. The regents' records of that war period are bare of references to the lease, but the alumni were beginning to stir. The alumni were ready to do the spade-work that the regents, managing the university in a difficult season, simply could not do. And what the alumni did could not have been done without the regents' knowledge and encouragement.

In the summer of 1944, the board of trustees of the alumni association—the new president a thirty-eight-year-old printing company executive, R. Mort Frayn—approved appointment of a committee to study the history of the leasehold for the information of alumni and as background for any exploration of policy that might come later.[1]

The wartime university was carrying on in a state best described as one of suspense between the recent deprivations of the Depression and the dislocations caused by the war effort. The enrollment was down (below 10,000), the campus once again was heavily involved in military training, and scores of faculty members were on leave, war-related research absorbing many who stayed. There was enough to keep a board of regents busy with matters at hand. President Sieg, by 1944, had served for a decade. It had been his destiny to be the university's executive as the institution moved through one set of historic difficulties into another. Sieg had been a strong president in an era in which the greatest strength was a firm and patient optimism. He had provided that kind of leadership and was helping to lay the groundwork for his successor. Already there was talk of establishing new medical and dental schools to round out health training efforts represented until then only by nursing and pharmacy. The university visualized four schools linked in a health sciences program built around a new teaching hospital. There would be additional buildings and facilities, long denied, for other disciplines. The legislature knew of, and even sympathized with, such ambitions. Whatever was being thought about financing, among the regents or in the legislature, it was not escaping attention that additional income would be coming, in due course, from the Metropolitan Center.[2]

The alumni studies of the Metropolitan lease proceeded into 1945 under the auspices of a five-man committee headed by Roy G. Rosenthal, proprietor of a University District printing firm. Members of Rosenthal's committee were Joseph E. Gandy, a law graduate and prominent businessman who was already widely identified with community activities; Arthur E. Simon, a Seattle attorney soon to become president of the alumni association; Judge Lloyd Black, who had served on the federal bench since his appointment by President Roosevelt in 1939; and Raymond Davis, who had recently resigned as comptroller of the university to become vice-president of a Seattle-based insurance company. When the committee report was published in August 1945 in a sixteen-page booklet, *The University's Ten Acres*, the text was wholly historical, a short review of the story of the tract with due attention to the occasional disputes that had provided highlights. Not yet were there any alumni recommendations, but there were suggestions on the directions the future should take. The committee thought that something would have to be done to amend or revoke the 1923 law that bound the regents to take no action without legislative approval. How could rational negotiation on a new lease be conducted with the knowledge by all concerned that every term or condition would be subject to legislative debate and public scrutiny? And there was bound to be public scrutiny. The committee concluded its report with a discreet call to action tempered by understanding:

It seems apparent that the whole question of the further administration of the Metropolitan Tract is likely to be in the forefront of public attention in the immediate future. How should this property be handled? That question deserves careful, honest and deliberate consideration, since the issues involved are of very great importance to the University and to the cause of higher education. Deep prejudices with regard to the relative economic and political desirability of the public or private operation of a real-estate enterprise will, no doubt, be aroused. . . . In whatever way the matter is settled, it is to be hoped that the people of the state, by maintaining a continuous and intelligent interest in the problem, will encourage a solution which will be honestly arrived at and which will result in a proper return to the University of Washington.[3]

Thus the alumni committee, certainly with the knowledge and approval of the regents, put the Metropolitan lease question into the realm of public discussion. But even before that happened, the legislature had taken an initiative that must have been similarly inspired, and other events were piling up almost too rapidly to count.

The 1945 legislature approved the bill—Senate Bill No. 6—authorizing establishment of the medical and dental schools. The act was signed into law in the spring of 1945, just before the war ended in Europe, by the newly elected governor, Mon C. Wallgren, who had defeated Republican Arthur Langlie in the election of the previous November. The realization of that cherished plan not only affected in the short term the university's thinking about its administration, particularly in regard to the kind of president who should succeed Sieg, but altered significantly the course of the university's growth. Suddenly, in 1945, health sciences facilities were to be designed and new deans selected when everything including the university presidency was in a state of prospective change.

But the session of 1945 passed another university-related measure, and this was House Joint Resolution No. 16 creating a joint legislative interim commission of seven members (called invariably thereafter the legislative interim committee) to look into the Metropolitan tract lease "and all the facts and conditions relating to the said property and tending to affect the future policy of the state" in dealing with it. The committee was directed to make findings and recommendations to be reported in 1947 "for the assistance of the legislature in dealing with the property herein referred to" under the provisions of the 1923 law. The chairman of the committee was Senator M. T. Neal, of Des Moines, and the vice-chairman Representative George F. Yantis, of Olympia, who had introduced the resolution. By mid-1945 the committee was organized and at work, preparing to hold meetings with the regents and with representatives of the Metropolitan Building Company. A meager clue to contemporary thinking was contained in the Seattle *Times* report of the organization: "Because of the magnitude of the [lease] problem and its effect on future finances of the University, the Legislature ordered the study to begin now. Some believe the property should be re-leased to a private corporation; others think the University should operate it, probably under a management arrangement with a real-estate firm."[4]

Wallgren's election brought changes in the board of regents, for the terms of several members were about to expire. Balmer was president in 1945 and White was vice-president, but in the ensuing months four new regents came to the board to succeed Shemanski, Rupp, Macbride, and Anderson. The new members were Clarence J. Coleman, an Everett attorney; Joseph Drumheller of Spokane, head of a chemical concern; Captain John M. Fox of Seattle, an influential labor leader; and John L. King of Seattle, research director for the Washington State Grange. And when White's term expired in March 1946, Wallgren's choice to succeed him was Dave Beck of Seattle, vice-president of the Teamster's Union.[5]

The regents of 1946–47 made a most interesting group—Coleman president, Drumheller vice-president, and Miller, Fox, Balmer, King, and Beck—with Balmer and Miller the veterans who had, between them, some thirty-five years of experience on the board.

Balmer was well into his second decade, a busy railroad executive who had long since established himself as a strong man in his approach to university policy. But Miller was something of a miracle, a living link to the scarcely remembered days before World War I when, with Gaches and Fechter, he had battled the Metropolitan Building Company over the Arena. Miller was over seventy-five in 1946, patriarch and patrician, erect in carriage, impeccably dressed, passionately devoted to the university in all its aspects, including its varsity rowing program, which he beheld as the finest expression of the amateur spirit in collegiate sports. Not counting the years of his exile during the Hartley regime, Miller had been a regent for about twenty-four years. He loved the university campus. He served term after term as chairman of the regents' buildings and grounds committee. Now that there was talk about a new Metropolitan lease, he would turn his attention downtown again.

The newcomers were of great diversity of background. King was a native of Minnesota who had won his bachelor's and master's degrees from the University of Washington and whose career, already turning toward management in radio, and soon television, would include twenty years as a regent. Fox, who had served as a member of the War Labor Board and who was, among other things, president of the CIO Inland Boatmen's Union of the Pacific, somehow failed to be confirmed by the state senate, although he served as a regent until 1947. Among the newcomers, Drumheller and Coleman, both graduates of the university, were those with the closest ties there. Coleman, active in politics since his student days, had served four years as Democratic state chairman and two as national committeeman, but he was also a lawyer tapped frequently for state and national bar association assignments. Drumheller, a former state senator and Democratic national committeeman, had even older links to the university, for his mother had been a graduate and his grandfather was Leonard J. Powell, who had been the university's president from 1881 to 1887. But Dave Beck was the best known of them all, a national figure and rising.[6]

Beck was a self-made man among self-made men, once a laundry truck driver and secretary of a laundry workers' union who had become in twenty years (supplementing his high school training with university extension work in law, business administration, and economics) a leading figure in the International Brotherhood of Teamsters. Beck was, in 1946, on the verge of appointment as executive vice-president of the Teamsters under Daniel J. Tobin, a position said to have been created for the man who already was tabbed as Tobin's successor. Beck brought to the board of regents some forthright ideas. Upon his appointment in April 1946, he said he would advocate a survey of university facilities to see what was needed to accommodate postwar enrollments. He said it was his hope that the campus, with new buildings coming at last, might become the "showplace of Seattle." Beck also believed that regents' meetings should be open to press and public "because the people pay the bills and they have a right to know what's going on."[7]

With the regents thus assembled there were others who would have parts in approaching events relating to the Metropolitan property. One of these was Mort Frayn, a graduate of the university in 1929, who had been a printer and printing salesman for fifteen years before becoming president of the Frayn Printing Company of Seattle in 1944. Frayn's interest in the downtown property might have remained simply that of an alumni association president if he had not become a candidate for the legislature in 1946. He won handily a seat in the house from Seattle's Forty-third District, motivated primarily by a feeling that political action on behalf of the university would be important. In that year, too, George V. Powell was elected to the house. Powell, a graduate of Princeton University and the University of Washington Law School, was a young attorney just home from service in the navy. Neither then nor later was Powell active in alumni affairs, nor had he any alliance with Frayn, but he took to Olympia a determination to serve on whatever committees were handling university bills. It was not unimportant, certainly, that Powell was the son of John H. Powell, that regent during the first days of the Metropolitan lease and the adviser to the board in 1925.[8]

And there were some whose influence may have been felt, more directly if less obviously, all along. A member of Frayn's alumni board was Charles F. Frankland, who was from a family that had come to Seattle in the 1880s. Frankland had been a university basketball and track star, and by the early 1930s he had become the director of athletics and then, for a time, the comptroller of the university. He had also been in and out of banking, but by 1936 he had joined the Pacific National Bank as vice-president and in 1946 had become president. For a long time—from his university comptroller days —Frankland had been trying to help improve the effectiveness of the alumni association, and it was he who had been instrumental in bringing to the campus, as the association's executive secretary, R. Bronsdon Harris.[9]

Harris, known everywhere as Curly, was a graduate in forestry who had served his apprenticeship in 1931–35 as traveling secretary of his national fraternity. Curly had been coxswain of the Washington crews of 1929–31, and it was with a coxswain's hand that he steered the alumni association after he joined it in 1936. He planned activities, and entertained with polish, but he never dominated the scene. He knew alumni all over the world, the prominent and the merely loyal. He also knew the state and its people, and every member of the legislature, term after term; and they, university alumni or not, knew him. He moved easily, almost casually, in political and social circles, planting ideas. He brought people together. There can be no doubt that it was Harris who helped mobilize legislative support for the 1943 measure that gave the regents of the state's institutions of higher education protection, at last, from arbitrary removal for political purposes. It could only have been Harris who, when the university regents were beginning to think about a new Metropolitan lease, became the quiet link between the board and the alumni association, stimulating the alumni committee studies and beginning to make preliminary soundings of legislative views on the Metropolitan lease question.[10]

In the university's administrative staff there had been shifts, and certain faculty members were being called in as consultants. All of this was relevant to the kind of advice the regents would be getting. When Raymond Davis resigned as comptroller in 1944, he had been succeeded by Nelson A. Wahlstrom, an experienced and knowledgeable manager of business affairs, who had been with the university since 1928, when he joined the staff as an accountant, three years after his graduation, to help straighten out tangled finances in the Associated Students organization. Wahlstrom was acting comptroller for a time, but by 1945 he had been confirmed in the post and was beginning a fifteen-year period in which he not only handled the university's financial affairs during the great postwar expansion but became a leader among the business officers of major universities. The new assistant comptroller and business manager was Ernest M. Conrad, a young man from the Eastern Washington farming country, a 1940 graduate in business administration who for four years had been manager of the University Student Cooperative Association. The faculty members to whom the regents were turning for advice included Dean Judson Falknor and Professor Alfred Harsch, of the Law School (Falknor had helped prepare the bills relating to the medical and dental schools), and others.[11]

There was, in short, a newness in the assemblage. Five of the seven regents were new; Frayn and Powell, among others, were going to the legislature as freshman representatives; and university staff and faculty members were addressing Metropolitan lease matters far outside usual experience. And by 1946 there was a new university president, Raymond B. Allen, a man selected with care, for his energy and breadth, to lead the university into the period of unprecedented growth.

Raymond Allen was a big, expansive, happy man, just forty-three, dean of the University of Illinois Medical School and head of that university's branches on its Chicago campus. Allen fitted ideally, in training, background, and characteristic confidence, the specifications of a university that was ready to burst out in all directions, physically and academically, even as it prepared for the monumental task of adding a new health sciences division embracing medicine, dentistry, nursing, and pharmacy. Allen held both Ph.D. and M.D. degrees, he was a successful administrator, and his experience ranged from small-town medical practice to medical deanships in New York and Detroit. Above all, he was—as Suzzallo had been so long before him—a Western man with Eastern connections. He was a native of North Dakota and had practiced in Minot. He was a graduate of the University of Minnesota and had taught there on a Mayo Foundation Fellowship. He even had family ties to the university, where two brothers and a sister had been students, and to Seattle, where another brother was a contractor. Even so, Allen's selection had been a process taking many months. He had first been offered the deanship of medicine in 1945, but had declined that. Meanwhile, President Sieg had told the regents that he wished to be relieved, and so in February 1946 Allen was offered the presidency and accepted. By September 1, he was in office. The job ahead of him, a large one, was only peripherally concerned with what would be done about the Metropolitan tract, but there was reason to believe that, with new leadership, the university—and the legislative interim committee—could move forward constructively on that front as well.[12]

In and about the Metropolitan Center itself there had been premonitory stirrings. Early in 1945, William Edris, who already controlled the Olympic, had submitted to the Metropolitan Building Company an offer to buy the company's principal assets—the lease having slightly less than ten years to run—for $5,023,407. The company's stockholders voted overwhelmingly (409 of 437 responding) to reject the offer. Shortly before that, on January 2, 1945, Edris had resigned as a director and treasurer of the company, and he was succeeded by Frank S. Bayley, Sr., an attorney and widely known civic leader who, the company said, "has represented the principal welfare and religious institution stockholders." Bayley himself held no Metropolitan stock, but was simply the spokesman for the benevolent institutions having company stock in their endowment portfolios. In that year the company reported a net income of $348,908.55, equivalent to $1.60 a share, which it said represented a 31 percent decrease from 1944.[13]

With the end of the war, the Metropolitan Building Company was beginning to think about the needs of the Metropolitan Center for rehabilitation and construction. The company had done all it could in the war years to keep the buildings in condition, but now major development would be necessary if the Center was to hold its position. Andrew Steers was still secretary and manager of operations, and the vice-presidents were L. C. Henry, J. F. and J. H. Douglas, O. D. Fisher, and E. A. Hart. But the leadership of the company was slowly changing. New names were appearing in the lists of directors: Norton Clapp, secretary of the Weyerhaeuser Timber Company; Ben B. Ehrlichman, president of the United National Corporation; and Stanley N. Minor, president of the Pacific Northwest Company. The president was William G. Reed, who had been the young member of the board in the late

1930s. It was Reed who outlined some of the needs of the tract in a letter to Balmer in January 1946.[14]

Reed was president of the Metropolitan because there had been a feeling at the end of the war that young blood was needed at the top. Reed qualified on that score—he was only thirty-seven in 1945—but he had other and more important qualifications, not the least of which was that he was ready to resume a career in investment management after wartime service with the navy, his last station in the Aleutians. Reed was a graduate of the University of Washington with additional work at the Harvard School of Finance. Like his father, Mark Reed, who had been a stalwart in Republican politics, Reed had been active in party affairs and had served before the war both as treasurer of the Republican state central committee and as national committeeman during the 1940 campaign. Reed was familiar with the Metropolitan, its senior leaders, and with most of the other men who made up the financial and political elite in Seattle and elsewhere in the state. So when in 1945—Reed just home from the war—"Cully" Stimson indicated that his health probably would not permit him to continue as president, the choice as Stimson's successor was Reed. He would hold the office just two years, resigning in 1947 because of the pressure of other affairs, but it was Reed who represented the company in the first discussions of the lease question and who stayed with the company as a director during the later negotiations.[15]

Still among the directors was Elbridge H. Stuart, president of the Carnation Company in which J. F. Douglas now served as chairman of the finance committee. But the founder of the Carnation empire was no longer about. E. A. Stuart, whose dramatic life had begun in North Carolina before the Civil War, had died in 1944 at the age of eighty-seven. The Stuart Building in the Metropolitan Center was but one of the monuments to that indomitable merchant-adventurer.

There began, after the creation and organization of the legislative interim committee in 1945, an increasing flow of activity and communication on the part of the regents with respect to the Metropolitan leasehold. As early as September 1945, the interim committee group, headed by Neal and Yantis, visited the regents—Balmer was president—for an introductory discussion in which President Sieg and others participated.* Early in 1946, while the regents were preparing to offer the university presidency to Raymond Allen, other meetings were held and, in response to Senator Neal's request for a "more permanent arrangement" for consultations, the regents authorized the executive committee, with Balmer as chairman, to continue the contacts. Wahlstrom, as comptroller, was called on for information helpful to the committee. Harris wrote to the regents offering the assistance of the alumni committee "in all matters pertaining to the re-leasing." By March 1946,

---

* Besides Neal and Yantis, members of the committee were Senators W. C. Dawson, Seattle, and John N. Todd, Mercer Island, and Representatives Edward F. Riley, Seattle, Herbert M. Hamblen, Spokane, and W. J. Beierlein, Auburn.

Balmer and the executive committeemen, meeting with Neal and his associates, agreed that within the next sixty days they should be nearing a "more definite opinion" on the future of the leasehold. And it was at that meeting, on March 16, that the executive committee decided to ask Dean Falknor and Wahlstrom to make a fact-finding trip to universities in the East that had experience in the leasing or management of metropolitan real estate or business properties. Falknor and Wahlstrom made the trip, including in their sweep a series of interviews with financial officers at Columbia, Chicago, and Northwestern universities and incidental talks with representatives of other institutions. Columbia, of course, held the lease on the Rockefellers' giant Radio City, but the university also managed directly some two hundred other properties in the New York area. Northwestern managed more than one hundred parcels in Chicago and Evanston, Illinois, and the University of Chicago operated properties on LaSalle Street and elsewhere in the metropolitan area. By May 16, Falknor and Wahlstrom had submitted to Balmer an extensive written report of their findings. The report reflected the views of the Eastern financial officers that direct management of such properties by a university, from the institution's own offices, was a feasible alternative to other kinds of lease-management plans. On May 18, 1946, Falknor reported in person to the regents on the details of the Eastern visits, and Wahlstrom was instructed to set up another meeting with the legislative committee and to discuss the matter with the alumni. Rosenthal's alumni association committee soon was asked, in fact, to follow up its earlier historical work by preparing a set of recommendations.[16]

For that moment the thought existed that the University of Washington might become, at the expiration of the Metropolitan lease—or sooner if possible—the operating landlord of the Metropolitan Center.

At the core of the consideration was the tax question. It was not absolutely sure that the university, as landlord, would be free of tax obligations (and Professor Harsch seemingly had not been conclusive in opinions that he had drafted, upon request, for President Sieg and Balmer), but the presumption was that it would be. The Metropolitan Building Company was subject to the current federal income tax on corporations of 38 percent of net earnings, and its tax bills had been large. According to the information given the regents, the company's federal taxes from 1929 to 1945 had totaled $2,250,000 ($1,748,000 in the last five years, the years of the war). Whatever the taxes in the future, a private lessee would have to pay them. But an educational institution presumably would not. The Eastern universities had never been subject to taxation, and one of their spokesmen, Falknor told the regents, had said that "no question of income tax liability ever had been raised, even where the institution was directly managing and operating a property." It was true that Columbia and the other institutions were private, not public, but the tax exemption would seem to apply equally to institutions whose funds were acquired for educational purposes. The University of Washington would have to go to its legislature, of course, for approval of any arrangement it proposed, but the approval should be directed at giving the university the right to receive proceeds from the Metropolitan tract as "local funds," not subject to appropriation. The prospect of tax-free income was a tempting one, and if the university could buy out the Metropolitan Building Company before the lease expired in 1954—why not immediately, for that matter?— the sooner that income would be available. At the very least, a calculation of the income that might be coming to the landlord university would provide a base line for negotiations with private corporations if a new lease seemed the better way to go.[17]

An "artist's conception" of possible tract development from the alumni report of 1949

The idea of university operation of the tract persisted. It was covered in the newspapers. On August 15, 1946, the Seattle *Star* used stories headed "Hot Legislative Debate Looms on Metropolitan Tract's Future" and (over a story with a photograph) "Will University Take Over This Rich Area?" In March 1946, in their written report to the regents, Falknor and Wahlstrom had urged immediate action toward an arrangement anticipating university management. By June 12, 1946, Rosenthal's alumni committee had developed the recommendations asked of it, and in them university management was a third and last choice. As reflections of the current thinking—not only among the regents but also among others with intimate knowledge of the tract and considerable experience in business affairs—the recommendations are illuminating.

Falknor and Wahlstrom concluded their report with these summary suggestions: (1) That negotiations be initiated with the Metropolitan Building Company looking toward a "tentative agreement" on acquisition of the company's interest by June 30, 1947. (2) That any such agreement be submitted to the legislature for approval, "along with bills . . . which will permit the financing of the purchase of the leasehold and which will facilitate the businesslike operation of the project directly by the Board of Regents. . . ." (3) That, with acquisition of the leasehold, the regents, "with the necessary expert assistance and advice," begin to prepare a comprehensive plan for development of the tract, including new construction. (If new construction proved necessary, "prudent handling . . . might very well require the shifting of the burden and hazard of such new construction to lessees under long term ground leases.")

The alumni committee, working at the request of Senator Neal's interim group, had produced a report in which a number of considerations and options were built about three principal recommendations:

1. That the subject of the lease and disposition of same be made a matter of immediate attention and action.

Arrangements for future development of the tract needed to be made soon, the committee said, to stabilize property values, even if the regents had to issue revenue bonds to acquire the Metropolitan leasehold.

2. That the most satisfactory arrangement would be a lease to private operators, providing, however, a sum could be realized as a net rental commensurate with the value of the property.

Rentals of $1,000,000 a year seemed possible to the committee, but the rental level should be, in any case, not far below the level of tax-exempt income expectable under university operation. Long-term leases should be adjustable at intervals or percentage leases considered. "We believe," the committee said, "there are . . . advantages in leasing the tract to private operation, including the relieving of the Board of Regents . . . of the risks of large capital outlays in the future development of the property." Finally:

3. That if a satisfactory arrangement cannot be effected with private operators, the Board of Regents of the University should operate the tract itself.
    a. Representatives of the University who went back East to study similar holdings report that University ownership is feasible and profitable in other places.
    b. Full exemption from government taxes would be an important financial consideration.
    c. If this plan is entered into, the managing body should be free of political control, which should be assured by adequate legislation.
    d. If this plan is decided upon, then the matter of immediate purchase [of the leasehold, even with a sale of bonds] becomes the more imperative.[18]

It is to the credit of all who participated in this flow of thinking—the regents, the faculty and staff consultants, the alumni, the legislators, and, soon, the representatives of the Metropolitan Building Company—that a full range of alternatives was explored, even to the possibility of the sale of the tract, an alternative quickly rejected by the board. There had been some speculation even then that the university might do well to put the tract on the market (as the regents of 1900 had been expected to do) and invest the proceeds in a permanent endowment that might be somewhat easier for the regents to manage than a metropolitan site covered with buildings already inviting modernization or replacement. No one was ready to fix a market price, although a newspaper report said the tract might be worth $18,000,000. In any event, the coming months—from the autumn of 1946 until the legislature of 1947 was in session—not only were filled with meetings, exchanges of correspondence, and preliminary testings of views, but actually produced the first offer by the regents to buy out the Metropolitan Building Company.

Coleman, by late 1946, was president of the board, Drumheller vice-president. But Balmer, Drumheller, and Beck were the members of the Metropolitan lease committee, and it was Balmer, as chairman, who, moving carefully but persistently, was setting the pace of negotiations. Some pressure for movement was coming from the direction of the legislative interim committee, which had to make its report and recommendations to the 1947 legislature, but there was nothing of the kind from the Metropolitan Building Company, which had already turned down Edris's $5,000,000 offer for the balance of its lease and which could only wait now for some proposal to come from the university.

By August 3, 1946, Balmer and his associates had prepared a draft report to the interim committee for consideration by the regents.[19] The report was discussed by the board that day and approved unanimously for transmission to Senator Neal. The regents' communication, devoted in its early paragraphs to a review of the tax situation faced by the Metropolitan Building Company, then proceeded through the recommendations to a request that the board be permitted to negotiate for purchase of the Metropolitan Building Company's lease balance. The board's views of the choices before it were as follows:

3. From the foregoing it is apparent that any plan which subjects the revenues of the Metropolitan Tract to federal income taxation involves the surrender of an advantage to which the University is entitled by present federal laws. . . . Accordingly, any future plan of operation should preserve this valuable immunity to the University. The Board believes this could be accomplished by:

a. The direct operation of the Metropolitan properties by the Board of Regents through the medium of a capable and experienced staff.

b. The direct operation of the Metropolitan properties by the Board of Regents through the medium of a competent real estate management company acting for the Board of Regents under an agency contract, and receiving a suitable fixed or percentage fee for its services.

c. Operation of the properties by a lessee paying as rental a percentage of *gross* income to University [regents' emphasis], subject to a fixed annual minimum.

It may or may not be significant that in this statement of management alternatives the regents presented first the idea of direct operation by the board—the idea that to the alumni committee was an if-all-else-fails solution. In any case, the idea certainly was still alive. As for the action, the board report continued as follows:

4. The Board suggests to the Legislative Committee that it be legally empowered to deal with the property in any of these ways as may appear desirable from time to time in the light of conditions then prevailing.

5. The Board also suggests that it be empowered to negotiate with the Metropolitan Building Company for the purchase of the unexpired portion of the term of its lease, and concurs in the view of Dean Falknor and Comptroller Wahlstrom that there is ample opportunity for the successful negotiation of such a purchase upon terms favorable both to the University and to the Metropolitan Building Company.

6. The Board is of the opinion that it is out of the question to consider either a sale of the property or a new lease at a fixed rental such as that now held by the Metropolitan Building Company. The obvious reason for this view is that any private operator, whether as owner or lessee, would be subject to federal income taxation . . . and would be forced to take this obligation into account. . . . In other words, the property and the use thereof are more valuable to the University than they can possibly be to any private owner, or any lessee paying a fixed rent.

Senator Neal's response on behalf of the interim committee, prepared on September 11 and considered by the regents on September 28, 1946, pointed out that the regents' proposal was notably short on specifics and that "it would probably be pretty difficult to get the legislature to confer" a blanket authority on the regents for action on a time-to-time basis. Neal wanted a concrete proposal for management or specific proposals for legislative action. The interim committee, after all, had to go to the 1947 legislature with something more than a set of undeveloped contingency plans. Neal said in part:

We respectfully suggest to the Board of Regents that if this matter is to be disposed of by proper approval or authority from the next legislature, it will be necessary for the Regents to submit to the legislature

(a) A proposal for acquisition by the University of the remainder of the Metropolitan Building Company's present lease, which has been worked out in detail between the Regents and the Company involving a commitment by both parties, subject to legislative approval. (This, of course, is on the assumption that the Metropolitan lease is to be terminated prior to expiration.)

(b) Proposals for future operation and capital improvements by such method as the Regents deem best calculated to serve the public interest. (We note with concern that your report is silent on the matter of the necessary capital outlay needed to develop the tract.)[20]

The parenthetical comments in paragraphs (a) and (b) seemed to present the key questions. What were the regents actually going to do about acquiring the balance of the leasehold? And what were their plans—their calculations of cost—for developing the property? The interim committee wanted the regents to get into specifics, but it was also nudging the regents toward face-to-face negotiations with the Metropolitan Building Company.*

Soon the face-to-face meetings were taking place between university and Metropolitan Building Company representatives—Balmer and Wahlstrom on the one hand, Reed and Steers on the other. The meetings could scarcely be called negotiations, for that stage had not been reached. The meetings could not have been uncordial, either, for the participants undoubtedly were as familiar with each other as with the issues and political considerations involved. But it was fairly clear from the first that the company had no wish to leave the tract, was making its own plans for rehabilitation (including major construction on the site of the White-Henry-Stuart Building), and was anticipating a long-term extension, not an abandonment, of its leasehold. The scope of the company's thinking may have stunned Balmer and Wahlstrom a little.

The first meeting with Reed and Steers was held on October 18, 1946—perhaps in Balmer's Great Northern office at 404 Union Street—and the second, a month later, on November 15. The Metropolitan spokesmen were firm, even a little blunt. The company did not want to make an offer for cancellation of its lease. It did not want to become a "mere operating agency." It would think of surrendering the lease only if it could "at the same time make a new profit-sharing arrangement," and the outline of this was already in mind. The company would provide the capital needed for comprehensive tract development, and the revenues from the property would then go to operating expenses, to amortization and interest, to payment to the university on a ground rental exactly equivalent to a management fee paid the company and, after that, to a division of the profits—although not necessarily an even division. Certain figures were mentioned by Reed and Steers in an exploratory way, and then the matter of amortizing the improvements: "As to the term of the new lease or agreement, we would suggest 99 or 100 years. If it were of such a length of time, the university should have an opportunity to get out or have a revaluation. The precedent of the Rockefeller Center lease in New York might be a good guide to the procedure for revaluation." * Fifty years would be the minimum term acceptable.[21]

---

* It is of some interest that when it was learned that the regents might ask for authority to manage the tract, the Washington State Federation of Labor, meeting in Spokane, adopted a resolution saying, "the Board of Regents . . . should be empowered, upon the expiration of the above mentioned lease, to assume full control of and operate the properties. . . ." A copy of the resolution, endorsed by the Executive Board of the Federation, was forwarded to Balmer on August 22, 1946. A similar resolution commending the regents for proposing plans "looking toward recovery and operation" of the property was adopted by the Washington State Federation of Teachers at the state convention in Seattle on November 23 (Balmer Papers, 14-4, University of Washington Library).

* Falknor and Wahlstrom had reported that Columbia University's Radio City lease provided for three successive terms of twenty-one years each, rental for the first term fixed at $3,600,000 a year and for the succeeding periods by mutual agreement (or arbitration) but never less than the basic figure (Falknor and Wahlstrom to Balmer, May 16, 1946).

There had been hints for years, at least since the Metropolitan company had asked in 1921 a nineteen-year extension of its lease on land to be occupied by the community hotel, that the company would press when the time came for a new "main lease" based on a reevaluation of the property. No one, so far as is known, had thought of ninety-nine years, or of fifty years as a minimum. But as a matter of fact, Falknor and Wahlstrom were not the only ones who had gone east to get advice on leasing alternatives. Reed had been there too. Reed had gone off to New York some time after becoming president of the company and had talked to people in several real estate investment houses—all of them familiar, undoubtedly, with Columbia University's lease-management operations. So Reed and Steers had their own thoughts about what was possible, and Balmer and Wahlstrom could only go back to the regents and the interim committee and attempt to regroup.[22]

When the regents met again on December 2, 1946, Senator Neal and all members of the legislative committee were present for the consultation. Balmer reported the results of the two discussions with the Metropolitan Building Company representatives, and the situation was reviewed at length. The result was a series of determinations summarized in the regents' minutes. The university, first, should seek appropriate legislation rather than "attempting to force a sale at the present time." The legislation should authorize the regents to finance major construction on the tract by sale of bonds and to enter into lease contracts limited in duration. The regents in the meantime should prepare a "final report" to be given the interim committee while Wahlstrom sought more help from the Law School consultants—Falknor and Harsch—in the drafting of proposed legislation. Balmer and his Metropolitan lease committee associates were authorized to continue contracts with the interim committee and the Metropolitan Building Company directors.[23]

It was time, Balmer thought, that all this was put in writing and considered at a general meeting of all parties—the regents, the Metropolitan Building Company representatives, and perhaps one or more members of the interim committee. In mid-December, Balmer called such a meeting at his downtown office for December 27, on the eve of the opening of the 1947 session of the legislature. President Allen, now four months in office, would be attending. Reed had already said that the Metropolitan would have a written statement of its position, and Balmer thought that the university should also have a statement. He asked Wahlstrom and Falknor to draft, on behalf of the university, "a written offer (subject to legislative approval) of the price it is willing to pay" for the balance of the tract lease. In his call for the meeting, in a note addressed to Coleman, Drumheller, and Beck, Balmer concluded: "The interchange of these written statements . . . will undoubtedly throw the entire subject into the realm of public discussion, both before the Legislature and in the press. We should, therefore, make a fair and clear offer which we can readily explain and justify."[24]

The regents' offer and the company's proposal were, as Balmer had fore-

seen, immediately in the realm of public knowledge. The Metropolitan
had put in writing its long-term-lease and profit-sharing plan. The regents
had made an offer reflecting projections of income based on figures the company itself had supplied. The regents proposed to pay $4,643,696.65 for the
remaining eight years of the leasehold.

On December 31—New Year's Eve—the details, announced by Coleman
on behalf of the university, were in the newspapers. The *Star* and the *Times*
used five-column headlines, the *Times'* "U.W. SEEKS TO BUY LEASE ON MET-
ROPOLITAN CENTER," and the *Star's* main story accompanied by an analytical
report headed, "METROPOLITAN LEASE PROFITS AVERAGE $646,000 PER YEAR."
What the regents had done, as the news stories explained, was to establish a
figure that carried to the end of the lease term the average of the company's
earnings for the previous six years, adjusting this by subtracting rental and
leasehold and income tax obligations, adding amortization requirements,
and making allowance for the taxes the company would have to pay on the
sale price. Coleman had noted that any offer was contingent upon approval
by the legislature, but that the regents pledged their best efforts to secure it.[25]

It is easy, even years after the events of 1946, to appreciate both the intensity
of the public interest in matters touching the Metropolitan Center and the
feeling of utter confidence, on the part of the Metropolitan company, that it
alone was supremely and uniquely qualified to carry forward the management and development of the property. For forty years, ever since J. F.
Douglas had scurried about among Seattle's capitalists to assemble its original
financing, the company had been a dominant force in the development of the
city's downtown area. The company's management experience and its long
association with the university—however strained upon occasion—were elements of the city's history. But more than history was involved. Now, eight
years before the lease was to expire, the negotiations for the future were of
immediate and explicit interest to every tenant of the tract and to the owners
and tenants of all the other commercial buildings within the tract's environs.
Would the company sell? Would the university's board of regents become a
downtown landlord? Would every tenant's sublease have to be renewed? Not
to the university and to the state only, but to hundreds of lumber, railroad,
insurance, transportation, and retail companies, a decision on the Metropolitan lease appeared a crucial one.

The Metropolitan Building Company's letter, signed by Reed, put into
the record the company's profit-sharing proposal, the plan suggested earlier
to Balmer and Wahlstrom but with all details now left to later negotiation.
But it was to the company's grasp of the management challenge that the letter
was chiefly addressed:

As you know, Metropolitan Building Company has created a thoroughly sound
operation—a "going concern." Under the Company's stewardship, Metropolitan
Center has been built from an unimproved and neglected area to one of the nation's
leading business centers. The property has not only been conserved, but developed
for the University. In this the Company feels a justifiable pride.

Metropolitan Center cannot remain stationary. Its facilities must be enlarged and modernized if it is to continue to serve the community adequately. This requires experience, skill, initiative and planning, plus willingness to risk the money necessary for expansion. Metropolitan Building Company is ready with the actual plans, the needed skill, the experience and capital for a larger and more modern development.

Of the profit-sharing idea, Reed said:

This formula would, in our opinion, result in the highest possible continued revenue to the University, consistent with future security of Metropolitan Center. . . .

This plan also recognizes the fact that the field of office building management is highly competitive, hence better suited to private than political handling. We believe you will agree that in the past the Metropolitan Building Company has thoroughly demonstrated its capabilities along this line.[26]

There, between the regents' offer and the company's proposal, the question hung suspended as 1947 arrived. Senator Neal had been defeated for reelection in November, but he was still working with his colleagues on the report that was expected from the interim committee when Washington's thirtieth legislative session was convened in Olympia in January.

In the world at large the year 1947 was a year of transition, a year that did not everywhere fulfill the expectations associated with peace. In warsick Europe, war criminals were beginning to pay for their crimes, but Great Britain's economy was in disarray, American forces occupied Japan, and General George Marshall, newly confirmed as secretary of state, was developing his Marshall Plan for the nourishment of Western Europe while urging, at home, a system of universal military training that would give muscle to the nation's foreign policy initiatives. And disturbing forces were at work. There was worry about communism and about how to preserve the "secrets" of atomic energy. David Lilienthal, nominated to be the first chairman of the new Atomic Energy Commission, had been literally put on trial at his confirmation hearings in the United States Senate.

Remote such things were, perhaps, from what was going on in the state of Washington and in Seattle, especially in regard to the university and its Metropolitan Center. There the mood, in 1947, was not an unhappy one. The city had grown: the population of "Greater Seattle" was now 615,000, the Chamber of Commerce said. The Boeing Airplane Company had opened a new propulsion laboratory near Renton to develop ram-jet engines for what was still, until the armed services were unified that year, the Army Air Force. In the Washington legislature, as throughout the state, there was a feeling of warmth toward the university, where thousands of war veterans were crowding the classrooms, and where much-needed new buildings were being planned and constructed at last—buildings for engineering, music and art, a new classroom and office building, a student union, an administration building (the regents were still meeting in a conference room near the president's office in Education Hall), and an expansion of the Suzzallo Library. Some of these projects were in the drawing-board stage, but there was an exhilarating feeling of growth on the campus. In a state that had never possessed a medical school, the development of the health sciences division was particularly exciting, and there was satisfaction in the thought that all this planning and building was going forward under the leadership of a well-liked new president, Raymond Allen. Seattle's view probably was well expressed in a Seattle *Times* editorial of February 9, 1947, headed, "It's Regrettable that Dr. Suzzallo Couldn't See It":

Seattle and the state have reason for genuine satisfaction at present and forthcoming progress toward completion of "the university of a thousand years" on the campus of the University of Washington.

That hope, once a dream for the distant future, is assuming visible form . . . following the interruptions of war, and with the added momentum provided by large postwar enrollments. . . . Good friends of the University's late president, Dr. Henry Suzzallo, will regret that he could not have lived to see this rapid consummation of his dreams. For he was the author of these plans, and though their realization is being hastened somewhat by fortuitous circumstances, his original vision of the University of the future, in the beautiful setting with which it was endowed by the state a half a century ago, has been but little altered.

An especially pleasing aspect of the campus development was, as the *Times* pointed out somewhat anticlimactically, that most of the costs of the new construction would come not from state tax funds but from the accumulations of tuitions and fees and from the "University's own income"—the University of Washington Building Fund, that is, into which had been going both the fees and the rentals from the Metropolitan Center. So the regents were busy in 1947 not only with the question of what to do about the Metropolitan lease but with the manifold details of the building program—examining budgets, approving sites, picking architects, reviewing plans, and so on. A satisfying time it was, but not an easy one. And a further problem, as yet unperceived, was on the horizon. Late in 1946 certain conservative members of the legislature, Republican and Democrat, had held a political caucus that led in 1947 to the creation of a Joint Legislative Fact-Finding Committee on Un-American Activities, soon to be known as the Canwell Committee because its chairman was Albert Canwell of Spokane. The university—a state university with some seven hundred full-time and tenured faculty members and about the same number of part-time teachers and subfaculty—was a prime target of inquiries of the Canwell kind. By 1948 the university had indeed been touched by the inquiries and thereby plunged into a prolonged and wrenching internal (but very public) struggle—a struggle which, because at its core was the issue of academic freedom, went to the nature of the university. The struggle, when it erupted, dwarfed all else for months, testing the new administration of Allen's time even more savagely than those of earlier days had tested Suzzallo's.[27]

But in 1947 the regents still could press for, and the legislature consider, a resolution of the Metropolitan tract matter. The legislation of 1947 represented, in the end, not more than a small crack in the 1923 restriction on the regents' powers to take action on the lease. It was nevertheless a recognition that action was becoming imperative, and thus it was a small victory.

The bill that went before the legislature on February 10 (H. B. 268) embodied the recommendations of the legislative interim committee. It would have supplanted the act of 1923 and given the regents full power to negotiate for or decide upon the future management of the Metropolitan property, denying the board only the power to sell the tract, or to negotiate, without legislative approval, any lease longer than twenty years. (The measure repealed sections 7 and 8 of chapter 122, *Laws of 1893*, providing for sale of the land.) The board might determine to manage the tract itself, or to do so through an agent. It was empowered to improve the tract, to remodel, enlarge, or replace existing buildings, and to issue warrants or bonds to pay for such improvements. The act, introduced by Republican House Speaker Herbert M. Hamblen of Spokane, had strong bipartisan support.[28]

The interim committee's report accompanying the bill recommended termination of the Metropolitan Building Company lease—by purchase, clearly. Of this the committee said: "Your Committee is convinced of the necessity for developing a new arrangement . . . [to] preserve for the University of Washington . . . all profits, income, and benefits derived from said property free from federal income taxation. . . . To ignore and forgo the benefits of such exemption . . . would appear to be less than businesslike. If the foregoing analysis is correct, it would appear that any new arrangement . . . could be on the basis either of a percentage lease, an operating agreement for fixed or percentage fees, or direct operation and management by the University."[29]

There was support in the legislature. R. B. Harris was in Olympia, of course, keeping in touch with developments. And there was support elsewhere for early passage and early action. A *Post-Intelligencer* editorial of February 28, "Delay Dangerous to Metropolitan Tract," asserted that letting the old lease run to expiration would be "disastrous," that there was an "imperative need for new and larger buildings on the site if the property is to be saved from obsolescence." The editorial said that there would be a safeguard: "It has been argued that the plan would concentrate too much power in the hands of the board of regents. But this objection seems to be met by the proposal from the house committee on colleges and universities that any action on the lease be subject to approval by a 21-member joint legislative interim council, which would be ready to act at any time."

There were, of course, amendments to the legislation. By March 1 the house had passed an amendment authorizing immediate action by the regents for purchase of the lease balance. But when, by March 9, the bill had been passed by both house and senate and sent to Governor Wallgren for signature, it was a far less liberal measure than the interim committee had proposed. There was no reference to the regents' power to execute a lease of up to twenty years. The senate's amendments limited the regents' power to merely negotiating for a new arrangement—although that was more than the regents had had since 1923—and on March 22 Governor Wallgren vetoed the final, vital section of the act, section 5, because he declined to have any part of the approval of the regents' action vested in a new agency, the State Legislative Council.[30]

The State Legislative Council had been created only the month before, the bill establishing it passed by the house and senate in February and permitted to become law without the governor's signature. The council was to become a permanent body having "all duties and functions customarily delegated to special interim legislative committees" and operating in its own fashion through subcommittees. It was to this body that the legislation on the Metropolitan tract would have conferred major responsibility for approval of the regents' actions, and this idea Governor Wallgren could not abide. When the university bill reached his desk he vetoed all parts referring to the council and, after reviewing the somewhat ambiguous language of section 5, said in his veto message: "It is more than likely that section 5 of the act could be construed as providing that any agreement for the lease or private operation of the tract would be finally concluded upon being approved by a 2/3 vote of the Legislative Council and that any other arrangement for disposal of the tract must be submitted to the Legislature. I am unwilling that the Legislative Council should be given any final authority as to disposal of the tract. I believe that the final approving authority should in all instances be in the Legislature as is provided in chapter 44 of the Session Laws of 1923."[31]

When the Metropolitan Building Company prepared its annual report to stockholders for fiscal year 1946–47, it included a brief review of its conferences with the regents and the legislature's action. Of the latter it said: "The State Legislature at its 1947 session passed House Bill No. 268 defining the powers of the Board of Regents with respect to the Metropolitan Lease. However, portions of this bill were vetoed by the Governor, leaving the lease status practically the same as it had been before the legislature acted."[32] For all practical purposes, that summed it up.

But whatever it all meant, everyone—legislators, regents, university staff members, legal advisers, alumni representatives, spokesmen for the Metropolitan Building Company, the newspapers, and numberless private citizens with public-interest motivations—had come out of the experience with a better understanding of the problem and a realization that a solution would not be an easy one. Whatever Governor Wallgren thought of the Legislative Council, the council existed and it was ready to supply a subcommittee to continue the work begun by the former legislative interim committee. The regents, empowered now to "negotiate," were determined to do that in further talks with Reed and Steers. William Edris was soon writing the regents to make a proposal involving the Olympic Hotel. The Metropolitan Building Company, not averse to letting the public know that it had its own plans for improving the tract, soon announced that it was projecting construction of a new thousand-car garage under the White-Henry-Stuart Building if, as the newspapers reported, "the regents consent to an extension of the company's present lease." The lease still had seven years to run, but the clock was ticking.[33]

The Metropolitan Building Company did indeed have extensive plans—ideas, at least—for improving the tract. These included replacing the White-Henry-Stuart and Douglas buildings, so that the former would yield to a new building covering the block between Fourth and Fifth avenues and there would be a new Douglas Building extending along Fourth Avenue, from Union Street, as far as the Cobb. What the company was implying in its public announcements was, "Once we have an extended lease, we'll go ahead with our modernization and the city won't have to wait for the regents to make their own plans and issue bonds and decide about management and all that."

There was reason for concern about potential obsolescence in the tract, as the *Post-Intelligencer* had pointed out, if no modernization could go ahead until after the lease expired in 1954. But this was not to say that in 1947 the Metropolitan buildings were shabbily maintained or decaying. This would never be true. The buildings were far from new—the White was forty years old, and the newest, the Skinner, was more than twenty—but the Metropolitan company, even after depression, war, and changes in management, kept alive the old spirit of "White Building service" that had been inspired by J. F. Douglas. It was just that if no major rehabilitation or replacement was realized in a reasonable time, Seattle's business center might shift slowly north into the new buildings and business centers that would mark the city's postwar development.

In any case, the problem from the regents' standpoint was in several parts: (1) how and when to get control of the leasehold for the years still remaining; (2) how to decide what management plan was best; and (3) how to get the Metropolitan Center rehabilitated and improved for the protection of the values there. The parts were interlocking and each involved complicated questions of policy and management technique. And for the balance of 1947, after the adjournment of the legislature, the regents were considering the issues and mulling over suggestions.

There was one change in the membership of the board that year. George R. Stuntz, a Seattle lawyer and a graduate of the university active in political affairs, was appointed by Governor Wallgren to succeed Captain Fox, whose earlier nomination had not been confirmed by the senate.[34]

One of those most immediately concerned with the future of the tract was, understandably, Edris. By April 1947 Edris had developed a proposal. In a letter to the regents on April 11 he said:

Modification of the University lease appears to be stalemated between yourselves and the Metropolitan Building Company. We are vitally interested because of our position in the Olympic Hotel, which property is in need of refurbishing not practical under the present arrangement.

Without reference to all the ramifications involved, but having in mind the interim committee's report, the action of the past legislature and various reports in the press, we recognize you are seeking for the University:

First: An enhancement and preservation of value, and

Second: The utmost financial return for the University.

We, in turn, are seeking a solution of the problem which will meet your requirements and at the same time permit us continuance of proper operation.[35]

The Edris proposal was then outlined. The regents would create an "authority" to issue 2 percent tax-free serial bonds, to be retired at 2 percent per year, in an amount to cover the purchase of the Metropolitan leasehold balance and the stock—the "A" and "B" stock—of The Olympic, Incorporated. The Edris organization, Wm. Edris Company, would buy at par enough of the bond issue to fund the purchase of both the Metropolitan lease and the hotel stock and development of a lease or management agreement for future operation. The initial earnings would go to the bond service, the next portion to the university, the next to the company for "executive expense." All further earnings would be divided equally between the company and the university. The levels of financing were impressive. The Edris company would buy $10,000,000 of the 2 percent bonds to permit acquisition of the Metropolitan lease (for about $7,000,000), the balance to reimburse holders of the hotel stock. The first $400,000 of earnings would go to the initial bond service; future earnings of at least $400,000 would be guaranteed by a $1,500,000 deposit of bonds subject to forfeiture. The university would receive the next $1,000,000 of earnings and, after the $100,000 allocation for executive expense, its half of all future income. "We would expect suitable arrangements whereby the tract could be properly developed, subject to your approval," Edris wrote, "by issuing additional bonds."

The Edris proposal may have been superficially attractive because it put into one package a solution to both the Metropolitan and the Olympic Hotel leases. But by late in May—and perhaps after a conference that was held with Edris, by Balmer and Drumheller, on the same day that additional talks were held with Steers—the Edris idea was put aside for reasons that appear in an undated draft memorandum. (No formal records of the Edris proposal appear in the regents' minutes.) The Edris offer was considered "unattractive and unacceptable" because:

1. The Edris offer suggests the purchase of the Metropolitan and Olympic Hotel leaseholds at a price of $10,000,000. Mr. Edris has stated to members of the Board of Regents that $7,000,000 of the $10,000,000 would go to the Metropolitan Building Company, and $3,000,000 to the holders of the A and B stock of the Olympic Hotel. The University has already calculated that fair compensation for the unexpired portion of the Metropolitan lease would be $4,643,696.65 as of June 30, 1947, and has offered that amount. . . . It therefore appears that the payment of $7,000,000 to the Metropolitan Building Company would be some 2½ million dollars more than the leasehold is deemed to be worth. . . .

2. The offer of the Wm. Edris Co. to purchase $10,000,000 of bonds issued by

University authority, bearing 2% interest and retirable at the rate of 2% per year, offers nothing which the University could not obtain on the open market. . . .

3. The proffered guaranty of $400,000 per year is $260,000 per year more than the University is now receiving. . . . [But] $260,000 per year for 7½ years . . . amounts to $1,950,000. At the end of 7½ years the University will come into possession of the Metropolitan buildings and the Olympic Hotel without cost. Obviously the University cannot afford to pay $10,000,000 in order to collect $1,950,000, even if guaranteed.[36]

There was more. But the answer was no. The Balmer touch seems evident in this, for Balmer was the kind of man who would examine a question from all sides, cautiously, and then be as economical as possible in phrasing his answer. In this case, the Edris proposal simply was turned against itself. The Edris company was assuming no risk, and offering to divide the income after the university had provided for rehabilitation of the tract "by issuing additional bonds." This was not to attribute to Edris a wholly personal motive. Edris appears to have had a rather large appreciation of the regents' opportunity as related to the problem. He apparently told them, in the May discussions, that their opportunity was "to change the status of Seattle from that of a town to that of a major city." He said that the planning for further development of the tract was beyond the powers of any planners then in Seattle and that "it would be essential to bring in experts such as the architects who had planned the Rockefeller Building in New York."* Edris seems to have had a large vision of what the tract could become. But the answer of the regents—certainly correctly—was still no. Why pay $7,000,000 for a leasehold balance that the regents had valued at $4,643,696.65 when the whole property would come to the university at no cost in 1954? Any other answer would have been difficult to justify, particularly to a legislature.

Yet by the time Balmer and Drumheller met with Edris they already knew that the Metropolitan Building Company might be willing to ask its directors to approve a sale of the leasehold for $7,873,000, some $3,000,000 more than the regents had offered, payable annually or semiannually out of earnings. There probably had been preliminary communications on this. In any event, Balmer scheduled on May 29, 1947, a series of three hour-long discussions, the first with Reed and Steers, the second with Edris, and the

---

* It is interesting to observe how often the Columbia University–Rockefeller Center relationship was used as an example of the Metropolitan tract deliberations, even when the New York situation was imperfectly understood. Reed and Steers, in their first discussions with Falknor and Wahlstrom, had said that the Rockefeller Center lease concept might be a "guide." They were referring correctly to the Columbia University lease of the Center property, not to the university's management of other parcels. When the *Post-Intelligencer* was commenting later on the need for legislative action, it spoke of the opportunity before the regents to "take over direct management and operation of the property—as, for instance, Columbia University has done successfully with much larger real estate holdings." But of course Columbia, leasing Rockefeller Center, was not itself managing any single "holding" larger than the University of Washington's. Edris, using the New York example in his talk with the regents, was saying simply that planning for the university tract should be of that caliber—and his instincts certainly were right.

third with a Seattle investment man who had no offer to make but wanted to explore possibilities. Steers just then was succeeding Reed as president of the company and thus was the principal spokesman. In this conference Steers explained that the company anticipated earnings much higher than those projected by the university and that the $7,873,000 figure was to cover $6,324,000 in earnings during the balance of the lease and $1,549,000 in capital gains tax. Reed and Steers still plainly preferred, however, the profit-sharing arrangement they had suggested in December 1946. Certain other ideas were explored, but there the matter rested.[37]

The regents in these months must have been subjected to all kinds of private advice. Some of the advice was public. In June 1947, Hugh B. Mitchell, the former U.S. senator from Washington, proposed the organization of a "business and professional committee on the university tract," which he visualized as a research-liaison-public information agency that would help all parties come together on an agreeable solution. The regents, at least, seemingly wanted none of this. The city of Seattle, in a letter to the board, asked the regents to be prepared to make payments to the city in lieu of taxes from the income resulting from any new lease that might be consummated. By June 1947 Balmer seems to have had enough. The board approved Balmer's report that the Metropolitan lease committee "had decided not to recommend any further immediate consideration of any proposals made to the committee to date in regard to the disposition of the Metropolitan Building Lease."[38]

The regents of 1946 had been dealing with the legislative interim committee in preparation for the legislature of 1947. The regents of 1947 now were dealing with a subcommittee on the Metropolitan lease of the newly organized State Legislative Council, the body of which Governor Wallgren took such a dim view. The chairman of the subcommittee (as of the council itself) was L. J. Shadbolt, whose associates were Edward F. Riley and Thomas Montgomery. By autumn 1947 the subcommittee was ready to address the lease question, not merely to prepare for the legislature of 1949 but to see what it could do to move off dead center the negotiations for the balance of the Metropolitan lease.

The regents of 1947–48 (Coleman, Drumheller, Miller, Balmer, King, Beck, and Stuntz) must have reflected now and then, as others had before them, that service on a University of Washington board was of its own demanding kind. Whatever their backgrounds, and however diverse their experience, they were after all just seven men who were serving the state without pay while they attended to their own business and professional responsibilities. They were doing all the usual things that regents do—approving faculty appointments, building plans, budgets, even the employment of football coaches—and in addition were now charged with making decisions about a multi-million dollar commercial property in the full view of constituencies and interests that were themselves not often in agreement. There was a rather general appreciation of the delicacy of the regents' situation, but even the regents' staunchest supporters, notably the alumni, were far from having a single mind about the course the board should take.

That autumn of 1947 the regents met for the first time with Shadbolt and his fellow subcommittee members for a preliminary discussion of the lease question, the meeting also attended by Arthur Simon, the member of the alumni association committee, and—somewhat unusually—by a single newspaper reporter, Douglass Welch of the *Post-Intelligencer.* The alumni committee of 1944–45 was still standing by to be of help, but Simon was the author of an article in the fall issue of the *Washington Alumnus,* in which, in the most sympathetic fashion, he had said that it was time to get on with a decision about the lease, and the regents might do well to hire a qualified technician or staff assistant to help them gather information and analyze the choices ahead of them. Of such things Simon had written: "There is much work to be done—much work. Time marches on. The responsibility rests primarily on the Board of Regents. Properly discharged, that responsibility will mean an enormous boon to the cause of higher education in this state for many years. Since the Metropolitan Lease is so urgent, I believe that the Board of Regents should employ some competent person to devote his full time and attention to the matter. It may be that some member of the faculty could be relieved of his other duties and assigned to the task."[39]

The regents thus far, in seeking a "proper discharge" of their responsibility, had made what they thought was a fair offer for the balance of the Metropolitan lease; had received, discussed, and put aside a proposal from Edris; had coaxed an offer from the Metropolitan Building Company; and had tried to determine how to "negotiate" some new arrangement under the limited authority granted them by the 1947 legislature. But a board consensus—a policy, really—had been forming all along, and, in view of the public and legislative feeling that early action was essential, the regents were showing some independence of mind.

The regents had decided that, even though time was running, more would be gained by waiting than by rushing forward. A proposal by the Legislative Council subcommittee soon put this policy to test. On January 19, 1948, two months after the initial talk, the subcommittee sent to the regents a proposed plan for acquisition of the Metropolitan lease. The subcommittee said that its figures were to be considered simply "starting points for negotiation." Some of the figures—to the regents, at least—must have seemed familiar.

The subcommittee suggested that the university issue $10,000,000 in 2 percent tax-free income bonds to acquire the leaseholds of the Metropolitan Building Company and The Olympic, Incorporated—$7,000,000 for the one, $3,000,000 for the other—executing new leases to the two companies for continued operation for at least twenty-five years. With $400,000 per year set aside for bond service and retirement, the university would then receive $1,000,000 a year plus the $140,000 currently being paid in rent by the Metropolitan. After these payments, the balance of income would be divided between the university and the lessee companies.

However arrived at, the subcommittee's figures were remarkably similar to those proposed by Edris nine months before. It was not coincidence, however, but the mathematics of the proposal that concerned the regents' Metropolitan lease committee. The executive committee of the board held a meeting on January 28, 1948, to consider the lease committee's recommendations, and these were contained in a long analytical report—drafted primarily by Balmer, without doubt—that was, in its own measured way, devastating.

Using the legislative subcommittee's formula, the report demonstrated that the university would actually be losing $1,360,000 over the remaining years of the leaseholds and making thereafter what would amount to second payments to the lessees for their continued management of the properties. The report opposed absolutely the suggestions that the university tie itself to lease arrangements concluded without open competition.

Balmer had constructed a simple table to show how the $1,360,000 loss had been calculated. The $10,000,000 price plus bond interest until 1954 indicated a university expenditure of $10,675,000. But, even accepting the subcommittee's estimates of earnings—"the highest in the history of the property and . . . a dangerous basis to use in estimating future income"—the net annual return would be $1,380,000, or a total for the balance of the leasehold period of $9,315,000.* A legislative subcommittee was suggesting that the university pay $10,675,000 to realize $9,315,000. And, as analyzed by Balmer, the suggestion came out in tatters.

The price was too high. "Bearing in mind that the University will come into exclusive possession of the property and all of its income after November 1, 1954, the only question is what the University would be justified in paying for the right to collect this income during the 6¾ years," the report said. "What the tract may produce after that time has no bearing . . . because the University will get it without having to buy it from anyone." As for future leases:

The Regent's Committee does not believe that any settlement made with the Metropolitan Building Company or the Olympic Hotel Company should be combined with an extended lease or profit-sharing contract with either of these parties. The present leaseholds, if bought at all, should be bought and paid for at a fair price, in cash, and without entangling future commitments. After November 1, 1954, the rights of the Building Company and the Hotel Company will absolutely cease and terminate. There is no reason why their tenure for the coming 6¾ years should give them any preferential position on the property beyond that time. Without the slightest criticism of either of the two companies, it is nevertheless obvious that the University should keep itself in position to obtain competitive offers for the tract after the present lease expires.

---

* The subcommittee had calculated income to the university of $1,000,000, the basic payment, plus $140,000, the current rental, plus $380,000 in profit sharing—an equal division between the university and the lessees—for a total of $1,520,000. Since the university already was receiving its $140,000 in annual rent, the net was $1,380,000.

And why pay twice? On this:

If, however, purchase of the present leaseholds is to be accompanied by new 25-year contracts in favor of the same lessees, then obviously these parties should not be paid twice for giving up their present leases. They should not be paid in full for loss of future earnings and then be allowed to share for a second time in these same earnings. The $10,000,000 payment suggested by the Legislative Subcommittee will buy nothing for the University . . . other than the earning power of the property during the coming 6¾ years. But the University can hardly be expected, first, to pay $10,000,000 for this earning power, and then to turn the property back to the sellers.[40]

There was more. But the point had been made—at necessary length, but respectfully: "The members of the Metropolitan Lease Committee are appreciative of the counsel and the advice of the Legislative Subcommittee. . . . They also share the view of the Legislative Subcommittee that a settlement for the outstanding leaseholds should be negotiated whenever it is possible to make such a settlement at a fair price. . . . They are convinced, however, that the price and plan suggested by the Legislative Subcommittee would involve excessive and duplicate payments." The report, as it appeared in the regents' minutes, was signed by Coleman as president of the board, Balmer as chairman of the committee, Drumheller, and Stuntz—the latter signing as "alternate" for Beck. Miller had moved adoption and, as the minutes put it, the motion "prevailed." If this meant that the approval was not unanimous, the position nevertheless had been established. The board, as a board, was not going to be pushed into a bad deal, even by a legislative group. It could afford to wait.

By mid-1948 the regents were ready to make another offer to the Metropolitan Building Company for the balance of the leasehold. The first offer of eighteen months before was for $4,643,696.65. On June 12, 1948, in a letter signed by Drumheller, who was now president of the board, the regents offered $4,901,005.21 for the six years and four months after July 1, 1948. The regents had increased the amount for the term, but the offer was far short of the $7,873,000 proposed by the company the year before.[41]

It was of small moment that the company's offer no longer existed. On February 18, 1948, Steers had sent a long memorandum to the company's directors in which he recommended that since the offer had not been accepted, it should be withdrawn. Steers had stated fairly that, based on the company's own studies, the state would gain "substantial dollar benefits . . . on the assumption that the State could operate the property so as to produce the same gross and net income before Federal Income Taxes as it has under private management." But Steers, the experienced property manager, hooted at the idea that university management in any form—directly or through an agent— could expect the results attained by a private lessee. The agent concept might work, he conceded, if the agent was offered a minimum fee and a share in the profits, but the thought of university-as-landlord was absurd on its face. "This concept is entirely erroneous," he wrote, "and denotes a pitiful lack of

knowledge of how these results were obtained under private management."
Private management was the answer, under whatever terms ultimately were
developed. Steers noted, too, what certainly was a weakness in the university
position. The regents had as yet no discernible plan for development of the
Metropolitan Center even if the lease was acquired.[42]

The regents, nevertheless, were making a serious offer. There had been
consultations in the intervening months with the company, with Edris, with
the legislative subcommittee, with the Municipal League. Nelson Wahlstrom
had been busy compiling data on probable earnings and taxation, and this
time, under the instruction of the regents, he had made an earnings forecast
on a base of six years ending June 30, 1947, the formula the same as for the
first offer but the base covering a period of higher earnings. The regents'
letter of June 12 said in part: "The Board of Regents offers, subject to the
provisions of existing law, to purchase the unexpired portion of your lease, as
of July 1, 1948, for the sum of $4,901,005.21; such purchase to be effected so
as not to affect further the rights or obligations of tenants under existing subleases expiring at or before the end of your present lease." The offer was
contingent, of course: "Our offer, as you know, depends upon legislative
approval as required by Chapter 44 of the Laws of 1923 and Chapter 284 of
the Laws of 1947 and upon provision by the Legislature of funds necessary
to complete the transaction. You have our assurance that we shall use our best
efforts to secure legislative approval."[43]

For months the offer hung in midair. These were the months, in 1948,
in which the Canwell Committee inquiries into alleged communist activities,
having led to the campus among other places, were fraying the spirit of unity
that had seemed so well established under the new Allen administration.
While the regents carried on with the flow of business they were also awaiting
a report of the university's faculty committee on tenure and academic freedom, which was considering the cases of six persons whose names had sur-
faced in the Canwell hearings. And in the election of November 1948, Arthur
B. Langlie was returned to the governor's chair, and Wallgren was out, and
the change in administration would change before long the composition of
the board of regents. It was possible that the legislature of 1949 would take
some positive action with respect to the regents' powers in the lease quandary.

When the regents submitted their biennial report to the governor and the
legislature in December 1948, they recounted the course of negotiations
on the lease and stated flatly the policy that had become their fixed guide:

. . . the Board of Regents believes that its June 12, 1948, proposal is the maximum
that it can offer.

In dealing with this valuable property, the Board has felt that its prime responsibility is not to make a premature capture of its earning power, but to avoid the possibility of its deterioration. Such deterioration might result either from the neglect of
maintenance by the lessee, or from the competition of newer competitive buildings. . . . There is no evidence of either of these conditions. . . . The Board feels
that, while it is justified in offering the Metropolitan Building Company a price

equivalent to the prospective earning power of the property . . . it is not justified in paying a premium to secure immediate possession. . . . Its [the board's] policy is to obtain unqualified control of the property, either by outright purchase . . . or by lapse of time until the lease expires, and then to invite competitive tenders for future operation.[44]

The legislature of 1949 made no substantive move to solve the dilemma— either to redefine the regents' powers or to fix a term within which they might negotiate with independence. Not that there were no efforts along these lines. Several bills were introduced, friends of the university were active, and R. B. Harris was there to represent the university. There was newspaper pressure for action, at least in Seattle. The *Post-Intelligencer*, in an editorial published shortly after the legislature convened, was saying that a resolution of the lease impasse "constitutes one of the most urgent tasks" confronting the 1949 session. A solution was to "reclothe" the regents with the authority "taken from them by the legislature more than a quarter of a century ago." There were other choices, but in any case: "As matters now stand, the University of Washington is losing upwards of half a million dollars a year which the lessees . . . are paying the federal government in income taxes. . . . But what is more serious still, the whole city is being held back because of the uncertainty surrounding the future of the 10-acre tract in the heart of downtown Seattle. . . . Admitted that, from a political standpoint, it's a 'hot potato.' But it isn't going to get any cooler by 1951."[45]

The task, however, was not accomplished, and little more than five years remained before the lease expired. Two developments had occurred, nevertheless, one deserving mention although it was purely functional, the other the product of the slow evolution of the regents' policy.

At the functional level, the regents turned to the university's own faculty— at President Allen's suggestion—for broad-based professional studies of the Metropolitan Center. The result was the organization of a team of a dozen specialists in business, engineering, sociology, and planning, brought together under the aegis of the College of Business Administration to prepare a comprehensive report on the status and probable future of the downtown tract. A participant in this effort was Arthur M. Cannon, associate professor of accounting, who filed his own elaborate analysis of tract operations.* Neither of these efforts—the team report or the study by Cannon—seems to have been of much help while the lease issue was in stalemate. The time came, however, when Cannon had a more direct part in the story.[46]

---

* Members of this faculty team also included Henry A. Burd, then acting dean of business administration; Grant I. Butterbaugh, associate professor of statistics; Joseph Demmery, professor of business fluctuations and real estate; Nathanael H. Engle, director of the Bureau of Business Research; Robert G. Hennes, professor of civil engineering; Edgar A. Loew, dean emeritus of engineering; Calvin F. Schmid, professor of sociology; William J. Stanton, associate professor of marketing; Joshua H. Vogel, consultant on planning and public works; Bayard O. Wheeler, associate professor of business administration; and Nelson A. Wahlstrom, university comptroller.

By far the more significant development was that the regents had come to realize finally that the university-as-landlord idea simply would not work. Perhaps, by simply declining to scrap the idea, they had kept their options open. But there were many sincere friends of the university who had long ago decided that such a solution would not do. George Powell, who, like Mort Frayn, had been returned to the legislature in 1949, was one of these. Every argument for university management of the tract was really an argument against it. If it was said that the regents might maintain a broad supervisory control over management, the answer was that the regents, serving part-time, already were consumed by details of university management without also having a downtown property to worry about. Was the university to set up a special office for management? If so, from where would come the top-level management experience? Was the tax saving all that relevant? What would be saved if the university faced the expense of establishing and operating a rental office—with a staff of legal specialists, accountants, designers and draftsmen, buyers, and securtiy and service personnel—to meet the needs of the hundreds of tenants? Who would do the planning for the rehabilitation and replacement of aging buildings, the job the regents had not yet faced? How could anything be done expeditiously and profitably, much less with the old Metropolitan flair, if every idea, proposal, decision, or expenditure had to be subjected to legislative oversight or after-the-fact review?

These were considerations at the practical level. But there was another. What would university management of the tract do to the university itself? What would happen to a university president who had to defend every presumed lapse in management judgment or to explain every failure to keep the property in repair? What would happen to the board of regents? Would the time come when a regent was selected more for business acumen than for willingness to bring his best judgment to the service of higher education? The regents of 1947–49 had answered the questions at last. When they decided to wait for "competitive tenders of future operations," they had given up any thought of managing the tract themselves.

In the spring of 1950, when the terms of Drumheller and Coleman were expiring, Governor Langlie appointed two new members to the board of regents. One, Coleman's successor, was Dr. Donald G. Corbett, a Spokane physician, the other Grant Armstrong, a Chehalis attorney.

In retrospect, the year was, as far as the Metropolitan tract was concerned, a year of mobilization for an historic decision. There would have to be careful preparation, everyone realized, for the legislature of 1951. But there was forward motion elsewhere, particularly in the realm of the health sciences, where Corbett's judgment was expected to be valuable. The university's building program had reached the astonishing level, in overall cost, of $45,-000,000, and a faculty building needs committee—an Allen-encouraged innovation—had reviewed the whole spectrum of building priorities and had approved a schedule in which the top position was assigned to a new teaching hospital that would cost $10,000,000 without equipment.[47]

Corbett and Armstrong joined a board which, with Beck now president and Stuntz vice-president, also included the veterans Miller, Balmer, and King. The secretary of the board was, as he had been for years, the much-loved Herbert T. Condon. But Condon was almost eighty, and so he had been given an assistant, John Spiller, the assistant attorney general assigned to the campus, who also was the board's counsel. It was this team, with Balmer still chairman of the Metropolitan lease committee, that devoted what time it could to the tract question and, later, to legislative strategy.

Corbett was the elder of the two new regents. He had entered the university initially in 1917, but then had gone off to war service and had won his B.S. degree in 1923. His M.D. degree was from the University of Pennsylvania (1927), and he had done advanced medical studies at Johns Hopkins and the University of California. He had practiced in Spokane since 1933 and he had been a member of the advisory committee of the university's medical school. When he became a regent, he also became, almost simultaneously, president of the Washington State Medical Association.[48]

Armstrong's ties to the university were somewhat closer. A graduate of the university's Law School in 1929, Armstrong had been admitted to the state bar in 1930, had established his law practice in Chehalis (where he had attended high school), had briefly been a police judge, and had served with the navy in World War II. After the war, and back in Chehalis, he had resumed his successful practice. Although he had been mildly involved in Republican politics, he was above all an attorney widely known in the state, especially in Seattle, where he had university friends and professional connections. It would be Armstrong's destiny to serve only one term as a regent, but to be president of the board when all the years of policy-making and preparation came together in the execution of the new leases and agreements that fixed for decades the future of the tract after the Metropolitan Building Company was no longer in charge.[49]

For most of the remaining months of 1950 the tract question simmered, not at the center of the regents' attention, but far from forgotten by them or by the Metropolitan Building Company, the alumni, or members of the legislature. The focus was 1951, and it was Beck who ignited a small burst of fireworks as the legislative session approached.

The alumni committee on the lease had been continuously in touch with developments of 1947 and 1948 and disappointed that no assistance had come from the legislature of 1949. By late 1949, the committee, with Arthur Simon now its chairman, was ready to come forward with a recommendation that the legislature simply scrap the 1923 law that was proving an impediment to progress. In October, the committee published a second report, *The 'Old University Grounds' in 1949*, in which it stated the alumni position and put into the record again the history of the tract and the recommendations of 1945. Noting that four years had already passed since its earlier call for action, the committee said:

> Since prompt action is necessary, the Committee of the Alumni Association has unanimously arrived at the conclusion that the responsibility for the administration of the Metropolitan Tract should be returned to the Board of Regents . . . without the requirement of legislative ratification of their acts. . . . The Committee has concluded that the Board of Regents cannot effectively bargain with the present tenants of the property . . . and cannot effectively discuss commitments for long range improvement of the tract, if all of the proposals of the Boad of Regents continue to be, as they are now, purely tentative and subject to legislative ratification under the provisions of Chapter 44 of the Laws of 1923. Accordingly, the Committee strongly urges that this statute be repealed.[50]

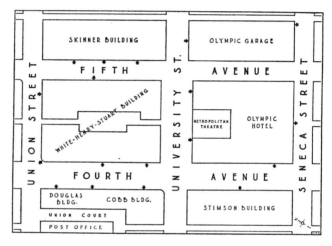

Plat of the tract as it was when new lease negotiations were nearing, displayed in the university alumni association's publication, *The "Old University Grounds" in 1949*

Whether or not it was a university policy objective, repeal of the 1923 law presumably was, to the regents, a consummation devoutly to be wished. The idea was in the background during 1950, but by November the regents were meeting with Curly Harris and William H. Ferguson, the Seattle attorney who was then president of the alumni association, to discuss "proposed repeal of the 1923 Legislative Act." In December, three regents, Balmer, Armstrong, and Corbett, accompanied by Wahlstrom, went to Olympia to get Governor Langlie's views. The results of the conference with Langlie were reported to the board at a meeting later that same day, December 20. The governor, Balmer said, was opposed to "outright repeal" of the 1923 law but might consider "some amplifications" of the regents' powers. Balmer was authorized by the regents to prepare a draft of proposed legislation to come to the board later through the Metropolitan lease committee.[51]

Something in all this seems to have rasped the nerves of Beck, who was, after all, president of the board. The meeting of December 20 may not have been one of total harmony. A week later, in any case, Beck had given to the newspapers a long statement in which, while it implied that Governor Langlie was "playing politics with the University," also showed rather plainly that Beck had objected to the Balmer-Armstrong-Corbett approach to the governor: Corbett was not a member of the Metropolitan lease committee and Stuntz, a member, was not invited. Beck had not been invited either, although the president of the board was, as he pointed out, an ex officio member of all committees.

Beck's statements made headlines, of course. The Douglass Welch story in the *Post-Intelligencer* was headed "Beck Charges Langlie with U. of W. Politics" (December 28, 1950), and Beck was quoted as saying:

In my position as a member of the board of regents, I insist that no branch of state government should attempt to exert pressure upon the regents in the discharge of their trusteeship. I object to the injection of politics into the management of the University. . . .

Secondly, I recognize that the regents do not now possess the authority to enter into a lease or make other disposition of the Metropolitan Tract unless such agreement is first approved by the state legislature. It is now generally recognized that some additional legislation is necessary. . . . I have studied various proposals for amending the law. . . . I am convinced that the plan offered by the alumni is the best. The alumni plan calls for an amendment to the law making the regents solely responsible for the transaction of University business, including the matter of the tract.

Beck disclosed the other regents' meeting with Governor Langlie, saying that he had been informed "that the governor at that meeting vigorously opposed the alumni plan." Then he said: "I insist that discussions of this question should be conducted by the governor, out in the open, with the authorized Metropolitan Committee of the regents."

When Governor Langlie was asked for his comment, he said that he had simply been candid with the delegation of regents: "There never has been anything secret about my views and I never have tried to inject myself into the University's problems. But I have to veto or accept whatever legislation is decided upon. Anyone who wanted to discuss the problem was entitled to my views. . . . I feel that the University regents should have every latitude in the management of the tract, but if it comes to a long-term lease . . . any arrangements should be subject to the checks and balances that normally apply . . . , and the legislature should confirm any long-range program. . . . This is the way all public business should be handled."

There the exchange ended. Beck was on record as supporting the alumni position. Balmer was considering possible legislation, and it remained to be seen whether he and his committee would recommend outright repeal of the 1923 law. In a position of such ambivalence the regents and the alumni awaited the opening of the 1951 legislature.

CHAPTER 9

The Second Era Begins:
1951 to 1953

No one knew how or even whether, as the year 1951 opened, the parts of the Metropolitan lease puzzle could be fitted together passably well before the lease expired on October 31, 1954. Something had to be done, for it was no use saying again that time was getting short. The regents bore a heavy responsibility, but it could not be said that the initiative was theirs alone, for the hand of the legislature was upon them. The regents were Beck, president, Stuntz, vice-president, and Miller, Balmer, King, Armstrong, and Corbett. Under a surface calm, much groping was going on.

Tenants of the tract—some eight hundred—were understandably restive, their plans for the future in abeyance during months of waiting to find out who was to be their landlord. Certain of the tenants, including such star sub-lessees as Littler's and I. Magnin and Company, also had plans for expansion that were in suspense. If the 1951 legislature did nothing—neither expanded the regents' authority nor found some other solution—there would be only the 1953 session to look to, and 1953 would be late in the game to make major decisions affecting Seattle's central business district. The Metropolitan Center still stood at the core of the urban entity, but for years that entity had been flowing out over the hills and into the valleys of the region, southward beyond the Duwamish industrial tangle to the Seattle-Tacoma Airport, eastward about Lake Washington, and northward into new residential communities and business centers. The automobile had made it all possible, and had induced the construction of a marvelous floating bridge across Lake Washington. But the interestingly difficult Seattle topography was dotted by traffic choke points, especially downtown. There was no guarantee that, with the emergence of new patterns of transportation and business activity, Seattle's commercial center would not be moved slowly away from its historic locus.

One response to the traffic situation had appeared by 1951, a response not only significant in its originality but touched by a certain second-generation inevitability. Eight miles north of the Metropolitan Center, in what had been mostly forest land when the White Building was constructed in 1908, a new company, the Northgate, had built an $18,000,000 shopping mall, a sixty-acre plaza where stores and shops were surrounded by vast expanses of parking space. This development, the first of its kind in the United States, was prepared to serve a population of 275,000 persons living within a five-mile radius. At Northgate, the automobile was welcome, and the suburban mall was on its way. The president and manager of the Northgate Company was James B. Douglas, the son of J. F. Douglas, and many of J. F. Douglas's thoughts about doing things in "the Metropolitan way"—controlling the use of overly ostentatious signs, for one—went into the planning of Northgate. J. F. himself, now past seventy-five, had been in failing health for about three years, and in November 1951, he would resign as a director and chairman of the finance committee of the Carnation Company. Nevertheless, he was still a vice-president of the Metropolitan Company that he had founded—the company that expected to win, before long, a renewal of its downtown lease.[1]

Yet the downtown lease problem was a set of problems. The regents of the university, given whatever latitude the legislature might provide, had to make arrangements not for a single "ten-acre" tract but for a property of three interlocking elements, the Olympic Hotel, the Metropolitan Theatre, and the main part upon which stood middle-aged and aging buildings and annexes, including two structures, the Douglas Building and the Olympic Garage (the old Arena), which were growing old far from gracefully. Furthermore, the problems were enveloped by uncertainties. The Korean War was now six months old. On July 25, 1950, North Korean forces had struck south across the 38th parallel, and once again (even though the incursion was characterized for a while as an "incident") the armed forces of the United States were in action, civilian rationing was in prospect, steel and other building materials were in short supply, and the nation was thinking nervously about civil defense, but this time in the new age of the atomic bomb. In the state of Washington, the budget was in trouble, and Governor Langlie was worrying in public about this. At the university, an unhappy period of retrenchment was looming, just as the administration was preparing to ask the legislature about funding the new teaching hospital. And although the signs were perceptible only within the university, a change in the university administration itself was possible.

That, in January 1951, was the situation. Three years and four months before a fifty-year deadline it could not be predicted with confidence that Metropolitan lease questions of great complexity could be worked out in time, even if the regents' authority was to be duly delegated.

But it happened, and the pieces were fitted into place. By mid-1953, the regents, clothed with authority, had executed new agreements covering the Olympic, the Metropolitan Theatre, and the main body of the tract. By early 1954, plans for improvement of the tract were being put into action. Holding the new "main lease" was a company headed by a New York and Detroit entrepreneur who had never seen Seattle until that moment. And the Metropolitan Building Company still lived. When it became essential to solve the three-part puzzle, the puzzle was solved. But the solutions were of kinds not readily imagined in 1951.

First, there was the legislature. The Metropolitan stakes were high in 1951, and the tensions as well, but of political trading there was none. The trading was in ideas, and the issue was simplicity itself: what could a legislature do— what language could it put into a bill—to assure that the Metropolitan tract became at last a profitable endowment? It would have been helpful if the university people most familiar with the question—the regents and the alumni association representatives in particular—had been in agreement in the beginning on a proposed solution. But they were not, and thus they invited proposals by others. It might have been better too, if the regents had not let the idea persist that they might choose to manage the tract themselves. They had forsworn the thought, but they never had said so in public. Because they had not clarified their view of the management choices, they soon found themselves facing legislative misunderstanding.

Ten bills relating to the tract or to the powers of the regents' were introduced during the 1951 session. The number is deceptive. Two of these were place-saving bills—bills numbered, but without texts—and two obviously were out of step with prevailing sentiment. One of the latter would have authorized the sale of the tract for not less than $90,000,000 (the sponsors said knowledgeable appraisers put the value as high as $120,000,000), the proceeds to go into a trust fund to support university construction. The other would have placed management of the tract under a nine-member commission headed by the governor, only two of the nine members to be appointed by the regents. Such proposals at least tested the outer limits of the possibilities. But while almost no one considered seriously an effort to sell the tract, the commission idea apparently attracted some momentary support. In any case, President Allen, obviously with the approval of the regents, eventually sent to the key committee chairmen in house and senate (with copies for all concerned) a long and judiciously worded letter pointing out the danger inherent in removing responsibility for the tract from the regents, the historic and duly constituted custodians of university property.[2]

Other bills there were—the critical bills, the serious bills. It is dangerous, and perhaps unnecessary, to try to draw too narrowly the account of what was going on in the legislature that year. But in the legislative journals, the contemporary newspaper accounts, and the regents' minutes (seldom rich in detail), it is possible to glimpse the events in sequence.

The legislature convened on January 8, 1951. But before that, on January 2, Balmer had brought to the regents, as he had been asked to do, a draft of a proposed bill modifying the 1923 law that limited the regents' authority. Balmer's suggestions fell somewhat short of outright repeal of the 1923 law, the alumni association's recommendation supported by President Beck. Balmer, who had talked to Governor Langlie and knew that the governor was not ready to think of repeal, may simply have been practicing the art of the possible, searching for some middle position. But Balmer was also thinking of the tenants of the tract—of the need to assure them a continuity of occupancy and sublesseeship—and was trying to assume a statesmanlike position that would avoid a legislative hang-up on total repeal, preparing to make some compromise if a compromise were necessary to protect the tenants against legislative stalemate. In any case, since the regents' and alumni views obviously needed reconciling, the board could only ask Balmer and his fellow members of the Metropolitan lease committee to set up an early meeting with the alumni. That meeting was held on January 6, 1951, two days before the legislature was to convene.

The meeting went on all day. Balmer, Armstrong, and Stuntz were there from the Metropolitan lease committee, and the alumni were represented by a ten-man group including Donald Douglas, current president of the alumni association; William H. Ferguson, the former president (he was president when the association's 1949 recommendations were developed); Philip Macbride, the former regent; Arthur Simon, Raymond Davis, and Joseph Gandy, from the alumni lease committee; and others—R. B. Harris among them, of course. This long session produced a proposal that was submitted to the regents the following week and became, for a time, an official position. It was indeed a compromise. The university would favor repeal of the 1923 law while yielding to the legislature the right to ratify any sale or lease effective after November 1, 1954, when the old lease expired. Such a solution would empower the regents to try to negotiate purchase of the Metropolitan Building Company's waning leasehold while they worked with the tract tenants, regardless of any settlement with the Metropolitan company, to write new subleases or agreements extending beyond the lease expiration dates. These objectives were incorporated in a bill introduced on January 12, shortly after the legislature convened, by Mort Frayn and Bernard Gallagher, a Spokane Democrat. Surprisingly, the bill specified, as the first among three options for management, that management of the tract might be "directly by the Board." The bill also stipulated that no sale of the tract or extension of the existing lease or "a new lease or combination of leases . . . shall be valid or effective unless it shall have been first approved by statute enacted by this legislature."[3]

There the lease matter rested while university spokesmen appeared before the senate and house appropriations committees to ask funding for the teaching hospital. Such funding was not in Governor Langlie's proposed budget, and the request, in such a year, may have seemed somewhat unrealistic. Questions about the program in medicine—particularly about the number of medical students being admitted—were fielded before a joint meeting of the committees by Dean Edward L. Turner, but it was Nelson Wahlstrom who had an idea about financing. A $5,000,000 appropriation from the state's general fund might be matched, Wahlstrom said, by money from the federal government. Inevitably it would occur to someone that part of the funding might come from the millions of revenue that the university would be getting from the Metropolitan tract, even though the millions were far from in hand. The idea soon took its own twist. On January 25, a week after the Turner-Wahlstrom testimony, Senators Robert Grieve and Albert Rosellini introduced a bill that would permit the university to issue $5,000,000 in bonds against Metropolitan tract income to provide basic financing for the hospital.[4]

The weeks until late February were filled with speculation and efforts to correct misunderstandings. Balmer seems to have scored heavily at a legislative hearing of late January when he outlined his personal views of the tract dilemma, describing the plight of the tenants if they were left in limbo and the regents' desire to achieve some flexibility in handling such interim questions. Balmer said that the tract might be "vacant" in November 1954 if restrictions on the regents were not relaxed, but he was not in favor of removing final authority from the legislature. He said that the whole tract property should yield $2,250,000 a year for the university and another $250,000 to the city in lieu of property taxes. Certain legislators seemingly were nervous about a solution resulting in two leases, one to the Olympic Hotel, the other to the tract itself. But that was what Balmer advocated, or would, at least, regard with equanimity. The hotel, he thought, was a separate problem, and he would favor a lease of not more than seven to ten years, or long enough for a proprietor to amortize the costs of improvements. But Balmer confessed that his fellow regents were not unanimously behind his "plan." Balmer was quoted in the *Times*, "Some regents want the legislature to relinquish all control." One such regent undoubtedly was Beck.[5]

If the regents were not agreed, and if they had not publicly disclaimed their interest in direct management, it was small wonder that confusion arose. Soon there was newspaper talk of a possible "deadlock" over the issue—which would throw the whole matter over to 1953, if not into a special session—or of a fear that, if some last-minute compromise brought "ill-advised legislation," the resulting bill would be vetoed by Governor Langlie. Any general legislative mood seemed firm on two points. The committees were searching for some neat leasing package embracing the whole of the property, and they were opposed to management by the regents or by the university. As a *Times* report put it, the legislators felt that "the university should be prevented" from operating the tract. The phrasing was revealing. But by mid-February there had come from the house committee on colleges and universities a bill that would give the regents leeway they apparently had not even contemplated.

The new bill (H.B. 516) would give the regents power to work out leases of the tract, without legislative approval, for any period up to twenty-five years. The bill had the weight of a committee bill, but it was not to go unchallenged even though the sixteen members of the committee included several who were known to have particular knowledge of the tract and the alternatives for its development. In the chair of the committee was Jeanette Testu, one of Washington's experienced women legislators, and with her was that educator, historian, and former regent of the university, Eva Anderson, now a legislative activist. Frayn was a member, as was L. J. Shadbolt, who had been chairman of the legislative council's subcommittee on the lease. Frayn, who had said that the Frayn-Gallagher bill had been designed simply to give the regents "interim authority," now favored the twenty-five-year concept.[6]

How the concept arose is not altogether clear, but it apparently resulted as a compromise among proponents of three viewpoints: (1) those who wanted a single lease for the whole tract, but with a time limit; (2) those who would have given the regents broad authority, except to sell the tract or manage it themselves, but this authority would also be limited in time; and (3) those who would free the regents entirely from legislative or time limits, but who felt the university should be able to "recapture" the property if the regents' arrangements proved unsatisfactory. From some such mixture the twenty-five-year idea came to the surface. In any case, the twenty-five-year limit was the theme of the committee bill, and it was a theme that the regents regarded at first with mixed feelings.[7]

On February 28, only a week before the legislature was to adjourn, the regents held a special meeting in Balmer's office—although Beck and Corbett were absent—to review their position. President Allen and Wahlstrom also attended, as did Dean Edwin Guthrie of the Graduate School and Donald K. Anderson, director of university relations. Stuntz, presiding in Beck's absence, asked Balmer and Wahlstrom to "check him in his statement about the present appearance of the University's interests at Olympia." Of this the regents' minutes say:

The discussion hinged around the attitude of the Board as to several points, one being the insistence upon a lease not to exceed 25 years in length, and also as to the opposition of numerous members of the Legislature to the University Regents operating the properties covered by the lease. The consensus of those present was that while there was considerable doubt as to the wisdom of a lease as short as 25 years (40 to 50 years possibly preferable), the difference was not of great enough importance to demand any great sacrifice. . . . As to the operation of the lease, the Regents felt that it was largely a misunderstanding upon the part of the members of the Legislature as no Regent cares to have the detailed responsibility of operating the properties under the lease. In fact, they are opposed to such.[8]

As for the twenty-five-year limit, the regents had looked the gift horse in the mouth and found it sound, if marginally. They asked Balmer to go to Olympia soon to express their support of the committee bill. As for their management of the tract "directly," the regents finally had said—although not in public—that they were "opposed to such." It is just possible that the legislature's continuing doubt about the regents' position was, ironically, the element that worked to the regents' advantage after all.

The committee bill had passed the house on February 23 by a vote of 86 to 0, thirteen members absent or not voting. It was in the senate that the challenge came on March 6, virtually on the eve of adjournment. The senate committee on higher education had introduced an alternative bill that would give the regents unlimited authority as long as neither they nor the university attempted to manage the property. At 4 P.M. the senate debate began, tempers frequently flaring, the newspapers said. When the house bill was sustained, it then faced a series of proposed amendments, all eventually voted down. But the debate went on until after midnight, when the clocks were stopped to permit the senate to finish. The final vote was 36 to 8, two senators not voting. The house version had won. In a special report from Olympia, Ross Cunningham, the *Times*'s associate editor wrote: "Politically the situation was unusual. The bill mainly was of Democratic origin, since the Democrats control the house where it was drawn and first passed. In the Senate, the Republicans applied the pressure to pass it, with the Senate Democrats putting on the steam to amend it."[9]

The regents had been given freedom to act. They could negotiate for the Metropolitan leasehold. They could make new leases up to twenty-five years. The inhibitions of the old 1923 law were at last removed. The legislature also approved and sent to the governor the bill (S.B. 113) authorizing the university to issue $5,000,000 in bonds against future Metropolitan tract income to support construction of the teaching hospital.

Balmer had his thoughts about what the next steps should be. In a statement issued immediately after the legislature's adjournment he expressed the regents' appreciation of the outcome and said that the board would seek expert advice on how best to open the property to competitive proposals for leasing and management: "The Regents are gratified by the passage of this bill, which gives them latitude for business-like management of the property that they have not enjoyed under the Act of 1923. . . . The Regents' first step probably will be the preparation of a pamphlet containing photographs of the property and an accurate description of the buildings. . . . The next . . . to advertise in nationally-distributed publications inviting inquiries . . . and proposals for the operation of the property upon the expiration of the present lease . . . whether that expiration occurs by lapse of time or prior settlement upon some agreed basis with the Metropolitan Building Company."[10]

The course thus plotted was sensible, certainly, although it gave scant encouragement to the Metropolitan Building Company, which could only wait for another offer on its leasehold or prepare to bid against others for a new agreement. The course was followed, but not quite the way Balmer visualized it.

A change in the membership of the board was to be expected in the spring of 1951, because Stuntz's term was expiring and Governor Langlie would have a place to fill. The new regent, who joined the board in April, was Charles Frankland, the banker, who had been close to the university all along. What was not anticipated was that there would be another change. In May, Dave Beck resigned, after finishing his year as president of the board. In the annual reorganization John L. King had been elected president and Beck had not been appointed to the Metropolitan lease committee, which now was composed of Balmer, Frankland, Armstrong, and Corbett. Thus there was not only a change in the board, but for a year the board had only six members. Not until June 1952 did Governor Langlie name Beck's replacement.

Beck resigned on May 9 with a letter to Governor Langlie and another to

King in which he protested the regents' decision to increase the fees of university students. His feeling about the fee increase was linked to his feeling about what should be done at the Metropolitan tract, and he elaborated on his views in an interview with the press. The increase in fees would not be dramatic—from $138 to $165 for the academic year—but why charge the students, Beck asked, when the university very soon would be receiving vast new amounts of rental income from the tract? In Beck's eyes, the prospect of larger income from the tract made many of the university's traditional financial improvisations subject to reexamination. Beck thought the regents should move at once to begin to make arrangements with tenants beyond 1954— from the Olympic Hotel to Magnin's, Littler's, and others—as they had been empowered by the legislature to do. (Beck's interview came on the very day that the president of Magnin's, Hector Escabosa, was visiting Seattle to explore plans for expansion, including a possible move away from the tract.) But Beck also thought that the regents should review the historic policy by which tract income was assigned to the university building fund. When the university's rental was only $140,000 a year, such a conservative use of modest resources might be defensible. But now the income might be millions. Apart from the matter of the fees—or even including that matter—Beck's remarks touched issues that would indeed have to be faced. Still, by resigning, Beck had withdrawn from the position where he might have been able to influence decisions. In his statements to the press the reason seemed to come clear. Beck had been a board member five years, one year as president. He thought that he should be a member of the Metropolitan lease committee and he was not. "I felt when the new subcommittee was set up without me," he said, "that if my experience with the tract problem was not sufficient for me to be continued on a subcommittee, I didn't belong on the Board of Regents." Beck was gone. His questions remained.[11]

But within a month Balmer had moved to get the expert assistance that he was sure the regents would need if they were to move forthrightly on the leasing problems. On June 8, 1951, he asked the board to approve the establishment in the Metropolitan Center of a university office headed by an "administrative assistant" who would be the regents' representative in all things pertaining to the tract—the pivot man in the complicated game that was about to start. The board approved the idea unanimously. Balmer described the kind of man he had in mind, but it was Frankland who found him.[12]

A downtown office under full-time direction was essential. No part-time board could begin to involve itself in the studies and negotiations that were coming. The "administrative assistant" would have to possess, nevertheless, an almost unrealizable combination of premium qualifications—a record of success in business, experience with leasing and leasing philosophies, a knowledge of property management and maintenance, an analytical mind, an ability to represent the regents in contacts with corporate executives at any level, a sensitivity for the liaison role (especially in the context of university processes), an ability to move quickly and effectively within the limits of the authority delegated by the regents, a knowledge of Seattle and of the importance of the tract therein, an awareness of the political overtones associated with leasing decisions, and an instinct for knowing when not to talk, particularly to representatives of the press. Any other attributes a candidate might bring would be his own, and welcome. When, a month later, Balmer had developed a draft "Directive to Administrative Assistant"—this before the choice was made final—the position looked no less formidable. In a preamble, Balmer said, "The broad policy of the Board of Regents is to obtain the maximum revenue from the Metropolitan Tract consistent with its maintenance, improvement, and progressive development as a property of the highest class." The plans were open, the regents receptive to all "constructive" and "responsible" proposals. In the context of such anticipations the new man would serve the Metropolitan lease committee with an office in the White-Henry-Stuart Building. His "clerical help" would be "as authorized by the President of the University." On financial matters he would confer with the comptroller, Nelson Wahlstrom, and on legal matters with the assistant attorney general, John Spiller. He would assemble in his office all possible data bearing on the tract—rentable space, rentals, records of tenancies, floor plans, probable future rental values. He would study the needs for modernization or replacement. He would be prepared to deal with the Metropolitan Building Company or with Edris, forwarding his recommendations with regard to leases. He was to deal similarly with major tenants. He was to prepare literature describing the tract for "persons desiring to submit proposals for the future operation of the property." He was to analyze all proposals, conduct correspondence about them, and report his recommendations to the lease committee. He was to be the counsel to the committee and subject to its direction. The administrative assistant had to be, in short, a man of broad experience with enough sensitivity to work effectively at the center of the action without trying unduly to direct the outcome.[13]

The man who came to that position was Arthur T. Lee. He was not long the "administrative assistant," however, for quite soon Lee became, by title and in fact, representative of the Metropolitan lease committee. The special quality that Lee brought to the job was a philosophical outlook—an easy, confident, good-humored approach to an assignment that he took absolutely seriously. He had not asked for the position, and he was reluctant to accept it when it was offered, saying that he knew little about the Metropolitan tract and even less about the university's policies or expectations with respect to it. Lee had only recently retired from business, as a partner in James Farrell and Company, a Seattle-San Francisco merchandising firm, and he was young enough—not yet sixty—to be enjoying it. But he was a long-time friend of Charles Frankland's, and it was Frankland who talked to Lee on several occasions and described the regents' need for a man with a sure hand in a very complicated business-university-legislative situation. When Lee agreed in mid-1951 to open the Metropolitan lease committee's downtown office, he was stepping into a role entirely new to him. The salary was scarcely more than a retainer for a man who, as Balmer said, had to be "conversant with matters of the nature of this one, which involves many millions of dollars." But the role would have been new to anyone at any price. Lee assumed it.[14]

The regents' determination to open the leases to all "responsible" offers meant that the bidding, at least for the hotel and probably for the tract itself, would be national. The regents intended, as Balmer had said, to publish calls for offers in nationally distributed journals and to support these with literature describing and illustrating the property upon which lease bids were invited. Simply assembling data on the buildings would be an exacting undertaking. Making comparative analyses of the resulting offers would be even more so. It was a solid, unblinking business judgment that the regents wanted when they employed Lee. And if Lee's career was not of the kind to have won national attention, the regents were sure that he had the judgment. He was, furthermore, a Seattle man of more than local scope.

Lee had been born in the Seattle of the 1890s in a small home on Taylor Street (near the spot where the Space Needle would one day rise). He was one of seven children of a Presbyterian minister and the grandson of the William B. Lee, pastor of the First Presbyterian Church of Olympia, who had delivered the invocation at Washington's statehood ceremonies in 1889. Lee's father had taken his family to Cincinnati early in the century, but Lee attended high school in Seattle before going off to Whitworth College for a year and then on to Whitman. He graduated from Whitman just as the United States declared war on Germany in 1917. From college Lee went to officer training in San Francisco and then to France, where he was seriously wounded, spent months in hospitals, and was awarded the U.S. Army's Distinguished Service Cross by General John J. Pershing, and the Croix de Guerre with Palm by the governments of France and Belgium, the French award signed by General Philippe Pétain, the hero of Verdun. For a while, after the war, Lee accumulated business experience in New York, but he soon returned to Seattle to become in time a part owner of James Farrell and Company. Since 1949 he had been a trustee of Whitman College. His wife was a graduate of the University of Washington, as were a son and a daughter.[15]

Lee went to work in a small office in the Cobb Building, but by autumn 1951, his quarters had been established in room 1031, White-Henry-Stuart Building. There were no lease offers yet, of course, but there were some inquiries. The Hilton and the Statler groups were said to be interested in the Olympic—as was Edris, naturally—and an unnamed insurance company and a California financier apparently had thoughts about development of the tract as a whole. The regents had considered the development question and had decided that nothing was more important. And as they were approving the employment of Lee they approved a letter from King to President Allen, asking him to explain to Dean Turner that income from the tract could not then be bonded for construction of the teaching hospital, even though legislative authority existed, because the regents had to put first the "conservation and improvement of the income producing potentialities" of the property.[16]

Yet even as Lee was busy with his initial inventories downtown, the wheels of change were grinding on the university campus. It was of sentimental as well as of immediate and functional significance that Herbert T. Condon retired in August 1951. The kindly, loyal Condon, so long the secretary of the board of regents, had not much longer to live, but his presence still had meaning, for if Edmond Meany had been the keeper of the university's history, Condon, no less than Meany, had been the keeper of its spirit as well as of its official records. In a long and happy life Condon had served as bursar, comptroller, registrar, and dean, friend of students and regents alike, and he retired as dean emeritus of students and secretary emeritus and "adviser" to the board. But it was not long before President Allen submitted his own resignation as president of the university. Once again a board of regents—this time a board of six—would be searching for a new president when certain large problems, among them the leasing of the tract and the funding of the teaching hospital, were on the agenda.[17]

Raymond Allen's five years as president had been years of tremendous growth on the campus. Allen was an enthusiast, and in that period when federal funding of university reasearch was just coming into flower, Allen had been the fast-moving spokesman for expansion, development, and improvement of facilities. He was often in Washington, D.C., both for the university and in national service: he was on leave in 1949 as the first director of medical services for the Department of Defense and in 1951 as first chairman of the U.S. Salary Stabilization Board. But the years had been frustrating in the stalemate over hospital funding, and, in the protracted sequel to the Canwell inquiries, bruising. Whatever the elements that went into his decision, Allen was ready for change. Late in 1951 he accepted an appointment by President Truman as director of the Psychological Strategy Board, an arm of the National Security Council, but even then it was thought that Allen would be invited soon to some other major post in higher education, perhaps another university presidency. Allen's new assignment was to begin on January 2, 1952, and thus there had to be an interim administration of some kind. Late in December 1951, the regents acted on this. "Pending selection of the permanent president," the board approved the appointment of H. P. Everest as acting president and chairman of an administrative executive committee. The committee was composed of four deans, Lloyd S. Woodburne, of Arts and Sciences; Harold E. Wessman, of Engineering; Edward L. Turner, of Medicine; and Gordon D. Marckworth, of Forestry.[18]

It may reveal something about the mood of the time to note that even as he departed Allen had the Metropolitan tract on his mind. In his final remarks to the alumni he spoke of the work of the Metropolitan lease committee in helping to assure passage of the 1951 legislation. And Everest, coming in as acting president, was about to begin a long and—somewhat later—direct connection with the tract and the changes that were coming. For the moment, Everest had his hands full.

Everest was the second man to come to the president's chair from the field of journalism, for he had been a Kirkland newspaper publisher from 1924 to 1938 (when he sold his paper to complete the university education that had been interrupted by World War I), and by 1944 he was director of the School of Journalism and by 1950 head of the new School of Communications. The appointment was generally welcomed, for Everest was not only widely known throughout the state but also known as a skillful administrator whose natural political talents had been sharpened by short-term service on two occasions, in 1944 and 1949, as administrative assistant to Governor Langlie. Whatever else Everest's appointment meant, it meant that until the new president was selected and installed the university's problems would get the direct, daily, and unremitting attention of a man who, with a team of four deans, would try to effect a consolidation of the growth that had come under President Allen.[19]

Events came in a tumble in 1952. Lee had been busy, and by mid-January the Metropolitan tract was being offered for lease in advertisements in the *Wall Street Journal* and other publications of national circulation. By February, the regents were preparing to make another offer for acquisition of the remaining years—the final thirty-two months, actually—of the Metropolitan Building Company leasehold. By March, the new president of the university had been named.

Lee's advertisement in the *Wall Street Journal*—the text checked and approved by the regents, of course—was a model of calculated simplicity. It said, tersely:

THE UNIVERSITY OF WASHINGTON
ANNOUNCES AN INTERESTING OPPORTUNITY
IN SEATTLE'S FAMED METROPOLITAN CENTER

Present lease of the University of Washington's highly developed 10-acre tract with 8 major office buildings, hotel and garage, in the business heart of Seattle, expires October, 1954. New lease or other business arrangement for management and operation will be made. Your interest is invited in the tract as a whole, or the Olympic Hotel (Seattle's finest) and office buildings, separately or in a group. (Sale of property not contemplated.)

There could not have been such an advertisement before—ever—for a property of such value in so singular a place. To provide information for respondents, Lee had put together a sixteen-page brochure, "The University of Washington's Metropolitan Properties: In the Heart of Seattle—a Growing City," with photographs and data on every building and annex from the Olympic Hotel to the antique Douglas Building—a priceless record of the tract as it was in 1951. In the booklet was a perspective map of the

Seattle area with the tract highlighted in the center of the metropolitan land-scape. "It is our hope," the regents' invitation said, "that prospective lessees and others interested will themselves make a study of the situation and sub-mit to us their ideas and proposals. No fees, commissions or brokerage will be paid by the University."[20]

Offers did not come pouring in. But there were preliminary inquiries. One was from Norman Tishman, president of Tishman Realty and Construction Company of New York, which operated more than twenty office and apart-ment buildings in New York, Chicago, Los Angeles, and elsewhere. But the regents, and Lee, were moving quickly in the meantime to try to acquire the balance of the Metropolitan leasehold. They had tried twice before without result, but now the effort was in a different setting. No proposal for extension of the lease had come from the Metropolitan Building Company, and even if one should come, it would be measured against any others that might be received. The regents wanted to clear the deck. They wanted overall manage-ment by a single lessee company except for the Olympic Hotel, which they regarded as a separate matter. They did not want to have to deal individually with each of the hundreds of tenants of the tract, and they thought that a new lessee should be able to do that from a position uncluttered by the remnants of the old leasehold.[21]

During January 1952, Balmer and his Metropolitan lease committee asso-ciates—Armstrong, Corbett, and Frankland—had been in conference with Steers and others of the Metropolitan Building Company leadership. Philip Macbride was participating as attorney for the board. The result was an agreement, approved by the board on February 1, under which the university would acquire the leasehold balance on March 1, 1952, for $2,666,500 payable in four installments, $366,500 on consummation of the purchase, $775,000 on March 1 of 1953 and 1954, and $750,000 on January 1, 1955. The purchase would include the ground lease of the Olympic Hotel without affecting the management. The Metropolitan Building Company would continue to oper-ate the tract to the end of its lease, subject to cancellation on notice, receiving reimbursement for operating and administrative expenses and half of all net operating income above $120,000 per month, the amount the university needed to make its payments. Only one aspect of the arrangement was in doubt. Would the rentals derived by the university continue to be exempt from federal taxation? The regents instructed Macbride to obtain a ruling from the Commissioner of Internal Revenue.[22]

There was wide interest and a general feeling of jubilation in Seattle when this agreement became known, especially among tract tenants. Newspaper reports, covering the development at length, included calculations that the university would be receiving some $800,000 more, in the final months of the lease, than under the old $140,000-a-year schedule. The Metropolitan stock-holders still had to approve the agreement, but approval seemed assured. It was merely the tax ruling that was awaited. By February 20 the tax question seemed to have been cleared when the federal bureau ruled that the university's supplemental income would be exempt—the ruling subject, however, to certain "technical reservations." On February 29 the Metropolitan company's stockholders approved at a special meeting (unanimously by holders of the 74.7 percent of shares represented) the proposal to accept the university's offer. But the Metropolitan company was agreeing to the sale only if the proceeds were subject to long-term capital gains taxes. A federal ruling on March 27 declared some items subject to capital gains and others to ordinary income taxes.* For months no clarification came despite the company's repeated requests. The original agreement languished. Finally it became obsolete.[23]

Serious talks nevertheless had been going on about major leasings, particularly with regard to the hotel. Talks were also under way with Norman Tishman, who had refined his planning somewhat and approached individual regents in March 1952 with ideas for a development—again, a Rockefeller Center—costing perhaps $50,000,000. Tishman had produced a scale model of his tract concept, and he was thinking tall. He visualized the White-Henry-Stuart replaced by a forty-story structure and others by two buildings of twenty-five stories. The new center would also be served by a garage for seven thousand cars. Tishman himself told the press that the regents wanted to "listen to all comers," but it was his interest, perhaps, that sparked the national attention the regents' efforts now were getting. *Business Week* magazine covered the situation with a report, "For Rent: The Best Business Section of Seattle," in which Tishman's model was given appropriate attention. There was as yet no move from the Metropolitan Building Company, but the hotel question certainly was nearing resolution. By the spring of 1952 proposals had been submitted by The Olympic, Incorporated—the Edris lessee company—and by the Hilton Hotels Corporation, the Sheraton Corporation of America, the Hotels Statler Company, Western Hotels, Incorporated, and Allied Properties. A Texas man, L. F. Corrigan, also outlined a proposal. All of these Lee and the Metropolitan lease committee were weighing carefully.[24]

Amid all this the regents picked a new president for the university and, a short time later, Governor Langlie picked a new regent to succeed Dave Beck, who had been gone from the board for more than a year. The new president was Henry Schmitz, dean of the University of Minnesota's College of Forestry, Agriculture, Home Economics, and Veterinary Medicine in St. Paul. A graduate of the university in forestry in 1915, he was the first alumnus to become its chief executive. Not only was Schmitz of a pioneer Washington family—a family still prominent in the business and community life of

* In the University Archives is the text of a small memorandum by which Balmer transmitted to members of his Metropolitan lease committee (Armstrong, Corbett, Frankland) copies of the federal ruling of March 27, a long and circular statement that even Philip Macbride had found incomprehensible. With a flash of characteristic humor Balmer wrote: "For your information and mental exercise. Phil Macbride and I are looking for a genius who can interpret his ruling. Volunteers please step forward, T.B. 4-3-52" (Balmer Papers, 15-5).

Seattle—but he had received as recently as 1949 the highest honor the university conferred, its Alumnus Summa Laude Dignatus award. Schmitz, at fifty-nine, would bring to the presidency all the appropriate academic credentials—his professional activities had been in forestry, so important to the Washington economy—as well as a knowledge of the state, a lifetime familiarity with Seattle, and a deep affection for the university that went back to childhood recollections of the downtown campus when it was still a ten-acre pasture. The Schmitz inauguration was set for October 1952. As they invited Schmitz to become Allen's successor the regents also made Everest the vice-president, and this was a new position. It was expected that Everest would continue to handle the major financial matters that had engaged him during the interregnum, including matters at the Metropolitan tract.[25]

The regent who came to the board that June was Mrs. J. Herbert Gardner, of La Conner. Beatrice Gardner was the third woman, after Ruth Karr McKee and Eva Anderson, to be appointed a regent. She was also a second-generation regent, and this had happened only once before, when Howard Cosgrove, son of Governor S. G. Cosgrove, had followed his father to the board in 1910. Mrs. Gardner was the daughter of that soldier-regent-alumni leader Charles Gaches, Winlock Miller's friend and fellow freedom fighter in the old skirmishes over the Arena Building and the effort to save President Suzzallo. The Gardners lived in the historic Gaches home near La Conner where Suzzallo had been a frequent guest in earlier days. Both of the Gardners had been students at the university, and he had later been a member of the board of the alumni association. Now Beatrice Gardner would sit with Winlock Miller on a board that was trying to decide the future of the old university grounds.[26]

It was not unimportant as the year 1952 moved along that a new session of the legislature would be convening the following January. Lee was in full stride now, and in March he had been given a part-time assistant. This was Professor Arthur Cannon, of the College of Business Administration, the expert accountant who had made the careful study of the tract in 1948 and who was joining Lee two afternoons a week to work on financial analyses. But with the downtown office in full operation and Lee seeing himself directly responsible only to the Metropolitan lease committee—Balmer, Frankland, et al.—it became necessary to clarify the lines of communication from the downtown office to the campus itself. It was decided initially that periodic reports of developments should go only to the university president, Allen, and this system was continued when Schmitz became president. Somewhat later, when it had become apparent that proper liaison demanded more explicit attention at the university end, the assistant comptroller, E. M. Conrad, was given responsibility for staff support.[27]

The immediate question early in 1952 was the leasing of the hotel, on which there were seven bidders including the Edris organization. This was a matter on which the regents could not delay even if they wished to, and they did not. On June 28 they held a special meeting in Lee's office in the White-Henry-Stuart Building to review the prospects, particularly with respect to a late but interesting inquiry from L. F. Corrigan, the Texan. Corbett was now president of the board, Armstrong was vice-president, and the other regents were Balmer, Frankland, King, Miller, and Beatrice Gardner, who was attending her first meeting. Everest, still acting president of the university until the arrival of Schmitz, was also present. In a discussion that lasted for hours, all the proposals were laid out for comparison, including Corrigan's, on which Lee had rather detailed long-distance telephone notes. The choice thus far, Lee thought, was still between the proposals of The Olympic, Incorporated, and the Hilton Group. Finally, Balmer and the lease committee were asked to pursue the question further and, if the Olympic and Hilton offers still seemed best, to bring to the board, as developed by Macbride, two "tentative" lease drafts for final comparison.[28]

The winner in the end was The Olympic, Incorporated, the Edris organization that had controlled the hotel since 1943. But the decision did not come at once. On August 16, six weeks after the June meeting, the regents approved the Edris proposal in a resolution reciting the terms and noting that The Olympic, Incorporated, had offered to obtain from the Metropolitan Building Company by September 10 a "release of all right, title and interest in and to" the hotel property. The regents were persuaded, they said, that beyond the basic terms of the proposal, it was "in the best interests of the University that there be an uninterrupted continuity in the operation" of the hotel. Edris proceeded to work out the agreement with the Metropolitan Building Company (or perhaps he had already done so), yet in the meantime the Hilton people were back with an "additional offer" that Lee thought inadequate but also felt obliged to report. Thus when the regents met on September 8 to execute the final documents, they also held a special session in which they reviewed again the lease offers, including the new Hilton proposal, before confirming their action of August 16. When all questions had been cleared away, the lease was signed for the regents by Corbett and by Spiller as secretary, and for The Olympic, Incorporated, by Edris and John P. Garvin, the Seattle attorney who was secretary of the hotel company. The Metropolitan Building Company's interest in the hotel was assigned to the regents by Andrew Steers, president, and Frank Bayley, secretary. Edris had agreed not to sell or transfer before January 2, 1960, without the regents' consent, any of the stock of the hotel corporation, so Edris deposited with the Seattle-First National Bank a certificate covering the two thousand shares of capital stock. The stock deposit was executed on September 8, and the bank's acceptance as trustee was received the next day.[29]

The new lease was for twenty-two years, from September 10, 1952, to October 31, 1974. The university was to receive on a stipulated schedule $725,000 in cash advance payments representing rentals to the expiration of the Metropolitan leasehold on October 31, 1954. It would then receive two payments totaling $600,000 for the two-year period ending November 1, 1956. Thereafter the property was on a percentage-rental basis, with a minimum guarantee to the university of $400,000 per year and any additional amounts as percentages of gross receipts above the minimum—25 percent of the gross room rentals, 5 percent of the sales of food and beverages, and 50 percent of rentals from store and concession space. The Olympic, Incorporated, agreed to spend $1,225,000 in the ensuing four years in modernization and improvement and an average of 7 percent of the annual gross room rentals "for maintenance and related purposes." The company was to insure the property against fire and other damage, to execute a chattel mortgage on hotel furniture and equipment as a guarantee of performance, and to give to the university an option to acquire the furniture and equipment, upon expiration of the lease, at the then appraised value.[30]

Whether or not anyone had brought off a coup, all seemed happy about the results. The regents, with Lee's help, had analyzed every proposal to the bone. Edris was the winner, and the Edris management—the comfortably local management—would be continued. From the hotel alone, the university would finally be receiving the addition to the tract income so long desired—an annual income perhaps four times the $140,000 that was the maximum payment under the lease of 1907. And Seattle's major hotel—its "community hotel"—would be improved at a cost of not less than $1,255,000. Not for decades—not, at least, since the hotel had been put in place by Kerry and his associates—had there been such a time for congratulation. Only for the sentimentalists was there a prospect that might be viewed, perhaps, with regret. Any plan to improve the hotel almost certainly would involve the demolition of the Metropolitan Theatre. The prospect was mentioned nowhere in the new lease. It was implicit. Any plan for the hotel of 1953 would have no room for a theater of 1911.[31]

The new "main lease"—the lease of the rest of the tract—was still to be negotiated. Potential bidders were few, although Tishman seems to have been at the head of the short line. It was necessary for the regents to get their thoughts together, and so Lee, at Balmer's behest, had been busy with the development of a base-line plan. It was here that Lee's experience, reinforced by his enlarging knowledge of the tract, showed most clearly. When in October 1952 Balmer asked Lee to prepare a "sample lease plan," Lee responded with a memorandum that set out principles from which the regents never departed in all the negotiations that followed.[32]

Lee's basic philosophy was that both parties to a business arrangement should be able to profit—that a lopsided agreement defeated itself. Applied to leasing, Lee's principle meant that a lessor, while realizing satisfactory returns, should accord the lessee both an opportunity for profit and incentives to make the most of the opportunity for the benefit of all concerned. A lessee starving for profit would be forced to pare his operations to the critical point or give up his lease altogether, and no lessee worth talking to would put himself in such a position.[33]

From such ideas Lee started. But tangled thickets of special considerations lay ahead. For a Metropolitan lease neither Lee nor the regents had example or precedent. The Rockefeller Center case so frequently cited would not do, for there Columbia University held a long-term lease renegotiable periodically, a concept that Lee quickly rejected because he thought no responsible lessee of the tract would subject himself to the uncertainties of repeated calculations of rental terms. There was the case in New Orleans, where Tulane University was lessor of a major hotel, but in New Orleans as in New York the property was a single unit. In Seattle, and this was the nub of the matter, the property was a community of buildings diverse in character and age, the needs for improvement or replacement different in each case. A lessee would have to be enabled, or put under obligation, to effect improvements—the funds somehow to be provided—because the improvement of one building would increase the value of all. And the regents had to retain control over improvements and over the use of funds without being drawn directly into management.

Having mulled over these conditions with Balmer and with Frankland, Lee arrived at two broad recommendations which he incorporated in his "sample lease plan" of October 1952. One was the design of a lease in which the return to the university was a percentage, with a guaranteed minimum, of the lessee's gross receipts. The other was the establishment of a building fund extending over the life of the lease (Lee was still thinking of twenty-five years) and based on a percentage of the annual gross receipts, the fund applicable at the discretion of the regents for development and modernization. The calculations would be based on gross receipts, because if net income was the basis, the regents would indeed be thrust directly into management, forever having to decide if the lessee's net income was being maintained at reasonable levels.

Lee's figures were exploratory, but they pinned down the principles. Lee thought a lessee should make a $2,000,000 "down payment" on signing, then divide equally with the university the gross receipts, which he estimated at $2,400,000 per year. The lessee, from his $1,200,000 in gross annual receipts, would pay operating, administrative, amortization, and interest costs of $970,000, leaving him a net profit of $230,000. Out of the gross rental of $2,400,000, 20 percent—$480,000—would be set aside for the building and improvement fund, leaving 30 percent or about $720,000 per year "as income which could be taken from the tract and put to any University use the Regents desired." Adding interest on the $2,000,000 prepayment, and apportioning the fund over twenty-five years, might bring the university's annual income to $880,000, or $22,000,000 over the period of the lease—this in addition to the annual $600,000 expected from the hotel.[34]

If there was any question about the estimates, it may have been only that they seemed too low. If the hotel was bringing $600,000, why should the rest of the tract produce only $880,000? The figures, however, were only exemplary. Lee's plan dealt with the practical and political realities. The lease

Lee proposed could be short-term, thus avoiding a return to the legislature for additional authority. It would provide for a cumulative building fund, whereas under any other lease all improvement would have to be done in the early years, after being specified in the lease terms. The regents would be removed from participation in operation, and from the "continuous political pressures" that operation would entail, while the lessee "would have a chance to benefit proportionately to the merit of his operation." The lessee, profiting, and able to come to the regents with proposals for improvements, could bring to the tract capable and imaginative management. The regents could authorize improvements without incurring debt, which under law they could not do. And the more capable the lessee's performance, the faster the building fund would grow and the larger would be the university's income for its own purposes.

Into the late autumn of 1952 the situation simmered, Lee conferring with prospective bidders and the university preparing for the legislative session of 1953. In October, Henry Schmitz was inaugurated as president of the university. In the election of November—the election that made Dwight Eisenhower president of the United States—Arthur Langlie was elected to his third, his second consecutive, term as governor. In that autumn J. F. Douglas died.

Douglas died in Los Angeles on November 29, 1952. There was little shock in the news, for Douglas was seventy-eight, no longer with the Carnation Company, and twenty years beyond the time of his last direct and active management of the Metropolitan. Yet his passing was the passing of a well-remembered figure. Douglas was a vice-president of the Metropolitan at the end, occasionally visiting Seattle (less frequently after the onset of his illness), and still called "Major" Douglas. Douglas had been his own kind of pioneer, not of the bullwhip and bushwhacker days of Seattle's muddy beginnings, but of the days when Seattle was booming into its commercial development with White, Stimson, Henry, Backus, Stuart, Cobb, the Fishers, and such men at the controls. In a singularly improbable way the young lawyer from North Dakota had shaped a Metropolitan Center that was, first of all, the creation of his imagination. Douglas's pioneering had been in management ideas and in business style. But Douglas had never forgotten North Dakota. In 1933 he had been the speaker at the University of North Dakota's commencement, where he received an honorary degree. In 1949, in a talk to the Los Angeles alumni, he had recalled incidents of a boyhood on the North Dakota farm. And when the University of North Dakota polled faculty, students, and alumni to find the "ten greatest" men trained there, Douglas's name was fifth on a list that also contained the names of Maxwell Anderson and Vilhjalmur Stefansson. The directors of the Metropolitan memorialized Douglas thus: "A gentlemen in the best sense of the word, of the highest integrity and moral courage, and of rare personal charm and magnetism, he was endeared to all who were privileged to know him." A copy of the resolution went to Neva, who as a young wife in 1904 had called on lawyers, door to door, to sell copies of her husband's book on Washington corporations.[35]

The legislature of 1953 was quite prepared to take a liberal view of the regents' necessities in the sphere of their lease negotiations. The leasing of the hotel had been a constructive demonstration of the possibilities for increasing the income from the Metropolitan property and making early improvements. It was widely known that the regents, with Lee's help, were approaching other and even more far-reaching decisions with regard to a new "main lease." This time there was no stopping of clocks to accommodate final debate. This time few, if any, tempers flared. Eva Anderson was now chairman of the house committee on colleges and universities. Mort Frayn was chairman of the State Legislative Council. And although his name appeared nowhere, R. B. Harris was, as usual, watching developments in Olympia.

Before January was out, the regents were noting at their regular meeting that the twenty-five-year "restriction" on leasing might be extended to forty years. They hoped so, and said so in the minutes. Lee was present at that meeting to review the proposals thus far received. No details were recorded, but the minutes clearly suggested that the board hoped to hear something from the Metropolitan Building Company, from which no offer had been received. The regents expressed a wish for "local operation," and Lee was asked to discuss the prospects with "this group"—which certainly meant Andrew Steers and his associates. It was of some interest that the regents' minutes now were being prepared by Mrs. Helen E. Hoagland, who had been secretary to the university's presidents since Sieg's time and had been appointed, earlier in 1953, the assistant to John Spiller as secretary to the board.[36]

By mid-February the regents had more than they dreamed of in the way of freedom from "restrictions." They were not unhappy with twenty-five years. They were ready to welcome forty. What they got was sixty—an unequivocal authorization to negotiate a new lease for any term up to sixty years without the need to refer the terms for legislative ratification.

The bill came this time from the senate side (S.B. 159). The bill passed the house on February 25 and the senate the following day. It was signed by Governor Langlie on March 4. Frankland must have had a hand in this, for at a meeting on March 6 the regents commended him for his "masterful" presentation of the regents'—the university's—Metropolitan tract case before the legislative committees. But it was Balmer who had received a triumphant letter from Eva Anderson of the house committee. On February 27 she wrote:

Dear Mr. Balmer:

I am happy to report that today the Senate concurred with us in Senate Bill No. 159 which enables the Regents to negotiate leases with a *sixty* year period [Anderson's emphasis].

When the bill came to my committee in the House, the time read *forty* years. Our substitution of sixty years brought forth considerable interesting (and helpful) discussion. I only wished that the Regents might have heard it. Anyway, the matter is settled and you now have a little more "rope" if you need it.

Mr. Thompson [was it Frankland?] and Mr. Armstrong, along with Mr. Lee, made a fine presentation of the Regents' problems, and my committee was most receptive. We really welcomed the opportunity to lend what we believed might be a bit of help.

Thank you for your offer . . . to come to us. No one on that Board, I feel, has ever given more earnest or efficient help.[37]

So it was in March 1953—thirty years after enactment of the old 1923 law— the regents had all the "rope" they needed. Offers were before them, but none from the Metropolitan Building Company, and the Metropolitan leasehold was moving toward expiration.

It seemed, somehow, as if the Metropolitan Building Company was not around. But it was. Although there had been no Metropolitan offer for a lease renewal, the company was carrying on. At a meeting on March 28, 1953, the regents considered a matter relating to tract improvement. The city wanted to install new mercury vapor lights in the downtown sector, but it could not do so in the Metropolitan tract because "the streets have not been dedicated to public use." Nor had they been. Except for Fourth Avenue, the streets were, in fact, the streets put there by the Metropolitan Building Company, which was being asked by the city to pay a street-light bill of up to $15,000. The company went to the regents. The company said it was quite willing to reimburse the university for any position of the cost "assignable to its tenancy . . . either under the present lease or an extension," but it really should not, it thought, pay the whole cost when only seventeen months of its leasehold remained. The regents approved payment of the university's pro rata share, whatever that might be, the funds to come from tract receipts. But still the question hung in the air: was or was not the Metropolitan company expecting to make an offer for the renewal of its leasehold?[38]

At that moment—the March meeting of the regents—the bells began to toll for the old Metropolitan Theatre. Balmer reported that Lee was asking authority to develop with The Olympic, Incorporated, a supplemental lease agreement covering the theater and involving an additional rental of $24,000 a year. Lee was instructed to work out the details with Macbride, as legal counsel, and to present the proposal for approval at a later meeting. By the time the regents met again this had been done. A supplemental lease was approved for a term beginning November 2, 1954, and running to the end of the hotel lease on October 31, 1974. And the theater was to go. The Olympic, Incorporated, "will [the agreement provided] demolish and remove the existing theatre building and will, among other things, improve and employ the ground floor level of the site as a drive-in entrance and concourse to the Olympic Hotel to be connected with the main lobby by appropriate doorways, vestibules, escalators, and other convenient means for access and service usual to a first-class hotel." The theater was to be closed the day after the expiration of the Metropolitan company's lease, and when the word was out, in May, there was little surprise. The *Times* report noted that the closing had been a "foregone conclusion for several years," and that the operator, Hugh Becket, Jr., had been negotiating for another theater. Whatever changes might come after November 1, 1954, the loss of the "Met" would mean, in any case, a better hotel.[39]

It was time, in that university commencement season of 1953, for the board of regents to get on with a decision about the main lease. Sixteen months had elapsed since the regents had advertised in the *Wall Street Journal* and other publications their "Interesting Opportunity in Seattle's Famed Metropolitan Center." Eleven proposals had been received—none yet from the Metropolitan Building Company—and all had been analyzed, reanalyzed, compared, and discussed by Lee, with the help of Cannon (who was now devoting more than half his time to the project), and by Balmer, Frankland, and others. The tenants of the tract were still in a state of uncertainty, and Magnin's was already planning to move from the Skinner Building to a new and larger site outside the university property. There was increasing public curiosity about what would happen and when.

Yet the regents who would make the decision were not fully assembled in June 1953. Grant Armstrong had become president in the spring reorganization, Frankland vice-president. But John King's term had expired and a new appointment was expected. It was not until June 23 that the new member was seated, and he was Charles M. Harris, of Entiat. With the regents under intense pressure to make a judgment of epochal dimensions, Governor Langlie had sent into the game, at the last minute, a young man who was not even familiar with the plays.

The story of Harris's initiation is one of the remarkable stories of the leasing. Harris was young—just thirty-five—a graduate of the university in 1939, and an Eastern Washington lumberman and orchardist with interests in three family companies. But he brought to the board both an unassuming modesty and a determination to make up his own mind about university matters including the lease prospects. His university degree was in accounting (*magna cum laude*). He was a member of Phi Beta Kappa and of the Washington Society of Certified Public Accountants. He was perfectly capable of judging lease proposals, and he meant to. His first act as regent was to enroll in a cram course, under Lee, Cannon, and Balmer, on the lease proposals before the board. For two weeks he worked to make his own analyses and comparisons, and when he was through, he drafted a personal statement summarizing his conclusions. Harris, new though he was, approached the leasing decision on his own. And when Harris took his place on the board, the membership included not only one of the youngest regents ever to sit there (Gaches had been thirty-three), but also, the oldest, Winlock Miller, who had first become a regent years before Harris was born.[40]

Any review of the newspapers of the period will show how tensions were rising. The tempers that no longer flared in the legislature now tended to flare in Seattle. There was a disposition to believe that the regents somehow were working out a "deal" in "secret" meetings. The tract tenants, and particularly the owners of retail stores, were talking about organizing, and by July 1 the regents were having to decline an invitation from the tenants to attend a public meeting, saying that this merely would interrupt their work with the lease proposals. The regents nevertheless urged the tenants to elect a committee to consult with the board. Soon John King was quoted as charging that "all the regents had not been given the opportunity to see all the proposals," by which he presumably meant that most of the spadework was being done by Balmer and the Metropolitan lease committee. King's assertion was immediately denied by his former colleagues. Armstrong issued a statement describing the board's procedure for analysis and comparison of the lease offers. Perhaps most serious of all was a threat by Senator Albert Rosellini to propose a "legislative inquiry" if the board had not made a "complete disclosure of its position in the controversy" by July 18, when the State Legislative Council was to hold its quarterly meeting. Rosellini was the cosponsor of the 1951 bill enabling the regents to bond tract income to help finance the university hospital. Now he was the senate's minority (Democratic) floor leader and chairman of the council's subcommittee on commerce, trade, and industry. "The lease negotiations are of such magnitude," Rosellini said, "that if there is the slightest question it should be ironed out before the deal is concluded. There must be complete public confidence in whatever is done."[41]

What the newspapers knew—and thus what the public knew—was that the regents had received eleven proposals. What the newspapers were reporting was that the field had been narrowed to "three or four" bidders and that the prime lessee prospect was Roger L. Stevens, "a real estate promoter and developer in Detroit and New York." All of this was true, but the regents had reached no final decision or confirmed or denied the rumors that were going around.

What was going on, nevertheless, was a painfully protracted, morning-to-evening, closed-doors, shirt-sleeves movement toward a new lease—a process made particularly painful by the sudden death in the Olympic Hotel of one of the Stevens representatives. The Stevens proposal was without doubt emerging as the soundest, but the terms had to be made absolute—and absolutely specific in days and nights of face-to-face discussion—without, the regents would have been the first to say, a legislative council subcommittee calling for a review of the bidding. To Seattle at large, Roger Stevens was unknown. And where was the Metropolitan Building Company? To the regents, Stevens and his spokesmen were the men with the ideas.

It was on July 9, and late at night, that the death occurred. Charles J. Powell was president of Roger Stevens Associates, of Detroit. He was also a Seattle Powell, although not of the John H. and George V. Powell family. His father had been an army man, Brigadier General Charles F. Powell, and he had attended Seattle's Queen Anne High School and the University of

Washington. He had been away from Seattle since going to the army in World War I. After the war, he had stayed in the army for a while and then had managed properties for the Massachusetts Mutual Life Insurance Company. He joined Stevens just before the Detroit group acquired New York's Empire State Building in 1951. Powell still had many local connections—a sister and a daughter who lived in the state, a brother who was a Seattle school man, and a sister-in-law, Mrs. F. F. Powell, who was a member of the Seattle City Council. Powell was sixty-one, and the lease negotiations had brought him back to the city of his younger years. He died in the Olympic Hotel, of a heart attack, after a long day of lease conferences. Years later Lee, among others, still had vivid recollections of the shock.[42]

By July 11, when the regents assembled for their regular meeting, they were nearing decision. Neither then nor later did the board ever put into its record the names of bidders besides Stevens, although Tishman certainly was another. The regents must have been slightly surprised when they met to find among the spectators Senator Rosellini and Senator John N. Todd, who had been a member of legislative committees studying the tract. But when Balmer reported for the Metropolitan tract committee, he simply went briefly and directly to the point—to two points, actually. Balmer said that thorough analysis of the eleven proposals suggested that four "were deemed to offer the greatest potential," and that of the four the Stevens offer "appears to be the most desirable." But negotiations with the Stevens people were being resumed, Balmer said, following the death of Powell, "for the purpose of determining whether the Stevens proposal can be embodied in a written lease satisfactory to both parties." There was the Rosellini matter, too, and Balmer mentioned this, as Rosellini listened, saying that the board had received a letter from the senator asking that no final action be taken until the legislative council had been given opportunity to consider the prospects. "In our judgment it is impracticable to concur in this request," Balmer said. "The Board is acting under legislative authority and an early decision . . . is desirable so that the tenants of the tract may make their plans. We recommend that Senator Rosellini's request be declined." The board agreed. Rosellini went from the meeting to issue a statement in which he said he was "astounded that the board is planning final action on this lease, which involves millions of dollars of values belonging to the taxpayers of the state, without a full public disclosure of all the facts." Nevertheless, the news reports were confirmed now. The Stevens group was ahead as the field turned into the stretch.[43]

The race was, in fact, over. On Friday, July 10, copies of the articles of incorporation of a new Stevens organization, University Properties, Incorporated (the incorporation in Delaware) had been filed with Washington's secretary of state. Powell had been named president, but Powell had died only the day before. By the following week Stevens was in Seattle to be present during the arrangement of final details, and Stevens would be the president of University Properties. At that moment, too, Edris was quoted as stoutly defending the regents' procedures in the negotiations: "I say the citizens of the state can rest easy in confidence that care of their property is in good hands." He hoped that the lease would be signed soon because his own hotel modernization program was in suspense. And even as events moved toward conclusion, there was a moment of wonder that the Metropolitan Building Company was not among the bidders. The disclosure came on July 15 in an announcement by Andrew Steers, even as Balmer and his committee were meeting behind closed doors with the Stevens spokesmen, that Metropolitan was preparing an offer. Steers said that although there had been "preliminary and tentative" talks with the regents, "The building company is still studying the situation and will be prepared shortly to put in a formal proposal." As late as that, with the direction of the wind obvious to all, the company that had built the tract had not brought itself to realize that some other organization might take over. But the company finally acted. The next day it submitted an offer of undisclosed terms. The regents could only acknowledge, later, that they had received a "second tentative proposal" from the Metropolitan Building Company.[44]

The regents were on call for the formal approval and signing of the new lease, and the call was to a meeting on Saturday, July 18. Notices had been distributed to the media and the distribution certified by an affidavit, this in response to Washington's new law requiring the conduct of public business at open meetings. Assembled with the regents—Armstrong, Balmer, Corbett, Frankland, Gardner, Harris, and Miller—were the principals of University Properties, Incorporated, Stevens and Edward L. Rosling, secretary, and university administrators and tract office persons including President Schmitz, Nelson Wahlstrom, D. K. Anderson, John Spiller, Helen Hoagland, and, of course, Arthur Lee and Arthur Cannon.[45]

The meeting had three principal actions before it—approval of the report of the Metropolitan tract committee, approval of a resolution authorizing execution of the lease and related agreements, and, finally, the signings. The occasion was one well remembered by every participant, not only because it was the climax of a long process of policy formulation and negotiation but because for both the university and the city a page was turned. Copies of group photographs made that day were to be found for years in the offices or homes of those who sat that morning in the regents' room in the university's Administration Building. Yet one of the principals unfortunately missed being in the photographs because he was too busy with the lease papers. This was Rosling, who had carried much of the load to that hour.

Rosling was secretary of University Properties, Incorporated, because he was the Stevens legal counsel in the negotiations. Rosling was, however, of Seattle. A graduate of the University of Washington Law School (with World War I navy training on campus) and of the Harvard Graduate School of Law, he was a prominent attorney who would turn some years later to medical law and become the first chairman of the Seattle Artificial Kidney Center. Before 1953, Rosling had represented several local real estate investment interests, and he knew more than most about the Metropolitan situation. Eventually he had been approached by a Stevens representative, Nathan Potter, about handling the Stevens proposal, and thereafter Rosling had been totally involved in the Stevens leasing effort, and had drafted the language of the lease terms as they were worked out in the long face-to-face meetings.[46]

Spiller was there as secretary to the board, Mrs. Hoagland the assistant. Mrs. Hoagland was about to begin her own twenty-year career as secretary, the position held for such long terms by Markham and Condon.*

Balmer's Metropolitan tract committee report was a statement of some sixteen hundred words setting out in detail the "salient features" of the lease and the lines of reasoning behind them. When the statement had been read, Lee and Cannon were asked to comment, which they did. Balmer moved the adoption of the report, then read the resolution prepared by Spiller. Balmer's motion was seconded by Miller. The lease was signed, by Armstrong and Spiller for the board, by Stevens and Rosling for University Properties.[47]

The lease was for thirty-five years, well within the sixty-year term authorized by the legislature, and effective November 1, 1954, although University Properties had no thought of waiting sixteen months to go into action. Stevens announced immediately that he intended to institute negotiations with the Metropolitan Building Company toward acquiring the balance of the old lease. With Stevens as principals of University Properties were Alfred Glancy, Jr., of Detroit, and Ben Tobin, of Hollywood, Florida. Other key figures included H. Adams Ashforth and Donald B. Callender, of New York, and Potter, the astute Stevens spear carrier who was quoted as saying that the "mathematics" of the proposals clearly had tilted the decision to Stevens. One of the principals, had he lived, would have been Charles Powell, who in a few short weeks of hard negotiation had won respect as an enlightened, even a "brilliant," negotiator. If any Seattle purists viewed with dubious eyes a new Metropolitan tract management so predominantly "Eastern," they had Balmer's word that the regents considered the new men "of high repute and financial responsibility . . . skillful and aggressive." The university was "well satisfied with its choice."[48]

Ever since Lee had been asked to prepare his "sample lease plan," the regents had been setting down certain basic guidelines. They wanted a percentage lease with a guaranteed minimum. They wanted adequate financial guarantees. They wanted funds for modernization to come from the university's own revenues, so that they retained control over demolition and construction. They wanted a lessee of substance and reputation, financially

---

* Spiller soon left the university to reenter private law practice. He resigned as counsel and board secretary in September 1953, and the following month Mrs. Hoagland was appointed to succeed him in the secretary's position (Regents Minutes, 11:174–75, September 11, 1953, and 11:196, October 31, 1953). The new university counsel was Fred Harlocker, who would have his own part to play in ensuing developments.

sound, interested in property development rather than in speculation, expert
in management, and free of interests that might be competitive to his obligations to the tract. Stevens and the Stevens proposal passed on all points.

The University Properties lease provided for payments aggregating $6,800,-
000 in four years after November 1, 1954: $1,600,000 the first year, $1,700,000
in the second and third years, and $1,800,000 in the fourth. After November
1, 1958, the lease moved to a percentage schedule (the percentages calculated
at differing levels on the lessee's gross receipts from commercial and office
tenants) averaging about 50 percent of gross income with a minimum annual
guarantee of $1,000,000. Performance was assured by a deposit of $1,000,000
in cash or securities, returnable to University Properties when the $6,800,000
in fixed rent had been paid or forfeited in the event of default. The company
agreed to spend not less than 4 percent per year of the gross income of the
tract on the maintenance of the property, payments that would protect the
tract from deterioration to the end of the thirty-five-year term. As for modernization and construction, the regents would establish a building fund under
their control from which they would reimburse University Properties for
projects duly authorized. The fund would receive for the first four years 35
percent of the gross rental income from the tract, with a maximum of $800,000
a year, and thereafter 15 percent of the gross with a maximum of $450,000—
the larger figures in the early years to make possible immediate movement
toward modernization at a cost of $2,000,000.[49]

In sum, the Metropolitan Center had been leased for thirty-five years—
until 1989—for a minimum of $1,000,000 a year plus the office- and commer-
cial-space rental increments, whatever they proved to be. The regents would
be in control of funds for improvement, and the largest and most necessary
improvements were to be made in the ensuing four years. University Properties pledged to maintenance expenditures that would forestall deterioration
even in the last years of the lease. No new Rockefeller Center would rise where
the first university building had stood, but there would be new buildings
where the old ones should be replaced. Even though the legislature had authorized a term of up to sixty years, it had been the judgment of the regents'
Metropolitan committee that "since a satisfactory lease can be obtained for a
35-year term, the authority to make a longer lease should not be exercised."
When Balmer and Lee developed, for purposes of example, projections of
income to the university from the tract and the hotel, they limited the view
to ten years, to October 31, 1964. Their projected minimum income was
$17,565,000 for the decade ($12,800,000 from the new agreement, $4,765,000
from the hotel-theater site), or $12,565,000 after subtracting $5,000,000 in
payments to the building fund. In the years from 1907 to 1953 the total rental
payments of the Metropolitan Building Company had been about $3,900,000.
Of the new income, whatever it was, the regents were ready to obligate $5,000,-
000 for construction of the new teaching hospital.[50]

The *Post-Intelligencer* editorial of July 23, 1953 was headed, "A Good

Lease," and it seemed to sum up the Seattle reaction. In what appeared to be an oblique reference to the Tishman proposal the writer said, "Seattle isn't going to get anything as spectacular as Rockefeller Center out of the plan. But it is assured of the maintenance of this tract in the heart of its downtown district as first-class business property. . . . And that is a lot more desirable than a spectacular project which the community might find it difficult to support. . . . The members of the Regents Metropolitan Tract Committee and their executive assistant, Mr. Arthur T. Lee, are entitled to the gratitude of the community."

Yet Seattle suddenly realized that many things so long familiar might be—inevitably would be—changed. There was more excitement than apprehension in the realization that now all those buildings the city had known for so long —the White-Henry-Stuart, the Cobb, the Douglas, the Stimson, the Olympic Garage, the Skinner, and the Fifth Avenue Theater—would be under new management. Seattle knew Edris, and Edris was providing the "uninterrupted continuity" of hotel operation that seemed so desirable. But what was this new company? What would happen to the old Metropolitan Building Company? Above all, who was Roger Stevens?

Seattle's real estate investment and property management people knew about Stevens. So, too, did many in the city's theatrical sector. But each group knew little more than half of the man, and neither had any prior expectation that its half would appear in the flesh. Stevens even then, at forty-three—tall, husky, growing bald—was a man frequently referred to as an "almost legendary" figure, although the references were in the main to his successes in real estate ventures. But about that time, or very soon thereafter, the "almost" was being dropped.

Stevens had demonstrated a singular brilliance in acquiring or refinancing or putting into shape large properties. He was not a "developer." An associate once said that he did not have the patience for it. Nor was he a J. F. Douglas, with Douglas's dogged determination to devote himself to a single project. Stevens was a man who plunged fearlessly into any project that engaged his interest, business or theatrical, and his business affairs were in the multimillion-dollar range. To any who gave it thought it must have seemed ironic that the man behind the lease of the "old university grounds" was a university dropout who was in Seattle only by chance—a university dropout who was, nevertheless, an exceedingly broad, widely read, and genuinely cultured man.

Stevens was born in 1910 in Detroit. He attended Choate School, then the University of Michigan, which he left after a year, in the late 1920s, because, as he said, he "had no ambition." But he did have a passion for reading and, as he put it in an interview years later, "a sort of talent . . . for making deals." Stevens spent hours in the Detroit library reading Shaw, Shakespeare, general literature. He worked in a Ford assembly plant and as a gas station attendant. When he discovered his talent for "deals"—buying up bonds on Depression-troubled apartment houses and office buildings—he began to make money.

By World War II, which he spent at a naval air station in Florida, he had made half a million dollars, had taken a wife, and had become associated with Glancy and Tobin.[51]

Tobin was from a Russian immigrant family and got his start in business by selling newspapers, at age ten, in Lynn, Massachusetts. In due course, he became a successful investor in real estate and other kinds of property, particularly hotels. Glancy was the wealthy member of the trio, but he had had a taste of the Depression. Glancy's father, Alfred Glancy, had been a vice-president of DuPont when General Motors was established, then a vice-president of General Motors and president of its Pontiac Division. When young Glancy went to Princeton in the 1920s, he was a rich man's son, but when he graduated in 1931 (one of his classmates was George V. Powell, of Seattle), the Depression was at its bottom and there was no place for him anywhere. The Glancys had, nevertheless, a large deposit account at the National Bank of Detroit, and Glancy applied there for a job—any job, salary no object. So the bank made him a vice-president at no salary. Soon his vice-presidency began to pay, but in the meantime Stevens and Tobin had appeared. Glancy left the bank and joined Stevens, the fellow Detroiter, in what were becoming larger and larger enterprises. When World War II was over, the Stevens-Glancy-Tobin combination was investing heavily in real estate. Stevens, meanwhile, had found a concomitant interest.[52]

It is said that Stevens, the reader of plays from Shakespeare to Shaw, had not seen a professional production until after his marriage. But in 1949 he helped support a production of *Twelfth Night* at the Ann Arbor, Michigan, Drama Festival. Apparently intrigued by this dabble in the arts, he took the play to New York and lost $45,000 on it. Nevertheless he had found a new outlet for his restless mental energy. To his passion for real estate "deals" he added a passion for the stage.

Then and later Stevens was interested in hotels, including New York's Commodore, Gotham, Ambassador, and Carlyle. His purchase of the Empire State Building for $50,000,000 was a complicated financial undertaking that brought more suspense than profit, according to subsequent accounts (he put down $1,000,000 and promised to add $49,000,000 in six months). But he came out of that with a reputation for unswerving integrity in transactions of the most esoteric kind. About the time he became interested in the Seattle prospect he was engaged in a rare "development," the planning in Boston of a $75,000,000 commercial center designed to be somewhat more commodious than the Rockefeller in New York. From this he eventually withdrew, and the Prudential Life Insurance Company took it on. But he was also engaged in preparations for the New York opening of the play *Tea and Sympathy*, and was making ready to bring to America from Stratford-on-Avon the Shakespeare Memorial Theatre Company. *Tea and Sympathy* would be followed by Broadway productions such as *Sabrina Fair*, *The Remarkable Mr. Pennypacker*, *Ondine*, *West Side Story*, *A Man for All Seasons*—eventually by more than 125 productions in which Stevens was the "producing partner." How he did it all he explained in due course: "I worked on real estate in the morning, when the theater people were asleep, and on theater in the evening when the real estate people were relaxing." He had even found himself in politics after 1952. Because he was obviously a skillful fundraiser, the Volunteers for Stevenson made him chairman of their finance committee when Adlai Stevenson was opposing Eisenhower for the presidency. Stevens was a success, even though Stevenson lost, and four years later Stevenson would make him chairman of the Democratic Finance Committee. When Stevens went to Seattle in 1953, seeing the city for the first time, the regents of the University of Washington were satisfied that he and his associates were men of "high repute and financial responsibility." But who among the regents could have guessed that Stevens would one day become the chairman of the National Council on the Arts, chairman of the John F. Kennedy Center for the Performing Arts, and recipient of several honorary degrees, one a doctorate in humane letters from the University of Michigan?[53]

How had Stevens become interested in the Metropolitan lease in the first place? A profile of Stevens published in 1954 makes Charles Powell (although Powell was not named) the accidental agent. By this account, Powell, the former Seattleite, chatted with Stevens after a business conference, impressed him with the opportunities in Seattle, and was selected by Stevens to become his representative in the lease negotiations. Powell was indeed a central figure until his sudden death, but recollections point to a rather different set of circumstances in what Seattle came to know as the "Yale link." The link was in the thirty-year friendship of two Yale classmates: Ashforth, the New York investment man, and Lawrence W. Wiley, vice-president of Seattle's John Davis and Company. But others were involved. One was Irving Anches, a Seattle property owner and investment specialist, and another was Callender, of the Ashforth group. Even Governor Langlie entered the account, although obliquely.[54]

Early in 1953, Anches, a friend of Wiley's, was going to New York on private business. Wiley, learning of this, suggested that Anches carry to Ashforth a letter from Wiley describing the Metropolitan lease offering as of possible interest to Eastern investors. Anches, traveling east by train, found that a fellow passenger was Governor Langlie, bound for Washington, D.C., and the Eisenhower inauguration. Langlie and Anches were not acquainted, but they talked during the long ride, and it became evident that Langlie was following the lease question closely, and was, in fact, carrying with him a copy of the lease-offering brochure prepared by Arthur Lee. Finding that Anches was in real estate, Langlie pressed him for ideas about the kind of lease that might be expected. When Anches arrived in New York he talked first to Callender, not to Ashforth, but the Wiley suggestion soon set events in motion. The Ashforth staff was impressed both by Wiley's report and by the fact that the governor of Washington was keenly interested in encouraging proposals from capable and financially sound prospective lessees. Ashforth immediately thought of Stevens, with whom he had been associated in other projects and who was well known by then as the man who had bought the Empire State Building. Callender and Potter went to Seattle to get a preliminary view of the situation. Stevens soon followed, although not before assuring himself that Governor Langlie's interest was above politics.* When Stevens did finally decide to think seriously of a proposal, it was Charles Powell whom he sent west—Powell knowing Seattle—to become his principal.[55]

It never was Stevens's intention to move to Seattle, but with no resident agent on the scene, although Rosling was handling legal matters, Stevens was in the city frequently in the late summer of 1953. He had two immediate objectives. One was to organize a management team to be installed in headquarters that had been established in 301 White-Henry-Stuart Building. The other was to obtain control of the Metropolitan Building Company so that he could begin at once to make improvements that otherwise would have to wait until November 1, 1954.

The management question was pressing, for University Properties needed on-site representation, yet there really was nothing to manage—no new subleases could be signed with tenants—until the lease situation was clarified. By mid-August 1953, Stevens was meeting with Andrew Steers to see how negotiations might proceed. Just fourteen months of the old lease remained, but they could not be months of inaction. There were, however, complications. The Metropolitan Building Company was a majority stockholder in two corporations operating off-tract properties, the Exchange Building and the United Medical and Dental Building, the latter serving doctors and dentists and thus competing in the rental field with the Metropolitan Center's Cobb and Stimson buildings. If Stevens acquired the Metropolitan company he would be acquiring also two buildings outside the realm of his leasehold— buildings which, under the terms of his lease, he would have to sell.[56]

The university regents had tried three times to buy the unexpired portion of the Metropolitan lease. Stevens proposed to buy the company or the controlling interest therein. To do so he needed to ask the regents' permission, because the two off-tract buildings were involved. On September 18 he addressed a letter to Lee—a letter to be placed before the regents—outlining a stock-purchase plan and his proposals concerning disposal of the Exchange and Medical-Dental buildings. The Exchange he would sell as soon as possible, "within a reasonable period so as not to have the hardship of a forced sale." He asked, however, permission to operate the Medical-Dental Building until November 1, 1958, "because we believe that it is to the best interests of the Cobb and Stimson Buildings that we should control the Medical-Dental Building" to avoid a rash of competitive rentings. Stevens would agree to sell

---

* Anches was not directly involved in the lease negotiations, but he became more than a casual bearer of Wiley's letter. Inspired by Langlie's questions, he studied the Metropolitan offering and, as the first person to present the idea to Callender, became for a time an advisor. It was Anches who assured Stevens, in a subsequent meeting in New York, that his conversation with Langlie had been by chance, no political implications attached. Stevens's reply, as Anches recalled it, was: "That's what I wanted to hear."

the Medical-Dental Building on or before November 1, 1958, meantime renting to no one there, if space was available in the Cobb or the Stimson, without the regents' consent. The regents could not have been expected to demur, and they did not. Their approval went into the record on October 31, 1953. Meanwhile, Stevens had prepared for distribution to Metropolitan stockholders, as a printed folder with a letter of acceptance, his "Offer to Purchase" their holdings.[57]

Stevens was offering thirty dollars a share for 190,000 or more (two-thirds) of the 278,079 shares of Metropolitan common then outstanding.* The Pacific National Bank of Seattle was named depository, and Stevens deposited $200,000 there as his initial payment. Stockholders' letters of acceptance and transfer were to be received by the bank no later than December 1. Stevens reserved the right to extend the period by thirty days upon written notice, and the offer was cancellable if fewer than 190,000 shares were submitted.[58]

Stevens was prepared to pay at least $5,700,000 for the company and its off-tract buildings, which he was bound to sell, and this for the little more than a year remaining on the Metropolitan lease. The obligation would be reduced by receipts from the sale of the buildings and by interim income from rentals. By getting control of the company, however, he could start the improvements that would make his lease profitable. And, as some observers were noting, Stevens would acquire the Metropolitan books and records and thus a knowledge of the company's operating costs. The Metropolitan's officers were uncomfortable about all this, press reports indicate (the *Post-Intelligencer*'s Douglass Welch, who had covered the lease story for years, was particularly persistent in the search for information), and quite soon the officers were preparing their own recommendations to the stockholders even as the deposits of shares were beginning to appear at the Pacific National Bank "in increasing numbers." Meanwhile, Stevens had solved that other problem—leadership of the management team.[59]

The decision had been made early in October and the new head of University Properties, as president and general manager, was James M. Ryan. Whatever the choices that had been before Stevens, he had selected a Seattle man who was an alumnus of the University of Washington and whose whole career had been in property management. With Ryan would be Waldemar Karkow, of Chicago, as vice-president in charge of modernizations and construction, and J. L. (Jack) Dierdorff, who came from the Metropolitan Building Company—and who was known to every tenant of the tract—to take charge of tenant relations.

Ryan was not a native of Seattle. He was from Wisconsin by way of Montana, where he had attended high school. But he was as familiar with the Seattle property scene as anyone around, widely known in the Northwest,

---

* The Metropolitan's authorization was for 325,000 shares at a par value of ten dollars. The company held 60,134 of the 76,000 shares of Exchange common (par value one dollar) and 6,690 of the 7,120 shares (par value ten dollars) of the Medical-Dental Corporation (Roger L. Stevens, "Offer to Purchase," October 21, 1953).

and well acquainted elsewhere. Ryan was forty-five in 1953. He was leaving a position as general manager of the Vance Lumber Company, of Seattle, and manager and secretary-treasurer of Vance Properties, which operated three Seattle buildings, the Vance, the Lloyd, and the Tower, and five hotels, the Vance and the Camlin, in Seattle, and others in Spokane, Yakima, and Richland. He had been in Seattle since the late 1920s, when he had been a student at the university, and he had an appreciation of the Metropolitan Center as a university property. His experience included four years as manager of the Dexter Horton Building, a Seattle landmark. He brought to his new job an easy-going humor, a wide range of friendships in the Seattle business community, and a sense of excitement about the prospects for tract development. Stevens, with Ryan now president of University Properties, became chairman of the board.[60]

Events moved thereafter toward a totally unexpected denouement. It was predictable that there would be rumors—that the Douglas Building was to be demolished immediately and the Cobb converted to general office space—and these had to be denied by Ryan and Lee in a joint appearance before a meeting of the Seattle Building Owners and Managers Association at the Olympic. There was as yet no hint, however, that Stevens's stock-purchase plan would not be successful.[61]

The Metropolitan company's situation was peculiar and precarious. The company had not been an even mildly serious contender for the lease that Stevens had won, the directors apparently gripped by indecision when the bidding became so general. But there had been for years an internal division among the board members and major stockholders over the issues of expansion and diversification. William Reed had been the somewhat brash proponent of expansion, arguing that the company, whatever happened to its lease, could enlarge the off-tract operations then represented by the Exchange and Medical-Dental buildings. Although that idea was formally endorsed, there undoubtedly existed among the Metropolitan's directors a feeling against surrender of the tract lease, particularly to an organization that was not of Seattle or, at the very least, of the Northwest.[62]

A perfectly plain statement of the Metropolitan board's feeling was contained in a letter addressed to Balmer on October 26, 1953, by Frank S. Bayley, the director representing the stock interests of charitable organizations. Bayley had spoken to Balmer earlier, as the text of the letter shows, and now he put in writing, on the letterhead of his legal firm and in a statement almost four pages long, his—and undoubtedly the Metropolitan board's—protest at the regents' agreement with Stevens's efforts to buy the company's stock. The company could have had no better spokesman. Bayley, who owned no Metropolitan stock, had been for ten years the representative of a block of seventeen thousand shares given by C. H. Cobb to such agencies as the Children's Orthopedic Hospital, the YMCA and the YWCA, and the Washington Children's Home. Bayley said that Cobb had given the stock on the condition that it be held for fifty years after his death "unless the Company was liquidated within that period." He said that his organizations could not sell their shares and if Stevens acquired control they would be "minority stockholders in a Company . . . completely under the control of a man who is not a resident of Seattle and who presumably has no interest in the city." Furthermore, if the company was liquidated, his organizations would be completely dispossessed. Let Stevens have the leasehold balance. Steers and the executive committee had agreed with Stevens in September on a price—a net price to the Metropolitan of $277,400. Why not this, for the good of all? "It is highly desirable from the point of view for the Regents," Bayley wrote, "that acquisition of our lease be accomplished at the earliest possible date." The lease, but not the stock. But Bayley was already too late. When the regents met on October 31—in the meeting in which they approved Stevens's request to make his stock-purchase offering—they simply authorized Balmer to tell Bayley that the Stevens plan seemed in the best interests of the university.[63]

Stevens got the leasehold, at length, but not the company. And there was a bewildering aspect to the ensuing happenings. Suddenly, in November 1953, the Metropolitan did a strangely daring thing. It set up a stock purchase plan of its own.

Wherever the idea came from—perhaps it was only a flicker of the "old Seattle spirit"—the company offered to buy from its own stockholders (at thirty dollars a share, Stevens's price) all the shares that were surrendered to it by November 23, 1953, a week before the Stevens deadline. If the shares then on deposit were fewer than 140,000, the purchase would be made from the company's own cash, the maximum investment thus $4,200,000. If more than 140,000 shares were surrendered, the company would sell to Stevens or to any other buyer, presumably at the best price that could be obtained. The company might go, but it would go with flags flying.

With that announcement still another element was injected into the situation. The Stevens offer having been matched, the Transamerica Corporation, the large diversified holding company, suddenly took an interest in the Seattle prospect, and Transamerica soon was said to be "feverishly dickering" for the purchase of the 200,000 shares of stock the company claimed to have on deposit. Clearly a break was near. On November 23 the Metropolitan directors extended their stock-transfer offer a week. But by the next day all "dickering" was over. The company was owned by a new entity, Northwest Associates.[64]

No one knew what Northwest was or who the associates were. But Seattle—and Tacoma—knew well the man in charge. He was Norton Clapp, an executive of the Weyerhaeuser Company, president of several lumber and other companies in Washington and elsewhere, and, not incidentally, still a member of the board of the Metropolitan Building Company. Clapp was a wealthy man, a millionaire several times over, tall, friendly, of a commanding presence. He had made his calculations. He knew the company's assets beyond the fading leasehold—its off-tract buildings and, particularly, its cash reserves. He thought the assets—principally the cash—justified a reasonable risk. He was prepared to make an offer, and he made it at a meeting of the Metropolitan directors on November 24. Clapp simply laid on the directors' table a check for $250,000 and said "Gentlemen, I offer $30.50 a share for Metropolitan Building stock."[65]

Clapp's fellow board members were described later as stunned. But they were not too stunned to accept the offer instantly. Steers announced that all stockholders who had not yet deposited their shares might do so until December 15. Payment, he said, would be made "on or before January 8, 1954." What neither Steers nor the Metropolitan directors knew, however, and what they did not take time to discover, was that Stevens had authorized Ryan to offer up to $35 a share for the stock they were selling for $30.50. The opportunity to bid never came. The Metropolitan board, happy that the company would be going to one of its own, accepted Clapp's offer and put the company in familiar hands.[66]

The man who now owned the Metropolitan was not in the game simply to top Stevens, however, nor was he then a "legendary" figure. Clapp was a man who went his own way, but not remotely, for he was deeply involved in community activities of many kinds. Clapp was born in Pasadena in 1906 of transplanted New England stock, had won his A.B. at Occidental College, and had moved on to the University of Chicago (Chicago also was family territory) for work in law that led to a J.D. degree in 1929. Admitted to the bar in California and Washington, he had started his law practice in Tacoma, where he lived until 1942, when he went into the navy and served four years, becoming a lieutenant commander. In 1953, still spreading his interests, he was on his way to becoming vice-president of Weyerhaeuser, a life trustee of the University of Chicago, a chairman of the board of Tacoma's University of Puget Sound, an honorary vice-president of the Boy Scouts of America, and—in the fullness of time—the only man who had been president of the chambers of commerce of both Seattle and Tacoma.[67]

The details of the Stevens lease were public knowledge, but in the legislature there was a residual curiosity not only about the financial implications but about how, and over what competitive offers, the regents had decided that the Stevens proposal was best. The next session of the legislature—and the State Legislative Council in the meantime—had a right to ask how the regents had discharged their public trust. The regents were in fact required by the 1951 law to report biennially to the legislature all actions with respect to the tract. Yet in 1953, and so soon after the leasing, there was a need for delicacy. The regents were quite willing to supply information, but they did not want to go into the specific details of the proposals that had not been accepted. Such matters, in simple fairness to the bidders, they considered privileged.

There was no threat of a legislative "investigation." But in the early autumn of 1953, while the Stevens and Metropolitan stock-purchase plans were germinating, the legislative council asked for a preliminary report in as much detail as possible. Mort Fryan was chairman now and the council was meeting in Spokane on November 6. Lee, in response to Frayn's request and under the regents' authority, sent multiple copies of all pertinent documents with a covering statement describing the processes of analysis by which the regents had come to agree on the Stevens proposal. The other ten bidders were not identified and the terms they had offered were merely described, not revealed. So a report was made, but a report just then was, in any case, a little premature, for much of the significant action of 1953 was ahead. By the time Norton Clapp had bought the Metropolitan Building Company it was an open question whether Stevens could do much about his new lease until the old lease had died its lingering death.[68]

Waiting for the death, however, was not in Stevens' nature. Nor was it in Clapp's. Stevens and Ryan, and Rosling too, wanted to move forward. Stevens had tried to buy the Metropolitan stock (this, according to Bayley, after there had been substantial agreement on the price of the leasehold), and that had failed. Clapp had bought everything, including the old lease, but not for the lease itself. Clapp was interested in the Metropolitan's assets, including the cash reserves, which certainly amounted to a large fraction of the $4,200,000 the Metropolitan directors had thought they could spend to buy back the company's stock. Stevens now was willing to buy the tiny fragment of the old lease, and Clapp was willing to sell, confident that he could preserve the Metropolitan, with its off-tract building core, as a profitable enterprise—an enterprise for which he had, in any case, other plans. The president of the Metropolitan was A. H. Link, a Clapp associate.

Late in 1953, after the repercussions of Clapp's dramatic move had stopped ricocheting about Seattle's business community, Stevens was prepared to act. Through one of his companies, Rostev Realty, he made an earnest money deposit of $250,000 on the remnant of the old lease, the balance of the sale price to be determined. The negotiations, launched early in the winter—Ryan and Rosling on one side, Link and Metropolitan attorneys on the other—proceeded until the last days of December. Ryan was becoming increasingly desperate ("We finally were talking about mops and brooms," he said) to reach agreement before the end of the year on the price of the existing assets. The final moment was one that Ryan never forgot. To force a conclusion he had proposed that independent appraisers be asked to fix the value. As 1954 approached he went a step further, saying that if a price could not be reached, he was prepared to call a press conference to announce a breakdown in negotiations. With that, Metropolitan set a price. The price was $1,750,000, or $1,500,000 in addition to the earnest money, the funds to be paid immediately and in cash. Thus on the last day of 1953, and just fifteen minutes before the banks closed in New York, Ryan called Stevens to describe the requirements. Stevens "went through the ceiling," as Ryan recalled, but cut off the telephone call and began to make arrangements. Later that day, while the conferees were still meeting, a representative of a Seattle bank delivered to Ryan a check for $1,500,000. In that fifteen-minute interval Stevens had arranged the transfer of funds, saying, "We'll get it all straightened out next week."[69]

The announcement was made on January 8, 1954—the date that Steers had said that the Metropolitan stockholders would be paid for the stock they deposited with the company. But that was meaningless now. The stockholders had been paid $30.35 for each of their shares after the Metropolitan accepted Clapp's offer. If January 8, 1954, was not widely recognized as historic, it nevertheless was the date of an ending and a beginning. A long tenure was over, a new one coming.

Clapp had the Metropolitan Building Company, for a price never announced, and with it the cash reserves, the receipts from the sale to Rostev, and the Exchange and Medical-Dental Buildings, each worth perhaps $450,-000 or more. Stevens and Ryan, University Properties now in control, had freedom to begin the subleasing and improving that would make the leasehold profitable.

The university—the regents having watched these late developments from the sidelines—could hope, at last, for a respectable return from its downtown property.

CHAPTER 10

The Changes Come: 1954 to 1959

In January 1954, something called University Properties, Incorporated, held the place occupied for so long by the Metropolitan Building Company, and if University Properties was not exactly what Seattle had been expecting, so be it. The old lease still had nine months to run, but the new regime was in command. At that moment, the man in the center was James M. Ryan, and Ryan, in the vernacular, had his work cut out for him.

Ryan was, in a way, a latter-day J. F. Douglas, except that Ryan's task was not to create a Metropolitan Center but to recreate it, carrying along fifty years of history and tradition. University Properties had to rehabilitate and revitalize the center while bringing that half century of risk and investment to new levels of income in which the university would share. Seattle looked to this, as did the university. It was a measure of Ryan, as of Stevens, that University Properties began to demonstrate in its earliest days flashes of the daring that had marked the Metropolitan Building Company's best moments, while functioning with an extraordinary sensitivity to the public view of the Metropolitan Center as a university—and thus a public—property.

Through decades of alternating prosperity, depression, and war, the Metropolitan had represented a continuity in Seattle and in the state of Washington. University Properties represented the beginning of another. From 1907 to 1954 the Metropolitan had paid to the university less than $4,000,000 in rent, but it had developed a property conservatively valued at $25,000,000. University Properties, taking over, was committed to a lease under which the university's income was estimated at $17,500,000 for the first ten years after a heavy investment in modernization. What Nathan Potter had called the "mathematics" of the lease was the mathematics of an entirely new age.

There had been a continuity on the university's part, too, and of a peculiarly self-generated style, a blend of pragmatism and idealism. Sixty-two regents had served the university since that day in 1902 when Richard Winsor had moved that the board "adopt the policy of leasing the old university site." The Moore lease of 1904 had been approved by Winsor and by W. E. Schricker, James Z. Moore, Alden J. Blethen, George H. King, and John H. Powell. Who now remembered them? But in preserving for the university a valuable property, they had bequeathed to their successors a responsibility that would not stop. They had, in a fashion they could not have dreamed of, placed on later boards the unremitting burden of custodianship of a property that was as much monument as endowment, and a downtown monument at that.

Every regent who had served between 1904 and 1954 had shared, however fleetingly, a singularly layered set of obligations—to the university first, and thus to the state, but also, because the Metropolitan tract existed, to the city of Seattle, and to the historical origins as well as to the future of all. Had a University of Washington board of regents developed a special character because of this? Yes, without doubt. A regent of the university had always been under some pressure to look inward and outward—to the new and growing campus and to the old one. Because of the presence of the Metropolitan tract a regent of the university functioned in a particularly public way in the realm of policy making. But policies had been shaped over the years, and they had not been casually arrived at. In ways difficult to describe, the university had benefited, not because it was more independent, certainly, but because a part of the university's character derived from that early dedication of private lands to university purposes. The tract was a constant reminder of original intent. And the saving element had been that continuity of membership of the board. Even with the radical shifts in membership in the Lister and Hartley periods, and with the expectable numbers of early resignations and other changes that any board experiences, only sixty-two regents had served in fifty-two years, and some of the seats on that board of seven members had been occupied for long periods by such persons as Blethen, Rupp, Fechter, McKee, Macbride, Shemanski, and, of course, Miller and Balmer, the champions among them all. To become a regent was, by 1954, to join a remarkably small roll of men and women who had served the state in that capacity since the old campus became a leasehold. Now, in 1954, with a new lessee managing the Metropolitan tract, an era of more explicit responsibility was beginning.

The Metropolitan Building Company had cherished in its way its relationship to a university property hallowed as a first campus. Its buildings, however, had carried the names of the capitalists—White, Henry, Cobb, Stuart, Stimson, Skinner—who played the largest roles in putting them there. In 1954 the regents who had approved the new University Properties lease did something of the same kind, but on the campus itself and in honor of one of their own. They named a building for Winlock W. Miller.

The regents' impulse had nothing to do with the tract. The time simply had come to memorialize—even while he lived, and thus in contravention of established policy—a gentle, courageous, and almost timeless man whose peer would not soon be found. Miller had been the preeminent champion of the university's interests in the long-ago scuffles over the development of the downtown tract. But all that was over. What mattered was that Miller, as chairman of the board's buildings and grounds committee for thirty years, had done more than any other to shape the character of the campus. The campus architectural style had been predominantly Gothic since Suzzallo's time, a moment of aspiration in which Miller had been a new and positive force. The original theme had been Bebb and Gould's, and Miller, the old Yale man, was happy with it. Some thought the Gothic theme not really suited to the modern university. Yet in Miller, none could fail to see a man of unswerving dedication to the interpretation of the university ideal in its accommodations for learning. The regents decided that Miller's name should go on Education Hall, the Quadrangle building that not only was his in spirit but had been the meeting place of the regents until 1949. At their meeting of January 15, 1954, the regents unanimously—except for Miller—approved Balmer's motion to change Education Hall to Miller Hall. Miller demurred, saying that he thought the board, in naming the building for a living person, was violating its own sensible and necessary rule. Miller was eighty-three. No other living regent—and only Edmond Meany in his own time—had been so singled out.[1]

It was at that first meeting of 1954 that the regents adopted another resolution, and in this one Miller concurred. Citing chapter 118 of the *Laws of 1951* (the enactment of S.B. 113 introduced by Senators Robert Grieve and Albert Rosellini), the board resolved that it did "hereby agree to commit $5,000,000 of income to be derived from the Metropolitan Tract, after the needs of the Tract itself have been met, toward completion of the Teaching and Research Hospital of the Schools of Medicine and Dentistry."[2]

Questions were already being asked about the possible uses of the larger sums the university expected to receive under the new lease, and particularly how soon any benefits might accrue to the university itself. Members of the faculty were anxious about this, as were the alumni. There was fear that the legislature might be tempted to make the new funds available to the state at large by simply deducting from the university's appropriations the amounts of rental income. Friends of the university were said to be ready to mobilize to prevent this. The questions would not soon go away, but with regard to the teaching hospital the regents had felt free, at last, to make a long-delayed commitment.[3]

Within University Properties, the early months of 1954 were months of mobilization carried out in an atmosphere made harrowing by the need to conduct lease discussions with all the commercial and office tenants. These discussions almost invariably involved planning new space arrangements or improvements. Ryan and Jack Dierdorff, now the rental manager, worked around the clock on such problems, trying, not always successfully, to meet a target of eight signed leases each day. They were having to establish a new subleasing pattern as they went along, however, for not only did they not have access to Metropolitan Building Company records showing the overall levels of sublease income, but the needs of the tenants, put aside for so long, were exerting a pressure that would have made the records of little use.[4]

Ryan was facing larger problems, of course. It was not the formation of a new organization that was Ryan's principal concern, for that had been done. It was, rather, how to give the organization its own new identity and how to use it, quickly, to improve and enhance the attractiveness of the property. There was the $2,000,000 rehabilitation program to be planned, and this had to be carried forward in close conjunction with the university, as the terms of the University Properties lease demanded.

Except for Waldemar Karkow, who had come from Chicago to take charge of rehabilitation and construction, Ryan's staff was home grown, experienced, and drawn in large part from the Metropolitan Building Company. The local experience of the leadership was its strength. Dierdorff, although a native of Montana who had grown up in North Dakota, had been in Seattle since 1937 and was a 1940 graduate of the university in business administration whose whole career had been with the Metropolitan save for three years in the South Pacific in World War II. The new assistant general manager in charge of operations was A. G. (Tony) Schille, who had joined the Metropolitan immediately after his graduation from Oregon State College. He had worked his way to managership of the operating department, and his building management experience included a short stint with the Tacoma Building, in Tacoma, before he rejoined the Metropolitan in its rental department. In all, the University Properties organization included some 225 former Metropolitan employees who had been on the University Properties payroll since the Rostev corporation acquired the balance of the old lease.[5]

With his team in place and with a nine-month start on the projected operations under the leasehold, Ryan was prepared to move as fast as he could to get rehabilitation under way. There were, however, certain imponderables. Funds for the $2,000,000 rehabilitation, these from the university's rentals and under university control, would not begin to accumulate until the period of the new lease began on November 1, 1954. Some form of advance payment, by the corporation or the university, might be necessary. Furthermore, the simplest decisions about rehabilitation could not be made until a study of the tract had shown what improvements were most essential and whether or when certain of the buildings—the Douglas, for example—should be demolished and replaced rather than renovated. Above all, Ryan and University Properties were facing a procedural question that never had faced the Metropolitan Building Company in J. F. Douglas's time or later. They were bound by their lease to consult the regents on proposals for major improvements, because the regents controlled the funds. Consultation had to be close and continuous through channels of communication that had never existed before.

Arthur Lee's agreement to remain for a time at his Metropolitan Center station—he on a part-time basis and Arthur Cannon increasingly involved in financial calculations and liaison—was a decision of particular importance at that juncture. Because the Lee-Cannon office was nearby, Ryan could discuss his ideas, formally or informally, with the two men most familiar with the lease, the tract, and the regents' interest in proper development of the property. Ryan, keeping Lee and Cannon informed, was keeping the regents informed. The relationship thus established not only was an agreeable one but set the tone for the later contacts when University Properties was going to the regents with proposals for major projects.

There had to be, in fact, an understanding everywhere—on the part of the public as well as among the principals—of the relationship between the university and its lessee. University Properties was a lessee. The name had been chosen to suggest the special nature of the property the corporation leased, and no one in University Properties or at the university had thought this amiss. The name had been selected before the leasing, but with neither the name nor the concept was Ryan not at ease. He knew the university and its people. He was proud of the association through the leasehold. He meant to develop the tract as a reflection of its special status. Yet it soon became evident that emphasizing the university connection led to confusion. Was University Properties a lessee or an agent? The regents and members of the university staff were now more directly involved in the processes of consultation and approval, and newspaper reports of developments sometimes made it difficult to determine whether University Properties or the university was making decisions. Tenants with plans for expansion were disturbed when the plans seemed to require university action. Even the design of a University Properties symbol, or logotype, presented problems. The first trial designs emphasized a link between a "U" for the university and a "UP" for University Properties, and one even incorporated a four-columns device—the four columns of the university's original building—long the motif of the university's own seal. All such schemes were abandoned. There could be no suggestion that University Properties was an arm of the university. University Properties was a lessee, not an agent, standing independently and responsible for its own performance under the lease.[6]

For the regents as for University Properties the year 1954 might have been one of dress rehearsal for the new relationship, of tidying up essential procedures. It was not so, either for the regents or for Ryan and his associates. The regents soon found themselves having to answer, with Lee's help (this time in more detail), the State Legislative Council's questions about the lease and the way it was formulated. The regents also had to face the question of what payment in lieu of taxes—to the city, and perhaps to the county and other tax authorities—should be made by the Metropolitan Center for the services it received. Ryan, meanwhile, put his organization in gear and pressed ahead.

As early as January 1954 Ryan and Cannon had held a long talk in which they covered all the questions then in suspense, including how soon modernization and construction might begin. News stories about an expansion of the Littler's accommodations had suggested that the university itself was "financing improvements," as Cannon later reported to Balmer, and it was natural that other tenants wanted such treatment. Ryan and Cannon both thought that the tenants should know that improvements within the tract ranged from those authorized by the university from its building fund to those paid for by the university or University Properties but with costs recoverable from the tenants themselves. These, however, were questions to be adjusted. When, on the other hand, could University Properties begin on its $2,000,000 program of improvement? And when, looking farther ahead, would it be possible to think of replacing the oldest buildings? Karkow could foresee an expenditure of $2,000,000 on modernization as early as November 1, 1955, a year after the new lease term began, even without waiting for an assessment of the building-replacement situation. To meet such prospects for improvement the university would have to authorize advances substantially above the $800,000 that would be going into the building fund the first year. The university had that option under the lease, Cannon pointed out, and the income by mid-1955, including income from the Olympic, might amount to $2,500,-000—more than enough to cover the $2,000,000 commitment. Would the regents authorize advance payments? On the answer hung a hope for early action.[7]

While the long-range issues were in suspense, Ryan made the most of the opportunities before him. In his own way, and in an entirely different age, he set about to do what J. F. Douglas had done before him. He accumulated ideas. He generated his own, reaching into his years of experience in property management, his knowledge of Seattle, and his appreciation of what the tract meant to the university. The lease under which Ryan operated had been signed three months before he came to University Properties, but he understood quite clearly what his objective must be. His energy and ingenuity had to be focused on giving the Metropolitan Center a renewed vitality as Seattle's commercial core, and this at an extremely critical moment. The pressures were both direct and subtle. New buildings were being built or projected in other parts of the downtown area, particularly in the Denny Regrade area to the north of the tract. The opening of the Alaskan Way viaduct along the waterfront had created a new, fast north-south traffic corridor that both relieved the city center and encouraged avoidance of it. The decision of I. Magnin and Company to move from the tract to a new site at Sixth and Pine was a decision that undoubtedly would be weighed and analyzed by other prime tenants sensitive to the directions of long-term merchandising advantage. On the tract itself the only improvements were being made by William Edris, who had refurbished more than four hundred rooms in the Olympic and had spent most of the $1,255,000 he had pledged toward rehabilitation. (Edris also was known by then to be interested in selling his hotel lease if he could find a buyer who would take the furniture and equipment and acknowledge the value of the improvements.) Above all, the tract itself cried out for modernization—and modernization in ways that somehow would reflect the expertness that was supposed to be inherent in any enterprise undertaken by Roger Stevens, Alfred Glancy, and their associates. That expectation—that need to show progress even before the financial mechanisms were running smoothly—probably was Ryan's greatest burden. The property that Ryan now managed, always with reference to what the regents would approve, was by no means shabby. But it had to be made contemporary, at least, before it could be made appealing. The challenge was to eliminate at once any evidences of creeping antiquity and then to plunge, even at risk, into the major building projects that simply had to be done.[8]

University Properties' first moves were along two lines, one in the realm of policy, the other immediate and specific. Major merchandising tenants, the old and the new, were encouraged to expand their operations with the help of the company. This was the general theme. It was implemented by the early emphasis on development of Fifth Avenue between Union and Seneca streets as an avenue of "smart" specialty shops. In references to Seattle's Fifth Avenue there were allusions, of course, to New York's Fifth Avenue and Chicago's Michigan Boulevard. There was not much that could be done soon about the other part of the tract that included the Douglas Building next to the gray pile of the old post office, but Fifth Avenue was to become the glamour street. Early in 1954 the John Doyle Bishop ladies' specialty shop, which had its own distinctive clientele, decided to take the Skinner Building space being vacated by I. Magnin. The space would be "completely remodeled and renovated," Ryan announced, as a step toward what was called a "Seattle face-lifting." University Properties had to ask the regents to authorize its expenditures for such improvements, of course—$75,000 for the Magnin-to-Bishop change, lesser amounts for others. By June 1954 the tract was stirring. By autumn, the truly significant developments were beginning or were in the wind.[9]

On the part of the university, the regents (Charles F. Frankland had succeeded Grant Armstrong as president) were approaching decisions above the housekeeping level, and this led soon to a further adjustment of procedures for liaison with University Properties. Simply because of the flow of requests for tract authorizations, it was decided that routine approvals should be handled at the administrative level. H. P. Everest, as the officer concerned primarily with university finances, had become the pivot man, keeping in touch with Lee, Cannon, and Ryan and reporting to the regents or to Balmer and the Metropolitan tract committee on questions of policy. Everest soon developed a system of comprehensive monthly reports to the board on Metropolitan tract affairs. The reports were usually accompanied by financial statements and cumulative records of construction authorizations, so that the regents had before them at each meeting Everest's personal review of current affairs. But by fall 1954 Everest had worked up a draft of proposed accounting procedures that was a preliminary effort to sort out responsibilities at various levels. Central to this scheme was appointment of a permanent tract representative (Lee was not interested in a permanent assignment)—a representative "independent of the Comptroller's Office of the University" and having rather broad powers to certify expenditures, issue approvals, and monitor the lessee's performance. Such explorations were of a workaday kind, but they were shaping the future organization. Cannon would succeed Lee before many months had passed, and Ernest Conrad would become the staff member directly involved in accounting and reporting operations at the university end.[10]

It was to be expected that with a new lessee now in charge, the old, nagging question of the taxability of the university property and the "leasehold estate" should again arise. Not quite so expectable, but certainly no surprise, was the continuing curiosity in the legislature about how and on what grounds the regents had determined that the University Properties lease proposal was the best of the eleven submitted.

The tax matter was a tricky one that might require a ruling by the attorney general, legislation, or even a constitutional amendment. At least that was the early view. In article 8 of its lease University Properties agreed to pay property taxes or taxes imposed on the leasehold, and all local improvement district assessments and charges, but this was with the understanding that equivalent amounts could be deducted from the ensuing rental payments to the university. The central issue thus was whether taxes and assessments paid by University Properties and deducted from its rentals were not, in fact, taxes and assessments on the university, a state institution, and thus unconstitutional. There were other questions. Was the University Properties leasehold actually taxable? Did the regents have the right to consent to such taxation? If the attorney general ruled such taxes direct, what legislation might be necessary? Could the regents, as an alternative, agree to make payments in lieu of taxes? Had they the right and, if so, to what taxing authorities beyond the city of Seattle, if any (the county, the school district, the Port of Seattle), should payments be made?

The history of the issue was of little help. The Metropolitan Building Company had been paying personal property taxes on its leasehold since about 1910, and the value of the leasehold interest was repeatedly in dispute. By the late 1930s, when the land and buildings were assessed at just under $5,000,000, the valuations had been placed on a descending scale to recognize the diminishing value of the Metropolitan's interest. In 1947, after the regents had tried to buy the unexpired portion of the lease for $4,643,000, the then county assessor had pegged the assessed valuation at $1,200,000, and on that amount the Metropolitan had been paying $60,000 a year in personal property taxes.[11]

No one, and certainly not the regents, thought that the university property should not carry its fair share of the costs of the municipal services provided through general taxation. The city was vitally interested in the decision. So was the Municipal League of Seattle and King County, a widely representative study group that had given the question intensive examination in 1953 through its own Metropolitan tract committee. On October 29, 1953, the League had sent to the regents a copy of its committee study containing a resolution saying that "the University should be required to pay to those local governmental units whose boundaries include this tract annual sums in lieu of taxes which should approximate the sums those units would receive if the tract and its improvements were owned by private persons."* By 1954,

---

* On July 15, 1953, three days before the new lease was signed, Seattle's Mayor Allen Pomeroy had invited Arthur Lee to a conference in his office to discuss reimbursement for city services. In this letter Pomeroy said, "This particular problem of the Metropolitan tract is peculiar to Seattle. No other city in the United States offers the spectacle of the

examinations of the interlocking questions were involving the King County commissioners, the county assessor and the auditor, representatives of the Seattle school district, the State Tax Commission, and members of the staff of the state attorney general, most particularly Fred L. Harlocker, the assistant attorney general who had come to the campus from Olympia to succeed John Spiller as the resident legal counsel to the university. Balmer and the regents were more than casually interested, for the university was committed in the new lease to forgo in rentals the taxes and assessments that University Properties paid.[12]

In the end, it was legislation that cut the knot, but only the following year. The legislature of 1955, in another last-minute vote, approved a house bill authorizing the regents to enter agreements with the city of Seattle for annual payments of not more than $60,000 for services to the tract. The use of the $60,000 figure may have reflected the thought that the university should be expected to pay no more than had been paid in taxes by the Metropolitan Building Company. In any case, passage seems to have been in doubt until just before the legislature adjourned.* Under this legislative sanction the university began its $60,000-per-year payments in 1956, when the regents also authorized a payment to the city of $10,075 as the university's pro rata share of the cost of the city's street-light-improvement project referred to the board by the Metropolitan Building Company in 1953. All such payments by the university were now considered voluntary, and made by the university from its Metropolitan tract income.[13]

As for the lingering curiosity about the Stevens lease, this blossomed in mid-1954 in a hearing held at the request of the State Legislative Council subcommittee concerned with the Metropolitan tract, the leading member Senator Albert Rosellini. There was an impression at the time that the hearing was a politically inspired "fishing expedition" related to Rosellini's earlier call for disclosure of the details of the lease negotiations, and that the inspiration now reflected the unhappiness of one or more of the losing "bidders." Mort Frayn, still chairman of the council, could not deny that a hearing was proper, but he by no means wanted a hearing to become an inquisition. It did not, and the episode might be no more than a footnote to the leasing except that it did put to rest residual questions about the wisdom of the regents' decision in 1953.

Lee and Cannon were the principal witnesses at a legislative council meet-

---

dominant 10 acres of the central business district, devoted entirely to profit-making commercial business, actually classified as tax free" (Metropolitan Tract Office files, "Payment in Lieu of Taxes"). When the Municipal League conducted a nationwide survey to find out how other states handled such situations, the results showed that six states taxed and twenty-two exempted the income-producing property of state universities. Among the twenty-two states exempting such property, only Connecticut required payments in lieu of taxes and in five other states voluntary payments were made by the institutions (Municipal League, "Report of Metropolitan Tract Committee, October 2, 1953").

* The legislation (chap. 229, *Laws of 1955*) flowed from H.B. 472 introduced by King County Representatives Newman H. Clark and Frank Connor.

ing held in Lee's own offices in June 1954. Cannon described the financial considerations and Lee the elements that tilted the university toward the University Properties proposal. Cannon said the university had calculated that the property should yield an annual gross income of $2,400,000, that operating costs would be about $975,000, and that the problem had been to find a responsible lessee with a plan for operation and development that would leave the university as much as possible of the $1,425,000 balance. Development was important, hence the creation of the building fund, and so too were the guarantees of performance, upon which the final decision actually turned. Lee, taking up the Cannon account, said that the Stevens offer of a $1,000,000 guarantee was by far the largest, approached only by a "Seattle group" that had offered $500,000, and of course Stevens had also proposed an advance of $2,000,000 for immediate rehabilitation of the tract. The Stevens lease, Lee said, was expected to give the university an average annual yield of $1,307,000, whereas University Properties was expecting earnings of about $168,000 before payment of federal taxes.[14]

The "Seattle group" that had made a proposal was not identified, but it was at that legislative council hearing that the identities of the competing applicants came closest to being revealed. The council subcommittee was given data on the proposals, but no names. Some of the regents, the newspapers said, felt no qualms about releasing the names, but Lee resolutely resisted this, because the terms had been given in confidence. Lee was supported by Frayn and the Republicans on the subcommittee, the Democrats favoring disclosure. Frayn announced before the hearing was over that if a "disgruntled bidder or two" wanted to be heard, the subcommittee would be reconvened. That never was necessary. The applicants remained anonymous, the record closed.[15]

The large decisions about improvements in the tract were coming to the regents long before 1954 was out. By August, University Properties architects and engineers had drawn up a proposal for rehabilitating the White-Henry-Stuart Building at a cost of $1,300,000. There would be new lobbies, new automatic elevators, and a general overhaul of store fronts and office accommodations. Such plans the regents approved. By September they also had approved construction of a new two-level parking garage under the Stimson Building, a garage that would have a daily capacity of some six hundred cars, the upper level to be used by patients visiting doctors or dentists in either the Stimson or the Cobb. All such work would be going ahead in 1955. Ryan, his organization now up to speed, was saying that expenditures might exceed the $2,000,000 to which University Properties was committed by its lease.[16]

What significance surrounded that autumn day in 1954 when the old Metropolitan lease was to expire? October 31 was a Sunday, which gave the newspapers an opportunity to do a little Sunday-morning reminiscing about the history of the university tract. But most of the looking was forward, not backward. Monday, November 1, was the day the new leases—the University

Properties thirty-five-year lease and Edris's twenty-two-year lease on the Olympic—were to go into effect. But already University Properties was deep in improvement projects, and Edris, who had been rehabilitating the hotel, was trying to sell it to Western Hotels, Incorporated, which wanted to buy. The hotel sale required the approval of the regents, but a great many details had to be worked out.

Western Hotels had been hoping for some years to acquire the Olympic, which it viewed as a logical addition to its extensive chain, and Western had been one of the groups submitting proposals when the lease went to Edris in 1952. The company already operated four hotels in Seattle—the New Washington, the Benjamin Franklin, the Roosevelt, and the Mayflower—and eighteen other hotels in fourteen cities from Los Angeles to Vancouver, British Columbia. President of the company was S. W. Thurston, and with him was a team of five vice-presidents—Dewey Metzdorf, Edward E. Carlson, Lynn P. Himmelman, Willard E. Abel, and Gordon Bass—with substantial experience in Seattle and the Northwest. Metzdorf, Carlson, and Himmelman had attended the University of Washington and were prominent in Seattle's community life. Carlson, as Thurston's assistant and a member of Western's executive committee, was at the center of the effort to acquire the Olympic. When at length Western Hotels organized a subsidiary to take over Seattle's one-time "community hotel," the new organization was the Seattle Olympic Hotel Company, with Thurston as its president and Carlson its secretary.[17]

Edris wanted to sell, Western Hotels wanted to buy, but the transaction took a while, the discussions proceeding well into 1955. The details involved negotiations not merely for the improvements that Edris had insituted, which then had cost more than the $1,255,000 to which he was committed, but also for acquisition of furniture and fixtures and, of course, for assignment of responsibility for demolition of the Metropolitan Theatre and construction of the new hotel entrance that would replace it. While the preliminary bargaining was going on, the regents could only wait, but they soon became parties of the third part in a complicated process of proposal and review. The Metropolitan Theatre had been closed since December 1954, and the responsibility for its demolition would go to Western Hotels if that corporation succeeded in acquiring the Edris lease.

It was on July 23, 1955, that the regents approved assignment of the Edris lease to the Seattle Olympic Hotel Company, the new Western affiliate. The recommendation came from Balmer and his Metropolitan tract committee. On August 1 the stockholders of The Olympic, Incorporated (Edris the principal), approved by resolution the sale of the hotel for $3,500,000 "and adjustments in the sum of $177,000." On August 2 the Seattle Olympic accepted the transfer, and an agreement covering the sale was executed by the regents and the two hotel organizations. Beatrice Gardner, now president of the board, and Nelson Wahlstrom, acting secretary, signed for the regents. Edris and John P. Garvin signed for The Olympic, Incorporated. Thurston and Carlson signed for the Seattle Olympic.[18]

In the assignment of the lease and the accompanying agreements, the Seattle Olympic Hotel Company assumed until October 31, 1974, the rental obligations of The Olympic, Incorporated, the balance of the $600,000 due before November 1, 1956, the percentage rental, after that, with the $400,000 minimum, and the annual payments of $24,000 for use of the Metropolitan Theatre site. The company agreed in addition to spend within two years not less than $200,000 in further rehabilitation of the hotel, and to replace the theater with a new hotel entrance. It agreed to operate and maintain the Olympic "as the leading hotel in the city of Seattle, and in good faith [to] use its utmost efforts to keep the transient occupancy . . . as high as possible." But since Western already owned the other Seattle hotels, the agreement provided that operation of the Olympic by a Western affiliate would not be considered a conflict, although under certain conditions appearing in the future Seattle Olympic might ask the regents' permission to enlarge or alter its other establishments (specifically the Roosevelt or the Benjamin Franklin) under plans to be submitted for approval.[19]

Seattle had few tears left for the old Metropolitan Theatre. The city remembered, nevertheless, that many of the century's greatest actors and vocalists had appeared at the "Met"—Otis Skinner, Ethel Barrymore, Mary Garden, Jeanne Eagels, Galli-Curci, Antonio Scotti, Geraldine Farrar, Gertrude Lawrence, Katherine Cornell—and it was proud that one of the greatest, Helen Hayes, was playing there in Barrie's *What Every Woman Knows* when the last curtain went down on December 4, 1954. The papers noted that on that last night a Seattle architect, G. C. Field, had watched Miss Hayes from the same seat he had occupied when, forty-three years before, he took his bride to see Edna Wallace Hopper in *Jumping Jupiter* on the Metropolitan's opening night.[20]

The part of the Metropolitan Center most in need of modernization was that northwest sector at Fourth Avenue and Union Street where the Douglas Building was separated by an alley from the U.S. Post Office. The problem there was complex. The post office at Third and Union had stood for fifty years on a plot of land that included the small corner of the tract sold for $25,000 by the regents of 1902. The structure not only was old but it was of a federal-monumental style, wasteful of space inside and out, with front steps that jutted into the sidewalks, impeding pedestrian traffic. It was altogether unsuited to contemporary government requirements. As for the Douglas, no formal survey was needed to determine if it should be replaced, for despite occasional refurbishments it remained a squat and unattractive vestige of the tract's first tentative development. Furthermore, although the Douglas extended 140 feet along Fourth Avenue, its Union Street frontage was only 63 feet. Thus it occupied only a tiny fraction of the area between Third and Fourth, the area where rehabilitation was essential. It was impossible to think of replacing the Douglas with a new tall building on the small Douglas base and adjacent to the space-wasting federal antique. University Properties, with all else before it, could only look at the problem with a determination to do something later. The seeds of the solution nevertheless were planted in 1954.

The initial impetus came from outside the tract. Ryan had been with University Properties scarcely three months, and was involved in planning "Seattle's Fifth Avenue," when he was approached by owners of nearby off-tract buildings who were thinking of trying to build a parking garage on the post office site. There would have to be an accommodation with the government, probably an exchange of the post office property for another location offering more room for postal and federal facilities. Ryan had been asked if it would be possible for University Properties to join such a venture, and Ryan and Cannon had discussed this at their meeting of January 1954. They had agreed that the proposal was interesting, since it would place a parking garage adjacent to the tract—and better there than elsewhere—but there was a large question whether University Properties, participating in the project, would not be violating its lease clause prohibiting engagement in competitive business.[21]

There the matter rested while University Properties went ahead with its plans for the White-Henry-Stuart Building and for the new parking garage under the Stimson. But every review of the needs of the tract came back to the Douglas Building, and slowly over the ensuing months the idea of a comprehensive government-university solution took hold. The idea had only rough outlines at first. The outlines were gradually refined in consultations involving Ryan, Lee, Cannon, Everest, and Balmer and the Metropolitan tract committee. By December 1954 exploratory talks had been started with representatives of the federal agencies—the Post Office Department and the General Services Administration—and Seattle's Congressman Tom Pelly. No one knew yet what was possible under federal law or regulation—whether an exchange of property might be worked out (although the university itself had nothing to exchange) or whether University Properties might build a new building, with the permission of the regents, to be occupied by the government under lease. In any case, when the federal officials entered the discussion, the prospects of a major new tract improvement became public knowledge.[22]

With all the proposing and approving, the public announcements, and the planning for improvements, the Metropolitan Center was a lively place again. And Ryan was one who could see that the liveliness was at the community-participation level. In the Christmas season of 1954 a week-long Christmas Choral Festival, sponsored jointly by University Properties and the Seattle Olympic Hotel Company, was held in Victory Square, the University Street site of the bond-sale rallies and memorial services of World War II. A dozen choruses and choirs from churches, high schools, clubs—including Seattle's well-known Ralston Male Chorus—presented daily performances in a temporary pavilion erected near the marquee of the Metropolitan Theatre, still awaiting demolition. On the last evening all the choirs combined to close the festival in a program of 250 voices. Ryan tried to overlook no opportunity to make the Metropolitan Center a magnet. When tenants expanded their quarters, small ceremonies were planned for the openings. New tenants were welcomed, such as when Victor Rosellini, a leading Seattle restaurateur, prepared to open a new room, the Four-Ten, in the Stuart Annex across from the Olympic. The Seattle Olympic Hotel Company was pressing forward with its plans for the major overhaul of the hotel, and Carlson and Thomas Gildersleeve, the hotel manager, supported the general atmosphere of growth with promotional ideas of their own.[23]

Not all of the corners were being turned in 1955, but every turn was celebrated. The University Properties rehabilitation of the White-Henry-Stuart Building produced in time new automatic elevators and new lobbies, in addition to other interior refurbishments, each step marked upon completion by a ribbon-cutting or other program to which community leaders were invited.

Things were going well—so well that Arthur Lee now thought it time for him to withdraw as the regents' tract representative. He had discussed this with Balmer and Everest, who had hoped he would stay. But in March 1955 Lee wrote Everest to say that he wanted to be relieved at the end of the month. "The handling of the negotiations for new leases has been a most interesting experience for me," Lee said, "and I have appreciated the opportunity to do so." Interesting and, he might have added, exhausting. The regents approved Lee's decision reluctantly, hoping that he would continue to be available, on special occasions, as a consultant. Everest recommended that Arthur Cannon become tract representative until the end of the year, when the whole liaison structure might be reviewed. Cannon and Conrad worked together so smoothly, Everest said, that "I hate to disrupt the organization more than necessary." But on the University Properties side another kind of disruption, fortunately a temporary one, was coming.[24]

In April 1955, less than a month after Cannon had replaced Lee, James Ryan suffered a coronary attack. Ryan was in the hospital, his condition subject to conjecture, and Waldemar Karkow was carrying on in his stead. Karkow was competent, widely respected, and perfectly capable of moving forward the tract rehabilitation projects that were his responsibility. But he was not Ryan, nor could he be expected to have Ryan's touch in public and university relations. To Ryan, of course, the interlude was an agony of uncertainty, for his return, when that occurred, would put him under the strains that probably had induced the attack in the first place. When Everest prepared his April report to the regents, he could only say that Ryan was expected to be in command again, "perhaps," by June. That was how events turned out. Ryan returned, recovered and ready to go into action, at what was a critical point in tract development. It was with Cannon, as tract representative, that Ryan now conferred, but a new staff member joined University Properties that year, and he was Donald J. Covey, a graduate of the university in 1953. Covey helped ease the load.[25]

Seattle watched in those months the changes being wrought in the tract—
the creation of new storefronts on Fifth Avenue and construction of the
Stimson-Cobb drive-in garage—and absorbed the reports of the progress of
discussions with the federal agencies on the Douglas Building–post office
project. But Seattle was caught up in other visions as well. For as long as
anyone could remember, Seattle's highway connections north and south had
been routes of struggle. Particularly to the south, the highway that skirted the
new Seattle-Tacoma International Airport was marked by jogs, angles,
stretches of two-lane paving, and traffic-control lights at major intersections.
Suddenly there was talk of a new Tacoma-to-Everett expressway, probably
a toll road, that would be a six-lane, high-speed route passing through Seattle
and expediting the flow of commuter travel and heavy hauling as the Alaskan
Way viaduct never had been expected to do. What this meant to the Metropolitan Center was that major downtown exits or interchanges at University
and Union streets, at the east edge of the tract, might not merely create new
downtown traffic patterns but require further expansion of parking facilities.
Rogers Stevens, visiting Seattle in January 1955, had said he thought the
expressway idea a splendid one, and that any concomitant problems would be
solved. "It never ceases to amaze me how people in Seattle worry about parking," Stevens told the Seattle *Times.* "When you think what it's like in New
York and other cities, Seattle is well off."[26] But the Seattle of 1955 was not
worrying excessively about parking—at least not a certain small group of
community leaders. The idea had been advanced that Seattle should become
the site of a world's fair. The legislature was approached about this, for a
broad base of support and funding was essential. The legislature of 1955
created by statute a World Fair Commission. When the commission was organized, its chairman was Edward E. Carlson.

All such developments held meanings, subtle or otherwise, of importance to
the Metropolitan Center, where the long-range plans for the improvement of
the Olympic and the replacement of the Douglas Building were being spun
out in seemingly endless conferences in 1956 and later. There came a reminder of the special nature of the tract when the city began pressing for
acknowledgement by the state that University Street and Fifth Avenue were
owned by the city, as was Fourth Avenue, which had been duly condemned
and taken for public use in 1906. University Properties, naturally curious
about whether its leasehold included the two streets, asked its attorneys to
search the record, and the answer was that neither University Street nor Fifth
Avenue had ever been condemned. They belonged to the university and the
state and thus were properly within the leasehold. The city appeared to have
no ground for contending that the two thoroughfares had become public
property by "prescription." The Metropolitan Building Company had surveyed, graded, and paved the streets years before. The city had never pressed
a claim. It had, in fact, merely assessed against the property the costs of certain
improvements to those segments of the streets within the tract. In no other

city, certainly, were important parts of the downtown street system leased or leaseable to private operations by a nonmunicipal entity.[27]

By late 1956 the regents had authorized University Properties tract improvements totaling $3,802,315. The projects completed had cost $2,833,132, with $1,850,028 spent on the White-Henry-Stuart Building alone. The principal aspects of the early modernization thus were nearing completion within two years of the date the new "main lease" went into effect. Meanwhile, Western Hotels and the Seattle Olympic Hotel Company were enlarging their view of what was possible at the Olympic. Even as the Metropolitan Theatre was coming down, Seattle Olympic had completed work on a proposal, soon submitted to the regents, under which the hotel improvement would be enlarged in scope. The space freed by the demolition of the theater would be used not only for a new hotel entrance, with associated facilities, but for construction of a grand ballroom, a new dining room, a new "Palm Court" lounge, a "specialty" restaurant, and additional kitchen facilities. There would be adjustments in the rental payments: the minimum guarantees would be increased from $400,000 to $450,000, and the percentage rates would be extended but under a $650,000 ceiling related by formula to the cost of the improvements. For this, the Seattle Olympic asked a five-year extension of its lease to permit amortization of the added costs. On that issue the proposal turned, but only briefly. Under an agreement of September 15, 1956, Seattle Olympic was granted its five-year extension. The lease would now run to October 31, 1979. The action of the regents was not unanimous, however, and there was in this a faint suggestion of old times. Winlock Miller, who always had opposed so firmly any extension of the Metropolitan Building Company lease, even for the original "community hotel," voted against the five-year extension for Seattle Olympic. In this Miller was supported, a little surprisingly, by Thomas Balmer, who may simply have wished to stand beside an old colleague in his statement of principle. The agreement was approved, nevertheless, and signed for the university by Charles M. Harris, as president of the board, and Helen Hoagland, secretary. Thurston and Carlson again signed for the hotel company.[28]

The theater was gone. The whole city block where the Olympic stood would now hold only the expanded, vastly improved hotel. There would be a new ballroom above the new "carriage entrance" and, at the hotel's Fifth and University corner, a new restaurant, the Golden Lion. Work would be completed in mid-1957.

The solution of the Douglas Building question was years in its accomplishment. The solution was ingenious, yet no more ingenious than original, for it had no precedent. The essence of it was that the university and the federal government made a singular exchange. The university acquired the additional land it needed to erect a twenty-two story building, the Douglas replacement. For this, the university assumed the costs of construction for the government of a new three-story main post office. None could remember an arrangement whereby funds other than federal funds were used in construction of a federal building. And the arrangement was concluded, finally, when University Properties—which is to say Stevens and Ryan—assumed any risks of possible financial loss by the university or the government. That gamble seemed another measure of the quality of the new lessee.

The processes of negotiation, decision, and approval covered five years, from 1954 to 1959. These were, as it turned out, not only years of stress on the university campus but years in which the university selected and inaugurated a new president and the board of regents experienced a complete change in its membership. The state also elected a new governor, and the legislature held three sessions. It can only be wondered what might have happened if the regents, instead of leasing the tract, had attempted to manage the property themselves.

The University Properties interest in the Douglas Building problem, given an initial focus in 1954 and then put aside during Ryan's illness and all else that followed, was matched by that of the university, where by 1955 Everest's reports to the regents routinely contained his notes on exploratory conversations with Ryan, Karkow, Cannon, and federal officials, particularly with representatives of the General Services Administration in Seattle. The GSA wanted on Third Avenue a new tall building that would accommodate the post office and centralize federal offices scattered elsewhere in the city. Congressman Pelly was firmly opposed to construction on tax-free land of a building that would take tenants away from privately operated properties, and Pelly's view coincided with that of the university, which did not want a tall federal building occupying air space next to its own new Douglas Building and probably eliminating any chance to improve public parking. But at that moment the university simply wanted the best building it could get. It had no design in mind, even as to height. More ground area was needed, and the university hoped, at the very least, to be able to use that part of the tract sold off in 1902. Among the imponderables was that of cost, for the regents had committed the $5,000,000 of tract income to the teaching hospital. What role University Properties might have in all this was an open question.

A path through the thicket seemed to have appeared in 1955. Roger Stevens, visiting Seattle, met at lunch with Frankland, Corbett, and Everest and discussed with them, among other things, the Douglas prospect. Although any cost estimates were wholly preliminary, Stevens said he thought he could arrange $6,000,000 in financing—$2,000,000 to be paid to the university during construction and another $4,000,000, interest free, payable over five years. Stevens, having made the rounds of New York banks, soon confirmed this. The university would have to look closely at its building-fund projections, naturally, and Everest asked Cannon to try to work out a financial plan. Cannon, making all the necessary assumptions concerning rental income and revenue from the new building, said that the university might be receiving $5,810,000 by December 1960, and $14,520,000 by 1965. "As you will see from the calculations set out," Everest wrote the regents, "the schedule is a rather tight one and involves very definitely the arrangements for providing the $5,000,000 for the hospital and . . . a definite effect on any other moneys which might be forthcoming from the Tract for several years to come." As for discussions about the post office site, all was going well, Everest said. The GSA's view was somewhat more flexible (Pelly apparently had made his view public in a statement from Washington, D.C.), and there seemed room for proposal and counterproposal. "While the process of these negotiations is slow and time-consuming, it is nevertheless working even more rapidly than we had originally hoped," Everest wrote, "and it could well be that some conclusions could be reached early in the spring."[29]

That would be the spring of 1956. On March 29, 1956, Everest, on behalf of the regents, sent a letter to the Seattle office of the GSA putting the university's proposal and expectations in rather specific terms. The university wanted to acquire that part of the federal site lying west of the Douglas Building and east of the post office—land with a 105-foot frontage on Union Street and extending south to a depth of 235 feet—much of this originally the university's property. It had been suggested, Everest said, that "the State of Washington construct for the Federal government a new post office on the remaining westerly 70 feet on Union Street by 235 feet on Third Avenue, the cost of this new post office to be equal to the negotiated fair market value of the property to be acquired by the State." The university might be willing to pay cash, if a federal building was no higher than eight or ten stories. But it also had been suggested that a new post office of two or three stories might lend itself to roof parking to supplement the parking facilities the university was visualizing. To make the parking garage idea feasible, there would have to be a 35-by-70-foot easement through the ground floor of the new post office to facilitate joint access from the south. "Transfer of this property along the lines suggested" Everest urged, "would well serve the citizens of Seattle as well as the University while at the same time securing for the Federal government badly needed post office facilities with little or no cash outlay. We would expect this joint development by the State and the Federal government to have the support of our Congressional delegation, of downtown property owners, and the public generally."[30]

On the government side, the university's proposal went to the GSA's legal department for review, but in the meantime the regents had before them the matter of funding the teaching hospital, for which $11,418,948 was necessary. By March, Harris was president of the board, succeeding Gardner, with Miller vice-president. The question now was how, in view of the financial pressures at the tract and on the campus, to use to best advantage the $5,000,000 bonding authority granted by the 1951 legislature. In April the board considered a $4,000,000 bond issue with $1,000,000 transferred from the "Metropolitan operating account." By May, it had been decided to issue $5,000,000 in bonds, but the issue would fall short of solving the problem. The university would have to ask the 1957 legislature for $2,500,000. Even then—and even after assembling bits of financing from half a dozen "local" building and operating accounts, with "possible" additional help from the federal government—the construction deficit would be $713,948. The regents nevertheless plunged ahead, and at that May meeting they named as bond counsel a prominent Seattle attorney, Harold S. Shefelman. The choice was not by chance, for Shefelman's counsel was sought in many places and on matters quite apart from bond issues, but there was a premonitory air about it. Shefelman had been close to the university for more than a quarter of a century—ever since he had become a lecturer in law in 1930—and now he was serving the regents directly in a new capacity. Plans for the bond issue went forward in ensuing months, and on November 10, 1956, the regents authorized $5,000,000 of "University of Washington Teaching Hospital Metropolitan Tract Revenue Bonds." The bonds were sold in December, upon the bid opening, to Blyth and Company. There had been technical problems that Shefelman helped solve. The most difficult of these was the University Properties lease clause requiring university deposits in the tract building fund. Because this lease provision took priority over bond debt service, the regents created a Metropolitan Tract Special Reserve Fund, in which, until bond indebtedness was extinguished in 1969, the university would make deposits to equal the building fund deposits under the lease.[31]

But in all this time a final answer to the post office problem had come no nearer. It was, in fact, farther away. There had been occasional trips to Washington, D.C., by Ryan or Cannon. There had been conferences, exchanges of memorandums, and calculation and recalculations of estimated costs. There was even federal legislation. Since the university was attempting to acquire the post office site by negotiation, the question had arisen whether the GSA still held authority to dispose of surplus property by negotiation rather than through public advertising for bids. The GSA's authority was contained in the Federal Property and Administrative Services Act of 1949, which had been routinely extended periodically, most recently to June 1956. With the latest extension running out, it was necessary to get the Congress to approve another if the university negotiations were to go forward. By August 1956 this had been done, with the help of Congressman Pelly and certain others in the Washington congressional delegation. A House bill of 1955 (H.R. 7855), originally introduced by Representative McCormick, was passed by the House in a version extending the GSA authority to July 31, 1958, approved by the Senate only a week before the congressional adjournment, and signed by President Eisenhower on August 3, 1956. The June 11 report of the Senate Committee on Government Operations, which recommended passage, said: "In the sale of surplus property desired by States or by former owners—the two major classes of transactions covered by this bill—the circumstances occasionally are such as would make it inequitable or contrary to the public interest if those purchasers were required to bid competitively with private interests. . . . It is the intent of the committee, in recommending extension of the authority, that negotiated sales to States, local government, former owners, or others be made at the current market value of the properties, as established by competent appraisers."[32]

The act thus said that the GSA might continue to negotiate with states or former owners of property, and the Seattle negotiation would qualify on both points. Everest told the regents on September 4, 1956, that all signs were "hopeful." But the university could not even begin to think of plans for a new Douglas Building until the post office site offer had been accepted, possibly at a figure somewhat higher than the $420,000 offered by the university on the basis of independent appraisals. University Properties was restless, not only because sublessees were beginning to leave the Douglas Building but because University Properties was having to pay standby charges on bank credit arrangements for financing the new building.* Only a month later, in October 1956, Everest was reporting the post office situation "complicated and perplexing." There had been a turnover in leadership of the GSA—the new administrator was Franklin G. Floete—and new men were coming from Washington, D.C., to see what had been going on with respect to the post office proposal. This was not in itself discouraging, for neither Floete nor his representatives were hostile to the plans. But discussions were starting from the beginning with a new GSA team. The regional director in Seattle was retiring on January 1, 1957.[33]

Cannon had decided to leave his tract assignment to return to full-time duties on the campus. He submitted his resignation in July 1956, effective September 15. With that, Ernest Conrad was assigned to the downtown office to become familiar with procedures there and to establish his own working relationships with University Properties and with the contractor and auditing staffs.

Larger cyclical changes now began to occur. In July 1956, President Schmitz told the regents that he wished to retire in August 1957, when he would be sixty-five. In the election of November 1956, the state chose as its new governor a Democrat, Albert D. Rosellini. Rosellini would soon have vacancies to fill on the university's board of regents, for the terms of Armstrong, Corbett, and Frankland—all Langlie appointees—were expiring. The new governor was the Albert Rosellini who, as a state senator, had demanded a public accounting of the regents' actions with respect to the Metropolitan tract leasing and a "full disclosure" of the details of the eleven lease proposals. He was also, however, the Albert Rosellini who had been a cosponsor

---

* The university was still worried about tax questions. In that autumn of 1956, Edward L. Rosling, attorney for University Properties, was asked whether the university might incur "any possible tax liability under the present plans for construction of the new Douglas Building." Rosling's answer, in a letter to University Properties on October 26, 1956, was that the university would not be risking a tax liability if it would "continue to handle the New Building Fund in the same manner as it has handled the modernization of the tract and do so within the framework of the present lease" (Rosling to University Properties, Inc., October 26, 1956, Balmer Papers, 16–7, copy).

of the 1951 bill authorizing the regents to bond Metropolitan tract income for construction of the teaching hospital. The fact was that Albert Rosellini, governor of the state at forty-six, was an experienced legislator of keen political instincts who felt for the university the loyalty of a man who had struggled on his own to get a law degree.

Rosellini, born in Tacoma in 1910, had delivered newspapers and worked at odd jobs from the age of nine, and was still working when he graduated from Stadium High School in 1927. At the university he earned his way with jobs as a meatcutter and merchant seaman, getting his B.A. degree and then, in 1933, with employment as a law clerk, his degree in law. After graduation, Rosellini became a King County deputy prosecutor under Warren G. Magnuson, who was not far from election to the U.S. Congress. He was only twenty-eight when he was elected to the state senate, and he had served in the senate for eighteen years, repeatedly the Democratic floor leader, when he was elected to the governorship. Bills Rosellini had sponsored ranged across a wide spectrum—fair employment practices, improvements in the teacher retirement system, pensions for firemen and policemen, equal wages for women, and, of course, the university teaching hospital bond bill.[34]

It was a surprise to no one, except perhaps the nominee himself, that one of Governor Rosellini's first acts was to name Harold Shefelman to the board of regents. A quarter of a century before, when Shefelman, as a young lawyer with a feeling for teaching, was first meeting with his university law classes (always at 8 A.M.), Rosellini had been a Shefelman student. The careers of Shefelman and Rosellini had been utterly different, but ascendent. By the time Rosellini was governor, Shefelman was a man engaged in an astonishing array of city, state, and national programs, many of them related to education. In January 1957, when Shefelman's name was submitted to the senate, confirmation was immediate and unanimous, without even the customary reference to committee. Shefelman would succeed Charles Frankland as a regent in March, and there was an interesting sequence in this. Frankland, on becoming a regent in 1951, had resigned his seat on the State Board of Education, and to that seat Shefelman had been appointed. Now Shefelman had succeeded Frankland as a regent and he, too, had resigned from the State Board of Education to do so. Shefelman and Frankland were long-time friends, and Frankland was the first to applaud Shefelman's selection. By March, when Shefelman took his seat, Rosellini had made two other appointments to the board. John L. King, who had served his first term from 1946 to 1952, was returned as Armstrong's successor, and Lloyd L. Wiehl, a Yakima attorney, replaced Corbett.[35]

In a sense, Shefelman was of an earlier tradition—a man born and educated elsewhere who had made association with the University of Washington a large part of his life. A native of New York City, his youth spent in San Antonio, Texas, Shefelman was a graduate of Brown University (a scholar-athlete, Phi Beta Kappa, and captain of the wrestling team) and of Yale Law School, where he won his LL.B. in 1925. Shefelman had an eye on the

Northwest, and by 1926 he had been admitted to the Washington bar and had joined, as a very junior attorney, a well-established Seattle firm in which he soon became a partner. From his beginnings in Seattle, Shefelman's sphere of professional and community activity had expanded by the year. He was disciplined, energetic, an insatiable participant with a flair for leadership, and happy in a campus environment. Even as a young newcomer to Seattle, Shefelman had gone out to the university gymnasium to keep in shape as a wrestler and to help with the coaching. The 8 A.M. class he first met in 1930 he continued to meet, year after year for twenty-six years, until he became a regent. Long before 1957, Shefelman had become a man invariably thought of when large affairs, civic or educational, were in the wind. He had been called, frequently as chairman, to programs such as those of the Washington Child Welfare Committee and the Committee on State Government Organization. From 1948 he had been a member of the Seattle City Planning Commission, its chairman in 1950-52. In 1955, Shefelman had been chairman of the Washington state delegation to the White House Conference on Education, and the central figure and moderator at the statewide educational conference at Olympia that preceded the national assembly in Washington, D.C. Throughout it all, Shefelman was busy with his law practice, the work of professional organizations, and alumni and development programs at Brown and Yale.[36]

Three new regents had come to the board in 1957, but other changes were imminent. Wiehl resigned in October to accept a Yakima County judgeship, and to his place Governor Rosellini appointed Joseph Drumheller, the Spokane industrial chemist who, like King, had been a regent before. And on October 16, 1957, the day after his eighty-seventh birthday, Winlock Miller sent to Governor Rosellini a letter of resignation. The news of Miller's decision was announced by the governor on October 23 with a simple statement of thanks and appreciation for Miller's long service. Miller's absence was felt, now, because of what he stood for. His career had linked epochs of state and university history. He had been a regent for almost thirty-six years in a span of forty-three. He had served under six governors, Democratic and Republican, since Governor Lister had appointed him in 1914. A university building bore his name and, because of his love of intercollegiate rowing, a Washington racing shell was called the *Winlock W. Miller*. There really was nothing more to say. The monuments were in place. Miller would live until January 19, 1964, dying at the age of ninety-three.[37]

In the months that followed, the board had only six members—Balmer, again president, Shefelman, vice-president, and Drumheller, Gardner, Harris, and King. Nothing had been done about the search for President Schmitz's successor—Schmitz in the meantime had agreed to stay another year—but Shefelman soon was heading a regent-faculty committee that would get the search into an organized form. Shefelman also was chairman of the Metropolitan tract committee and thus busy becoming acquainted with developments downtown. The post office development still was in suspense.

Nowhere else does there exist a structural complex like that occupying the land south of Seattle's Union Street between Third and Fourth avenues. Its uniqueness is not in its architectural treatment, nor in the fact that it represents an unusual conjunction of office building, parking garage, and post office. The uniqueness is in the degree to which it represents a wedding of state and federal interests made possible by adjustment, compromise, persistence, and—by no means least—the calculation of necessary easements. That the wedding took place was something of a wonder, for the engagement almost collapsed after publication of the banns.

By the end of 1956 almost three years of conference and discussion seemingly had led to an impasse. The university had offered to pay $420,000 for the 105-foot strip of land west of the Douglas Building and to construct for the government, on Post Office Department specifications, a new three-story post office that would occupy the remaining 70-by-235-foot plot at Third and Union. This offer had not been accepted. The negotiations with the new GSA staff were at a standstill. It was also becoming clearer with every calculation that a large gap existed between the amount the university could pay for any part of the federal land—the figure certified by qualified appraisers— and the cost of the new post office that the university might build in exchange.

The calculations were intriguing. In March 1956, teams of appraisers from three leading Seattle firms (Davis and Darnell, Harry R. Fenton and Associates, and Yates, Riley and MacDonald) had certified that $380,000 represented a fair market value for the 105-foot strip that the university wanted to acquire. Demolition engineers estimated that razing the old post office and clearing the site would cost $60,000. The university thus arrived at a net of $320,000 as its basic offer for the land, and to this added $100,000 as the projected value of the right to use the post office roof as a supplementary parking area for twenty-five years. In such a way the university's original offer of $420,000 had been arrived at. In the interim, while estimates of the cost of a new post office were going up, other questions were being asked.[38]

Floete, the new GSA administrator, came from Washington, D.C., to attend a morning meeting at the Olympic on December 27, 1956, and he was raising basic issues. Was the post office site too valuable to hold only the three-story building proposed? What questions might Congress ask if so unusual an exchange was concluded? Where would the funds come from if the cost of the post office was more than the university could pay? Everest, Ryan, and others present at the meeting could only respond that the Post Office Department had already approved the proposal, the plan had wide support, and the university's offer was reasonable. Floete asked, in the end, that the university assemble cost estimates based on three possible alternatives: (1) purchase of the whole post office site in an outright sale; (2) purchase of the 105 feet with an easement, south of the post office, for access to Third Avenue; and (3) purchase of the 105 feet, with the easement and the right to use the post office roof for parking. The university, responding to Floete's first suggestion, ordered an appraisal of all of the federal property. On January 2, 1957, appraisers from the same Seattle firms reported a fair market value of $750,000 for the land, assuming the old post office would be demolished. Nothing more was heard of the idea.[39]

Yet Ryan and Everest, now assisted by Conrad, were grappling with cost calculations. The university, by late 1956, had visualized the office building–parking garage–post office concept in floor plans and perspective drawings prepared by its architectural firm of Naramore, Bain, Brady and Johanson. The office building would be of twenty stories and the ramp garage between the building and the post office would accommodate five hundred automobiles. The easement to the south of the post office would permit construction of a ramp driveway from Third Avenue to the parking spaces on the roof. It was not certain what the office building would cost—perhaps $9,000,000— but it was the cost of the post office that was of immediate concern.[40]

Early in 1957, before Shefelman, King, and Wiehl had come to the board, the regents had decided to see what could be done about narrowing the gap between the university's first offer and the cost of the post office. University Properties, desperate to eliminate the old Douglas Building, was quite ready to participate in the financing. By mid-February, shortly before the regents were to meet, it had been decided that the university would offer $380,000, the original appraisal, plus the $100,000 for the use of the post office roof and an additional $50,000—a total of $530,000 for the 105-foot plot. The cost of the post office was now estimated at $870,000, however, and the difference thus was $340,000. University Properties had offered to pay $150,000, but the difference even then was $190,000. The options were beyond university control and none was easy. University Properties might increase its participation, perhaps by the full amount. The Post Office Department might reduce its requirements by $100,000, or assume $100,000 of the cost, leaving $90,000 to be paid by University Properties. Or, finally, the Post Office Department might reduce the size of the post office building. The building as planned extended to a depth of 70 feet east of Third Avenue. What if this was reduced to 60 feet—reducing the cost and giving the university an additional 10-foot strip of the property? Post office architects were already at work in an effort to see if the solution was possible.[41]

Floete would have argued, as he had, that if the university could put together financing for a post office costing almost $900,000, and this while it contemplated construction of a new major office building, the simple course was to negotiate for purchase of all the federal property and begin the development afresh. Several circumstances combined to make this impractical. For one, the Post Office Department wanted to keep its main office on the site it had occupied for fifty years, and the department was cooperating in the attempt to reach a workable arrangement. For another, the university could have offered no more than the $750,000 certified as fair value by the appraisers on January 2, and there was no assurance that such an offer could be accepted by the GSA. There was also the element of momentum: everyone from local postal officials to Postmaster General Arthur Summerfield and

members of Washington's congressional delegation had participated in some
fashion in consideration of the case. Another consideration had not yet been
mentioned. If the university could make an offer on the federal land, why
could not a private citizen? When the regents met on February 16, 1957, they
authorized Everest to negotiate for the "easterly 105 feet" of the post office
site, then to build on the land remaining—60 feet, presumably—a post office
building costing "not more than $690,000."[42] Why a ceiling of $690,000?
The record fails to elaborate. Perhaps the Post Office Department's architects
had already come in with their plans for a building narrowed by 10 feet on
the east. Everest had authority to go back to the negotiating table, but soon
negotiation was not the way things would be done.

On March 15, 1957, Norton Clapp sent a letter to the board of regents,
copies to all members. Clapp's Metropolitan Building Corporation, successor
to the Metropolitan Building Company, was operating the Exchange and
Medical-Dental buildings and had other projects in mind, including a new
building at Second Avenue and Columbia Street, near the Exchange, that
would become the Norton Building. Clapp objected strongly to the regents'
approach to the post office solution, not only because it foreclosed any possibility of private investment but because the university's acquisition of the
site would represent a first expansion of the ten-acre tract given originally for
"school purposes." Clapp said that he himself had considered making an
offer on the land because he understood that the government planned to declare the property surplus. Quite apart from that, however, he asked the
regents to examine the implications of the action they were preparing to
take. No one objected to university operation of the tract "as a state owned
real estate development," Clapp wrote, but:

Now, however, for the first time, a new element has been injected, and this involves
a very fundamental question which I feel merits your most careful consideration. I
refer to the proposed expansion of the Tract itself. . . .

I wish to raise the important question as to whether or not the University should
expand its downtown commercial real estate operations at all. . . . I feel that there
is some real doubt as to whether the legislature really contemplated any such expansion. I wonder if the Board of Regents themselves, when they entered into the
present lease, ever intended that any of the funds received for rent would be used for
land acquisition. It, of course, can be argued that this is a relatively small parcel of
land, and that a portion of it is some land which the university once owned. Also,
it may be felt that the purchase is not a major move, but is merely incidental to the
proper rebuilding of the Douglas Building. However, it is nevertheless an expansive
move—the first in over fifty years; and, with the preferential position that the University of Washington enjoys with respect to having capital funds readily available for
building purposes, any move of this kind, no matter how small, will serve as a permanent threat to all building and land owners in Seattle.[43]

Clapp was correct in saying that expansion of the tract, however slight,
was still expansion and thus a question of policy. If the university acquired
the 105-foot strip of land, it would be buying back the 63 feet sold to the

government in 1902 and an additional 42 feet. Such expansion was, however, permitted by existing law. The legislation of 1947 setting out the powers of the regents with respect to the tract had granted them the right "to lease or to acquire, by purchase or gift, land and rights necessary or convenient for the maximum utilization and development of said tract." The university was sufficiently concerned about the point to check out the earlier legislation.[44]

Clapp had entered the case with a letter that did indeed raise important questions. Clapp was soon playing a more direct part in the events of that year and his presence had two significant effects. He asked that the post office property be opened to public bids, a request that the GSA could not deny. And when the bid date had been established and the advertising begun, Clapp won a postponement on the ground that the GSA had allowed him inadequate time for preparation. These developments occurred just as Ryan, simply by pledging that University Properties would guarantee the government against loss on buildings costs, had put together an agreement that seemingly had closed the negotiations in favor of the university.

When the regents in February had authorized Everest to resume discussions with the GSA and post office officials, Everest and Ryan had gone to Washington, D.C., to make the rounds again. The officials they visited included Irving Thomas, a graduate of the University of Washington, who was, by then, director of real estate in the Post Office Department's Bureau of Facilities. Again, however, the results were discouraging. The funds the university could commit were too small, the cost of the post office too high. After several days of consultations, Everest returned to the university while Ryan, also scheduled to go on to New York, delayed that trip and decided to make one more attempt on his own. By telephone and personal calls he put before Floete, Postmaster General Summerfield, Thomas, and others in the GSA and the Post Office Department an unambiguous proposition. University Properties, which already had pledged $150,000 to the university effort, would now assume any costs of post office construction above the $870,000 that was the current estimate. The university's offer would stand, University Properties would commit additional funds as necessary, the government would get its post office, and all risk—on the government's side— would be removed. On such terms agreement was reached, and Ryan seemed to have achieved a goal that had been elusive for three years. The Post Office Department was satisfied, and the agreement now needed only the approval of the GSA. On April 11 Everest addressed a formal letter to Floete presenting, on behalf of the regents, the university's offer.[45]

But elusive the goal was still to be. Clapp was not alone in his interest in the government property. Another Seattle man, a real estate owner and operator, was also said to have an eye on the site. Such developments, as well as the principal elements of the university's proposal, had been reported in the Seattle press. In the face of such openly declared interest on the part of at least two private organizations, one of them the Metropolitan Building Corporation, the GSA felt it had no choice but to follow a bid procedure. By mid-May a bid opening had been set for July 3 on what the newspapers called a "novel trade basis," actually the basis upon which the university had been trying for so long to acquire the property. The invitation, published as a display advertisement in the newspapers, was headed "Disposal of Government-Owned Land by Exchange: Portion of Post Office Site, 3rd Avenue and Union Street, Seattle, Washington," and the conditions were described thus:

Bids are invited for the disposal of the following Government property in accordance with the terms hereinafter set forth:

Southerly 235 feet of the easterly 115 feet of the above site fronting on Union Street. The Government will:

1. convey said parcel of land by quitclaim deed;
2. grant the right to joint use with the United States of the 24 feet at the rear of the remainder of the site as a means of ingress and egress to and from Third Avenue; and
3. grant the right to exclusive use of the roof of the new Post Office Building as an automobile parking facility for 25 years (optional).

In exchange for:

1. demolition of the existing Post Office Building;
2. construction of a new part-basement and three-story Post Office Building;
3. provision of space for use by the Post Office Department during construction of the new building; and
4. Payment of cash differential.[46]

There was more. Instructions were outlined. Each bid was to be accompanied by check or money order for $50,000. But the "cash differential" was a critical matter. Might not a private operator submit a bid which, whether or not it followed precisely the pattern of the exchange, offered an attractive cash inducement? As the *Times* put it, "The bid plan follows the line of the university proposal, but gives any bidder the right to compete by offering additional cash 'to boot.' "[47]

Whatever else the GSA invitation had done it had put into explicit terms the bases on which a decision would be made. Negotiation was over. The size of the property had been increased definitely from 105 to 115 feet on the Union Street frontage, which meant that the three-story post office would be 60, not 70, feet in depth, the successful bidder thus acquiring a site 115 by 235 feet. Ryan and Conrad went to work immediately to analyze the situation. On May 23, 1957, they sent to Everest a memorandum outlining the case. The 10-foot increase in the width of the property meant that the university, if it was the successful bidder, would gain 11,000 square feet of rentable area in its new office building. This translated into $20,000 per year or $1,200,000 of additional income over the building's sixty-year life. On the other hand, the enlargement of the site made it vastly more attractive to other bidders, for the 115-by-235-foot base was large enough to support a twenty-story building—a building larger than the university could build on the Douglas site. This could mean that the Metropolitan Building Corporation, for example, might be enabled to place a major new office building at that prime northwest corner of the tract that the university was trying to improve. There was the additional GSA requirement that the successful bidder provide housing for postal operations while the new post office was under construction, but that cost—probably $75,000—was an obligation that any bidder would face. Ryan and Conrad, reexamining all available figures and estimates, concluded that the cost of construction of the new (but slightly smaller) post office, plus $60,000 for demolition of the old and $75,000 for temporary housing, would total $941,000. Commitments by the university and University Properties stood at $770,000. The "Balance to be Resolved" was $171,000. It was perfectly possible to think that a private bidder who was contemplating constructing a major office building would consider it not unreasonable to offer something close to $1,000,000 for a choice site—actually a one-of-a-kind site—in the heart of Seattle's downtown area, a site made more valuable because it adjoined the Metropolitan Center itself.[48]

The University Properties commitment was substantial, as it had to be. Whereas University Properties had earlier agreed to invest $150,000, it had more recently proposed that its tract rental be increased by $240,000, payable in three $80,000 installments. Even so, the "Balance to be Resolved" was $171,000 if the university was to pay $530,000. In the calculations of that spring of 1957, it was considered a possibility that the university might increase its payment by $40,000 (because it was acquiring additional space) and assume the $60,000 cost of demolishing the old post office. University Properties would absorb the baalnce.[49]

From May until late summer—with Shefelman now chairman of the Metropolitan tract committee—developments followed a totally unpredictable course. Late in May there was an effort on the part of the Metropolitan Building Corporation to enlist the interest of the Building Owners and Managers Association of Seattle in the questions of policy and principle about which Clapp had written the regents. The response, on behalf of the association's trustees, was that "action was . . . deemed not within the scope of Association purviews." Before the month was out Congressman Pelly was asking for a review of plans for the post office. Pelly and others, including Postmaster General Summerfield and Senators Warren G. Magnuson and Henry M. Jackson (Jackson then in his first year in the United States Senate) had received communications from the Seattle Branch of the National Association of Postal Supervisors citing what were said to be deficiencies in the allocations of space, particularly for mail handling and the loading and unloading of postal trucks. The plans were reviewed, not altogether stilling certain criticisms, for by July a former Seattle postmaster was saying that the proposed exchange was a "Republican giveaway." But the former postmaster was by that time chairman of the King County Democratic Committee, and it was difficult to see why Republicans should be disposed to be generous, on political grounds, in an arrangement involving a state university and a lessee firm in which the major figure was Roger Stevens, a fundraiser for the

Democratic Stevenson-for-President campaign of 1956. In any case, on the eve of the July 3 bid opening the GSA decided to postpone the opening to a later date.[50]

As late as July 1, 1957, the bidding procedure seemed on track. The university and University Properties—Shefelman, Everest, and Conrad on the one hand, Ryan on the other—had been getting the joint bid in order. At a meeting on June 7 it had been decided that a figure of $974,000 was feasible, this the estimated cost of the new post office plus all accompanying charges including demolition of the old building, provision of interim postal facilities, architects' fees, and so on. The regents, in their meeting of June 22, had authorized such a bid at the July 3 opening. But Norton Clapp was pressing for delay, his office in touch with Congressman Pelly. The other potential bidder, as it developed, was in communication with local post office officials. Both were saying that the July 3 opening did not give them time to prepare their proposals, and the GSA could only reschedule. The bid opening was set for August 5, 1957, and then soon changed to September 30. Again the invitations to bidders appeared in the newspapers, and terms, this time, were much more specific. The "payment of cash differential" had become a "lump-sum of a monetary consideration," for whatever difference that made. But the property to be deeded no longer was a simple plot of 115 by 235 feet. It was a property extending 240 feet south of Union Street and described minutely in relation to the easements that were considered necessary to give the post office additional space, including a "subsurface" area of 6,020 square feet for an enlarged basement.* The new description reflected the thinking that had been going on with regard to complaints about the first post office designs. Now there was not only an easement to the south for the new Third Avenue parking ramp but also an easement to the east *beneath* the deeded surface to accommodate the expanded post office basement. (The new post office would have some 43,000 square feet of usable floor space.)[51]

The summer of 1957 was an anxious one for the regents and for University Properties, where Ryan, particularly, was haunted by the thought of a tall, new, highly competitive building occupying a position virtually inside the Metropolitan Center and dwarfing any building that could be erected in its shadow on the 63-foot Douglas site. Beside that specter was another—the loss of the five-hundred-car parking facility if the federal land went to an-

---

* The property was described as "comprising the Southerly 240 feet of the Easterly 184 feet fronting on Union Street except that portion thereof fronting 69 feet on the Southerly side of Union Street and extending of that width along the Easterly side of Third Avenue a depth of 161 feet, reserving in the Government in the portion to be conveyed by it hereunder a perpetual, alienable easement in and to an area of 6,020 square feet, more or less, of the subsurface of the land to be conveyed by the Government hereunder up and in which the basement of the building to be constructed hereunder will be situated together with a perpetual alienable easement in and to an area of 9,412 square feet, more or less, of the surface of the land to be conveyed by the Government thereunder, upon which the first floor, and maneuvering area on the Southerly end of the building, to be constructed by the successful bidder hereunder will be situated, as shown on plans available at the Regional office" (General Services Administration invitation to post office site bidders, September 1957).

other bidder. Such a loss would be felt even more keenly because the new Tacoma-Seattle-Everett express highway was under construction (it would be a freeway, not a toll road), and its route through Seattle was expected to eliminate about thirteen hundred parking spaces in the central business district. For the first time the Palomar property began to be mentioned. This was the Palomar Building and theater at Third and University, south of the post office and west of the Cobb Building.[52] Perhaps the Palomar could be acquired somehow for construction of the additional parking accommodations that the Metropolitan Center would require.*

As the September 30 bid opening approached, Ryan put in writing, in a letter to the regents through Everest, the assurances that were at the heart of the university bid. University Properties would build a new post office building at a cost to the university of not more than $870,000, and for the right to use the roof of the post office for parking for twenty-five years, University Properties agreed to make increased rental payments of $80,000 annually in 1960, 1961, and 1962. On September 26, just four days before the opening, Everest sent to the regents a long memorandum in which he discussed the university's expectations in relation to the post office site—"the nature of the overlapping type of construction which will be necessary if the Post Office Building and the New Douglas Building are erected"—and then dealt with a question that Balmer had raised. Balmer apparently had been worried about the costs of the new twenty-story building that the university was promising to build. Even as he signed the bid forms Balmer had asked if the university was committing itself to begin construction immediately, construction costs and the money market being what they were. Everest's reply put the situation in a nutshell, for the regents and for University Properties: "With respect to commitments, the Board is not committed to the building of a new office building. Actually the Board cannot be committed until such time as preliminary plans for a new structure are presented to them and, again, when final plans are presented. However, I think it should be clear in the minds of every member of the Board that the negotiations for the purchase of the Post Office site are all directed toward the ultimate construction of a new building. University Properties is moving forward with every hope and expectation that a new structure will be authorized by the Board. They are gambling on obtaining such approval." And, four days before the bid opening, Everest thought he knew how the bidding would come out. The GSA had received no other requests for plans and specifications on the post office. The university would be the only bidder and the GSA would make a "prompt award" so that a construction schedule could be developed at last.[53]

That is what happened. The regents held a special meeting, Shefelman

---

* The regents also accepted in July 1957, a proposal of The Olympic, Incorporated, the Edris organization, that for a payment of $200,000 the company be released from any contingent liability for performance under the hotel lease that had been exclusively the obligations of the Seattle Olympic Hotel Company since August 2, 1955. (See *Metropolitan Tract*, vol. 1, part 4, Current Metropolitan Tract Leases, pp. 247–59.) This payment ultimately became part of the funding of the new Faculty Center on the university campus.

presiding, on the morning of September 30. When the hour of the opening
came, only the university's $870,000 bid was on the table. At the regents' regular meeting of October 4 Shefelman announced officially that the university
had been the sole bidder. A month later, November 8, the board authorized
Shefelman, as chairman of the tract committee, to initiate at once the planning
for a new Douglas Building.[54]

Balmer and Shefelman had been, on the part of the regents, the principal
forces in carrying forward the climactic activities in the long struggle to
acquire space for the Douglas Building replacement. Everest, still vice-president of the University, had been supporting a major part of the load,
however, as he threaded his way through the political complexities of
the situation and, with Conrad's help, kept in touch with developments
on all fronts. But Everest, approaching sixty-five, was expecting to resign
as vice-president and devote his whole attention to the Metropolitan Center while keeping a half-time appointment in the School of Communications. Until that summer of 1957 there had been no progress at all in the
search for a successor to President Schmitz, even though Schmitz had hoped
to be welcoming his successor in August. Positive action had become essential,
and it was in this matter that Shefelman's presence had a catalytic effect, for
among the regents of that year—a board of only six after Miller's resignation
—Shefelman, although the regent with the least prior experience on the
board, was also the regent with the broadest and readiest acquaintance with
and within the community of higher education at large. Thus it was Shefelman, a close friend of Henry Schmitz, who had begun to carry much of the
burden of the search for a new president, flying off to other campuses to interview university administrators, to assemble suggestions of possible candidates,
and to compile dossiers and lists while keeping up a running consultation
with the other regents and with the faculty members of the search committee.
By the end of 1957 the choice was being made, and the selection was announced at a special meeting of the regents on January 29, 1958. The new
president of the University would be Charles Edwin Odegaard, the forty-seven-year-old historian and dean of arts and sciences at the University of
Michigan.[55]

Odegaard's appointment inspired a wide feeling of satisfaction, outside
the university as well as within. The feeling was shared genuinely and expressed with characteristic warmth by Henry Schmitz, who had done all that
he properly could to help the regents and the search committee reach a decision. Odegaard was known to be a scholar with a talent for academic administration, a graduate of Dartmouth with M.A. and Ph.D. from Harvard, a
navy officer in World War II, a former executive director of the American
Council of Learned Societies, dean at Michigan since 1952, and the youngest
ever to head Michigan's College of Arts and Sciences. Odegaard would succeed Schmitz on August 1, 1958, and soon plans were being made for inaugural ceremonies in the autumn.[56]

Amid all that had been accomplished and all that impended, the Metropolitan Center remained near the center of attention in 1958—the attention of the regents and the attention of the city. Seattle not only was getting its freeway but was looking forward to its world's fair, still scheduled (with a dashing optimism) to open the following year. But planning for the new post office and office building meant that dramatic changes were coming at the very core of the city—the first such changes in almost three decades. The monumental-style post office would go—demolition was to begin April 1—and so would the rickety Douglas Building, already more than half empty of tenants. In their places would rise the office building–garage–post office complex, full of layers and easements at its base, but functional and attractive.

The construction plan that soon emerged was for a twenty-one-story office building straddling the former westerly line of the Douglas site and linked by a six-level garage, three stories below ground, to the three-story post office. The base of the new building would incorporate, on Fourth Avenue, the two bottom stories of the old Cobb Annex, three stories of the annex removed to permit the design of a smooth façade at the Fourth Avenue entrance. The drawings were moved ahead by Naramore, Bain, Brady and Johanson and by Frederick M. Mann, the University's own chief architect, while Everest and Conrad conducted discussions with Post Office Department and GSA officials on the final post office requirements. A consulting member of the university staff involved in financial analyses was Julius Roller, professor of accounting in the College of Business Administration. An informal architectural consultant was a newcomer—although not really a newcomer—Minoru Yamasaki, of Detroit.[57]

Yamasaki, then forty-five, was from Seattle and a graduate in 1934 of the university's School of Architecture. But for twenty years Yamasaki had been away. He had been a student and instructor at New York University, an instructor at Columbia, a chief architectural designer for a number of firms, including Raymond Loewy's, a founder of his own Detroit firm. By 1957 he had received several of the many awards that would come to him, including an American Institute of Architects "First Honor" for his design of the St. Louis International Airport.[58]

In 1957, when Harold Shefelman and Edward Carlson were leading the planning for the Seattle fair, they asked Perry Johanson, of the Naramore, Bain firm, to become chairman of a Design Standards Advisory Board, a seven-member body—two members from out of state, one an architect, one a landscape architect—whose role was to give architectural unity to the fair buildings and to try to make sure that the permanent buildings would be functionally appropriate to a subsequent civic center. Johanson had been a classmate of Yamasaki's at the university, and it was Yamasaki whom Johanson suggested as the out-of-state architect, sending with his nomination a copy of a current architectural report describing Yamasaki's recent work, including his design of a U.S. pavilion for a fair at New Delhi, India. Yamasaki became a member of the Design Standards Advisory Board. From Yamasaki's association with Shefelman came, at the end of 1957, the creation at the university of a commission to advise the regents on the designs and plans for the university's own buildings as they were coming along. Yamasaki was a member of that commission too.[59]

But in 1958 the new downtown building was in prospect, and on February 14 the regents approved a resolution authorizing construction at a cost of $9,319,000. The post office was to cost not more than $870,000, which meant that University Properties would be underwriting any costs above $870,000. The level of University Properties participation in the financing was already high. The lessee not only was paying $240,000 of the post office costs in three years of additional rent but also was providing $4,000,000 of interim financing on the main building without interest charges to the university. Moreover, the search for temporary post office accommodations had led to the Jones Building, at 1331 Third Avenue, and thus in the immediate neighborhood. University Properties had executed an option for its use at $1,500 a month while the new post office was being built. Whether or not there would prove to be additional post office construction costs—costs that University Properties had pledged to assume—the lessee was paying in interest and other charges more than $700,000 above the requirements of its lease.[60]

The hope was, early in 1958, that the whole project would be in place in eighteen months. Before construction began, however, an unexpected adjustment had to be made in the design of the garage. To meet the expanded post office requirements it already had been necessary to reduce the projected garage capacity from 500 to 400 automobiles. In March 1958, soil tests at the site showed that much additional shoring and reinforcing would be needed for the garage to be sunk to the three-floor underground level. The regents, holding a special meeting on this problem, decided to eliminate the bottom floor—two underground, now, and three above—reducing the garage capacity to 350 cars. The saving in cost was placed at $230,000.[61]

The new building, of steel, aluminum, marble and glass, was designed to offer 223,000 square feet of rentable space. Economic studies conducted for the regents supported confidence that occupancy would be high and suggested a return of 6.1 percent on the total investment. The regents approved a schedule of transfers to the building fund which—apart from the commitment to the teaching hospital revenue bonds—would reach the $9,319,000 figure by December 31, 1961. As it turned out, the low construction bid (by Lloyd Johnson and Morrison-Knudson Company) was $350,000 below the architects' estimates.[62]

Shefelman became president of the board of regents at the annual reorganization on March 21, succeeding Balmer, who had been president for two years, and John King became vice-president. These shifts were expected. But Shefelman was president of a board that again had seven members, for on March 11 Governor Rosellini had appointed, at last, a regent to complete Winlock Miller's unexpired term. The new regent was Mrs. A. Scott Bullitt, president of the KING Broadcasting Company, a major Seattle television-radio organization. At the meeting at which he welcomed Mrs. Bullitt, Shefelman reminded the regents that the time was approaching when they should decide on a name for the new building that would replace the Douglas.[63]

If there was any surprise in Mrs. Bullitt's appointment, it was that it had taken so long. Mrs. Bullitt was a keen and knowledgeable businesswoman much involved in business and public affairs both because of her natural inclinations and because of her position as a television-radio executive. It had been no more than an act of public spirit when in 1951 she and her KING organization had given to the university the major components of television-station equipment that had made possible the establishment on the campus of KCTS-TV, the first educational television outlet in the region. But now Mrs. Bullitt had succeeded Winlock Miller, and to those who thought of such things there was an interesting appropriateness in this. Mrs. Bullitt was Dorothy Stimson Bullitt, the daughter of C. D. Stimson, the capitalist, lumberman, community leader, yachtsman, philanthropist, and former president of the Metropolitan Building Company who had been a major mover in the shaping of Seattle in the first quarter of the century. Mrs. Bullitt was also the woman who had married Scott Bullitt, the young Kentuckian who had become the political foe of Roland Hartley in the 1920s when Hartley was setting out to "reorganize" the university under Henry Suzzallo. Dorothy Bullitt brought to the board a business sense, but she also brought a sense of how Seattle and the university came to be what they were.

Dorothy Bullitt's life had been quite as full as her father's, quite as entwined with Seattle's history, yet even more her own. She had been born on Queen Anne Hill, but when the Stimsons lived in the big mansion on First Hill, Dorothy had grown up as C. D.'s active young daughter, loving horses and riding, among other things, and owning for a time one of Harry Treat's fine harness ponies, a gift to her. She did not attend the university, for in days when many young ladies went east to boarding school, Dorothy went east to boarding school in New York, where she studied languages and literature. Her marriage to Scott Bullitt was a happy one. She shared and supported his quick rise in law, business, and Democratic party politics. But when the personal losses came, Dorothy was about to begin her own career.

Within months of C. D. Stimson's death in 1929 the Depression made a shambles of his estate and of his arrangement for the division of it between Dorothy and her brother, and the brother was soon killed in an airplane accident. Early in 1932, the Bullitts were in Washington, D.C., where Scott Bullitt was conferring with James A. Farley and other party leaders on plans to swing the nomination to Franklin Roosevelt in the Chicago convention that summer. When Bullitt returned to Seattle, he was ill. By April he was dead of cancer. His wife was left with three children, real estate holdings that were in serious trouble, and an uncertain future.

What Dorothy Bullitt did, with no formal business training, was to decide to manage the property she had. In that summer of 1932 she was—as Scott

Bullitt's proxy—the Bullitt vote in the Washington delegation's solid support of Roosevelt at the Chicago convention. Then she took charge of her own life. She owned the 1411 Fourth Avenue Building, built by C. D. Stimson in the 1920s, being managed in 1932 by the Metropolitan Building Company and steadily losing tenants. She took over management herself, with the advice of friends. She mortgaged the building to rehabilitate it and devised her own campaign to win tenants. By the time the 1411 was succeeding, in 1939, Dorothy and a cousin, Fred Stimson, who was interested in radio, made a plunge in that direction. Together they bought a small Seattle radio station, KEVR, with offices in the Smith Tower. In 1948, Dorothy Bullitt bought Seattle's first television station, KRST-TV, this at a time when the nearest station was in San Francisco and there were said to be no more than six thousand television receivers in the Northwest. From such a start came KING Broadcasting. The "KING" was Dorothy Bullitt's own invention.[64]

The regents had been reminded in March 1958 that they should choose a name for the new building downtown. The reminder itself contained a hint that the building might not be a new Douglas, for Shefelman had noted that other suggestions were coming in. Why not Douglas? Why should not the new twenty-one-story tower at Fourth and Union carry the name of the man who had built the Metropolitan Center? There was, as soon became evident, a large segment of community support for this—a sentimental support rooted in a regard for the historical origins of the Metropolitan Center as a place apart. Yet another name would be chosen.

The colorations of feeling do not show in the record. They may be guessed. J. F. Douglas was remembered—by many with affection, by many more simply for the figure he was—because he had been in and about Seattle, coming up from his Carnation Company offices in Los Angeles, until his death just six years before. Yet Douglas had had no active association with the Metropolitan Center for a quarter of a century, and in any case the building that carried his name had been constructed in 1904, three years before there was a Metropolitan Building Company and many years before Douglas's name went on it. But above all, the new tower was not just a Douglas Building replacement but something large enough to erase old lines and to become the beginning of a new Metropolitan Center. Douglas would be memorialized, but in other ways.

The new building was called the Washington, but the decision came slowly and only after a small technical difficulty was solved. At their meeting of August 1958, five months after Shefelman's reminder, the regents were talking about the question again. Dorothy Bullitt reported that sentiment downtown seemed to be favoring retention of the Douglas name. There were then, apparently, special meetings or subcommittee meetings. On October 30, Balmer reported that in an "informal" meeting the regents had selected "Washington," only to find that there was another Washington Building in the city (a small office building north of the downtown area). It had been necessary to obtain the permission of the other owners to use the name.

This had been done, Balmer said, and University Properties approved the selection. Balmer moved that the new building be the Washington, but that in it there be installed a "suitable recognition" of J. F. Douglas and his place in the history of the tract. The regents approved and that was the way it was done.[65]

Charles Odegaard was in his first year as president of the university in 1959, already grappling with the financial problems of a growing institution and trying to describe to legislators and others his views of its needs. Odegaard's inauguration the previous November had been an occasion of a kind not experienced before by the university, the city, or the state—a three-day convocation of townspeople, university faculty, and academic guests at which distinguished speakers explored significant aspects of modern society and celebrated the contributions of the university to them. Amid it all, Odegaard had been preparing for the 1959 legislative session. The legislature was friendly and ready to welcome the new president, but it faced, nevertheless, difficult questions of state financing.

Two changes in the board of regents occurred at this time. With the terms of Beatrice Gardner and Charles Harris expiring, Governor Rosellini nominated, in December 1958, Dr. Albert Murphy, an Everett physician, and Judge Robert J. Willis, of Yakima, a native of Alaska who had won his J.D. degree at the university in 1930, had set up his law practice in Yakima County, and had been judge of the Superior Court in Yakima County from 1937 to 1957. As 1959 began, Thomas Balmer was the only regent who had participated in the leasing of the Metropolitan tract to University Properties in 1953. And H. P. Everest, vice-president emeritus of the university, had given up his half-time appointment in the School of Communications and was devoting his attention solely to the Metropolitan Center. He had helped build the School of Communications but he was ready to resign an academic position in which he had done no teaching since the university's business affairs and the work of the Metropolitan Center had begun to absorb him. Everest retired from the university in 1959. His last meeting with the regents was on June 19, when it was Balmer who presented a resolution citing Everest's career as faculty member, acting president of the university, and Metropolitan tract representative.[66]

The new post office was completed in 1959. It was three stories high and so constructed that it would always be a low shelf to the west of the tall new tower. By late that year the Washington Building, although far from ready for occupancy, had risen to its full height of 288 feet. Balmer watched the new tower rise only a short distance from his modest, second-floor offices at 404 Union Street, but he did not see the building finished. On August 1, 1959, Thomas Balmer died.[67]

Balmer was a big man and the gap he left in Seattle's leadership was a big one. Yet, at seventy-one, he had done all that he could. Some months earlier he had retired as vice-president and western counsel of the Great Northern Railway Company, but even then, in March 1959, he had been reappointed by Governor Rosellini to still another term on the university board he had served since 1934. As a lawyer in railroading, Balmer had been called to so many offices in business, banking, mining, and community work that it was pointless to count them. But for twenty-five years he had been a regent, and it was equally meaningless to count the years he had been president or vice-president of the board or chairman of the tract committee. He had been the strong man and the spokesman in all the most sensitive periods of the Metropolitan lease negotiations—always thoughtful, frequently maddeningly stubborn, never without a sense of humor. Balmer had done far more for the university than attend to its Metropolitan tract, but what the tract was becoming was undeniably his most enduring legacy.[68]

CHAPTER 11

Transition: 1960 to 1969

The Metropolitan Center's Washington Building was a showpiece in downtown Seattle in 1960, the tallest building in its vicinity and standing in shining contrast to that low brick structure at the opposite corner of the university property, the Olympic Garage, once the Arena Building. The Washington was dedicated on June 2, 1960. Not all of the interior construction was finished, for some of the offices were still being adapted to tenants' specifications, but in a ceremony in the new lobby, Harold Shefelman presiding, a plaque honoring J. F. Douglas was unveiled. The dedication of the Washington was, in short, a rededication to Douglas.

The plaque, a simple, handsome bronze bearing J. F. Douglas's features in bas relief, had been mounted on the marble south wall of the lobby, and it was unveiled by John L. King, now president of the board of regents. Those who witnessed the unveiling included James B. Douglas and a number of J. F. Douglas's old friends, some the widows of the financiers who had been among Douglas's earliest associates. The principal speaker was Joshua Green, and this inspiration was James M. Ryan's, the arrangements worked out by Ernest Conrad. Green, although never a stockholder in the Metropolitan Building Company, had known Douglas well and was the man best qualified to speak with disinterested authority of the Douglas era. Green was ninety, but still erect and vigorous, and with a long and unclouded memory of the Seattle of earlier years. Green spoke of the development of the city and of J. F. Douglas's part in it. "Major Douglas's memory will never die," Green said. "He was for forty years the most unselfish, useful citizen in Seattle." From the man who had known most of the most useful citizens for more than sixty years that judgment was sufficient.[1]

By autumn 1960 the work in the Washington Building was substantially finished, although some financial tidying up needed to be done. The cost of the whole project as then calculated, after deducting costs recoverable from tenants, was $9,837,820. The office building and garage had cost $8,920,874, the post office, $808,209, and the reconstruction of the Cobb Annex, $108,737. The funding would come through transfers of tract income to what was called the New Building Fund. The regents, having authorized $9,319,000 in December 1957, had authorized additional transfers of $519,574—enough to cover the new cost projections—in December 1959. By November 30, 1960, the transfers had reached more than $6,800,000, and the funding was expected to be completed by August 1962. Until then University Properties would be paying, without interest charges to the university, any bills that exceeded the cash in hand. The rental situation was almost improbably strong. It had been anticipated that occupancy would be 30 percent at the opening and 60 percent at the end of the first year. But by December 1960, 85 percent of the space was under lease to some seventy-five tenants and occupancy was calculated, modestly, at a steady 93 percent. At that level the gross annual rental income would be $1,326,149, the university's receipts $590,352.[2]

Much had been done to rehabilitate and modernize the other buildings of the tract—all, that is, except the Olympic Garage. The Seattle Olympic Hotel Company, committed by its lease to spend $1,500,000 on capital improvements, furniture, and fixtures for the Olympic, had instead spent $2,369,168, or $869,168 more than required. The company had removed the Metropolitan Theatre and replaced it with a new drive-in entrance, plaza, and grand ballroom, all costing $1,700,000, and had built at Fifth and University the new Golden Lion Restaurant, with grill room and kitchen, at a cost of $235,000. As for the rest of the center, University Properties, working with regents' authorizations of about $4,300,000, had expended by 1960 a total of $3,792,129 on modernization projects, more than $2,000,000 of this in the White-Henry-Stuart Building and most of the balance in the Skinner, Stimson, and Cobb. The Metropolitan Center, thus refurbished, was brighter and better, but it was far from transformed.[3]

The buildings immediately outside the boundaries of the Metropolitan Center were something of a miscellany in 1960. On Sixth Avenue, separated from the university property by the alley at its east edge, were—with parking lots adjoining—the tall and modern Washington Athletic Club and the old Plymouth Congregational Church, a landmark. To the south was the YWCA and nearby, on Fifth Avenue and Seneca Street, were low "business blocks." The building at Fifth and Seneca was owned by the Standard Oil Company, and behind it at Fifth and Spring (and also behind the Hungerford Hotel at Fourth and Spring) was a parking lot owned by the Northwest Bible College. On Third Avenue, below the Stimson Building, were the Northern Life Tower and the Pacific Telephone buildings. Across University, west of the Cobb and adjoining the Washington Building garage, was the Palomar Building, which contained the Palomar Theatre, originally the Pantages. As for the Union Street boundary, the center's across-the-street neighbors there were office buildings with street-level shops, from the Vance and the 1411 Fourth Avenue buildings between Third and Fourth avenues to the Logan at Fifth and Union. It was to the north, beyond Union Street, that commercial development would continue to be more probable. The impact of the new freeway remained to be seen, but it could not fail to be dramatic. The fast-traffic lanes, slicing through the hills above Seattle's business district, would be curving northward, only a block east of the Metropolitan Center, with ramps that would accept traffic from University Street and bring automobiles to the downtown area between Denny Way and Madison.

Neither University Properties nor the leasehold it managed was in a critical position in 1960, yet the situation called for careful planning. The lessee's income was derived from the operation of just six buildings, one of them new, one an antique, one incorporating a theater, the Fifth Avenue, and two devoted to serving doctors and dentists at a time when many doctors and dentists were moving to First Hill or the suburbs. Since October 31, 1958, when the company had completed its four years of fixed rental payments totaling $6,800,000, University Properties had been on a percentage rental basis, the guaranteed minimum $1,000,000 a year, and until 1962 it was paying the additional annual rental of $80,000 as its share of the Washington Building–post office financing. It had under its control a total of 976,093 square feet of rentable space—732,632 in offices, 164,411 in stores, and 79,050 in "basement" areas. The garages within the center—in the White-Henry-Stuart, the Stimson, the Cobb, and the Washington buildings and in the Olympic Garage itself—would accommodate 1,040 automobiles. The largest of these was the Olympic Garage, which would hold 400 cars, even more than the Washington. But the Olympic Garage, where the old trussed roof leaked and the fire protection system no longer met the city code, was past due for replacement. Something had to be done soon.[4]

Roger Stevens had made his small joke some years earlier about Seattle's preoccupation with its parking problem. Seattle could laugh too, but the fact was that it had no underground transportation and, in a city of such undulant topography, transit by bus was not altogether direct and rapid and the habitual use of the automobile would not be discouraged by the freeway. Tenants in buildings needed parking space. Shoppers, tourists, convention visitors, and doctors' patients needed places to leave their cars. The Olympic, even though it was Seattle's preeminent hostelry, was particularly vulnerable. Although major hotels in every other major city were expected to give free parking to guests, the Olympic was almost completely dependent on the Olympic Garage, which not only was not free but was inefficient, requiring a service staff of twenty-two. The problem before University Properties was to find a "highest and best use" for a choice downtown site occupied by a garage that had begun life forty-six years before as a skating rink—such a use certainly not merely another garage. The problem before the Seattle Olympic Hotel Company, which had invested millions in rehabilitation and improvement of the Olympic, was how to acquire or gain access to garage facilities that were essential to keep the Olympic the "leading hotel in the city of Seattle," as it was expected to do under its lease.

The two problems overlapped by half. They were, in a sense, one, for a University Properties solution seemed likely to jeopardize a solution for the Olympic. Any solution required, of course, the approval of the board of regents. The board was quite willing to listen to proposals, and about the time King became president the board again had acquired a seventh member. In March 1960, Herbert S. Little, a Seattle attorney, had been appointed by Governor Rosellini to fill the vacancy occasioned by the death of Thomas Balmer. Little thus joined a board that included King, Joseph Drumheller,

Dorothy Bullitt, Albert Murphy, Harold Shefelman, and Robert J. Willis. Little had been active for years in community, university, and alumni affairs. British by birth but an American citizen since 1920, Little was a graduate of the university, where he had received his LL.B. in 1923 and his A.M. in 1927. While rising in law, he had involved himself with many civic organizations— the Institute of Pacific Relations, the Japanese and International Trade Fairs, the YMCA, the Seattle Symphony, and the alumni association, which he had served as president in 1935–36. Along the way he had received the Seattle Civic Award for 1945.[5]

From 1960 through 1961 the planning went on downtown, by University Properties on one hand and by Seattle Olympic on the other. Edward Carlson, now president of Western Hotels, was developing ideas about what might be done for the Olympic, although as chairman of the World's Fair Commission he was deeply involved in preparations for the Seattle exposition, which would be called Century 21 and held in 1962 in the compact, architecturally transformed civic center area between Denny Way and Mercer Street, where the new 600-foot Space Needle was rising. James M. Ryan, looking for the highest and best use of the Olympic Garage site, was thinking about a new major office building. There were repeated consultations between representatives of the lessee organizations and with university representatives, particularly with Conrad, who, although business manager of the university, was also the regents' principal liaison officer for tract affairs following the retirement of H. P. Everest. Associated with Conrad was Ernest J. Riley, formerly with the property management firm of Yates, Riley and MacDonald, now the university's real estate officer.[6]

But while plans for the new downtown buildings had been germinating, the university itself had been bringing to culmination other plans directed at expressing what it had become in the years since its beginnings in what was now the Metropolitan Center. The university was celebrating its centennial.

Thinking about how the centennial should be observed had been going on since the early years of the administration of Henry Schmitz, whose affection for the university ran deep. Yet there never had been a disposition to devise a centennial program that would become an orgy of commemorative activities. A history of the university would be published, perhaps, and the founding and the founders remembered in a simple, and primarily local, convocation. By the time the anniversary year was approaching, with Charles Odegaard now the university's president, the decision had been made to follow that theme of simplicity. The events of 1961 would be centennial events, and the period of observance would run from February 22 to November 4. On February 22 it would be one hundred years since Daniel Bagley had been elected chairman of the board of commissioners that set out to create the territorial university, and November 4 was the traditional university birthday, the anniversary of the day that classes were first held in the original building on Denny's knoll.[7] Charles M. Gates, of the university's history department, an authority on the history of the Northwest, was at work on the centennial volume.*

On February 22, an hour-long KING-TV documentary, "The Hundred Years," was presented in an initial showing. The project was sponsored by the Boeing Airplane Company, and that first showing was followed in ensuing months by periodical showings on the campus and elsewhere. The coverage was not only of the university's beginnings but included wide-ranging interviews with faculty members working in the sciences, the arts, medicine, and engineering, and with some of the 18,000 students then enrolled in undergraduate and graduate programs. (It was predicted that the enrollment would rise to a staggering 29,000 in the next decade.) In those months the alumni activities as well as the university's own regular programs, including the commencement, had a centennial flavor.[8]

But the observance was not ended on November 4, but on November 16 in a convocation at which the speaker was President John F. Kennedy. The young president had been in office less than a year. Arrangements for his visit had been proceeding for several months, the prospect encouraged by Washington's U.S. senators. It was not irrelevant that 1961 was the twenty-fifth anniversary of Senator Warren Magnuson's election to Congress. But even as the arrangements went forward the world was gripped suddenly by tension when, in August, the Berlin Wall went up and the East-West confrontation became direct, explicit, and dangerous. The president came to Seattle to congratulate a great state university, but his address was related inescapably to the national concern.[9]

President Kennedy, arriving at Boeing Field on a bright November morning, was met by a delegation that included Mayor Gordon Clinton, Governor Rosellini, and Joseph Gandy, president of Century 21. He was taken through the central city by motorcade along Fourth Avenue, then to the site of the exposition that would be opening in a few months, and finally back to University Plaza and the Olympic. The university program that afternoon was held in Edmundson Pavilion, where the president, robed, joined President Odegaard and Governor Rosellini in an academic procession composed of members of the faculty, the regents, and distinguished guests, including a sprinkling of U.S. senators who had come west with Kennedy for the ceremonies and for a later political gathering in honor of Magnuson.† A "Cen-

---

* For a number of years Frederick E. Bolton, dean emeritus of education, had been compiling in his retirement an extensive manuscript history of the university that by 1960 was considered unready for publication. Dean Bolton's work was acknowledged by the university in a special historical booklet, *Vision on the Knoll.* His manuscript is preserved in the university archives.

† Welcomed to Seattle by Mayor Clinton on the morning of November 16, the President had smiled and replied, in Kennedy fashion: "It is a great pleasure to come here on this occasion—the 100th anniversary of the University of Washington, Senator Magnuson's twenty-fifth anniversary in Congress, and the first anniversary of my election to the presidency." Soon thereafter, as preparations were made for the centennial processional, the question of academic robing came up. President Kennedy held a recent honorary Ph.D., but not

tennial Fanfare" was played by the university's symphony orchestra under the direction of its composer, Stanley Chapple, director of the School of Music.

Kennedy's allusions to the function of higher education were in reference to the need for the "light of wisdom" in the cause of freedom. But he was thinking more specifically of Berlin and of the delicacy of the balance, at the Wall, between diplomacy and force and of the rise in some quarters of a "suicide or surrender" attitude that might bring the world to war. The president's centennial address became one of a series of statements on the position of the United States in relation to the crisis.

It was a touch much welcomed by those who cherished university history that the Denny bell was rung that day—the bell that had hung in the old first building, that had tolled at President Lincoln's death, and that for almost a century had welcomed distinguished guests, including other presidents. The university awards no honorary degrees, but Kennedy took away with him two gifts. One was a commemorative medallion. The other was a copy, in a special binding, of Charles Gates's centennial volume, *The First Century at the University of Washington.*

By 1962 the Seattle Olympic Hotel Company and University Properties had perfected proposals for the developments they felt were essential at that neglected southeast corner of the Metropolitan Center. On February 8, Carlson sent to Conrad a long letter containing proposals that would combine a solution to the garage problem with a plan to provide, adjacent to the Olympic, new and much-needed downtown airport transportation terminal facilities. On February 13, Ryan outlined in a similarly detailed letter a University Properties proposal to raze the Olympic Garage and construct on the site a ten-story office building for which preliminary studies had already been made and about which discussions were proceeding with a prospective major tenant. Implementation of either proposal would require a lease extension— of fourteen years for the garage and airline terminal, of twenty years for the office building—to permit amortization. The Seattle Olympic proposal would involve, as had the Washington Building–post office project, acquisition of property outside the university tract. On February 15, 1962, Conrad and Riley sent to President Odegaard two memorandums analyzing the proposals, transmitting copies of the original letters with attachments, and suggesting that the regents be asked to approve in principle the key aspects of the proposals so that further planning could proceed. Specific approval could be considered when additional data were ready.[10]

The scope of the thinking that had gone into the proposals was evident.

---

the earned doctorate, from Harvard. He had with him, in any case, no academic gown or hood. In those hours before the ceremony at Edmundson Pavilion, two decisions were made —the first that Kennedy was entitled to wear the black and crimson of the Harvard Ph.D., the second that the robe and hood he wore would be those of Professor Edwin Hewitt, of the University's Department of Mathematics, whose doctorate was from Harvard and who had been a friend and classmate of Kennedy's there.

There had been, as the correspondence said, repeated bilateral and trilateral conferences on the financing and timing of the projects, which had to be synchronized if they were to be feasible at all. And although the plans involved considerations that had once been bugaboos (the lease extensions, the acquisitions of additional property), in neither proposal, Seattle and the Metropolitan Center being what they now were, did the consideration seem unreasonable. If the Olympic Garage gave way to an office building, the logical building for such a site, the Olympic would have to look elsewhere for the parking it needed to survive as the "leading hotel." No one in Seattle wanted the Olympic to go into a decline simply because its position in the center of the city denied it elbow room. The university's income would be enlarged, certainly, if University Properties built a new building and Seattle Olympic a new garage and airline bus terminal. The prospect of increased income was demonstrable. But at the heart of the matter were the questions of how the Metropolitan Center should be developed and whether that development required, as in the case of the Washington Building, an addition to the original area of the tract. Nothing in the Washington Building arrangement established a precedent, really, but the regents and the Seattle of the early 1960s could look at these new questions without choosing up sides. And both Seattle Olympic and University Properties had worked out their proposals with due regard for certain immutable university requirements: the projects must be self-funding, there must be no "significant reduction" in income from the tract, and the university must not be required to incur indebtedness.

The Seattle Olympic proposal was possible at all only because property adjacent to the hotel could be purchased—the Standard Oil–owned building across Seneca Street and the Northwest Bible College land beyond, the small parking lot at Fifth and Spring. The two parcels comprised half a block directly across from the Olympic, 28,400 square feet obtainable at a cost of $690,000 plus a real estate commission of $13,850. In that area of 120 by 240 feet Seattle Olympic would build a reinforced concrete structure consisting of two below-ground levels, a main level, and eight parking levels capable of handling 787 automobiles. The structure would include a parking area for airport buses and a waiting room for airport passengers. The garage would be served by automatic elevators and connected to the hotel by a pedestrian overpass above Seneca Street. There would be an escalator connection to the hotel lobby and a conveyor system for baggage. The total cost, including purchase of the site and $75,000 for contingencies, was estimated at $2,959,950.[11]

As for finances, Seattle Olympic would assume all costs, mortgaging its leasehold interest to do so, and then would pay the university 80 percent of the net profit on garage operations. But the lease extension was essential.

Seattle Olympic's lease then ran to October 31, 1979. The company proposed the extension to 1994 to give it a thirty-year management term beyond the time the garage was expected to be in place, the minimum term considered necessary for favorable financing. Upon execution of the lease revisions, the

Arthur A. Denny

Daniel Bagley

Charles C. Terry

Edward Lander

(*Top*) The territorial university building, surrounded by its picket fence, overlooking the Seattle of 1878; (*bottom*) the building of 1861 still standing on its original site in 1909, fourteen years after the university had been moved to its new campus

Alden J. Blethen

Richard Winsor

John P. Hoyt

Manson F. Backus

Chester F. White (*from the* Cartoon, *1911*)   Horace C. Henry

E. A. Stuart

Charles H. Cobb

(*Left*) James A. Moore; (*right*) J. F. Douglas (*both photos from the* Cartoon, *1911*)

John Mead Howells   O. D. Fisher (*from the* Cartoon, *1911*)

(*Above*) The site of the White Building, at Fourth Avenue and Union Street, being cleared in January 1908; (*below*) Seattle's Federal Building at Third and Union, just five years old when this photograph was made by Asahel Curtis in 1909; beyond it, the Post-Intelligencer, first building on the university tract, and the just-completed White Building, soon to be joined by the Henry

(*Above*) The Henry Building going up in 1909, with the old university building moved from its original site and placed on an empty lot above Fifth Avenue, and the site of the Cobb Building (foreground) being cleared (*courtesy of UNICO*); (*below*) the White and Henry buildings, first units of the Howells and Stokes "master plan," in place by August 1909

(*Left*) The Cobb Building, first buildin[g] in the West to be designed exclusivel[y] for doctors and dentists, occupied i[n] June 1910; (*below*) a steam shovel an[d] horse-drawn wagons working abov[e] Fifth Avenue in 1911 to finish the grad[ing] ing of the university tract

(*Left*) The Cobb Building (left) and the White-Henry, dominating Fourth Avenue in 1911; behind the planked sidewalk in the foreground are two temporary buildings, the Anti-Tuberculosis Society headquarters (columns), financed with the help of Horace C. Henry, and the American Music Hall (*photograph by Asahel Curtis*); (*below*) the new Metropolitan Theatre, opened in 1911, still draped in bunting when this photograph was made some months later by Asahel Curtis; in the foreground, the new planted plaza of "University Place"

METROPOLITAN-LUMBERMEN'S CLUB LOUNGING ROOM   COLLEGE CLUB DINING ROOM   SEATTLE PRESS CLUB BILLIARD ROOM

WOMEN'S UNIVERSITY CLUB—PORTION INTERIOR   AUTOMOBILE CLUB   METROPOLITAN INDOOR GOLF CLUB

(*Top*) Seattle's Fourth Avenue, north of Seneca Street, in the World War I era, the Cobb and the White-Henry-Stuart buildings and the Metropolitan Theatre standing amid the temporary structures; (*bottom*) the interiors of clubs occupying quarters on the university tract, as displayed in a Metropolitan Building Company promotional booklet of about 1917–18

(*Above*) The Arena in its earliest phase, as ice skating rink and public auditorium, Totem Gardens in the right foreground; (*below*) the University Place of 1918, containing not only the small planted plaza in front of the Metropolitan Theatre but the "gas station" standing in the widened University Street between the Stuart Building and the temporary Neyhart Building (right); behind the Stuart is the one-story Whitson Building, above Fifth Avenue is the Arena (center), and beyond is the Plymouth Congregational Church, the tower visible in the background

Charles E. Gaches (*courtesy of Beatrice Gardner*)

D. E. Skinner (*courtesy of David E. Skinner an*
Seattle Times)

Albert S. Kerry (*courtesy of A. S.*
Kerry, Jr.)

C. D. Stimson (*courtesy of Doro-*
thy Bullitt)

John H. Powell (*courtesy*
George V. Powell)

By 1921 the old Post-Intelligencer Building, refurbished and linked to the Cobb Annex, had become the Douglas, named for J. F. Douglas, secretary of the Metropolitan Building Company; the building stood at Fourth Avenue and Union Street until replaced by the Washington in 1959 (*courtesy of* UNICO)

The Arena Building at Fifth Avenue and University Street had been converted to a garage in 1924, shops lining the Fifth Avenue side; not yet had the roof been raised to make the structure "permanent" (*courtesy of* UNICO)

(*Top*) Excavating for the Olympic: in August 1923 ground was being cleared around the Metropolitan Theatre for construction of the new community hotel; to the right is the new Stuart Annex and back of the theatre are the Cobb and White-Henry-Stuart buildings (*courtesy of* UNICO); (*bottom*) the steel frame of the new Olympic displays Community Hotel Corporation notices to participants in the financial campaign (*courtesy of A. S. Kerry, Jr.*)

(*Top*) The Metropolitan Center as the scene of a rush of construction in June 1924, the Olympic Hotel rising about the Metropolitan Theatre, the Stimson Building going up (foreground), and the Arena being converted to a garage (*courtesy of* UNICO); (*bottom*) the Olympic in place by 1925, its Seneca Street façade standing where temporary buildings had lined the south edge of the Metropolitan tract

(*Above*) The sumptuous interior of the Olympic fulfilled Seattle's hope that its community hotel would be one of the finest in the West; (*bottom*) construction of the new Skinner Building, which would house the spectacularly beautiful Fifth Avenue Theater, was well under way in June 1926 (*courtesy of* UNICO)

(*Above*) The Fifth Avenue Theater was conceived, in the detail of its design and decoration, as an authentic replica of the Ming dynasty throne room in Peking's Forbidden City; this is a view of the rotunda when the theater was opened in 1926; (*left*) the lobby of the theater at the time of the opening (*both photos courtesy of* UNICO)

(*Above*) The Stimson Building, the second of the Metropolitan Center's medical-dental facilities, extending along Fourth Avenue between University and Seneca streets opposite the Olympic Hotel, about 1926 (*courtesy of* UNICO); (*below*) the university regents of 1925, whose ultimatum to the Metropolitan Building Company led to the rapid remodeling of the Arena; (from left) Roger R. Rogers, Werner A. Rupp, John T. Heffernan, James H. Davis, Ruth Karr McKee, Winlock Miller, and Oscar A. Fechter

Robert C. Reamer

J. F. Douglas (*portrait by Louis Betts, 1938, courtesy of Neva Douglas*)

Winlock W. Miller

Thomas Balmer

(*Above*) Changes in membership were coming, and Henry Suzzallo was nearing the end of his presidency of the university, when the regents posed for this photograph in August 1926; in the front row, A. H. B. Jordan, Ruth Karr McKee, President Suzzallo, and Oscar A. Fechter; in the back row, Paul H. Johns, John T. Heffernan, Sidney Lewis, and Roscoe A. Balch; (*below*) Joseph Drumheller was president of the board when the regents of 1948 made a second effort to acquire the balance of the Metropolitan Building Company lease; this photo of the regents and members of the university staff includes (from left) John L. King, George R. Stuntz, Dave Beck, Clarence J. Coleman, Dean Edwin R. Guthrie, Drumheller, Raymond B. Allen, president of the university, Nelson A. Wahlstrom, comptroller, Winlock Miller, Thomas Balmer, and Herbert T. Condon, secretary to the board

R. Bronsdon Harris

R. Mort Frayn

Charles Frankland

Eva Anderson (*courtesy of the Wenatchee World*)

University Properties, Inc., a new corporation headed by Roger L. Stevens, became lessee of the Metropolitan tract on July 18, 1953; here Stevens is signing the lease, which was signed for the university by Grant Armstrong (left), president of the regents, who watches with Thomas Balmer, chairman of the Metropolitan tract committee; standing are John Spiller (left), secretary to the board, and Arthur T. Lee, the regents' Metropolitan tract representative

Persons present at the signing of the University Properties lease included the regents, university staff members, and principals and advisers who had been active in the long negotiation; seated (from left), Charles F. Frankland, Beatrice Gardner, Charles M. Harris, Grant Armstrong, president of the board; Roger L. Stevens, Thomas Balmer, Professor Arthur Cannon, Arthur T. Lee, Metropolitan tract representative, Helen Hoagland, assistant secretary to the board, Donald G. Corbett, University President Henry Schmitz, Nelson A. Wahlstrom, comptroller, and (front) Winlock Miller; standing (from left), John Spiller, secretary to the board, Edward L. Rosling, secretary of University Properties, H. Adams Ashforth, Lawrence W. Wiley, Irving Anches, Nathan Potter, and Donald K. Anderson, director of university relations

Arthur T. Lee

H. P. Everest

Ernest M. Conrad

The historic old Metropolitan Theatre was gone by 1955, replaced by the new motor entrance to the Olympic Hotel
(photo by Roger Dudley, courtesy of Naramore, Bain, Brady & Johanson

(*Above*) The regents of 1959–60 had been continually involved in the planning for the Washington Building and the new U.S. post office; this group photo—the last in which Thomas Balmer would appear—includes (from left) Albert Murphy, John L. King, Balmer, University President Charles E. Odegaard, Harold S. Shefelman, president of the board, Helen Hoagland, secretary, Dorothy Bullitt, Joseph Drumheller, and Robert J. Willis; (*below*) before the demolition of the Stimson Building began, commemorative ceremonies attended the opening of the cornerstone in March 1970, when a guest of honor was Dorothy Bullitt, former university regent and daughter of C. D. Stimson for whom the building was named; Mrs. Bullitt stands beside the bronze plaque honoring her father and with her are James M. Ryan, of University Properties, Inc., and (partly hidden) Harold S. Shefelman, of the board of regents

(Left) Roger L. Stevens *(courtesy of* UNICO*); (right)* Minoru Yamasaki *(photo by Balthazar Korab)*

(Left) James M. Ryan; *(right)* Donald J. Covey *(both photos by Grady-Jentoft, courtesy of* UNICO)

By 1977, when the Rainier Bank Tower had reached its full height, demolition of the White-Henry buildings was proceeding; in this photo the tower stands above the rubble of the White Annex on Union Street (*courtesy of Seattle* Times)

Harold S. Shefelman (*photo by Grady-Jentoft*)

Robert F. Philip

James R. Ellis

Three regents served as chairmen of the university's Metropolitan tract committee in the two decades of tract development after 1959; Shefelman had been chairman for fifteen years when he left the board in 1975; Ellis, who served for two years, was succeeded by Philip in 1977

(*Left*) The IBM Building, 1964, the Plymouth Congregational Church to the left (*photo by Dudley, Hardin & Yang, Inc.*); (*center*) the Washington Building, 1970, the U.S. Post office at the lower right on Union Street (*photo by Dudley, Hardin & Yang, Inc.*); (*right*) the Financial Center, 1972, the rounded corner of the historic Cobb Building at the right (*photo by Grady-Jentoft*) (*all photos courtesy of UNICO*)

(*Above*) The university regents of 1974 ordered environmental impact studies of Rainier Square and eventually approved the plans; in this group photograph are (from left) Robert L. Flennaugh, R. Mort Frayn, Robert F. Philip, University President John Hogness, Jack G. Neupert, president of the board, Harold S. Shefelman, James R. Ellis, and George V. Powell; (*below*) the Rainier Bank Tower, finished in 1978, shown here from the IBM Building plaza, the corner of the Olympic Hotel at the left, the Skinner Building at the right (*photo by Balthazar Korab, courtesy of* UNICO)

(*Above*) Mary Gates was president of the regents when the board met on December 8, 1978; others present are (from left) Robert D. Larrabee, R. Mort Frayn, Gordon C. Culp, University President John R. Hogness, Dr. J. Hans Lehmann, Taul Watanabe, Robert F. Philip; (*below*) the new Urban–Four Seasons lease on the Olympic Hotel was signed for the university on January 18, 1980, by Taul Watanabe, president of the board of regents, and Barbara Zimmerman, secretary; witnessing the signings are Regents Robert F. Philip and Gordon C. Culp and (standing, from left) James M. Hilton, a legal consultant during the drafting, James F. Ryan, the university's vice president for business and finance, and James B. Wilson, senior assistant attorney general and the university's legal counsel

(*Top*) The Olympic Hotel, its University Street motor entrance still occupying the space where the Metropolitan Theatre once stood, awaiting in April 1980 the processes of restoration that will assure its continued life as Seattle's classic and much-loved "grande dame"; (*bottom*) downtown Seattle, spring 1980, with the Metropolitan Tract circled (*courtesy of Aerolist Inc.*)

company would pay $2,960,000, approximately the estimated cost of the project (the figure subject to final adjustment), as an advance on the rent for the thirty-year period, and for this it would pledge its leasehold interest to a mortgage firm that would have the right, in the event of default, to take over the garage and its management. Both the mortgagee and any such transfer would be subject to approval by the regents. Amortization of the mortgage was calculated at twenty-four years, the annual debt service $233,000. For twenty-four years Seattle Olympic would pay the university 80 percent of the net profit above the $233,000, and thereafter, until 1994, the full 80 percent. Three separately developed projections of potential earnings suggested that the income from the garage might range from $248,000 to $302,000 a year, more than enough to cover the debt service. Furthermore, while the hotel company was paying a minimum annual rental of $400,000, plus $24,000 for the theater site, it was thought that, with the general increase in the hotel's business attributable in part to the new garage facilities, the university would be receiving almost $300,000 a year more in rent.[12]

There were other lease changes that Seattle Olympic thought important. The Olympic was the only major hotel in Seattle that did not offer free garage space to guests, and the company proposed that the university allow up to 50 percent of the costs of free parking, as a credit against the rental, when the hotel adopted a free-parking policy. And, because the company's responsibility for the payment of leasehold taxes might prove an impediment to favorable financing, Seattle Olympic asked that it be given a lease modification offering the same protection against real estate tax liability that had been accorded University Properties. Such questions would have to receive extended study by the university staff and by the regents, but Seattle Olympic had worked out what was, at the least, an ingenious solution to the hotel parking problem and one that would permanently establish the Olympic as the downtown terminus of Seattle-Tacoma International Airport bus traffic. The preliminary plans for the garage-terminal had been prepared by John Graham and Company, architects and engineers, designers of the Space Needle for the Seattle fair.[13]

The office building proposed by University Properties required no off-tract space, but its realization demanded coordination with the Seattle Olympic project and a financial plan based on the twenty-year lease extension and certain other basic modifications of lessee performance requirements. Under the original ten-story concept, the building was to provide about 170,-000 square feet of space, about 100,000 square feet of which—six floors—would be leased to an as-yet-unnamed tenant of national stature. There was the thought that additional floors might be added later. Very soon, however—certainly by April 1962—the decision had been made to design a building of twenty stories, eight stories to be leased to the national firm. The firm, with which Ryan had been conducting negotiations for several months, was the International Business Machines Corporation.[14]

The cost of the ten-story building had been estimated at $5,500,000. The new estimate was $8,000,000. The design work was proceeding under the direction of Minoru Yamasaki and Associates, and the plans were being produced by Naramore, Bain, Brady and Johanson. The structure was visualized as a tall office tower—the height emphasized by vertical lines, graceful arches at the base—that would be placed at the high south end of the half-block on Fifth Avenue. There would be a garage for two hundred cars beneath and an open plaza, lined by shops, at the street level space adjoining. The name, not surprisingly, would be the IBM Building. The architects' studies of the placement and character of the new structure and of the requirements of the IBM Corporation had run parallel with studies by University Properties of economic factors, based on its experience with the Washington Building, and these with regard to surveys and long-term projections developed by the Building and Managers Association, the Central Association of Seattle, and the City Planning Commission. Every study reinforced the feeling in University Properties that the twenty-story office building represented the best use of the Olympic Garage site, where, because of the shortage of shops and offices, the pedestrian traffic was lower than in any block in the downtown area. Planning Commission and Central Association studies indicated that within twenty-five years Seattle's downtown would need at least eight more buildings of the size of the Washington Building to accommodate the demand for office space and retail stores. The Metropolitan Center itself, as Ryan pointed out, badly needed a pinion at its southeast corner, a building that would anchor there, as the Washington Building did at the northwest corner, the commercial activity the center was attracting. The Washington Building was already 98 percent occupied and the White-Henry-Stuart Building, which had lost some tenants to the Washington, was again at its normal level of occupancy.[15]

But, as with the garage-airline terminal, the questions of lease extension and financing remained. University Properties was proposing an extension to the year 2009 of the lease that otherwise would expire in 1989. It was prepared, if the extension was granted, to seek financing for a twenty-five year prepayment of rent of $8,000,000, the cost of the building. The arrangements —a mortgage of leasehold interest, university approval of the mortgagee and of any contingent assignment—would be substantially like those asked by Seattle Olympic. For the purposes of calculating its rental payments to the university, University Properties would count as commercial space, rather than office space, that part of the building occupied by the IBM Corporation, thus raising the rental rate from 38 to 80 percent and increasing the payments to the university by $57,492 a year or by $1,437,300 for the twenty-five years.[16]

In addition to the twenty-year extension, the University Properties lease modifications would have to include approval of the plan for financing and certain other changes. One was a revision of article 10 of the lease that gave the university the right to cancel the agreement if the university was at any time "threatened with liability" for taxation on its Metropolitan tract income. The open-ended right of cancellation would make exceedingly difficult, University Properties thought, any borrowing on its leasehold from usual sources. University Properties also asked a reduction of $547,000 a year in its rental payments to the university for the twenty-five year term, the $547,000 representing the amount needed to amortize the $8,000,000 in twenty-five years at an interest rate of 4.75 percent. Since the estimated rental from the new building was $549,545, including the adjusted rental from the IBM space, the difference was only barely covered. On the other hand, University Properties was gambling that financing was possible at the 4.75-percent rate—by no means a sure thing—and making its proposal accordingly. Finally, University Properties asked to be relieved for twenty-five years, as far as the IBM space was concerned, of its lease obligation to spend a minimum of 4 percent a year on repairs and maintenance. IBM had already agreed to take care of such costs in its own quarters.[17]

The Seattle Olympic was asking the regents to approve plans for a new off-tract garage and airlines bus terminal. University Properties was proposing a twenty-story office building where the Olympic Garage, first the Arena Building, had stood for almost half a century. Conrad, Riley, Ryan, Carlson, and others had been in months of repeated meetings over details, and the regents had been informed of the general shape of the proposals. By June 1962, the studies had been completed, the estimates of cost and income prepared, and the necessary modifications of the leases drafted. For the special meeting of the regents on June 30, 1962, Conrad had sent to President Odegaard, with copies for members of the board of regents, the university business office recommendations for approval with copies of the letters of proposal, the projections of cash flow, the plans and architects' sketches of the garage and the IBM Building, and the reports of the certified public accountants (Touche, Ross, Bailey and Smart) on studies of costs, revenues, debt service, and net income. The projected benefits to the university were impressive. Looking only to 1969, the revenues from the Olympic would be increased by $2,090,000—to $8,756,000 over $6,666,000—while net revenues from the Metropolitan Center as a whole, the garage and office building in place, would rise from $11,346,000 to $13,436,000, an increase of more than $2,000,-000 for the decade.[18]

Warranty deeds conveying to the university the two plots of land needed for the new garage were executed late in June by the Standard Oil Company of California and the Northwest Bible College. At a special meeting on June 30, 1962—two members filing their approvals by letter—the board of regents, with Dorothy Bullitt now president, authorized the Seattle Olympic Hotel Company and University Properties to proceed with their projects.[19]

Century 21, that exposition designed to provide a glimpse of the future, had been awaited by Seattle with an excitement that contained an almost apprehensive anticipation of irrevocable change. "Look about you now," people had said, "for you'll never see Seattle like this again." That the fair was a complete success financially was due to a disciplined management—Carlson, Gandy, and their associates, and a general manager named Ewen Dingwall, had seen to it—but the larger achievement was that the change the fair brought was of the happiest kind. The Alaska-Yukon-Pacific Exposition of 1909 had transformed and shaped permanently the campus of the University of Washington at a time when it was still a somewhat remote academic grove overlooking Lake Washington and Lake Union. Century 21 left a similarly significant community heritage in a Seattle Center which would now have not merely such mechanical trappings as a Space Needle and a monorail connection to the central city but also accommodations for drama, music, and learning in a setting of courtyards, fountains, restaurants, and shops. From the beginning there had been a conscious effort to make the fair a contribution to the city's cultural composition. The fair visitors and tourists came and, for the most part, went. The Seattle Center remained. And the enveloping changes had been coming all along in the spread of the population to Bellevue and other communities east of Lake Washington, in the construction of the new freeway and the floating bridges across the lake, and in the development at strategic points of new shopping malls. Growth was implicit. Century 21 helped shape it.

Preparations for the new construction at the Metropolitan Center proceeded during 1962 while the lease amendments were executed and approved and IBM Building site studies were made by Naramore, Bain, Brady and Johanson. The old Olympic Garage was scheduled for demolition in March 1963, so until then—during the year of Century 21 and later—it continued to be the Olympic's parking facility. The new garage was to be rushed to completion by December 1963, and in that nine-month interval the Olympic would have to rely on space made available by arrangements with other parking-lot operators.[20]

As a result of business stimulated by Century 21, and particularly of the activity in the Olympic, the university's income from the Metropolitan Center that year was the highest in history—a total of $3,017,000 in payments of $1,087,000 from the hotel and $1,930,000 from University Properties. Hotel payments were expected to level off at about $950,000 even after the garage was completed, but those from the tract itself would be, it was thought, not less than $1,938,000. Yet the financial prospect was both bright and complicated. New cash flow projections had been made in the expectation that the university would receive each biennium $3,000,000 for campus construction or other capital requirements and thus would be putting aside $1,500,000 each year for such purposes. In addition to this, however, were other annual demands—payments of $100,000 for city services (up from the $60,000 that had been paid since 1956); $200,000 for tenant alterations and modernizations; and $30,000 for operation of the Metropolitan tract office. By February 1963 it was clear that major modernization would have to be scheduled soon for the Cobb and Stimson buildings, where the facilities for the doctors and dentists were becoming so obsolescent that tenancy was a serious problem.

The Cobb and Stimson projects were outside the normal flow of alterations, and Ryan's staff had estimated the cost at $285,000, of which only $4,500 was available from previous modernization authorizations. Finally, the teaching hospital bonds—the bonds of the $5,000,000 issue of 1956—were scheduled to be retired in annual blocks of $700,000 beginning January 1, 1963, and that annual demand would continue until 1969. All of this meant, particularly with respect to the determination to devote $3,000,000 each biennium to campus projects, that the regents would have to defer deposits into the New Building Fund until December 31, 1966, and that University Properties would have to continue to advance funds of up to $350,000 for tenant alterations with no immediate prospect of reimbursement and no compensation for the advances it made.[21]

There was no sorrow when, in 1963, the Olympic Garage, so long a not-very-attractive landmark, was razed to make room for the IBM Building. But while even the new building presented certain problems, at first, its construction was accompanied by two singularly fortuitous developments.

Soil tests at the IBM site had revealed almost at once that the original designs would have to be modified—the two-hundred-car garage reduced in size, the plaza altered—or the cost of the project raised from $8,000,000 to $8,750,-000 or more. There seemed three choices for the university: construct a building costing no more than $8,000,000, whatever the sacrifices in garage or tenant space; let University Properties build an $8,750,000 building and increase by $60,000 or so the $47,000 that the company was allowed as an offset in its rental payments; or ask University Properties to proceed with the $8,750,000 building while advancing the additional costs from its own funds—again without compensation—until the teaching hospital bonds were amortized in 1969 and the university could begin to put the $700,000-a-year-bond commitment into the New Building Fund.

It was the third alternative that Conrad recommended, Riley concurring. It was a proposition that meant another uncompensated advance by University Properties, this time of perhaps $750,000, and it was a commitment that Ryan alone could not make. But on January 23, 1963, Ryan discussed the question with members of the University Properties board. They approved. University Properties would advance the additional funds without interest. Construction of the IBM Building would proceed with only such design changes as were imperative to accommodate the subsurface realities of the site. What University Properties was doing was to make it possible for the university to continue to use its tract income—perhaps $3,000,000 per biennium—for campus projects, and to receive the other funds it needed for reimbursement of leasehold taxes, payments to the city for services, and so on.[22]

It was here that there began to occur concomitant developments of striking importance to the character and value of the area. The Plymouth Congregational Church, a massive, rather squarish edifice topped by a tower, had stood for decades facing Sixth Avenue in the half block behind the Arena-turned-garage. The church building antedated the old Arena, for it had been erected in 1910–12 to replace an earlier Plymouth church at Third and University. But by the early 1960s the trustees and members of the church were determining to replace the old building by a new one, and because the church site and the IBM site were contiguous, a certain amount of coordination seemed indicated.

By 1962 a Plymouth church study group had been examining for many months the alternatives—whether to erect the new building on the old site or to seek a new location, possibly on First Hill—and the considerations touched both finances and the long-term advantages or disadvantages of continuing church activities in a downtown location that was being brushed by the freeway. The idea of moving was dropped rather early, history and tradition arguing against flight from the central city. Yet the questions before the church were formidable. Not the least of them was how to design and build a church that would offer some limited parking accommodations for members. Studies of these questions led to consultations, about the time the IBM plan was in the making, with Ryan and others in University Properties. For the church, the principals were members of the board of trustees, including particularly Kenneth Fisher, now head of the Fisher Mills and other properties, and R. Mort Frayn, who had a long-standing familiarity with Metropolitan Center developments. The early talks were, in the main, no more than exploratory and without involvement by university representatives. One of the thoughts, soon abandoned, was that there might be an exchange of property whereby the university would acquire the church site—thus having the whole block between Fifth and Sixth avenues—and the church would build on the Standard Oil and Northwest Bible College plots, south of Seneca, which were being purchased for the new garage. But while such ideas proved impractical, the talks nevertheless had several interesting results. One was related to the dimensions of the university tract.[23]

From the time of its construction the Plymouth church had been separated from the tract by a twenty-foot alley, an alley extending from Seneca Street to Union and thus also separating the Skinner Building from the Washington Athletic Club. For all those years it had been assumed that the east boundary of the Metropolitan tract lay at the west boundary of the alley—that the alley was outside the tract. When it came to planning access to the IBM Building's underground garage, it seemed desirable to use the alley area for the new ramps, and Ryan, pursuing this idea, approached the church board to see if the alley might be vacated. The conversations led naturally to a search of the records, and this to the discovery that no existing survey confirmed the presumption with regard to the boundaries. Ryan instituted a new survey, and this placed the Metropolitan tract boundary at the east line of the alley, which meant that the land between the church and the tract had been the university's all along. The line was the one that had been thrown into a state of uncertainty when the regents of 1873 had permitted neighboring property owners to put a street above the old campus—the rather casual permission that had necessitated the clarifying court decisions of 1910. With the new survey in hand, University Properties applied to the Washington Title Insurance Company for a title policy covering the alley. The Plymouth church, although it might have had contestable rights, had no wish to press them. The city gave University Properties a permit to excavate the space for the garage entrance, and certain adjustments in utilities connections had to be made. But the outcome was that the property line had been reestablished and the university was in possession of a strip of land that it had not realized it possessed—a strip that extended the 600 feet of the original Denny gift and was, in area, some 13,000 square feet.[24]

A further development involved the design of the new Plymouth church— the design still in a state of suspense when construction of the IBM Building was begun. It was a rare thing, and perhaps unprecedented, that construction of a church and an office building should be contemplated virtually at the same time and in the same block in a city's busy downtown area. The IBM Building had a head start, but the church would be placed, somehow, beside it. The two structures would have to be entirely different creations, distinct in function and feeling, but the feelings should not clash, and the challenge to the architects was to design a church that could stand beside a twenty-story tower without being diminished or sacrificing its essential character as a religious center.

Perry Johanson, chief of the Naramore, Bain, Brady and Johanson design team, was the one who worked out the solution. It was a solution perfected not solely in regard to architectural composition but also in relation to the requirements and future plans of the church itself, which had to do with finances, and, inevitably, the needs for automobile parking of a congregation assembling at a downtown center. In 1963 it was arranged that Johanson, who had been totally involved in the IBM Building design, should develop the theme of the church. By the time the IBM was nearing completion, Johanson had designed a gleaming white structure to occupy that other half of the block-square site—a structure with a street-level chapel, a sanctuary seating six hundred, a fellowship hall seating four hundred, an education unit, and administrative offices. The church would be contemporary but timeless in style, utterly unlike the IBM Building but complementing it without loss of dignity or identity.[25]

With coordination being achieved in such ways, all stemming from the 1962 consultations between the Plymouth board and University Properties, it was not surprising perhaps that coordination should also involve church financing. And that development came—could it be guessed?—by way of the parking problem.

The need of the church for parking would be only occasional, principally on Sundays and at times of special observances and activities. The cost of the church as well as its design depended, nevertheless, upon the nature of the accommodations to be provided, and with such questions University Properties was gaining considerable experience. By 1964, with the IBM Building nearing readiness for occupancy, University Properties had devised a plan to satisfy the need of the church and to augment somewhat further the parking requirements of IBM tenants. University Properties proposed to lease the full half block under the church, for the period expiring with its own lease in 2009, and to construct therein a ninety-stall parking garage to be operated as a commercial facility on business days but reserved for members of the Plymouth congregation on weekends. University Properties then also arranged a $400,000 bank loan on the site—actually another advance payment of rent—and this became a part of the financing of a structure that would cost about $1,500,000. The church garage, with its own separate entrance on University Street, was incorporated into the Johanson design. University Properties lease amendments covering the Plymouth garage proposal were approved by the regents in September 1964.[26]

From mid-1963 to late 1964, while the new garage was being completed and linked to the Olympic by the Seneca Street pedestrian overpass, construction had proceeded on the IBM Building. The time had brought, but not for Seattle alone, one overwhelming event. In November 1963, while Seattle was still looking about at itself in the wake of the fair, John F. Kennedy was assassinated and the city shared the nation's shock, and in a particularly personal way, remembering that it was almost exactly two years before that the president had been conducted along Fourth Avenue in a motorcade much like that tragic one in Dallas. At the university there had been changes, among the regents and in the primary administrative staff. Dr. Murphy, a regent since 1958 and vice-president of the board for 1962–63, died in December 1962, and his successor was Dr. E. A. Addington, a Seattle radiologist, a graduate of the University of Minnesota, and since 1948 a clinical assistant professor of radiology in the university's medical school. But before 1964 was out Addington, too, had died (also while serving as vice-president of the board), and to his place Governor Rosellini had appointed Dr. Leo J. Rosellini, a Seattle surgeon. Dr. Rosellini was a cousin of the governor, and he not only was prominent professionally—a member of the staffs of six Seattle-area hospitals—but he had worked years before, when Albert Rosellini was a state senator, to help achieve passage of legislation establishing and providing for funding of the university's medical school. Ernest Conrad was now a university vice-president. Conrad, the staff neophyte of 1944 and the participant in Metropolitan tract affairs since about 1951, had become increasingly involved in tract studies and liaison, first as assistant comptroller, then as business manager. By 1960, Nelson Wahlstrom, a leader for years in studies of university financial procedures, had left the university for Washington, D.C., to establish a national office for a committee representing major universities in consultations with federal agencies on problems of management in federally sponsored research. In subsequent shifts of staff assignments, Conrad had carried larger responsibilities on the campus and at the tract. In June 1963, he was appointed vice-president for business and finance.[27]

The IBM Building was dedicated on November 17, 1964. The building, the towering, fluted pillar of reinforced concrete, quartz aggregate, aluminum, and marble, had been erected in just nineteen months, the design the work of architectural teams headed by Yamasaki and Johanson.* The building had cost something over $8,500,000, and the original concept—an office building rising from an open plaza—had been preserved. The building occupied only half of the block-long site between University and Seneca streets, and the plaza contained a sculptured fountain of black bronze, created by Seattle artist James FitzGerald, and places for shrubs and flowers. The dedication ceremonies, begun outside and followed by a luncheon in the building, brought together those who had been most closely involved. The IBM Corporation was represented by H. Wisner Miller, president of IBM's Real Estate and Construction Division, and the board of regents by Harold Shefelman, still chairman of the Metropolitan tract committee. Roger Stevens was accompanied by Alfred Glancy, of Detroit, vice-president of University Properties, and directors Ben Tobin, of Hollywood Beach, Florida, and Nathan Shulman of New York. These were the men who had agreed to assume the costs over $8,000,000 so that construction could proceed as planned. Ryan was there, of course, with the principal members of his management team—Jack Dierdorff, A. G. Schille, and Donald J. Covey, all now vice-presidents—and the architectural and engineering firms were represented. It was appropriate that among the speakers was Minoru Yamasaki and inevitable that some attention should be focused on him.[28]

The IBM Building was the product of a high level of architectural, engineering, construction, and management teamwork, as Yamasaki said that day. Yet none doubted that the basic concept was Yamasaki's, for while the IBM was unlike any other office building in Seattle, it had a touch that Seattle could readily recognize. For almost eight years Yamasaki, the university alumnus who had been known to Glancy for his work in Michigan and to Shefelman from the World's Fair Design Standards Board days, had been more and more heavily involved in Seattle projects. When the Washington Building's Fourth Avenue façade was under discussion, incorporation into it of the old Cobb Annex had been suggested by William J. Bain, the Naramore, Bain partner in charge. Yamasaki had supported the Bain idea. Then had come the design of the Century 21 Science Pavilion, later the Pacific Science Center, for which the Yamasaki firm and Naramore, Bain were associate architects. Yamasaki had continued his interest in the work of the university's architectural commission, even as he continued to win prizes—in-

---

* The general contractor was the Howard S. Wright Construction Company. Engineering was by Worthington, Skilling, Helle and Jackson and mechanical and electrical engineering by Bouillon, Christofferson and Schairer.

cluding new AIA First Honor awards—for buildings from Detroit to Saudi Arabia. By 1964 Yamasaki had placed his imprint on Seattle.[29]

In the mid-1960s a period of consolidation seemed ahead for the Metropolitan Center. The University Properties organization, running smoothly, had achieved a quite remarkable transformation with two new major office buildings and extensive and continuing rehabilitation of the other buildings, notably in the White-Henry-Stuart but also in the Stimson and the Cobb, which now were called the Stimson and Cobb Medical Centers. The Seattle Olympic Hotel Company, which was looking forward to the benefits that were coming with the new garage, also was continuing to improve facilities in the hotel. Commercial and office tenancies were gratifyingly high, the Washington Building with an occupancy of an almost unprecedented 99 percent, the IBM Building at 70 percent and rising, the White-Henry-Stuart at something above 90 percent. The Washington and IBM were not and would not be the only new buildings in town, for the Norton Building on Second Avenue, erected by Norton Clapp's Metropolitan Building Corporation, had been for five years a part of the skyline, and in 1965 two other major buildings were in prospect. The Seattle-First National Bank had announced plans for a new $25,000,000 tower to be erected a block south of the Metropolitan Center between Third and Fourth avenues, and a new $25,000,000 federal office building was being proposed, the location not determined. If such developments were to be regarded as competitive, it could only be remembered that the projections of Seattle's growth had anticipated them.[30]

Another somewhat sidelong addition to the Metropolitan Center had been proposed and approved late in 1964. This was the acquisition of the old Palomar Building at Third Avenue and University Street, below the Cobb and south of the Washington Building garage as it angled about the new post office. The idea was, again, to gain an additional automobile parking facility. If that refrain was an old one, the logic was that the satisfaction of Metropolitan Center parking needs approached, after all the effort, a net in automobile stalls of little more than the 375 in the Washington garage. The Olympic's new garage accommodated some 610 cars, not the 787 first planned. Even when the Plymouth Church garage was added to the IBM space the total would fail to equal the space in the old Olympic Garage, now vanished. Parking below the White-Henry-Stuart was difficult and limited. Only the Palomar Building, the Palomar Theater not even used regularly, represented a solid prospect for a parking garage addition of the kind required, and it had been seen as a prospect since planning for the Washington Building was going forward in 1957–59. University Properties had inquired about purchase of the Palomar in that period, thinking that the Washington Building garage (which had lost its lowest subsurface level because of the soil conditions) might be extended along Third Avenue to University Street. The purchase was not possible in 1957. It had become so by 1964.[31]

University Properties, making its calculations of cost and income, presented the question to the regents. There had been months of negotiations and feasibility studies. The Palomar Building would be razed, and the new garage that would replace it would be linked to the Washington Building garage, which it adjoined, and incorporated into a single operating unit. It would have a capacity of three hundred cars, serving the Metropolitan Center as a whole but particularly the tenants and visitors of the Cobb and Stimson Medical Centers. There would be direct access to the Cobb through a new pedestrian entry from the garage level. The proposal was approved by the regents on September 22, 1964—at the same meeting in which they approved the University Properties arrangement with the Plymouth church—the appropriate lease amendments to be prepared. University Properties was authorized to buy the Palomar Building from its own funds, to demolish the old building and replace it with the new garage, and to operate the property, paying the real estate taxes on it, until the expiration of its own lease in 2009. In August 1965, the regents reviewed and approved the plans and specifications of the project, which was then estimated to cost $1,181,000 with completion scheduled for February 1966. Again, the architectural firm was Naramore, Bain.[32]

The Palomar arrangement was another of those instances in which University Properties, faced by a contemporary need, helped work out a solution that would enhance the future value of the tract—in this case by both enlargement and ultimate reversion of physical improvements. University Properties would buy the Palomar site and the building, replace the building with a garage, and operate the garage until the expiration of the lease in 2009. In acquiring the Palomar site, University Properties would be making a gift to the university—a future gift. The title to the property would be placed in escrow so that the land and garage would go to the university in 2009. Until then, University Properties was the owner, the property still on the tax rolls.

By 1965, Seattle Olympic had been the university's lessee for ten years and University Properties for more than eleven. Physically, the results were in a brightened, immensely improved tract that was reaching upward in new buildings, a tract somewhat larger than the original ten acres but meshed in new ways, thereby, into the central city. There had been a heavy emphasis on modernization, but provisions for this had been built into the leases. Financially, the operation was at a level of many millions of dollars, and the university itself was not without immediate benefits even though the more substantial ones presumably would be coming at some time in the future.

In the autumn of 1965 the regents received a comprehensive report, prepared by the university staff, that included a summary of receipts and expenditures under the hotel and tract leases from their inceptions (or from the inception of each authorized project) to June 30 of that year. There also were projections for the bienniums ending June 30, 1973.[33]

The receipts to 1965 would have been astonishing to any who remembered the old days, the expenditures even more so. Rental incomes and certain miscellaneous receipts totaled $37,712,789. This included (with prepaid rentals) some $25,500,000 from University Properties and about $11,500,000 from the Olympic, the Olympic Garage, and the $24,000-a-year Metropolitan Theatre lease. Expenditures had reached a total of $37,872,227, and of this sum more than $21,000,000 had gone to new construction and $5,500,000 to modernization and related studies.* But what had the university received, and what would it receive in the future?

The regents had decided in 1961 that Metropolitan Center operations should be producing $3,000,000 per biennium for university purposes, such receipts to be deposited in the university's own plant fund. By 1965 the transfers had approximated this goal: the total was $5,938,570 for the two most recent bienniums. There had been, in addition, allocations for debt service on the $5,000,000 bond issue that had helped finance the teaching and research hospital, these totaling $3,973,320. Center operations by 1965 thus had contributed almost $10,000,000 to university plant funding. This was a considerable fraction of the total expenditures and more than twice the income the university had received between 1907 and 1953 under the old fixed-rental lease.[34]

As for the future—the future limited to the eight years to 1973—the staff could see rather dramatic increases in funds available for university purposes, both because certain commitments would end (teaching hospital debt service costs would cease in December 1969) and because deposits into the New Building Fund would be scheduled to assure availability of the $3,000,000 per biennium for university purposes. Whereas income from tract operations might exceed $5,000,000 per biennium for a total of $22,241,000, the expenditures also might fall below $7,000,000, leaving perhaps as much as $15,000,000 to be transferred to the university.[35]

The projection by the staff was by no means a forecast, as was pointed out, and within it were various imponderables, including those related to long-range studies of the needs of the Metropolitan Center. Long-range studies were coming up shortly.

Two new regents had joined the board in June 1965, and these were the appointees of Daniel J. Evans, the Republican who had come to the governor's chair to succeed Albert Rosellini. The newcomers were Seattle attorneys of prominence, George V. Powell and James R. Ellis, and they were the successors to Dorothy Bullitt and Herbert Little, whose terms had expired. Shefelman was president of the board again, and with him were John King, vice-president, and Joseph Drumheller, Robert Willis, Leo Rosellini, and

---

* To put the costs of new construction in exact figures, the total was $21,274,628: Washington Building, $9,001,494; post office building, $809,694; Cobb Annex remodeling, $114,486; Olympic Garage, $3,512,483; and IBM Building, $7,836,471.

Powell and Ellis. At the university, growth was not now merely inescapable—enrollments were exceeding the predictions, thus imposing demands for additional faculty and space—but the university under President Odegaard was growing in stature as an institution. The university long since had become one of the perennial leaders among institutions conducting federally sponsored and other research. Its biennial operations were at a record level of about $230,000,000. But the university was feeling, too, the early manifestations of the activism that would make the 1960s turbulent on campuses everywhere.

Powell was the son of the John H. Powell, who as a regent of 1907 had been a signer of the Metropolitan Building Company lease and, later, legal counsel to the board in the wake of the 1925 Arena matter. Powell himself, having attended Seattle's Garfield and Broadway high schools, had gone on to Phillips Exeter Academy, then to Princeton, where he was graduated in 1931, and to the University of Washington Law School, where he won his LL.B in 1934. His experience in the legislature, from 1947 to 1953, had covered almost exactly the years the university was endeavoring to establish a base of authority and policy for the future leasing of the Metropolitan tract. Powell was always sympathetic to university views in general but consistently opposed any of the earlier plans for direct management by the regents themselves. He had served on the board of governors of the Washington State Bar Association and on the Commission on Uniform State Laws.[36]

Ellis, not yet forty-four, was a man just getting into full gear in a career that would bring him national recognition as an eloquent spokesman for enlightened, planned growth in American cities. Ellis's roots were in early Washington. His parents, both from the Spokane region, had attended the university, and his father, Floyd E. Ellis, had been the first president of the associated students organization in the World War I era. Ellis had attended high school in Seattle, then had gone on to Yale University where he received his B.S. degree in 1942 before serving three years in the Army Air Force in World War II. In 1948, he had won his J.D. degree at the university, and was admitted to the Washington bar the following year. He was a past president of the Municipal League, a member of the Washington Planning Advisory Council, and president of Forward Thrust, Incorporated, a community-action program of which he was a principal organizer. Believing that Seattle and other cities were being choked by the freeways that brought more and more automobiles into their core areas, Ellis was an advocate of rapid transit and of parks and greenbelts that controlled urban congestion. For Seattle he was urging a $500,000,000 program to build the parks and greenbelts, to improve major arterials, to construct a world trade center, and to make the city a center for research and education. He would say of Seattle, "We can build here one of the great cities of man." Ellis had been for some months an occasional unofficial adviser to Governor Evans.[37]

The planning that was about to begin was in the Metropolitan Center itself, and under the authority of the regents. The product would be a study, subject to frequent amendment, called Plan 2009 in obvious reference to the terminal date of the University Properties lease.[38]

It was time to make appraisals of the future, and the IBM Building was suggesting new directions. None of the older buildings on the tract was younger than forty years, and the oldest, the White, was more than fifty-five. The White-Henry-Stuart block—the original buildings and the annexes—was an impressive mass, and central to the tract. But its age showed, even after all the rehabilitation. The Skinner, including the Fifth Avenue Theater, was sound and attractive, but it nevertheless presented peculiar problems with respect to the improvement of office space simply because the theater was there. As for the Stimson and Cobb Medical Centers, there seemed somehow a redundance, since so many doctors and dentists, the new generations particularly, were conducting their practices in medical centers established in virtually every new neighborhood in the widening urban area. What—in the light of changing economic conditions and modes of living—should come next?

Plan 2009—the scope of it—was the result of repeated conferences in 1965 and 1966 between representatives of the university and the University Properties, the principals Conrad on the one hand and Ryan on the other. But early in 1966 the conclusion was that the planning should be professional, the judgments on the needs for further developments, and the timing of them and their nature, coming from architects who were familiar with the University Properties management philosophies and sensitive to the expectations of the university. The choices for such planning were, inevitably, the firms of Naramore, Bain, Brady and Johanson and Minoru Yamasaki and Associates.[39]

Plan 2009 was to be evolutionary. Calculations were to be made in relation to other studies of Seattle's probable future development, including those of public transportation, office rentals, demographic trends, and retail merchandising prospects. A scale model of downtown Seattle with related schematic drawings was constructed, and all were submitted to the university's architectural commission for review and comment and, of course, to the regents' Metropolitan tract committee. As the months went by and the studies proceeded, the conclusion at the heart of the effort took shape: the time was very near when the older buildings of the tract would have to be replaced. The questions were how and in what order the replacements should come and what their character should be.[40]

In 1966, meanwhile, the regents had approved an amendment to the hotel lease that was, in a way, a suggestion of things to come. Under the lease assignments of the 1950s Seattle Olympic and Western International had been restrained from undertaking other local hotel improvements that might represent competitive developments. Now, however, Western International desired to enlarge its Benjamin Franklin Hotel (operated by another subsidiary, Benjamin Franklin Hotel, Incorporated) to increase the number of guest rooms from 286 to 731 and to augment dining, retail, and parking facilities. There had been extended discussions of these proposals before the regents at length approved them on March 18, 1966. For permitting the Benjamin Franklin enlargements, all carefully set out in the lease amendment of that date, the regents obtained agreement to an additional modernization program in the Olympic itself at an estimated cost of $1,650,000 and an increase in the annual minimum rental of from $400,000 to $500,000.[41]

While this was going on, the new Plymouth Congregational Church was taking its place alongside the IBM Building. The old church, the landmark, had been demolished early in 1966, and for the ensuing months, under arrangements with University Properties, church services were held in the Fifth Avenue Theater. The cornerstone of the new structure was laid on January 22, 1967, and the building opened the following September.

There was a surprise, perhaps, in the decision that the Stimson should be the next of the old buildings to go. The Stimson was far from the oldest. Construction had begun in 1924 before the Olympic's first units were completed and the improvement of its garage facilities had been among the first major projects undertaken by University Properties. Yet the years and the changes in Seattle had made the decision logical. The Stimson was the larger of the two medical centers (with four acres of floor area, it was said), yet while occupancy in other buildings was rising, occupancy in the Stimson had fallen by 1967 to 70 percent and seemed certain to fall farther because of the movement of medical services to other parts of the city, especially the area of the hospitals grouped on First Hill. The architectural studies had shown that there was no economically feasible prospect for converting the building to general office use. Above all, Fourth Avenue itself was maturing. The Washington Building had started this and the $25,000,000 Seattle-First National Bank Building was rising. A new building on the Stimson site, across from the Olympic, would take advantage of this new growth, contribute to the development of a major thoroughfare, and help to keep the Metropolitan Center at the heart of it all.[42]

The approach to the decision was appropriately deliberate, the final approval coming only after two years of review. The decision was made by the board of regents, which by then had two new members, appointed in 1968 to replace the veterans Joseph Drumheller and John L. King. One was Mort Frayn, the other Robert F. Philip, of Kennewick.

The retiring regents were among those who had served the longest. Each had been involved for years in determinations concerning the Metropolitan tract, yet neither, simply because of the order of events, had been a board member when the University Properties lease was signed in 1953. Drumheller had come to the board in 1945 and had served again from 1957 to 1968, in that last year as president of the board for the fourth time. King had been appointed in 1946, and with Drumheller had come back in 1957. Their service had been long, though interrupted, and had included most of the years of the university's phenomenal growth after World War II.

As for the new regents, neither needed introductions. Frayn, the Seattle printing company executive, had been intimately associated with university affairs since, as a recent alumni association president, he had won a seat in the legislature in 1946. From the State Legislative Council's Metropolitan tract hearings of the 1950s to the more recent negotiations with regard to the Plymouth church, Frayn had been a steady, respected, and judicious participant in the unfolding events. Philip, a newspaper publisher, had been close to university affairs since his student days in the late 1930s. He was president of the *Tri-City Herald* in Kennewick, a newspaper serving the important Richland-Pasco-Kennewick community adjacent to the Hanford nuclear plant in southeast Washington. In the 1950s, Philip had been a local leader in the move to establish in Richland the Center for Graduate Study at Hanford, a center operated by the university with the cooperation of Oregon State University and Washington State University. He was president of the Tri-City Industrial Council, a member of the regional advisory council of the Small Business Administration, and a member of the governor's advisory council to the State Department of Commerce and Economic Development. Philip was also a member of the visiting committee of the university's Medical School and a district governor of the alumni association.[42]

After the months of study and preparation, University Properties gave to the university staff in April 1968 an initial report on the plan to replace the Stimson Building, a report relating the proposed development to the concepts of Plan 2009. The projection was followed in November by another one covering the economic aspects of the proposal. This was soon accompanied by a financial study conducted by an accounting firm (Touche, Ross, Bailey and Smart) indicating that a new building on the Stimson site would earn in rentals, in the next decade, some $4,000,000 more than could be expected from the Stimson itself. The Stimson had simply outlived its time.[44]

The amendments to the University Properties lease authorizing construction of a new building were executed on February 28, 1969. University Properties agreed to demolish the Stimson and to erect a new building of approximately thirty stories with a basement garage. The university agreed to make deposits in the New Building Fund, until University Properties had been reimbursed for its costs, of all tract and hotel rental income above $1,250,000 per year and above whatever amounts were required to cover the payments for city services and the costs of operating the university's Metropolitan Tract Office. On April 24, 1969, the regents approved the preliminary plans for the new building and authorized University Properties to proceed with final plans and working drawings.[45]

In the autumn of 1969, although the contracts for construction had not yet been awarded, Seattle saw in the newspapers the architects' perspective drawings of the thirty-story tower that would stand where the Stimson had stood since 1924. Major tenants would be the Unigard Insurance Group and the Pacific National Bank (Charles Frankland, formerly a university regent, was now chairman of the board of Pacific National). The building would be called the Financial Center. The cost was expected to be $15,000,000 and the building ready for occupancy by December 1971.[46]

When the regents met on February 13, 1970 (Leo Rosellini had succeeded Willis as president), they formally approved the final plans, stipulating now, however, that the cost was not to exceed $16,900,000. That, at the Metropolitan Center, was how the new decade began.[47]

CHAPTER 12

The Tower: 1970 to 1975

Since 1925 the Stimson Building, more recently called the Stimson Medical Center, had stood in dignified association with those other older buildings of the Metropolitan Center, a companion of the Cobb, a contemporary of the Olympic, and a neighbor of the historic White-Henry-Stuart. Yet when the new Financial Center rose on the Stimson site something more than mere replacement occurred. The Financial Center was the third tower, after the Washington and IBM buildings, to stand at a corner of the university property. None approached in height the giant fifty-story Seattle-First National Bank Building that had been erected southwest of the center between Third and Fourth, but the movement now was upward—the Olympic was flanked by towers, east and west—with a saving element, the regard for open space. Neither the IBM Building nor the Financial Center occupied the whole of its half-block site. Each had a plaza at its base. University Properties was visualizing more of this—the construction of tall buildings positioned to admit light and to invite pedestrians to a parklike environment below—and was beginning to refer to the Metropolitan Center as the Metropolitan Plaza. There was significance, too, in the fact that Plan 2009 was commonly referred to, by 1970, as Project 2009. The use of "project" suggested the determination to put plans into action.

The Stimson Medical Center had disappeared by July 1970, smashed down by wrecking balls, the basement of the new building excavated. But before that happened the Stimson had its moment of remembrance in the opening of the cornerstone on March 5, 1970. There was a commemorative ceremony at the entrance of the building, planned by James M. Ryan. The guests included representatives of the Unigard Insurance Group and the Pacific National Bank, the companies that would occupy major areas of the Financial Center, and other persons associated with University Properties and the architectural and construction firms, among them William J. Bain and Perry Johanson, of Naramore, Bain, Brady and Johanson, the Financial Center design firm in which Johanson was the partner in charge. The principal guest was Dorothy Bullitt, daughter of C. D. Stimson and lately a regent of the university. If few others present had personal memories of C. D. Stimson, one who did was Dr. Roscoe S. Mosiman, who had been one of the first tenants of the Stimson. Dr. Leo Rosellini, soon to retire as president of the university regents, was also there, as was Harold Shefelman, again chairman of the regents' Metropolitan tract committee. It was Shefelman who, with the help of Donald Covey, of University Properties, pried open the copper box that held the mementos of forty-five years before—the photograph of C. D. Stimson, the copy of the text of Stimson's remarks when the cornerstone was laid, the photographs of the building when it was new, rosters of the officers and trustees of the Metropolitan Building Company and of the members of the "junior board" (Stimson then president of the company and Scott Bullitt among the junior advisors), and a copy of the Metropolitan's *Directory of Tenants* for 1925. Ryan presided at the ceremony, Shefelman spoke of the development of the tract and of the regents' commitment to it, and Mrs. Bullitt expressed the gratitude of the Stimson family.[1]

It may seem off the point to recall what was happening at the university campus in those early months of 1970. The significance, if any exists, is that the climate on the campus was a reflection of the climate in American higher education, which was the product of the several interrelated social revolutions that had occurred in the 1960s with the passage of federal civil rights and education legislation and the spread of angry moods inspired by the Vietnam War. The University of Washington had achieved by 1970 a position that would have been beyond the outer limits of the dreams of earlier administrators, not merely in the size of the faculty, student body, physical plant, or instructional facilities, but in the sheer scope and influence of its teaching, research, and service programs. Yet in years when there was violence on many campuses across the nation, the university had not escaped. In 1968 the explosion of a bomb in the Administration Building had caused damage estimated at $291,000. The explosion was at night, fortunately, and caused no injuries to students or staff. By 1970 a special session of the legislature had considered it necessary to pass a law imposing criminal penalties on any persons interfering with faculty members or administrators in the conduct of their duties. The regents of those years—Leo Rosellini, George Powell, Robert Philip, James Ellis, Mort Frayn, Robert Willis, and Harold Shefelman—had been confronted by questions totally unlike any presented to regents before them or to any earlier university administration. It was a reflection of the time that it was necessary for Charles Odegaard to go to Olympia that spring to testify before the legislature's Interim Committee on Higher Education on the university's need for help from the state in the control of campus disorders. By autumn, when a measure of calm appeared to be prevailing, President Odegaard announced two major changes in the administration. Dr. John R. Hogness, the young former dean of the Medical School and for a year the university's executive vice-president, was returning to the health sciences to become director of a new Health Sciences Center and chairman of its board. The new executive vice-president was Philip W. Cartwright, a professor of economics who had been dean of the College of Arts and Sciences since 1966 and who thus was a man with his own store of experience with university administration in troubled years.[2]

The board had been joined meantime by two new regents, appointees of Governor Daniel Evans to fill the places of Rosellini and Willis, whose terms had expired. One was Dr. Robert L. Flennaugh, a Seattle dentist, the other Jack G. Neupert, a Spokane businessman.

Flennaugh went to the place on the board assigned by custom in recent years—that is, since establishment of the university's Division of Health Sciences—to such professionals from the health fields as Corbett, Addington, Murphy, and Rosellini. But Flennaugh's appointment was historic in several ways. Flennaugh was a black—the first black graduate of the university's School of Dentistry and the first black regent. He also was, at thirty-two, the youngest regent ever appointed. A native of California, he had attended high school in Fairbanks, Alaska, and after two years at the University of Alaska had enrolled for his dental training at the University of Washington, earning his way with summer jobs in Alaska construction and playing saxophone with small dance groups during the school years, when he was also the drum major of the university's marching band. By the time he became a regent, Flennaugh was a consultant to the Head Start program, an inner-city service agency, a member of the Model City advisory board, a part-time teacher in the School of Dentistry, and a member of the Health Sciences Committee to Encourage the Recruitment of Black Students.[3]

Neupert was a Stanford graduate and, at forty-nine, a veteran of World War II with a long association with the Consolidated Supply Company, of Spokane, a firm of which he had been president and owner since 1956. He had left Stanford in 1943 to serve with the army in Europe, where he won the Bronze Star and the Air Medal. He later returned for a year of graduate study. He was prominent in community affairs and a member of the boards of a bank, an insurance group, and an investment company.[4]

As the new regents took their places, Powell became president of the board for 1970–71. Ellis, the vice-president, would take the chair the following year. In those years and the next, as the Financial Center was being completed and occupied, the regents then sitting, while facing heavier loads of regular business, found themselves drawn further toward what proved to be critical decisions about the future of the Metropolitan Center in relation to Project 2009.

The Financial Center was by no means dwarfed by the nearby Seattle-First National—"SeaFirst"—Bank Building. The Financial Center contained 300,000 square feet of rentable space, and its tower, placed on a central core, was supported on each side by two columns, each carrying a load of 11,000,000 pounds. Twelve elevators, one a service lift, served the thirty floors, and the below-ground garage accommodated 175 automobiles. Some 34,600 cubic yards of concrete went into the structure, and the exterior surfaces were of rough-textured concrete aggregate. The statistics were impressive, certainly, but perhaps not unusual for a thirty-story building. One circumstance, however, was extraordinary. More than sixty years before, in Seattle's younger years, the Great Northern Railroad had dug far below the slopes of the downtown area a tunnel that curved northward from Fourth Avenue under the southwest corner of the university property. The intrusion, if that is what it was, had been unnoticed and seemed immaterial at the time. Never in the life of the Stimson Building had a question been raised about the tunnel, not even when the parking garage had been inserted under the building in 1955, and the Northern Life Tower (later renamed the Seattle Tower) had been built directly over it. But with the coming of the Financial Center the security of the foundation made a difference. Engineering investigations disclosed that it would be necessary to put under the new building a caisson that was, in depth and volume, the largest in the world. One of the caissons supporting the tower was sunk to a level below the tunnel through which Great Northern trains, now mostly freight trains, passed each day. Another went to a depth of 158 feet—to 16 feet below sea level from the Financial Center's grade level of 142 feet. Though less spectacularly obvious, the stabilization of the Fourth Avenue slope was an achievement approaching in calculated daring the grading of Seattle's hills early in the century.[5]

Project 2009 was meant to be an evolving thing, capable of being reshaped and revised in relation to whatever economic, social, commercial, demographic, or "people-moving" requirements Seattle might eventually be heir to. The Washington and IBM buildings, already in place when the project was initiated in 1967, were fixed points in the pattern, and now the Financial Center had joined them. But "people-moving" was a well-recognized term in the language of the planners by 1972, and it reflected a recognition of the delicate balance of factors inherent in the development of a midcity commercial area—the relation of buildings to buildings, of buildings to space, of space to commercial requirements, and in Seattle, as the case in point, the need for covered walkways, sky bridges, escalators, gallerias, or underground passages to expedite pedestrian movement from place to place. A clue to what would become an increasing public interest in the nature of the problem had appeared as early as 1971, and, somewhat peculiarly, in respect to sky bridges.

The design of the Financial Center included a covered walkway over Fourth Avenue to link the Center to the Olympic at the mezzanine level as the Olympic's garage-airline terminal was linked to the hotel by a bridge over Seneca Street (and as the Bon Marche and its adjacent multilevel garage had been linked some years earlier by a high bridge over Third Avenue). The Seneca Street connection seemingly had occasioned no comment, but such use of airspace over publicly owned thoroughfares was subject to approval by the Seattle City Council, and this time, when the Fourth Avenue bridge was proposed, there not only had been some council discussion but approval had been granted by a somewhat-short-of-unanimous vote of 7 to 2. Members of the council were familiar with the model of Project 2009 in its current phase and with the prospect that other sky bridges would be coming along. They were beginning to be interested in where all this might lead, and early in 1971 they had asked the Department of Community Development to draw up "criteria," covering both the physical appearance and the "people-moving" necessities of sky bridges, so that they might better judge proposals in the future.[6]

The evolution of Project 2009 was by no means clandestine. The gradual changes in plan and projection were as public as the newspapers and frequent community presentations could make them. It was no secret, even in 1971, that University Properties and its architectural planners—that is, Naramore, Bain, Brady and Johanson and Minoru Yamasaki and Associates—were thinking of tall buildings. These included a new, high-rise Olympic Hotel, a "University Plaza" where the White-Henry-Stuart Building stood, a tall office building to replace the Skinner (perhaps with a new theater nearby to succeed the historic, and cavernous, Fifth Avenue), and even such alternatives as an office building on the Olympic garage–airlines terminal site or apartment hotel accommodations in the upper floors of one or more of the tall office buildings. Project 2009 was preserving its fluidity. But the thinking had to be, after all, for a distant future and a future city. The planning was not for the Metropolitan Center alone, or at least the anticipations were not. Planning was in relation to present and future environmental developments—to the presence of the SeaFirst Tower and the other buildings known to be coming, to possible future retail, hotel, or governmental office groupings, and even to the prospect of new rapid-transit channels including a subway under Third Avenue with branches to the main traffic centers. In short, planning had to incorporate concepts of what Seattle might be forty years hence. The planning had to be brought along with the city's own plans and with the ideas that were being filtered through such organizations as the Central Association. Ryan and University Properties were trying to keep in touch with all, but the watchword was "Forward!" By the year 2009 the White-Henry-Stuart's original segments would be one hundred years old, as would the Cobb Building; even the new IBM Building would be forty-five, almost as old as the Stimson had been.[7]

It was somehow remarkable that the Cobb, alone among the older buildings, was the building not marked for demolition in the near future. Old the Cobb was, and a little quaint, having about it the flavor of 1909. It also had a singular past in a record of service going back to its conception by J. F. Douglas as one of the first completely specialized medical-dental buildings in the nation. But such circumstances alone, in 1972, probably would not have saved it. The Cobb was given a reprieve—an indefinite reprieve—simply because it was indispensable. It had been kept up to date. It was convenient, linked to the parking garage on the old Palomar site behind it. With the Stimson Building gone, the Cobb represented a necessary continuity. Both the Stimson and the Cobb had suffered declining occupancy in recent years, but when the Stimson was coming down many of the prime tenants moved to the older buildings across University Street. By late 1970 the tenancy in the Cobb had risen from about 81 percent to almost 96 percent. The Cobb was saved not by sentiment but by the economic soundness of its place in the spectrum of foreseeable requirements in the Metropolitan Center.[8]

When Ellis became president of the board of regents in 1971, Frayn now vice-president, affairs at the university itself remained demanding. Ellis, Shefelman, Powell, and Frayn—the Seattle regents—were those with the closest views of developments downtown, but all members of the board were kept in touch with the planning by the reports of Ernest Conrad, who was the principal link between the regents and the planners. As vice-president for business and finance, he was also heavily involved in the university's own problems of budget and construction. Ellis, not incidentally, was a man now widely recognized as a dynamic exponent of carefully calculated community growth. He had received a number of local and national honors, among them the First Citizen awards of Seattle and of King County and national and state conservation awards. By 1970 he had been a leader for some years of Seattle's Forward Thrust (its president since 1966), the Washingtgon Planning Advisory Council, and the council of the National Municipal League, which had named him a Distinguished Citizen. By that time he was also a member of the National Water Commission, a member of the Urban Transportation Advisory Council of the U.S. Department of Transportation, and a trustee of the Ford Foundation. Ellis was a man much looked to, and soon he would be on center stage, as a regent, in a crucial decision about the course of future development nearer home.[9]

It was noteworthy that at the end of 1971 there had been a change in the office of secretary to the board. In December, Helen Hoagland retired from the position she had held since becoming an interim "assistant secretary" at the time of the University Properties lease signing in 1953. She had been, as secretary, something apart from traditional patterns. Occupying a position held in earlier years by such university pillars as Edmond Meany and Herbert Condon, she had come to it because, as administrative assistant to the university's presidents, she was at once capable, gracious, and knowledgeable in the realms of university administration. After 1953 her signature had been on the regents' minutes, the memorandums that flowed to board members, the downtown lease amendments, and university bonds. But she also remained in the president's office. By the time she retired, she had served five presidents— Sieg, Allen, Everest, Schmitz, and Odegaard. Her successor, Barbara (Baker) Zimmerman, was a 1949 university graduate—her B.A. in English after two years at Mount Holyoke—who, married and the mother of two daughters, had begun her university staff experience as a part-time secretary in the Office of University Committees. Mrs. Zimmerman knew the university well and was practiced in the kinds of staff support that her new position demanded. She was also one of those rarities, a third-generation Washingtonian.[10]

Project 2009 had gone through several phases by 1972. Scale models had succeeded scale models, each introducing rearrangements of the initial concepts—a graded plaza here, a tall building there. Essentially it was a matter of working with blocks to demonstrate overall relationships. But there were growing efforts to put the ideas into more exact architectural dimensions—

to make calculations of elevations and gradients, to do the basic engineering, and to prepare working drawings and perspectives, all looking to the next movement forward, the transformation of the block that was central to the whole downtown tract, the block occupied by the White-Henry-Stuart Building. The architectural firms were busy at the drawing boards, and Minoru Yamasaki was in the process of designing a tall office tower to go in the southeast corner of the White-Henry-Stuart site. As the months went by the planning did become firm, and the prospect for new construction was enlarged when University Properties reached preliminary understandings with the Seattle bank that might become the principal new tenant, the National Bank of Commerce.

The movement of Project 2009 from plan to proposal had been a progression. And a proposal by University Properties was, after all, just that, and subject to approval by the regents, although time was on the march. The regents had not been permitted to sit and await developments, for another proposal had come to them from the direction of the Olympic. This proposal was, in a way, the other side of the coin. The Olympic was having financial problems.

The problems had been in evidence before 1970 and they had been suggested to the regents, then and later, by representatives of the Seattle Olympic Hotel Company and its parent, Western International Hotels. Finally, in October 1971, the lessees had put before the regents a request for modification of the hotel lease. The modification, in addition to making adjustments in the financial arrangements, would cover a period of only ten years, cutting back the terminal date from 1994 to 1982.

The Olympic was still first among Seattle's hotels—still the "grande dame," as the newspapers called it—but the realities of the hotel business had changed. Large central-city hotels all across the country, faced by airport-motel competition and new transportation modes and habits, were having difficulties of varying degree. The older hotels were particularly vulnerable, and the Olympic was getting old. It needed further rehabilitation, and the lessees were still bound to maintain it as the leading hotel in Seattle. Seattle Olympic and Western International could show that the hotel income was scarcely sufficient to cover their inevitable maintenance costs and the percentage rentals owed the university. They asked relief. The request raised questions of economics, law, and public policy. To the regents it also raised the question of their obligations to lessees who, managing a property of such significance, were saying that the economic load was too heavy. An element in the consideration was that decision of the regents of 1966 to permit Western International to enlarge the old Benjamin Franklin Hotel. Where the Benjamin Franklin stood there had arisen the Washington Plaza Hotel, and the round tower of the Washington Plaza was now a part of the hotel scene.

For more than a year, while work with Project 2009 was proceeding on other fronts, consultations went on between the regents and university staff members on one hand and hotel lessee representatives on the other. Shefel-

man, Powell, and Ellis–Shefelman for the Metropolitan tract committee—
were heavily involved, as was Lynn P. Himmelman, chairman of the board
of Seattle Olympic. Much of the staff work was done by Conrad, who now
had the assistance of Professor Warren W. Etcheson, of the College of Business Administration, who developed economic data. Soon the regents brought
to the staff as special consultant an Olympia attorney, John S. Robinson,
who made analyses of alternatives as proposals and counterproposals shaped
an ultimate agreement. The agreement, finally drawn up on November 1,
1972, was approved by the regents on December 14, signed for the board by
Mort Frayn, as president, and for Seattle Olympic by Himmelman. In essence, Seattle Olympic would pay, over a term shortened to 1982, a minimum
annual rental that would be increased from $500,000 to $750,000 plus 25 percent of all gross room rentals above $3,200,000. The university's anticipated
income from the hotel would be reduced, for the ten years, by about $350,000
a year, from $1,230,000 to $880,000.[11]

As for Project 2009, it was inevitable that, with all the changes in mind,
questions about directions and choices should begin to be asked publicly.
Project 2009 had been moving the blocks around in 1972—an office tower
and a small theater where the Skinner Building was, a new hotel south of
Seneca Street with plazas and a galleria on the White-Henry-Stuart site, and
ramps, escalators, sky bridges, and underground walkways providing pedestrian connections. The ideas were exciting, but they also led to thoughts
about old issues. What was the university getting out of all this? Why not—
again that question—sell the property and put the proceeds into endowment?
In answer to the first question, Shefelman was quoted as saying that of about
$50,000,000 thus far received under the hotel and University Properties
leases, some $20,000,000 had gone to the university campus. (The university
not only had used Metropolitan tract income at the teaching hospital and
in retirement of the hospital bonds but had spent about $10,000,000 in ac-
quisition sites near the campus for new architecture, law, and oceanography
buildings and for other facilities including the new student services center,
Schmitz Hall.) As for selling, no one was sure that the university itself had
an unrestricted right to sell (legislative authority certainly was necessary),
or what a proper price would be ($50,000,000? $100,000,000?). Such matters
never reached the stage of serious discussions, but they hovered about. The
questions were those that the regents, or usually Conrad, were having to answer. They hovered because city and the state officials had an instinctive feeling that the Metropolitan Center was at a turning point.[12]

Questions that continued to be of some moment, however, were those related to university payments for city and county services to the tract and
those related to the amounts of leasehold property taxes. The overall answer
was that payments to local governments had amounted to about $2,084,000
over a period of seventeen years, but the courses of events needed separation
and clarification.

As for the governmental services, the history went back to 1956, when the legislature had authorized annual payments of not more than $60,000. Through 1971, direct payments to the city of Seattle had reached a total of of $980,000 (the payments were lowered to $45,000 from 1963 to 1966). By 1972 a special session of the legislature had replaced the 1956 ceiling by a new formula contained in a bill (H.B. 142, sponsored by the university itself) authorizing the university to pay for services in amounts not to exceed what would be payable as real and personal property taxes if such taxes were regularly levied. Thus for 1972 the university was paying $149,917 to the city and $63,287 to the county, the sums prorated from the effective date of the new law. For 1973, the university would pay to the city and county a total of $127,917.[13]

As for the leasehold property taxes, the question went to the terms of the University Properties lease with a background of court rulings from the days of the Metropolitan Building Company. Beginning in 1911 the State Supreme Court had handed down four decisions with regard to assessed valuations of the Metropolitan tract. These held, in brief, that the value of the leasehold for assessment purposes was the value of the leasehold less the rent reserved. When the University Properties lease was being developed in 1953, the university agreed to assume the obligation to pay any future property taxes imposed on the leasehold—such taxes to be deducted from University Properties rental payments—a device which, by reducing the tax risks of the lessee, gave the university more favorable lease terms while keeping control in the hands of the regents. By 1963, the county had begun to make regular assessments of the University Properties leasehold—assessments from which the city of Seattle would receive its proportionate shares—and the annual payments were being deducted by University Properties from its university rents. By 1973 these leasehold tax payments had reached a total of about $843,000.[14]

By summer of 1972, even before the Financial Center was completed, the city knew that the White-Henry-Stuart was targeted for replacement, probably by a forty-story tower flanked by a shopping galleria, and that the National Bank of Commerce might be the major tenant. There was a tendency to applaud, or at least to withhold judgment. The idea had drama. Such a development would give Seattle a central focus something like those in cities such as San Francisco, Minneapolis, and Houston. It would be a high-style development especially suited to Seattle's matchless site.[15]

But by autumn, and from the campus itself, there came an announcement of an entirely different kind. Charles Odegaard would be leaving the university presidency at the end of the 1972–73 academic year. There was more than a touch of drama in this, too, and not simply because even the regents were, as one of them said, "stunned." Odegaard's decision to resign had not been reached swiftly, nor was it a product of the pressures that had been focused on the presidency in recent years. He had simply decided it was time —after more than fourteen years—to give over the management of the university to a new executive. It was noteworthy that he had served longer than any other president. He had defined the university as no president since Suzzallo had been able to do. The historian had been a demanding administrator, absorbing detail, recognized instinctively on the campus and elsewhere as a man who spoke with eloquence both for the university and for the higher education of which it was a part. Odegaard's achievements included the enlargement of graduate training, the fulfillment of the objectives for the health sciences, the expansion of library and other facilities (the construction of a new Suzzallo Plaza was under way), all for a student body that now numbered about 34,000. But Odegaard's announcement of his impending retirement meant that the faculty and the regents would have to turn after so many years—and at a time when so many questions of finance and policy still abounded—to the task of finding a successor to a president of such stature. Nothing else, in the succeeding months, was of greater importance.

Among the regents of 1972–73, only Shefelman, who had headed that earlier search committee, had been serving when Odegaard was selected in 1958. Now the new search committee was under the chairmanship of Robert Philip, and by April 1973 the committee was ready to report. This it did at a meeting of April 28, and its recommendations were unanimously approved. The next university president would be John Hogness, who, although he had gone off to Washington, D.C., in the meantime, as president of the Institute of Medicine of the National Academy of Sciences, was well remembered both for his services to the Division of Health Sciences and for his handling of university affairs during his brief term as executive vice-president. There was wide satisfaction at the announcement of the choice. Since Hogness was expected to arrive October 1, the regents granted Odegaard a terminal leave and appointed an acting president to serve until then. The acting president was Philip Cartwright, who had been a steady and respected figure in the administrative councils. As events turned out, it was months before Hogness could disentangle himself from his Institute of Medicine obligations, and Cartwright continued to serve until April 1974.

None of this was related, even marginally, to developments at the Metropolitan tract. The regents, facing the paperwork and files of staff memorandums and recommendations that constituted their normal fare—faculty appointments, contracts for campus construction, amendments of policy and regulation, budget approvals—had also been engrossed with the presidential search. Shefelman and his Metropolitan tract committee were in touch with proceedings downtown and were kept informed by the regular reports from Conrad, who was increasingly divided between his campus and downtown activities. Shefelman and other regents had been present at the dedication of the Financial Center on February 15, 1973—a ceremony at which Dorothy Bullitt again was a guest and in which a copy of the Project 2009 folder was placed with other documents in the cornerstone. There had been a general sense of pleasure at the progress of Metropolitan modernization. It seemed time for the next step.

The step forward would be the project now formally proposed by University Properties in a letter from Ryan. The project came to the regents in the form of a covering resolution presented by Shefelman, for the Metropolitan tract committee, at a special meeting held May 5, 1973, in the university's Metropolitan Tract Office in the White-Henry-Stuart Building. Only the four Seattle regents attended the special meeting, for the general nature of the proposal had been examined fully by the board at earlier sessions, including the meeting of the week before at which the regents had elected Hogness to the presidency. The proposal contemplated demolition of the White-Henry-Stuart Building and its replacement by a $35,000,000 office building–shopping plaza complex in which the dominant element would be a tower to be called Commerce House—twenty-eight floors of offices rising from a 127-foot pedestal. The "Commerce" was drawn from the name of the tenant bank, the National Bank of Commerce.[16]

The tract committee's resolution recited the principal elements of the proposal. University Properties had submitted a "tentative" Commerce House design developed by Minoru Yamasaki and Associates in collaboration with Naramore, Bain, Brady and Johanson. There would be an underground pedestrian concourse—a "people-mover"—linking the retail plaza to parking on Sixth Avenue. Financing was adequate, and the necessary easements had been obtained. The action of the regents on May 5 was to give approval "subject to all the provisions of this Resolution." Demolition and construction were approved, as were University Properties' contracts with the architects. But the regents reserved final decisions. Advancement of the project was "with the understanding that both the schematics and final plans . . . and the contract for construction . . . will be subject to final approval by the Regents," and any necessary lease modifications were to be prepared "for submission to the Board of Regents for final approval."[17]

Final decisions and authorizations were in suspense, but at least the general character of the proposed development could be revealed. The announcement was made in news releases by the regents and by University Properties. The latter was a joint announcement by Ryan and by T. Robert Faragher, president and chief executive officer of the bank. Commerce House would be placed in the high, southeast corner of the White-Henry-Stuart block, where the Stuart Annex stood. The rest of the site—about 75 percent of it—would incorporate, in what was being called a "podium," two or more levels of small shops, specialty stores, restaurants, and travel and airlines offices. Over the shopping area would be a "two-acre park complete with landscaping, reflecting pools, seating clusters, a Japanese tea house, and additional food facilities." There would be an "underground conveyance" of some kind by which pedestrians could be moved—under Fifth Avenue and under the Skinner Building and the recently built Hilton Hotel—from Commerce House to a new seven-hundred-car parking garage east of Sixth Avenue (near the freeway) on the National Bank of Commerce property. Underground walkways might be constructed, later, to take pedestrians westward under the Cobb Building to the Palomar-site garage and to Third Avenue. The total rentable area would be 600,000 square feet. Of the 500,000 square feet in the tower, 200,000 would be occupied by the bank, which also would use 50,000 at the podium levels. Funds for construction of Commerce House would be advanced by University Properties, which would be reimbursed from future rental receipts, the $35,000,000 to be amortized over a thirty-year term by university deposits into the New Building Fund from general Metropolitan Center income.[18]

Such planning was impressive. Commerce House would not be as tall as the SeaFirst, but it would be a commanding structure in the downtown scene, a beacon above an attractive plaza that admitted light to the central district and was designed for people, not automobiles (although a sixty-car parking garage would be incorporated). The most striking aspect of the plan was the tower's design. The twenty-eight office levels would rise floor by floor above a stark-white, twelve-story pedestal that was smaller at the base than at the vertical elevation. The building would seem to be suspended above its foundation. Within the pedestal would go the lobby, the elevators, and the ramps or escalators to adjacent lower levels, but its smooth facings, curving up and out, would be unmarred by surface designs, hidden arches, or functional supports.

The name, Commerce House, was a name with an interesting flavor—even vaguely eighteenth-century. But Commerce House was a Yamasaki design, a Yamasaki looking to the twenty-first century. The design seemed to strike again the Yamasaki themes of simplicity and elegance. Faragher was quoted as saying: "The influence of Far Eastern architecture on Mr. Yamasaki's design is important to the bank and to Seattle as the city becomes more and more the gateway to the Orient." For that moment, in 1973, Seattle—at least that part of it that watched such matters—was more intrigued by the Commerce House design than disturbed by the prospect of losing the venerable White-Henry-Stuart. The moment soon passed.[19]

Nothing about the planning had been unduly precipitate. With the approval of the regents, University Properties had talked to the National Bank of Commerce in 1971 about the bank's possible occupancy of a building on the university property—on the Skinner site, perhaps, and thus closer to the garage and other structures owned by the bank between Sixth Avenue and the freeway. But no design for the Skinner site offered the room the bank needed, so the design teams then worked with various plans for a building where the White-Henry-Stuart stood, all this going forward in 1972. The original idea thus had grown considerably by 1973, but it had behind it more than a measure of careful deliberation. There lay ahead, nevertheless, a year of public review and criticism and public hearings by the board of regents before the Commerce House design would win final approval.

The Seattle newspapers covered thoroughly and commented favorably on the Commerce House announcement as it came from that special meeting of the regents on May 5. Three days later, however, the *Times* departed momentarily from the hymnal to deliver a mild rebuke to the regents for appearing to have violated the spirit of the state's open-meeting law. The *Times* was not unhappy with the project or the approval ("The new building . . . will be a handsome addition to the city's downtown skyline," it said), but it noted that the regents, while giving their approval in what was technically an open session, the public notices duly given, had acted in a meeting that precluded the possibility of "meaningful discussion." The law required public agencies to conduct their business "in a manner open to public scrutiny—and, if need be, to public challenge." [20]

Challenges were coming, but not of kinds that the regents could have handled just then. If their action seemed abrupt, the regents had not thought of it as such, much less as secret, for the planning had been proceeding for months, major elements explicitly exposed to public view, and the idea now was to get the proposal on the table so that open discussion and eventual final approval or disapproval could follow in train. The action of May 5 nevertheless had been a large one. The regents had indicated that they looked with favor on a plan that would transform a square block in the very center of the city, replacing the venerable White-Henry-Stuart with a new structure of striking contemporary design. The potential impact was somehow greater than the sum of the parts, and each part invited comment.

Involved in the situation, too, were additional elements to which the regents felt obliged to devote attention. One was a not-so-new movement, national in scope and with strong attachments in Seattle, to preserve or find new uses for the best of the old buildings of the nation's heritage, of which the White-Henry-Stuart certainly might be considered one. The other was the requirement that final approval of a project such as Commerce House be preceded by a statement of its environmental impact. The requirement in the Commerce House case was only implicit in 1973, but the impact-statement rules derived from the National Environmental Policy Act of 1969 and, in the state of Washington, from the 1971 State Environmental Policy Act for which implementation guidelines had been published in 1971 by the Washington State Department of Ecology. [21]

Whether or not it was surprising, the first comments critical of the Commerce House plan came from architects. Some were from members of the faculty of the university's own Department of Architecture and some were from other professionals. In letters to the newspapers they raised questions about the Commerce House design—the diminished base, the contrasts in heights between the building and the plaza, the general tone of the project and its "people-moving" concept. There was not a flood of such criticisms, but in the next several months they had not abated, and in August 1973, questions about alternatives were raised for the first time in organized form. The questions came from what was called the Seattle Chowder Society, an informal discussion group composed of architects, lawyers, and others concerned with the quality of life in Seattle. In a letter distributed to Mayor Wes Uhlman, the Seattle City Council, and the board of regents—a letter signed by sixteen members—the society suggested reconsideration of Commerce House planning and asked if it would not be better to combine a new tower with the old buildings, the "humanly scaled" buildings, rather than to place a "shopping-center-like" development at the city's center. The society also urged establishment of a "design zone" for the downtown area, a zone wherein building proposals would be subject automatically to rules for disclosure and public review. To an approach such as this, James M. Ryan, at least, felt compelled to respond, and he did so, with copies of his letter also going to the mayor, the council and the regents. Ryan noted that the various stages of Project 2009 up to and including Commerce House had been offered for inspection by the public at large and shown particularly to persons or organizations presumed to have immediate interest in them—to officials of the city and the state, to architects in Seattle and elsewhere, to members of the Allied Arts of Seattle, and to Seattle businessmen including, specifically, those whose shops on Fifth Avenue would be most directly affected. The Chowder Society had requested an environmental impact statement. Ryan said such a statement was being prepared.[22]

Whatever the currents then running, they were widening by 1974. The year was scarcely begun when two occurrences showed the trend. On January 18, the regents authorized the preparation of a "tentative draft of an environmental impact statement," this to be based on work already started by the university staff. There was to be wide distribution of the document, upon which there would be public hearings, prior to issuance of a final statement. Meanwhile, no demolition of the White-Henry-Stuart was to proceed. Almost immediately, the city's Landmarks Preservation Board entered the case.[23]

On February 13, 1974, the Landmarks Preservation Board, a twelve-member tribunal created by the city ordinance in May 1973, voted unanimously to "consider" creation of a landmark district on Fifth Avenue between University and Union streets, the block lined by the Skinner Building to the east and the White-Henry-Stuart annexes to the west. This was a proposal which, if brought to culmination, would prevent any demolition where the tower and the Fifth Avenue side of the plaza were to be placed, sending the whole Commerce House project back to the drawing boards, and possibly canceling it. There would have to be a public hearing within sixty days on the landmarks board's decision, and any prolonged delay of a final verdict on Commerce House was a delay that no one involved with the project cared to face. At the aesthetic level, postponement or abandonment of the Commerce House amounted to an adverse comment on the designs developed so carefully by Yamasaki and the associate architects in Naramore, Bain, Brady and Johanson. In the realm of economics, further delay invited serious troubles—rising costs (construction estimates appeared to have risen already to $37,-000,000) and the prospect that the National Bank of Commerce would have to drop its plans for a new central headquarters in the Metropolitan tract.[24]

The views of various public-interest groups—the views enunciated by the spokesmen—became very public in succeeding weeks. Arrayed with the Chowder Society in reflecting views critical of the Commerce House plan or with the Landmarks Preservation Board in concern for the White-Henry-Stuart's Fifth Avenue façade were groups such as Allied Arts, with a membership of about one thousand individuals and fifty organizations, and another called Choose an Effective City Council for Seattle City Government (the acronym, CHECC), which claimed two hundred members. There were others: the Friends of the [Pike Place] Market were concerned, the Metropolitan tract subcommittee of the environmental law committee of the Young Lawyers Section of the Seattle Bar Association was studying the legal background. Although there was some overlapping of membership among these organizations, they formed a substantial force. Supporting Commerce House—in principle, at least, and more specifically, undoubtedly, its validity as a planning concept—were the owners of neighboring businesses as well as the Downtown Seattle Development Association, successor to the Central Association, which claimed a membership of some six hundred businessmen, property owners, and developers.[25]

The Landmarks Preservation Board's potential interdiction soon was ended by the board itself. On April 16, 1974, the board, by a vote of 9 to 2, decided against creating a landmark district on Fifth Avenue. James Wilson, the assistant attorney general at the university, had told the regents in the beginning that the landmarks board had no jurisdiction. He said that the board, responsive to the city council, had no power to create a district on state property. But in the public hearing itself this opinion was not even mentioned (Ryan was quoted later as saying that he "wanted to win this one on its merits"), and the Commerce House idea simply prevailed in a board action that the newspapers said "cleared the way" for demolition of the old and construction of the new.* But it was not to be that easy. Three days after the landmarks board hearing, the regents were to release the draft of their environmental impact statement.[26]

In the events that were to follow, two men would be in the vortex. One, James M. Ryan, was already there. The other, James R. Ellis, would soon join him. They would represent divergent points of view on what should be done at the White-Henry-Stuart site, not as antagonists—they were, in fact, good friends—but as spokesmen for alternative concepts, Ryan for the Commerce House plan as it existed, Ellis for a variation of it.

Ryan had a depth of development experience unequaled in Seattle. All of the building and planning at the Metropolitan Center, before and after the

---

* There had been, during this period, mobilization of support both for the tower and for the historic-district idea. The Seattle *Argus* had carried advertisements by a new group calling itself the Committee to Save White-Henry-Stuart, these in the form of petitions upon which supporters (who were also invited to send donations) could choose the message they wished to send the regents, urging them either to vote against razing the building, and direct its rehabilitation, or to vote to require a redesign of the Commerce House proposal "so as to preserve the 5th Avenue exterior of White-Henry-Stuart *without any alterations whatsoever* [emphasis in the advertisement] in a form that exemplifies architectural excellence and sensitivity to existing design."

inception of Project 2009, had proceeded under his direction. For just over twenty years he had devoted himself totally to the university tract in ways that not only reflected his natural impulses but also resulted from the conditions of a University Properties lease requiring him to function in a special relationship to the university—to make proposals, to ask approvals, frequently to take risks in the solution of funding problems—while keeping in touch with every other commercial development in the city and its environs. Ryan had stood always in the center, but actively, imaginatively, and with a willingness to back his judgment. Ryan's judgment was respected. He was a founder of the Central Association, a member of the board of its successor, a past president of the Building Owners and Managers Association, long a moving figure in the Chamber of Commerce. He had been a director and member of the steering committee of the Seattle fair. He had been a consultant on more than seventy-five office building and merchandise-center construction projects, including several in South America for the U.S. government. In sponsoring Project 2009 he had tried to make planning both flexible and visible. The planning still was flexible, for University Properties had in its files some twenty potential modifications of the basic tower-plaza design—one that would put a three-hundred-room hotel over the plaza. But Ryan was eager to press ahead, and he was trying to do so. Wind tunnel tests of a model of the Yamasaki tower, centered in a scaled replica of downtown Seattle, were being conducted in the spring of 1974 by a Buffalo, New York, research firm. First work at the White-Henry-Stuart site was scheduled for July. Ryan felt strongly that if the central theme was rejected—if all planning was to begin again—the ramifications, economic and otherwise, would be incalculable.[27]

In the passing months, however, James Ellis had come to regard the Commerce House–plaza plan with a somewhat more critical eye. Ellis had watched with a personal interest the evolution, in Project 2009, of the Commerce House proposal, getting glimpses of the kinds of planning he had espoused. Ellis had been one of the regents who approved Commerce House in May 1973. But it was Ellis, too, who urged most strongly the resolution of January 1974, authorizing preparation of the draft environmental impact statement. Between May and January, Ellis had made it a point to talk to the architects and others who were critical of Commerce House and to the leaders of the organizations seeking to preserve as much as possible of the White-Henry-Stuart. Ellis had not been disturbed at first by the Yamasaki design. He had expected, as he recalled later, a building of the "pristine" character that was Yamasaki's mark. But his view of this had changed somewhat, too, and he made a trip to the Midwest to talk to Yamasaki and to inspect other buildings for which Yamasaki had been the architect. But beyond the design, two aspects of the case worried Ellis. He had become increasingly concerned with the possible implications of recent environmental law—the extent, that is, to which the law applied to central-city developments such as Commerce House. Furthermore, Ellis was by nature sympathetic to preservation. He was disposed—committed, actually—to listen to those who thought that the old White-

Henry-Stuart, or part of it, at least, should be saved. A long-time fighter for urban planning and civic grace, Ellis came to believe that some modification of the primary plan might serve both. Ellis moved in those months to such a position. By mid-1974, he was standing alone among the regents in advocating an alternative plan that involved an act of preservation.[28]

The draft environmental impact statement was ready on April 19, 1974. On that day and a week later the newspapers published legal notices by the regents announcing that copies of the document were available for inspection at the university's Metropolitan Tract Office in the White-Henry-Stuart, that written comments were invited within thirty days of first publication, and that a public hearing would be held by the regents on the evening of May 20 to receive additional statements or written materials. The notices described the nature of the Commerce House proposal (noting that the "most visible" impact was the demolition of the White-Henry-Stuart) and said that nineteen alternatives were presented for consideration. The statement was distributed that week in scores of copies to libraries, to federal, state, county, and city offices, and to fifteen or so of the groups, committees, or leagues that had been most prominent in the widening public discussions.[29]

The draft document had been prepared under the direction of John S. Robinson, the Olympia attorney who had been brought to Seattle by the regents as a consultant in the 1972 Olympic lease modification. He had been retained to work with the impact statement because of his experience with environmental law. Assisted by William Daniel, of Naramore, Bain, Brady and Johanson, Robinson had to put into manageable form a vast amount of information ranging from the history of the tract and its buildings to the topographical, engineering, and design considerations involved in the proposed Commerce House plan. The draft became a publication of 241 pages plus 30 pages of introductory material and 60 of tables, photographs, perspective drawings, and maps showing the relationship of the Metropolitan Center to other elements of the downtown scene. Some of the peculiar difficulties surrounding an effort to prepare a statement for a project such as Commerce House were noted by Robinson in a brief foreword:

To anyone who has closely studied the evolution of Environmental Impact Statements, it is clear that these documents are now required in a much wider variety of situations than could ever have been contemplated by the lawmakers who enacted the original Environmental Policy Act. The rules for the content of the Statement were probably first formulated with the thought that they would be applied to dams, highways, bridges, nuclear submarine bases—large federal projects whose impact on the natural environment would be substantial, irrevocable, permanent, and very often severely detrimental. When one attempts to apply identical rules to a project such as that with which the present Statement is concerned—the demolition of an urban office building and the construction of another in its place—one may discover that they do not precisely fit. The result is continuing uncertainty as to just how the rules should properly be applied.[30]

In short, an impact statement for a Commerce House had to be worked up under rules governing a statement for something else. But a statement was required by law. That had been the position of the regents. This statement had to be exceptionally thorough and complete to withstand successfully a legal challenge—a challenge which opponents of Commerce House had indicated their intention to mount. In the mid-1970s, the rules for the content of such statements were still in flux, spelled out in individual court decisions rather than in legislative guidelines. Robinson, in preparing the Commerce House draft, was exceedingly conscious of the many instances in which judicial interpretations of the National Environmental Policy Act (upon which the Washington act was based) had postponed or halted projects because of alleged deficiencies or omissions in the impact statements prepared for them. Delays in the Commerce House proposal resulting from protracted litigation over the contents of the statement might become the longest and most damaging delays of all. With such considerations behind it, the draft statement as it appeared laid out for public inspection (usually with illustrative charts or tables) pro-and-con treatments of the potential implications, within the central-urban context, of such matters as air quality, wind conditions, noise impact, shadow patterns of the tall buildings, visibility factors, energy consumption, social-cultural-historical elements, pedestrian and automobile traffic, and potential uses of space. Copies were examined with deep interest, and the text, despite the care with which it had been prepared, was subjected immediately to challenging questions. The regents' hearing would put these into the record.[31]

The May 20 hearing was the first at which proponents and opponents of Commerce House had an opportunity to come before the regents to state their positions. Shefelman presided at the evening meeting, which went on, finally, until 11 o'clock, and with him were Ellis, Powell, Neupert, and Frayn. Thirty-two speakers were heard, each within stipulated time limits, five minutes for individuals, eight for representatives of organizations. Robinson, Ryan, and Perry Johanson were asked to present first the basic considerations: Robinson discussed the impact statement's scope and organization, Ryan the policies and objectives of University Properties as lessee, and Johanson the architectural and engineering concepts embodied in Commerce House. After that the speakers who had asked time were called in turn to the microphone to express their views. Proponents were for the most part businessmen sympathetic to Commerce House (the newspapers said that proponents predominated in the audience), and opponents included spokesmen for organizations already identified: Allied Arts, CHECC, the Young Lawyers' committee, the Committee to Save the White-Henry-Stuart. There were only touches of acrimony. Before the hearing adjourned Shefelman announced that since written comments had been few, and since some speakers obviously had wished to say more, the regents would receive any further communications submitted within seven days.[32]

Throughout June and into July 1974, questions simmered. Early in July, however, Allied Arts, CHECC, and other principal organizations had narrowed their counterproposals to four alternatives that they asked the regents to consider, these ranging from a remodeling of the White-Henry-Stuart to the design of a tower without the pedestal to make it "more compatible with the surroundings." On July 8 the regents held a further "information review" hearing during a special meeting on the campus. Critics of the project had asserted that the nineteen alternatives incorporated into the draft impact statement still had not covered the field and that some of the alternatives outlined had been given insufficient consideration. It was to such objections that the regents now directed their attention while Robinson and others were working into July toward publication of a final statement. Additions to the list of alternatives, or modifications of those already presented, meant the compilation of much new information. The task was complicated by the fact that some of the public comments had not come in by the May deadline (some not until late in June), although all were accepted.* Allied Arts had been prompt in its response, however. On May 22 the trustees had approved a statement, transmitted to the regents, saying that the Commerce House design would "deaden the entire area" and urging further attention to two of the draft statement's alternatives: (1) modernization of the White-Henry-Stuart with a tower in the interior court or (2) modernization of the annexes, demolition of the older elements, and construction of a Commerce House and low-level retail structure on Fourth Avenue. Yet as Robinson and his associates examined the proposed new alternatives they could see them really only as modifications of certain of the original ones, deserving of consideration, with all applicable data, but only to be isolated as specific responses to the four clearly identifiable public proposals. As the final environmental statement was shaped up, these were incorporated into what was called the VH Series, "Alternatives Developed in Further Detail." One called for the remodeling of the White-Henry-Stuart with a galleria and additional rentable space, another for the insertion of the tower in the center of the White-Henry-Stuart block, and still another for a redesign of the tower to eliminate the pedestal base, the site remaining at Fourth Avenue and University Street. But it was the fourth, VH3 in the series, that soon emerged as the proposal upon which the Commerce House issue—to accept the University Properties plan or to modify it—would be decided.[33]

The final environmental impact statement was published July 22, 1974, again announced in the regents' legal notices but distributed this time not only to offices and agencies that had received the draft statement but also to more than thirty persons who had reacted strongly to the draft. The new

---

* On June 10, 1974, CHECC sent a letter to the Board of Public Works and to the Superintendent of Buildings asking those offices, before they issued any demolition or street-use permits, to publish and circulate for thirty days their own environmental impact statement "disclosing the impacts on the Central Business District created by the proposed actions, and in particular the impacts of ultimate development of this property and the University Tract as a whole" (copy of letter sent to regents, University Metropolitan Tract Office file).

document, of 444 pages plus the expanded introductory and illustrative materials, was organized into eight sections and six appendixes. Special attention was given to the "new" (VH Series) alternatives. One of the appendixes was devoted to responses by the university staff, on behalf of the regents, to key questions raised at the May and July hearings. A full transcript of the May 20 hearing was included. Added later, on July 30, was a report by Touche Ross and Company, the accounting firm, containing estimated projections of rental receipts and income under each of the alternatives on which attention was now focused.[34]

The long-awaited meeting for decision, a special meeting, was scheduled by the regents for August 2, 1974, eleven days after publication of the final statement. If the interval seemed short, time itself was becoming a costly commodity. The date already was past on which, under the original expectations, the first phases of the project were to begin, and Ryan was estimating that additional delays might cost $1,000,000 in rising costs and interest charges. There had been a year of public examination of the basic plan, three months of opportunity for public response, first to the draft statement and, in that summer, to the final statement and the alternatives expanded therein. And the thinking had been, at least, narrowed. No one had ever thought that the White-Henry-Stuart should simply be further rehabilitated and preserved, but responsible segments of the community thought that parts were worth preserving. The irony was that as discussion developed, the possibility of preservation came to be focused, not on the White-Henry-Stuart originals, the buildings erected between 1909 and 1915, but on the annexes built in the 1920s—low-rise elements of small architectural distinction but considered by some as essential to the ambience of Fifth Avenue.

It may be wondered whether, if Yamasaki's design of Commerce House had been of a less challenging kind, the tempest would have taken the course it did. But the reactions to the pedestal had been cumulative and sustained. Whereas the IBM Building had been generally welcomed as a logical and elegantly restrained "highest and best use" of the site occupied by the antique Olympic Garage, Commerce House would be regarded, both by preservationists and by those with other views of modern planning needs, as either a violation of an early twentieth-century vision that had been unique to Seattle or a rather cold use of a precious site that needed not just "people-movers" but warmth. Objections to the design flowed into and merged with feelings that a decision of such magnitude—a decision that would cast the future of the central city far beyond the year 2009—should rest on something more substantial than a novel architectural concept, even Yamasaki's.

It was to be expected that the issue would attract attention elsewhere, and by late July 1974, on the eve of the regents' meeting, it had done so. Wolf Von Eckhardt, of the Washington (D.C.) *Post*, an architectural critic of repute (he held the AIA Critics' Medal), discussed in a biting article both the Yamasaki design and its relation to modern thinking about what should be done to make cities inviting and comfortable. The article was republished by the Seattle newspapers. Von Eckhardt, referring to the "pointless point on which the pin-striped 'Commerce House' is to be perched," said in part:

That free-form perch, veneered in beige marble and gracelessly curving outward in the manner of Detroit's outdated automobile styling, is higher than the surrounding buildings on Seattle's Fifth Avenue and Union Street.

Eventually this shocker is to pop out of the 10-acre, University-owned tract as a three-acre, double-decked "retail plaza," one of those slick, presumably Muzak-doused suburban concrete oases with potted plants, look-alike store fronts, fountains, chain restaurants, a skating rink, and lots and lots of pavement.

In suburbia, these plaza cliches replace pastures or potato fields. In Seattle, the Yamasaki complex will replace the turn-of-the-century White-Henry-Stuart Building, which is less than a great historic landmark, to be sure, but something at least equally precious: The last single block left in downtown Seattle where pleasantly scaled buildings add up to an attractive and elegent shopping street.[35]

The comment was harsh. But Yamasaki had already discussed his thoughts about the design in a letter to the regents, and the statement by the Allied Arts trustees on May 22 had provided the opportunity. Because the Allied Arts analysis had seemed particularly penetrating, the regents had asked it be referred to Yamasaki for response. Yamasaki's reply was not defensive. He said, simply, that he was designing buildings for "one of the most beautiful cities in the United States." As for the pedestal, "The Tower with its upwardly curved base" would create a space which would complement the plaza diagonally opposite (the IBM space). He said that the space provided at the corner of Fifth and University would be a "complete and delightful surprise as you walk along the street, either north or south." There would be room for trees as well as pedestrians.[36]

In the weeks before the August 2 meeting James Ellis had been busy with the calculations of the aesthetic and economic balances presented by the fourth new alternative, VH3, by which the old Fifth Avenue façade would be incorporated into the new galleria design. Its realization would mean that the Commerce House tower would be at Fourth Avenue, not Fifth. The cost would be greater, perhaps $44,000,000 according to the final impact statement, and with a lowered projection of income. Ellis, however, had asked for more figures, and it was in response to his questions that the Touche Ross and Company projections had been prepared late in July as an impact statement addendum. The projections had to take into account not merely the differences in revenues from office and commercial space but also the complicated management maneuvers by which tenant occupancy would be handled during demolition and construction. The Touche Ross analysis thus had been made on what was called alternative VH3A. But Ellis's view had become firm. He was convinced that additional costs in the beginning would be more than compensated by the income gains over the long term to 2009 and beyond. He was willing to take his stand on that premise.[37]

There was a strange final matching of plans in those last moments. On August 1, Seattle got a look, in the press, at what Ellis had been advocating. A ground plan of the VH3 alternative had been prepared by Naramore, Bain at Ellis's request, and this showed how Commerce House would look with the tower moved to Fourth Avenue and University Street and the White and Stuart annexes kept in place, converted to a modernized block-long retail section, and linked to the new construction by a glass-enclosed galleria. But University Properties also had a version of its own. As a "compromise" with the Ellis plan, University Properties said, it would be possible to build north of the Commerce House tower a six- or seven-story building containing hotel rooms—complementing the Olympic's facilities—a building that would not require a shift in the tower site. This building would not incorporate the old annexes, but would place on Union Street and Fifth Avenue expanded accommodations above the new shopping levels.[38]

That was the position as the regents prepared to meet. The special meeting had been called for 2 P.M. in the Regents Room of the Administration Building on the university campus, but that small room would not accommodate the seventy or more persons who attended. Within minutes, the meeting had been adjourned to an auditorium in Kane Hall, one of the new buildings across the brick-paved Suzzallo plaza, and there the meeting was called to order by Jack Neupert, the Spokane regent who was president of the board for 1974–75. In the audience were university people, President Hogness and the principal administrators, the chairman of the faculty senate, and the presidents of the alumni association and the associated students organization. With them were persons who had strong interests in the Commerce House issue, including those who would express personal views, pro and con, or speak for their organizations. The regents—Neupert, Flennaugh, Ellis, Frayn, Shefelman, Philip, and Powell—would make the final decision.

The discussion, when it came, was on two motions, one by Shefelman, the other by Ellis. Shefelman had first moved that the board adopt the final impact statement, but deferred to Ellis, who asked that the motion be put aside until the board had acted on the Commerce House proposal. Shefelman then spoke to the main point, citing in a comprehensive statement both the weight of the decision the regents would make and the pressure that time was imposing on it:

Probably the most important thing to emphasize today is the urgent necessity to make a decision on this matter. The Commerce House proposal has now been before the public for well over a year. Perhaps no building ever proposed for Seattle has been so thoroughly analyzed. . . . The Board of Regents . . . has complied with the State Environmental Policy Act down to the smallest detail. . . . The proposed project has been analyzed by every public agency which has anything to do with it. No public agency has disapproved it. The Board has encouraged everyone interested in the project to communicate his views. Many have done so. . . . No one with any interest in the project itself or in the future of downtown can now claim that he has not had a chance to be heard. . . . We must now move ahead.[39]

When he had finished, Shefelman moved, Powell seconding, that the board accept the proposal of University Properties "for the demolition of the White-Henry-Stuart Building and the construction on the site thereof of the Commerce House development substantially as set forth in the Final Environment Impact Statement." The motion stipulated that the immediate construction should include the tower but only those parts of the podium needed for "related banking facilities." The initial cost to the university was not to exceed $30,500,000, and the balance of the construction, estimated to cost $6,200,000, would be subject to later approvals.[40]

When Shefelman had concluded, Ellis asked to speak to the motion and to offer, as a substitute, a motion of his own. Ellis knew that his position had no support among his fellow regents—all of them his friends, with some of whom he had worked since 1965. He spoke, nevertheless, to review his personal studies of the Commerce House plan and the alternatives and to urge consideration of the VH3, now the VH3A, compromise. When Ellis offered his substitute motion, there was no second until Neupert, as president, offered his second to get the proposal before the meeting. Ellis's motion, of 450 words tracing the history of the regents' movement toward resolution of the case, concluded by saying that the board "states its preference for the development of Commerce House substantially in the form of VH3B as same has been presented to this meeting, provided that University Properties, Inc., can secure adequate financing therefor." University Properties—that is, Ryan, and the university's vice-president for business and finance, Conrad—would be directed to prepare plans for financing and construction, to submit these with necessary lease amendments to the board, and "to give such tenant notices as required to permit such development to proceed at the earliest practicable date."[41]

There remained the public statements, including statements by each of the regents, and the questionings. The proceeding took more than two hours. Twelve speakers addressed the regents that afternoon. Some had been heard before, at the May 20 hearing or on other occasions: Ryan, Johanson, and Robert F. Buck, a senior vice-president of the National Bank of Commerce; James B. Douglas, president of Northgate Centers, Incorporated; Lloyd Nordstrom, of the Nordstrom Company; Professor Victor Steinbrueck, of the university's Department of Architecture; and Armen Odabashian, a leader of the Committee to Save the White-Henry-Stuart. Others were those whose interest in the issue was no less: Robert Block, representing Allied Arts; Laurence G. Fry, president of Littler's, Inc.; Professor Val Laigo, of Seattle University, who supported the University Properties proposal; Pamela Bradburn, chairman of CHECC (a leader of CHECC's activities from the beginning but this time "speaking as a private citizen"); and Roger Stevens, chairman of the board of University Properties, who had come west again for this climactic hearing.

The speakers were heard, and at the end the regents themselves, in turn, stated their positions. The board had agreed that Ellis, as the proposer of the substitute motion, should be permitted to make the final statement, but Ellis had heard his colleagues and he spoke only briefly. When Neupert called for the vote on the substitute motion, the count was 6 to 1 against. Shefelman's motion to approve the University Properties proposal was passed by the same margin. When Shefelman moved approval of the final impact statement, Powell again seconded and the motion passed unanimously. The special meeting was adjourned at 5:45 P.M.[42]

Commerce House had been approved, after all those months, as it had been described in Ryan's letter of proposal that the regents had before them in May 1973. But in that time much had been learned, clarified, put in writing, and tested in the court of public reaction. That had been Ellis's contribution. There was coming, however, the long-expected legal challenge that introduced yet another uncertainty.

In legal notices of August 9 the regents announced their decision, setting out the Shefelman motion in full and saying, "Any action to set aside, enjoin, review, or otherwise challenge such action on the grounds of noncompliance with the provisions [of the State Environmental Policy Act] shall be commenced within sixty days or be barred." Four days later such an action was filed in King County Superior Court by four critics of Commerce House who, as members of a group calling itself CITY (Citizens Interested in the Transfusion of Yesteryear) named as defendants in their suit the regents, the city of Seattle, and the city's Superintendent of Buildings, who was in the process of issuing permits for the White-Henry-Stuart demolition. CITY charged that the regents' approval of the Commerce House resolution of May 5, 1973, amounted in reality to final approval before the impact statements had been prepared; that insufficient attention had been given to environmental considerations as mandated by the State Environmental Policy Act; that the impact statement was deficient in several respects; and that not enough attention had been given to alternatives, particularly to the Ellis alternative. Almost concurrently CHECC came into the case again by asking the Board of Public Works (as it had asked once before) to deny to University Properties the street-use permits that were essential to the White-Henry-Stuart demolition, this as the plaintiffs in the suit sought an injunction forbidding the regents to allow demolition to proceed.[43]

August 20 and 21, 1974, were the crucial days for proponents and opponents. It was then that the request for injunction was heard in King County Superior Court, and it was recognized on all sides that the granting of the injunction, carrying the implication of successive appeals and delays, might simply end the Commerce House project. On August 21, however, Judge Erle Horswill denied the request for injunction, and on that day the demolition of the White-Henry-Stuart was begun at the University Street side of the Stuart Annex.[44]

The suit itself continued, although by the time it eventually reached the State Supreme Court, the Stuart Annex had long since vanished and the base of the tower was already in place. On January 6, 1976, the Supreme

Court, speaking through Justice Robert C. Finley, unanimously held that the action had been improperly instituted and was, therefore, a nullity.[45]

What meanings were to be found in the whole proceeding? The long public review of plans and alternatives had been costly in dollars, some of the dollars the university's. University Properties estimated later, without quarreling at all with the propriety of the procedures, that the postponement of construction, coming at a time when costs were rising at a rate of 1 percent a month, had added $5,000,000 to the price of the building, to which might be added another $5,000,000 in losses of rental revenue. Yet the process of review, if trying and sometimes bitter, had been healthy. If some or many were dissatisfied with the outcome, there also were some or many of these who found themselves, later, not unhappy with the result. Shefelman had said, when the regents approached final decision, that "perhaps no other building proposed for Seattle had been so thoroughly analyzed." He need not have said "perhaps." No other such project had been so scrutinized, and this was the product of Ellis's persistent study of the choices. Ellis had been a missionary, devoting countless weeks to the Commerce House issues and willing to stand alone, finally, in disagreement with his colleagues and friends. It was largely because of Ellis that the proceedings took the course they did, and it was because they took such a course that, when the legal actions came, the regents' decision was sustained. When the regents' decision had been made, Ellis supported it wholly. Quite soon, as the details of the Commerce House development were being worked out, it was Ellis who fought for a concept that went beyond mere "people-moving" and into making the underground concourse a people-attracting place.

The demolition of the White-Henry-Stuart was accomplished in the scheduled phases, first the Stuart Annex, then the Stuart. The White-Henry and the White Annex were left standing and occupied until the Commerce House tower was in place. Thus the new construction only gradually erased the old. When the wrecking ball attacked the Stuart Annex on August 21, 1974, with University Street blocked to automobile traffic, it was at the noon hour and the lunchtime crowds were watching. There may have been an intuitive feeling among the watchers that the moment was a significant one in Seattle's history. But it would have been too much to expect that, even among those who most cherished the old buildings, there could be more than indistinct impressions of the men for whom the buildings were named: C. F. White, the lumberman who had first staked J. F. Douglas's old Metropolitan dream; Horace Henry, the railroad builder whose art collection was housed in a university building that also carried his name; and E. A. Stuart, the North Carolina-Indiana-Kansas-Texas merchandising impresario who had built a worldwide Carnation organization from a few experimental cans of condensed milk. The wrecking ball simply went to work, and down came walls that had been there since before most of the spectators could remember.

The Stuart Annex had vanished within days, and heavy machinery was making the deep excavation where the new tower was to stand. By February 1975 the concrete "pad" had been put in place. A month later the pouring of the twelve-story pedestal had begun, the concrete 12 feet thick at the base and 6 feet thick to the fourth-"floor" level where the walls were flaring outward. Not until September 1975 would the steel frames of the office floors begin to rise above the pedestal. Before that, changes of other kinds occurred.

As far as the regents were concerned, it was not enough simply to let events take their course. They still had before them approval of University Properties proposals for completion of the Commerce House plaza, in addition to general monitoring of the costs of construction of the whole program. Thus by October 1974, a decision had been made to make Ernest Conrad the university's full-time representative at the Metropolitan Center Office in the White Building. On October 1, 1974, Conrad was appointed vice-president for Metropolitan tract affairs.

No one knew more than Conrad about tract affairs. No one at the university had been more consistently in touch with them. For almost twenty years, while regents came and departed and university administrations changed— from the Washington Building negotiations of the 1950s through the years after 1963 when, as vice-president for business and finance, he was the university's chief financial officer—Conrad had been at that point where lessee proposals were reviewed and financial data assembled and reports prepared, including the regents' reports to the legislature. Conrad had not only a university experience that went back to President Sieg's time but an instinctive feeling for university relations, external and internal, especially with the faculty. He had a talent for problem solving. He was a thoroughly knowledgeable spokesman for the university. He not only was busy with various community affairs but was active in professional organizations, regional and national. It was inevitable that, after Everest's retirement, Conrad should become, among other things, the staff counselor to the regents and their Metropolitan tract committees, because the controls that were given the board under the tract and hotel leases made financial analysis imperative. Now, with Commerce House coming along, Conrad was to give full time to the task.

Conrad's successor as vice-president for business and finance was James F. Ryan, who had been with the university since 1965 and, since 1969, its vice-president for planning and budgeting. A 1950 graduate of Marquette University, Ryan earlier had served as supervisor of research for the Washington State Tax Commission, executive secretary of the Tax Advisory Council, and chief budget analyst for the Washington State Central Budget Agency.

But Commerce House would not much longer be called that, and another change in name was coming. The directors of the National Bank of Commerce had been seeking for many months a new name for the bank—a name both distinctive and suggestive of the Northwest—for city after city across the country had a National Bank of Something. The board had suggested and the stockholders had approved the name Rainier National Bank. A change had been anticipated in the bank's leasing of Commerce House, for a lease clause gave the bank an option to ask a new name for its headquarters if the bank's name was indeed changed. Approval of this, however, as of other things, rested in the board of regents, and a great many variations of the "Rainier" theme—"square," "plaza," "place," "block"—had been discussed in meetings involving bank representatives, Ryan, and members of the Metropolitan tract committee. By December 20, 1974, the recommendations were ready for the regents' action. On that day the block occupied by the White-Henry-Stuart became Rainier Square, and the office building on it would be the Rainier Bank Tower.[46]

And with respect to names, University Properties had been itself increasingly uncomfortable with the name it bore. From 1953, when Roger Stevens had organized the corporation that would assume the tract lease, the name had been subject to misunderstanding. The thought in the beginning had been, not unreasonably, to emphasize the nature of the corporation as lessee of a historic university property, to underline the university connection. But even after two decades it had not become unmistakably clear, even in Seattle, that University Properties, Incorporated, was a lessee and not a special-status management arm of the university's board of regents. Long before 1975, University Properties had been planning to act, and in May 1975 it did so. By amendment of its articles of incorporation, University Properties, Incorporated, became UNICO Properties, Incorporated. At the same time, Ryan was made chairman of the board, a position held since 1953 by Roger Stevens. Donald Covey, who had come to the corporation twenty years before as a young management assistant, succeeded Ryan as president.

As for the regents themselves, a somewhat emotional time was approaching in that spring of 1975. Early in the year, with the Stuart Annex excavation barely finished, the historical implications were on Robert Philip's mind. In a memorandum to Shefelman, still chairman of the Metropolitan tract committee, Philip suggested that the board consider establishing, perhaps in the Rainier Square plaza, when that was finished, a "historical display commemorating the first site of the University of Washington." The idea was for the future, but it was a sound one, for by 1975 there were generations of Washington people—and countless thousands of recent Seattle arrivals—who did not know that the Metropolitan tract had once been the university's campus and that Rainier Bank Tower would be rising near the site of the old first building. Soon thereafter, in any case, the regents approved the schematic drawings for the "low-rise portion" of Rainier Square, and with Conrad's help they were keeping an eye on the cost estimates.[47]

Yet a moment with historical overtones of a more personal nature was arriving. At the annual reorganization of the board of regents in March 1975, Robert Flennaugh, the first black regent, became the first black president of the board. And at that meeting the regents said farewell to Harold Shefelman, who was leaving the board after eighteen years. The symbols affected everyone who sat with the regents that day.

Flennaugh came to the presidency in the normal rotation of board seniority, but the young professional, only eleven years out of dental school, had been through all the pressures that had surrounded the regents since 1970—on the campus, in the prolonged dispute over Commerce House—and had given to the board the judgments of a man sensitive to community problems. But what could be said of Shefelman? Or, rather, how? The regents tried. They adopted a resolution praising Shefelman for the "wise counsel" he had brought to the board, but this was after they and others in the Regents Room had stood to express their feelings in spontaneous applause.[48]

Harold Shefelman's service as a regent was not the longest. The terms of Winlock Miller and Thomas Balmer were longer. But such record-keeping was immaterial. Shefelman's imprint on the university was an accumulation, a history of busy participation in university affairs, small and large, from the time he became a young law lecturer in 1930. As a regent, he had served in his turns as president of the board and had been so long the chairman of the Metropolitan tract committee that his work spanned all of the new developments downtown, from the Washington Building to Rainier Square. He possessed, above all, an expansive view of the university itself, a view that was with him whether he was helping to select a new president, or mobilizing an architectural commission to keep an eye on university building, or speaking for the university at the legislature or elsewhere. Shefelman, the incurable participant, had been a regent committed. The applause on his last day acknowledged it.

The new regent, Shefelman's successor in May 1975, was Mary Gates, a graduate of the university, wife of Seattle attorney William H. Gates and mother of three children, a woman busy with community affairs—United Way, the Children's Orthopedic Hospital—and a director of the National Bank of Washington and the Unigard Insurance Company. Mary Gates, the appointee of Governor Daniel Evans, was the fifth woman regent, and she was plunged immediately into the committee work of a board which, with Flennaugh president and Powell vice-president, also included Ellis, Frayn, Neupert, and Philip.[49]

At the Metropolitan tract the demolition and construction proceeded at Rainier Square in 1975, and by autumn, while the steel frames of the Rainier Bank Tower were rising, the regents authorized the demolition of the rest of the White-Henry-Stuart. This was to be accomplished by 1977, and soon the walls of the Stuart Building were coming down. By March 1976, when the nation was warming up to its Bicentennial celebration and the Rainier Bank Tower was about to be given its white cap, UNICO Properties conducted a noontime ceremony on University Street in which a red, white, and blue "Bicentennial beam" was raised to the top of the tower to signal its completion.

Rainier Square remained to be finished, but certain questions also remained in 1976. There was the Cobb Building, the last survivor of the original "master plan," and the Skinner, which still had within it the Fifth Avenue Theater with that ornate domed ceiling that had been called the most authentic Chinese interior in the Western world. What would be done there? And what with the Olympic, which was under lease to 1982?

Project 2009 still provided a framework. Studies of the Olympic were already in process, and they included analyses of Seattle's historical growth and projections for the future. But the year 2009 was beginning to seem not so far away.

CHAPTER 13

Toward the New Century

Rainier Square was finished in 1979. The Rainier Bank Tower, by now a familiar image, had been joined at its base by the multilevel shopping plaza and linked to its automobile parking garage on Sixth Avenue by an underground pedestrian concourse that widened under Fifth Avenue to accommodate shops and restaurants. The concourse had been made a gallery of history. On the illuminated walls of the long hallway were displayed bits of Metropolitan memorabilia and enlarged photographs from the earlier days of Seattle and of the University of Washington. The gallery was in the spirit of Regent Robert Philip's 1975 suggestion that Rainier Square contain a place dedicated to the story of the tract as a university property, but UNICO Properties had modified the theme and expanded the concourse displays to include panels illustrating Seattle's commercial and industrial growth. A walk through the concourse was a walk through Seattle's past.

Five years had slipped by since that climactic meeting of 1974 in which the regents had authorized construction of what then was called Commerce House. Final plans and bids on the remaining construction had been approved in 1976. But much besides building had been going on in that five-year span. With change so strikingly evident at Seattle's commercial center, old questions had come to the surface again—questions about building costs, rental income, taxation and payments for city services, management policy, future plans. But this time, from studies of kinds not attempted before, answers were coming. The future of the Olympic was not quite revealed, but the UNICO Properties lease, the "main lease," had been extended five years to October 31, 2014. Long-range planning was going forward, even though the program no longer could be called Project 2009.

In the mid-1970s, the state of affairs at the Metropolitan tract was reflected, in large part, in the status of the leases—the "main lease" on the one hand and the Seattle Olympic Hotel Company's lease on the other. The question of the future of the Olympic was pressing. The regents of 1972, after negotiations lasting more than a year, had entered that agreement with Seattle Olympic (the terms now guaranteed by Western International Hotels, Seattle Olympic's parent company), in which, for appropriate adjustments in rental arrangements, the lease on the hotel was cut back from 1994 to 1982. Thus, long before 1982, fundamental decisions about the hotel would have to be made. By early 1975, studies had been initiated. After a call for proposals from professional consultants, the regents had selected, as prime contractor, Peat, Marwick, Mitchell and Company, the national accounting and management consulting firm with offices in Seattle. The study team also would include representatives of the Richardson Associates, a Seattle architectural and engineering firm handling physical planning and cost estimates, and Harry Weese and Associates, of Chicago, an organization experienced in urban design and restoration projects including, specifically, hotels. The team was asked to identify and describe—without making recommendations—the restoration or new-construction alternatives that would seem appropriate and reasonable, before 1982, for a hotel of the Olympic's age, location, and historical and sentimental significance.[1]

But though the hotel lease had been shortened, the UNICO lease had been extended. In the UNICO case, as in that of the hotel, the reasons were financial, but the pressures were of an entirely different magnitude. In little more than a decade the new construction accomplished and planned under the UNICO lease had been of impressive proportions. The IBM Building of 1964 and the Financial Center of 1972 were followed by the Rainier Bank Tower and its associated podium. The costs represented many millions of dollars borrowed at interest by UNICO and advanced to cover construction until the university, as the lease provided, could make reimbursement by authorizing transfers from its tract rental income into the New Building Fund. The IBM Building, which finally cost $8,415,000, was financed by a prepayment of $8,000,000 in rent to be amortized in twenty-five years. But the costs of the Financial Center and Rainier Square were larger—in the second case, far larger—than anticipated. The Financial Center had cost $16,990,000, an increase of $1,490,000 over the original estimate. The costs of Rainier Square had risen during the months of the environmental impact hearings and legal actions (and because of later strike-related delays), much as James M. Ryan had predicted they would. In 1974, construction of the tower and the Rainier Bank part of the podium had been authorized at a cost not to exceed $30,500,000. When, in 1976, the regents approved the final construction, they specified that the total cost to the university of Rainier Square—the costs of the tower and the podium, all ultimately to be reimbursed through the New Building Fund—should not exceed $42,718,000. Ryan estimated that the sixteen-month delay in construction had meant losses to UNICO and to the university of $10,000,000 in rising building costs and unrealizable rental income.[2]

These were the circumstances underlying the decision of the regents, in 1976, to extend the UNICO lease to 2014. When the cost of the Financial Center climbed above the estimate, the regents had authorized accelerated deposits into the New Building Fund of up to $1,250,000. By late 1974, when the regents finally had before them the supplemental lease agreements implementing their decision to proceed with the Rainier Bank Tower, they approved these and at the same time authorized UNICO to increase its leasehold mortgage to a maximum of $62,500,000, which was the amount that UNICO had borrowed and would borrow to cover the remaining costs of the

IBM Building and the additional obligations incurred in building the Financial Center and Rainier Square. UNICO could borrow, but it had to wait for reimbursement from the New Building Fund, the authorizations under the regents' control. On both sides—on the university's and UNICO's—there had to be time for rental income to pay for it all.[3]

The solution was complex, and it came slowly. For the initial period of Rainier construction UNICO had arranged intermediate financing, and the regents in their early calculations had agreed, by way of easing the pressure on UNICO—particularly with regard to the financing costs UNICO was incurring—to allow UNICO to anticipate a $1,000,000-a-year reduction in rental payments by the last five years of the leasehold, from 2005 through 2009. By 1974 it was becoming clear that a leasehold to 2009 probably provided not enough time to amortize borrowings at the $62,500,000 level. Two factors then had to be considered. It might become necessary for UNICO to ask for a lease extension, because UNICO's New York banks could not, under New York law, execute a mortgage for a term longer than 75 percent of the leasehold period after the buildings were in place—that is, not more than twenty-four of the thirty-three years remaining after 1976–77. Yet the lease could not be extended beyond the year 2014, because that was believed to be the outer limit of the sixty-year leasing authority granted by the legislature of 1953. The limits left scant room for comfort.

An extended lease was a possibility—perhaps more than a possibility—and the regents in 1974 had left the door open a bit. As they approved the Rainier Square lease adjustments they also agreed that UNICO might have the extension if this became necessary and if UNICO would waive its rent reduction of $1,000,000 a year from 2005 through 2009. For two years the lease extension remained an option while Rainier Square construction delays sliced months off the leasehold balance. But on December 17, 1976, the regents, at UNICO's request, approved the bargain of 1974. The lease was extended to October 31, 2014. UNICO sacrificed its future savings in rent, assuring the university of $5,000,000 in additional income after 2005. In the agreements as again revised, the regents established new schedules of payments to the building fund and of rental income to be retained for campus use. The lease extension moved to 2014 the date on which UNICO's parking garage on the former Palomar site, south of the post office, would become the property of the university.[4]

A most interesting and unexpected result of the considerations of the lease extension was the subsequent clarification of the regents' power to execute leases of up to sixty years. It was realized during the discussions—suddenly, apparently, because there had been no occasion to consider the matter before—that the language of the 1953 act was perplexingly ambiguous. Had the 1953 legislature given the regents the power to award single, one-time leases of not more than sixty years? Or had the legislature conferred a continuing and renewable authority which permitted the regents to execute such new leases at any time? Whatever the relevance of the questions to the UNICO case, the answers obviously would be important when the regents approached any new leasing of the Olympic. The doubt had to be cleared away, and soon it was, by the legislature in its first 1974 extraordinary session, at the university's suggestion. The act of that year (chapter 174, *Laws of 1974*) authorized the regents "to lease said land, or any part thereof or any improvement thereon," for "not more than sixty years beyond the effective date of this 1974 act." Thus the authorization of 1953, permitting leasing to 2014, had been rolled forward to 2034. By 1977 even this act had been amended to extend the authority sixty years beyond December 31, 1980, to December 31, 2040. Such a period would embrace, it was hoped, any possible arrangements that might be made for the future of the hotel.[5]

The years from 1974 to 1977 were the years of questioning and of efforts to get, or to begin to get, a perspective on tract operations. With the university being pressed harder and harder financially, members of the faculty tended to look with jaundiced eyes on "downtown" projects requiring seemingly interminable funding. But there was a wide public interest, too. Because the future of the Olympic was in suspense, concern was growing about what might happen to the "grande dame." The concern also extended to the Cobb Building, the Skinner, and the Fifth Avenue Theater, all regarded as significant elements of Seattle's cultural heritage.

A stocktaking was inevitable. It began about the time the regents' report to the legislature of 1977 showed that for the tract year ending October 31, 1975, no part of the university's rental income had been reserved for campus purposes. There were calls for explanation, and pointed reports and comments in the Seattle press. When new regents came to the board, they had questions. So did the legislature itself. Soon there would be hearings by the Senate Ways and Means Committee.

Until early in 1977 the regents, except for Mary Gates, who had succeeded Harold Shefelman, were those who had sat through the whole course of the Commerce House–Rainier Square development period. Robert Flennaugh was president for 1975–76, and he was followed by George V. Powell. The other board members included James R. Ellis, Jack Neupert, Mort Frayn, Philip, and Gates. Upon Shefelman's departure, Ellis had become chairman of the Metropolitan tract committee in May 1975. He continued as chairman until he himself left the board, when Philip succeeded to the chairmanship. Ernest Conrad, as vice-president for Metropolitan tract affairs, was directing the efforts to develop background data while maintaining liaison with lessees. Staff support activities were heavily involving James F. Ryan, Conrad's successor as vice-president for business and finance, and—because so many of the questions before the regents were as much legal as financial in nature— James B. Wilson, senior assistant attorney general. Staff consultants were Professor Warren Etcheson, whose knowledge of tract affairs was available to faculty committees, and John Robinson, the Olympia attorney who had been called in when the Commerce House impact statements were in preparation.

For all concerned—not least for members of the Metropolitan tract committee—it was a time of meetings, hearings, staff reporting, and quick changes of scene. The hotel issue was very much alive. In September 1975, Peat, Marwick, Mitchell and Company had submitted to the regents a voluminous draft report which set out twenty-six alternatives for the hotel's future. A month later, copies having been distributed for review, the regents held a public hearing on the report. Ellis presided at the evening meeting, which was held in the Georgian Room of the Olympic and was attended by about thirty persons. But much also was in suspense or in the process of change. Payments for government services to the tract—fire and police protection, street lighting, and street and sewer repair—were higher, as were the leasehold taxes paid by UNICO and covered, as the lease provided, by deductions from UNICO's rental payments to the university. These adjustments, which required legislative authority, had been encouraged by the university itself in recognition of the demands of the modernized and expanded property. There was continuing consideration of questions of landmark preservation, the university denying the city's right to apply its landmarks ordinance to buildings on state-owned land.[6] Soon there would be a development that no one had foreseen—one that threatened to establish a landmark of another kind.

During that time came the decision that brought future reckonings. The regents approved that schedule of increased payments to the New Building Fund to reduce at a more rapid rate the debt being incurred, through UNICO's advances, for the new construction. They also scheduled annual reserves for the campus. But for that first year, the lease year 1975, the campus funding showed, as it turned out, a negative balance—presumably a "loss"—of $202,635. The episode deserves reconstruction because it triggered the inquiries that led to the most comprehensive analyses of tract management and policy ever conducted.

The regents' decision was based on the knowledge—Conrad having supplied the figures—that the flow of rental income to the campus exceeded, at that juncture, the possibilities of expenditure for campus purposes. In the twenty years after 1955 the revenues from the "main lease" and from the hotel and its garage had totaled $67,477,000. Of this sum, $23,075,000—more than $1,000,000 a year—had been and was being devoted to developments at the university campus. Tract income had paid off the $5,000,000 bond issue on the teaching hospital. Beyond this, however, tract funds had been used for the acquisition of off-campus properties rather than for additional construction. The income had made possible the purchase of lands on which had been erected new buildings such as those for the School of Law and the College of Architecture and Urban Planning. Tract funds had purchased older buildings near the campus for housing university activities. The policy was rooted in history and precedent, and in 1975 the university's tract rental accounts contained funds for which no such uses were imminent. In approving an accelerated payment to the tract's New Building Fund the regents were making it possible for the university to realize sooner the larger increments of income in later years, for while UNICO was financing the construction, the buildings would be the university's and the ultimate beneficiary would be the university, not UNICO. This commitment was made, however, as the regents were to find, just as certain large bills, including larger assessments for government services and leasehold taxes, were coming. Until 1971 the university's payments for services had been no more than $60,000, although under recent legislation, supported by the university itself, the payments had leaped up, to almost $590,000 by 1974.* Cost rises were converging from elsewhere as well, including the costs in professional fees for the hotel studies and for the preparation and publication of environmental impact statements. In the lease year 1975 the tract operating costs rose from $844,880 to $1,010,-641, more than half of this, $635,641, in payments for government services and leasehold taxes. In that year the amount reinvested in the tract through the New Building Fund was $2,714,080, the second highest in history.[7]

The regents' actions with respect to the "downtown" funding had been discretionary and totally within the concept of the lease, which put the university in control of developments. There was no "loss" of income, but rather a new apportionment of it. With nothing left over for campus purposes, however, the situation demanded explanation. It was easy for an observer to think that the university's returns from its property were insufficient or that the interests of UNICO, the lessee, had weighed too heavily in the balance.

Explanations would have to come, but the mood of the time is revealed in the regents' further decision in 1976 on the seemingly simple matter of the width of the pedestrian concourse. That "people-mover" under the Skinner Building and Fifth Avenue had been visualized initially as little more than a lighted and carpeted tunnel, 13 feet wide and about 380 feet long, connecting Rainier Square to the Rainier Bank's property east of Sixth Ave-

---

* From 1956 to 1971 the university had continued to make its voluntary payments of up to $60,000 a year for services provided by the city of Seattle. By 1963, the county had instituted assessments of UNICO's leasehold interest, these leasehold tax payments by UNICO being assumed by the university, as the lease provided, as deductions from rent. The whole question of leasehold taxation was made subject to review, however, when a State Supreme Court decision of 1970, in *Pier 67, Inc.* [Edgewater Inn] v. *King County*, reversed all prior decisions on the status of tax-exempt land. So complex were the issues that the legislature of 1971 declared a three-year moratorium while studies were conducted by the State Legislative Council. In this period, in the legislative session of 1971 and the special session of 1972, the university sponsored the introduction of bills that would have authorized substantial increases in the university's payments for government services. It was the 1973 legislature that changed the system, however, with passage of an act (chap. 137, *Laws of 1973*) providing for payment by the university of an in-lieu excise tax of 14 percent of gross rental income from the tract leaseholds. By 1976, an amendment had placed the tax at 12 percent of contract rent, the payments going to the Department of Revenue, which would make disbursements to local governments. Whereas the university's payments to city and county had totaled only $2,094,731 by 1973, the new and combined payments through the Department of Revenue were $589,284 for 1974 and $635,641 for 1975.

nue, where a parking garage provided spaces for three hundred automobiles.* Rainier's lease with UNICO gave the bank an annual rent reduction of $100,000 for as long as such parking accommodations were available to tract tenants and their clients. UNICO also had worked out a separate financial arrangement with the Hilton Hotel, adjacent to the tract, for use of another three hundred spaces in the hotel garage. All necessary easements had been acquired, and the concourse plan seemed firmly established. But by early 1976 the regents were discussing with UNICO a proposed widening of the concourse at the Rainier Square end, a plan to make the concourse a corridor of access to below-ground shops and eating places, an underground mall with its own attractions for shoppers. The idea had come from Ellis, and it was Ellis, the regent who had stood alone when the board voted to proceed with Rainier Square, who now stood alone, again, for the wider concourse. This time Ellis won.

The wider concourse would be costly, perhaps adding $250,000 to construction estimates. The regents were thoroughly conscious of costs, as was James M. Ryan. No one could quite imagine a corridor having the appeal Ellis saw there. But Ellis, so long devoted to the idea of designing cities with room for people, believed that even such an underground area should provide interests for the people who came downtown—space, but not "sterile" space, as he put it later. By May 1976 the Metropolitan tract committee had decided to recommend that $200,000 be earmarked for the widening of the concourse under Fifth Avenue to 55 feet. By June, when the regents authorized an increase in the costs of Rainier Square to $42,718,000, the sum was to incorporate the costs of the widening. The final figure, approved on September 17, 1976, was $224,684. When at last the concourse was functioning, by 1978, Ellis had been proved right. The shops and the restaurants, and the historical displays, had made the underground corridor one of the bright spots in the downtown area. And by April 1978, to assure the university's future rights there, UNICO assigned to the university its concourse easements in perpetuity and its parking rights for the balance of the lease term.[8]

But in the autumn of 1976 many questions were unresolved. One was whether there would be a revision of the city's landmarks preservation ordinance in which the university had an interest. The Seattle City Council had declined earlier in the year to adopt the recommendation of its Landmarks Preservation Board that the Cobb Building be given a landmark designation, but a proposed revision of the ordinance might make possible a test of the city's power to assign landmark status to the Olympic Hotel and to the Skinner Building and the Fifth Avenue Theater. Then, even as the staff was assembling the data for the regent's report to the 1977 legislature, that unexpected development occurred. In October, the Internal Revenue Service

---

* The Rainier Bank's property, encompassing most of the block between Union and University streets and a small triangle east of Seventh Avenue, was called the "Rajah tract" and was so identified in contemporary reports. The bank had purchased the property from the Rajah Investment Company, which specialized in automobile parking developments and which had acquired the various pieces in the 1960s.

instituted a detailed examination of the mechanisms of the tract lease to determine whether rents paid to the university, a tax-exempt educational institution, represented income unrelated to the purpose for which exemption was granted—that is, debt-financed business income subject to federal income tax. The years under study were 1974 and 1975. The issue went to the heart of the tract lease—to the provisions for financing buildings and improvements through the New Building Fund—for if the rental income was held to be business income, it would be taxable just as ordinary corporate income was taxable. The university staff began to assemble information and the Seattle office of the Internal Revenue Service began to prepare a "Technical Advice Memorandum," a request for a final determination, which would go to the national office with statements of the IRS and university positions. The procedure would take months. The possible implications for the university were of kinds the regents hesitated to contemplate.[9]

It was in that December of 1976 that the regents approved the extension of UNICO's lease to 2014. The Metropolitan tract committee, Ellis still the chairman, had recommended this. In the elections of November, the winner of the governor's race had been Dixy Lee Ray, formerly a marine biologist member of the university faculty, who would become Washington's first woman chief executive. Changes in the membership of the board of regents were certain. The terms of Powell and Ellis were expiring. Flennaugh and Neupert had been appointed to new terms by Governor Evans in March 1976, but they had not been confirmed by the senate. Four appointments would be made by the new governor.

It was to be expected, in the legislative year 1977, that the broad question of the university's need for financial support would be touched, however glancingly, by the questions that had arisen about the Metropolitan tract, upon which so much attention had been focused. The regents who came to the board that year were sharing responsibility for the direction of a major educational institution, but they—as had the regents they joined and so many regents before them—were also accepting responsibility for the management of that "downtown" property with its New Building Fund, its new buildings, and its tax, government-services, and landmarks problems. The questions the new regents had were the questions they brought with them upon appointment.

The four regents were Taul Watanabe of Bellevue, Dr. J. Hans Lehmann and Gordon Culp of Seattle, and Robert D. Larrabee of Clarkston. Watanabe was the first, in January, and Larrabee the fourth, in August. Not solely because the board was changing in composition, but certainly in part because of that, the search for perspectives on tract operations was about to begin. The experience of the new members covered a wide and interesting spectrum.

Larrabee, the grandson of Idaho pioneers, was prominent in business, banking, and civic affairs in his small southeastern Washington community near the Idaho border. He was owner and operator of a funeral home and of a cattle and wheat ranch. For his public services he had been given several awards.[10]

Culp was an attorney specializing in utilities and business law. A graduate of the university's Law School (J.D., 1952), he was senior partner of his Seattle firm and a man whose advice had been sought frequently by state and national committees and commissions, among them the National Science Foundation's Advisory Committee on Energy Facility Siting, the U.S. Public Land Law Review Commission, and the U.S. Senate Subcommittee on Territories and Insular Affairs when that body was drafting the Alaska and Hawaii statehood bills.[11]

Lehmann was the physician member of the board, a specialist in internal medicine and cardiology who had been a member of the clinical faculty of the university's School of Medicine since 1950 and a clinical professor since 1963. Lehmann had been born in Germany and trained in universities in Germany and Italy, but he had fled to the United States in 1935 as a refugee from the racial persecutions that eventually sent members of his family to Nazi concentration camps. After establishing his practice in Seattle, he had been a cofounder of the Ballard Community Hospital and, apart from his professional involvements, was a member of the board of the Seattle Symphony and an officer or trustee of other cultural and educational programs.[12]

Watanabe was a railroad executive and economist whose outlook was, because of his heritage and personal experience, international. A native of Salem, Oregon, Watanabe already was a graduate of Willamette University and living in Seattle when, after Pearl Harbor, he was interned with other Japanese-Americans in a detention camp at Puyallup, Washington. By simple persistence even as an internee, Watanabe gained permission to continue his schooling, and in 1943 he won his J.D. degree at the University of Denver. Persistence and ingenuity soon took him farther. He was a founder, in Los Angeles, of the nation's first Japanese-American bank, then president of the Los Angeles Harbor Commission and a member of the city's Human Rights Commission. While the Japanese economy was moving into high production in the decades after World War II, Watanabe became a figure in international trade. When he returned to Seattle in 1969, as vice-president of the Burlington Northern Railroad and a director of the Burlington Northern Airfreight Company, Watanabe was for a time a consultant to the Port of Seattle and a member of the State Oceanographic Commission, where a fellow member was the future Governor Ray. Watanabe had been a trustee of his alma mater, Willamette University. As Watanabe became a regent he also was appointed chairman of the Governor's Board of Economic Advisers, a position in which he was close to the processes of state financing and economic planning.[13]

Many currents were running in 1977. There would come in the autumn what would be called a "probe" of the tract in hearings conducted by the

Senate Ways and Means Committee. But thoughts about the Olympic were germinating meanwhile in the wake of the Peat, Marwick-Richardson-Weese reports. At the request of the regents the Seattle Olympic Hotel Company produced a plan, this calling for complete refurbishment of the hotel with many of the rooms enlarged and the total reduced from 764 to 560. Soon another proposal was under study. This would entail use of property to the south of the tract, the half block adjacent to the Olympic Garage and occupied in part by the elderly Hungerford Hotel. The idea was to build in what was being called the "Hungerford block" a combination hotel and office tower that would augment both the accommodations of the Olympic and the office space available in the banking and business sector of Fourth Avenue. There would have to be another acquisition of off-tract property—by UNICO, as the long-term lessee—and UNICO was ready to proceed. A draft environmental impact statement was prepared early in 1977 and a public hearing held on May 31, but by the time the final statement was published in June the hotel-tower idea had faded. UNICO and Western Hotels joined in recommending that the property be used only for a new office tower, UNICO obtaining purchase options from four separate owners. Such a proposal was approved by the regents when they held an August meeting at the university's marine laboratories at Friday Harbor, but the "Hungerford block" idea soon was dropped, and UNICO disposed of the interests it had acquired in the site.[14]

In ways that were difficult to comprehend in their entirety, issues of policy with regard to the tract's status as a public property were being tested. At their simplest levels, the questions concerned the university's cash returns from its holdings—the returns on the "investment," the amounts of money available annually for campus purposes. The hearings before the senate committee would be devoted principally to such matters. The larger question, the question for the next century, was how far a lessee, UNICO, should be permitted to broaden the base of its leasehold to improve the university's investment in the future. Implicit in any proposal to permit a lessee to acquire and manage property outside the tract was a relaxation of the lease clause prohibiting it. There was also the matter of the expansion of the tract—the matter that had brought a protest from Norton Clapp twenty years before. Clapp, who in 1957 had opposed the university's acquisition of additional land for the Washington Building, was among those opposing the regents' decision on the "Hungerford block" in 1977. On issues of that kind the answers lay more in the realm of community consensus than within ordinary property management guidelines. As far as the off-tract tower idea was concerned, consensus ultimately weighed against it.[15]

By the time Larrabee became a regent in August 1977, the "new" board was assembled: Frayn was president, and the others were Larrabee, Culp, Lehmann, Watanabe, Philip, and Gates. Philip was chairman of the Metropolitan tract committee. Conrad, nearing retirement, had moved to a slightly, but only slightly, lower level of involvement, while James F. Ryan was assuming a larger measure of responsibility for staff support. Thus Philip and Ryan were the principal spokesmen for the university when the Senate Ways and Means Committee held its hearings on the tract in October of that year.

The senate committee hearings did not actually constitute a "probe" of tract management and policy. They were preceded by statements that the committee intended to find out why the university's rental income seemed less than adequate, and they gave focus to the curiosity about tract finances that had arisen in the legislative session earlier in the year. By that time it was known that the rent retained for campus purposes for 1976 was only $55,098, which seemed an absurdly small gain following the presumed "loss" of $202,635 in 1975. Watanabe himself was quoted in the press as saying that the $23,000,000 accumulated for campus use since 1955 appeared to be something short of a return that might be expected from a property of such value. When the committee hearing began on October 7, 1977, Philip testified at length in a prepared statement, covering again the terms of the UNICO lease and the financial dispositions that had been authorized by the regents for the construction of tract buildings, the support of the health sciences bond issue, and the acquisition of lands and buildings needed for campus expansion. The university's Ryan, following, pointed out that the $23,000,000 received by the university as cash in hand was only a third of the total return, since more than $44,000,000 had been put back into the tract to assure the larger rental income later. From the university representatives the committee also received as a background document a history of the tract leasings to which was appended a table showing an estimate of "net spendable income" expected to be generated through the year 2014. The total was $153,984,000, the average per year, $4,052,000.[16]

The inquiry by the senate committee remained open that autumn of 1977, with further hearings or requests for information possible. But what the regents were realizing that they themselves wanted—in part for the senate committee, but rather more for their own guidance—was an independent and professionally competent assessment of the university's record of management of the tract over the years. Earlier, in connection with the hotel studies, the regents of 1976 had commissioned Keith Riely, of the Seattle real estate appraisal firm of Shorett and Riely, to prepare an appraisal of the land occupied by the Olympic Hotel and the Olympic Garage. (In May 1977, Riely had reported the hotel land, assuming it "vacant and unoccupied," worth $4,150,000, the garage land $1,725,000.) By the time the Metropolitan tract committee met on October 14, 1977—Philip the chairman, the members Watanabe and Culp—the thought was occurring to the regents that a similar appraisal of the whole tract, land and buildings, might be useful, the appraisal perhaps accompanied by a study of the rates of income return on the property from the 1953 past to the 2014 future. The idea took hold. The board approved it and opened the invitation for proposals as wide as possible in order to find a firm that had the proper credentials and also had no previous contact with the tract. By the spring of 1978 the search for rate-of-return analysts was under way. So, too, was a search for a firm to help the regents solve the puzzle of the Olympic. Little more than four years remained until the Seattle Olympic lease on the hotel would expire in October 1982.[17]

The issues on the line in the spring of 1978 need not be underscored for dramatic effect. The whole course of the tract's development to that year was up for confirmation or reevaluation. The Internal Revenue Service was continuing its exhaustive examination of the university's position as lessor to determine a possible tax liability. Pressure was rising for positive action toward solution of the hotel dilemma, and the landmarks issue was very much alive. When the city's Landmarks Preservation Board voted in April to assign landmark status to the Skinner Building and the Fifth Avenue Theater therein, the university response was a King County Superior Court suit for injunction and for a declaratory judgment denying the city's right to exercise such authority over state-owned property. Amid all this, the regents were looking for a consultant firm competent to approach the largest question of all: were the leasing paths the university was following the best paths that might have been chosen?[18]

The firm selected to perform the rate-of-return study was Bowes and Company, of Denver, one of two finalist respondents to a request for proposals developed by Philip and his Metropolitan tract committee with the assistance and approval of the Management Services Division of the state's Office of Financial Management. The Bowes firm—a family firm of a father and three sons—was new to the Seattle scene and sound in experience. The senior and president, Eugene G. Bowes, was a real estate appraiser and property management counselor who had been working with projects throughout the West since 1937. The assignment was detailed and explicit, but it could be summarized rather simply. The Bowes company was to evaluate the university's financial performance as lessor, in the tract and hotel leases, to October 1977. It was also to project the expectations of performance under those leases, financially, to the expiration of the hotel lease in 1982 and the UNICO lease in 2014. Bowes estimated completion of the reports by September or October 1978, the cost to be $97,000. The proposal was approved by the regents on May 12.[19]

On the question of the Olympic, the Peat, Marwick-Richardson-Weese report had suggested twenty-six alternatives for remodeling or reconstruction, selecting six for detailed financial analysis. The options were narrowed, but no more than that. The regents had tested the "Hungerford block" waters and found them cold, and the regents themselves could not, in the short time remaining, work through the other alternatives one by one. The solution they came to was the selection of a firm to manage the search for qualified hotel companies with ideas about the hotel and interest in leasing it after 1982. The firm the regents chose to help them was the Jack N. Hodgson Company, of Seattle. By July 1978, the search for prospective lessees was proceeding.[20]

The Hodgson Company was local, but this, as it would not have been in the Bowes case, was an advantage. Hodgson was not to make a study but to become the regents' agent in the hunt for qualified proposers. Hodgson was a graduate of Dartmouth and Stanford whose career included real estate investment and economic analysis positions in Milwaukee and Los Angeles and five years as a development officer for Western International. Since 1972, when he established his own firm, he had been a consultant on dozens of hotel projects from Hawaii to New York, three of them involving hotels of historic interest. Hodgson's community activities included membership on the Puget Sound Land Use Committee.

Proposals for the hotel were to be received by the regents until March 1, 1979. Meanwhile, work was begun on a new environmental impact statement. This statement would not be limited to analysis of the impact of a single proposal. It would display, instead, the probable impacts of four alternatives ranging from doing nothing at all—thus condemning the hotel to early demise—to replacing the old structure with a new "convention" hotel of perhaps nine hundred rooms. The Hodgson Company, soliciting inquiries, soon was placing advertisements in national publications. The notice in the *Wall Street Journal* was reminiscent of 1952, when the "main lease" had been up for proposals. Its text, in part, stated:

The Board of Regents of the University of Washington, acting for the State of Washington as owner of the subject property, has issued a Request for Lease Proposals to a selected list of hotel operators and developers seeking a new lessee to rehabilitate the 766-room hotel or to rebuild a new high-quality hotel of from 450 to 900 rooms on the present 55,000 sq. ft. site in downtown Seattle. . . . Proposals are due March 1, 1979. Information is available from . . . the Regents' consultants on this project. . . .[21]

While the regents—and Seattle—waited for the ideas that might clarify the future of the Olympic, other tensions suddenly fell away. In September 1978, the Internal Revenue Service ruled that the university had no income tax liability. In November, the report of Bowes and Company confirmed fully the wisdom of the leasing course the regents had adopted in 1953, the nature of the lease terms developed then, and the quality of the management of the tract thereunder. In each instance, questions of the most fundamental character had been examined by agencies completely outside the university. In neither instance had fault been found.

The Internal Revenue Service decision came in a five-page memorandum from the national office ending with two simple conclusions. Amounts received by the university were (1) excluded from unrelated business tax computations as defined by the IRS code, and (2) "not characterized as debt-financed income under Section 514." It was Philip, as chairman of the Metropolitan tract committee, who announced the news to the regents in a memorandum of October 2. "It is a pleasure to bring you some good news," he wrote. "This morning's mail brought the enclosed material from the Internal Revenue

Service. . . . This ruling should reassure the current members of the Board as to the soundness of our leases with respect to Federal tax liability. The ruling will be especially satisfying to those former Regents who worked so long and hard on our leases, not only as to the economic return to the University, but also on the difficult and unique tax consequences."[22]

The Bowes analyses were presented to the regents on November 15, the data contained in three large "volumes." Volume 3 was devoted to summaries and conclusions. The report arrived in time to permit volume 3 to be incorporated as an appendix to the regents' biennial report to the legislature that December—an answer, two years later, to questions first raised in the 1977 session.

The Bowes study incorporated estimates of the market value of the tract lands and buildings at periodic intervals after 1954 and projections of these to 2014. Corrections were made for diminishing indebtedness and increased obsolescence. All such calculations and projections were intended to get answers to the old questions: Would the university have been better off financially if the regents of 1953 had sold the tract and invested the proceeds? Would it have been preferable to write a "net lease" contract with an independent management firm allowing the university to anticipate a "recapture" of the 1953 value of the improvements over a period of twenty years? Or was, in fact, the 1953 lease the best option?

The calculations were at length, and hypothetical, necessarily, with regard to the sale and "net lease" alternatives. The answer nevertheless was unequivocal. The course the regents chose in 1953—the lease with the university's firm participation in the decisions—had been, and was proving to be, the proper one. The tabulations told the story. Whereas the university had received a return for campus purposes of only $23,900,000 (beyond tract reinvestments) by 1977, this net would rise to $400,800,000 over the full sixty years of the lease term, and the net earnings and increases in the value of the property would total $595,800,000 by 2014. The annual average gain would be $9,930,000. The sale of the property would have produced, on the other hand, with prudent investment over the sixty years, not more than $234,200,000 in net earnings and increases in value, the gains less than $4,000,000 a year. The net lease option was not even close.

The value of the tract in 1954—the market value of the land and improvements—was placed by Bowes at $26,940,000. By 1977, this had risen to $102,780,000. In 2014, the value would be $221,900,000. The "rate of return" for the balance of the UNICO lease—thirty-seven years—would be 12.275 percent, the rate for the full sixty years, 7.675 percent.

The Bowes conclusions were cast in simple statements, all figures aside. The third option, the lease as of 1953, was the proper one:

1. It will produce more net dollars in the long-term than would the other options. . . .
2. It promised to satisfy, and it has satisfied, the objective of The University that the Tract be further improved in its commercial standing and prestige, to benefit the City of Seattle and its central areas.

The lessees, Bowes thought, had been well chosen:

The choice of basic Lessees . . . was good. In large measure, they have represented the University of Washington in its Tract relations with Seattle's central commercial, civic, and cultural interests.

The basic Lessees have brought important immediate capital dollars and financing credibility to the Tract, together with specialized management, maintenance, rehabilitation, and development skills. . . . These promise to continue in UNICO properties, and perhaps through lease year 1982 in the Olympic properties.[23]

The Bowes judgment was in. Could the regents of 1953, who had signed a thirty-five-year lease with Roger Stevens and University Properties, have visualized the lease extended to sixty years with a cumulative earnings–property value approaching $600,000,000? Not likely. In any case, 1982 and the decisions about the Olympic were drawing nearer and UNICO was deep in studies of what to do about the Fifth Avenue Theater. There was much to be decided in 1979.

The basic decisions did come, although implementation was for the future. The Fifth Avenue, soon listed by the National Register of Historical Places, would be anticipating new life as a center for the performing arts. As for the Olympic, the deadline was pressing, and considering the magnitude of the hotel project and the intensity of public interest surrounding it, the movement toward decision flowed with considerable smoothness, although a second call for proposals became necessary. By the time this happened, Watanabe had succeeded Mary Gates as president of the regents, Philip continuing as chairman of the Metropolitan tract committee. But three years before the expiration of the Olympic lease a new course was established. The Olympic would be restored, reoriented, and improved in accommodation and service. The instrument of the transformation would be a development team composed of a Canadian firm, Four Seasons, Limited, of Toronto, and the Urban Investment and Development Company, a wholly owned subsidiary of the Aetna Life and Casualty Company. Seattle's Naramore, Bain, Brady and Johanson would provide architectural services.

In January 1979, while the regents awaited any proposals that might follow the Hodgson company's initial call, Western International indicated to the regents its willingness to surrender its lease before 1982—at a sacrifice in profits of about $500,000 a year—both to give the regents latitude in dealing with a new lessee and to free the hotel company of the restrictive covenants of 1952, 1966, and 1972, particularly the covenant against conducting competitive hotel operations, as in a further expansion of the Washington Plaza, once the Benjamin Franklin Hotel. The regents authorized the Metropolitan tract committee to study this suggestion and then, in mid-February, approved the committee's recommendation that the board accept Western's proposal, the details and releases to be worked out only after a new lessee was preparing to take over.[24]

But with the arrival of the March 1 deadline only one solid proposal had been received. This was from a Seattle group, Olympic Center Associates, the plan involving expenditure of $20,000,000 to convert the Olympic into a "luxury class" hotel, particularly by combining smaller rooms to make larger ones, reducing the total to about 530, and introducing a new glass-domed galleria, with restaurant and retail space, into the University Street space long occupied by the automobile entrance. Three other companies or development groups had sent letters expressing interest, one of them Four Seasons, which was thinking about demolishing the hotel and building a new one on the site. By the time the regents met on March 19, however, the decision was to issue a second call for proposals. It was not simply that a single proposal seemed not enough. It was being realized that $30,000,000 or more, rather than $20,000,000, might be required to recreate the Olympic, and that a sixty-year lease term, as asked by Olympic Center Associates, probably was too long for an old hotel that would receive anything less than total rehabilitation. Beyond such considerations was another. The original call for proposals had contemplated possible demolition and replacement of the hotel. The regents knew, now, that only restoration would do. Like the Fifth Avenue Theater, the Olympic had been nominated, in January, for the National Register of Historic Places. Soon thereafter the public hearing on the environmental impact statement had disclosed a unanimous sentiment for preservation. By March, resolutions of the state senate and house urged the regents to give first consideration to any proposal assuring the retention of the Olympic Hotel. Thus there would be no "new" Olympic. But although the Olympic Center Associates plan had anticipated rehabilitation, the regents now felt that the ground rules were more clearly defined and that other rehabilitation ideas should be received. On April 19, the regents, through Hodgson, issued a supplemental call for proposals. The new target date was June 29, 1979.[25]

Three proposals were received this time—from Four Seasons, Olympic Center Associates, and the Hyatt Corporation of Chicago—and each was analyzed in succeeding days by the Metropolitan tract committee in consultation with Hodgson and in long interviews with representatives of the proposing firms. When the regents met on July 13, Philip presented the recommendation of the tract committee that Four Seasons–Urban be the group with which the committee would negotiate the terms of a lease for forty years. Moving down its checklist, the committee had made its choice.

Because all proposals were for strengthening and rehabilitating an existing hotel, not replacing it, the regents' judgment now had to be exercised within a narrower range in which, assuming that architectural and planning concepts were of equal excellence, decision would turn on financial considerations, including the levels of direct investment by the proposing firms and, of course, on the long-term financial return to the university. In their aesthetic aspects the design proposals, although different, were not strikingly so. Each suggested an architectural treatment that respected the Olympic's familiar form. Each provided for reducing the number of rooms to offer larger and more luxurious accommodations to guests: Hyatt proposed 600 rooms, Olympic Center Associates 532, and Four Seasons 448. The financial proposals were of a different order, however. Four Seasons would spend $38,000,000 on the project, Hyatt $38,300,000, and Olympic Center Associates $28,400,000. But Four Seasons and Urban were also prepared to invest $12,000,000 of their own resources in the project. The Metropolitan tract committee was "especially impressed" by this commitment, as by Four Seasons' record of ownership and management of luxury hotels, by Urban's financial strength ($570,000,000 in "owned and managed" assets), and by the closeness of the relationship between Four Seasons and Urban as exemplified by their operation of another luxury hotel, the Ritz-Carlton in Chicago's Water Tower Place. Four Seasons would pay the university $450,000 a year for two years—the projected preparation and construction period—and thereafter a base annual rental of $1,260,000 plus a percentage of room rents or gross receipts. The regents approved the tract committee's recommendation unanimously.[26]

The Olympic would live, renewed, improved, still in character. Seattle wanted it that way. The details of the Urban–Four Seasons lease were to be worked out, but almost at the moment the regents approved the Urban–Four Seasons proposal they were informed that the hotel had been accepted for listing by the National Register of Historic Places. The regents had supported this. A month before, on June 8, 1979, Philip, as chairman of the Metropolitan tract committee, had sent a letter to the Keeper of the National Register saying that the board was anticipating execution of "an appropriate lease calling for restoration of the Hotel," and that a national listing would enhance this prospect.[27] All of the elements seemed to be coming together as the process of drafting the lease terms began.

The lease with Urban–Four Seasons was approved by the regents on January 18, 1980, signed for the university by Taul Watanabe, president of the board, and Barbara Zimmerman, secretary. The lease actually was a part of a package of agreements signed that day. Since the Seattle Oympic–Western International lease was not due to expire until October 31, 1982, the negotiations for early termination had covered matters ranging from the termination itself to the releases of covenants, the financial settlements, and the provision for payment of the mortgage balance on the Olympic Garage, this obligation assumed by the new lessee. The principal financial specifications followed closely those of the original Urban–Four Seasons proposal, the project to cost just over $38,000,000 (the lessee's equity at least 25 percent), the rentals $450,000 a year for two years and not less than $1,260,000 a year thereafter. The major change was in the postponement from April 1 to October 1, 1980, of the date Urban–Four Seasons would take over the hotel, the restoration then to begin within sixty days and operations resumed within two years. The Urban–Four Seasons plan called for complete closure during the construction period, and the six-month delay was considered necessary to permit orderly shifts of advance convention bookings. For the costs of inflation in the six-month period, as well as for additional seismic work, the university assumed responsibility. More significant than these immediate arrangements, however, was the term of the lease, which projected operations far into the next century. Urban–Four Seasons had proposed a term of forty years with four five-year renewal options. The term as agreed was of sixty years—to October, 2040—but with cancellation options at five-year intervals during the last twenty.[28]

There would be time until the autumn of 1980 for the people of the Northwest to accumulate reminiscent glimpses of the Olympic before the renovation began, but soon the changes in orientation and accommodation would come. The automobile entrance of 1955 and the ballroom above it would be replaced by a new main entrance on University Street. The number of guest rooms would be reduced to 448, as Urban–Four Seasons had proposed. Across Fifth Avenue, meantime, the matchless theater in the Skinner Building would be launched on a new life.

The career of the Fifth Avenue Theater was following a different course. For years, until 1978, the theater had been a motion picture house, the beauties of its Chinese decor usually hidden in darkness. The beauties were there, nevertheless, and a strong public sentiment supported their preservation. In December 1978 the theater and the Skinner Building were placed separately on the National Register of Historic Places, this while UNICO Properties, studying possible uses for the theater, was moving toward a

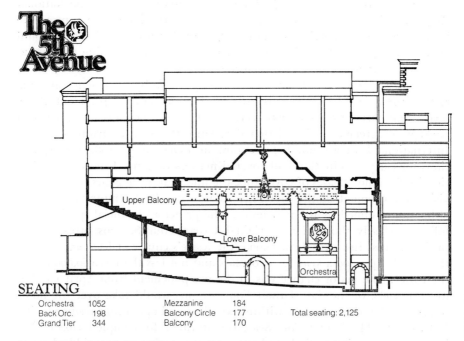

SEATING

Orchestra	1052	Mezzanine	184	
Back Orc.	198	Balcony Circle	177	Total seating: 2,125
Grand Tier	344	Balcony	170	

Cross section view of the Fifth Avenue Theater as restored and converted to a center for the performing arts (*plan by R. F. McCann and Company, courtesy of* UNICO)

recommendation that the Fifth Avenue, restored and modified only as necessary to improve its function, become a Northwest center for the performing arts. The theater had been examined with that thought in mind by consultants from New York, Los Angeles, and San Francisco. UNICO representatives visited similarly converted theaters in San Francisco, San Diego, and Washington, D.C., and it seemed another of those predestined circumstances that one of the consultants could be Roger Stevens. The performing arts idea had begun to take shape in mid-1978, although it was not until autumn 1979 that problems associated with it had been solved. The solution made the project a community affair.[29]

The cost of the theater conversion was estimated at up to $2,600,000, sources of funding at that level not immediately discernible. By November, however, a new nonprofit corporation had been organized to accept the pledges of business firms offering to guarantee financing in the form of a loan by a consortium of Seattle banks. More than twenty such firms were on the original list, the number soon forty, plus two individual participants. The incorporator and president of the nonprofit association was D. E. (Ned) Skinner, grandson of the D. E. Skinner for whom the building was named (and head of the Skinner Corporation, which still had its offices in the building), other officers including Edward E. Carlson, vice president, James R. Ellis, secretary, and W. J. Pennington, president of the Seattle *Times*, treasurer. Trustees and members of the executive committee were Robert F. Buck, general counsel of the Rainier Bank; Stanley Little Jr., vice president of the Boeing company; Morris J. Alhadeff, president of the Washington Jockey Club; William Jenkins, chairman of the board of the Seattle–First National Bank; I. M. Trafton, president of the Safeco Insurance Company; James M. Ryan, of UNICO; and, from the university, Solomon Katz, professor emeritus of history. By early 1980, the financing assured, the convention was proceeding under the supervision of Richard McCann, a Seattle architect experienced in such projects, the work to be completed well ahead of a July opening of a first performing arts season. In the first years, income from operations would go to repay the guarantors, after that to support other cultural activities throughout the state of Washington. As its contribution to the nonprofit nature of the financing, UNICO would forgo for ten years the rentals it might have received, all such income going to the university.[30]

Before the Fifth Avenue reopened there came, as something more than a footnote, an answer to the question of the city's authority to exercise landmark control over state-owned buildings located in the Metropolitan Center. On April 5, 1978, the city's Landmark Preservation Board had approved the nominations of the Skinner Building and the Fifth Avenue Theater. The action implied authority that the regents had consistently rejected, and on April 28 a suit in King County Superior Court asked a permanent injunction and a declaratory judgment that the city had no jurisdiction. When, in November, the Superior Court sustained the university position, the city immediately asked the State Supreme Court for a review, and oral arguments in the case were heard on February 19, 1980. When the Supreme Court's ruling came, some months later, the answer was the same. The buildings, as the state's, were beyond any landmark jurisdiction the city might assert.[31]

Thus it was in 1980. The university itself had a new president, William P. Gerberding, who had come from the University of Illinois to succeed John Hogness. Gerberding, a fifty-year-old political scientist, had left the chancellorship at Illinois to take the university presidency, but he was in fact, like certain of his well-remembered predecessors, a "Western man" in experience and viewpoint—from 1961 a member of the faculty of the University of California at Los Angeles, professor and chairman of his department by 1970; for two years, 1973 to 1975, dean and vice president for academic affairs at Occidental College, Los Angeles; then once again at UCLA, until 1978, as executive vice chancellor. Gerberding was welcomed as a man of keen mind, of good humor and wide-ranging interests, and of firmness in administrative style. His inauguration on January 31, 1980, was a happy occasion, seen at the university as a proper beginning of what certainly would be an important if perhaps also a particularly demanding, new decade.

Whatever the future would bring, the Metropolitan tract had reached by 1980 a point at which its history could be seen as a remarkable continuity. From the 1860s to the 1980s the University of Washington's first campus had been a place where the histories of the state, the university, and the city of Seattle converged and flowed together. The ten-acre plot donated by Arthur Denny, Edward Lander, and Charles Terry had been accumulating history, layer after layer, since the day Denny and Daniel Bagley had climbed through the woods to select it as a university site. Denny and Bagley had planned a university, but what they had also done, unknowingly, was to pick the site of what would become the commercial center of one of the great cities of the world.

The dedication of that land to the support of a public educational institution was the essence of it, and not merely in a technical sense. The leasing policy had taken shape almost accidentally after 1900, and in the face of legislation that had anticipated sale of the land. Yet it was a policy that preserved the old campus virtually intact (except for the small fraction sold for the post office). The presence in Seattle of property that called for development as a whole was a circumstance that shaped not only the city's growth but the city's viewpoint. The property was public, and thus a shared interest. It awaited a developer with the nerve and imagination to make it economically productive. When young J. F. Douglas organized his Metropolitan Building Company in 1907, employing the New York architectural firm of Howells and Stokes to prepare a "master plan," the main directions of development had been established for the next century even while the university's first building still stood there.

Looking back over eighty years it was possible to see how the tract had been throughout its history a testing ground for ideas in the fields of leasing, prop-

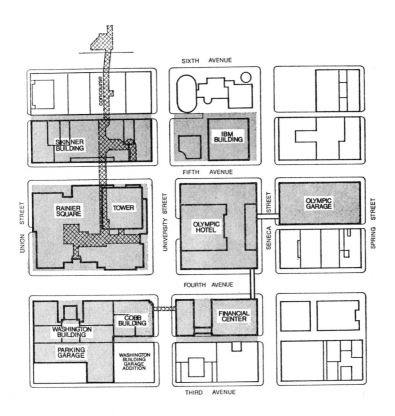

The Metropolitan Center of 1980, with the underground pedestrian concourse extending from Sixth Avenue to Rainier Square, sky bridges linking the Olympic Hotel to its garage and to the Financial Center, and of the earliest buildings only the Cobb remaining (*plat by Edgar L. P. Yang*)

erty management, public oversight of private ventures, and comprehensive planning. No other site in any other city had offered quite the same opportunities for planning—or had so demanded it—whether in the early transformation of a campus to a "city within a city" or later, in the days of environmental impact calculations, in the replacement of aging buildings by towers, courts, and plazas. The original J. F. Douglas plan was never fully realized, but the tract bore the Douglas stamp. Douglas had graded raw land and placed ten major buildings on it in his time. His Metropolitan company had put its name there. Modified as his plan was, and improvised for years in the construction of temporary buildings, Douglas still gave the tract a Metropolitan style—a style perfectly attuned to the business, professional, and social patterns of the Seattle before World War I and into the booming days of the 1920s. He had created and polished the mold.

If it was fortunate that there was a J. F. Douglas to shape the tract in its beginnings, it seems no less so that there should have been a Roger Stevens to take up the development after 1953. Although Stevens, then a theatrical entrepreneur as well as a prospector in real estate, was years away from the time he would become chairman of the Kennedy Center for the Performing Arts in Washington, D.C., he brought to the tract new kinds of daring and determination—the daring to enter a lease of the most singular nature and a willingness to back up his judgments all along the way, frequently with advance payments, mortgages, borrowings, or guarantees that seemed sometimes no more than gambles on a distant future. Stevens, although not of Seattle, had a feeling for the tract and the university's proprietorship, and in forming University Properties, which became UNICO, he had the judgment to give it, in James M. Ryan, a Seattle man who knew the city and the university and who could function effectively, with his own willingness to take risks, between these differing constituencies.

The lease under which the Metropolitan Building Company operated had been a torture to the university. Not until 1942 had the university received as much as $140,000 a year from property that had multiplied steadily in value. In the forty-seven years before 1954 the cumulative return in rentals had not reached $4,000,000. The multiplications in value had come, however, not alone because of Seattle's growth, but because Douglas, with the help of Seattle's capitalists, had pursued his private vision of the tract as a showcase. When the new era began—when in 1953 the winner of the new "main lease" was University Properties—the significance was not solely in the increases in rentals that would come, although these would be large, with guaranteed minimum payments augmented by percentages of gross income. Equally significant were the lease terms putting the regents in charge of events as they never had been before. The regents assumed responsibility for every development at the tract. Through the New Building Fund they had control over the allocation of the university's income, whether for the improvement of the property endowment or for the support of campus projects. The 1953 lease demanded liaison and staff work at unprecedented levels, hence the creation of the Metropolitan Tract Office downtown. The lease asked future boards of regents to make decisions of epochal kinds, as in the complicated post office negotiations of the 1950s that cleared the way for construction of the Washington Building or in the planning, environmental hearings, and approvals that produced Rainier Square. In such ways, among others, the lease itself was epochal.

What had it all meant to the university, this history? The question seemed unanswerable by 1980, even in monetary terms. The rentals and reversionary values of the improvements were at levels undreamed of by the regents of 1900, yet the rentals were only small percentages of the funds needed to sustain an institution of the university's caliber and the question of reversions was for the future. To put the question another way, what had been the costs? Successive boards of regents had participated, decade after decade, in the management of that endowment. In eighty years just eighty regents had served for periods longer than a year, the value of their contributions incalculable. Was their attention to the tract a cost to the university as well as to the regents themselves—the time devoted to committee meetings, negotiations, public hearings, review of architectural plans, bid openings, consultations with alumni, staff, or lessees, and testimony before the legislature? Had there been a dilution of their efforts? Was the university itself something less or other than it might have been if the regents had faced no such obligations? It was difficult to say, the university being what it was. Whatever form the endowment might have taken, the regents would have been responsible for it, and the form selected in 1953 had been found to be the best one. Beyond that, it could be believed that the university, preserving as an endowment the place of its 1861 beginnings, had preserved its unique identity and thus was strengthened in ways that were not to be found in tabulations of income.

The tract was larger than ten acres in 1979—about eleven acres, in fact. Some of the land sold to the U.S. government in 1901 had been regained in the complicated post office negotiation of the 1950s that cleared the way for construction of the Washington Building. Then had come the purchase in 1964 of the half block on Fifth Avenue on which had been built the Olympic Garage and Airlines Terminal. There would be a further addition when, at the expiration of the UNICO lease, the university would take title to the parking garage on Third Avenue where the Palomar Theater once stood. The boundaries of the tract had been changed, and would be changed further, but the movements were not aggressively expansionist. The tract was integrated into its metropolitan surroundings. The major additions were, in their times, simply responses to the perpetual problem of where to put automobiles.

The history of the tract had been one of experiment, of risks with large stakes—a history at the center of a history. Seattle itself was an assured and confident city in 1980, characteristically proud of its setting and content with its past without being content to remain there. And while no samplings of community sentiment certified it, there seemed to be a blend of pride and contentment in what had happened to the tract in later years: the Washington, Financial Center, and IBM buildings were old friends; Rainier Square was a shopping place; and the Cobb and Skinner buildings were standing reassuringly while the Olympic was made ready for a new life. The Metropolitan was not a Rockefeller Center and Seattle's Fifth Avenue was not New York's. But who cared? Even the original Rockefeller "Radio City" designs had been declared, in their time, "aberrations and monstrosities." What Seattle had was crisp, clean, and its own—and it owned it. The shopper on Seattle's Fifth Avenue was walking along a street laid on public land. On the University Street side of the Olympic was the fifteen-foot setback created in 1911 when the Metropolitan Theatre looked out on a widened "University Place." In the modern city such traces of old times remained—good to recognize, good to remember. Despite the buildings and the changes, the view from Denny's knoll was still a grand one.

It was the view that mattered in a symbolic, perhaps even in a prophetic, way. It was a view of a university that should share in the future of its "old grounds." The university, even as it lived elsewhere, had so shared. As a public institution it had been more public than others, its story inseparable from its city's and its state's.

APPENDIX 1

Denny Deed Dated April 16, 1861

(Deed from Arthur A. and Mary A. Denny [husband and wife] to Territory of Washington conveying eight-plus acres to be used as a site for the Territorial university with reversion over to the Town of Seattle as a site for a university, high school, or college in the event the land were not so used by the Territory. Recorded in Vol. ABC of Deeds, page 461, records of King County, Washington.)

This Indenture made the sixteenth day of April in the year of our Lord, one thousand eight hundred & sixty one between Arthur A. Denny & Mary A. Denny his wife of Seattle in the County of King & Territory of Washington of the first part & the Territory of Washington of the second part whereas, the Legislative Assembly of the Territory of Washington having by act passed at the eighth session of said Assembly begun & held at Olympia on the 5th day of December A.D. 1860, located and established the Territorial University at Seattle in King County—Provided a good and sufficient deed to ten acres of land eligibly situated in the vicinity of Seattle be first executed to the Territory of Washington for University purposes. *Now This Indenture Witnesseth* that the said party of the first part in consideration that the said University shall be permanently located and built at Seattle as aforesaid and that the following described tract lot or parcel of land shall be used as a portion of the ten acres required by the act aforesaid as a site for the said building *Hath* for themselves their heirs executors administrators and assigns remised released and quitclaimed and by these presents *Doth* remise release and forever quitclaim unto the said party of the second part all his and their right title and interest whatsoever both at law and in equity in and to all that part or parcel of land lying and being in King County Washington Territory in Township 25 North Range 4 East Willamette Meridian and more particularly described as follows: Beginning at the fractional corner of the donation land claim of the said party of the first part, it also being the N.W. Corner of Carson D. Boren's claim from which the corner post to sections 31 and 32 bears S 10°E 27.79 chs thence east 8.61 chs thence north 57 ¾°E 2.72 chs to the S. E. Corner of the tract of land conveyed thence N 32 ¼° west 10.00 chs to the northeast corner of the site thence S 32¼° E 5.40 chs to the S.W. Corner and place of beginning containing eight and $\frac{32\ 14/25}{100}$ acres of land to-

---

* Source: *The Metropolitan Tract of the University of Washington*; pp. 25–27.

gether with all and singular and tenements hereditaments and appurtenances there unto belonging or in any wise appertaining and the reversion and reversions, remainder and remainders rents issues and profits thereof. And also the estate right title interest property possession claim and demand whatsoever as well in law as in equity of the said party of the first part in and to the same and every part and parcel thereof with the appurtenances. To have and To hold the same...
....with all and singular the appurtenances unto the said party of the second part forever. Provided Always and these presents are upon this express condition that if the said Territorial University by act of the Legislative Assembly or otherwise should not be located and built upon the ten acre lot of which the above described tract lot or parcel of land shall form a part according to the true intent and meaning of these presents then the said tract lot or parcel of land shall revert to and immediately vest in the Town of Seattle in King County aforesaid for the use and benefit of and as a site for a University, High School or College and for no other purpose. And the said party of the first part and his and their heirs executors administrators and assigns the said premises in the quiet and peaceable possession of the said party of the second part against the said party of the first part his and their heirs, executors, administrators and assigns and against all and every person and persons whomsoever lawfully claiming or to claim the same by from or under him of them or either of them shall and will warrant and by these presents forever defend. In Witness Whereof the said party of the first part have hereunto set their hands and seals the day and year first above written.

(signed)

Signed Sealed and Delivered in   ARTHUR A. DENNY   [SEAL]
            presence of   MARY A. DENNY   [SEAL]
J. W. JOHHNSON   L. C. FRYE

APPENDIX 2

Regents of the University, 1900 to 1980

Listed here are the men and women who have served as members of the University of Washington's board of regents from the time of the earliest leasings of the former campus. Circumstances affecting lengths of service are indicated where these are known. Terms of presidents are noted.

Dr. E. A. Addington, Bellevue, 1962–64 (died while serving)

Eva (Mrs. L. O.) Anderson, Chelan, 1942–46

Grant Armstrong, Chehalis, 1950–57; president, 1953–54

Manson F. Backus, Seattle, 1909–11 (resigned)

Roscoe A. Balch, Spokane, 1926–33 (resigned)

Thomas Balmer, Seattle, 1934–59 (died while serving); president, 1938–39, 1939–40, 1945–46, 1957–58

Dave Beck, Seattle, 1946–51 (resigned); president, 1950–51

James E. Bell, Everett, 1901–04

Alden J. Blethen, Seattle, 1897–1904 (resigned); president, 1902–03

Dorothy (Mrs. A. Scott) Bullitt, Seattle, 1958–65; president, 1962–63

Clarence J. Coleman, Everett, 1945–50; president, 1946–47, 1947–48

Howard G. Cosgrove, Seattle, 1909–13 (resigned); president, 1912–Dec. 1, 1913)

S. G. Cosgrove, Pomeroy, 1905–08 (elected governor of state)

Dr. Donald G. Corbett, Spokane, 1950–57; president, 1952–53

Gordon C. Culp, Seattle, 1977– (present term to October 1982)

James H. Davis, Tacoma, 1922–26; president, 1924–25

George Donworth, Seattle, 1923–24 (resigned)

Joseph Drumheller, Spokane, 1945–50, 1957–68; president, 1948–49, 1949–50, 1961–62, 1967–68

Charles M. Easterday, Tacoma, 1897–1902

James R. Ellis, Bellevue, 1965–77; president, 1971–72

John D. Farrell, Seattle, 1926–29 (resigned)

Oscar A. Fechter, Yakima, 1914–26 (resigned); president, 1914–15, 1915–16

Dr. Robert L. Flennaugh, Seattle, 1970–76; president, 1975–76

John M. Fox, Seattle, 1945–47 (not confirmed)

Charles F. Frankland, Seattle, 1951–57; president, 1954–55

R. Mort Frayn, Seattle, 1968– (present term to October 1980); president 1972–73, 1977–78

Charles E. Gaches, Mount Vernon, 1914–17 (entered military service); president, Dec. 1, 1916–Mar. 12, 1917

Beatrice (Mrs. J. Herbert) Gardner, La Conner, 1952–58; president, 1955–56

Mary (Mrs. William H.) Gates, Seattle, 1975– (present term to October 1981); president, 1978–79

Lincoln D. Godshall, Everett, 1898–1900 (resigned)

Charles M. Harris, Entiat, 1953–58; president, 1956–57

John P. Hartman, Seattle, 1905–09; president, 1906–07

F. A. Hazeltine, South Bend, 1904–05 (not confirmed), 1908–13 (resigned); president, 1909–10, 1910–11

John T. Heffernan, Seattle, 1924–26 (resigned)

John C. Higgins, Seattle, 1909–13 (resigned); president, 1911–12

John P. Hoyt, Seattle, 1898–1902 (resigned); president, 1901–02

D. L. Huntington, Spokane, 1906–09 (resigned)

Paul H. Johns, Tacoma, 1926–33 (resigned); president, 1930–33

Alvah H. B. Jordan, Everett, 1926–30 (resigned); president, 1926–27, 1927–28, 1928–29, 1929–30

George H. King, Seattle, 1897–1905; president, 1897–98, 1898–99, 1899–1900

John L. King, Seattle, 1946–53, 1957–68; president, 1951–52, 1960–61, 1966–67

Ward G. Kumm, Seattle, 1932–33 (resigned)

Joseph E. Lease, Centralia, 1927–30 (died while serving)

Robert D. Larrabee, Clarkston, 1977– (present term to October 1983)

Dr. J. Hans Lehmann, Seattle, 1977– (present term to October 1893); president, 1980–81

Sidney B. Lewis, Seattle, 1926–28 (resigned)

Herbert S. Little, Seattle, 1960–65; president, 1964–65

Philip D. Macbride, Seattle, 1933–45; president, 1935–36, 1936–37, 1942–43, 1943–44

Alexander F. McEwan, Seattle, 1909–13 (resigned); president, 1913

Ruth Karr (Mrs. J. S.) McKee, Hoquiam, Vancouver, 1917–26 (resigned); president, 1923–24

Winlock W. Miller, Seattle, 1914–26, 1933–57 (resigned); president, 1910–20, 1941–42

Robert Montgomery, Puyallup, 1933–36 (died while serving)

James Z. Moore, Spokane, 1898–1904; president, 1903–04

Dr. Albert B. Murphy, Everett, 1958–62 (died while serving)

Frank D. Nash, Tacoma, 1905–10; president, 1908–09

Jack G. Neupert, Spokane, 1970–77; president, 1974–75

James V. Paterson, Seattle, 1928–33 (resigned)

William T. Perkins, Seattle, 1914–22 (resigned); president, 1917–18, 1918–19

J. M. Perry, Yakima, 1926–33 (resigned)

Robert F. Philip, Pasco, 1968– (present term to October 1980); president, 1973–74

F. A. Post, Spokane, 1904–05 (not confirmed)

George V. Powell, Seattle, 1965–77; president, 1970–71, 1976–77

John H. Powell, Seattle, 1902–09 (resigned); president, 1905–06

Joan A. Rea, Tacoma, 1910–22; president, 1921–22

Albert L. Rogers, Waterville, 1909–13 (resigned)

Roger R. Rogers, Spokane, 1922–26 (resigned); president, 1925–26

James T. Ronald, Seattle, 1905–09 (resigned)

Dr. Leo J. Rosellini, Seattle, 1964–70; president, 1969–70

Werner A. Rupp, Aberdeen, 1921–26, 1933–45; president, 1926, 1940–41

Edward P. Ryan, Spokane, 1933–42; president, 1934–35

A. P. Sawyer, Seattle, 1905–09 (resigned); president, 1907–98

J. F. Saylor, Spokane, 1905–06 (resigned)

William E. Schricker, La Conner, 1902–05 (resigned); president, 1904–05

Lewis B. Schwellenbach, Seattle, 1933–34 (elected to U.S. Senate); president, 1933–34

Dr. William A. Shannon, Seattle, 1914–23; president, 1922–23

Harold S. Shefelman, Seattle, 1957–75; president, 1958–59, 1959–60, 1965–66

Alfred Shemanski, Seattle, 1933–45; president, 1937–38, 1944–45

Charles P. Spooner, Seattle, 1911–13 (resigned)

George R. Stuntz, Seattle, 1947–51

George H. Walker, Seattle, 1913 (resigned)

Taul Watanabe, Bellevue, 1977– (present term to October, 1982); president, 1979–80

Eldridge Wheeler, Montesano, 1913–21; president, 1920–21

Eugene A. White, Tacoma, 1942–46

Lloyd L. Wiehl, Yakima, 1957 (resigned)

William Neal Winter, Medina, 1930–33 (resigned)

Robert J. Willis, Yakima, 1958–70; president, 1963–64, 1968–69

Richard Winsor, Seattle, 1898–1905; president 1900–01

APPENDIX 3

Financial Records

The financial records given in the three tables following were adapted from data supplied in Metropolitan Tract, Report of the Board of Regents to the Legislature, December 31, 1978.

Lease Year*	Income from Rentals		
	UNICO Properties	Olympic Hotel	Total Rentals
1955	$ 1,600,000	$ 324,000	$ 1,924,000
1956	1,700,000	324,000	2,024,000
1957	1,700,000	1,005,085	2,705,085
1958	1,748,815	819,415	2,568,230
1959	1,361,203	883,884	2,245,087
1960	1,463,479	881,478	2,344,957
1961	1,852,421	903,013	2,755,434
1962	2,010,922	1,076,549	3,087,471
1963	1,981,953	867,702	2,849,655
1964	1,689,687	846,480	2,536,167
1965	1,991,835	959,291	2,951,126
1966	2,168,571	1,160,598	3,329,169
1967	2,265,400	1,303,897	3,569,297
1968	2,378,022	1,401,938	3,779,960
1969	2,327,707	1,528,153	3,855,860
1970	2,237,966	1,269,736	3,507,702
1971	2,279,078	1,127,282	3,406,360
1972	2,304,234	1,204,462	3,508,696
1973	2,894,421	1,005,237	3,899,658
1974	3,035,510	1,195,261	4,230,771
1975	2,366,252	1,155,834	3,522,086
1976	1,532,572	1,344,071	2,876,643
1977	1,614,689	1,576,728	3,191,417
1978	2,545,678	1,937,772	4,483,450
1979	3,126,865	2,372,466	5,499,331
Totals	$52,177,280	$28,474,332	$80,651,612

* Lease year ends October 31.

Deductions, Operating Costs			Total Net Income to University
Taxes and Services†	University Management‡	Total Expenses	
$	$ 15,000	$ 15,000	$ 1,909,000
60,000	21,000	81,000	1,943,000
60,000	28,000	88,000	2,617,085
60,000	30,000	90,000	2,478,230
60,000	30,000	90,000	2,155,087
60,000	28,000	88,000	2,256,957
60,000	28,000	88,000	2,667,434
60,000	28,000	88,000	2,999,471
72,442	28,000	100,442	2,749,213
98,777	82,000	180,777	2,355,390
98,343	54,000	152,343	2,798,783
100,070	55,000	155,070	3,174,099
126,362	56,000	182,362	3,386,935
128,674	65,000	193,674	3,586,286
130,845	93,000	223,845	3,632,015
145,186	86,000	231,186	3,276,516
140,296	94,000	234,296	3,172,064
281,416	117,000	398,416	3,110,280
252,725	136,000	388,725	3,510,933
678,880	166,000	844,880	3,385,891
635,641	375,000	1,010,641	2,511,445
175,000	274,000	449,000	2,427,643
429,822	220,029	649,851	2,541,566
536,136	462,107	998,243	3,485,207
787,917	393,948	1,181,865	4,317,466
$5,238,532	$2,965,084	$8,203,616	$72,447,996

† Totals include leasehold taxes and payments for local government services as authorized by the legislature.

‡ University expenses include salaries, professional fees, insurance, printing, office supplies and other costs associated with management of the tract.

DISTRIBUTION OF NET RENTALS, 1955–79

Lease Year	Total Net Income to University	To Tract Improvement, Construction	To University for Campus Purposes
1955	$ 1,909,000	$ 1,612,312	$ 296,688
1956	1,943,000	1,528,682	414,318
1957	2,617,085	548,952	2,068,133
1958	2,478,230	2,410,511	67,719
1959	2,155,087	2,155,087	
1960	2,256,957	1,959,444	297,513
1961	2,667,434	2,018,293	649,141
1962	2,999,471	2,230,585	768,886
1963	2,749,213	1,343,454	1,405,759
1964	2,355,390	524,866	1,830,524
1965	2,798,783	657,080	2,141,703
1966	3,174,099	600,656	2,573,443
1967	3,386,935	875,480	2,511,455
1968	3,586,286	1,521,270	2,065,016
1969	3,632,015	1,988,234	1,643,781
1970	3,276,516	2,347,583	928,933
1971	3,172,064	2,001,547	1,170,517
1972	3,110,280	1,897,362	1,212,918
1973	3,510,933	3,105,884	405,049
1974	3,385,891	2,614,146	771,745
1975	2,511,445	2,714,080	(202,635)
1976	2,427,643	2,372,545	55,098
1977	2,541,566	1,673,947	867,619
1978	3,485,207	1,619,934	1,865,273
1979	4,317,466	1,582,568	2,734,898
Totals	$72,447,996	$43,904,502	$28,543,494

NEW CONSTRUCTION, 1960–1980

Building	Initial Occupancy	Total Cost to University
Washington Building	1960	$ 9,925,674
IBM Building	1964	8,415,736
Olympic Garage	1964	3,495,053
Financial Center	1972	16,989,978
Rainier Square	1977	42,724,684
Total		$81,551,125

Notes

Sources used in the preparation of this history are original as far as possible in the tracing of events related to the evolution of the Metropolitan tract itself. In this category are the record materials such as the minutes or reports of the board of regents, the official reports of the university, and the letters, reports, clippings, and publications preserved in the Archives and Manuscripts Division and the Northwest Collection of the University of Washington Library.

For general background, information comes in the main from standard or secondary sources such as the various histories of Seattle, King County, and the state of Washington, from certain early publications of biography, and from magazines, newspapers, directories, or lessee publications reflecting developments in the various periods. Much information was gained in conversations or correspondence with a number of persons—former regents, university officials, lessee representatives, and others—having recollections of tract developments.

Minutes and records of the university's board of regents form a central thread. Citations from these are by volume, page number, and date (for example, Regents Minutes, 3:112, March 15, 1901). Other files in the Office of the Board of Regents at the University of Washington are designated as regents' files.

The basic documents—deeds, laws, conveyances, agreements, and so on—have been assembled and reproduced in the two volumes of *The Metropolitan Tract of the University of Washington* (1961 and 1976). The references are by volume, part, and page number; the office of record of the original document is shown in parentheses.

Two unpublished manuscripts representing detailed studies of tract developments to the 1920s are used extensively. One is the "Metropolitan Building Company Lease: Document History, 1898–1921," which is cited simply as "Document History" with page number. The other is the "Chronology of Events and Facts Relating to the University 10 Acre Tract in Seattle," a report prepared by Roy H. Dodge, who was employed as a special consultant to the board of regents in 1925. These manuscripts and other materials concerning the Metropolitan tract are contained in four boxes (boxes 46 to 49) of the Regents Records in the University of Washington Library's

Archives and Records Center. The Thomas Balmer Papers are found in the Library's Manuscript Section (identified by box and folder numbers: e.g., 14–5).

Notes on the university's own development are taken primarily from Charles M. Gates's centennial history, *The First Century at the University of Washington, 1861–1961*, published by the University of Washington Press in 1961.

Some details, particularly biographical, have been drawn from early city and county histories or directories. These include Clarence B. Bagley's two works of narrative and reminiscence, *History of Seattle* (1916) and *History of King County, Washington* (1929). A third such work is *A Volume of Memoirs and Genealogy of Representative Citizens of the City of Seattle and County of King, Washington*, published in 1903.

CHAPTER 1. *The Knoll: 1854 to 1894*

1. Charles M. Gates, *The First Century at the University of Washington, 1861–1961* (Seattle: University of Washington Press, 1961), pp. 7–8.
2. *Pacific Wave* (University of Washington student newspaper), May 5, 1905.
3. *The Metropolitan Tract of the University of Washington*, 2 vols. (Seattle: University of Washington Department of Publications and Printing, 1961 and 1976), vol. 1, part 1, Laws Relating to the Metropolitan Tract (*Laws of 1860–61*, act of December 12, 1860, act of January 11, 1861), pp. 5–6. Gates, *First Century*, p. 10. Clarence B. Bagley, *History of Seattle from the Earliest Settlement to the Present Time*, 3 vols. (Chicago: S. J. Clarke Publishing Co., 1916), 1:136.
4. *Metropolitan Tract*, vol. 1, part 2, Basic Conveyances, pp. 25–28.
5. Bagley, *Seattle*, 1:136.
6. Ibid., p. 137.
7. Gates, *First Century*, p. 12.
8. *Metropolitan Tract*, vol. 1, part 1 (*Laws of 1875*, act of November 12, 1875), p. 6.
9. Ibid. (*Laws of 1891*, act of March 7, 1891), pp. 6–8.
10. Ibid. (*Laws of 1893*, act of March 14, 1893), pp. 8–9.
11. Gates, *First Century*, p. 55.

CHAPTER 2. *Years of Decision: 1895 to 1902*

1. Gates, *First Century*, pp. 56–58.
2. *Metropolitan Tract*, vol. 1, part 2, Basic Conveyances (vol. 123, p. 315, *Deeds*, Records of King County), pp. 31–33.
3. Ibid., part 1, Laws Relating to the Metropolitan Tract (chap. 122, *Laws of Washington, 1893*), pp. 8–9.
4. Gates, *First Century*, pp. 62–63 and 66–67.
5. Roy H. Dodge, "Chronology of Events and Facts Relating to the University 10 Acre Tract in Seattle," p. 6, Regents Records, box 47, University of Washington Archives: State of Washington, *Report of the University Land and Building Commissioners, 1892* (Olympia: State Printer, 1892), p. 5.
6. Polk's *Seattle City Directory*, 1900; Seattle Chamber of Commerce, *A Few Facts About Seattle, the Queen City of the Pacific*, 1898.
7. Ibid.
8. Seattle *Post-Intelligencer*, "Bicentennial Biographies: Col. Alden Blethen," February 13, 1976.
9. Seattle *Post-Intelligencer* (John P. Hoyt), June 17, 1919.

10. *Washington Standard* (Olympia), "Constitutional Convention, Pen and Ink Sketches of Its Members: J. Z. Moore," August 23, 1889.

11. Gates, *First Century*, pp. 67–70; Regents Minutes (Lincoln D. Godshall), 4:84, May 2, 1898, and 4:86, May 11, 1898; Seattle *Times* (obituary, George H. King), March 27, 1931.

12. Seattle *Post-Intelligencer* (obituary, Richard Winsor), December 2, 1923; *A Volume of Memoirs and Genealogy of Representative Citizens of the City of Seattle and County of King, Washington, Including Biographies of Many of Those Who Have Passed Away* (New York and Chicago: Lewis Publishing Co., 1903), pp. 113–18.

13. Regents Minutes, 4:129, July 25, 1899, and 4:130, August 7, 1899.

14. Ibid., 1:146, March 15, 1884, and 1:148, April 15, 1884; *Report of the Board of Regents of the Territorial University* (Goldendale: Goldendale Publishing Co., 1889), p. 9.

15. Regents Minutes, 4:56, September 16, 1897, and 4:130, August 7, 1899.

16. Ibid., 4:130, August 7, 1899; 4:135, September 8, 1899; and 4:133, September 12, 1899.

17. Ibid., 4:147, December 27, 1899.

18. Seattle *Times*, January 6, 13, 20, and 27, 1900, and Seattle *Post-Intelligencer*, January 5, 12, 19, and 26, 1900.

19. Regents Minutes; 4:151, February 14, 1900.

20. *Volume of Memoirs* (James A. Moore), pp. 747–49; Polk's *Seattle City Directory*, 1889 to 1901; Seattle *Times* (obituary, James A. Moore), May 22, 1929; Sophie Frye Bass, *When Seattle Was a Village* (naming of Capitol Hill) (Seattle: Lowman and Hanford, 1947), p. 140.

21. Abstract of Title to University Ten Acre Tract, Osborne, Tremper & Co., Inc., Seattle, December 20, 1921. Agreement June 24, 1899, J. C. Levold, H. P. McGuire, and Clarence W. Carter, in Regents Records, box 47, University of Washington Archives.

22. Regents Minutes, 4:156–57, April 11, 1900.

23. Ibid., 4:164, June 25, 1900.

24. Ibid., 4:166, August 13, 1900; 4:166–67, August 24, 1900; and 4:176, March 25, 1901.

25. Seattle *Post-Intelligencer*, April 13, 1900; W. B. Stratton to Secretary, Board of Regents, November 20, 1902, in Washington Attorney General, Letters, 1888–1946, Regents Records, box 6, folder 41, University of Washington Archives.

26. *Callvert* v. *Winsor*, 26 Washington 368 (1901).

27. Regents Minutes, 4:177, April 11, 1901.

28. Seattle *Post-Intelligencer*, July 16, 1901; *Callvert* v. *Winsor*.

29. Dodge, "Chronology," p. 14.

30. *Metropolitan Tract*, vol. 1, part 1 (vol. 297, p. 473, *Deeds*, and vol. 311, p. 191, *Deeds*, Records of King County), pp. 39–42; Regents Minutes, 4:210, October 30, 1901.

31. Frederick E. Bolton, "A History of the University of Washington, 1855–1953" (manuscript), chap. 14; "Lease of the Metropolitan Tract," Bolton Papers, University of Washington Archives.

32. Regents Minutes, 4:209, November 5, 1901; Dodge, "Chronology," p. 12.

33. William F. Prosser, *A History of the Puget Sound Country*, 2 vols. (New York and Chicago: Lewis Publishing Co., 1903) (William E. Schricker), 2:420–22.

34. Regents Minutes, 4:220, January 21, 1902, and 4:222, January 22, 1902.

35. Seattle *Post-Intelligencer*, January 6, 9, and 19, 1900; Seattle *Times*, December 7, 1902; Polk's *Seattle City Directory*, 1901, 1902.

36. Regents Minutes, 4:224, March 13, 1902; 4:228, April 25, 1902; and 4:230, May 7, 1902; Dodge, "Chronology," pp. 14–15.

37. Seattle *Times*, C. T. Conover, "Dignity and Conviction Characterized John Powell," February 18, 1950; (obituary, John H. Powell), March 10, 1930. Regents Minutes, 4:237, June 6, 1902.

38. Stratton to Markham, Secretary, Board of Regents, December 2, 1902, in Washington Attorney General, Letters, 1888–1946, Regents Records, box 6, folder 41, University of Washington Archives.

39. Regents Minutes, 4:278, December 9, 1902.

40. Ibid., 4:280–81, December 10, 1902.

41. Portland *Morning Oregonian*, "Levold Loses His Claim," November 16, 1904; "Metropolitan Building Company Lease: Document History, 1989–1921" (manuscript, 875 pp.), pp. 50–53, Regents Records, box 46, University of Washington Archives.

42. Regents Minutes, 4:283 (University Site Improvement Company lease text, pp. 283–95), December 22, 1902, and 4:296, December 23, 1902.

CHAPTER 3. *Call It Metropolitan: 1903 to 1907*

1. Seattle *Times* (obituary, M. F. Backus), February 16, 1935.
2. Seattle *Post-Intelligencer* (obituary, W. D. Hofius), February 28, 1912.
3. Polk's *Seattle City Directory*, 1901, 1902.
4. Bagley, *Seattle*, 3:377–78 (Stirrat), 3:389 (Goetz).
5. Regents Minutes, 4:300, January 27, 1903; 4:302, February 11, 1903; 4:304, February 25, 1903; 4:307, March 25, 1903; 4:317, June 9, 1903; 4:325, June 27, 1903; 4:375, June 14, 1904.
6. Metropolitan Building Company, *The Douglas Building: On the Site Where Seattle History Was Made*, promotional booklet, ca. 1925.
7. *Seventh Biennial Report of the Board of Regents to the Governor of Washington*, 1903, pp. 14–16.
8. Regents Minutes, 4:357, January 29, 1904; 4:361–62, February 25, 1904. See also Seattle *Post-Intelligencer*, January 30, 1904.
9. Regents Minutes, 4:363, February 25, 1904.
10. Ibid., 4:357, June 14, 1904.
11. Ibid., 4:388, October 28, 1904; Dodge, "Chronology," p. 17.
12. Regents Minutes, 4:384–404 (Moore lease text, pp. 391–401), November 1, 1904; 4:405, November 25, 1904. See also Moore lease text in *Metropolitan Tract*, vol. 1, part 3, The Moore Leases, pp. 53–63.
13. Regents Minutes, 4:404 (undated note).
14. Ibid., 4:384, November 1, 1904, and 4:405, November 25, 1904.
15. Dodge, "Chronology," p. 22.
16. Seattle *Times*, C. T. Conover, "James A. Moore Had a Spectacular Career," September 26, 1954; Polk's *Seattle City Directory*, 1901 to 1908; undated newspaper clipping (ca. 1902), "Mr. James A. Moore a Prominent Figure in the Upbuilding of This City," Edmond S. Meany Pioneer File, Northwest Collection, University of Washington Library.
17. Ted Van Arsdol, "Big House on the Columbia," *Franklin Flyer*, Franklin County [Washington] Historical Society, October 1974.
18. Conover, "James A. Moore"; Polk's *Seattle City Directory*, 1904; Seattle *Post-Intelligencer*, September 25, 1904.
19. *Where to Go in Seattle and the Puget Sound Country*, Seattle Chamber of Commerce, ca. 1904–5, Seattle Public Library; Seattle *Post-Intelligencer* (waterfront controversy), December 31, 1902; Clarence B. Bagley, *History of King County, Washington*, 4 vols. (Chicago and Seattle: S. J. Clarke Publishing Co., 1929), 1:310–30; Seattle *Times* (shipping "war"), December 10, 1902; Seattle *Sunday Times*, Fifth Anniversary Issue, February 10, 1907.
20. Dodge, "Chronology," pp. 68–70.
21. Van Arsdol, "Big House on the Columbia"; Conover, "James A. Moore."
22. Tacoma clipping (obituary, Frank D. Nash, undated), Meany Pioneer File, Northwest Collection, University of Washington Library; Seattle *Post-Intelligencer* (S. G. Cosgrove), September 10, October 18, 1908.
23. *Volume of Memoirs*, pp. 421–24; Seattle *Times* (obituary, John P. Hartman), October 30, 1945.
24. Bagley, *Seattle* (James T. Ronald), 2:837–40.
25. Ibid., (A. P. Sawyer), 3:924–27; Spokane *Spokesman-Review* (J. F. Saylor), March 22, 25, 1935.
26. Regents Minutes, 4:456–57, March 29, 1906.
27. *The University's Ten Acres*, Report of the Metropolitan leasehold study committee, University of Washington Alumni Association, August 1945; Regents Minutes, 4:480, November 6, 1906.
28. Regents Minutes, 4:488, January 25, 1907.
29. *Metropolitan Tract*, vol. 1, part 3 (vol. 21, p. 231, *Leases*, under receiving no. 492753, Records of King County), pp. 64–73.
30. Regents Minutes, 4:491, March 7, 1907.
31. *University's Ten Acres*.
32. Dodge, "Chronology," pp. 22–23; *Metropolitan Tract* (assignment of Moore lease to Metropolitan Building Company, December 3, 1907), vol. 1, part 3 (vol. 22, p. 86, *Leases*, Records of King County), pp. 73–75.

33. Dodge, "Chronology," p. 23; Regents Minutes, 4:551, March 31, 1908; "Document History," pp. 158–60.

CHAPTER 4. *The Transformation Begins: 1908 to 1911*

1. *Seattle and Western Washington: A Statement of Resources*, Seattle Chamber of Commerce, 1907; *Polk's Seattle City Directory*, 1908; Seattle *Times* (Valdez road), November 27, 1904, and (Valdez boom), September 2, 1907.
2. Seattle *Post-Intelligencer*, March 1, 5, 14, 29, and April 2, 3, 1908.
3. Seattle *Post-Intelligencer* (Seattle Symphony), March 1, 1908; (university graduates, faculty), March 5, 15, 1908; (Pioneer Place improvement plan), October 7, 1908; Regents Minutes (Curtis gift), 4:564; Gates, *First Century* (AYP funding), p. 124; Frank Calvert, ed., *The Cartoon: A Reference Book of Seattle's Successful Men* (Seattle: n.p., 1911) (Pantages) *Polk's Seattle City Directory* (theaters), 1906, 1907.
4. UNICO Properties, Inc., "Metropolitan Building Company: Factual History," informal summary, ca. 1965.
5. Dodge, "Chronology" (original Metropolitan stockholders), p. 23; conversation with James B. Douglas, November 1, 1976; Neva B. Douglas, "A Biographical Sketch of John Francis Douglas and Neva B. Douglas," unpublished memoir, ca. 1960.
6. Seattle *Post-Intelligencer* (obituary, Chester F. White), April 28, 1917; *The Cartoon* (White).
7. Bagley, *King County* (Bordeaux), 4:198–201; Seattle *Times* (obituary, Patrick McCoy), December 1, 1938.
8. Seattle *Times* (obituary, Charles Henry Cobb), November 16, 1939; Cornelius H. Hanford, ed., *Seattle and Environs, 1852–1924*, 4 vols. (Chicago: Pioneer Historical Publishing Co., 1924), 1:481–83.
9. Bagley, *Seattle*, 3:41–42; Seattle *Times* (obituary, Warren Danforth Lane), January 10, 1938.
10. Seattle *Times*, May 28, 1959, and (obituary, Richard D. Merrill), October 25, 1965; *The Cartoon* (Austin E. Griffiths).
11. Bagley, *King County*, 4:158–61.
12. Bagley, *Seattle*, 3:5–7.
13. Neva B. Douglas, "Biographical Sketch"; conversations with Neva Douglas (daughter), August 2–3, 1978.
14. Ibid.; Seattle *Times* (obituary, J. F. Douglas), November 30, 1952; John Monk Saunders, "A Western Builder Who Changed the Face of a City," *American Magazine*, November 1924, pp. 16–17, 177–83.
15. Neva B. Douglas, "Biographical Sketch," and conversation with James B. Douglas, 1976.
16. Neva B. Douglas, "Biographical Sketch."
17. Metropolitan Building Company, *Metropolitan Bulletin*, July 18, 1908; Saunders, "Western Builder"; conversation with James B. Douglas.
18. Neva B. Douglas, "Biographical Sketch."
19. Ibid., and Saunders, "Western Builder."
20. George H. Emerson as quoted in Howells & Stokes, Architects, "Some Work, Away from New York," *American Architect*, June 21, 1916, p. 404.
21. New York *Times* (obituary, John Howells), September 23, 1959; *Who's Who in America* (Howells, John Mead), 1922–1923; *Biographical Dictionary of American Architects (Deceased)* (Los Angeles: New Age Publishing Co., 1956) (Stokes, I. N. Phelps); Seattle *Times* (report of Howells death, incorporating note on Albertson), September 23, 1959.
22. Seattle *Post-Intelligencer*, March 8, 1908.
23. Ibid.; Douglas to Sawyer, March 25, 1908, "Document History," p. 166.
24. Howells & Stokes, "Some Work, Away from New York," pp. 402–3.
25. Seattle *Post-Intelligencer* (Fourth Avenue grading), June 14, 1908; Seattle *Star*, "Metropolitan Leasehold Assessment Is Sustained," August 18, 1909; Howells & Stokes, "Some Work, Away from New York."
26. Regents Minutes, 4:558, June 1, 1908, and 4:564, June 24, 1908.
27. Ibid., 4:585, January 26, 1909, and 4:587, February 10, 1909; Tacoma newspaper clip-

ping, unidentified (obituary, Frank D. Nash), Meany Pioneer File, Northwest Collection, University of Washington Library.

28. Regents Minutes, 4:629, October 26, 1909, 4:641, January 7, 1910; 4:651–52, February 23, 1910; and 4:668, April 26, 1910.

29. Seattle *Star*, "A. E. Parish Assesses Leasehold," August 2, 1909, and "Metropolitan Leasehold Assessment Is Sustained," August 18, 1909.

30. Regents Minutes, 4:547, February 27, 1908.

31. Letter report (copy), "Statement as to the University Tract and Parcels Taken Therefrom," Professor Leslie J. Ayer to Regents, July 19, 1929, Regents Records, box 47, University of Washington Archives.

32. Ibid.

33. Regents Minutes (Meany request), 4:564, June 24, 1908.

34. A. H. Albertson, Howells & Stokes, "Old University Building," report (copy), March 24, 1910, Regents Records, box 47, University of Washington Archives.

35. Regents' files, membership by year; Polk's *Tacoma City Directory* (John A. Rea), 1909.

36. Seattle *Post-Intelligencer* (Howard G. Cosgrove), November 20, 1913; Hanford, *Seattle and Environs* (John C. Higgins), 2:640; Seattle *Times* (obituary, A. F. McEwan), August 21, 1945; Extract copy, *Senate Journal, 1911*, "Regarding Appointment of Regent M. F. Backus (Confirmed)," Regents Records, box 49, University of Washington Archives.

37. "Metropolitan Building Company, Factual History": Metropolitan Building Company, *Metropolitan Bulletin*, January 1 and 29, February 26, and March 12, 1910.

38. Seattle *Post-Intelligencer*, "Plans for a Big Department Store," July 31, 1909.

39. Neva B. Douglas, "Biographical Sketch"; conversation with James B. Douglas, 1976, and correspondence, 1977; "The Highlands, Seattle," booklet, articles of incorporation and bylaws, 1908; Seattle *Times* (obituary, C. D. Stimson), August 30, 1929.

40. *Metropolitan Bulletin*, December 4, 1909.

41. Ibid.

42. Conversation and correspondence with James B. Douglas.

43. Metropolitan Building Company, Prospectus (offering of $500,000 in 6 percent sinking-fund bonds), 1910 (copy), "Document History," pp. 189–93.

44. Herman Steen, *The O. W. Fisher Heritage* (Seattle: Frank McCaffrey Publishers, 1961); Seattle *Times* (obituary, O. D. Fisher), January 2, 1967.

45. Douglas to Regents, March 21, 1911, "Document History," pp. 229–30; Dodge, "Chronology," p. 26.

46. Seattle *Post-Intelligencer*, "The New Metropolitan Theatre," October 1, 1911.

47. *Metropolitan Tract*, vol. 1, part 3, The Moore Leases, pp. 76–77, 66.

48. Dodge, "Chronology," p. 34.

49. Ibid., p. 35.

50. Regents Minutes, 4:694, October 25, 1910.

51. Ibid., p. 698, November 29, 1910, and pp. 699–700, December 6, 1910; Seattle *Post-Intelligencer*, "Klaw & Erlanger Theater Will Be Started at Once," November 17, 1910.

52. Dodge, "Chronology" (transcript of Douglas's letter to Regents, December 8, 1910), p. 39.

53. Regents Minutes, 4:694.

54. Seattle *Post-Intelligencer*, "Klaw-Erlanger House to Open," August 21, 1911, and "The New Metropolitan Theatre," October 1, 1911.

55. Seattle *Post-Intelligencer*, "The New Metropolitan Theatre," October 1, 1911.

56. Ibid.

57. Ibid.

58. *Metropolitan Bulletin*, "Golden Potlatch, 1912," October 21, 1911, and "A Letter from J. F. Douglas," December 30, 1911.

Chapter 5. *To Build a Center: 1912 to 1917*

1. Gates, *First Century*, pp. 130–31; Spokane *Spokesman-Review*, "University Lands Worth Millions Leased in Seattle for Sums Less Than Taxes Would Bring to the State," June 27, 1909, and A. P. Sawyer response in *Spokesman-Review* as reprinted in the *Metropolitan Bulletin*, Metropolitan Building Company, July 31, 1909.

2. "Document History," copy of "Report upon the University Grounds Prepared by the

Taxation Committee of the [Seattle] Chamber of Commerce," pp. 201–2, and copy of Senate Bill 127, "An Act Relating to or Affecting the Leasing of What Is Known as the 'Old University Tract' in Seattle" (January 30, 1911), p. 225, with summary of legislative history, pp. 226–28.

3. *Metropolitan Tract*, vol. 1, part 3, The Moore Leases (Modification Agreement of January 8, 1912), pp. 80–82.

4. Dodge, "Chronology," pp. 26–27; "Document History," pp. 260–61, 262; Regents Minutes, 5:19, March 27, 1912.

5. Dodge, "Chronology," pp. 30–31.

6. Regents Minutes, 5:39, July 23, 1912; Regents Records ("Gist of statement made by Mr. J. F. Douglas . . . July 23, 1912"), box 47, University of Washington Archives.

7. Neva B. Douglas, "Biographical Sketch."

8. Transcript (copy) of analysis of Metropolitan Building Company financial status and management (by unidentified brokerage or credit firm), Regents Records, box 47, University of Washington Archives.

9. Neva B. Douglas, "Biographical Sketch."

10. Ibid., *Metropolitan Bulletin* (management meetings), March 12, 1910, and (company employment), June 17, 1911.

11. Bagley, *King County* (James Doster Hoge), 3:724–27; Seattle *Times* (obituary, Joshua Green), January 27, 1975.

12. Conversation with Loyal Treat Nichols (and notes from scrapbooks), August 7, 1978; *Advance Bio-Bulletin* (New York: Co-Operative Press, 1914) (Harry Whitney Treat); Seattle *Post-Intelligencer* (the Treat tallyho), January 29, 1955, and "Picturesque Coaching Days of Old England To Be Revived for Ten Days in Seattle by H. W. Treat," May 29, 1910; Seattle *Times*, "H. W. Treat Meets Death!" July 31, 1922, and Dorothy Brant Brazier, "Distinguished Name Saluted," August 14, 1972.

13. Conversations with Dorothy Stimson Bullitt, July 6 and November 17, 1978; "The Highlands, Seattle"; Seattle *Times* (obituary, C. D. Stimson), August 30, 1929; Seattle *Post-Intelligencer*, Northwest Magazine, "Dorothy Stimson Bullitt: She's as Contemporary as the Next TV Newscast," November 5, 1978.

14. Regents Minutes, 5:96–97, May 14, 1913; *Metropolitan Tract*, vol. 1, part 3, Modification Agreement of May 14, 1913, pp. 82–84.

15. Gates, *First Century*, pp. 131–40.

16. Lister to Cosgrove, August 13, 1913, Washington Governor, Incoming Letters, 1888–1944, Regents Records, box 7, folder 34, University of Washington Archives.

17. Seattle *Post-Intelligencer*, "Cosgrove Quits as Regent and 2 May Follow," November 20, 1913; "Regents Do Not Get Resignation of Dr. T. F. Kane," November 26, 1913; "F. A. Hazeltine First Regent to Drop Out," December 29, 1913; University of Washington *Daily*, October 2, 1913, and January 5, 1914.

18. *Metropolitan Bulletin*, February 14, 1914; Polk's *Seattle City Directory*, 1913; University of Washington *Daily*, January 5, 1914.

19. Yakima *Daily Republic* (obituary, Oscar A. Fechter), February 25, 1935; Fechter on "University Control," *Washington Alumnus*, November 1914.

20. Seattle *Times*, "Winlock Miller Quits U. W. Regents Board," October 23, 1957, and (obituary, Winlock W. Miller), January 20, 1964.

21. Lloyd Spencer and Lancaster Pollard, *A History of the State of Washington*, 4 vols. (New York: American Historical Society, 1937) (Charles Ernest Gaches), 3:71.

22. Dodge, "Chronology," pp. 24–25.

23. Douglas to Regents, "Improvements Required for the Extension of Permit Time on Temporary Buildings," April 24, 1914, "Document History," p. 279.

24. Regents Minutes, 5:170, April 24, 1914; "Document History," pp. 276–77.

25. Regents Minutes, 5:173, May 20, 1914; "Document History," p. 281.

26. Regents Minutes, 5:195–96, June 16, 1914; "Document History," pp. 279, 285–87.

27. *Washington Alumnus*, November 1914 and January 1915.

28. B. C. Forbes, *Men Who Are Making the West* (New York: B. C. Forbes Publishing Co., 1923), pp. 76–96; Carnation Company, *Fifty Years of Progress, 1899–1949* (1950).

29. Regents Minutes, 5:239–40, May 8, 1915; "Document History" (Bebb & Gould reports, August 19, 1914), pp. 295–96, (November 19, 1914), pp. 298–300; Dodge, "Chronology" (cost of Stuart Building), p. 34.

30. Gates, *First Century*, pp. 142–45.

31. Regents Minutes, 5:260–61, June 14, 1915.
32. Dodge, "Chronology," pp. 44–46.
33. Regents Minutes, 5:262, June 16, 1915.
34. Ibid., 5:267, July 23, 1915.
35. Ibid., 5:274, September 24, 1915; Dodge, "Chronology," pp. 47–49; *Metropolitan Tract*, vol. 1, part 3, Modification Agreement of September 29, 1915, pp. 84–86.
36. Dodge, "Chronology," p. 50; "Document History," pp. 335–42 (Gaches to Miller, October 8, 1915; Markham to Gaches, October 9, 1915; Markham to Gaches, October 12, 1915; Gaches to Miller, October 18, 1915; Markham to Miller, October 20, 1915; Miller to Gaches, telegram).
37. Dodge, "Chronology," p. 50.
38. Regents Minutes, 5:281–82, October 29, 1915.
39. Ibid., 5:284–85, October 30, 1915.
40. *Washington Alumnus*, "Billy Visits the Judge," December 1923.
41. *Washington Alumnus*, "Alumni to the Regents," December 1915.
42. Ibid.
43. *Washington Alumnus*, "A Decision with Consequences," November 1915.
44. Regents Minutes, 5:291, December 27, 1915; Seattle *Times*, "Regents Won't Accept Arena as Permanent," December 28, 1915; Dodge, "Chronology," pp. 52–55.
45. Dodge, "Chronology," pp. 53–54 (and texts of letters in "Document History").
46. Chap. 66, *Laws of 1915* (act of March 15, 1915: Providing Funds for New Buildings for University of Washington); *Washington Alumnus*, "Collegiate Tudor Is Type of New Building," November 1915, and "The University Building Fund," December 1915.
47. Metropolitan Building Company, *Development of the University Tract* (Seattle: Lumbermen's Printing Co., n.d. [ca. 1917]), Northwest Collection, University of Washington Library.
48. Neva B. Douglas, "Biographical Sketch"; Seattle *Times* (first Seattle–New York long-distance telephone service), September 29, 1936.
49. Douglas to Suzzallo, December 14, 1916, meeting of February 20, and Douglas to Regents, March 12, 1917, "Document History," pp. 414, 420, 421.
50. Douglas to Suzzallo, April 16, 1917, and Henry to Suzzallo, April 19, 1917, "Document History," pp. 423–24, 426–27.
51. Suzzallo to Douglas, April 20, 1917, "Document History," p. 425.
52. Seattle *Post-Intelligencer*, Walter Evans, "The Mercer Girls"; Regents Minutes, 5:452, August 23, 1917.

CHAPTER 6. *The Center in Place: 1918 to 1925*

1. Gates, *First Century* (campus in wartime, Suzzallo activities), pp. 153–55; *Fifteenth Biennial Report of the Regents to the Governor of Washington* (campus military training, Boeing gift), 1919.
2. Neva B. Douglas, "Biographical Sketch."
3. Conversations with Miss Neva Douglas, August 2–3, 1978.
4. Saunders, "Western Builder," p. 183.
5. Metropolitan Building Company, *Development of the University Tract* (see chap 5, n. 47, above).
6. Saunders, "Western Builder," p. 178; *Metropolitan Bulletin*, October 15, 1926.
7. *Metropolitan Bulletin*, February 14, 1914.
8. Conversation with James B. Douglas, November 3, 1976; Saunders, "Western Builder," p. 179.
9. Saunders, "Western Builder," pp. 180, 16.
10. Neva B. Douglas, "Biographical Sketch"; conversations with Miss Neva Douglas.
11. Seattle *Post-Intelligencer*, "Moore Decides Against Locating in Northwest," September 3, 1918; Seattle *Times*, C. T. Conover, "James A. Moore Had a Spectacular Career," September 26, 1954.
12. Regents' files (collected notes on McKee); *Washington Alumnus*, "Interesting Alumni: Ruth Karr McKee," May 1915.
13. Regents Minutes (joint meeting of regents with Metropolitan Building Company

trustees), 5:720, September 4, 1920; and (Metropolitan lease committee meeting), 5:736, November 26, 1920.

14. Stuart and Douglas to Regents, May 13, 1921, Regents Records, box 49, University of Washington Archives.

15. Seattle *Argus*, "A New Hotel," May 21, 1921.

16. Regents Minutes (Perkins in Washington, D.C.), 6:14, May 26, 1921.

17. Seattle *Union-Record*, "Would Upset Decision," May 30, 1921.

18. Regents Minutes (text of statement on hotel proposal), 6:10–22, May 26–27, 1921.

19. Seattle *Post-Intelligencer*, May 28, 1921.

20. Stuart and Douglas to Higgins, May 24, 1921, Regents Records, box 49, University of Washington Archives.

21. Seattle *Times*, "Would Force Regents' Hands in Hotel Row," May 31, 1921; Seattle *Argus*, "A Fair Offer," June 4, 1921.

22. Stuart and Douglas to Regents, in Dodge, "Chronology," p. 93; Regents Minutes (acknowledgment of letter) 6:27, July 8, 1921.

23. Dodge, "Chronology" (Community Hotel incorporation), pp. 94–95; Seattle *Times* (advertisement, "Seattle's New Hotel Project"), June 29, 1922; Community Hotel Corporation prospectus, "Seattle's Own New Hotel," 1922, Olympic Hotel file, property of A. S. Kerry, Jr., Seattle.

24. Seattle *Times* (page one obituary, Frank Waterhouse), March 20, 1930.

25. Seattle *Times* (oil boom in Alaska), July 12, 1922; (Klondike gold rush anniversary), July 15, 1922; (construction on university tract, elsewhere), July 16, August 15, 1922; (Boeing aircraft work, opening of Public Market), August 15, 1922.

26. Seattle *Times* (hotel campaign preparations and opening of drive), July 1–25, 1922.

27. Seattle *Times* (Ellzey and the Olympic), September 1–2, 1922.

28. Roy H. Dodge, "The University '10 Acre Tract' in Seattle," chap. 10, pp. 10–11, Regents Records, box 47, University of Washington Archives; Seattle *Times*, "Lease for Seattle's Great New Hotel Signed!" October 20, 1922; "Olympic Hotel Company," descriptive folder, October/November 1922, Kerry file.

29. Seattle *Times* (preparations for hotel construction), October 31, 1922.

30. Community Hotel Corporation, "Annual Report of President Waterhouse and Financial Statement," December 4, 1923, Kerry file.

31. Communtiy Hotel Corporation (letterhead list of directors), January 1923, and "The Olympic Hotel, Seattle," announcement of public inspection, June 14, 1924, Kerry file.

32. Kerry to Halsey, Stewart & Co., Chicago (management concept, steel problems, sale of bonds), December 10, 1923, and to Roy Carruthers (organizational problems), October 24, 1924, Kerry file.

33. Seattle *Times* (obituary, A. S. Kerry), April 28, 1939, and C. T. Conover, "Albert S. Kerry—Civic and Business Leader . . . ," November 16, 1950.

34. A. S. Kerry (text of talk when hotel was turned over to the Olympic Hotel Company), October 31, 1924, Kerry file.

35. Seattle *Times* (activities at completion of hotel construction, with photographs), November 1, 1924; photographs of signs on hotel structure during construction, Kerry file.

36. Kerry (text of talk, October 31, 1924), Kerry file.

37. Regents Minutes (free use of Arena), 6:71, February 27, 1922; (White Annex approval), 6:73, February 27, 1922; (Arena modification plans) 6:82, April 21, 1922; (amended Arena plans, Stuart Annex), 6:89, June 17, 1922.

38. *Metropolitan Tract*, vol. 1, part 1, Laws Relating to the Metropolitan Tract (chap. 44, *Laws of 1923*), p. 10.

39. Dodge, "Chronology" (Arena reconstruction permit, Albertson letter), p. 59; Regents Minutes (conditional approval of plans), 6:136, May 26, 1923.

40. Dodge, "Chronology," p. 62.

41. Ibid. (Metropolitan letter on change in Arena plans, City Building Department report), pp. 62–65; Regents Minutes (new Arena plans to buildings and grounds committee), 6:182, March 14, 1924; (buildings and grounds committee report), 6:188, March 29, 1924; *Metropolitan Bulletin* (garage plan), March 7, 1924.

42. Regents Minutes (Arena plans ordered filed), 6:188, and (lien bond question), 6:188–89, May 28, 1924; *Metropolitan Bulletin* (officers, "junior board"), January 12, 1924.

43. Regents' files (Donworth resignation, Heffernan appointment); Seattle *Times* (Heffernan as "capitalist"), June 21, 1925.

44. Regents Minutes (Condon acting for Markham), 6:214, October 17–18, 1924, and (Condon succeeds Markham), 6:260, February 26–27, 1925; (Markham on leave to attend Custer regimental reunion), 6:132, May 25, 1923.

45. Seattle *Post-Intelligencer* (general developments of 1925), miscellaneous issues, June 1925.

46. Regents Minutes (authority for negotiating Dodge agreement), 6:289, March 20, 1925; (authorizing resolution), 6:300–302, April 24, 1925; (agreement between regents and Dodge, Heffernan for regents), 6:315–17, May 15, 1925.

47. Roy H. Dodge, letter-report to Regents, "In re Metropolitan Building Co. Lease," March 12, 1925, Regents Records, box 47, University of Washington Archives.

48. Roy H. Dodge, undated report, Regents Records, box 47.

49. Dodge, "Chronology" (Proctor letter, extract of building permit), pp. 65–66.

50. Regents Minutes (regents' resolution on Arena as temporary building), 6:324–27, June 16, 1925.

51. "Builders Race Against Time—Make Record," *Pacific Builder and Engineer*, July 24, 1925.

52. Condon to Regents McKee, Rupp, Rogers, Davis, and Fechter (letters on Powell appointment), June 23, 1925, and regents' responses, June 24–28, 1925, Regents Records, box 49, University of Washington Archives.

53. Seattle *Times*, "University Regent Explains Arena Lease Inquiry," June 27, 1925; Seattle *Post-Intelligencer*, "Arena Site Under Roof Against Time," June 28, 1925; Seattle *Star*, "U. of W. Lease Fight On," June 27, 1925.

54. Regents Minutes (Powell report and text of opinion), 6:341–50, September 20, 1925.

CHAPTER 7. *Good Times, Hard Times, War: 1926 to 1943*

1. UNICO Properties, Inc., "Metropolitan Building Company: Factual History," informal summary, ca. 1965.

2. Metropolitan Building Company, *The Stimson Building*, promotional booklet, 1926.

3. Metropolitan Building Company, *The White-Henry-Stuart Building*, no date, and *The Cobb Building*, 1926; *Metropolitan Bulletin*, February 9, 1924, and October 15, 1926; *The Stimson Building ("You may be proud . . .")*.

4. *Metropolitan Bulletin* (railroad, lumber offices), March 7, 1924; Carnation Company, *Fifty Years of Progress, 1899–1949* (see chap. 5, n. 28, above).

5. Neva B. Douglas, "Biographical Sketch"; *Seattle Times* (obituary, D. E. Skinner), December 28, 1933.

6. *Metropolitan Bulletin* (Metropolitan administrative staff), September 25, 1925; Seattle Public Library biographical file (Robert C. Reamer), December 1978.

7. Seattle Public Library biographical file (Eustace P. Ziegler), December 1978.

8. Seattle *Times* (obituary, Roland H. Hartley), September 22, 1952; Gates, *First Century* (Suzzallo and Hartley), pp. 165–67.

9. Regents Minutes (resolution supporting Suzzallo), 6:292, April 24, 1925.

10. Henry Suzzallo, "The Student's Part in the University," address to students at first fall assembly, 1915, *Washington Alumnus*, November 1915.

11. Henry Suzzallo, inaugural address, *Washington Alumnus*, May 1916.

12. Regents Minutes (Fifth Avenue Building and regents), 6:341, September 26, 1925; (Skinner Building plans, bond), 6:355–56, November 6, 1925; (Miller elected secretary of board), 6:363, January 9, 1926; (Powell report on insurance, Bebb & Gould on Skinner Building plans, new Dodge contract), 6:371, February 1–2, 1926; (Skinner Building plans approved, Henry gift of art collection, 6:388–89, March 12–13, 1926.

13. Gates, *First Century* (Hartley appointments, Supreme Court ruling on right of appointment), p. 170. Hartley appointees: Polk's *Spokane City Directory* (Balch), 1926; regents' biographical files (Lewis); Polk's *Everett City Directory* (Jordan), 1926–27; Polk's *Tacoma City Directory* (Johns), 1927. Regents Minutes (Hartley and Dunbar letters, election of officers), 6:397–402, May 7, 1926.

14. University of Washington *Daily* report of regents' meeting, "Hartley Changes Will Be Contested," May 7, 1926; "Regents Retain Suzzallo for Year," June 3, 1926; ("anti-Hartley" mass meeting), June 8, 1926.

15. Regents Minutes (dismissal of Suzzallo), 6:468–69, October 4, 1926; University of

Washington *Daily*, "Regents Oust President," October 5, 1926. Hartley appointees: Polk's *Yakima City Directory* (Perry), 1926; Seattle *Times* (obituary, J. D. Farrell), November 17, 1933; Centralia *Daily Chronicle* (obituary, Joseph E. Lease), October 15, 1930.

16. Regents Minutes (Spencer's selection), 6:555, July 25, 1926; Seattle *Times* (obituary, J. V. Paterson), May 20, 1947.

17. Dodge to Rupp (letter concerning payment of fee including expression of appreciation of help offered by Winlock Miller, Herbert T. Condon, and Leslie J. Ayer), April 20, 1926, Regents Records, box 47, University of Washington Archives.

18. Dodge, "Chronology" and "University '10 Acre Tract,'" Regents Records, box 47; Regents Record, 6:373–74, February 1–2, 1926.

19. Dodge, "University '10 Acre Tract,'" chap. 2: "Early Lease Negotiations from 1899 to 1907," pp. 10–13.

20. Dodge to Regents, "In re Metropolitan Building Co. Lease," March 12, 1925, Regents Records, box 47.

21. Dodge, "University '10 Acre Tract,'" chap. 7, pp. 16–17.

22. Leslie J. Ayer, "The Metropolitan Lease" ("original opinion," undated, but accompanying statement of July 19, 1929), Regents Records, box 47.

23. Dodge, "University '10 Acre Tract,'" chap. 8: "Condemnations Affecting the 10 Acre Tract," pp. 11–12; Regents Minutes (Powell to Regents), 6:340–42, September 26, 1925; Ayer, "Metropolitan Lease."

24. Regents Minutes (Powell to Regents), 6:340–42.

25. Dodge, "University '10 Acre Tract,'" chap. 5: "The Metropolitan Theatre Modification and Widening of University Street," p. 8.

26. Ayer, "Metropolitan Lease."

27. Regents Minutes (Powell to Regents), 6:340–42; Dodge, "University '10 Acre Tract,'" chap. 9: "Conditions and Covenants of Lease and Discussions of Compliance or Non-Compliance Thereof by Lessee," pp. 15–16; Ayer, "Metropolitan Lease."

28. Dodge, "University '10 Acre Tract,'" chap. 9 (analysis of insurance at Metropolitan Center), pp. 7–10.

29. Ibid., chap. 10: "Miscellaneous Matters Including the Community Hotel, Taxation, and the Metropolitan Corporation," pp. 5–8; Dodge to Rupp (Dodge on the quality of his work).

30. Seattle *Times*, "Metropolitan Company Rivals Press Tax Suit" (on "competitors" and stockholders with "a grouch on"), August 28, 1925.

31. Bagley, *King County*, 3:748–53; Seattle *Times* (obituary, A. Scott Bullitt), April 11, 1932.

32. Roland H. Hartley campaign folder, "Scott Bullitt and the Metropolitan Building Company," November 1928, Seattle Public Library, unclassified Northwest materials, box 6.

33. Jordan to Douglas, letter request (copy) for reimbursement for state's share of Union Street condemnation award, April 29, 1929, Regents Records, box 48.

34. Donworth to Jordan, May 2, 1929, Regents Records, box 48.

35. Paterson to Donworth, November 10, 1929, and Donworth to Paterson, November 22, 1929, Regents Records, box 48.

36. Seattle *Times* (obituary, James A. Moore), May 22, 1929; (obituary, C. D. Stimson), August 30, 1929; and Conover, "James A. Moore Had a Spectacular Career," September 26, 1954.

37. Metropolitan Company, Minute Book (book 1), June 28, 1929, to March 30, 1935 (Norton Clapp, Metropolitan Building Corporation, Seattle).

38. Seattle *Times* (obituary, Clarence D. Martin), August 12, 1955, and biographical file, Seattle Public Library.

39. Seattle *Post-Intelligencer*, "Spencer May Lose Presidency of Institution," January 26, 1933.

40. Ibid., and Seattle *Post-Intelligencer*, "University of Washington Regents Rush Work of Reorganization," January 28, 1933.

41. Seattle *Times*, "Death of Lewis B. Schwellenbach Ends Distinguished Career," June 10, 1948.

42. Edgar I. Stewart, *Washington: Northwest Frontier*, 4 vols. (New York: Lewis Historical Publishing Co., 1957) (Edward Patrick Ryan), 3:237–38.

43. Seattle *Times* (obituary, Alfred Shemanski), August 17, 1966.

44. Seattle *Times* (obituary, Robert L. Montgomery), May 4, 1936.

45. Seattle *Times* (obituary, Philip D. Macbride), April 9, 1965.

46. Regents Minutes (executive committee to get legal opinion on use of rentals from tract), 7:47, January 27, 1933; (executive committee report), 7:48, February 4, 1933; (Miller proposal), 7:52, February 5, 1933; and (proposed agreement with bank), 7:129, October 16, 1934.

47. Gates, *First Century*, pp. 180–82.

48. Seattle *Times*, "Gilman Retires as G. N. Chief," December 30, 1936, and (obituary, Thomas Balmer), August 3, 1959.

49. Seattle *Times* (obituary, Edmond S. Meany), April 22, 1935.

50. Neva B. Douglas, "Biographical Sketch"; Polk's *Seattle City Directory* (officers of Metropolitan Building Company), 1933.

51. Neva B. Douglas, "Biographical Sketch."

52. Seattle *Times* (obituary, Walter T. Douglas), May 1, 1936.

53. UNICO Properties, Inc., "Metropolitan Building Company: Factual History."

54. Ibid.

55. Price, Waterhouse & Co., December 31, 1938, report noting reorganization and transfer of assets of Metropolitan Company and Fifth Avenue Building Company to Metropolitan Building Company, in Historical Files, box 1, University Metropolitan Tract Office.

56. Seattle *Times* (obituary, Andrew Steers), January 26, 1962, and (obituary, C. W. Stimson), October 2, 1953; Metropolitan Building Company (officers, directors, and department heads), *Directory of Tenants*, 1942.

57. Seattle *Times*, "Metropolitan Probe Ordered," February 28, 1939; University of Washington *Daily*, "University May Get Large Added Rents . . . ," February 28, 1939; Regents Minutes (Condon on legislative committee action), 7:391, January 13, 1940.

58. *Washington Alumnus*, "Washingtonians You Should Know: Eugene A. White," April 1943.

59. Seattle *Times* (Anderson and White join board of regents), June 14, 1942.

60. Regents Minutes (war damage insurance), 9:509, June 26, 1942, and 9:510, July 31, 1942; (extension of lease on the Olympic denied), 9:538, November 28, 1942.

61. Chap. 59, *Laws of 1943* (Removal of Regents of Institutions of Higher Learning), March 3, 1943; *Washington Alumnus*, "Safeguards for University Regents," March 1943.

62. Seattle *Times*, "Wm. Edris Gets Olympic Hotel," July 15, 1943; "Metropolitan Building Company: Factual History."

CHAPTER 8. *Moving Toward Decision—Again: 1944 to 1950*

1. *Washington Alumnus* (Frayn elected president), June 1944; University of Washington Alumni Association, *The University's Ten Acres*, August 1945.

2. *Twenty-eighth Biennial Report from the Board of Regents to the Governor of Washington* (enrollments, campus in wartime), December 2, 1944.

3. *University's Ten Acres*.

4. House Joint Resolution No. 16 (by Mr. Yantis), Twenty-ninth Legislative Session, 1945; Seattle *Times* (organization of legislative interim committee, "Interim Group Opens Study of U. Met Problem"), July 15, 1945.

5. Regents' files, board membership by years, 1945-1947.

6. Seattle *Times* (obituary, John L. King), August 29, 1973; news report, "Captain Fox Named on U.W. Board," July 12, 1945; Seattle *Post-Intelligencer* (obituary, Joseph Drumheller), April 30, 1970; (Clarence J. Coleman), *Who's Who in Washington*, 1962, and *Washington Alumnus*, November 1946.

7. *Current Biography*, 1949 (Dave Beck), and *Who's Who in America*, 1958–1959; Seattle *Times*, "Beck Tells Plans for U.," April 23, 1946.

8. *Who's Who in Washington*, 1962 (Mort Frayn); conversations with George V. Powell, January 31, 1978, and Frayn, February 3, 1978.

9. Seattle *Times* (obituary, "Charles F. Frankland, Banker, Regent, Dies"), December 7, 1973, and *Who's Who in Washington*, 1962; conversation with Frayn (Frankland's interest in alumni association).

10. Seattle *Times* (obituary, R. B. Harris), June 23, 1968; conversation with Frayn (Harris's probable role).

11. Regents Minutes (Wahlstrom, Conrad appointments), 9:654, July 15, 1944, and 9:686,

May 3, 1945; (Falknor bill on medical and dental schools), 9:679, October 31, 1944; Seattle *Times* (obituary, Nelson A. Wahlstrom, October 20, 1972; *Who's Who in Washington*, 1962 (Ernest M. Conrad).

12. Regents Minutes (Allen offered presidency), 9:777; *Washington Alumnus*, "Dr. R. B. Allen Elected University President," March 1946; Seattle *Times*, "R. B. Allen Takes Post on Sept. 1," February 24, 1946.

13. Metropolitan Building Company, *Annual Report to Stockholders*, 1944–1945, 1946–1947.

14. Reed to Balmer, January 2, 1946, Thomas Balmer Papers, box 14, folder 3, Archives and Manuscripts Division, Manuscripts Section, University of Washington Library (box and folder numbers hereafter abbreviated: 14–3).

15. Seattle *Times* (biographical note on William G. Reed), November 10, 1941; conversation with Reed about presidency of Metropolitan Building Company, February 23, 1978.

16. Regents Minutes (interim committee meeting with regents), 9:736, September 29, 1945; (additional contacts), 9:764, January 5, 1946; ("more permanent arrangement" for consultations), 9:776–77; (Harris offer), 9:796, April 13, 1946; (Falknor-Wahlstrom trip east), 9:788, March 16, 1946; (Falknor's personal report on eastern trip, Wahlstrom's instructions on early conferences), 9:803, May 18, 1946; (text of Falknor-Wahlstrom report of May 16, 1946), Balmer Papers, 14–4.

17. Balmer Papers, 14–4; Regents Minutes (report of the board to legislative interim committee, corporate tax on Metropolitan Building Company), 9:823, August 3, 1946.

18. University of Washington Alumni Association, memorandum (copy), "To the Legislative Interim Committee on the Metropolitan Leasehold," June 12, 1946, Balmer Papers, 14–4.

19. Regents' report to interim committee, August 3, 1946.

20. Neal to Regents (copy), September 11, 1946. Balmer Papers, 14–4; Regents Minutes (Neal's letter before board), 9:833, September 28, 1946.

21. Balmer and Wahlstrom, joint memorandum for the record (carbon copy, signed), of meeting with Reed and Steers on November 15, 1946, Balmer Papers, 14–5.

22. Conversation with William G. Reed (visits to New York investment houses).

23. Regents Minutes (meeting with legislative interim committee), 9:846, December 2, 1946.

24. Balmer to Coleman, Drumheller, and Beck (memorandum, "Metropolitan Tract," calling meeting of December 27, 1946), December 19, 1946, Balmer Papers, 14–5.

25. Seattle *Star*, "U.W. Offers to Buy 'Met' Tract Lease" and "Metropolitan Lease Profits Average $646,000 per Year," December 31, 1946; Seattle *Times*, "U.W. Seeks to Buy Lease on Metropolitan Center," December 31, 1946.

26. Reed to Regents, letter (carbon transcript) transmitting Metropolitan Building Company profit-sharing proposal, December 26, 1946, Balmer Papers, 14–5.

27. Gates (Canwell Committee background), *First Century*, pp. 196–97.

28. House Bill 268, Thirtieth Legislative Session, 1947; Seattle *Times*, "Bill Would Add to Regents' Power," February 10, 1947.

29. *Report of Legislative Interim Committee on "Old University Grounds" Metropolitan Leases, as Authorized by House Joint Resolution No. 16* (n.p., 1947), p. 17; Seattle *Times*, "Solons to Get New 'Met' Plan," February 7, 1947.

30. University of Washington—Board of Regents, chap. 284 (H.B. 268), *Session Laws, Washington, 1947*.

31. State Legislative Council, chap. 36 (H.B. 115), *Session Laws, Washington, 1947*; Governor Mon C. Wallgren (veto message on H.B. 268), March 22, 1947, *House Journal*, January 13, 1949.

32. Metropolitan Building Company, *Annual Report*, 1946–1947.

33. Seattle *Times*, "Met Company Plans Garage for 1,000 Cars," May 21, 1947.

34. Regents' files, board membership by years (Stuntz replaces Fox), 1947–1948.

35. Edris to Regents (original letter to Wahlstrom, copy to Balmer), April 11, 1947, Balmer Papers, 14–5.

36. Memorandum response (draft), "Re: Offer Concerning Metropolitan Tract Made by Wm. Edris Co., in Letter Dated April 11, 1947," and "Report and Summary of Meeting of the Metropolitan Lease Committee with Mr. Reed and Mr. Steers of the Metropolitan Building Company, Mr. William Edris, and Mr. Charles Clise," May 29, 1947, Balmer Papers, 14–5.

37. "Report and Summary of Meeting . . . with Mr. Reed and Mr. Steers."

38. Hugh B. Mitchell, Incorporated, preliminary report, "The University Tract: Key to Seattle Development," Northwest Development Council, July 1947; Regents Minutes (city resolution on payment in lieu of taxes and board action on Metropolitan lease committee policy), 9:892, June 28, 1947.

39. Regents Minutes (meeting with Legislative Council subcommittee), 9:919, November 22, 1947; Arthur E. Simon, "Our University Is Big Business," *Washington Alumnus,* Fall 1947.

40. Regents Minutes (meeting of executive committee), 10:7–10, January 28, 1948. Text also reproduced in the *Washington Alumnus,* "Old Campus Lease Makes Headlines," Winter 1948.

41. Regents Minutes (second offer by regents to buy balance of lease), 10:35, June 12, 1948.

42. Steers to Metropolitan Building Company directors, "Memorandum re Metropolitan Lease," February 18, 1948, UNICO Properties, Inc. file (copy).

43. Regents Minutes, 10:35, June 12, 1948.

44. *Thirtieth Biennial Report from the Board of Regents to the Governor of Washington,* December 31, 1948.

45. Seattle *Post-Intelligencer,* editorial, "Action Vital on Metropolitan Tract," January 21, 1949; State of Washington, Thirty-first Legislative Session (bills introduced), Senate Bill No. 55 (McCutcheon) and No. 269 (Davidson), House Bill No. 85 (Beierlein and Paulsen), No. 123 (Powell), and No. 553 (Riley).

46. Regents Minutes (Allen proposes faculty studies), 10:48, August 13, 1948; Cannon memorandum to board of regents, "Metropolitan Tract Studies: Analysis of Financial Position and Results of Operations with Estimates of Future Expenses," copy, undated (ca. November 1948), UNICO Properties, Inc.

47. Regents Minutes (faculty building needs committee report), 10:151–52, March 24, 1950.

48. Regents' files, Donald G. Corbett, board service and biographical notes.

49. Regents' files, Grant Armstrong, board service and biographical notes; *Who's Who in the West,* 1976.

50. University of Washington Alumni Association, *The "Old University Grounds" in 1949,* October 7, 1949.

51. Regents Minutes (discussion of 1923 law with alumni representatives), 10:183, November 25, 1950; (report of Armstrong-Balmer-Corbett meeting with Governor Langlie), 10:186, December 20, 1950.

CHAPTER 9. *The Second Era Begins: 1951 to 1953*

1. Seattle *Times,* C. T. Conover, "Like Father, Like Son Is Rule in Douglas Family," March 13, 1950; Neva B. Douglas, "Biographical Sketch."

2. *Legislative Bills, House, 1951,* H.B. 44, authorizing sale of Metropolitan tract for not less than $90,000,000 (Representative Young and Wedekind); *Senate, 1951,* S.B. 314, providing for management of tract by commission (Senator Zednick); Raymond B. Allen (memorandum on commission plan) to Jeanette Testu, chairman, House Committee on Colleges and Universities, and Asa Clark, chairman, Senate Committee on Higher Education and Libraries, February 21, 1951 (copy). Balmer Papers, 14–6, University of Washington Archives.

3. *Legislative Bills, House, 1951,* H.B. 46, authorizing regents' negotiation for lease and management "directly" or otherwise (Representatives Frayn and Gallagher).

4. Seattle *Times,* "Legislators Hear U.W. Plea for Hospital," January 19, 1951; *Legislative Bills, Senate, 1951,* S.B. 113, authorizing $5,000,000 in tract income bonding for hospital (Senators Grieve and Rosellini).

5. Seattle *Times,* Ross Cunningham, "Balmer Strikes Responsive Chord in Legislature with Proposals on Met Tract," January 26, 1951.

6. *House Journal, 1951* (membership, committee on colleges and universities), *Legislative Bills, House, 1951,* H.B. 516 (read first time, February 16, 1951).

7. Seattle *Times,* Ross Cunningham, "Passage of Met-Tract Bill by Senate Ends Six-Year Controversy," March 7, 1951.

8. Regents Minutes (special meeting to review legislative position), 10:192–93, February 28, 1951.

9. Seattle *Times*, Ross Cunningham, March 7, 1951, and news story, "Solons Stop Clocks to Delay Bill Deadline," same date.

10. Balmer statement (copy of text as reproduced in the *Washington Alumnus*, March 1951).

11. Seattle *Post-Intelligencer*, Douglass Welch, "U. Regents Will Meet Soon on Met. Lease," May 11, 1951; Seattle *Times*, "Metropolitan Review Asked by Dave Beck," May 11, 1951.

12. Regents Minutes (approving employment of "administrative assistant"), 10:206, June 8, 1951.

13. Balmer to King, Corbett, and Armstrong, draft memorandum (copy), "Directive to Administrative Assistant," July 11, 1951, Balmer Papers, 14–24.

14. Conversations with Arthur T. Lee, August 5 and 25, 1976; Regents Minutes (employment of Lee), 10:214, July 6, 1951.

15. Conversations with Lee; Seattle *Times*, "Arthur T. Lee to Aid Regents on Met. Tract," July 22, 1951.

16. Regents Minutes (King letter to President Allen), 10:210, and (employment of Lee), 10:214, July 6, 1951; Seattle *Times*, July 22, 1951.

17. Regents Minutes (Condon retirement), 10:220, August 24, 1951.

18. *Washington Alumnus*, "President Allen Thanks Alumni," December 1951; Regents Minutes (appointment of Everest), 10:239–40, December 22, 1951.

19. *Washington Alumnus*, C. B. Lafromboise, "Trouble Shooter," Spring 1952.

20. Metropolitan Tract Committee, "The University of Washington's Metropolitan Properties," lease prospectus, 1951, University of Washington Metropolitan Center Office.

21. Seattle *Post-Intelligencer*, "Big N.Y. Firms in Negotiation for Met Lease," February 14, 1952; Seattle *Times*, "Significant Questions in Regard to Metropolitan Tract Lease Are Answered," February 17, 1952.

22. Regents Minutes (approval of offer to acquire Metropolitan leasehold), 10:247, February 1, 1952; joint news release, Arthur T. Lee for Metropolitan lease committee and Andrew Steers for Metropolitan Building Company, February 9, 1952, Balmer Papers, 15–3.

23. Seattle *Post-Intelligencer*, "U.W. Regents Bid $2,666,500 for Metropolitan Lease," February 10, 1952; Seattle *Times*, "Metropolitan Co., U.W. Regents Agree on Sale of Lease to University," February 10, 1952; Metropolitan Building Company, *Annual Report to Stockholders*, 1951–1952.

24. Seattle *Post-Intelligencer*, Tishman plan ("Multi-Million Met. Tract Plan Bared"), March 26, 1952; *Business Week*, May 24, 1952; Regents Record (special meeting on hotel offers), 10:299, June 28, 1952.

25. Regents Minutes (Schmitz named president, Everest vice-president), 10:255, March 16, 1952; Seattle *Times*, "Dr. Henry Schmitz, Dean at Minnesota, Named U. of W. Head," March 17, 1952.

26. Regents' files, Beatrice Gardner (biographical notes).

27. Regents Minutes (Cannon to tract office), 10:248, March 8, 1952; conversations with Lee, Conrad (clarification of lines of communication), 1976–77.

28. Ibid. (special meeting on hotel offers), 10:299, June 28, 1952.

29. Ibid. (resolution authorizing lease of hotel to The Olympic, Inc.), 10:333–34, August 16, 1952; *Metropolitan Tract*, vol. 1, part 4, Current Leases: Minutes of the Special Meeting of the Board of Regents, September 8, 1952, p. 157; Assignment of Sub-Lease on Olympic Hotel to Board of Regents, September 8, 1952, pp. 157–61; letters on The Olympic, Inc., stock assignment to Seattle-First National Bank, pp. 191–93.

30. *Metropolitan Tract*, New Olympic Hotel Lease, September 8, 1952, pp. 161–91.

31. Seattle *Times* magazine section, Herb Robinson, "Theatrical Landmark's Days Are Numbered: Colorful Past of Seattle's Famed 'Met' Recalled," November 2, 1952.

32. Lee to Balmer (memorandum on sample lease plan), October 23, 1952, Balmer Papers, 15–5.

33. Conversations with Lee.

34. Lee to Balmer, October 23, 1952.

35. Neva B. Douglas, "Biographical Sketch"; Seattle *Times* (obituary, J. F. Douglas), November 30, 1952; Metropolitan Building Company, *Annual Report to Stockholders*, 1952–1953 (memorial resolution).

36. Regents Minutes (Mrs. Hoagland to be assistant secretary), 11:20, January 24, 1953; (Lee's review of tract proposals), 11:40, January 31, 1953.

37. Chap. 69, *Session Laws, Washington, 1953*; Anderson to Balmer (report on committee action), February 27, 1953, Balmer Papers, 15–11.

38. Regents Minutes (street lights in Metropolitan tract), 11:62, March 28, 1953.

39. Ibid. (preliminary authority for theater lease), 11:62, and (supplemental lease, Metropolitan Theatre site), 11:75, April 25, 1953; Seattle *Times*, "Announcement of Closing of 'Met' Awaited," May 8, 1953, *Metropolitan Tract*, vol. 1, part 4, Supplemental Lease (theater site), May 8, 1953, pp. 194–99.

40. Regents' files, Charles M. Harris (biographical notes); Balmer Papers, 15–10 (Harris memorandum on lease); personal communications from Harris.

41. Seattle *Times*, " 'Met'-Lease Field Cut to Three or Four—Says Regent," and "Rosellini Requests Clarification on 'Met' Tract Deal," July 1, 1953.

42. Seattle *Times*, "Powell, Bidder on Met Tract, Dies Suddenly," July 10, 1953; conversations with Lee.

43. Regents Minutes (Balmer report on progress in lease negotiations), 11:134–35, July 11, 1953; Seattle *Times*, "Balmer Favors Detroiters' Met Tract Bid," July 12, 1953.

44. Seattle *Times*, "Balmer Favors . . . ," July 12, 1953, "Detroit Real Estate Man 'Ready to Close Deal' to Lease Metropolitan Tract," and "Edris Backs Regents, But Hits Delays," July 14, 1953; Seattle *Post-Intelligencer*, "Lessee Has Not Yet Presented Formal Bid on Tract," July 16, 1953.

45. Regents Minutes (meeting for signing of the new tract lease), 11:136–41, July 18, 1953.

46. Conversations with Edward L. Rosling, April 24, 1978; Seattle *Times* (obituary, Edward L. Rosling), May 24, 1978.

47. Regents Minutes, July 18, 1953.

48. Ibid.; Seattle *Post-Intelligencer* (Stevens intent to acquire Metropolitan leasehold balance), July 19, 1953; "The Metropolitan Tract: A Report to the Legislature . . . of the Leases and Transactions Entered by the Board of Regents" (comments on principals of University Properties, Inc.), December 31, 1954.

49. Regents Minutes, July 18, 1953.

50. Ibid.; regents' report, December 31, 1954.

51. Duncan Norton-Taylor, "Roger Stevens, a Performing Art," *Fortune*, March 1966; E. J. Kahn, "Closings and Openings," *New Yorker* (Profiles), February 13 and 20, 1954; Tom Kelly, "A Mild Tycoon Named Roger L. Stevens is the Capital's Cultural Pooh-Bah," *People Magazine*, June 9, 1975.

52. Kahn, "Closings and Openings"; conversation with James M. Ryan (on Glancy), May 24, 1978.

53. Norton-Taylor, "Roger Stevens."

54. Kahn, "Closings and Openings."

55. Seattle *Post-Intelligencer*, "Yale Link in Lease Deal," July 20, 1953; conversation with Irving Anches, April 27, 1978, and conversation with Lawrence W. Wiley (by telephone), January 6, 1979.

56. Seattle *Post-Intelligencer*, "Metropolitan Lease: Negotiations on Unexpired Portion to Open Soon," August 25, 1953.

57. Stevens to Lee, September 18, 1953, Balmer Papers, 15–12; Regents Record (approval of Stevens proposal to buy Metropolitan stock), 11:196, October 31, 1953; Stevens stock-purchase invitation, "Offer to Purchase: To Stockholders of Metropolitan Building Company from Roger L. Stevens," October 21, 1953, Balmer File, folder 15–12.

58. Stevens, "Offer to Purchase."

59. Seattle *Post-Intelligencer*, Douglass Welch, "Met Building Offer Rejection Possible," October 27, 1953, and "Stockholders Selling Met Shares," October 30, 1953.

60. Seattle *Post-Intelligencer*, "Seattle Man Named Manager of Met Tract," October 7, 1953; *Who's Who in Washington*, 1962 (James M. Ryan); conversations with Ryan.

61. Seattle *Post-Intelligencer*, "Lessees Spike 'Rush' Rumors," October 27, 1953.

62. Conversation with William G. Reed, February 23, 1978.

63. Bayley to Balmer, October 26, 1953, Balmer File, folder 15–13; Regents Minutes (action on Bayley protest), 11:196, October 31, 1953.

64. Seattle *Post-Intelligencer*, "Met Stock Transfer Date Extended," November 24, 1953.

65. Conversation with Norton Clapp, March 2, 1978; Seattle *Post-Intelligencer*, "Wealthy Seattle Group Buys Metropolitan Co.," November 25, 1953.

66. Seattle *Post-Intelligencer*, November 25, 1953; conversations with James M. Ryan (authority for bid on Metropolitan stock).

67. Conversation with Norton Clapp; *Who's Who in America*, 1976–1977 (Clapp).

68. Lee to Balmer (letter report of preliminary meeting with members of legislative council), October 20, and Frayn to Lee (request for report and documents), October 19, 1953; Balmer Papers, 15–13; Seattle *Times*, "U.W. Regents to Give Legislators Details of New Tract Lease," November 1, 1953.

69. Seattle *Times*, "Stevens Buys Unexpired Part of Met Lease," January 9, 1954; conversations with James M. Ryan, 1978.

CHAPTER 10. *The Changes Come: 1954 to 1959*

1. Regents Minutes (renaming of Education Hall), 11:230–31, January 15, 1954.

2. Ibid.

3. Seattle *Times*, Ross Cunningham, "Increased Metropolitan Tract Revenue for University Poses a Question of Disposition," November 5, 1953.

4. Conversation with James M. Ryan, April 10, 1978.

5. J. L. Dierdorff and A. G. Schille (biographical notes), UNICO Properties, Inc., 1978.

6. Cannon to Balmer, "Memorandum of Conversation with University Properties, Inc., January 23, 1954" (trademark, publicity, etc.), January 28, 1954, Balmer Papers, 15–15.

7. Ibid.

8. Lee to Balmer, memorandum report (modernization of the Olympic and Edris's possible interest in a sale), January 14, 1954, Balmer Papers, 15–15.

9. General Seattle newspaper coverage of University Properties, Inc., announcements, January to June 1954.

10. Everest to Balmer, letter report and attachment, "Draft of Proposed Report to the Board of Regents . . . Covering Accounting and Auditing Procedures Under the Lease Between the Board of Regents and University Properties, Inc.," October 22, 1954, Balmer Papers, 15–19.

11. Municipal League of Seattle and King County, "Report of Metropolitan Tract Committee, October 2, 1953," transmitted to Board of Regents on October 29, 1953, Balmer Papers, 15–13.

12. Harlocker to Balmer, June 4, 1954, transmitting correspondence, "Taxability of New Metropolitan Lease," from John Thomas, assistant attorney general, and Ralph S. Stacy, King County assessor, Balmer Papers, 15–16.

13. Board of Regents, "The Metropolitan Tract: A Report to the Legislature of the State of Washington" (second biennial report), December 31, 1956.

14. Seattle *Times*, Ross Cunningham, "Met-Tract Lease May Yield U. of W. $1,307,000 Annually," June 22, 1954.

15. Ibid.; Seattle *Post-Intelligencer*, Stub Nelson, "Legislators Recess Met Lease Quiz," June 23, 1954.

16. Regents Minutes (authorization for White-Henry-Stuart Building rehabilitation), 11:303, June 26, 1954; 11:341, September 11, 1954; and (Stimson Building parking garage), 11:341, September 11, 1954. Seattle *Post-Intelligencer*, E. B. Fussell. "Two New Leases on Metropolitan Tract to Take Effect; Improvements Set," October 31, 1954.

17. Western Hotels, Inc., "Proposal to the Board of Regents, University of Washington for 25-Year Lease of the Olympic Hotel by Western Hotels, Inc." undated (1952).

18. *Metropolitan Tract*, vol. 1, part 4, Current Metropolitan Tract Leases, Excerpts from Minutes of Board of Regents Meeting, July 23, 1955 (approval of Olympic Hotel lease transfer), p. 202; Resolution of Stockholders of The Olympic Incorporated, August 1, 1955, p. 203; Resolution of Board of Directors of Seattle Olympic Hotel Co., August 2, 1955, pp. 203–4; Agreement of August 2, 1955 Between the Board of Regents, The Olympic Incorporated and Seattle Olympic Hotel Co., pp. 204–10.

19. *Metropolitan Tract*, Agreement of August 2, 1955.

20. Seattle *Times*, Louis Guzzo, "Live Theater Dies a Little Here as Metropolitan Goes," December 6, 1954, and "Man Has Same Seat at 1st, Last Met Show," December 5, 1954.

21. Cannon to Balmer (confidential attachment to memorandum report), January 28, 1954 (see note 6 above).

22. Seattle *Times*, "Plans Discussed to Give Seattle Postoffice, with Ten-Story Building," December 10, 1954.

23. General Seattle newspaper coverage, December 1954.

24. Lee to Everest (copy of letter of resignation), March 11, 1955, and Everest to Regents, "Report on Metropolitan Tract Activities," March 1955, Balmer Papers, 16–1.

25. Everest to Regents, "Report on Metropolitan Tract Activities" (Ryan's illness), April 1955, Balmer Papers, 16–2.

26. Seattle *Times*, "Tollway Hailed by Met Tract Operator," January 6, 1955.

27. Joseph J. Lanza to Ryan (status of University Street and Fifth Avenue), November 9, 1955, UNICO Properties, Inc., and (copy) University of Washington Metropolitan Center office.

28. Everest to Regents, "Metropolitan Center Report," December 2, 1955, Balmer Papers, 16–1; Board of Regents, "The Metropolitan Tract: A Report to the Legislature," December 31, 1956; *Metropolitan Tract*, vol. 1, part 4, Current Leases, Agreement Dated September 15, 1956 with Seattle Olympic Hotel Co. and The Olympic Incorporated, pp. 224–39; conversation with Charles M. Harris (by telephone) on Balmer's role and Balmer's vote on the lease extension, May 19, 1978.

29. Everest to Regents, December 2, 1955.

30. Everest to O. C. Bradeen, regional director, General Services Administration, Seattle, March 29, 1956 (copy), Balmer Papers, 16–3.

31. Regents Minutes (financing second unit of University Teaching Hospital), 12:257–58, April 14, 1956, and ($5,000,000 bond issue, Shefelman as bond counsel), 12:282, May 19, 1956; Board of Regents, "The Metropolitan Tract: A Report to the Legislature" (teaching hospital bond issue), December 31, 1958.

32. U.S. Senate, 84th Congress, 2nd Session, Calendar no. 2222, Report no. 2199, "Amending the Federal Property and Administrative Services Act of 1949, as Amended," June 11, 1956 (To Accompany H.R. 7855).

33. Everest to Regents, "Metropolitan Center Report," memorandums of September 4 and October 17, 1956, Balmer Papers, 16–6 and 16–7.

34. State of Washington, *Historical Highlights*, Secretary of State (Albert D. Rosellini, Fifteenth State Governor), 1959.

35. Conversations with Harold S. Shefelman, 1978; Regents' records, appointments to board of regents.

36. Harold S. Shefelman (biographical notes), *Who's Who in America*, 1976; Seattle *Times*, Robert Heilman, "Harold Shefelman: The Balancer," Sunday Magazine, May 30, 1976.

37. Seattle *Times*, "Winlock Miller Quits U.W. Regents Board," October 23, 1957, and "Winlock W. Miller Dies at 93," January 20, 1964.

38. Report of appraisers (Davis & Darnell, Harry R. Fenton & Associates, Yates, Riley & MacDonald) to James M. Ryan, University Properties, Inc., March 22, 1956.

39. Ernest M. Conrad, memorandum minutes of meeting with GSA officials in the Olympic on December 27, 1956 (copy), and report of appraisers (Davis & Darnell, Harry R. Fenton & Associates, and Yates, Riley & MacDonald) to Everest, January 2, 1957 (copy), UNICO Properties, Inc., file 280.35—Post Office.

40. Everest, "Proposal of the State of Washington Acting Through the Board of Regents of the University of Washington for Purchase of East 105 Feet of Federal Post Office Site, Third and Union, Seattle, Washington" (summary of correspondence, reports, exhibits), December 26, 1956, UNICO Properties, Inc.

41. Ryan to Stevens (letter report of status of post office negotiations), February 11, 1957, UNICO Properties, Inc., file 280.35.

42. Regents Minutes (Everest's new authorization to negotiate for post office site), 13:112–13, February 16, 1957.

43. Clapp to Regents (letter regarding projected offer on post office site), March 15, 1957, Balmer Papers, 16–17.

44. Harlocker to Conrad, letter citing legislative authority for acquisition of land outside tract (chap. 284, *Laws of 1947*: RCW 28.77.360), June 5, 1957.

45. Conversation with James M. Ryan, May 24, 1978; Everest to Floete (letter of proposal for acquisition of the post office site), April 11, 1957 (copy), UNICO Properties, Inc., file 280.35.

46. Seattle *Times* (General Services Administration advertisements for bids on post office site), May 1957.

47. Seattle *Times*, "Firms Seek Right to Bid Against U.W. on Post Office," July 1, 1957.

48. Ryan and Conrad to Everest (memorandum: "Bid Proposal of General Services Administration for Disposal of the East 115 Feet of Third and Union Street Post Office Site"), May 23, 1957 (copy), UNICO Properties, Inc., file 280.35.

49. Ibid.

50. A. H. Link, president, Metropolitan Building Corporation, to Building Owners and Managers Association of Seattle (letter urging attention to post office exchange), May 24, 1957, and response by Eugene E. Dootson, May 27, 1957 (copies), UNICO Properties, Inc., file 280.35; Seattle *Times*, "Pelly Seeks Review of P.O. Plans," May 28, 1957; Van R. Peirson to Senator Henry M. Jackson (letter citing alleged deficiencies in post office plan as determined by Seattle branch of National Association of Postal Supervisors), May 29, 1957 (copy), UNICO file; Seattle *Times*, "Starr Raps Plans for Postoffice," July 3, 1957.

51. Agenda, meeting of June 7, 1957 (Shefelman, Everest, Ryan, Conrad) on bid proposal, UNICO Properties, file 280.35; Regents Minutes (authorization of bid in GSA opening of July 3, 1957), 13:208, June 22, 1957; Seattle *Times*, July 1, 1957, and (General Services Administration advertisements for September 30 bids on post office site), September, 1957.

52. Seattle *Times*, E. B. Fussell, "Proposed New Postoffice Building Would Provide Advantages for City," July 17, 1957, and E. B. Fussell, "Some Complaints and Answers Voiced on New-Postoffice Plan," July 18, 1957.

53. Ryan to Regents (letter confirming agreements on construction and rental for post office site), September 13, 1957; Everest to Regents, "Metropolitan Center Report for Regents' Meetings of September 30 and October 4, 1957" (copy), September 26, 1957, UNICO Properties, Inc.

54. Regents Minutes (special meeting on post office bid), 13:278, September 30, 1957; (university announced as sole bidder), 13:296, October 4, 1957; (authorization of Douglas Building planning), 13:339-40, November 8, 1957.

55. Ibid. (Odegaard appointment), 14:25, January 29, 1958.

56. Seattle *Times*, "Historian Will Replace Schmitz Next August," January 29, 1958, and "Odegaard, New U.W. President, to Visit Campus Within Month," January 30, 1958; *Who's Who in America*, 1974-1975.

57. H. P. Everest, Metropolitan Center reports to regents (general progress, consultations), January 6 and February 5, 1958, Balmer Papers, 16-13.

58. Minoru Yamasaki (biographical notes), *Who's Who in America*, 1976-1977.

59. Perry Johanson (Yamasaki's appointment to Design Commission), personal communication, September 7, 1978; Regents Minutes (resolution establishing university's Architectural Commission), 13:354, December 14, 1957.

60. Regents Minutes (authorization for construction at a cost of $9,319,000), 14:84, February 14, 1958; Board of Regents, "The Metropolitan Tract: A Report to the Legislature of the State of Washington" (third biennial report), December 31, 1958; Ryan to T. B. Jones, letter offer for optional lease of Jones Building (copy), June 27, 1957, UNICO Properties, Inc., file 280.35.

61. Regents Minutes (special meeting on change in garage design), 14:50, March 7, 1958.

62. "The Metropolitan Tract," December 31, 1958.

63. Regents Minutes (Shefelman reminds regents that name for new building will be needed), 14:84-85, March 21, 1958; regents' files, appointment of Mrs. A. Scott Bullitt.

64. Conversations with Mrs. A. Scott Bullitt, July 6 and November 17, 1978; Seattle *Post-Intelligencer*, Northwest Magazine, Jane Estes, "Dorothy Stimson Bullitt: She's as Contemporary as the Next TV Newscast," November 5, 1978.

65. Regents Minutes (Mrs. Bullitt reports growing sentiment for Douglas name), 14:233, August 15, 1958, and (approval of "Washington" as name for new building), 14:357, October 30, 1958.

66. Regents' files, appointments of Murphy and Willis; notes on Willis, *Who's Who in America*, 1976-1977; Seattle *Times*, "Everest to Keep One Job at U. of W.," February 21, 1959; Regents Minutes (regents' resolution on Everest's service), 15:164, June 19, 1959.

67. Board of Regents, "The Metropolitan Tract: A Report to the Legislature of the State of Washington" (fourth biennial report), December 31, 1960; Seattle *Times*, "New Process Speeds Building," April 7, 1959, and "Last Rites for Thomas Balmer," August 1, 1959.

68. Regents' files, Balmer appointment to new term, 1959; Regents Minutes (regents' resolution memorializing Balmer), 15:356, August 14, 1959.

CHAPTER 11. *Transition: 1960 to 1969*

1. Seattle *Times*, "Washington Building Dedicated," June 3, 1960; conversations (by telephone) with Harold S. Shefelman and James B. Douglas, and with Ernest Conrad, 1978.
2. Board of Regents, "The Metropolitan Tract: A Report to the Legislature of the State of Washington," December 31, 1960; Regents Minutes (authorization of additional transfers to New Building Fund), 15:332-33, December 19, 1959.
3. Board of Regents, "The Metropolitan Tract," December 31, 1960.
4. Ibid.
5. Regents' files, appointment and biographical notes, Herbert S. Little.
6. Conrad and Riley to Odegaard, memorandums, with attached transcripts of proposals and exhibits, on Seattle Olympic Company plan for new garage and University Properties, Inc., plan for new office building, February 15, 1962, University Metropolitan Tract Office file.
7. Seattle *Times*, "Fete to Run from February 22, 1961 to November 4, 1961," December 11, 1960.
8. KING-TV script, "The Hundred Years: A Television Panorama of the University of Washington," centennial documentary program sponsored by the Boeing Airplane Company (bound copy presented by President Odegaard to Mrs. A. Scott Bullitt).
9. Seattle *Times*, November 16, 1961; program of the Academic Centennial Convocation, same date.
10. Conrad and Riley to Odegaard, February 15, 1962 (see note 6).
11. Ibid.
12. Ibid.
13. Ibid.
14. University of Washington Metropolitan Tract, Proposals for New Garage Building and New Office Building (memorandum from Conrad to Odegaard), background study, for the information of the regents, with exhibits, June 30, 1962, University Metropolitan Tract Office file.
15. Ibid. (Ryan to Conrad, June 19, 1962).
16. Ibid.
17. Ibid.
18. Ibid.
19. Regents Minutes (approval of Olympic Garage and IBM projects), 19:69-73, June 30, 1962; *Metropolitan Tract*, vol. 2, part 2, Basic Conveyances (Continued), (warranty deeds by Standard Oil Company and Northwest Bible College), pp. 25-27; Seattle *Times*, "$11,000,000 Commercial Project Announced for Metropolitan Tract," July 1, 1962.
20. *Metropolitan Tract*, vol. 2, part 4, Current Metropolitan Tract Leases (Continued) (regents' authorizations of lease amendments for construction of IBM Building and new Olympic Garage Building), pp. 43-45; Conrad to Odegaard, Report on Metropolitan Tract (memorandum with exhibits), February 27, 1963, University Metropolitan Tract Office file.
21. Conrad to Odegaard, February 27, 1963.
22. Ibid.
23. Conversation (by telephone) with R. Mort Frayn, July 19, 1978.
24. Conrad to Odegaard, February 27, 1963 (Ryan to Conrad, February 25, 1963); conversation (by telephone) with James M. Ryan, July 19, 1978.
25. Conversation with Ryan; Seattle *Times*, "Plymouth Church Will Rebuild," January 14, 1965.
26. Ibid.; *Metropolitan Tract*, vol. 2, part 4, Current Metropolitan Tract Leases (Continued) (regents' authorization at meeting of September 22, 1964, of University Properties lease amendment covering Plymouth Church parking garage), pp. 56-59.
27. Regents' files (appointments and biographical notes); Seattle *Times*, "Dr. Leo Rosellini Named U.W. Regent," December 16, 1964.
28. University Properties, Inc., "University Properties Presents the IBM Building" (promotional brochure), 1964; Seattle *Times*, "Architect for I.B.M. Building Thanks City,"

November 17, 1964, and Seattle *Post-Intelligencer,* "$8.5 Million IBM Building Is Officially Opened Here," November 18, 1964.

29. Regents Minutes (architectural commission established), 13:354, December 14, 1957, and (adoption of preamble and statement of function of architectural commission), 17:356, August 25, 1961; (Yamasaki), *Who's Who in America,* 1976–1977.

30. Metropolitan Tract Operations: Report to the Board of Regents, University of Washington, October 22, 1965, University Metropolitan Tract Office files.

31. Conversations with James M. Ryan.

32. Metropolitan Tract Operations: Report to the Board of Regents, October 22, 1965.

33. Ibid.

34. Ibid. (table 1).

35. Ibid. (tables 2 and 3).

36. *Who's Who in America,* 1976–1977 (George V. Powell).

37. Ibid. (James R. Ellis); Seattle *Argus,* "In the Argus Eyes," June 21, 1965, and Philip Bailey, "As I See It," November 5, 1965; conversation with Ellis, August 11, 1978.

38. Board of Regents, "The Metropolitan Tract: A Report to the Legislature," December 31, 1970.

39. Ibid.

40. Ibid.

41. Ibid.; Regents Minutes (hotel lease amendment), 21:839, March 18, 1966; *Metropolitan Tract,* vol. 2, part 4, Current Leases, pp. 192–98.

42. Board of Regents, "The Metropolitan Tract," December 31, 1970.

43. Seattle *Times,* "Robert F. Philip, Tri City Herald Official, Is Regent," March 29, 1968.

44. Board of Regents, "The Metropolitan Tract," December 31, 1970.

45. Ibid.

46. Seattle *Post-Intelligencer,* "New $15 Million Structure," October 5, 1969; Seattle *Times,* "Financial Center: 30-Story Replacement for Stimson Building," October 6, 1969.

47. Board of Regents, "The Metropolitan Tract," December 31, 1970; Regents Minutes (University Properties, Inc.—The Financial Center bid opening), 24:572, February 13, 1970.

CHAPTER 12. *The Tower: 1970 to 1975*

1. University Properties, Inc., "Cornerstone Removal Ceremony, the Stimson Medical Center Building, December 12, 1924–December 26, 1969" (looseleaf folder of photographs and information prepared for board of regents, October 1, 1970), regents' files.

2. Seattle *Times* (bombing on campus), July 1, 1968, and "U.W. President Wants Police-Protection Plan," March 26, 1970.

3. Regents' files (Flennaugh appointment); Seattle *Times,* "Black Dentist Named to U.W. Regents," and "New Regent Is 1st Black U.W. Dentistry Graduate," March 25, 1970.

4. Regents' files (Neupert appointment); Seattle *Times,* "Spokane Man Is New U.W. Regent," March 26, 1970.

5. Conversation with James M. Ryan, May 24, 1978; University Properties, Inc., "Fact Sheet: The Financial Center" (Merry, Calvo, Lane & Baker, Inc.), September 30, 1969; Seattle *Times,* Polly Lane, "Financial Center: 30-Story Replacement for Stimson Building," October 5, 1969.

6. Seattle *Times,* Jerry Craig, "Skybridges Form Integral Part of Downtown Core Planning," May 7, 1971.

7. Ibid. (news photograph of Project 2009 model); James M. Ryan (note on ages of original buildings), August 9, 1978.

8. Board of Regents, "The Metropolitan Tract: A Report to the Legislature," December 31, 1970.

9. James R. Ellis (biographical notes), *Who's-Who in America,* 1976–1977.

10. Mrs. Barbara Zimmerman (biographical notes), personal communication, September 2, 1978.

11. Background studies, Olympic lease amendment, 1971–1972, Metropolitan Tract Office file; conversations with Warren W. Etcheson and John S. Robinson, February 1979; *Metropolitan Tract,* vol. 2, part 4, Current Metropolitan Tract Leases (Continued), "Excerpt from

Board of Regents Meeting of December 15, 1972," and "Third Supplemental Lease Agreement of November 1, 1972," pp. 201–11.

12. Seattle *Post-Intelligencer*, Solveig Torvik, "UW Having Landlord Headaches," December 20, 1971; Seattle *Times*, Polly Lane, "Project 2009 Ponders Highrise How, Where"), July 9, 1972.

13. Board of Regents, "The Metropolitan Tract: A Report to the Legislature," December 31, 1974.

14. Ibid.

15. Seattle *Argus*, David Brewster, "40-Story Bank Tower and Shopping Galleria Proposed to Transform Metropolitan Tract," June 30, 1972; Seattle *Times*, Polly Lane, "40-Story Office Tower Proposed," July 2, 1972, and Polly Lane, "Saving Yesterday for Tomorrow," February 11, 1973.

16. Regents Minutes (initial approval of Commerce House), 26:337–41, May 5, 1973; news releases, for regents, May 5, 1973, and by University Properties, Inc., May 7, 1973 (copies in University Metropolitan Tract Office files).

17. Regents Minutes, May 5, 1973.

18. University Properties news release, May 7, 1973.

19. Board of Regents, "The Metropolitan Tract," December 31, 1974; Seattle *Times*, Polly Lane, "Pedestal Design—Light and Air," May 6, 1973; Seattle *Post-Intelligencer*, Walter A. Evans, "NB of C Plans New Structure," May 6, 1973.

20. Seattle *Times*, editorial, "U.W. Regents and Open-meeting Law," May 8, 1973.

21. John S. Robinson (notes on environmental impact statements), foreword, *Commerce House: Draft Environmental Impact Statement*, April 19, 1974.

22. Seattle *Times*, Polly Lane, "Letter Urges New Look at Building Plan," August 20, 1973, and Polly Lane, "Developer Defends Plan for Project," August 27, 1973.

23. Regents Minutes (resolution authorizing preliminary environmental impact statement), 26:664–65, January 18, 1974.

24. Seattle *Post-Intelligencer*, Michael Sweeney, "A Threat to Bank Tower," February 14, 1974.

25. Seattle *Post-Intelligencer*, Susan Chadwick, "A Blast at 'Opposers' Is Fired Downtown," March 7, 1974.

26. Seattle *Post-Intelligencer*, Michael Sweeney, "Office Tower Is OKd; 'Landmark' Plea Is Rejected," April 18, 1974.

27. James M. Ryan (biographical notes), UNICO Properties, Inc.; Seattle *Post-Intelligencer*, Darrel Glover, "Wind Tunnel Tests Made for New 40-story Building," March 31, 1974.

28. Conversation with James R. Ellis, August 11, 1978; Seattle *Argus*, David Brewster, "Ellis's Last-Minute Effort to Modify Commerce House," July 12, 1974.

29. Board of Regents (legal notices in Seattle *Post-Intelligencer* and *Times*), April 19 and 26, 1974.

30. Robinson, foreword, *Draft Environmental Impact Statement*.

31. Conversation with and personal communications from John S. Robinson, February 1979.

32. Board of Regents, *Final Environmental Impact Statement: Commerce House*, July 22, 1974, section VIIIC, "Hearing on Draft Environmental Impact Statement" (transcript of remarks); Seattle *Post-Intelligencer*, "3-Hour 'Battle' on Building Plan," May 21, 1974.

33. Seattle *Post-Intelligencer*, Michael Sweeney, "Regents Rapped on Tower Plan," July 2, 1974; Allied Arts of Seattle, "Commerce House" (statement approved by Board of Trustees, May 22, 1974), section VIII, "Comments on Draft Environmental Impact Statement," *Final Environmental Impact Statement*.

34. Board of Regents, *Final Environmental Impact Statement*.

35. Seattle *Times*, "Commerce House Shows Need for Control—Critic Says" (republication of Wolf Von Eckhardt comment), July 28, 1974.

36. Yamasaki to Board of Regents (letter in response to Allied Arts statement), section VIII, *Final Environmental Impact Statement*, pp. 325–26.

37. Touche Ross & Co., appendix F, "Economic Analysis of VH Series of Alternatives," *Final Environmental Impact Statement*, July 5, 1974, and addendum to appendix F, July 30, 1974.

38. Seattle *Times*, Polly Lane, "White-Henry-Stuart Bldg. Preservation Plan Offered," August 1, 1974; Seattle *Post-Intelligencer*, Michael Sweeney, "Another Commerce House Plan Proposed," August 2, 1974.

39. Harold S. Shefelman, text of remarks on August 2, 1974, in personal communication, December 1978.

40. Regents Minutes (special meeting), 26:867–71, August 2, 1974.

41. Ibid.

42. Ibid.; Seattle *Post-Intelligencer*, "Michael Sweeney, "Original Commerce House Design OKd," and Seattle *Times*, Polly Lane, "U.W. to Tear Down White-Henry-Stuart," August 4, 1974.

43. Board of Regents (legal notices in Seattle *Post-Intelligencer* and *Times*), August 9, 1974; Seattle *Post-Intelligencer*, Michael Sweeney, "Suit to Block Commerce House Filed," August 14, 1974; Seattle *Times*, Polly Lane, "Building Demolition Is Closer," August 16, 1974.

44. Seattle *Post-Intelligencer*, "Wrecking Ball Suspended," August 16, 1974; "Building Demolition Delayed," August 17, 1974; Michael Sweeney, "White-Henry-Stuart Bldg. Razing Could Begin Today," August 21, 1974; "Hammer Falls on White-Henry-Stu . . . ," August 22, 1974; and "Challengers Quit, Demolition Prevails," August 23, 1974.

45. Conservations with John S. Robinson and James B. Wilson, senior assistant attorney general, University of Washington, February 1979; *Citizens Interested in the Transfusion of Yesteryear et al. v. The Board of Regents of the University of Washington et al.*, 86 Wn. 2d 323, 544 p. 2d 740 (1976).

46. Board of Regents, Metropolitan tract committee (recommendation of "Rainier Square" with supporting narrative), December 20, 1974.

47. Philip to Shefelman (memorandum on creation of historical display in Rainier Square), January 6, 1975, University Metropolitan Tract Office files; Regents Minutes (approval of schematic plans for low-rise portion of Rainier Square), 27:110, January 17, 1975.

48. Regents Minutes (election of Flennaugh, retirement of Shefelman), 27:212, March 22, 1975, and Seattle *Times*, "Board Change," March 22, 1975.

49. Regents' files, Gates appointment, May 2, 1975.

CHAPTER 13. *Toward the New Century*

1. Regents Minutes ("tentative" selection of Peat, Marwick, Mitchell & Co. and associated consultants), 27:175, February 28, 1975.

2. Ibid. (authorization of increase in cost of Rainier Square from $41,000,000 to $42,718,-000), 27:752, June 11, 1976; Ryan to Philip and members of Metropolitan tract committee (estimate of losses through construction delays), memorandum request for review of tract costs, June 3, 1977, Metropolitan Center Office files.

3. Board of Regents, "The Metropolitan Tract: A Report to the Legislature . . . for Lease Years November 1, 1976–October 31, 1978, and a History of Metropolitan Tract Developments," December 31, 1978.

4. Ibid.; conversation with Ernest M. Conrad and James M. Ryan, April 13, 1979.

5. James B. Wilson to Regents (memorandum review of "rights and restrictions" of board), August 22, 1977, Metropolitan Center Office files; conversation with Wilson (by telephone), April 5, 1979.

6. Regents' files (board and committee memberships), 1975–1976; Peat, Marwick, Mitchell & Co., "Economic and Planning Study of Potential Restoration and New Construction Alternatives for the Olympic Hotel Property," draft report, September 19, 1975; Metropolitan tract committee minutes, 1975 (record of public presentation of hotel studies, October 23, 1975).

7. Board of Regents, "The Metropolitan Tract: A Report to the Legislature," December 31, 1978 (see note 3 above); conversations with Ernest M. Conrad, March 1979.

8. Regents Minutes (authorization of increased costs of Rainier Square with concourse), 27:752, June 11, 1976; Metropolitan tract committee minutes, September 17, 1976; conversation with James R. Ellis, December 14, 1978; "The Metropolitan Tract: A Report to the Legislature," December 31, 1978.

9. Board of Regents, "The Metropolitan Tract: A Report to the Legislature," December 31, 1978.

10. Regents' biographical files (Robert D. Larrabee).

11. Ibid. (Gordon C. Culp).

12. Ibid. (John Hans Lehmann).

13. Ibid. (Taul Watanabe).

14. Board of Regents, "The Metropolitan Tract: A Report to the Legislature," December 31, 1978; Metropolitan tract committee minutes (UNICO request for second mortgage), October 14, 1977; "Olympic Hotel: Draft Environmental Impact Statement," May 4, 1977, and "Olympic Hotel: Final Environmental Impact Statement," June 16, 1977; Seattle *Post-Intelligencer*, "Regents OK Downtown Tower," August 13, 1977.

15. Seattle *Post-Intelligencer* (Norton Clapp letter to regents on off-tract tower), August 13, 1977.

16. Seattle *Post-Intelligencer*, "Donahue Pursues Probe of UW Tract Management," October 8, 1977; "Review of the Metropolitan Tract: History, Leases, and Building Program" (regents' background paper for Senate Ways and Means Committee), October 7, 1977.

17. Shorett and Riely (Keith Riely) to E. M. Conrad, "Olympic Hotel Block and Olympic Hotel Garage Half-block" (report of appraisal), May 1977, Metropolitan Tract Office files; Metropolitan tract committee minutes (projected appraisal and rate of return study), October 14, 1977.

18. Board of Regents, "The Metropolitan Tract: A Report to the Legislature" (university landmarks suit), December 31, 1978; Seattle *Post-Intelligencer*, "Plan Spurs UW Suit," April 28, 1978.

19. Regents Minutes (selection of Bowes & Company), 29:302, May 12, 1978; Bowes & Company, "Proposal: The Metropolitan Tract" (outline of rate-of-return project and background data), April 10, 1978.

20. Regents Minutes (selection of Jack N. Hodgson Company), 29:352, June 9, 1978; Jack N. Hodgson, "Proposal for Providing Consulting Services . . . ," April 26, 1978, and Hodgson Company, "The Olympic Hotel Block and Parking Garage: Request for Lease Proposal," November 3, 1978.

21. Board of Regents, "Olympic Hotel Alternatives: Draft Environmental Impact Statement," January 19, 1979; Jack N. Hodgson Company (advertisement), *Wall Street Journal*, December 1, 1978.

22. Internal Revenue Service, Artura A. Jacobs, district director, Seattle, to James F. Ryan, transmitting National Office Technical Advice Memorandum, September 29, 1978; Philip to Regents, "I.R.S. Ruling of Metropolitan Tract," October 2, 1978.

23. Bowes & Company, "Rate of Return Study: The University of Washington Metropolitan Tract," vol. 3: Comments and Conclusions, November 15, 1978.

24. Regents agenda (addendum), Metropolitan tract committee ("Olympic Hotel/Western International Hotels—Release of Covenants"), February 9, 1979, with attachments: addendum of January 12, 1979, and letter proposal, Harry Mullikin, Western International Hotels, to Philip, January 4, 1979.

25. Barbara Krohn, president, Washington Trust for Historic Preservation, to Mary Gates, president, Board of Regents (notice of Olympic Hotel nomination for National Register), January 31, 1979, regents' files; Seattle *Times*, Polly Lane, "Save Olympic Is Word at Hearing," February 8, 1979. Washington Legislature, Senate Resolution 1979–21 (preservation of Olympic), March 8, 1979; Seattle *Times*, Polly Lane, "Only One Full Plan Offered on Olympic," March 2, 1979; Polly Lane, "U.W. Regents Reject Hotel Plans," March 19, 1979. Seattle *Post-Intelligencer*, Wayne Jacobi, "Hearing's Single Voice: 'Save the Olympic,' " February 8, 1979; Charles Dunsire, "One Bid for Olympic Conversion," March 2, 1979; Carol Perkins, "Olympic to Get Facelift, Not Demolition," March 20, 1979. Jack N. Hodgson Company, "The Olympic Hotel Block and Parking Garage: Request for Lease Proposal," supplement, April 19, 1979.

26. Regents Minutes (approval of Four Seasons proposal), with addendum, Metropolitan tract committee, "Olympic Hotel and Garage—Selection of Proposer," 30:313–16, July 13, 1979; Seattle *Times*, Polly Lane, "Redeveloper Selected for Olympic Hotel," July 13, 1979; Seattle *Post-Intelligencer*, Charles Dunsire, "Local Firms Lose Bid to Renovate Olympic Hotel," July 14, 1979.

27. Jeanne M. Welch, deputy state historic preservation officer, to Board of Regents (Olympic Hotel on National Register of Historic Places), June 28, 1979, regents' files; R. F. Philip, chairman, Metropolitan tract committee, to William J. Murtaugh, Keeper of the National Register, June 8, 1979, Metropolitan Center Office file.

28. Board of Regents, "The Metropolitan Tract: A Report to the Legislature" (Legislative Year 1980), February 29, 1980.

29. Donald J. Covey to James F. Ryan (review of Fifth Avenue Theater studies and pre-

liminary recommendations), June 19, 1978, Metropolitan Center Office file; Seattle *Times*, Polly Lane, "5th Ave. Theater to be Revived for Performing Arts," September 19, 1979.

30. Articles of incorporation, 5th Avenue Theatre Association, November 19, 1979; Seattle *Times*, Polly Lane, "Group Underwrites Theater Renovation," November 20, 1979, and "Much of Fifth Avenue Theater Work to be 'Hidden,'" February 3, 1980; Seattle *Post-Intelligencer*, Michael Sweeney, "Cash Infusion for 5th Avenue Theater," November 21, 1979.

31. Board of Regents, "The Metropolitan Tract: A Report to the Legislature," February 29, 1980.

Index

Wahlstrom, Nelson A.: career at university to comptrollership (1945), 230; consultant to regents (1946), fact-finding trip to Eastern universities, 232–33; suggests federal funding for teaching hospital (1951), 261; at "main lease" signing (1953), 282; signs Olympic Hotel transfer agreement (1955), 305; to Washington, D.C. (1960), 346; mentioned, 238, 239, 240, 252, 253*n*, 263, 266

Waldorf Hotel, 63, 72, 184

Walker, George H. (regent), 118

Wallgren, Mon C. (governor), 227, 244

Washington Alumnus: on regents' stand in Arena case (1915), 137, 138; supports regents in hotel controversy (1921), 157–58; urges full-time staff on lease effort (1947), 249

Washington Art Association, 140

Washington Building: replaces Douglas (1959), 330; dedication, costs, rentals (1960), 332–33; mentioned, 337, 338, 340, 348, 353. *See also* Douglas Building–post office project

Washington Hotel, 53, 106

Washington Plaza Hotel, 362

Washington Trust and Savings Bank, 200

Washington Trust Company, 62

Watanabe, Taul (regent), 392, 393, 399, 402

Waterhouse, Frank: president, Community Hotel Corporation (1922), 161; career, 162; death (1930), 216; mentioned, 166, 167

Wessman, Harold E., 268

Western (International) Hotels, 305, 400

Wheeler, Eldridge (regent): joins board (1913), 118; career, 119; on Women's University Club Building issue, 124; leaves board (1921), 151; mentioned, 132, 134, 138, 149, 150

White, Chester F.: incorporator, president, Metropolitan Building Company (1907), 62; career, 68–69; capital participation, name on first building, 75; death (1917), 140–41; mentioned, 54, 88, 97, 106, 116, 121

White, Eugene A. (regent), 222, 225

White-Henry-Stuart Building: construction begins (1908), 79; cost (White),

81; White-Henry completed (1909), 90; Stuart in place (1915), 129–30; amenities, conference rooms, library (1918), 146; White Annex (1922), 169; targeted for demolition (1972), 364; demolition begun (1974), 379–80; mentioned, 183, 245, 307, 308, 310, 333, 340, 345

Whitson, M. J., 92

Whitson Building (temporary), 112, 163, 169, 201

Wiehl, Lloyd L. (regent), 315, 316

Wiley, Lawrence W., 287

Willis, Dr. P. W., 161

Willis, Robert J. (regent), 330, 335, 350, 357

Wills, C. S., 161, 166*n*

Wilson, James B., 370, 388

Wilson, Katherine, 187

Wilson, Worrall, 161, 166*n*

Winkenwerder, Hugo, 215

Winsor, Amos, 26

Winsor, Richard (regent): career, 26; defendant in *Callvert* suit, 36; motion (1902) fixes tract leasing policy, 42; on University Site lease, 45; approves Moore lease (1904), 51; leaves board (1905), 56; death (1923), 182; mentioned, 27, 37, 38, 41, 47, 50, 52

Woodburne, Lloyd S., 268

Women's University Club Building (temporary), 124–25

World's Fair. *See* Century 21

Yamasaki, Minoru: consultant on Douglas Building–post office design (1958), career, links to Seattle, 326–27; speaker at IBM Building dedication (1964), impact on Seattle of architectural style, 347–48; designing Commerce House (1972), 362; comment on Commerce House design (1974), 376. *See also* Minoru Yamasaki and Associates

Yantis, George F., 227, 232

Young Lawyers section, Seattle Bar, 370, 373

Young Naturalists, 18

YWCA (temporary building), 112, 140

Ziegler, Eustace P., 188

Zimmerman, Barbara, 361, 402

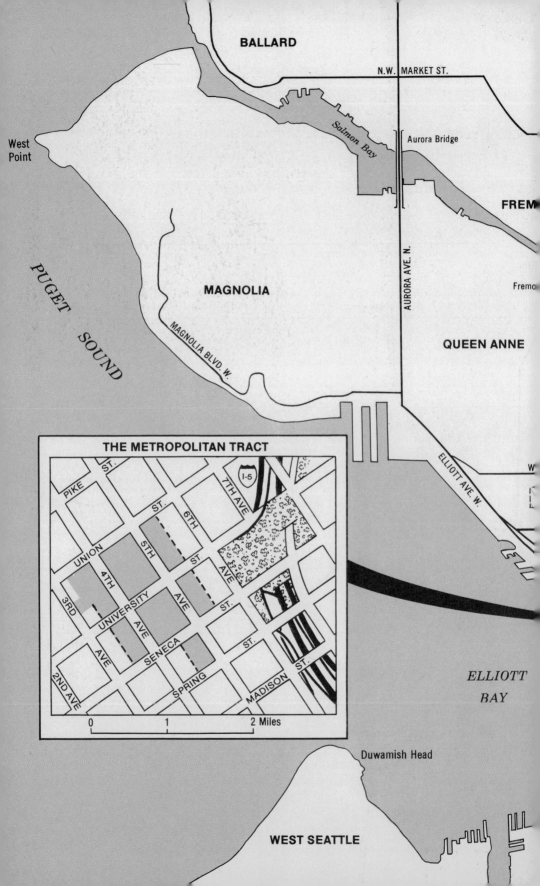

BALLARD

N.W. MARKET ST.

Salmon Bay

Aurora Bridge

West
Point

FREM

Fremo

PUGET

MAGNOLIA

AURORA AVE. N.

QUEEN ANNE

SOUND

MAGNOLIA BLVD. W.

ELLIOTT AVE. W.

W

THE METROPOLITAN TRACT

I-5

PIKE

ST.

7TH AVE

6TH

5TH

ST.

ST.

UNION

4TH

AVE

ST.

3RD

ST.

UNIVERSITY

AVE.

AVE

2ND AVE

AVE

SENECA

ST.

ST.

SPRING

MADISON

ST.

ST.

0   1   2 Miles

ELLIOTT

BAY

Duwamish Head

WEST SEATTLE